A Rose
for
Mrs. Miniver

A Rose

for

Mrs. Miniver

The
Life of

Greer Garson

Michael Troyan

THE UNIVERSITY PRESS OF KENTUCKY

Publication of this volume was made possible in part by a grant
from the National Endowment for the Humanities.

Published by The University Press of Kentucky

Scholarly publisher for the Commonwealth,
serving Bellarmine College, Berea College, Centre
College of Kentucky, Eastern Kentucky University,
The Filson Club Historical Society, Georgetown College,
Kentucky Historical Society, Kentucky State University,
Morehead State University, Murray State University,
Northern Kentucky University, Transylvania University,
University of Kentucky, University of Louisville,
and Western Kentucky University.

Editorial and Sales Offices: The University Press of Kentucky
663 South Limestone Street, Lexington, Kentucky 40508-4008

03 02 01 00 99   5 4 3

Frontispiece: Greer Garson in 1943. *Opposite foreword
opening page:* as Elizabeth Bennet in *Pride and Prejudice.*
Both A.M.P.A.S. © Turner Entertainment Co. All rights reserved.
Act 1 photo courtesy of Greer C. Murray. Acts 2 and 3 photos
© Turner Entertainment Co. All rights reserved.

Library of Congress Cataloging-in-Publication Data

Troyan, Michael, 1968-
    A rose for Mrs. Miniver : The life of Greer Garson / Michael Troyan.
        p.   cm.
    Includes bibliographical references and index.
    ISBN 0-8131-2094-2 (cloth : alk. paper)
    1. Garson, Greer, 1908-1996. 2. Motion picture actors and actresses
—United States—Biography. I. Title.
PN2287.G393T76   1999
791.43'028'092—dc21
[B]   98-37542

Manufactured in the United States of America

Contents

*Illustrations follow pages
50, 178, and 306.*

Foreword

HALF A CENTURY AGO, in a world where the primary form of entertainment was the black-and-white motion picture and the movie star was of magical interest, the advent of Greer Garson was of major importance.

Some actors achieve stellar position due to talent, a particular original persona, exploitation, and good fortune. Then there are others who embrace all of this, but also walk hand in hand with another component: a special need of society at a given moment—Will Rogers, Shirley Temple, Jean Harlow, James Dean are a few of these. And Greer Garson.

Just three years after her auspicious film debut in *Goodbye, Mr. Chips*, she became a legend in her sixth screen appearance, as "Mrs. Miniver." All of her unique accomplishments fused with the peak of World War II, and she became the personification of female courage, dignity, grace, humanity, and stamina. She was a stunning figurehead during very bleak days.

Besides being a highly accomplished actress, she is endowed with other precious gifts: a translucently beautiful Irish complexion, Titian hair, charming wit, and a wryly elegant tone which sets her deliciously apart from any other leading lady. Plus that husky, beautifully modulated speaking voice, which has always provided compassion and distinction to every word she has uttered. And her permeating warmth that radiates comfort and empathy in all directions.

Greer has a dash of the charming naughty Edwardian about her: elegant, stylish, humorously imperious—her twinkling eye full of a provocative innocent waltz that suggests romantic implication but threatens, if her words are misinterpreted, censure with the snap of an invisible fan. Lace, lavender, and a dash of paprika . . . like "Mrs. Parkington."

One brief look at the signature of Greer Garson is a gleeful invitation to the pulse of her nature: bold, original, generous, opulently romantic, and perky. She is a rare one!

The imprint of her philanthropy, friendship, and artistic accomplishment will echo continuously to bolster the rousing affection with which she is held by all who know her. This is compounded by the merciful preservation of her canon of screen work, especially in that nearly two decades when she was one of the rarest prizes in the galaxy of stars at Metro-Goldwyn-Mayer during those halcyon days of motion pictures . . . days which have provided us with a score of performances that are living proof that Greer Garson is a rare indelible, both in her art form and as a human being.

—Roddy McDowall

Preface

A radiant rose of a woman, Greer Garson scatters her delightful personality like a handful of petals. "But that's my symbol—the rose," said Miss Garson, resigned to being everybody's Mrs. Miniver forever.

IN THE FALL OF 1994 when I first began the research for this, my first book, I thought of Greer Garson—as most cinema audiences and film scholars do—as a rose-colored creature of celluloid, the very incarnation of the English lady: graceful, witty, beautiful, and courageous. She was known to me then as Mrs. Miniver, Paula Ridgeway of *Random Harvest*, Edna Gladney of *Blossoms in the Dust*, Madame Curie, and Eleanor Roosevelt in *Sunrise at Campobello*. Because of these performances alone, I decided to start working on a book entitled *The Films of Greer Garson*. While studying her movie and television roles, I discovered that the noble characterizations of this accomplished actress were deceiving. I discovered hints that there was far more to Greer Garson beneath the glossy Hollywood surface, such as her delightful Scottish Highlands musical number in *Random Harvest*, her witty, beautifully modulated performance as Elizabeth Bennet in *Pride and Prejudice*, her spellbinding portrayal of purest evil in *The Little Foxes*, and her delightful slapstick routines in *Julia Misbehaves*. I was both intrigued and inspired by what I began to uncover and chose to expand my work into a full biography.

The facts that I learned were impressive. At the height of her career, there were more than two hundred official Greer Garson fan clubs around the world. Her witty remarks at parties or in interviews were quoted nationwide, her movies broke box-office records and played an unequaled eighty-three weeks at Radio City Music Hall in

New York, and during World War II her performance as Mrs. Miniver was cheered by Allied leaders around the globe, from President
Roosevelt to Winston Churchill. But the real woman seemed elusive.
There had never been a book of any kind published about Greer
Garson's life and films. More than fifty years have passed since the
heyday of her movie career, and most of her Hollywood contemporaries are gone. Turning to newspapers and magazines, I found that,
because she could be as evasive as Greta Garbo in interviews, very few
film historians and journalists had been able to penetrate the image
of "Metro's Glorified Mrs." that was carefully designed for her by
Louis B. Mayer. Diane Jennings of the *Dallas Morning News* described
a typical interview: "'You're not who I thought you were,' people used
to say to her. 'I don't know,' Greer replies. 'Who do you think that I
am?' 'You're not . . .' they continue. 'Mickey Rooney?' she answers.
'You're right. I'm not.'" In 1994 she was still alive, but very ill in Dallas
Presbyterian Hospital and therefore unavailable for in-depth interviews. When she died two years later, journalists complained about
this lack of information about her and noted that she had not made
a film since 1967. "So," Henry Sheenan wrote in the *Orange County
Register,* "perhaps it's not surprising that the write-ups were somewhat involved in a process of self-justification, trying to explain just
who this actress was and why she deserved a long obituary."

   This project came to life only because of the generous assistance
of a number of Greer Garson Fogelson's relatives, friends, and coworkers who generously allowed me to interview or correspond with
them. They are Edward Ashley, Bob Banner, Dr. B. Clayton Bell Sr.,
Dr. Eugene Bonelli, Carol Burrow, Arthur Cantor, Col. James P.
Caston, A.J. Carothers, Betty Christenson, Van Cliburn, Sheila
Collings, Tim Considine, Malcolm Disimone, Joseph Dispenza, Jack
and Marilyn Evinger, Commodore Robin W. Garson CBE. RN.,
Sydney Guilaroff, Ann Harper, Bobbie Hill, Marsha Hunt, Herbert
and Julie Hutner, Janet Leigh, Francisca Lucas, Roddy McDowall, Dr.
Greer C. Murray, Margaret O'Brien, Gilbert Ortiz, Robert Osborne,
Gregory Peck, Jean Porter, Ann Rasor, John and Laura Roach, Lillian
Burns Sidney, Dr. Sophia Sloan, Keester Sweeney, Zann Taylor, Dr.
William O. Tschumy Jr., and William Tuttle.

   The administrative staff and faculty of The College of Santa Fe
were also extremely helpful, specifically President James Fries, Brother

Cyprian Luke Roney, John Weckesser, Walter Burke, Randolph Mann, Sherry Erickson, Bill Turner, Lisa Nichols, Michael Santopollo, and especially Nancy Bachlet, who provided innumerable research materials and organized my memorable tour of that unique institution. Bill Torres, at the Pecos National Historical Park, provided me with a thorough and informative tour of the Forked Lightning Ranch outside Santa Fe.

With the insight that I had gained, and in the midst of research, I became like a gardener who, confronted with an overgrown rosebush, begins to chop away the excess foliage of legend, carefully trims the Hollywood half-truths, clears and searches through the rubble that was Louis B. Mayer's Hollywood empire, and finally discovers the true rose that was Eileen Evelyn Greer Garson: "a romantic, tempestuous beauty, with dancing blue-green eyes, startling energy, a versatile acting technique, and overflowing humor." I found the Scotch-Irish girl running barefoot on her grandparents' Irish farm who became the chatelaine of Hollywood's grandest motion picture studio and earned an astounding seven Academy Award nominations for Best Actress. A voluble conversationalist, she was at the same time an intensely private woman who managed to keep much of her past in shadows for all of her ninety-one years. She preferred to dabble in witty comedies such as *Pride and Prejudice* and unsheathe her fingernails in stage melodramas such as *Old Music,* yet inadvertently was catapulted to the top of her profession playing stoic heroines. She sought to escape the impressive but lonely throne as Queen of Metro-Goldwyn-Mayer by becoming the woman she portrayed on screen, with the companionship of a husband and the security of a home and children, but the driving ambitions of her youth prevented it until it was almost too late.

Garson often found her life intertwined with roses, both symbolic and real, and I have incorporated this into the book. There were the roses at her childhood home in Ilford, the prize-winning garden at her Bel Air estate in California, the famous Mrs. Miniver Rose, and even a rare breed that carries her own name. The comparison is significant. Religious writer Frances Gumley once remarked, "A rose is a visual paradox, a flower of great beauty, but on a stem of thorn. And that paradox is like a metaphor or allegory of life—almost like light and dark. It has petals of great softness, but symbols of suffering on the side." Roses are as emblematic of England as she is and also, as actress Jane Asher referred to them, as "desperately romantic . . . with a hint of the purity not being totally steadfast; there's fire beneath the ice."

The fact that you are holding this book in your hands right now I also owe to the consistent support of a team of researchers and good friends. Elizabeth Jones, who was involved in every phase of this project, is the most conscientious and authoritative collector of Garson memorabilia that a biographer could hope for. David R. Smith, director of the Walt Disney Archives, generously provided much assistance and advice. Julia R. Hodges undertook research for me in Atlanta and Los Angeles and accompanied me on research and interview sessions in Dallas and Santa Fe. Pam Pagels provided invaluable historical material from the University of Wisconsin archives. Caroline Frick undertook research at the British Film Institute. Jackie Marvin and Lois Spradlin transcribed the interviews for me. Patrick Murphy provided an insightful background of Irish history. Amy Stone, Larissa Moskalo, Tony Romani, and Barbara Summers, who brought me into contact with my agent, Carol Schild, helped improve and polish my manuscript. I owe a special note of thanks to Dr. Greer C. Murray, who provided me with photographs from his family's collection; Dr. Philip and Barbara Williams for their wonderful hospitality in Dallas; and Craig Blanchard for his assistance concerning the history of Greer Garson's home in Bel Air. I would also like to thank my friends at the Turner Entertainment Company and Warner Bros.

I am indebted to the following libraries and special archives for their generous assistance: Stacy Behlmer, Sam Gill, and the staff of the Academy of Motion Picture Arts and Sciences Margaret Herrick Library; Sam Ratcliffe, head of the Special Collections archives of Southern Methodist University in Dallas; the British Film Institute; Melanie Christoudia of the British Theatre Museum; Richard Mangan, administrator of the Raymond Mander and Joe Mitchenson Theatre Collection; Ruth F. Vyse, archivist for the University of London; K. Higgins at the Central Library in Birmingham, England; Richard M. Harvey of the Guildhall Library, London; Robert Bonar at the Presbyterian Historical Society in Belfast, Ireland; the New York Public Library for the Performing Arts; the Los Angeles and Burbank public libraries; Donna Ross at the UCLA film archives; Ned Comstock and Stuart Ng at the University of Southern California; Robert C. Eason Jr. of the Fine Arts Division of the Dallas Public Library; Judy Klinger of the Santa Fe Public Library; Harry Max Hill of the Fort Worth Public Library; Vivian Montoya and Marie St. John at the library of the California Thoroughbred Breeders Association; and Carol Burrow and Pat Standlee of Dallas Presbyterian Hospital.

By the time I polished my last chapter and placed my last period, I had uncovered the story of a remarkable woman whose life was more colorful and inspirational than any of her motion pictures. I have divided the book into three parts, named for the cities that most profoundly affected her life. I bridged them with the two most significant journeys in her lifetime: from England to America aboard the *Normandie* in 1937 and from Los Angeles to Santa Fe aboard the *Santa Fe Super Chief* in 1949. The first brought her the successful career she had sought since childhood; the second a marriage to Col. E.E. Fogelson, which she dubbed "the greatest adventure."

I wish to dedicate this book to my family.

Prologue

ON THE EVENING OF MARCH 4, 1943, as waiters in the Ambassador Hotel began serving dinner to the attendees of the fifteenth annual Academy Awards ceremony, Louis B. Mayer glanced at his watch. It read 8:15. Sitting with Ronald Colman and Walter Pidgeon and their wives, Benita and Ruth, the most powerful mogul in Hollywood looked around the glittering Cocoanut Grove. His guest of honor was late. The orchestra was playing one of the nominated songs of the year, and L.B. recognized it as "How About You" from Metro-Goldwyn-Mayer's own *Babes on Broadway.*

America was halfway through its World War II engagement in 1943. In a continued effort to boost the country's morale, President Franklin D. Roosevelt proclaimed, "The Axis powers knew that they must win the war in 1942 or eventually lose everything. I do not need to tell you that our enemies did not win the war in 1942!" While men were fighting overseas to free the South Pacific and Aleutians from the Japanese, women's importance to the nation was greater than ever before. Female integration into the workforce had increased from 24.3 percent in 1940 to 34.7 percent by the time the war was over. By March 1943, 1,160,000 women were running munitions factories, preparing food parcels for the Red Cross in Europe, and filling the Women's Army Auxiliary Corps. Ever-on-the-move First Lady Eleanor Roosevelt was their inspiration.

In Hollywood a woman had captured the hearts and minds of moviegoers in a picture that the Academy was honoring with twelve nominations this evening. Her portrayal of a courageous British mother who protected her family from the horrors of war had inspired audiences on an unparalleled international scale. The Queen of England wrote to the actress: "You made us feel more brave than we actually were by your performance. To you, we will all be eter-

nally grateful." The film was *Mrs. Miniver,* and the actress was Greer
Garson. Already the recognized Queen of MGM, she had become
Hollywood's most important heroic wartime icon. Her latest film,
Random Harvest, was grossing millions around the country and was
in its eleventh week at "The Showplace of the Nation," Radio City
Music Hall.

Suddenly L.B. Mayer and his party saw a flurry of activity at the
entrance as cameramen and celebrity well-wishers surrounded the
latest arrival. It was Greer, dressed in a simple black gown, her bright
red hair shining in the scattered light from flashbulbs. Clutching the
hand of her mother, Nina Garson, she slowly made her way to the
official MGM table. As she sat down, she confessed to the gathering
that she had a splitting headache and was too nervous to eat. She had
spent a long day before the cameras portraying Madame Curie in the
studio's most expensive picture of the year.

It was past eleven o'clock when Gary Cooper approached the
stage to introduce the first of the acting awards for the evening. By
then *Mrs. Miniver* had earned four Oscars: Best Picture, Director,
Screenplay, and Cinematography. The director, William Wyler, was
not present to receive his award. He was in England with the Air
Force 91st Bomb Group, flying an air raid over Germany. Since producer Sidney Franklin was also absent, ill at home, Louis B. Mayer
received his Irving G. Thalberg Memorial Award and the Best Picture
Oscar. "If *Mrs. Miniver* keeps up like this, the government will put a
ceiling on statuettes!" Bob Hope quipped as L.B. stepped down.
Cooper began by reminding the audience, "It's possible to have this
banquet only because men in uniform are being shot and killed on
foreign battlegrounds," bringing a solemn hush over the crowd. Pri-
vates Tyrone Power and James Stewart then brought in an enormous
American flag bearing the names of all 27,677 Hollywood enlistees.

As the clocks throughout the Ambassador Hotel rang midnight,
Joan Fontaine took the podium and announced that Teresa Wright
had earned the Supporting Actress award, as Carol Beldon in *Mrs.
Miniver.* "It was a very emotional evening," Teresa recalls of her tearful acceptance speech. "I'd like to have won Best Actress for *Pride of
the Yankees,* but at the same time my heart, and everyone else's, was
with *Mrs. Miniver.*"

Greer held her mother's hand as Joan Fontaine read off the candidates for Best Actress: Katharine Hepburn (*Woman of the Year*), Greer Garson (*Mrs. Miniver*), Rosalind Russell (*My Sister Eileen*), Bette Davis (*Now Voyager*), and Teresa Wright (*Pride of the Yankees*). She did not expect to win and had not prepared an acceptance speech. Suddenly the envelope was opened and the announcement was made: "Greer Garson, for *Mrs. Miniver*."

Amid thundering applause and a standing ovation from many, Greer stood and approached the microphone. When Joan Fontaine, who had become Hollywood's archetypal English rose for her performances in *Suspicion* and *Rebecca,* handed over the statuette, she was passing on this mantle as well. Greer quickly apologized for being unprepared ("I feel just like Alice in Wonderland"), and then launched into a five-and-a-half-minute speech that would become legendary. It seemed as though she thanked everyone who came to mind, from her Hollywood peers at MGM to the doctor who delivered her into the world in London. As one who had suffered the anti-British prejudice in the United States before the country entered the war, she made a point of congratulating the Academy for honoring artists who were not originally from America. She was well aware that murmurs of controversy were swirling around the room that evening. Gossip columnist Hedda Hopper was among the most prominent critics who did not believe in bestowing so many accolades upon a picture that was not about Americans. She challenged her audience with words that reflected her pride in her adopted country. "I came to this country as a stranger five years ago," she said. "I've been very happy and very proud to be a member of this community and of this industry all that time. And from everybody I met or worked with, truly, I have received such ready kindness that for quite a long while I couldn't believe it was true. I may never win another statuette, but tonight is a memorable one; one that officially places the welcome mat for me. I shall cherish this evening and the kindness of my many friends forever."

Eileen Evelyn Greer Garson, who dubbed herself "The Little Girl Least Likely To Succeed," had achieved Hollywood's crowning glory; a triumphant moment of fairy-tale proportions. Auntie Mame, the character she would re-create on Broadway, once said: "Life is a banquet, and most poor suckers are starving to death." Greer was now at the head of that banquet table. But few in the Cocoanut Grove that evening were aware of the high price she had paid for it. From an early age, as a bedridden invalid, she had taken hold of her mother's favorite motto, "Keep faith in your star," and with a stubborn persistence that destroyed her first marriage, threatened to alienate her family, and ruin her health, sought an acting career. Like Marie Curie, she had reached "to catch a star on her fingertips" and achieved it. "I suppose I always believed in fairy tales," she once said. "They do come true. This one did, certainly."

Act One

London (1904-1937)

Destined, as I was, for an academic life or a safe matrimonial harbour I often feel that, in going on the stage, I
am a throwback to my renegade and lusty ancestors; it
was as if the taint of some wandering Scotch minstrel or
Norse scald had come to the surface in me.

CHAPTER 1

"TEA WITH GREER GARSON," a visiting journalist once remarked, "is one joyous afternoon with an elusive sprite who deflects hard questions with peals of laughter. But, push her beyond the punch line, try to get her to say something deeper . . . and she pulls rank on you. The imperious Garson is suddenly in charge." Among the inquiries most frequently asked by interviewers, and seldom answered by Greer, were questions about her birth. Typically, she attempted a diversion with an offer of a second cup of tea or a Scotch scone from her silver tea service. She might mention her astrological sign. "I was born under the sign of Libra," she would remark. "Libra is supposed to mean balance. But it is an uncomfortably high-tension balance and the slightest thing sets it swinging. I am very impatient by nature, quick-tempered, and high strung with a tendency to want things done at once, or not at all." An exasperated writer, after some diligent research, might come up with the birthdate of September 29, 1908, from a contact at MGM. Greer would recall that the birth occurred, "rather horridly, and three days ahead of time, which may account for my unpunctuality through life," in a nursing home in Belfast, Ireland. She was born a redhead, which surprised her mother, nineteen-year-old Nancy Sophia Garson, but Greer would later say with a smile, "Mother seems to have outgrown her initial displeasure at the sight of her first child."

On April 9, 1996, the *Belfast Telegraph* reported, "Legendary film star Greer Garson went to her grave in Dallas today—believing the great myth about her origins was still intact." Although newspaper obituaries around the world published her birthdate as 1908, as journalists and film historians had done for years, the discovery of her birth certificate in London only a few months before had lifted the veil on the shadowed origins of one of Hollywood's most secretive stars.

It was on September 29 that a baby girl was born to George and Nancy Garson. But the newly christened Eileen Evelyn Greer Garson was not born in Ireland, nor was the year 1908. It was in the Garsons' modest London home, in 1904, where she was laid upon a ceremonial pink satin pillow that had been in the Garson family for generations. When he notified G.E. Morgan, registrar of the subdistrict of North East Ham in the county of Essex, of his daughter's birth, thirty-nine-year-old George Garson listed his profession as commercial clerk in a London importing business.

His ancestors were adventurous Scandinavian seafarers who, beginning in the eighth century, had sought out more temperate conditions than their homeland. They crossed the 170 miles from Norway to the isles of Shetland, Caithness, and Orkney off the coast of Scotland. Among these colonists were the Garsons, members of the Clan Gunn, who settled in Orkney. After several generations, some of the Orcadians filtered down into the southern, coastal section of Scotland and then to England, becoming respectable Scotch Presbyterian members of their communities. Such was the intention of George's father, Peter Garson, a very fine and popular cabinetmaker who married Jane Firth in Kirkwall, the capital of Orkney, and shortly thereafter moved to London. George was the third child of a family that would swell to nine, born on June 15, 1865, with an older sister, Alexina Logie, and brother, James. An industrious young man, George quickly became independent, managing lucrative government commissions and running branch offices as far distant as Shanghai. He also found time to court a petite, beautiful young woman, recently arrived in the city, who was seeking employment as a city magistrate.

Her name was Nancy Sophia Greer, but she preferred "Nina." If George found that her career was an unusual one for an eighteen-year-old woman at the turn of the century, it was just one in a string of disclosures that surprised him during their courtship. Her petite size and soft, Scotch-Irish brogue thinly disguised an assertive, forthright nature. She had refused to follow the family pattern to attend Queen's University in Belfast and get married. Instead, she took the civil service examination for women, passed with honors, and moved to London despite family disapproval.

If Nina was a rebel in the ranks of her staid Presbyterian relatives, she came by that quality honestly. For she was a descendant of one of the most infamous families in Scotland. The wealthy and powerful Clan MacGregor of Glen Orchy owned land in Perthshire and Argyll in the volatile Highlands. They were a complex people—outspoken, hot-tempered, ambitious, and violent, yet honorable, proud, and fun-loving. J.M. Barrie, playwright and author of *Peter Pan*, once observed, "You Scots are such a mixture of the practical and the emotional that you escape out of an Englishman's hand like a trout." The MacGregors' bold family motto was "Royal Is My Race," for they claimed royal descent from Gregor, the third son of Alpin, King of the Scots. When the MacGregors suffered a devastating defeat by the Colquhouns in 1602, the families dispersed, and many became outlaws, including Rob Roy MacGregor, the legendary Scottish Robin Hood. Crossing the North Channel, some members of the persecuted family settled in the North of Ireland, hiding their past behind a new name—Greer—utilizing the Irish contraction of Gregor. Gradually, the hot-blooded clan of warriors and cattle thieves cooled into a respected assemblage of parsons, teachers, doctors, and barristers. Among them was David Greer, an honored sergeant in the Royal Irish Constabulary who retired as an estate agent in the province of Ulster. There he settled on a farm in Castlewellan, County Down. The small market village was surrounded by a vast windswept pastureland of dark, lonely moors and bright streams, bordered by the Irish Sea to the west, Belfast Lough to the north, and the majestically beautiful Mourne Mountains to the south. His wife, Sophia, bore him a son, Robert Francis, and three daughters: Elizabeth Laura, who died in infancy, Nancy Sophia, and Bertha Eveline.

The tranquil, green countryside in which Nina was reared belied the country's more infamous aspects, for the Ireland of the 1880s was a country as torn by bloody conflict as Scotland had been for the MacGregors. Ulster was a center of violent dissension, where the wholly Scottish Presbyterian community opposed Home Rule, creating "Orange Lodges" to protect the union with Great Britain and terrorizing opposing Catholics with the "Peep O'Day Boys." The Fenians, protesting English domination, struck back by scattering about the countryside murdering pro-British landlords and looting and burning their homes. In the middle was Charles Stuart Parnell, the Irish MP for West Meath, who was a champion of these restless, landless Irishmen impoverished by the Potato Famine of 1845-49 and agrarian competition from abroad.

As a respected elder in the Castlewellan Presbyterian congregation, David Greer instilled religion in his daughters from an early age. "Prayer is your strength," he told them. He also passed on his belief in family pride: "Always remember 'Archdoille,'" he told Nina. The Greer family motto translated as "To the Top of the Hill. Nothing Is Beyond Your Grasp!" Little did he realize how profoundly Nina—and later her daughter—intended to live up to that standard.

George and Nina married, and the newlyweds indulged in their favorite pastime together: travel. After their European honeymoon, they settled in a home outside London, only two streets away from the home in which George had grown up, at 88 First Avenue, Manor Park, Essex. "From the composite picture I have formed of my father since I have grown up," Greer would recall, "I think he was the kind of man with whom I, too, could have fallen in love. He had a profound appreciation of music—I think my love of music comes from him—spoke three or four languages, could recite whole pages from Goethe, Schiller, Shakespeare and the Bible, and satisfied his wanderlust by visiting a different country in Europe every year." Eileen, their firstborn, was a dangerously fragile infant who developed pneumonia within her first two months of life and showed indications of a heart malady, which worried the family doctor. Despite Nina's constant ministrations, he prepared the Garsons for their daughter's early death.

Two years later, Eileen was still alive. But Nina's triumph was short-lived. In 1906 her husband suffered an attack of appendicitis, was rushed to a London hospital, and died from surgical shock during the operation. The families were devastated and listened in numbed silence as the will disclosed that George Garson was, in his daughter's words, "one of those charming men who live generously but leave very little when they die." The blow was terrific and one for which Nina was unprepared. She could only sit in shocked silence in her darkened house holding her sniffling infant as many of the lovely, exotic furnishings from their numerous trips abroad went out the door for debt payments.

Despite her parents' wishes, Nina intended to stay in London.

She did not want to become a poor relation, nor did she want her daughter treated as an invalid as she feared her family would do. So she went to work, managing a row of old townhouses that she inherited from her husband and raising her child independently. Almost immediately the Garson aunts, most notably Mrs. Alexina Logie Cathles, swept into their lives. "Aunt Alexina was a very strict Scotch Presbyterian," Greer recalled, "a most excellent woman, a so-called Tower of Strength, a very present help in time of trouble. Aunt Alexina was so fearful lest mother, because of her youth and beauty, became a 'Merry Widow' that she did everything in her considerable power to guard against it, including the gift of a widow's toque with a crepe veil so long and heavy it would have blacked my poor, little mother out."

Despite her mother's efforts, little Eileen Garson's earliest memories of this dreary environment were not pleasant. She remembered the house at 88 First Avenue as "small, dark and narrow and in a dreary part of London. But beauty-loving as she is, and resourceful, mother made the inside of our house as attractive as possible." Nina painted the rooms in bright colors. The bathroom was done in red and yellow, and the curtains throughout were scarlet and blue. They lived in "genteel poverty," a phrase that, Greer quipped, "is more attractive than the experience."

Nina's finances were worsened by her daughter's constant illnesses, including chronic bronchitis. Following the doctor's advice, Eileen was confined to bed every winter and for six weeks every spring and autumn. She was wrapped in blankets, clothed in flannel underwear and mufflers, and fed a variety of medications, cough syrups, and cod-liver oil. Not only was she prone to colds and bronchitis but to fainting spells as well. "By the time she was fifteen," Nina recalled, "she had enough illnesses to fill most lifetimes."

Despite the gloom of her home and her constant sickness, Eileen was not an unhappy child. From her insular existence sprang a remarkable imagination, and from close relationships with adults, rather than children, came a vibrant precocity. She knew her letters by the age of two and could read by the age of four. Nearby, at 3 Tower Hamlets Road, Forest Gate, Grandfather Garson read constantly to the bedridden little girl. "I lived the characters in every book he read," she recalled. "When I was first on the stage, I could memorize pages of dialogue quite effortlessly and veteran actors would ask me, 'Where did you learn that sense of timing?' I often felt like telling them, 'By talking to myself,' but feared I might be misunderstood. Nevertheless, the mechanics of the craft came very easily to me and I do believe I have long hours in the Land of Counterpane to thank for it."

Dismissing Grandmother Greer's dire observation ("Early precocity, early decay"), Nina was determined that Eileen would receive her education in a schoolroom and not at home as an invalid. So early one cold September morning, Nina dressed her weeping five-year-old with special care and stuffed pills and lozenges in with her lunch. Walking her to the door of Essex Road Elementary School, she sharply admonished the frightened Eileen to "keep your mouth closed, lest you catch a germ." That first day confirmed all the nightmarish visions that the child's considerable imagination could conjure up. Surrounded by children her own age, she became shy, withdrawn, and self-conscious. She was particularly embarrassed about her bright red curls and endured endless nicknames of "Ginger," "Copper Knob," and "Carrots." "I think I was pretty until I lost my teeth," she recalled. "After that, I was pale-faced, spindly and very earnest; had a lot of freckles, a huge smile and a perfectly understandable phobia against being photographed."

Sensitive about her looks and prim and scholastic in her behavior, she did not make many friends. "I was an odd kid, a 'queer 'un,' and no mistake," she said. Her studies became paramount. In the afternoons while other children were playing games, Eileen rode her bicycle far into the countryside with a small black tin of cookies to do field work for her botany class. On weekends, she studied music and singing. "I loved my Saturday mornings," she recalled, "and thought of them, priggishly, as 'Dedicated to the Arts.'" Her absorption in her studies did not endear her to the local children. Years later she recalled an edition of the school paper that revealed her caricature of young Eileen surrounded by a sea of books and studying an oversized volume "with my brow furrowed like the Grand Canyon of the Colorados." Concerned about Eileen's fragile health, inability to socialize, and tendency to sequester herself in her room with her books, Nina consoled herself with an ever-strengthening belief that her daughter's future lay in the sheltered world of academia.

CHAPTER 2

THE SCENE IS THE OPULENT MANSION of a steel magnate in Pittsburgh, Pennsylvania, during the spring of 1873. In the dining room the youngest member of the Scott family is teasing a newly arrived Irish maid named Mary Rafferty. "I've never been in Ireland," Ted Scott declares to Mary. "Is it true or just a fable about 'pigs in the parlor'?" With an impish smile, Mary replies, "We only have 'em in at night, sir. You sing 'em to sleep and never a grunt out of 'em till mornin'." The scene is from Metro-Goldwyn-Mayer's *The Valley of Decision*, and the players are Marshall Thompson and Greer Garson. Throughout her career on stage and in films, Greer always insisted that Ireland was her birthplace, due to a great nostalgia for her happy childhood days in County Down. "We had some kind neighbors in London," she would later recall, "but we lived very much to ourselves and longed for the summer months when we escaped back to Ireland for heavenly long visits to my grandparents' home in the sweet green countryside."

A visit to the annual county fair outside Castlewellan was an event little Eileen Garson always looked forward to. No single experience in her childhood world fascinated her as much as observing the animals for sale or staring in rapt attention as David Greer patiently imparted his knowledge about the crops and cattle from his farmlands. Once, when she was four years old and her grandfather was engrossed in an auction, she quietly slipped away to join observers of a talent contest. Watching the performers with growing curiosity, her shyness left her; and during a brief intermission between acts, she stood before the crowd. Although uninvited, she was heartily welcomed and launched into an enthusiastic recital of "Shamus

O'Brien's Speech Before the House of Lords." Even as she had opened with: "My lords, if you ask me, if in a lifetime I committed a treason or thought any crime . . ." the laughter and applause engendered by the delightful contrast between poem and speaker began. Only the appearance of her disapproving grandfather could stop her from repeating the performance.

Three years later she tried again. Volunteering to join a band of traveling actors in a competitive display, she was pleased to accept a box of chocolates as first prize. Just as she was begging to join the troupe, David Greer turned up, horrified, and led her away. "Although Celtic by birth and temperament, I was brought up in an English environment, with the English training in reserve, dignity, and the stiff upper lip," she recalled. "These are fine things but they do not make for an uninhibited nature and an expressive countenance—the two first essentials for an actor."

Although she looked forward every year to her summer vacation in County Down, "running about like a happy little ragamuffin" in the country twilight, fishing in the lake, or exploring her grandparents' dairy, the mischievous Eileen found the Greers' household to be even more strict than the Garsons'. She was allowed to explore the secret places where the parsley, thyme, and small spring onions grew and visit the farm tenants, who gave her cups of the good, black tea that smelled of peat, but her public performances were frowned upon. Each summer Sophia Greer would eye with suspicion and increasing disapproval her maturing granddaughter's fondness for entertaining the family.

Often Eileen would return from an afternoon in the park with her mother and act out the parts of people she had observed. Her favorite parlor trick was to portray a fat policeman quarreling with a thin young man. The adventures of her uncle, Robert Francis Greer, an administrator for the Crown in the Sheen States of Burma, and his scimitar, which was a prized family heirloom, were sources of inspiration for the imaginary stories she dreamed up for herself. While the family was amused and applauded and encouraged Eileen's talents, Grandmother Greer took her childish dreams more seriously. "No granddaughter of mine will ever lift her skirts on the stage," she said with a finality that no one dared to question. Instead, Eileen was encouraged to engage in household duties, and, although she displayed very little interest in them, she enjoyed watching Sophia Greer make blackberry wine and crochet. "If Grandmother had been of this generation," she recalled, "she would have been a Schiaparelli or a Chanel. She crocheted yards of the most exquisite stuff, and her quilted bedspreads were things of skilled beauty." Often Eileen would escape her grandparents' scrutiny to dabble with writing. From her earliest years, the mill horn, which roused the family from sleep, was a source of fascination. One contemplative afternoon, she wrote her first poem, an ode to the horn entitled "The Siren." "I remember playing under blue skies in County Down and even today, when I hear Irish music, tears well in my eyes," she said.

These idyllic Irish vacations came to an abrupt end when David Greer died. Sophia subsequently sold the gray stone house in Castlewellan, packed up her things, and crossed the sea to Scotstown, near the industrial port of Glasgow, to live with her daughter Evelyn, who married Dr. James Campbell-Murray in 1918. Uncle James was the father Eileen had never had, "a great fur, fish and feather man, a genius with a rod and reel, a born sailor, and the most completely integrated and humane man I have ever known." With his skill as a doctor, he sought to improve her health. He discovered that she had a heart murmur, the first sign of heart disease. "On two occasions, when I had heart attacks, which were rather bad, he saved my life," she said. Aunt Evelyn, with her infectious sense of humor and complete devotion to her family, was, in her niece's opinion, "unconsciously great."

Eileen also enjoyed the company of the children of James and Evelyn, Greer, David, and Sophia. "She was not a very good sailor," Sophia recalls, "but she and her mother came with us on our holidays on our yacht, the Tarka, in the summer. We always had to anchor some place where there was a hotel where she and her mother slept at night." In the years to come, Eileen would shyly explain that "it's rather mortifying that although I boast of being descended from Viking robbers and bold cattle rustlers, I'm a rotten sailor and terrified of cows!" She found fishing to be "a gentle sport without offense to God or man, and as I practice it, very little offense to the fish either."

One summer, when Nina was unable to join the family yacht trip, teenage Eileen wrote of their adventures: "Ahoy! This is mail from the good ship Tarka! You should see me hoist the jib sail or twiddle the wheels in the engine room. There are nine of us aboard and two sets of bagpipes. I'm disgraced this evening because when lunch for the entire party was laid in the salon, I happened to be at the wheel. I was so busy watching the buoys ahead that I didn't notice the wash from an overtaking steamer, and took the waves at just the wrong angle. And was there a commotion down below, even when I tried to point out that I wasn't so unlucky, because though every other thing, including the soup, had shot off the table, we hadn't spilled the salt. Oh well, sailors don't care. I am no yacht woman, more like the understudy to the cabin boy."

Christmastime was Eileen's favorite time of the year, despite the threat that winter posed to her health. With mounting excitement she would wait anxiously to see whether she would spend her holiday in Scotland with the boisterous Murrays or in London for a more worldly and elegant celebration with the Garsons. In Scotland she would watch hungrily as the house filled up with gifts from Uncle James's patients: hothouse fruits, bottles of wine, and delicious candies. When she was well enough to attend, she joined the family in their hunt for a tree in the snowy woods above Loch Lomond. "It always smelled wonderful," she would recall, "and had strings and strings of tinsel and brightly colored balls and other ornaments, treasured for years, with which we decorated it. We hung tinsel up, too, in the windows, behind the lace curtains, and it was lovely, watching the snow falling outdoors, feeling so warm and loved indoors. On Christmas day itself after church all the relatives and neighbors gathered around my uncle's festive board and how we ate. The special treat was haggis, that honorable symbol of Scotland, along with thistles and bagpipes." Afterward, Eileen would present a play for the family. "Consistent with the biographies of all actors," she said, "I would make up the plays and cast myself in the star parts."

In England, the highlights of the holiday were more austere. Aunt Alexina or Aunt Annie or Aunt Jean or Aunt Lilian would prepare roast goose with chestnut dressing and a mammoth plum pudding cheerily set ablaze in brandy. Afterward, the Garson children would be treated to a London pantomime. Robin Garson, son of George's younger brother Peter, remembers those holidays with his cousin. "My two brothers and I—much younger by sixteen years than

Greer—frequently among ourselves referred to her by our pet name, 'Eggy,'" he recalled. "This was because her initials were 'EEGG' and we young boys thought her magnificent red hair was the colour of a rich egg yolk. As you can imagine, Greer heartily disliked this 'pet name.' Auntie Lilian, a Garson widow, took us to the theater. She was a very grand lady who lived throughout our young days in various hotels in London or on the South coast. Whenever in London, particularly during the winter, she took us to pantomimes, the zoo, and Bertram Mills circus at Olympia." Sitting in the theater watching the entertainment, Eileen frequently got carried away. "I would throw myself into the whole cast's emotions so completely that I'd be exhausted for weeks afterwards," she admitted.

Meanwhile, Eileen's experiences with school were gradually improving. Her fellow classmates admired her feverish desire to learn and remarkable ability to excel in everything save mathematics. "She was always brilliantly clever," Sophia recalled, "head of the class and very athletic, winning the high jump at that school. She also enjoyed hockey, tennis, and fencing. Everything she did, she did well—she sang beautifully, played the piano, could draw and paint." Eileen's school recitations and amateur theatrics won special praise. The first play in which she starred was *The Merchant of Venice.* Years later, she would recall, "I wish you could have seen my Shylock! What a beard and what a deep voice. I sounded like a breaking heart in a cellar!" In 1914 she passed with honors the scholarship exam to attend East Ham Secondary. She credited Nina with much of her accomplishments. From her earliest childhood her mother had taught her that she could achieve any goal—despite illness. "Follow your star," she would say. "I must have looked over a cloud before I was born and picked my mother out for me," Eileen often marveled. "She was so patient, so dedicated to a most tiresomely delicate child, who was constantly ailing, always getting sick on trains and busses and, what a nuisance, needing large hankies passed. Mother never let go of the dream of making me healthy, and the vitality I later enjoyed was the triumph of mind over matter."

CHAPTER 3

IT WAS AT A HOUSE PARTY in London in 1917 that the fourteen-year-old Eileen first attracted the attention of a Cambridge law student named Edward Alec Abbot Snelson. His family also lived in Essex, and the two young people met frequently at local events. To Eileen he was "dark and powerful looking, with a determined chin, rather heavy black eyes and beautiful hands." He was a brilliant student and had a particularly fine singing voice. The vaguely sentimental friendship was encouraged by both families. "It was delicately understood that Alec admired me," Greer recalls, "and his mother told mine that he was waiting for me to grow up." Snelson continued to write increasingly ardent letters and to dedicate his published poems to her even after his family moved from the neighborhood. When Eileen did not return his attentions, the young man, her first beau, finally grew discouraged and stopped his correspondence.

Driven by her scholastic work and a growing desire to become an actress, Eileen had no time for romance or anything else. Of those years she would later recall in 1954: "Only the very young who are trying to make their way, who are riding the crest of the first burst of ambition are allowed to be self-centered." The desire was strengthened as she began to see plays regularly in London. "I was an introvert because of my shut-in life," she said, "and I longed to break out of it, to do something exciting for a change, something glamorous, something to throw me in contact with thousands of people, the people I was starved for." Her Uncle Peter Garson was a particular inspiration. "Acting was in the family," recalled his son Robin, "my father being a vaudeville artiste in addition to a professional artist of considerable merit."

Eileen's senior certificate from East Ham Secondary was tenable at Cambridge, Oxford, or the University of London. She wanted to try for a scholarship at the Royal Academy of Dramatic Art instead, but her mother refused to consider it. "Mother had given my childish talk of being an actress the amused attention one gives to a little boy who wishes to be a fireman or a tram conductor," she said. The family proposed that she become a teacher. "My grandmother Garson thought I was too delicate to earn a living and hoped I would marry some 'deserving young man,'" she recalled. "What a thing to wish upon a deserving, young man! I sat for my university scholarship and then I had to wait a year before proceeding. I remember being very grumpy about the whole thing because I really wanted to try for the RADA." In the interim Eileen was prodded to teach at a young girls' school within bicycling distance from the house. "Apparently I 'gave satisfaction,'" she said, "for the headmistress told my mother that I had a lively way of imparting knowledge, no trouble with discipline and was a 'born teacher.' Words of doom. Teaching is, along with nursing, one of the finest professions. But I knew it was not for me."

Eileen entered the University of London in September 1921. She had chosen it over the others because "to be in the city, shops, people, offices, theatres, above all theatres, appealed to me more than an academic backwater, however beautiful." Fellow collegians at the University of London labeled her "a unique blend of La Belle Sans Merci and Goldilocks and the Three Bears" in the college yearbook. She was something of a mystery. Certainly she was an earnest and devoted student who studied intermediate arts in her first year's apprenticeship before entering King's College in October 1923. It was apparent to students and faculty, as she earned a subsidiary BA in French in 1925 and took a number of accelerated courses in literature, classical history, and botany, that she wanted to complete her curriculum requirements as soon as possible. She rarely participated in school activities. She had few friends. Just exactly where she was outside the classroom was anybody's guess.

Her first stop after classes was the British Museum on Great Russell Street, for within the east wing was housed one of the world's finest libraries. With her special reader's tickets that granted her entry into private study rooms, the young scholar could study among the original manuscripts of Shakespeare, Dickens, Austen, Swift, and

Pope. Afterward, she could be found in Madame Tussaud's on Marylebone Road gazing at the famous personages enshrined in wax, or following the adventures of Charles Chaplin and Ronald Colman in the silent movie theaters. But no portion of London captured her heart like the West End. Beginning at Piccadilly Circus, the glamorous night world of London branched off to the northeast along such legendary thoroughfares as Haymarket, Charing Cross Road, St. Martin's Lane, Shaftesbury Avenue, and Leicester Square. Although bold and exciting experimentation in German stagecraft had shifted the spotlight away from London as the theater capital of the world, the city's four-hundred-year theatrical tradition was still widely renowned. And Eileen attended every play her budget would allow, gazing with a mixture of awe and envy at the actors.

In November 1926 Nina purchased a new, spacious home at 5 Tillotson Road in Ilford, ten miles from London. The contrast with "that hateful neighborhood" of boardinghouses was a dramatic and happy one. Nina transformed the modest old country house into, in her daughter's words, "the prettiest in Ilford . . . with brasses, chintzes and garden flowers." There was an apple and pear orchard, a small rose garden that Eileen tended, a Scottie dog to run about the yard, and ready access to Valentines Park and the bus route to Ilford Station.

In her last year at the university, Eileen cautiously relaxed her terrific concentration on study and took advantage of the faculty dances. The first one was a milestone. She experimented with face powder, cut her hair short, and bought high-heeled, Continental-styled shoes and a turquoise blue taffeta dress. "So thrilled was I," she recalls, "by the dancing and the music and the attentive young men that I seldom missed a faculty dance thereafter. It was a charming, lighthearted time of a kind I had never had before. The fun most girls have in these years, parties, beaux, dancing, mother had, and rightly, in view of my health, forbidden me." She took a job as art editor and supervisor of the Administration Department for *Encyclopedia Britannica*. Years later, Hollywood journalists became fascinated with her knowledge of arcane trivia. "Marguery sauce on the fish summons up the chef situation in Paris in 1869," observed one awestruck journalist, "with the reason why oysters happened to be included in Marguery's masterpiece. A Rhine wine elicits a geographical skirmish in the Palatinate, first crush or second crush, and the annual rainfall for that year."

Eileen graduated with her Bachelor of Arts and upper second class honors in English in 1926. It was conferred, however, not by the chancellor of the university, but by proxy. After purchasing a satin-lined and fur-trimmed robe for the impressive rite, making an appointment to be photographed in it, and having invited her family and friends to witness her "scholastic and sartorial triumph," she was stricken by pneumonia and missed the entire ceremony. "There is inspiration surely in receiving one's diploma in the company of class-mates and professors at an impressive ceremony," she said. "There is no glory in accepting it in a cardboard roller handed over by the mailman."

That fall Eileen Garson's life was at a crossroads. Her goal was a career in the theater, but she faced some formidable obstacles. She had little money, no influence to open magic doors, and a thoroughly disapproving grandmother. Eileen's cousin Sophia Murray was a regular guest at the Garson home in Ilford. "I often visited there and observed that they were more like sisters than mother and daughter. As I recall, Eileen always wanted to go on the stage, but in those days acting was not considered a fitting career for a young lady. As long as our Grandmother Greer was alive, she could not go on the stage." Nina then suggested that it would be good for her twenty-two-year-old daughter to do postgraduate work at the University of Grenoble. "I did not go to Grenoble with a definite scholastic aim in mind," she said. "I went—for the first time in my life—to major in fun, and a very happy year it proved to be; fruitful too, in fun and color and romance and companionship, if not in any solid additions to my academic credits."

Between her classes in ecclesiastical architecture, she managed to study French theater and engage in more amateur dramatics. Eileen shared a large, sunny room in a villa just outside the town with three other female students. The quartet often cut their classes to revel in French cinema, the university dances, hiking trips in the mountains, or long motor trips along the Rues des Alpes, visiting monasteries for wine tasting. It was the first time that she had lived with a group of girls her own age. "I like women," Eileen wrote to her mother, "and because so much is expected of them (they must be domestic angels, chic, poised, able to accept responsibility, yet seem to be unconscious of it, all roses and sunshine and frou-frou) I admire them enormously."

However, the most long-reaching consequence of her French sojourn was an unfortunate dive into a swimming pool. She damaged the lumbar vertebrae in her spine. A chiropractor in London was able to ease her pain and heal the resulting nerve damage, but the injury would continue to haunt her throughout her life.

Returning to London, Eileen was hired by LINTAS, the advertising branch of Lever Brothers in London, to run the research library for five pounds a week. LINTAS advertised its range of cleansing and household products in seventy-three countries, so Eileen's job of interpreting figures and percentages for the sales department was formidable. But she was a proficient employee, managing the department and handling six telephones and several assistants. "I played the part of the young business executive to the hilt," she recalled. "I dressed for the part, too, with nice, white linen suits, crisp shirts, and every hair in place." She became especially popular with her male coworkers. Her self-proclaimed ugly duckling years were over. No one agreed with this assessment as much as George Sanders, a coworker in the office next door, whose fame as an actor also lay in the future. "I never lacked for excuses to wander into the office of that gorgeous redhead," Sanders recalled, "where I could feast my eyes on her and enjoy her brilliant conversation."

It was not long before Eileen discovered that the head of the market research department had a connection to the theater. His sister was an actress who had recently returned from a Canadian tour, so Eileen arranged a meeting over lunch one wintry afternoon, and the result was a letter of introduction to Cyril Phillips, general business manager of the Birmingham Repertory Company. At the thought of joining this cradle of theatrical art that formed the burgeoning talents of Cedric Hardwicke, Laurence Olivier, Edith Evans, and Ralph Richardson, she recalled "a thousand little candles lit up inside me." Eileen appeared at Mr. Phillips's office in London and was granted an interview. Although pleasantly polite, Cyril Phillips was completely unimpressed by Eileen Evelyn Greer Garson, who admitted, "With my hair smoothed back and covered by a hat, and very little makeup, I did not look very spectacular. People who are unpro-

fessional look so unpromising to people who are professional."
Phillips informed her that casting had already been completed for the
coming season and showed her out. "I hear you have an excellent job
with an excellent firm," he told her. "If you take my advice, you will
stick to a good wicket." "Then," she recalled, "quite unconscious that
his next words were to give me my long-awaited passport to the stage,
he added, 'Emile Littler, our manager in Birmingham, is coming
down this afternoon and he would tell you the same thing."

Determined never again to be detoured from her ambition,
Eileen waited in the outer office for Mr. Littler to appear. Finally, a
door opened from an unexpected angle and a voice in back of her
said, "Where is the girl who has been waiting two hours to see me?
You? Come in. I have five minutes." Within an hour Eileen Garson
was traveling home in a state of wide-eyed elation. "I can't promise
you anything specific," Littler had told her, "but if you want to come
to Birmingham on Saturday, I'll see that you get an audition."

CHAPTER 4

IN DECEMBER 1931 an anxious Eileen Garson hurried down Station Street, clutching a new silver fox coat her mother had presented as a congratulatory gift. By the time she arrived at the door of the Birmingham Repertory Theatre, she was late. It was a habit that Nina had tried to curb by awakening Eileen at an especially early hour, but to no avail. As she scurried inside, she had little time to gaze upon the theater's exterior. It was, in the words of alumnus Sir Cedric Hardwicke, "a trim little theatre . . . its exterior walls beautifully kept, in sharp contrast to the dingy buildings around it, which were smeared with Black Country grime." Without pretension, the small theater seated an audience of only 464 people in a steeply raked auditorium. But its appearance belied the company's national status. For Sir Barry Jackson, who had founded the theater in 1913, also presented his productions through one of three theaters—the Kingsway, the Royal Court, or the Regent—and through a three-company, international touring circuit. As director of the Birmingham Repertory, Sir Barry strove for the highest ideals for his theater. Its mission was "to enlarge and increase the aesthetic sense of the public . . . to give living authors an opportunity of seeing their works performed, and to learn something from the revival of the classics; in short to serve an art instead of making that art serve a commercial purpose." The theater opened on February 15, 1913, with Shakespeare's *Twelfth Night*. A string of hits followed, including *Abraham Lincoln*, *The Barretts of Wimpole Street*, and *The Farmer's Wife*. George Bernard Shaw became an important contributor, and in 1929 Jackson's enthusiastic appreciation for the works of the playwright eventually transformed the quiet, neighboring West-of-England town of Malvern. As Stratford held annual theatrical tributes to Shakespeare, Sir Barry was determined that the Malvern Festival be devoted to Shaw. Consequently, many Birmingham players performed at the festival as well.

Eileen was met in the lobby by Emile Littler. The manager and licensee in Birmingham had recently returned to the Repertory after a four-year stay in New York, stage-managing *Yellow Sands.* Upon his reinstatement in autumn 1931, he had begun an earnest program of reorganization and renovation to improve the theater's uneasy financial situation. Even as he met with Eileen, he was planning price reductions, redesigning the program covers and auditorium, and returning the theater to the original repertory system, in which new plays were introduced two or three times a week. "A constantly changing repertory encourages a much more living and critical spirit among playgoers of all kinds," Sir Barry said with approval.

Littler introduced Eileen to Maxwell Wray, the Repertory's producer. After some peremptory questions, she was asked to step onto the stage. Walking away from them, her nervousness turned to dismay when she overheard Wray remark "Another red-head? I have engaged a red-head for the company already. I don't want another and you know it." Once on the stage, Eileen performed a few character sketches that had proven successful in Grenoble and impressed the company not only with her dynamic personality but with her looks as well. Removing her hat and gloves, and dressed in a costume provided for her, she was a beautiful twenty-seven-year-old with expressive blue-green eyes and striking red hair. Concluding with a recitation ("probably very bad," she later recalled, "for the producer scowled as if in pain and the stagehands went into a corner and chuckled in their beards"), she was asked to read for the role of a middle-aged Jewish schoolteacher, Shirley Kaplan, in Elmer Rice's *Street Scene.* Finishing her lines, she heard Wray grumble, "There will be no standing her. Too ladylike. Too brainy. A business woman with a B.A., too!"

The two men retired to the office, leaving Eileen alone on the stage. "It was a bad half-hour," she said, "one of the worst I ever spent." But finally Mr. Littler reappeared with orders to report for rehearsal in three weeks' time for *Street Scene.* The salary was three pounds a week. Eileen bargained for four pounds and got it.

Resigning from the Lever Brothers agency, Eileen moved out of her mother's home and into a theatrical boardinghouse in Birmingham. The staff at LINTAS presented her with a jade-green dressing gown and a black tin makeup box as farewell gifts. The precious black box was under her arm when she arrived at the Birmingham theater for her first day. With her gift for dialects, Eileen played the Jewish schoolteacher most convincingly in rehearsals. Only Maxwell Wray was unimpressed with the newcomer, who kept to herself and was forever wrapped in the silver fox for warmth. "He tried in every way to make me unhappy, but failed," she later said. "Many a laugh was had at my expense. If an argument arose, he would point at me and say, 'Let's ask the Big Brain to decide the question for us.' When the company assembled for rehearsals, he never failed to ask loudly, 'Is the Duchess of Garson present? Two o'clock and time to begin—if it's all right with you, Your Grace.' In those first months at the Birmingham, I was immune to every slight. Since I am of the school of thought that believes one must suffer for one's art I not only expected martyrdom, but rather enjoyed it."

January 30, 1932, was opening night, a thrill Eileen Garson never forgot. "The first-nighters laughed and cried in the right places," she recalled. "My big scene got a hand and Henry Fielding, who played my father, came up to me in the wings and congratulated me!" She made another friend that night. Character actress Winifred Hindle, who played Greta Fiorentino in the play, gave Eileen a hug. As she was leaving the theater after her performance, Jewish families began crowding around her with invitations to their homes for dinner. At the final performance Eileen was even more pleased to hear that her contract was being renewed.

If theater life was not as glamorous as Eileen had supposed, it was certainly a busy and rewarding one. She was presented in a new play on an irregular monthly basis. The Victorian comedy *Ten Nights in a Barroom* opened on March 5, followed by Margaret Kennedy and Basil Dean's *The Constant Nymph* on the twenty-sixth. Monckton Hoffe's *Many Waters* opened on April 23; and *Jane's Legacy*, Eden Phillpotts's "comedy of laughter," followed on May 21. "I lived like a troglodyte," she recalled. "We worked constantly, dashed out for a bite of lunch, went back to the theatre, dashed out again for the evening meal then back for the evening performance and never saw the sunlight or breathed a lungful of air except on Sundays. But no matter— I was an actress!"

For his part, Emile Littler was pleased with his new actress and the healthy profits that his modifications had brought about. By the end of Eileen's first season, he was proud to declare to the company that the Birmingham Repertory Theatre had enjoyed the highest attendance of any previous year.

During her second season, Eileen fell in love. The actor was Michael Barry, a handsome, six-foot-three Repertory player whose intensity and dedication to his craft matched her own. He had appeared with her in *Street Scene* and *Jane's Legacy,* and the pair played lovers in *The Constant Nymph.* She considered him "a very poetic young man. He would go off alone on Sundays, a book of verse in his hand, the wind in his hair—until I came along, then we went off together. The whole company was in a seethe of sentiment over our romance. It got as far as the wedding ring and a promise from Sir Basil Bartlett, who played the character roles with the Repertory, to act as best man." Disturbed with the notion that her daughter might marry an actor, Nina encouraged Alec Snelson to correspond with Eileen once again. But preoccupied with her work and Michael, she barely skimmed the letters that began to come on a regular basis and described his graduation from Cambridge, subsequent two-year term at the Inns Court in London, high marks on the Indian Civil Service examination, and his position in India as a junior judge. He wrote that he had seen her at a distance a few times at the University of London but had not approached her fearing his presence might not be welcome. Then suddenly, in May 1932 during the run of *Jane's Legacy,* Alec wrote that he was coming home on leave to marry her. In his letter, he enclosed photographs of engagement rings from Cartier's. "I'm flattered by your proposal, naturally," Eileen wrote in return, "but also flabbergasted. It's quite impulsive of you to propose to a girl you have not seen for ten years. It is also fantastically idealistic of you, for how could you possibly know what kind of person I have become. I will not possibly be able to see you at the moment in any case. The theatre is my one real interest, which would make me a very unsatisfactory wife." When she received no immediate reply, Eileen assumed their uneasy relationship was over.

Meanwhile, George Bernard Shaw's latest play, *Too True to Be Good,* had opened at the Malvern Festival on August 6, 1932. The bizarre fantasy, incorporating religion, the medical profession, and the evils of postwar society, subsequently ran in Birmingham for the usual pre-London three weeks. On September 13 it opened at the New Theatre in London for fifty-five performances. London producer H.K. Ayliff planned to take the show on an international circuit to Oxford, Bournemouth, Brighton, Sheffield, Liverpool, Edinburgh, and Glasgow. Entranced with Eileen's performance as Tana in Robert Sherwood's *The Road to Rome,* which opened at the Birmingham Rep. in September, he offered her the leading role of the patient in *Too True to Be Good.* The offer was irresistible—except for the thought of leaving Michael Barry behind. Eileen turned to her friend Winifred Hindle. "Experience is what you need," the older woman told her. "All kinds of experience, as much of it as possible, as quickly as possible and touring is what will give it to you." Her engagement to Michael Barry was shortly dissolved. "Michael was someone with whom I might have been very happy," she recalled. "But for an early and romantic marriage to come along, hand in hand with a career, does not seem to be in the cards for most actors. We are attracted to the theater because of our emotional natures yet find it harder to fit marriage into the pattern of our lives than do people in any other profession. No wonder so many of us are neurotic. We find any kind of a complete and satisfying personal life is our major problem."

The tour of *Too True to Be Good* lasted for twelve weeks. Significantly, it was the first time Eileen requested that her name be printed in the program as Greer Garson ("She had never really liked the name Eileen," Robin Garson recalled). In a letter to her mother, she wrote: "In Oxford, among the academic set, we interpreted Mr. Shaw's play (Not one of his best; 'Too Bad To Be True' we call it) as cerebrally as possible. In Bournemouth and Brighton, our audience was mostly retired Army officers and their wives, genteel, elderly people, and invalids; in Sheffield, which is a lively industrial town where the people are very quick in their reactions, we speeded up our tempo, and were on our toes. Then to Liverpool, which is frankly proletarian, with audiences that want their entertainment plain-spoken and no nonsense or 'uppity,' if you please. From there to Edinburgh, the aristocratic and cultural center of Scotland where we read our lines with all the finesse possible, and then across to Glasgow, lusty and stimulating and liking its plays and players to be the same. Thus, week to week, fast and slow-paced performances, then forthright and nuanced performances until we felt like lightning change artists of characterization." Her opening in Glasgow, where she performed before the Murrays, was an especially rewarding treat. "I'll never forget when she entertained me and my pals—about half the school—to the best seats in the stalls in the Theatre Royal," recalls her cousin Greer, "and a special visit backstage afterward. A memory cherished by all."

Greer found that her learning experiences were not restricted to the stage. "There is a tradition in the English theatre," she wrote to her mother, "that the stars of plays on tour do not stay in the big hotels but in much recommended 'digs' (boarding houses) because they prefer 'home cooking.' A novice going out for the first time is told, 'Now, be sure when you go to Sheffield to stay at Mother Bradbury's, her gooseberry tart melts in your mouth!' You stay at Mother Bradbury's and it turns out to be the most pestilential week you have ever spent. The gooseberry tart is a short cut to dyspepsia, the bathroom is a mile away, the hot water is exiguous and everything is horrid. But the mantelpiece and walls are covered with pictures of noted actors and actresses gratefully and eloquently autographed 'To Mother Bradbury—We Had A Wonderful Time,' 'From Home To Home,' 'So Cosy, All My Thanks,' and so on. You read the fading inscriptions more carefully and realize that Miss Gladys Cooper has not been there for seven years and just as you are wondering how she could have, even then, you are enlightened. For less than fifteen minutes before your train leaves, Mother Bradbury comes in, lets you know how delightful it has been having you with her, and asks for your photograph, 'With a nice inscription, please, dearie.' You would miss your train if you tried to put her off and you think that, anyway, it would be nice to be up there between Gladys Cooper and Dame Sybil Thorndike and you say to yourself, 'I shall not pass this way again, any good deed that I can do, therefore . . . ' So you write your terrific recommendation as others have done before you and still others, alas for them, will do after you, and are on your way. It is not easy, but even the hardships are fun, living in drab 'digs,' hardly large enough to turn around in, cooking over a single gas burner, washing stockings in a community basin, and stretching four pounds a week to the limit."

What Greer did not tell her mother was that she became seriously ill. Her dual role as the patient in the first act and a native girl in the second act was the most physically demanding one that she had ever played. Between acts there was always a hurried commotion backstage as her maid used wet sponges to remove her makeup and then blackened her face and body and applied a wig and numerous bracelets, anklets, and jewels. Then, suddenly, the call-boy would shout, "One minute more—You're on, Miss Garson!" and she was onstage with the opening line, "Oh, the monotony of it here!" "Somehow I managed to deliver that line with a straight face," she recalled, "and then went through the set, every pore open and shivering uncontrollably because the body makeup was still damp. Although my understudy's eyes grew brighter and brighter when she heard my racking cough, and watched me painting my raw throat with iodine, I never missed a performance."

When she returned to Birmingham with pneumonia and strep throat, Greer was still ill but was the proud bearer of a letter from George Bernard Shaw that she showed to her mother. "Sarah Bernhardt broke one's heart," it read. "Ellen Terry mended it. You, Miss Garson, are the new Ellen Terry. Never leave the theatre. I shall be very disappointed indeed if you go to Hollywood to work with magic lanterns." Through sheer will and determination and despite Nina's numerous protestations, she managed to appear in *Musical Chairs, When the Crash Comes,* and *Infinite Shoeblack* through the spring of 1933. But the persistent illness developed into bronchitis and tonsillitis. Surgery was required, so Nina called for her brother-in-law. "As soon as my infection had subsided enough to make surgery safe, they sharpened their manicure scissors and slit my throat," Greer recalls. "Because of my heart, I could not take an anesthetic and if Uncle Jim had not come down for 24 hours and held my hand, I should have died of fright." Despite Dr. Murray's success, she convalesced very slowly. "Then, the nurse made the horrible mistake of giving me a glass of lemon juice," she recalls. "My throat hemorrhaged for days, and for weeks I couldn't talk at all. Garson, speechless, was Garson in a brand new role!"

One afternoon when Nina brought her a tea tray, two letters and a bouquet of red roses were lying on the napkin. One envelope was addressed from Birmingham. Emile Littler wrote that, despite her promising performances, the Birmingham Repertory Theatre had no choice, in view of her long and unfortunate illness, but to cancel her contract. The other letter and the roses were from Nagpur, India. Alec Snelson had heard of her illness through a correspondence with Nina and was coming home to visit her.

CHAPTER 5

"WHEN A YOUNG MAN HAS MONEY and leisure and determination, he can do quite a bit with a girl who is ill, and discouraged," Greer remarked of that fateful summer of 1933. By the time Alec Snelson arrived, Nina had taken rooms for her recuperating daughter at Kiln Cottage, Piddinghoe, Sussex, at three guineas a week. He took rooms at a nearby hotel. The sick young woman that he encountered, who tried to impress him with a few Birmingham press notices, made him all the more determined that marriage and not acting should be her future career. "There I was in bed, trying to look soignee in my frilliest bed-jacket," Greer recalled, "but succeeding only in seeming what I was, a thin, sick girl, pale and spiritless. 'Poor little thing,' he must have thought. 'Trying to make good on the stage. Well, I will press my suit during her convalescence and then there will be no more of this.'"

When she was well, Alec took Greer for long, leisurely drives through the countryside in his sports car. There were walks in the flowering lanes, long talks, and picnics. In the evenings he played the piano and composed a song for her. She found him endlessly patient and kind and thoughtful and, although he did not appeal to her romantically, their tastes and educations were similar. "We were very congenial," Greer would recall, "and anyone who is very much in love with you takes on a glow. He had a sort of dark humour which he managed to keep under cover and everyone thought him delightful and what a 'fortunate girl I was!'" Aunt Alexina wrote to Greer: "You've proved that you can entertain an audience, but you see what a hard life it is. How are you going to get in again? I do hope you marry this young man." As the summer came to an end and Greer still refused to give up acting, Alec offered a compromise. She could go to India with him immediately after they were married and come back to London in the fall to appear in a play. Faced with a decision that she could not make, Greer delayed her response to him by inviting him to the Malvern Festival. His face dark with prejudice, Alec acquiesced and attempted to be friendly to her Birmingham friends despite his disapproval of their profession. Winifred Hindle drew Greer aside and whispered, "Is this 'India'? Oh Greer, oh no!" "But as evening went on," Greer recalled, "and Alec got Winifred's coat for her, closed a window because of the draught and later, played the piano and sang for us, she changed her opinion. It carried a great deal of weight with me; more than it might have done, perhaps, if I had not been in so dispirited a state of mind." It seemed that everyone was advising her to marry the ambitious young judge. On September 28, 1933, in the parish of Westminster, she did.

Her doubts about her compatibility with Snelson proved to be correct on their two-week honeymoon. She had suggested France as their destination, but when Alec discovered her fluency with that language, he chose the Harz Mountains in Germany. "You will be dependent on me there," he said. "The country was beautiful," Greer wrote. "A Hansel and Gretel landscape, the houses looking like toys made of gingerbread and brown sugar against the dark mountains. And the little village where we stayed was something of a holiday center, the people wore bright clothes, were childlike, and gay. We should have had great fun but almost at once I realized that Alec and I were—shall I say 'temperamentally unsuited'?"

As an only child, Greer had become used to a great deal of privacy. Alec never left her alone for an hour. He was, in her estimation, "possessive to the point of being medieval." He cross-examined her about the men who had been "in love" with her and refused to take her out dining in the evening because, he insisted, tourists and students had stared at her. He tried to persuade her to come to live in India permanently and perform in the amateur theatricals produced by the officers' wives in Nagpur. She would be Queen of the Dramatic Clubs, he argued. Appalled at the thought, Greer refused, recalling the words of Alec's friend, Peter Stales-Corernam, who had written to her: "India is a damned lovely, un-Christian-like country and I am longing to get out of the place." Alec's enjoyment of outdoor exercise also strained their marriage. One five-hour hike, on which he insisted she accompany him, inflamed her spinal injury.

When she returned to London, weak and ill, Greer nearly collapsed in Nina's arms on the dock. "That two weeks was the best piece of acting I have ever done," she confided to her family. On November 13 Alec departed for India, accepting his wife's wish to stay behind for the winter. Greer drove from the pier at Southampton to Ilford, where a concerned Nina put her immediately to bed. Not only was she seriously ill with pneumonia, but her back injury had worsened, affecting the sciatic nerve in her left leg. "Skeleton gone a little wrong," the family doctor said, which struck Greer as "an idiotically understated diagnosis." In agonizing pain, she fainted whenever she attempted to stand up. She lay in bed as an invalid for four months.

In desperation, Nina transported her daughter to the seaside resort of Brighton, hoping that its famous salt baths might help. "Pleasing decay is a very English taste," observed Britain's *Independent*. "It is best indulged in at the seaside, especially off-season, when wind and rain enhance the melancholy romance of cracked stucco, rusting ironwork, and boarded-up shops. Brighton is a supreme example, with its faded glamour combined with raucous vulgarity." The town owed its fame to Dr. Richard Russell, known as "Dr. Brighton," who had published a book in 1750 praising seawater for its medicinal virtues. Like many fellow sufferers, Greer was lodged at Dr. Brighton's Tavern. She found it to be a particularly depressing site for a family Christmas. Nina tried to enliven her daughter's spirits by gathering every morsel of reading material that she could find. Among the newspapers and magazines was a copy of *British Weekly*, which contained a special holiday supplement. A touching short story by a little-known writer named James Hilton was featured. Its title was "Goodbye, Mr. Chips."

By early January Greer was able to walk along the Palace Pier. "Nobody was ever lower in luck, funds and spirit than I was," she recalled. One morning she came to an open booth that advertised: "Madame Stella—Fortunes Told by Tea Leaves, Cards, Crystal Ball and Modern Miraculous Methods—Two and Six." She went in. A gypsy woman took a chair opposite her, collected her fee, and bent over the crystal. She proceeded to give Greer a hair-raisingly accurate account of her past, describing George Garson's death "from the knife it was, and you a babe in arms at the time." The woman saw two more reverses in Greer's health ahead, then good health and a long lifeline. She also saw a marriage, "full of jealousies, but divided like a fork," and added that her heart line was not a happy one, criss-crossed with incidents. The crystal revealed another marriage in the future, which would be happy. She complained that the crystal was crowded with people—which meant that Greer would be much in the public eye; perhaps a great dancer, a great speaker, or a politician. She foresaw a long journey across the water and living and working in another land. She saw two shining objects—Success and Gold—and a scandal many years hence.

Feeling encouraged, Greer began writing letters to the various London managements again, and within a month she returned to London with her mother. "I don't think there was anything super-natural about Madame Stella's divinings," she said. "I just think she read my mind—and what I wanted was so ever-present at the front of my mind. And because I wanted it so badly, of course I got it, bad back, sore throat and damp spirits notwithstanding." Her chance came in the form of an interview with producer Sydney Carroll one May afternoon at his office on Charing Cross Road. Greer, like any stage hopeful, was well aware of Carroll's distinguished standing in the English theatrical world. A noted drama critic for the *Sunday Times* and the *Daily Telegraph* with his own theater troupe, Carroll was busy inaugurating a series of lavish productions at the Open Air Theatre in Queen Mary's Garden in Regent's Park. Entertainments at the 1,187-seat amphitheater had been initiated by Ben Greet, whose Woodland Players entertained in Edwardian times. Now Sydney Carroll intended to resurrect the tradition.

"A striking girl with exquisitely red hair and the unusual name of Greer Garson came to see me to ask for an engagement, " he re-called. "I was struck by the depth and richness of her voice. It made music for me. It was soft and yet penetrating. Her elocution was, if anything, a little too precise, almost pedantic in its accuracy. With a singularly sweet smile the young woman quickly convinced me of her possibilities. Very well educated and of unusual intelligence, she sug-gested, in her poise and authority, a future tragedienne." Immediately signing her to a summer-long contract, he arranged an audition with his producer, Robert Aikens, who promptly employed her as an extra in Shakespeare's *The Tempest,* which opened on June 5. Although billed thirty-second on the program as Iris, Greer was thrilled to finally be back on the stage—and for the first time in London. A week later, she was cast in *The Comedy of Errors*—starring Dennis Hoey, Ben Greet, and Andrew Leigh—as a "Courtesan" with Iris Hoey. The director was her old nemesis Maxwell Wray.

With little to do, Greer laid siege to Sydney Carroll's office regularly, urging him to give her a chance in a featured role. Carroll finally acquiesced, casting her, despite assistant director Maxwell Wray's protestations, as Hermia in *A Midsummer Night's Dream.* With less than a week to memorize her part, Greer spent every moment preparing for her featured debut on June 19. After waiting a few days to receive her summons, she went down to the theater. To her utter surprise, she found the company already in rehearsals. Catching sight of her, Wray yelled out, "Where the hell have you been?" in front of the startled company. Taking her aside, he insisted that he had been unable to contact her and had recast Margaretta Scott as Hermia. She could work as the understudy or not at all. Needing the money—and too nonplussed to defend herself—she swallowed her pride and accepted the part, which included a walk-on role carrying garlands of roses—the female equivalent of a spear-carrier.

Despite her best efforts to convince Sydney Carroll to give her another chance, she continued playing walk-ons for the rest of the summer. Thus she could be found playing "spear-carriers" at the daily matinees and evening performances of Shaw's *Androcles and the Lion* and *The Six of Calais.* When *Calais* closed on July 21, Greer was temporarily out of a job. Carroll was not able to find another part for her until Shakespeare's *Romeo and Juliet* opened on August 7. Again she would be an extra. On July 31, haunting the backstage dressing rooms before *Romeo and Juliet,* she found her coworkers clustered together around the latest copy of the *Daily Telegraph.* Louis B. Mayer, head of Metro-Goldwyn-Mayer, America's most powerful motion picture studio, was in London, planning to build an Anglo-American film industry alliance.

Under the terms of the Cinematograph Act of 1928 created by the United Kingdom Board of Trade, all foreign film studios were expected to subsidize British productions or at least produce their own series of films utilizing local filmmakers and actors. Although

L.B. Mayer had managed to pull some diplomatic strings and avoid financing a full 20 percent of the British film industry, as required, he did indeed want to make films in England. The *Telegraph* reported that Mayer intended to open a studio outside London and stock it with promising English talent. But to Greer, as she returned to her gloomy flat, the fairy-tale world of Hollywood seemed a million miles away. "It was well for me that I was not interested in films at the time," she said, "for you had to be of doll-like beauty to photograph at all well in British films then and someone with an odd face like mine might have fared disastrously."

In September, Sydney Carroll attempted to get Greer the lead in a Winter Garden Theatre presentation of *Androcles and the Lion,* but Shaw demanded that a "name" play the part. Once again, Greer played a "spear-carrier." On October 13, as the play's run concluded and the Shakespearean season drew to a close, Greer was freed from Carroll's contract. "This sort of thing might easily have gone on for the rest of my life," Greer later told London's *Sunday Express,* "for listening to English actors tell their thousand and one hard luck stories made me realize, more keenly than ever before, how rare a bird is success in the theatre, and I was afraid to try for greener pastures lest they prove to be only a mirage. I had begun to believe that my family and friends were right when they insisted that the theatre was a closed circle not to be penetrated by the use of legitimate means." Her mother could only offer the same advice, "Keep faith in your star."

Greer moved back into the University of London's Women's Club. Dining one evening alone at the club, certain that her illness at the Birmingham Rep. had forever destroyed her chance for a stage career, she read her mail. There was a letter from Alec, enclosed with a ticket to Nagpur, which entreated her once again to give up acting and join him. As she picked up the University's Appointments List, it occurred to Greer that she had not seen her husband for over a year. Like her career, her marriage was in shambles. As she drank a toast of sherry to her "Last Night as an Actress," wavering between a desire to rescue her marriage or to accept the tutorship at Cambridge that the List offered, she was spotted by a well-dressed woman at the opposite end of the restaurant. After staring at her intently for some time, she approached Greer's table and introduced herself as Sylvia Thompson.

She was a playwright who had recently finished a comedy for the stage called *The Golden Arrow* and, with her collaborator, Victor Cunard, was currently casting the feminine lead. She invited Greer to come to an audition the following morning at ten o'clock at the Whitehall Theatre near Trafalgar Square. Greer immediately accepted and spent the night reading the play. As envisioned by Thompson and Cunard, Fanny Field was a vivacious American mistress to an important English politician. When he refuses to take her on a train (named *The Golden Arrow*), she impetuously books passage for herself and embarks on an affair with a dashing Frenchman. When the politician realizes his mistake, the lovers are happily reunited.

At the audition next morning were Sylvia Thompson, Victor Cunard, Maurice Brown, the producer of *The Golden Arrow,* and the play's star and director, twenty-seven-year-old Laurence Olivier. Recalling a young American couple she had met at dinner during her Birmingham days, Greer borrowed some of their inflections of speech for her reading and won Thompson and Olivier over completely. Greer Garson and Fanny Field were one and the same: beautiful, willful, sometimes capricious, but strong and compassionate. Maurice Brown, however, was not impressed. He wanted Carol Goodner, the actress who had played the part in New York, for the role.

Of her theater years, Greer often complained that producers seemed to be allergic to her, one way or another. Maurice Brown, like Maxwell Wray, was such a case. During one afternoon session the first week of rehearsals, he suddenly interrupted the actors by pointing at Greer and saying aloud, "Kind of odd charm, but I ask myself—does she attract me sexually?" Greer soon realized that this odd bit of behaviorism was the opening gun in a campaign against her. "He was a strange one," she recalled, "with one earring and whips on the wall. I'm sure I was too young and wholesome for him." After a week of criticizing everything from the gown that she wore to her hair, he suddenly announced that he could not take responsibility for a production with an unknown girl named Greer Garson in the lead. The company was dismissed.

The following afternoon, Laurence Olivier telephoned his cast and crew, requesting everyone to report for rehearsal the next day under a new management. He explained that he alone intended to produce *The Golden Arrow.* Thereafter, Greer and her costar developed a swift rapport. "Having Larry as a friend was the luckiest thing that ever happened to me," she declared. Not since Michael Barry had she met a man who intrigued and inspired her, whom she admired and immediately felt at ease with as a director. She was impressed with his experimental acting methods: "To try out little things on our own. There were always little exercises he invented, adventures of the imagination, to keep the material fresh." Observing that his part as the rather stuffy politician was not as good as hers, Greer was grateful to find that "with his usual enthusiasm for whatever seems most worth the doing, he subordinated his job as an actor to his job as a director and went out of his way to build up my performance." Nina and cast members began to suspect a romance. For her part, Greer did nothing to allay their suspicions. She could not deny her attraction to this talented man who resembled Michael Barry in many ways.

They met frequently after hours, often at the Ivy, a popular theater restaurant near Covent Garden. Greer was eager to share Olivier's belief that the theater was the ultimate expression of an actor's art. She also learned to mistrust Hollywood and motion pictures when he related his own unfortunate experience. Summoned to America in 1931 by Metro-Goldwyn-Mayer to make *Queen Christina* with Greta Garbo, he was fired when Garbo chose John Gilbert for the part. Attempting a career at the RKO studio, he made only three pictures in two years. After that discussion, Greer thought of Hollywood as "Babylon-on-the-Pacific, a citadel of make-believe and meretricious values."

One last-minute costume change nearly destroyed the morale of the company. In the third act, Greer wore a sparkling white dress with an upstanding collar ("like a whiskbroom," she remembered). Examining his costar, Olivier was furious at Sylvia Thompson, who had chosen it, declaring that it was lacerating Greer's neck and that only a masochist would enjoy playing farce in a straitjacket. Much to Miss Thompson's consternation, the costume was exchanged for a soft, white, collarless crepe gown.

After a tryout at the New Theatre, Oxford, *The Golden Arrow* opened at the Whitehall on Thursday, May 30, at 8:40 P.M. That evening, Greer approached the theater from the back, unwilling to look at the glowing marquee, which she thought of as "a signature on a promissory note I might not be able to pay." Entering her dressing room, which was overflowing with flowers, she found a note from Olivier: "To say thank you would be a hopelessly inadequate way of telling you what I really think. Even hard-boiled financiers weaken and become full of gratitude and admiration. I am sending you flowers in the hope that they will tell you over and over again that the management and whole cast rejoice in the great success you will be tonight. Your success in the Birmingham Repertory Theatre will be only a stepping stone to far greater triumphs in which I shall rejoice."

That evening's performance moved like clockwork until the close of the first act, when panic erupted backstage. Greer had lost her glamorous nightgown, especially styled for her by Sulka of Bond Street. Everyone, from the stagehands and actors to the electricians, searched for the costume in vain. As the call-boy made his second rounds, Olivier threw a pair of his own pajamas at his tearful leading lady and instructed her to play the scene for comedy instead of chic. As it turned out, the scene was such a hit that Greer wore the pajamas until the end of the play's run—even after her nightgown was discovered under boxes of flowers and congratulatory notes. When the curtain came down at the end of the performance and Olivier appeared to greet the applauding audience, his admiration of his protégée was apparent to everyone. "It is a pleasure to introduce to you Greer Garson, who is—I won't only say promising—but already a very polished young actress, who, tonight is making her London debut. You will, I am sure, be seeing a great deal of her." In his *Sunday Times* review, James Agate wrote: "In his capacity as impresario, [Olivier] invited us to welcome a young actress 'in whom there are undeniable and obvious potentialities.' The ears nearly fell off my head at hearing the title of transcendent greatness specifically declaimed for a newcomer!"

Staying awake until the morning papers were delivered, Greer and Nina read the laudatory reviews while clutching their robes in the misty morning chill. "Miss Garson is to be congratulated," *The Bystander* opined, "on having got through the immense monologue with success and without manifestly boring people on both sides of the footlights. She has a pleasant personality, a voice that one can hear, and little tricks of gesture which will be most profitable if she does not allow them to develop into mannerisms. If she is to become a stage star—and I believe she will—I suggest changing that not very euphonious name. If, however, the films snap her up—and I suppose they will—doubtless a Christian name beginning with 'Gre' and a surname beginning with a 'Gar' will be an immense asset." The play that Greer described as "too slender to survive" ultimately ran three weeks. Her brief romance with Olivier ended just as suddenly when he moved on to more ambitious projects and fell in love with another ambitious young actress who had just made her own stunning West End debut. Her name was Vivien Leigh. Suddenly lonely and in need of a change, Greer rented a new, beautifully appointed flat closer to the West End at 81 South Audley Street and invited her mother to move in with her. Now more intent than ever to concentrate on her career, she consoled herself with the thought that, although *The Golden Arrow* was a flop, she was now a West End celebrity.

CHAPTER 6

AFTER THAT TRIUMPHANT OPENING NIGHT of *The Golden Arrow,* Greer found her life to be "exactly like a film that, running backwards, is suddenly reversed and begins to run forward." James Bunting, one of the producers of *Golden Arrow,* was the first to offer her a screen test. On June 18, 1935, he wrote: "I have made arrangements with my company, and we would be very glad to give you a full and comprehensive test on Friday afternoon of this week, if that is convenient to you. The test would be made in the vicinity of Wardour Street, and would be in the nature of a try-out for your suitability as lead in my next picture, which starts in the middle of next month. With regard to 'Golden Arrow,' you may have heard that my backers and myself considered it inadvisable to stage a transfer, with the theatre business in the state it is at the moment, but, at the same time, I have asked the Daniel Mayer Company and my own agents to try and find a suitable play for yourself which, in consideration of your really magnificent performance in 'Golden Arrow,' we should be very happy to put on in the West End, if that meets with your approval."

Although she declined the screen test, Greer was delighted to accept the lead Bunting secured for her in the London production of Samson Raphaelson's American play *Accent on Youth.* But since rehearsals were not due to begin until August and she was anxious to follow up her overnight success, Greer impulsively signed on with Sir Seymour Hicks in his revival of *Vintage Wine* with only four days to spare. Her featured role was that of Nina, a naive young woman who marries Charles Popinot, a wealthy wine-grower in Rome who is actually much older than she supposes. His grown sons initially disapprove, but Nina wins everyone over with her charm and diligence and even converts her husband from his capricious ways. Sir Seymour opened *Vintage Wine* at the large, opulent Victoria Palace Theatre on Victoria Street on June 22, 1935. When Greer emerged triumphantly opening night, he rewarded her with a bouquet of flowers nine feet high.

"Sir Seymour was a terror," Greer recalled. "A well-beloved comedian and a master craftsman of farce and timing (I learned about timing from him) it was a liberal education to play the long, two-hour scenes with him, and something of a torment, too, for he was both a martinet and a rascal." She could barely control herself from bursting into laughter when the actor would ad-lib his lines or make quiet, sarcastic remarks about the audience or her performance while they were on the stage. He delighted in her surprised reactions when he put cracker crumbs down her back in one scene and splashed toast into her coffee in another. "Although I lost eight pounds while I was with him," she said, "and was a candidate for a psychopath ward when I left, he gave me an invaluable training in developing that double-track mind which an actor must have in order to cope with extraneous disturbances and yet play out a scene."

Of *Vintage Wine*, the *Daily Telegraph* declared, "Greer Garson is a most important newcomer. In the part previously played by Claire Luce she gave a splendid performance." The *Daily Mail* commented, "The revival which Mr. Seymour Hicks presented at the Victoria Palace on Saturday night offered us once more the double pleasure of deft comedy and in authorship and acting. . . . The audience, enthusiastic throughout, applauded when Mr. Seymour Hicks paid due tribute to Miss Garson's skill in learning her part in four days." The *London Times* added, "Miss Garson . . . keeps up her end with gay and sparkling versatility."

In her London column, "The Stage of the Present Day," Dorothy Drake wrote of the West End's latest sensation: "Miss Greer Garson has a personality which is arresting on account of its vitality and originality, her coloring is unusually attractive with hair of that light auburn that artists call Florentine red and the pose of her figure, a shade too tall perhaps for perfection is full of repose and graceful lines. A friend told me that it was while she was at a party A.K. Lawrence saw her, asked her who she was and said, 'I want to paint her just as she is looking now with her head thrown up like that.' The result was a very striking portrait of her in the season's exhibition at Burlington House. . . . It will be interesting to see her in the new American play 'Accent on Youth.'" In her new play Greer played the part of Linda Brown, a beautiful young stenographer in love with her boss, a middle-aged celebrated playwright. Completely oblivious to his secretary's romantic inclination, the writer becomes aware of her affection only after producing a play about an older man in love with a younger girl. Nicholas Hannen, known as "Beau Hannen" for his good looks and elegant dress, was her costar. He was one of Greer's most diversely talented leading men, popular as bigger-than-life heroes in *The Dynasts* and *The Conquering Hero* as well as comedies with actress-wife Athene Seyler. Greer would later recall: "He had a little of the quality of Ronald Colman and we worked together as harmoniously and effortlessly as I did later with Ronald Colman in *Random Harvest*."

When *Accent on Youth* opened at the Globe Theatre on September 3, theater critics were reaching for new superlatives to describe Greer Garson. *Stage* reported, "By the first word she spoke, Greer Garson arrested the attention of the whole audience. All through the play her elocution continued to be a delight and as she showed interacting, that she could express any mood and make it seem real, her success was complete." Said the *London Times:* "Miss Garson and Mr. Nicholas Hannen, working in genuine collaboration, treat the love scenes with enough dash and seriousness to make them persuasive for just as long as the play requires it, and move off from passion to pattern-making with unfailing judgement. There is, too, a theatrical swing in their combined performance that gives to the whole evening an exceptional liveliness." The *Star* made note of the star's wardrobe: "The lovely young red-blonde actress in 'Accent on Youth' at the Globe Theatre has some very original color schemes for the red-haired woman. In the last act of the play she wears an exquisite long-sleeved velvet dinner gown in a very rich and very dark shade of maroon . . . it provides a dazzlingly effective foil for her bright hair and fair skin, as does a claret-colored dressing gown, another daring choice." Greer's tendency to defy accepted fashions and colors for redheads, on and off the stage, attracted considerable attention and provided her with the opportunity to write an article in the *Star* entitled "Rules For Red Heads." "Experiment—don't be content to stay

faithful to one safe color scheme," she wrote. "I do all my experiment-
ing with scarves and try all sorts of daring color combinations that
way, before I venture out with a complete outfit."

"I have always regretted my oversight and neglect of Greer
Garson," wrote Sydney Carroll in his review of the play. "It is impossible to give every likely debutante the chance she deserves. It is sufficient, I think, to say at the moment that Miss Garson now that she
has, under other auspices, sprung into a celebrity thoroughly deserved, has no warmer well-wisher, and certainly no one who better
appreciates the performance she is now giving in 'Accent on Youth.'
Miss Garson's surprising skill as a self-suppressing secretary with a
capacity for emotional outbursts converts unreality into vivid truth,
makes electric with the fire of genuine passions situations which,
critically examined, are stupid and theatrical. To be able to give conviction to the unconvincing, to render serious the preposterous, to
inflame an audience with pity and anger over trivialities, these things
are only possible to the genuine actress; and Miss Garson fully quali-
fies herself in this part for the description . . . go now to see her in
'Accent on Youth'—for you will then have a chance of watching a future star in the making." In her theater scrapbook, Greer commented:
"A very backhanded compliment to me written in self defense. Carroll
did not enjoy being referred to as the man who let a star slip through
his fingers. Soon after this both he and Mr. Atkins offered me several
plays."

Accent on Youth, despite the glowing reviews, proved to have
little box-office success and closed on October 5. The producers,
Stanley Hale and Harold Gosling, threw a party for the cast that last
evening. "It was a sprightly comedy that deserved a better fate if only
for the aplomb of its star," remarked the *Daily Mirror.* "Greer Garson
is one of the few young actresses for whom one can safely prophesy
lasting success. She's delightfully frank and modest and does not, as
so many do, regard the theatre as a personal playground. She has
worked hard in repertory theatre and knows her job."

Two weeks into the run of the play, Greer returned home one
evening to a surprising discovery. Nina had made inquiries about
their lodgings and received an explanation for their bargain rates.
Their neighborhood was, in fact, the heart of the high-class prosti-
tute district. "It seems my white-haired, lady-mother was considered,

undoubtedly, a prop," Greer would later recall with amusement, "and a 'front' for a place not quite . . . Within an hour we were out of it, bag, baggage and, we devoutly hope, our respectability intact!" They settled in Mayfair at 26 Conduit Street, neighboring Hyde Park and Kensington Gardens.

Greer's career brought her into contact with a great variety of people, which she found "kept my interests varied and elastic, my sympathies warm, and my perceptions wide awake." She joined various literary and artistic clubs, including the Tomorrow Club and a food and wine society. She enjoyed Sir Thomas Beecham's famous Sunday-afternoon musical concerts at Covent Garden, featuring the Philharmonic or BBC Orchestra and the works of Sibelius and Delius. There were operas like *Prince Igor* at Covent Garden and ballets like *Barn Dance* by Miss Littlefield's Philadelphia Ballet at the Hippodrome, or the Blum Monte Carlo Ballet at the Coliseum.

As secretary of the Tomorrow Club, she spent many evenings at the home of the chairman, Trevor Blakemore. "He and his sister had a delightful, exotic house facing Hyde Park," she recalled, "where I was a frequent guest. Trevor had travelled all over the world. He was a connoisseur of the Arts, a noted gourmet and was called the 'Last of the Edwardians,' having known everyone most worth knowing in London's literary, artistic and court circles for half a century, so I learned a great deal from him and his friends, not only about painting, poetry, literature, sauces and vintages, current scandals and political intrigues, but when Trevor reminisced about the manners and machinations of an era that ended when I began."

Mr. Blakemore tried to persuade the rising young actress to speak before the Tomorrow Club and was both surprised and intrigued by the horrified look and quick refusal that she gave him. She was too shy, she protested, and terrified of standing up before her peers. When Trevor reminded her that she was after all an actress and should have lost her fear of audiences, she smiled mischievously and explained her refusal as "a most beautiful example of feminine inconsistency." Years later she said, "When you are on stage, or before a camera, you are not yourself. You are, you devoutly hope, Mrs. Chips, or Mrs. Miniver or Paula in *Random Harvest*, or whomever you are playing." But finally she gave in to her mentor's numerous entreaties and gave a quick speech entitled: "Is Pleasure What It Was." "After only a brief consideration of the title of this discussion," she began, "as light-heartedly suggested to your secretary, and so ruefully contemplated afterwards, I soon came to the conclusion that the word 'Pleasure' as Mr. Pickwick said of the word 'Politics' comprises in itself a study of no inconsiderable magnitude. And so, automatically I found I had happened on that inevitable self-starter for our discussion." Within her discussion she argued against a growing passivity among audiences seeking entertainment. "Radio is very largely to blame for encouraging this general passivity," she declared. "I do think that its resources tend to make people who should be aggressively seeking their pleasure end up sitting drowsily at home letting a flood of highly organized entertainment trickle across their semiconsciousness. This constant drugging leads to a state of comatose satiety in which natural appreciation of pleasure is dulled. If it isn't radio, then it's the gramophone, or worse still the cinema. Thousands of people know nothing of romance but the vicarious thrills provided by Garbo and Colman, Bankhead, and the others. More vicarious sensations—more passivity."

During the run of *Accent on Youth,* Greer was pursued by an increasingly large number of theatrical agents, producers, playwrights, and even members of the motion picture industry. She hired an agent, Herbert de Leon, and acquired a publicist, Jean Wilson, but continued to cast a suspicious eye upon moviemakers. "It's no good," she complained, "they just can't photograph me. My face is all wrong for the screen." However, in August 1935, when Vivien Leigh signed a contract for fifteen hundred pounds in the first year for films with Alexander Korda, her opinion softened. The money was tempting, and the attention she received from moguls such as Adolph Zukor, of America's Paramount Studio, and Korda himself was flattering.

The problem was timing. During the run of *Accent on Youth,* she had accepted the lead in E.G. Hemmerde's 1911 divorce courtroom drama, *Butterfly on the Wheel.* There was scarcely time to consider movies. Nina, who acted as Greer's unofficial manager throughout her career, told reporters: "Greer always had and still has a tremendous energy for study, that she always works terrifically hard. In the university she took honors in English and French, and she lives every part she takes on. My job is to keep her from over-doing it." Greer earned two more backstage nicknames. She was known as "U.P.," the

Universal Provider, always ready to help a fellow actor with her ready
supply of safety pins, mints, and threads, and "Ca-reer Garson." "She
started rehearsing *Butterfly on the Wheel* the moment she had recovered from the Playhouse first night," remarked *Play Pictorial*. "It is
only six months since she swam into the ken of the West End, and in
six months she will be, who knows? Watch Ca-reer Garson!"

Greer played the challenging role of Peggy Admaston in *Butterfly*, a married woman who is persecuted in court—a trapped butterfly on the wheel of justice—by her husband who accuses her of
infidelity. But despite the *Observer*'s reaction that "Miss Greer Garson,
writhing, cool, and hysterical by turns, gives the butterfly histrionic
life" and praise from the *New York Times* ("Greer Garson lent her
vivacity to the butterfly and touched off a brilliant display of emotional fireworks in the witness box"), the play was another flop.
Trevor Blakemore offered this consolation:

> My Dear,
> To say you are first-class is now a platitude, but remem-
> ber I had never seen you do more than a rather reluc-
> tant speech at the Tomorrow, before last night. It was,
> of course, a revelation to me.
>   You see you have brain and quality, coming not
> from being a dramatist's "content," but from a superb
> sense of emotional values. That I have noticed in you
> before, you are one of the few people who can be real,
> artificially. But what has at once lifted you out of the
> ruck is your intellectual force behind the words, which
> gives a drive to all you do, and that drive illumines your
> part. I lay stress on this coefficient of mental potential,
> because it is so rare, you can get plenty of physical
> loveliness or you can get people like Flora Robson, who
> are intellectual, but, physically, knobby. You have both,
> and it squares the circle, dramatically. I long to see you
> in some much more worthy play.

He did not get his wish with Greer's next effort, *Page From a
Diary*, which was an absurd melodrama set in a faraway British fort.
She played Vivienne Maitland, the indiscreet wife of an officer who

is accidentally shot by her husband, and then her daughter Vivienne Glennie who pursues her mother's seducer in murderous revenge. "Have you a nice, simple taste in plays, with no silly ideas about subtlety, or dramatic construction, and above all, no obstinate insistence on a probable plot?" questioned the *Bystander.* "If so, do go and see the good, hearty English melodrama at the Garrick Theatre. Greer Garson . . . [as the] wife, a frail being in exquisite negligee . . . behaving in a quite impossibly idiotic manner . . . has deservedly made a meteoric flight to stardom and plays with great sincerity and admirable restraint."

That summer Greer was even more disappointed with her next play, Nicholas Monsarrat's *The Visitor,* produced by actress-turned-producer Ellen Pollock, and costarring Louis Borell. She played the naive daughter of rich, accommodating parents who expresses her philanthropic instincts by bringing home, and falling in love with, a penniless tramp with an unwritten play. "Mr. Monsarrat's play is better in design than in execution," declared critic W.A. Darlington after the opening at the Daly Theatre on July 7, 1936. "Still, his characters do provide Mr. Borell and Miss Garson with parts in which they can be attractive and alive. Miss Garson is improving all the time, and shows a much bigger range than in her previous parts." "Miss Garson's intelligent and persuasive charm glosses a character that is witless," remarked the *London Times.* "She has all the guns for a more admirable campaign than this. It is a pity to see such talent so wasted."

CHAPTER 7

GREER'S METEORIC STAGE CAREER confounded London's theater critics, who pointed out her less-than-inspired choice of plays. *Star Spotter Backstage* remarked: "Fame built on failures, extraordinary, but Greer Garson's must be unique, discovered as a new star in 'The Golden Arrow' at the Whitehall which failed, she then played in 'Vintage Wine' with Hicks, but only for a few weeks. Then looked like having a winner in 'Accent on Youth' at the Globe, that failed too. Then followed the ill-fated 'Butterfly on the Wheel' at the Alhambra. Shortly after, 'A Page from a Diary' at the Garrick was also short-lived. Three flops and two revivals and yet Greer Garson is one of the most sought after young actresses in London!"

"Of course I'm disappointed," Greer told the *Daily Express,* "but I'm not sad. Every part I have played has been entirely different, a long run would be good for the bank balance, but in these plays I have had experience that would have taken me years in the ordinary way. Since I began rehearsing for 'The Golden Arrow' last May, I have only had five free days from the Theatre. Long contracts terrify me a little, but I may go to America on Broadway and I would like to act in different languages."

In August, Noël Coward began casting for his new play, *Mademoiselle,* by Jacques Deval, which was being adapted by Audrey and Waveney Carten. It was the story of a spoiled society belle named Christianne Galvoisier who is, unbeknownst to anyone save her governess, about to become an unwed mother. Because her family is too busy to take note of her problem (her father complains that the Galvoisier household "is a railway station, where nobody takes the same train!"), it is up to the governess, Mademoiselle, to help Christianne

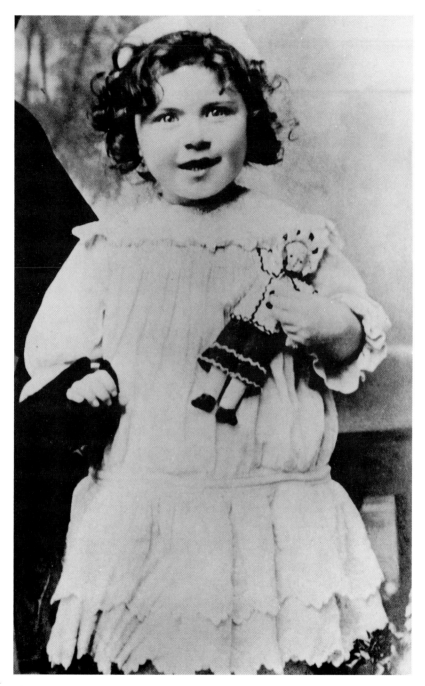

Eileen Evelyn Greer Garson at about age five. A.M.P.A.S. © Turner Entertainment Co. All rights reserved.

Left, Nina Garson and her daughter strike a pose. *Below*, David Greer rests from his duties managing "The Rovans," the Irish estate of Lord Stratheona in Castlewellan, to enjoy tea with his wife, Sophia, daughter Nina, and granddaughter Eileen. Photos courtesy of Greer C. Murray.

Above, Aunt Evelyn Campbell-Murray, the model for her famous niece's portrayal of Mrs. Miniver, with her children Greer, David, and Sophia. *Right*, Uncle James Campbell-Murray, "the most completely integrated and humane man" and the only father Greer knew. Photos courtesy of Greer C. Murray.

Above left, The aspiring actress graduates from the University of London in 1926. A.M.P.A.S. © Turner Entertainment Co. All rights reserved. *Above right*, An autographed portrait from *Madamoiselle*. Courtesy of Elizabeth Jones. *Below*, Greer (third from left) in *Jane's Legacy* at the Birmingham Repertory Theatre, with her first love, Michael Barry (top left). Sir Barry Jackson Trust, Birmingham, England.

Left, Greer with mentor
Madge Titheradge in
Mademoiselle.
Below, Eileen (far left)
becomes Greer Garson in
George Bernard Shaw's
"Too True To Be Good."
She referred to it as "Too
Bad To Be Good." Photos
courtesy of Mander and
Mitchenson Theatre
Collection.

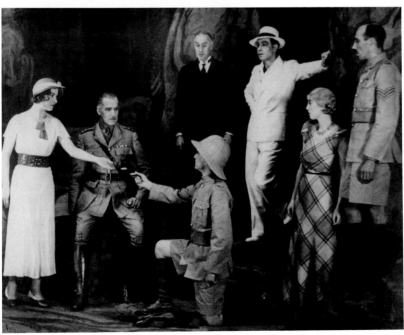

Greer in Cassis, on the Cote D'Azur, during a holiday with the Murrays in 1931. Courtesy of Greer C. Murray.

Old Music, the play in which Louis B. Mayer saw Greer at the St. James Theatre. Within twenty-four hours he offered her an MGM studio contract, which she initially turned down. Mander and Mitchenson Theatre Collection.

Greer Garson, London's "Most Sought After Star," in a thoughtful pose in 1937. From the author's collection.

with her predicament. Rescuing the girl from suicide, Mademoiselle whisks her off to the country for the birth and then adopts the child as her own.

Although Greer was intrigued with the role of Christianne, it was the opportunity to work with Noël Coward that brought her to an audition at Wyndham's Theatre, between St. Martin's Lane and Charing Cross Road. Laurence Olivier had described Coward as a brilliant playwright, actor, director, librettist, composer, and an inspiring mentor. Unfortunately, the audition did not go well.

"She is so piss-elegant that it hurts!" Coward proclaimed before the mortified young actress in the stage lights to his stage director, Gerard Clifton. "Too mannered. Too old. Too tall. And her voice is too deep. But . . . that woman's hair would set fire to every line I say!" So despite his reservations, he was willing to give her a try. By the second rehearsal, Greer had dropped the unwanted mannerisms, piped her voice up to a childish treble, and won Coward over completely. "I never have to tell you what to do, Greer," he once told her, "only occasionally what NOT to do, which is so much easier."

Over the subsequent weeks, Coward further refined Greer's technique. "Noël was a very exacting and painstaking taskmaster," she informed the London press, "but the grind always glitters for he never loses his subtle, glancing humor nor allows those who work for him to lose theirs. Noël would put us through a scene so many times we were ready to scream with nerves and boredom, then flick our spirits by saying drolly, 'Now, tots, run along home, papa is very pleased with you.'"

Madge Titheradge, who played Mademoiselle, quickly became Greer's friend and staunchest supporter. "Let me tell you," she told the *Evening Times* in her dressing room, "Greer Garson will be a very great actress, not mind you, not just a great actress but a very great actress. Take it from me and remember I told you so. I can't think of any other young actress I'd like opposite me in this play. Neither of us has a sympathetic character to portray. We have to follow on after those two great people Isabel Jeans and Cecil Parker, and it takes something out of both of us to switch the audience from laughter."

On opening night, September 15, 1936, Noël sent Greer a box of roses with a note: "If being directed by me has been half as exciting and interesting as directing you has been to me, then this is a very happy evening for both of us!" There were other gifts as well. In an article entitled "Just for Luck" the *Evening News* reported, "It is not so long ago that Greer Garson first became known in the West End, but she has already quite a large following among the fans. For the opening of 'Mademoiselle,' this week they sent her a doll of baby size, some coat hangers for her dressing room prettily decorated, and a miniature Japanese garden. The crew of her uncle's yacht, on which she had a holiday recently, sent her a big horse shoe of white heather from Scotland for good luck."

Mademoiselle was an instant hit that broke Greer's uncomfortably long string of unprofitable plays. The production even attracted Queen Mary, who attended an evening performance with her daughter-in-law, the Duchess of York, and her granddaughter Princess Elizabeth. Another evening, Greer received a card backstage in her dressing room from matinee idol Douglas Fairbanks Jr. and an American film director named Tay Garnett. "She responded that she would be happy to meet me and my associate in the lobby of the Dorchester for tea the next day," Garnett recalled. Greer arrived with her agent, Herbert de Leon. As tea was poured out, Fairbanks got right to the point. They had been searching the West End for a leading lady for an upcoming adventure film called *Jump for Glory* at Criterion, their British film studio, and had been "struck 'all in a heap' by her personality and talent." Would she consider testing for the part? Although Greer was hesitant, de Leon was convinced that this was the opportunity for his client to finally break into the movies.

"We promptly arranged for a comprehensive screen test," Tay Garnett recalls. Uncomfortable in the gown that had been chosen for her and the strange makeup required for the camera, Greer was, in Fairbanks's estimation, "flustered and fluttery as a young girl at her first dance." But the results were impressive. "It was a smash," Garnett recalled. "The girl's image lit up the projection room like summer lightning." Greer did not take the proceedings seriously and found the experience "all very lighthearted and charming," She preferred instead to hear Garnett's fascinating tales of Hollywood and his English-styled estate in the canyons of Bel Air. He described the drive beyond high wooden gates, the ancient sycamores, the sweep of lawn, the flags by the brook, and the gardens. It was just the sort of home Greer intended her mother to have one day.

When she saw the screen test a few days later, her hopes for a film career collapsed. In a letter to Douglas Fairbanks Jr., who was not at the screening, she wrote: "It was so nice of you to help me through that test Monday. I only wish the results were more gratifying. The only moment that didn't make me prickly with shame was when I thought they had cut and giggled something spontaneous. I rushed out of the building protesting wildly that never, no—never, unless your make-up and camera wizards could mitigate the full horror of my countenance, could I think of making your picture. My cheekbones stood out like crags, and my eyes looked too light. I thought I resembled a Zombie. [Herbert] seemed to think I had said quite the wrong thing, so perhaps he did his diplomatic stuff and maybe it will be possible to have another try. I'd ask you please to want me for another picture later on when 'Mademoiselle' is finished, only that I'm afraid you might go and find some other fair [actress] in the meantime who might be pretty-and-all-that but won't be half as amusing as I am—And, anyway, *Jump For Glory* would be fun to play."

But Douglas Fairbanks was not about to lose his discovery at this point. He argued that Criterion already had two film projects lined up for her and that her future was in pictures, so the sooner she got started the better. When she explained that, leaving her prejudice against a camera out of it, she had a contract with Noël Coward, which would, of course, prohibit her doing anything else, Fairbanks replied that he would give Noël a ring and fix it.

They summoned Herbert de Leon and began to negotiate a contract. Fairbanks offered one thousand pounds per picture, three pictures a year for five years. In the first year she would make five thousand pounds with options that would increase the salary to seventy-five hundred in the second year and to ten thousand in the third year. What pleased Greer most was a clause that allowed a minimum of six months' freedom for theater work upon the completion of the required three pictures. Criterion had the option of renewing her contract after the third year on at least as good terms as any other film offer she might receive. Then Fairbanks and Garnett showed Greer their production plans. There were three pictures being prepared at the time: *Jump for Glory* with Fairbanks, a proposed historical epic in Scotland, and *Thunder in the City*, costarring Edward G.

Robinson. With a theater and a film career almost at hand, Greer was exhilarated. Now she would have the best of both career worlds. The news made its way into the papers. The *New Chronicle* reported: "Douglas Fairbanks Jr.'s company, Criterion Films, have just recently been testing Greer Garson, London actress, for the purpose of discovering whether she is suitable for the leading role in *Jump for Glory*, the next film on schedule. In one scene of this film Doug will have to jump from the balcony with the heroine in his arms, which is probably the reason for the title. It will certainly be a difficult athletic feat! Carrying eight stones of relaxed femininity is one thing, but jumping off a balcony!"

But neither Greer, nor anyone at Criterion, had counted on the formidable Noël Coward. Sitting in her dressing room one afternoon with the door slightly ajar, she heard Coward phone Fairbanks. "What?" he cried, "I don't know what you mean. What? It's all very silly. Trying to steal my star. Over my dead body! What? My dear fellow. What? No, certainly not. That's all. Goodbye." "Noël Coward was very angry," Greer later related, "and said he would wring my neck if I gave up London for Hollywood." To ensure his point, Noël penned a letter to Douglas Fairbanks on October 28, 1936.

> My dear Douglas,
> Miss Greer Garson came to see me yesterday afternoon and explained to me that your Company had made her an offer to star in a film under your management. Miss Garson was extremely anxious to accept this offer, but I am afraid we have, quite firmly, had to refuse permission as it would, obviously, be quite impossible for us either to release her from the Cast of "Mademoiselle" at Wyndham's or to allow her to play in a film at the same time. Her part there is a very strenuous one and it would be quite out of the question for her to give eight performances a week if at the same time she were playing a leading part in a Film Production.
> Miss Garson was, naturally, very upset at our decision and I promised I would write to you and explain the reason she has been unable to accept your offer. Kindest regards.

A film career seemed a distant dream to Greer Garson now. But her friends were not willing to let her give up so easily. She received a letter from Samson Raphaelson, who was now a Hollywood screenwriter. "I have spent my time profitably in films and will be able to buy some leisure for myself this year," he wrote. "I have two new plays ready to be written, and both are promised for production in the fall. I think one of them will have a part along the lines of Linda, only stronger and more important. The play is on an important theme— but done in a comedy vein like *Accent*. If it goes to New York, will you take a chance on another play of mine in London? Is there any possibility of your coming to Hollywood? Or is there anything I can do to help create such a possibility? I want to see you so much that I think I'd do it even at the risk of feeding you into the maw of the movies."

Greer celebrated her hundredth performance in *Mademoiselle*— and the news from Noël Coward that he was planning to take the company on tour—by giving a tea party for the twin grandsons of her dresser, Kate. The continuing success of the play, as its run continued into December, eased Greer's disappointment. But not all of it. As the Criterion affair continued to haunt her, everything else suddenly seemed to go wrong. When she sat for the obligatory publicity photographs that month with Messrs. Claude Harris, she was nearly killed when a heavy floodlamp crashed down, just missing her head, tearing her dress, and badly cutting her back. But she insisted on playing her part that evening and then fainted away as the curtain came down.

Another blow came mid-month when she returned to 26 Conduit Street one frosty evening, laden with holiday postcards from Scotland and found her husband there. Alec Snelson had made holiday visits to London in the past, but because they had become increasingly unpleasant, Greer had attempted in her correspondence to discourage a meeting this Christmas. "If you have any choice," she wrote, "please try to postpone your leave a little longer. I am working so hard I will have very little time to spend with you and if I should be on tour when you arrive, may miss you entirely. I have promised to visit you as often as possible during our separation, but doctors have told me I could not live in India permanently. I feel you should know what I have known from the beginning—that our marriage was a mistake. I am deeply, deeply sorry for whatever distress or embarrassment this might cause you but the plain truth is you do not make me happy, and I cannot make you happy. The best, indeed the only thing to do is to meet and discuss the situation sometime in the future rationally and amicably."

"But it was not to be settled as simply as that," Greer testified in a crowded courtroom four years later, in 1940. "There were many months of unhappy negotiations and meetings and discussions which always ended in deadlock, and got us nowhere at all. And then Alec went back to India vowing he would never give me a divorce. Our encounters became more painful and stormy than the last. He began watching my comings and goings so closely that I finally had to see lawyers about an injunction to prevent him from molesting me."

Greer received another surprise on December 11 during a performance of *Mademoiselle.* For months she had listened to the backstage gossip about Edward VIII, whose coronation in May was jeopardized because he had fallen in love with American divorcée Wallis Simpson. Although a royal abdication and subsequent marriage seemed inevitable, the world was nonetheless shocked when, on December 11, the official radio announcement was made. "The night he made his abdication speech," Greer recalls, "I remember the curtain stayed up at the end of the second act. A microphone and loudspeaker were set up just behind the footlights, the cast remained on the stage and cast and audience listened to that moment of history in the making together. Madge was led offstage, sobbing, and it was very difficult to finish the third act of our make-believe play that night."

George VI, Edward's younger brother, was to be Great Britain's new monarch. The controversy threw the economy of the West End into an uproar. *Mademoiselle* suffered along with the rest and barely lasted another month. After closing at the Wyndham Theatre on January 23, 1937, Noël Coward fulfilled his promise and took the cast on the road through many of the cities that Greer had visited during her *Too True to Be Good* tour. "Some of the towns remembered me from that first tour," Greer recalled, "and I was always touched and pleased when I read in a local paper, 'Greer Garson is Here Again.' To be remembered made me feel that I was no longer a newcomer but belonged by virtue of continuity. The whole engagement, in fact, made me happier and prouder than ever before that I belonged in the theater and that its people were my people." The *Manchester Guardian* declared, "Miss Garson brilliantly defines the minx, Christianne, who seizes her rare and lucky chance to make light of travail and ignores its obligations. She gives the most precise and vivid portrayal of the sort of daughter who is both spoiled and neglected." The *Sunday Mail* remarked, "Noël Coward's production of 'Mademoiselle,' which comes to the King's Theatre, Glasgow, this week is distinguished, smart and beautiful. Greer Garson, a Scots girl from the Orkneys will be the star. This is the 'Ace' spot this week."

By April Greer was back in London, which was preparing for the coronation of George VI at Westminster Abbey on May 12. She wrote to Trevor Blakemore: "I'm enjoying a rest after 'Mademoiselle' which expired last week amid handsome plaudits. Still seeking that elusive romantic comedy. I'd have a shot at writing myself, but I'd have no friends left!" Temporarily unemployed, Greer was enjoying lunch with her mother at the Ivy when she spotted Michael Barry dining with Cecil Madden, the program organizer and senior producer of the British Broadcasting Company. She invited them to her table and listened with interest to their enthusiastic conversation about working at the BBC and the future of television. Michael informed her that the Birmingham Repertory has already televised its first play, *Delicate Ground,* with Muriel Forbes-Robertson from the BBC facility at Alexandra Palace. Nina, however, was skeptical of the new visual medium. Janet Flanner, English correspondent for the *New Yorker,* reported: "To date, televisionary results are more interesting than satisfactory. Twenty-five miles is about as far as the pictures carry without blurring; the frames are too small to contain a crowd; the electrical apparatus belonging to doctors on Harley Street, though nowhere near Alexandra Palace, has interfered with transmission. The promised rooms in which the public may view television are still scarce." There were other problems. The sets themselves cost one hundred pounds, about the price of a new car. Therefore, there were only around four hundred sets at that time. Many theater companies, fearing the new technology, forbade their players from performing at Alexandra Palace.

But Greer decided to take the risk. She made her live debut on May 14, 1937, in "Twelfth Night," as part of the popular *Play Parade* series. It was produced by George More O'Ferrall and featured Henry Oscar, Hilary Pritchard, and South African actress Dorothy Black. The *Evening Times* remarked, "Miss Garson gives an entirely original rendering of the parts of both Viola and Sebastian. In the final scene both characters appear on the screen at once, an effect obtained by the use of mirrors and skill-acting of Greer Garson. She has to change her voice to suit the different characters." Her television appearances continued into the summer of 1937. She appeared in another *Play Parade* episode: Richard Brinsley Sheridan's "School for Scandal" on May 19, again produced by George More O'Ferrall, with Campbell Gullan, Denys Blakelock, and Earle Grey. In June she was featured in "Hassan," a colorful fantasy by James Elroy Flecker that costarred Frank Cellier, John Wyse, D.A. Clarke-Smith, and Ivan Samson, that played in two parts on June 8 and 14. The production's most notable feature was the beautiful musical score by Frederick Delius. On July 7, she appeared in *How He Lied to Her Husband,* which garnered extra publicity with an appearance by the author, George Bernard Shaw. Like her earlier efforts, it was produced by George More O'Ferrall and costarred D.A. Clarke-Smith and Derek Williams. It was the first Shaw play to be televised from Alexandra Palace.

By the time she accepted *How He Lied to Her Husband,* Greer was commanding the top television pay of the time: seventy-five to one hundred guineas, or $520.80, a show. Years later, she recalled that the work was excellent practice for moviemaking. "The camera technique is much the same," she observed, "and teaches, most importantly, naturalness, restraint, and poise. In television, at least at that time, if an actor moved around too much and got out of focus, one side of his face would suddenly puff out like a balloon. I discovered that in front of either a television or movie camera, the worst fault of which a player can be guilty is over-acting."

CHAPTER 8

"LONDON'S HOTELS, SNACK BARS, theatres, cinemas, tubes, buses, flatlets, lodging houses, art shows, antique dealers' shops, bridle paths, and sidewalks are full," reported the *New Yorker* in the summer of 1937. "London is now unlike any London since the war. The city's passion for going to the play has particularly profited." It was a wonderful time to be on the stage, and by August Greer was riding the crest of her theatrical success. The *London Express* continued to call her "The Most Sought After Young Actress in London." Her portrait by A.K. Lawrence now hung in the Royal Academy. Songs and poems were composed for her. A rose and a supper dish at the Savoy Grill—the famous dining spot of theatrical clientele since Sarah Bernhardt's patronage—were named after her.

She considered three plays in early July. Tyrone Guthrie offered her the part of Viola in an Old Vic presentation of *Twelfth Night*. Firth Shepard wanted her to appear in his new play, *The Magic Age*. But she ultimately picked the starring role of Geraldine in Keith Winter's nineteenth-century melodrama, *Old Music*. It had not been a difficult decision, for there were a number of attractions. Since 1918, Gilbert Miller had presented a number of successful plays at the St. James Theatre, the last of which had been Jane Austen's *Pride and Prejudice*. The producer was the talented Margaret Webster, an actress and director who had made a name for herself in England and America. Her parents were noted professionals in the theater as well, Benjamin Webster and Dame May Whitty. *Old Music*'s noteworthy cast included Celia Johnson, who had received rave notices as Elizabeth Bennet in *Pride and Prejudice*.

Best of all, Greer found Geraldine Decker, a beautiful but cold-blooded murderess, a fascinating character. Of all her stage portrayals, this became her favorite. Set in 1853, the play follows Geraldine's selfish pursuit of wealth, which culminates in a marriage to Lord Philip Tresham, played by Bryan Coleman. Quickly bored with her conquest, she falls in love with Tony Yale, played by Hugh Williams, who is married to her cousin Judith (Celia Johnson). The *London Times* described her as "a gold-digger of the fifties and in other respects a greedy little animal . . . who does not hesitate, when opportunity arises, to become Tony's mistress." When their extramarital tryst is discovered and Tony returns to his wife, Geraldine kills him. Judith, despite the humiliations and betrayals inflicted upon her by Geraldine, covers up the crime.

Of the nineteenth-century hoopskirted gowns that she wore in the play, Greer told the *Evening News*: "They're such fun. I've got a specially knit pair of corsets to wear, only nineteen inches. When I first put them on, I felt as if I couldn't breathe at all, it was agony. But that feeling is wearing off now."

The production of *Old Music* at the prestigious St. James, which had witnessed the first dramatizations of Charles Dickens, was by far the most lavish showcase in which Greer had appeared. The *London Times* observed, "The play is full of lesser pleasures by the way—a Victorian picnic, for example, complete with footman, top-hats, silver tea-pots, cakestands, and an armoury of knives, spoons and forks. Such elaboration is the making of the play as a 'period piece,' but it happens to be also an original comment on human emotion." On August 18, the curtain came up on opening night. But the public reception and reviews did not match Greer's hopes. "Why 'Old Music'?" questioned the *Observer*. "Why music at all? Would not 'Old Hokum' be as good a title as any other? I fear that, despite the fact that the cast could not be bettered, I found this tale of muddled marriages to be not actual or moving in the least. If Greer Garson seems to lay on the greedy folly of Miss Decker rather thick, such emphasis is, I think, merited by the story and is made with a first-rate artistry by an actress of great capacity."

James Agate blamed Greer for the play's box-office failure. "What is presently wrong with Miss Garson is that she is in two minds, not being yet decided whether to be a naturalistic player or a great actress. At the moment she is twice too big for the one school and twice too little for the other. If a word of advice be permitted, I would suggest that she go all out, because I cannot convince myself that her natural bent is to go all in. In the meantime and in this piece she puts herself grandly on to the middle of the St. James stage. But this is not enough; the business of the great actress is to play every-body else off the stage, including the corners thereof. Alternatively, Miss Garson should make her appeal with fewer effects." He added, "This new, young meteor, Miss Greer Garson, will remain with us because, heaven be praised, she is not extraordinarily beautiful. . . . I do not think she will ever become a goddess of that other world where some over-titivated ninny simpers in front of a camera until a director, cigar in mouth, yells 'Cut!'"

Concerned with finding a more successful play to follow *Old Music,* Greer paid little attention to the latest gossip that was coursing through the English theatrical world. Louis B. Mayer was back in London. He had arrived in the city on August 25 to observe the activities at the recently leased Denham studio, north of London. His promise in 1934 to create an MGM-British film studio was finally realized in November 1936. The alliance was registered as a £250,000 film company, and Loews Incorporated, which owned MGM, negotiated to lease the English studio facilities. Michael Balcon, former head of Gaumont-British studio, was put in charge of the new organization with Ben Goetz.

Besides his inspection of the new facility, Mayer was also on another of his famous talent hunts. Accompanied by a retinue of company brass, he was like visiting royalty. With him were Joseph Schenck, president of Loews; Benjamin Thau, head of the talent department, contract negotiations, and executive assistant to Mayer; Howard Strickling, head of publicity; Robert Ritchie, a publicist; and Mrs. Ad Schulberg, an agent for numerous European talents. Mrs. Schulberg had heard of Greer's accomplishments and suggested to Mayer that they attend an evening performance of *Old Music.* Assuming that the play would be the sort of old Viennese musical that he loved, Mayer agreed and the party alighted at the curb of King Street before the St. James for an eight-thirty performance. Once seated, Mayer was thoroughly disgruntled to find that the play was a costume melodrama, without music. But he was not disappointed with Greer Garson's performance.

During intermission, at Mayer's insistence, Robert Ritchie sent a note to Greer's dressing room, inviting her to dinner at the Savoy Grill after the show. Thinking that Mr. Ritchie was the silk hosiery man she was expecting, she sent word back: "I don't want any." A few moments later, the doorman was back. "Excuse me, Miss Garson, but Mr. Ritchie said to tell you he has a message from Mr. Mayer. Mr. Metro-Goldwyn-Mayer. Don't you think you ought to meet him?" "Hyphens and all?" Greer gasped. She telephoned Nina, who advised her to accept the invitation. "But don't sign anything tonight," her mother warned, "and don't be late because you have a matinee tomorrow." Greer felt inadequate when she met the glamorous MGM gathering dressed in a simple green woolen dress, Tyrolean red sport jacket, and hair still untidy from wearing a wig. But L.B. Mayer found her all the more intriguing in person. He admired her elegant manner and her affectionate tones when she described her mother. His legendary career had been forged by nurturing the careers of actresses with patrician manners such as Anita Stewart, Barbara LaMarr, Norma Shearer, and Jeanette MacDonald. And no pictures were held in higher esteem than women's pictures at MGM—especially when they had to do with mothers, because of Mayer's reverence for his own mother. But it appeared that Greer, who evidently had dealt with film producers before, was ambivalent about appearing in motion pictures.

Mayer invited himself over to 26 Conduit Street the following day and received a morning sherry and a polite refusal when he asked her to do a screen test at MGM's Denham studio. Appearing undisturbed, he shrewdly turned his attentions to Nina. The tactic of ingratiating himself with the mother of an actor he wanted had proven successful in the past, and in this case he was cannily aware that Nina managed Greer's affairs. He charmed her with his descriptions of Metro-Goldwyn-Mayer as a family that worked together to make the finest motion pictures in the world and convinced the Garsons to take a tour of the studio's fabulous new facility. Built in 1935-36, Denham had been the grandiose dream of Alexander Korda and was the largest and most lavish filmmaking factory in England. The studio covered some 165 acres with seven sound stages, eighteen cutting rooms, film vaults, and its own film labs, including one for Technicolor. From the full-size symphonic recording hall to the largest electrical generating plant in England, Denham was the best. Greer finally agreed to a test but, as she patiently turned from side to side for the cameraman, she considered the whole affair a waste of time.

The next day Mayer and Benjamin Thau invited Greer and Nina to see the test. On the way to the studio, Thau expounded on the abundant pleasures of life in sunny California. After viewing the test and declaring that she hated it, Greer was surprised when Benjamin Thau said: "We can do wonders with your face in Hollywood," and Mayer added, "There's nobody who can't be photographed!"

Greer ultimately sat down to negotiate a contract with Louis B. Mayer for two reasons. "What made up my mind was the hope that the California climate might help my mother's health, as Mr. Mayer promised it would, and there is a certain quiet charm about money. The studio made me a lucrative offer." At first the offer was not enough. Benjamin Thau presented her with the standard MGM five-hundred-dollar-a-week, seven-year contract. Although attracted by the lure of a greater salary—she was making sixty-five pounds a week for *Old Music*—Greer insisted on a thousand dollars a week. But Mayer was adamant—no more money. "Are you engaging me for a specific part?" she asked. Recalling Laurence Olivier's misadventures in Hollywood, she told him that she had heard of actors going to America under contract and doing nothing. She warned him that if she was lost, forgotten, or submerged in America, the London producers would lose interest as well. Mayer insisted that he already had suitable parts ready for her. "Lady parts," he added. But with negotiations in a deadlock over money, the frustrated MGM entourage moved on to France.

At once Greer began to doubt her forbearance. With so many commercial failures, she had begun to mistrust her judgment to choose a play, and there was not a promising one on the horizon. There had not been any word from studios such as London Films, Criterion, or United Artists, to which Herbert de Leon had recently sent her Fairbanks-Garnett screen test. The only reply had come from the David O. Selznick organization in September. "I can't tell you how awfully sorry I am," a secretary had written, "that Mr. Selznick is not keen on your test. I am going to be candid and tell you that in his opinion—and judging on the test—he does not feel you are 'photogenic.'"

She asked Gilbert Miller for a brief vacation from *Old Music* in order to fly to Paris and renegotiate with Mayer. He refused, so her agent went instead. In a few days she learned that her choice of ambassador had been disastrous. De Leon phoned to say that Mayer was in a temper, refusing her request for a salary raise and declaring that he did not want to have any further contact with her. Her agent was eager to report, however, that his office had begun negotiations with Paramount. Greer asked him to bring L.B. Mayer to the phone.

For the rest of her life, she never forgot that conversation. "I don't think you want to come to work for us," Mayer said belligerently. When Greer reaffirmed her desire to join Metro-Goldwyn-Mayer but expressed her doubts about her financial future, there was a long silence on the Paris end of the wire. "When does your play close?" he finally asked. "On the thirtieth of October," she said. "Very well, Greer, we will meet your terms. Sail on the sixteenth of November." All she could manage was a "Bless you." Over the long distance telephone between London and Paris, the deal had been made. As Mayer sailed from Cherbourg back to the United States, she sent a wire to the boat: "Heartfelt thanks. My dearest wish is to justify your confidence."

The European tour was a profitable one for the MGM executives. Traveling back to America with Mayer was Victor Saville, a distinguished director and producer from the Gaumont-British studio who carried a number of valuable screen properties with him, including A.J. Cronin's *The Citadel.* Also on board were two Austrian actresses named Hedy Kiesler and Rose Stradner, screenwriter Walter Reisch, and two singers, Hungarian Ilona Hajmassy, and Polish Miliza Korjus. While Mayer renamed Hedy Kiesler "Hedy Lamarr" and changed Ilona Hajmassy to "Ilona Massey," he was stumped when it came to Greer and Miliza Korjus. Ultimately, he settled with Howard Strickling to start a publicity campaign for Korjus ("her name rhymes with gorgeous!"), and left Greer's name alone. But for years he would continue to complain that her name was not feminine enough.

Benjamin Thau came back to London, and Greer signed the contract in Claridge's Hotel. Sitting in the lavishly appointed, turn-of-the-century dining room where a string orchestra serenaded them, the pair toasted Greer's new career with champagne. "It was all very gay and charming," Greer would recall, "and I felt, happily, that picture people make business such fun!" Not so pleasant was her parting from Herbert de Leon. When he voiced his disapproval of her MGM agreement, Greer penned a last letter to him. "You must naturally be feeling very disappointed that Paramount was too late in showing their interest, as of course the regular 10% commission would have been due you, and it is that feeling, I am sure, which makes you think the present undertaking very little worthwhile by comparison. This is unfortunate for you, and uncomfortable for me, but it is the luck of the game and cannot be helped. It is anyhow uncertain that any options will be taken up, and whether they are, and on what terms, will obviously depend entirely on my own efforts during the next twelve months."

On September 28, 1937, the *Daily Express* announced the news: "Greer Garson to Hollywood for Seven Years: Failures have won her film contract. Twenty-five-year-old [*sic*] red-haired Greer Garson, West End actress of only two years' standing, has signed to go to Hollywood on a seven-year contract with MGM, Hollywood's biggest film company, as soon as her part in the play 'Old Music' closes."

Greer's flat on Conduit Street was in complete disarray when she granted one last request, from the *Evening News*, for an interview on November 12. "We sold some of the furniture," she said, "and stored the things we cared about most. Mr. Louis B. Mayer has certainly done us well in matter of accommodations on board. We have sumptuous cabins with a verandah all to ourselves!"

Nina woke Greer earlier than usual on November 16, the morning of their voyage. The SS *Normandie* was not scheduled to depart Southampton until two o'clock, but she did not intend that her daughter should make them late on this day of all days. Their maid, Charlotte Harding, was already up and packing last-minute items into their thirty-two trunks. Everything was going according to Nina's strict timetable until the well-wishers began to arrive. "Around noon people began dropping in," Greer recalled, "telephones were ringing and not until friends who were at Southampton to see us off began calling did I realize that we were running late. Our departure was, decidedly, colorful. We made 90 miles an hour through towns, 100 miles an hour in the open country to arrive at the pier just in time." Of the ocean voyage, Greer recalled, "Mother was happy about going mainly because she said, in a country with more enlightened divorce laws, I might be able to obtain my divorce from Alec." A few hours later, a publicity representative of Metro-Goldwyn-Mayer in New York radioed the ship: "Is Miss Garson happy?" It was Nina who sent the reply: "Miss Garson is enchantingly happy except not a good sailor."

Act Two

Hollywood (1937-1949)

People are always asking me what it was like during the golden years of Hollywood. That was in the 1920s and '30s—which wasn't my period. My period, the '40s and '50s, is what I call the romantic years of Hollywood.

CHAPTER 9

IN THE BEGINNING OF THE 1954 FILM, *Her Twelve Men,* Greer Garson's voice is heard narrating a near autobiographical montage of colorful, dreamlike images. "When I was a child," she intones, "and given to daydreaming, I had many visions of myself as a grownup. . . . Always I was glamorous, heroic and beloved. But dreams have a way of ending quite suddenly. You can wake up and find yourself, as I did . . . starting life over again on my way to a place I'd never been, to do something I'd never dreamed of doing, and trying not to show . . . how scared I was."

Such was the situation of the thirty-three-year-old Englishwoman who stepped from the train at the Pasadena, California, station on December 4, 1937. Wearing a heavy fur coat, a dark winter hat, kid gloves, and dark shoes and stockings, she felt "like a hibernating bear" in the warm California sunshine. As Metro-Goldwyn-Mayer's Cinderella of the hour, Greer was met by a limousine escort that whisked her exhausted entourage off toward the Beverly Hills Hotel. Peering from the windows of her room overlooking Sunset Boulevard, she found Los Angeles to be "like a fairyland. A Dreamer's Land. A Lotus Land. The gardens of roses. The palm trees. The orange trees. The pools under a sky continually brimming over with sunlight. A promised land which, we felt, kept its promise extravagantly." Only a squib in the *Hollywood Reporter* noting that an Irish actor named *Mr.* Greer Garson had signed a contract with MGM and arrived in town brought a disappointing touch of reality. "My fame, I perceived, was still to be made," she recalled; "it had not preceded me."

Life had become a whirlwind of publicity interviews, photograph sessions, and brief tours since her arrival in New York City on Novem-

ber 22. The first stop had been a visit to the headquarters of Loews Incorporated, the parent company of Metro-Goldwyn-Mayer, at 1540
Broadway in midtown Manhattan. On the twelfth floor, the doors
opened upon the publicity department. A secretary pointed out the
waiting room and informed Greer and her mother that Mr. Howard
Dietz, director of Advertising, Publicity, and Exploitation, would not
be able to see them for two hours.

The Garsons spent their afternoon at Radio City Music Hall, the
five-year-old "Showplace of the Nation" a few blocks away at the famous corner of Sixth Avenue and Fiftieth Street. It was the dream child
of two of New York's most influential personages, John D. Rockefeller
Jr. and Samuel Lionel "Roxy" Rothafel. In October 1928 Rockefeller had
signed a lease for the acreage that became Rockefeller Center. As the
centerpiece for his "city within a city" he commissioned architect Raymond Hood and the combined architectural firms of Todd, Robertson,
and Todd Engineering and Reinhard and Hof-meister to construct a
theater. Donald Deskey was chosen as the interior designer. David
Sarnoff's Radio Corporation of America, which had recently acquired
the RKO Studio in Hollywood, was the tenant. The theater became
America's grandest launching pad for Hollywood's most prestigious
films. The massive marquee that greeted the Garsons advertised David
O. Selznick's Technicolor comedy, *Nothing Sacred*, starring Carole
Lombard and Fredric March. They were awestruck by the elegant
Grand Foyer, took a peek into the Grand Lounge, and then ascended
the famous staircase to the auditorium with its dramatic curved ceiling
that reached to a height of eighty-three feet. They were seated in the
orchestra section and gazed upon a huge screen, unlike anything they
had seen in London, seventy feet wide and thirty-five feet high. After an
elaborate musical variety show featuring the world-famous Rockettes,
the lights dimmed and the movie began. It was just the sort of witty, romantic comedy that Greer adored, and she was still talking about the
experience hours after the screening, sitting before the desk of Howard
Dietz. Was there any chance that she might make films like that and
have them shown in such a magnificent theater? "My dear Miss Garson,"
Dietz said, slightly perturbed at the conversational flood he was experiencing, "only the *biggest* stars ever play the Music Hall."

On their cross-country trip by train to California, Greer found
America "so much huger than we imagined, that we felt like atoms lost

in infinite space." When they were not enjoying the swiftly changing winter landscape from their windows, Greer and Nina were catching up with a bundle of the nation's newspapers. In a continuing attempt to avoid embroiling the country in the war spreading over Europe, President Franklin D. Roosevelt had signed the Neutrality Act that was warmly applauded nationwide. The fate of the Loyalists in the Spanish Civil War was the only international issue that seemed to concern the citizens of the United States. They preferred to hope that FDR's New Deal, now in full swing, would work, and they supported the five hundred thousand workers who were striking across the country against unfair labor practices. The radio was playing such top tunes as "My Funny Valentine," "In the Still of the Night," and "Whistle While You Work." Rodgers and Hart's FDR satire, *I'd Rather Be Right,* and Clifford Odets's *Golden Boy* were making money on Broadway. John Steinbeck's *Of Mice and Men* had recently been published, and *Gone with the Wind* had won the Pulitzer Prize. But it was the latest news from the world's film capital in southern California that seemed to fascinate Americans the most. In 1937 Hollywood produced Walt Disney's *Snow White and the Seven Dwarfs,* Frank Capra's *Lost Horizon* with Ronald Colman, David O. Selznick's *A Star Is Born* with Janet Gaynor, Sam Goldwyn's *Stella Dallas* with Barbara Stanwyck, and Jack Warner's *The Life of Emile Zola* starring the remarkable Paul Muni. Shirley Temple, Clark Gable, Bing Crosby, Fred Astaire and Ginger Rogers, Myrna Loy, and Gary Cooper were among the top ten box-office attractions.

The movies had made the transition to sound in the late twenties, and the "talkies" were booming. In less than a decade, incredible strides had been made in film recording and the use of music, and the studio system was bursting with talent and revenues. Despite the tragedies and upheavals that came with the end of the silent movie era, most of the studios had survived and, in fact, blossomed and expanded across the southern California landscape as never before: Paramount in the heart of Hollywood, Universal in North Hollywood, Warner Bros. and Walt Disney Studio just over the Hollywood Hills in Burbank, RKO at the corner of Gower Street and Melrose Avenue, and Twentieth Century-Fox on Pico Boulevard in Beverly Hills. Grandest of them all was Metro-Goldwyn-Mayer, south of Hollywood in Culver City. Its emblem of a shaggy lion was significant, for no studio roared like MGM. In 1937 the other Hollywood moguls could only look on with envy as

MGM netted a record profit, $14.5 million, with films such as *Maytime,
Topper,* and *Conquest.* Its stable of stars was incomparable: Norma
Shearer, Clark Gable, Greta Garbo, Robert Taylor, Joan Crawford,
Spencer Tracy, Jeanette MacDonald, Nelson Eddy, Eleanor Powell,
William Powell, Myrna Loy, Melvyn Douglas, Margaret Sullavan,
Mickey Rooney, Judy Garland—the list went on and on.

Metro-Goldwyn-Mayer Studio had been created by theater magnate Arthur Loew, head of Loews theater chain. By merging Metro
Pictures, Goldwyn Pictures, and Louis B. Mayer Productions, Loew
hoped to build a film empire to supply his theaters with a moneymaking product. Each of the studios brought benefits crucial to the
success of the new company. Metro Pictures, which had been formed in
1915 and had been supplying films to Loews theaters since 1920, con-
tributed a stable of stars. Goldwyn Pictures, whose founder, Sam
Goldwyn, had departed in 1922, brought an expandable Culver City
lot and the lion logo. Louis B. Mayer brought his considerable talents
of leadership, negotiation, and business savvy. He also brought with
him a young, dynamic vice president named Irving Thalberg, whose
artistic successes such as *The Big Parade, Grand Hotel,* and *Mutiny on the
Bounty* raised the studio's reputation to an unparalleled degree. With
the untimely death in 1936 of his brilliant young associate, Mayer ex-
ercised his formidable powers to keep Metro's lion roaring. He organized the various studio executives, which included J. Robert Rubin,
Alexander Lichtman, Edgar J. Mannix, Hunt Stromberg, Lawrence A.
Weingarten, Bernard Hyman, Harry Rapf, Samuel Katz, Benjamin
Thau, and Mervyn LeRoy, into a governing board known as the "College of Cardinals." Although MGM's official motto was "Ars Gratia Artis"
("Art for Art's Sake"), it was the studio's boast of "More Stars Than
There Are in the Heavens" that Mayer concentrated on. To compete in
the industry, especially among studios that owned more theaters in
which to show their films, Mayer knew he needed star power, and he
expected Greer Garson, Hedy Lamarr, Ilona Massey, and Miliza Korjus
to rise and sustain this star system.

Upon their first visit to the MGM lot at 10202 Washington Boulevard, Greer and Nina were escorted into the executive dining room on
the fourth floor of the recently completed Irving G. Thalberg administration building. There they met a different Mr. Mayer, whose friendliness as he welcomed them to America was tempered by the aura of

power that surrounded him. The plump, bespectacled, fifty-two-year-old mogul was in his element—the oversized, all-white office that was his home. No longer the charming negotiator he had appeared to be in London, this was the patriarch of MGM—the ultimate despot who guided the careers of his family members. Deviance from his wishes, they soon learned, was nothing short of mutiny and a breach of family etiquette. "Up to a certain point we can develop people," he once said, "but we cannot control their temperament. The organization must have the strength to sustain the individual, and the individual also has his obligation to the organization. There have been comparatively few times in our history that this hasn't been recognized, or when differences might not be sensibly bridged."

The illuminating, but altogether pleasant, luncheon came to an abrupt end when Mayer informed Greer, in fatherly tones, that the studio had no current motion picture for her. Instead, plans were underway for a publicity buildup campaign and a number of screen and makeup tests. Before the bewildered young immigrant could protest, an assistant appeared to escort them on a tour. Greer's and Nina's brief glimpses of English motion picture studios had hardly prepared them for their first look at L.B. Mayer's empire, which stretched over 117 acres in Culver City. Lot One, which contained the Thalberg building, was a concrete maze of sound stages (the studio had twenty-three in all), the world's largest film laboratory, rehearsal halls, a legendary commissary, and construction mills. Lot Two, across Overland Avenue from Lot One, was a beautiful fairyland of outdoor sets ranging from Andy Hardy's street and Verona Square to Copperfield and Wimpole Streets. Lot Three, on Jefferson Boulevard and Overland, contained an even larger area of outdoor facades, including a western street and Tarzan's jungle, bordered by a tranquil lake. By 1940 there were a total of six outdoor lots housing police and fire departments for the studio, a small hospital, a zoo, a stable, parking lots, and storage units. Greer was now one of over four thousand employees at Metro-Goldwyn-Mayer.

The publicity department was the heart of the studio, where Howard Strickling and his staff of more than one hundred fifty pumped out the stories that turned actors into stars and even B films into box-office winners. After Strickling gathered information from Greer, stories about MGM's new personality would be turned over to fan magazines.

She insisted that Ireland was her birthplace, a fact she had told the English press since the days of her early stardom in *The Golden Arrow,* and that 1908 was her birthdate. Strickling sent Natalie Bucknall from the research department on a search for interesting Irish trivia. She sent him a memo: "The earliest native word for Ireland is Eriu. It means 'the most beautiful woman in the world!'"

Among the first publicity notices released about Greer Garson were her opinions about the first film she saw in Hollywood. Of course it was an MGM film, and, significantly, it was about the sea, which had always fascinated her. The movie was *Captains Courageous,* costarring Spencer Tracy and Freddie Bartholomew. "Ranking high among my favorites," she said, "is that haunting scene where Manuel, rough seaman with the gentle heart, plays his old hurdy-gurdy and sings his odd little songs about the sunrise and the sea and the little fish, all the simple everyday things of the fisherman's life that are quite unfamiliar to the poor little rich boy. There is something infinitely touching and significant in the dawning affection and understanding between these two, so opposite in their origins and manners."

In the makeup department, headed by Jack Dawn, she was introduced to his assistant, William Tuttle, who had been with the studio since April 1934. "She called me, 'Professor,'" Tuttle recalls. "I made up a makeup chart for her that we both agreed on. It was the angular lines of her face that we wanted to emphasize. Her mother came with her and sat nearby to watch." Greer also met the studio's famous hairstylist, Sydney Guilaroff, who had also joined MGM in 1934, and was immediately put at ease by his gracious manner and English-Canadian accent. "What a magnificent creature she was," Guilaroff observed. "It was clear to me from the start that Greer Garson would be a major star." Despite the intense scrutiny and her own self-doubts about her screen image, Greer enjoyed the makeover. "Studio experts teach you to streamline yourself," she reported in fan magazines, "and certainly to have experts make you up (my eyebrows, for example, resembled fish hooks when I came here and are now sleekly arched half-moons), do your hair and design clothes for you adds, immeasurably, to self-confidence."

Ushered onto a half-lit soundstage for screen tests, she was introduced to cinematographer Joseph Ruttenberg, who was on a day off from his work on Julien Duvivier's *The Great Waltz.* She was handed a script and requested to play the part of a secretary, with a mouthful of American slang that she did not understand. She amused Ruttenberg's crew by asking, "What is a two-base hit?" The second test, in which she portrayed a chic aristocrat, elegantly gowned, bejeweled, and ornately coifed, was better. "The moment the light was put on Miss Garson it brought out her full charm," Ruttenberg recalls. "At once I became aware of her striking photographic qualities. For one thing, I remarked how beautifully she carried her clothes. Her poise was of great help to me. Her hair—the detail and color of it—showed to fine advantage. She was kind enough to say that the test was a fine photographic job."

The third test, however, proved to be even more significant. Greer's partner was another MGM newcomer, a handsome six-foot-three middle-aged Canadian gentleman who had been signed only a few months earlier. Used to wisecracking actresses like Tallulah Bankhead, with whom he had appeared on the stage, the actor was bemused by Greer's formal English manner. When the test was over, he attempted to break the ice. "Duchess," he said, "I'll bet we're starring together before you know it, and running this studio!" Everyone burst into laughter. The nickname stuck. Greer had a new friend at Metro-Goldwyn-Mayer.

The actor's name was Walter Pidgeon. Born on September 23, 1897, Pidgeon came from a well-to-do Canadian family in East St. John, New Brunswick, where a young Russian immigrant named Louis B. Mayer was also raised. From an early age Pidgeon sought adventure, dreaming of becoming a sea captain, and eventually enlisted in the Canadian army during World War I. With a fine, strong baritone singing voice, he joined the Copeley Players in Boston after the war. As a result, he earned a booking in New York's Aeolian Hall with Elsie Janis, who was on tour of the United States and Britain; a Victor Records contract in which he introduced such Irving Berlin standards as "What'll I Do?" and "Remember"; and film offers from Hollywood. He took the train ride to California in 1926 and made a number of films, including Universal's first talking picture, *Melody of Love*. Five years later, he married Ruth Walker. "She has a sense of humor, and she needs it," he once said of his wife. "Also, she can blitz me at backgammon. What more can a man ask?"

After a ten-year career and thirty-three undistinguished pictures for Paramount, First National, and Universal, Pidgeon was cast in a

Jean Harlow/Clark Gable picture, *Saratoga,* at MGM. Although the film was successful, its creation was marred by tragedy. Even as the cameras were still rolling, twenty-six-year-old Harlow was hospitalized with uremic poisoning and died of cerebral edema on June 7, 1937. Although the studio had lost one of its brightest stars, it gained a new one when Pidgeon signed a long-term contact three months later, on September 7, at $1,750 a week. At the age of forty, he was pleased to be under contract to the prestigious studio but doubted whether he could perpetuate his film stardom for long.

Sam Wood, who was directing the latest Marx Brothers comedy, *A Day at the Races,* was one of the first to see Greer's test. He decided that she would make an excellent villainess in his picture. But Greer was not about to become another Margaret Dumont. She marched up to L.B. Mayer's office and declared that she did not want to be a supporting character and a victim of the Marx Brothers' zany antics. Mayer glanced at the script, which included a sequence in which she would be literally wallpapered to a wall, and agreed with her. Esther Muir was cast in the role instead.

Although concerned that no other roles appeared immediately, Greer enjoyed herself that winter. Old friends such as Samson Raphaelson, Douglas Fairbanks Jr., and the Edward G. Robinsons invited her and Nina to teas and luncheons. The Garsons took special care in shopping for a new home. They found exactly what they were looking for in a modest one-story Spanish-styled house at 704 North Walden Drive in Beverly Hills. "It has a most beautiful garden of white oleanders," Greer informed Howard Strickling, "and Mother and I have indulged our mania for interior decorating, and hunting antiques." On the front lawn she placed a stone goose, followed by five little goslings. "It's an old English custom," she explained. "When a house is hard to find, the idea is to arrange a sort of landmark to help identify the place. The geese are ideal. They're no trouble at all. They don't cackle. And they don't demand corn." L.B. Mayer shipped a Christmas tree, fully decorated, to their home and invited mother and daughter to his beach house in Santa Monica for the holiday dinner. After the meal, while strolling the bright, cold sands with the glare from the Pacific dazzling her, Greer felt a surge of homesickness. As much as the beach might remind her of England, she found that the people were remarkably different. She noticed that all the other women at the party were dressed more colorfully and casually than she and decided that her trunks full of city clothes would have to go. "The palette of Nature in California does something for you," she said in an early MGM publicity release. "Like most girls, I still have one 'good' black dress and a few pairs of white kid gloves but otherwise I have discarded the contents of my thirty-two trunks and now wear strong, primary colors, scarlets, and greens and blues and yellows, silly play shoes, blue jeans, gay scarves and go without hats or gloves. It's all very relaxing!"

Much to their delight, Greer and Nina discovered that they were hardly the only Britons in town. A sizable colony of actors from the UK had arrived in Hollywood with the advent of talking pictures and starred in film adaptations of English classics such as *David Copperfield*, *Vanity Fair*, *Lloyd's of London*, and *A Tale of Two Cities*. Among them were Ronald Colman, Charles Laughton, Elsa Lanchester, Maureen O'Sullivan, Ray Milland, Herbert Marshall, Cary Grant, Errol Flynn, Leslie Howard, and Cedric Hardwicke. The steady stream would continue into the 1940s as actors fled the emerging storm of war over Europe. Laurence Olivier returned, with Vivien Leigh, and David O. Selznick lured Alfred Hitchcock. The growing number prompted British scenarist R.J. Minney to write: "The English colony is so large that Americans have been provoked into reviving their forgotten War of Independence sentiment in a song entitled 'The British are Coming! Bang! Bang!'"

Many, like the Garsons, were attracted by the temperate climate and physical beauty of southern California. "There is something in it all of that dream of Paradise," John Galsworthy, author of *The Forsyte Saga*, remarked upon visiting San Ysidro. Others were disenchanted. "There is more actual positive reality in one square inch of the beach at Scarborough than in the whole extent of Hollywood," observed Hugh Walpole. "In Hollywood itself . . . nothing else is talked about, morning and night, but [the movies] and similar efforts. No wars, no politics, no deaths, make any effect here. We are all on a raft together in the middle of the cinema sea! Nothing is real here but salaries." Constance Collier, who had made intermittent appearances in Hollywood since 1916, wrote to Walpole in 1935: "Hugh, this place is just like Donington Hall. When the German prisoners first went there they were amazed by its splendour and beauty. 'Aren't the English fools!' they said. 'Why, it's better to be prisoner than free.' Then after walking in the grounds for a few days they discovered the barbed wire. A month later all they did was to walk on the same track up to the barbed wire and back again."

The common language allowed the emigres to settle more easily into the Hollywood community than most Europeans and yet remain separate. Many in the colony held tight to their traditions. C. Aubrey Smith founded the Hollywood Cricket Club and chaired annual public school dinners. Ronald Colman's British tennis set became famous. In his book *Strangers in Paradise,* John Russell Taylor observed: "Everybody was always conscious they were English, even if they did not necessarily cling together in a coherent national group. Their bearing often seems, from contemporary accounts, to have been that of colonialists in some farflung part of the empire retaining from the old country their interests, their sports, their normal patterns of life, however inappropriate they may have been to the new circumstances."

On March 18, 1938, *Greater Amusements* published MGM General Sales Manager William F. Rodgers's outline for the studio's film output for 1938. Fifty-two A features were planned, with an expenditure of $35 million. Two pictures, James Hilton's *Goodbye, Mr. Chips* and A.J. Cronin's *The Citadel,* were to be made in England. Among the A pictures on Metro's roster was a Civil War drama entitled *The Toy Wife.*

In Hollywood and much of America, 1938 was the year of Scarlett O'Hara and a rebirth of interest in the War Between the States. David O. Selznick was attempting to produce a movie version of Margaret Mitchell's best-selling novel *Gone with the Wind,* and the nationwide "Search for Scarlett" had captured the country's imagination. At MGM, Louis B. Mayer was beginning to fear that he had made a mistake by not purchasing the movie rights. Aware that Warner Bros. was launching their own southern melodrama, *Jezebel* starring Bette Davis, Mayer intended to cash in on the Civil War too. *The Toy Wife,* a play by Zoë Akins, seemed a likely hit. It contained all the essential elements: a beautiful yet irresponsible southern belle named Frou-Frou, two suitors and a variety of duels, white-pillared plantation houses, and a dramatic death scene.

In an odd bit of casting, Viennese actress Luise Rainer was given the starring role. She was L.B. Mayer's most recent European success story. By 1938 she had won two Best Actress Academy Awards consecutively, for *The Great Ziegfeld* in 1936 and for *The Good Earth* in 1937.

While Melvyn Douglas and Robert Young were cast as Frou-Frou's lovers, a search began for an actress to portray her sensible and good-hearted sister, Louise. *The Toy Wife's* producer, Merian Cooper, became intrigued with Greer Garson's screen test, but neither Luise Rainer nor director Richard Thorpe thought that she was right. Greer heartily seconded their opinions. She told Cooper and Mayer, "I was a star in London. I did not come to Hollywood to play supporting roles! Please, don't harness me to the chariot wheels of another star!"

When the offers for Greer's services suddenly stopped coming, Benjamin Thau, concerned that her problem was her screen test, advised a meeting with Lillian Burns, the studio's expert in training actors for the camera. "She came to me after testing with Luise Rainer in *Toy Wife*," Miss Burns recalls. "One day in the commissary, the waitress came to me and said, 'Miss Garson is having lunch with her mother. She wondered if they might join you at your table.' I joined them. But there was no need to teach Greer how to act. She was a beautiful actress. But she was accustomed to really projecting from the stage. English actors and actresses know very well that the voice and the diction is the most important thing. But the camera magnified her habits on the screen. In our discussion I told her the problem was very simple, 'You're just over-doing your delivery. We can read some poetry together.' Of course, her problem was overcome very quickly." Reading the lines of Tennyson and Browning, Greer found that her accent softened and her delivery relaxed. As she put it, "the hot mush had cooled off." Miss Burns quickly became a friend and confidante.

While spending an afternoon in her garden a few days later, Greer was surprised to find Walter and Ruth Pidgeon at the side gate. "When are we going to do that picture together?" Walter called good-naturedly. It seemed that the Pidgeons, at 710 North Walden, were neighbors. While Nina fixed tea, Greer invited the couple into the kitchen. The Pidgeons were amazed that Greer had not made a film. Walter had finished *My Dear Miss Aldrich* and was currently costarring in the Jeanette MacDonald/Nelson Eddy musical *The Girl of the Golden West* and looking over the script for his next film, *Man-Proof*, to costar Myrna Loy. Ruth mentioned that Myrna was going to England at the end of the year to star in *Goodbye, Mr. Chips*.

The Pidgeons' friendly gossip only increased Greer's anxious worries about her career. Her new home was little comfort without work.

Although Miliza Korjus was cast in *The Great Waltz* in 1938, Greer found that Hedy Lamarr and Ilona Massey had also been ignored. The women christened themselves the "Neglected Imports" and wondered collectively if L.B. Mayer would ever fulfill his promises. "If you're a painter or writer, you do it," Greer complained. "But an actor can't be an actor all alone. He just becomes nothing." Ilona was finally given a supporting role in *Rosalie,* an extravagant musical comedy featuring Nelson Eddy and Eleanor Powell. Then Hedy was borrowed by United Artists to star in the exotic romance, *Algiers,* with Charles Boyer, and became an overnight Hollywood sex symbol. The triumvirate had broken up, and Greer was alone.

Wandering about the soundstages, observing the fast-paced, exciting activity as Spencer Tracy and Mickey Rooney cried in *Boys Town,* Robert Taylor and Margaret Sullavan fell in love in *Three Comrades,* Jeanette MacDonald and Nelson Eddy sang to each other in *Sweethearts,* and Joan Crawford clashed with Melvyn Douglas in *The Shining Hour,* Greer felt despondent and out of place. She was not even given a dressing room. William Tuttle could understand what she was going through. "A strange face was murder," he recalled. "I would go down to the stock room to pick up some office supplies or Kleenex, and I could stand there forever. The store clerk would wait on everybody before he would wait on me. I was an outsider. After I'd been there awhile they finally accepted me." "The trouble, I learned later, was that I didn't fit into any established category," Greer said. "No glamour girl, no cheesecake, the oddly-boned face and the tallness. It didn't charm people. It worried them. And worried producers do not cast you in parts. I was, presumably, invisible, and so utterly miserable, and dispirited, that when I did see producers, I was stiff with resentment. They did not know what to make of me and must have thought, 'What did L.B. bring that one over for!'"

Greer surprised Benjamin Thau one morning by announcing that she had gone shopping for roles herself and had found one she wanted at Twentieth Century-Fox. It was the role of a ne'er-do-well British aristocrat, Lady Esketh, in *The Rains Came,* which was being prepared by Darryl Zanuck. Based on Louis Bromfield's best-selling novel, the story concerned the love affair between Lady Esketh and an Indian surgeon, which, like nearly everything else in the film, is destroyed by a spectacular flood. Zanuck intended to make the production one of his biggest hits for 1939, casting his most popular star, Tyrone Power, in the lead and lavishing exorbitant amounts of time and a $2.5 million budget on the movie.

Greer had certainly chosen the right moment to announce her candidacy. The *Hollywood Reporter* was filled with news about contract star negotiations between Louis B. Mayer and Zanuck. At Norma Shearer's insistence, Mayer had requested Tyrone Power for *Marie Antoinette.* In order to get him, Mayer was willing to loan two of his own stars for Fox films. Already Spencer Tracy had been chosen for *Stanley and Livingstone,* and now Zanuck was eyeing Metro's female talent for the part of Lady Esketh. However, even at Thau's suggestion, Mayer refused to loan Greer to Fox. She was too much of a lady to play a role like that, he declared. Mayer offered Zanuck Myrna Loy, who had recently been named "Queen of the Movies" in a *New York Daily News* poll.

As the months went by, Greer's impatience turned to illness. She suffered neuritis and caught influenza. Attempting to diet, to achieve Hollywood's exaggerated slimness, she suffered malnutrition and anemia. The rest of the time she strained at the leash, pondering seriously a return to England. "During that disappointing, and disillusioning, and humiliating period," Greer said, "it was my mother who kept me alive." The fact that she was now in her thirties, at an age when most actresses are already well into their careers, haunted her the most. Garbo, Shearer, and Crawford, all in their mid-thirties, had twenty-six, fifty-three, and forty-six films to their credit, respectively, by the end of 1937. Of the newest pool of MGM talent in which Greer found herself, Hedy Lamarr was only twenty-four and Lana Turner, who had also joined the studio in 1937, was just seventeen.

She began to search for an agent. Benjamin Thau suggested Mrs. Ad Schulberg. But, instead, Greer chose the highly experienced Michael Levee, who represented some of Metro's biggest stars, including Joan Crawford, and British actors such as Leslie Howard. He immediately began negotiations with Edgar Mannix, overseer of the studio's operations, and was dismayed by the blunt dislike of Greer Garson that he encountered. The College of Cardinals had no interest in an apparently spoiled English actress with a haughty manner and an inability to understand that she must earn her Hollywood stardom. Look at Norma Shearer, Robert Taylor, Joan Crawford, and Clark Gable. Each of them had started humbly in B pictures, supporting roles, or worse. Others voiced an even more alarming opinion: "Let her go!"

There were promising proposals for George Bernard Shaw's *The Doctor's Dilemma* (which Metro eventually made in 1958) and a comedy entitled *Millionairess*, but Levee's negotiations with the studio ultimately faltered. One afternoon in mid-July, he drove over to 704 North Walden Drive and sat down with Greer and Nina. Mervyn LeRoy, whom Mayer had hired to fill the shoes of Irving Thalberg, was planning to make a film in September entitled *Dramatic School*. It bore more than a passing resemblance to RKO's highly successful *Stage Door*, which had won raves for Katharine Hepburn's portrayal of an ambitious actress. *Dramatic School*'s heroine was an ambitious drama student named Louise. It was a part for which Luise Rainer, Paulette Goddard, Virginia Grey, and Lana Turner had already been tested. LeRoy had seen Greer's test and was considering her for the leading role of Louise.

The chance to star Greer Garson in a production by one of Hollywood's hottest young filmmakers was just the opportunity Levee had been bargaining for. In his ten-year career Mervyn LeRoy had risen to prominence as one of the finest directors at Warner Bros, consistently turning out profitable and critically acclaimed pictures such as *Little Caesar, I Am a Fugitive from a Chain Gang,* and *Gold Diggers of 1933.* He attained a Hollywood pedigree early, as the cousin of film pioneer Jesse Lasky and the son-in-law of Warner Bros. executive Harry Warner. Impressed with LeRoy's record, Irving Thalberg had lured him to Metro in February 1933 for thirty thousand dollars to make *Tugboat Annie,* a box-office blockbuster with Wallace Beery and Marie Dressler. But Jack Warner and his brothers were not about to let LeRoy go, and his stellar career continued at their Burbank studio with *Sweet Adeline, Anthony Adverse, They Won't Forget,* and *The Great Garrick.*

It was not until February 15, 1938, that L.B. Mayer, with an offer of six thousand dollars a week, was finally able to secure the director with an exclusive MGM contract as a producer. Among the lineup of films that LeRoy was preparing for 1938-39 was a musical, *The Wizard of Oz,* and *Dramatic School.* The following morning Greer was seated in the waiting room outside the producer's new third-floor corner executive suite in the Thalberg building. The script for *Dramatic School* was gripped tightly in her hands. She had spent the night reading over the screenplay and memorizing Louise's key lines. The part fit her like a glove and remarkably paralleled her own situation at Metro. Invited into LeRoy's office, she was surprised to find the thirty-seven-year-old Hollywood veteran so strikingly young. He introduced her to Robert Sinclair, the film's director. Assured by her appearance and conversation, they offered her the role.

The next few weeks were a happy preproduction whirl of script readings, wardrobe tests, meetings with Lillian Burns, and more tests. Then one morning Mervyn LeRoy's office received a call from Good Samaritan Hospital. Miss Garson would not be in. She had taken a fall from a horse over the weekend and inflamed an old spinal injury. The physicians discovered that Greer's damaged vertebrae were grinding together. Exploratory surgery was recommended, and an operation had been scheduled for August 1. "At last," Greer told her mother grimly, "I have appeared in a picture in Hollywood: X-ray pictures of my insides." Mervyn LeRoy called an emergency meeting with his *Dramatic School* staff. Greer was out. Luise Rainer was in. Just as in Birmingham, it appeared that illness might destroy Greer's career at MGM.

A few days before the operation, Greer attended a dinner party at the Edward G. Robinsons'. Seated with her was Viennese director Josef von Sternberg, who was currently directing Hedy Lamarr's MGM film debut, *I Take This Woman*. The man who had discovered Marlene Dietrich and made her most stylish films at Paramount was impressed with the spunk of the young British actress. He attempted to distract her from her career troubles with merry tales of his beautiful new home in the San Fernando Valley, surrounded by a moat and with a garage especially-scaled to his Dusenberg. He sent orchids to her hospital room every day that she was there.

Another bouquet that arrived after the surgery was less welcome. Alec Snelson attempted to reach her in Hollywood through a mutual friend, Mrs. Cora Copp, who had a cousin, Mrs. C.E.C. Cox, in Nagpur, India. Fearful that he might find her, Greer sent the flowers back and refused to give Mrs. Copp her forwarding address. The surgery had revealed the spinal weakness the doctors had feared, as well as one kidney out of place and signs of malnutrition. On August 22 she was released from the hospital, in more pain than ever. Shortly thereafter, Michael Levee paid a visit. Declining the usual offer of tea from Nina, Levee got straight to the point. Eddie Mannix had informed him that Metro-Goldwyn-Mayer was terminating her contract—immediately.

CHAPTER 10

THE ROOM GREW SUDDENLY STILL. The warm late afternoon sun was beginning to fade, and gloom surrounded them. Nina broke the silence, noisily setting down her teacup and turning distressed eyes upon her daughter. Greer only stared blankly at Michael Levee, no longer listening to him as he continued to explain contract details. All her worst fears were realized; Laurence Olivier's unhappy tales of Hollywood suddenly came flooding back. Levee gently reminded them that Mayer did have the right to drop any of his actors every six months. It was all there in the fine print. The mogul had promised, however, to buy up the balance of her contract and leave her free to consider other studio offers.

"Suddenly I knew what I had to do," Greer later reported. "When you can't wait for your ship to come in, you've got to row out to it. I don't know how I wiggled out of my wheelchair next day, but I fixed myself up and got down to the studio, packing my scrapbook under my arms. All my best friends at MGM were away; Louis B. Mayer was in Europe. The only one I knew even slightly was Eddie Mannix. I marched into his office, like any green, stagestruck girl. Imagine, hoping to influence a veteran Hollywood executive with a scrapbook! Especially when you're up to be fired! But I knew what I wanted. I wanted my chance."

Mannix calmly motioned her into a chair. He had heard of this new contract player's redheaded temper, but this was his first personal experience. He admitted that the studio had indeed found it difficult to find a film role for her, especially since she had refused to accept supporting parts. He showed her a list of the last ten releases of Metro-Goldwyn-Mayer. Did she see a part for herself in any of them? No, she admitted. But she was not interested in the last ten pictures. She was only concerned with the next ten. When she left his office a few minutes later, she had what she wanted: a promise from the head of studio operations to keep her on the Metro contract list until the end of her first-year option in October. But she was only slightly mollified, fully expecting to sit out the remainder of her studio tenure.

And that is exactly what happened as summer turned to fall and she watched her time run out. When she asked for Mayer, Benjamin Thau explained that the mogul had developed a new passion that summer: horse racing. On the advice of physicians, who warned him that he needed relaxation and diversion away from the studio, Mayer had tackled his new hobby in a big way. He had purchased a stable of horses for seventy-eight thousand dollars and set them up on a six-hundred-acre property in Sarasota Springs that included a six-furlong racing track and stables. As his interest grew into an obsession, studio personnel began to joke that Metro had another back lot, named Santa Anita Racetrack. Hearing of this, Greer snapped, "Tell him that he has a mustang right here in Culver City, pawing the ground, anxious to go places!"

"Greer was having a very difficult time," William Tuttle recalls. "Her back was constantly bothering her. She complained to me once that she intended to leave MGM and return to her chiropractor in London." As the back pain worsened, Greer sought another American doctor—this time an orthopedic surgeon. He suggested a delicate operation in which her spine would be wired up to avoid the painful pressure on the nerves. But the outcome would incapacitate her for two or three months in the hospital and another seven to eight months in a plaster cast. There was also the concern that she would never be as active as before.

One cool October morning only a few days before she had to give her consent to the surgeon, the telephone rang. It was Mike Levee. He told her there was a part available for her in *Goodbye, Mr. Chips.* Myrna Loy's departure for Twentieth Century-Fox had left the part of Mrs. Chips available. Director Sam Wood, author James Hilton, and producer Victor Saville thought she was suited for the part. Would she come to the studio and make some more tests?

Greer's heart sank as she read the script. The role of Katherine Chipping was as small as she had remembered it when she read the

story that long-ago Christmas in Brighton. The screenplay, which began in 1870 at a fictitious English boys' school named Brookfield,
focused on the teaching career of Charles Chipping. A strict and over-
zealous disciplinarian, Chipping's future at the school seems bleak and
lonely until a fellow teacher, Mr. Staefel, invites him on a hiking trip
high in the Tyrol mists. There, on a mountaintop, he meets the beautiful Katherine Ellis, whom he later marries. With the help of her
charm, gentle humor, and devotion to his students and career, Chipping soon becomes the popular and revered "Chips" of Brookfield.
When Kathie dies in childbirth he struggles on, maintaining his unqualified success at the school and becoming headmaster. During
World War I he keeps the school running despite bombings and the
tragic losses of former students and friends on the battlefield. On his
deathbed soon after the war, Chips overhears a colleague mourn the
fact that he never had any children. "Ah, but I have," he insists, "thousands of them, and all boys."

Torn between her need to work and the indignity of accepting
what amounted to a supporting role, Greer turned to her only female
friend at the studio. "Greer came in," Miss Burns recalls, "and she was
in a red-headed fury because they had asked her to do a test for
Goodbye, Mr. Chips. She said to me: 'I haven't done any American films
yet. How can I go back to England? How can I do anything with that
sparrow of a woman? The role is a first act curtain. Have you read it?'
And I said, 'Yes, I have.' And she said, 'Do you understand?' I said, 'No,
because if you do that Christmas scene the way I know you can and
will, they will never forget you.'" Some fifty-odd years later, Miss Burns
insisted, "It must have put something in her mind because I did get a
telegram from her after the premiere that said: 'You were right.' She
asked me to look after her mother while she was gone. Nina was a most
charming lady. We would have dinner some nights or see a picture,
things of that kind. We became good friends."

Surprised that her friend believed so strongly in the picture, Greer
showed up for the required tests in a pensive, submissive mood. When
she was introduced to the Chips production team, producer Victor
Saville explained how they discovered her. With less than a month before his scheduled departure for the Denham Studio to begin Chips,
Sam Wood had spent his days screening tests of actresses for the role of
Kathie Chipping. His friend and fellow producer, Bernard Hyman,

had helped out now and then. The men were alone except for the camera operator, who sat in the projection room watching the tests through the glass window. When one formally dressed, bejeweled actress appeared on the screen, Wood scowled impatiently, recalling her as that stuffy English actress he had once considered for *A Day at the Races*. But Hyman suggested that he take another look. The regal wardrobe that she was wearing was entirely inappropriate for Kathie Chipping—and yet there was something. The little square window flew up, interrupting Sam's concentration. The operator announced that he had made a mistake. Greer Garson's name was not listed on his sheet.

"It's all right," Wood replied. "I think we have our Mrs. Chips."

But Greer could not share their pleasure or excitement. On that all-too-familiar film test set, a symbol of her failure over the past year, her emotions were in a turmoil. Uncomfortable as always in front of the camera, with her back aching, she was dressed for seemingly innumerable costume tests, reflecting the changing Victorian, Edwardian, and Georgian styles of the film. Other disturbing thoughts occurred to her. What if *Chips* resulted in another *Dramatic School* disappointment? Could she face her London peers in a supporting role after her triumphant departure? She could also imagine the raised eyebrows among her family at her appearance in a film about teachers. Suddenly the cameraman, George Folsey, gave the signal, and the bright lights were turned off for the day. Greer fled the sound stage.

Returning home, she vented her anger and disappointment at her mother. But Nina sided with Lillian Burns. The wife in this picture was not a sparrow, she argued, but a dove. It was a chance to play a character Greer had never played in London, revealing the warmth and gentle good humor of her nature for the first time. She would have the privilege of portraying a woman every man would like to marry. Nina added that playing Mrs. Chips would also provide an opportunity to see the family chiropractor in London. Stubbornly, Greer turned a deaf ear to such consolations.

Little did she realize what a breathtaking impact her screen tests made upon Victor Saville and James Hilton in the screening room that evening. She was summoned by Sidney Franklin to his office and told that she had the part. The MGM producer who had almost directed *Goodbye, Mr. Chips* himself and continued to act as a production advisor, struck her as "a small, elfin-like man, with an uncanny perception about what is, at once, good taste and entertainment in a picture." A consummate artist, and consequently one of the most admired and respected men at Metro-Goldwyn-Mayer, Franklin's impressive film credits included Noël Coward's *Private Lives*; *The Guardsman* with Alfred Lunt and Lynn Fontanne; *The Barretts of Wimpole Street* with Norma Shearer, Fredric March, and Charles Laughton; and *The Good Earth*. With Victor Saville at hand, he apprised Greer of the troubled history of *Goodbye, Mr. Chips*.

James Hilton had written the poignant tale "Mr. Chips" in November 1933, as a twenty-thousand-word Christmas story for *British Weekly*. Before his days as the esteemed author of novels such as *Lost Horizon, Knight without Armor,* and *Journey's End,* Hilton was a struggling young writer living with his wife and dogs in Wanstead, Lancashire. Subsisting on the two articles a week that he wrote for Dublin's *Irish Independent,* Hilton jumped at the opportunity to write a "long short" story for the *British Weekly's* special Christmas supplement. He was given two weeks.

His inspiration for Mr. Chips was his father, who was a British schoolmaster, as well as other teachers who had instructed him, including his classical master at Leys School, Cambridge, William H. Balgarnie. "I don't think I have ever written before so quickly, easily, and with such certitude that I needn't think twice about a word, a sentence, or a movement in the narrative," Hilton told *Picturegoer*. "I had been granted that curious 'lift' of the pen which . . . must be called 'inspiration.' It duly appeared and got some mildly favorable comment and I considered it a closed chapter."

Though not an initial success in England, the *Atlantic Monthly* made *Goodbye, Mr. Chips* an immediate success in America in April 1934. The popularity and eventual publication of the story in June as a novelette made English critics take another look and deem it a masterpiece. In America, Alexander Woollcott, the radio broadcaster known famously as "The Town Crier," devoted an entire program to the book, proclaiming it "the most profoundly moving story that has passed this way in several years."

Metro-Goldwyn-Mayer purchased the galley proofs to the story that spring at the instigation of Irving Thalberg. He invited James Hilton to Hollywood to write the screen adaptation with studio writers R.C. Sherriff, Claudine West, and Eric Maschwitz. It did not require much persuasion to convince Hilton to come. Soon after his arrival, he wrote to his British friends from Hollywood's most exclusive hotel, the Chateau Marmont: "I am optimistic about the cinema. It is pioneering, without perhaps being aware of it, into channels of human behavior which are to become increasingly important in the world of the future. And I am impressed—why not?—with the power and possibilities of its influence."

Work progressed slowly on *Chips* because of Thalberg's heavy production schedule. By 1936 he was busy making *Romeo and Juliet* with his wife, Norma Shearer, collaborating with director George Cukor on Greta Garbo's *Camille,* and preparing ambitious filmizations of Pearl Buck's epic *The Good Earth* and Jane Austen's *Pride and Prejudice.* But he did find time to position Sidney Franklin as the director of the film and to develop a cast list. Considering Lionel Barrymore or Charles Laughton for Mr. Chips, Franklin asked James Hilton for advice. The author surprised him by suggesting Wallace Beery. "I would rather have an American who can feel what it ought to be than an Englishman who is selected just because he has the English accent," he argued. "Wallace Beery has the warmth for it. I don't understand why so many people think of Chips as a little wispy man. I don't describe the physical features of any of my characters."

On September 14, 1936, when Irving Thalberg died, *Goodbye, Mr. Chips* was temporarily shelved, along with his other productions. Denham production chief Michael Balcon chose *A Yank at Oxford,* starring Robert Taylor and Vivien Leigh, to inaugurate MGM's British studios. Victor Saville's production of *The Citadel,* featuring English matinee idol Robert Donat and Rosalind Russell, was to follow. It was Sidney Franklin, promoted to a producer upon Thalberg's death, who finally reactivated *Chips* and efficiently reorganized the production team. Forced to bow out of *Chips* because of his new responsibilities, he hired Victor Saville to produce the picture and Sam Wood to direct it. Fifty-five-year-old Sam Grosvenor Wood had been in the motion picture business since 1915, prompting Hedda Hopper to comment, "Sam's been around so long he's a landmark." "Franklin and I worked over the script for a month," Wood recalled, "and agreed on every detail before I left for England. The script contained nothing that was not in the book, except to add and amplify those scenes and situations that could be read between the lines, principally the charming love story between Mr. Chipping and Kathie. We were fortunate in having many notes made by Thalberg, who had great faith in Hilton's novel."

Victor Saville wanted Robert Donat for the role of Mr. Chips. The swashbuckling star of *The Private Life of Henry VIII* and *The Count of Monte Cristo* enthusiastically accepted despite warnings from his close friends, who felt that the role was a threat to his virile, heroic image. In 1938 he told the English press: "MGM has been tempting me for years with promises of how happy they would make me and so far they've certainly carried them out. For a so-called romantic actor to get one chance like *The Citadel*, is rare. To get two running is almost unbelievable!"

With their lead in place, Victor Saville turned to the role of Katherine Chipping. He had initially chosen English favorite Elizabeth Allan, who had starred in *David Copperfield* and *A Tale of Two Cities*, but these plans went awry when Miss Allan shocked Hollywood by suing Metro-Goldwyn-Mayer. She had originally been cast by Saville in *The Citadel*, until director King Vidor decided he wanted Rosalind Russell instead. Elizabeth was furious, contending that the move was unfair and damaging to her career, since the publicity about her casting had already been released. Saville and Mayer tried to console her with full financial compensation, but she took her case to court and ultimately lost her contract with MGM.

Greer packed for the trip back to London, fully intending to stay there when *Goodbye, Mr. Chips* was finished, even if L.B. Mayer offered to renew her studio contract. She would look up Margaret Webster or Michael Barry and Cecil Madden. "I'm not coming back," she said. "This place has broken me." But Nina, although silent, was just as stubborn. She refused to accompany Greer to London; she said she intended to stay at the house on North Walden until her daughter's return. Their argument was suddenly interrupted by the ring of the doorbell. Charlotte Harding opened the door to reveal Hollywood gossip columnist Hedda Hopper. "Isn't Miss Garson ready?" the formidable writer demanded as she marched in, sat down, and took out her writing pad. Absorbed in the difficulties of the day, Greer had forgotten about the scheduled interview. It was not an auspicious beginning to her relationship with the American press.

They sat at the kitchen table while Nina scurried into the kitchen to make tea. As the hours passed, Greer wearied of this invasion of her privacy. Suddenly, the pressures and unpleasantness of the previous weeks overwhelmed her, and she burst into tears. She admitted that her film career was a disaster but, upon recovering, requested that her confession be forgotten. It was not until 1950 that Hedda Hopper related the incident: "She was heartsick. Greer added herself up that night as a failure in Hollywood, going back to face the homefolks and play what she thought then was a secondary, inconspicuous role in a mediocre picture."

With her back still troubling her, Greer spent nearly the entire voyage to England in late November taking salt baths, lying on the massage table, or roaming the decks alone. One evening, while looking over her few pages of script in the dining room, she met British producer and director Gabriel Pascal. Although unwilling to divulge the details of her "lost" year, she explained the difficulties of playing Mrs. Chips. Leafing through the script over dinner, Pascal found the character "womanly and warm" and advised Greer that "she is sure to endear you to the public, which is all one can ask of a first screen role." As the boat arrived at Southampton, he kissed her hand in farewell and promised to find her screen work in London if her Metro contract was canceled.

Greer's spirits began to rise as she was driven through the city along familiar roads. She was home. After checking into her room at the Dorchester, she was driven to the Tower Road office of Sam Eckman Jr., the managing director of the MGM Denham facilities. There she was welcomed by Eckman, Michael Balcon, Sam Wood, and Ben Goetz and given a tour of the twenty-three sets that were emerging on the soundstages for *Goodbye, Mr. Chips.*

At a press conference, Sam Wood announced his plans to cast the remaining 153 speaking roles locally. "London has the greatest reservoir of acting talent of any city in the world," he announced. "Lyn Harding, John Mills, Paul Henreid, Milton Rosmer, Austin Trevor, Louise Hampton, and scores of other top-rank players, many of them with their names in lights on theater marquees, were willing to play the smallest of parts, providing they offered an exceptional scene or two. That is why the supporting cast of an English picture is uniformly excellent." Then, averting his eyes to Greer meaningfully, he added, "The English actor takes the attitude that a role does not necessarily have to be big to be good." Of her first press conference, Greer recalled, "The publicists were wonderful to me, and there were headlines in the papers, amused but good humored about the girl who had traveled 12,000 miles to play her first screen part!"

Filming officially began on November 28, 1938. Greer's first scene—the one in which Mrs. Chips is introduced to the professors of Brookfield—was scheduled for a month later, on December 20. The meaning behind her first speech—"It's so nice to meet you all—and just a little terrifying"—went beyond the film's story. "Someone must have known I was going to play Mrs. Chips when that was written," she said. "It expressed my feelings perfectly."

Greer needed all the advice she could get, for she was distracted by the process of moviemaking. Frequently Robert Donat found his leading lady completely disoriented on the set. "He'd say, 'Look here, my lovely. The camera's over there,'" Greer recalled. Despite the helpful advice of Lillian Burns, she had problems adjusting to the various stop and go signals, emoting on cue, and dealing with extraneous disturbances on the set. She later commented, "Since there are split scenes and endless repetition of important scenes so that they may be photographed from different angles and at different range, and the last scenes are often shot first, there can be no steady, uninterrupted flow, and to achieve any kind of smoothness or continuity, one must have the patience and ingenuity of a mosaic worker."

Robert Donat provided constant support. The actor, who had been inspired as a youngster to become an actor by watching the cinematic adventures of western star William S. Hart, had been making films since 1932. He was not only familiar with camera technique (he had worked with Alfred Hitchcock in *The Thirty-Nine Steps*), he had performed in another James Hilton work, *Knight without Armor*, as well. "Bob was the dearest man," Greer recalled. "Although I knew him only while we were working together, I have the happiest memories of a very special human being with an exceptional talent."

Paul Henreid, who later became famous as Ingrid Bergman's idealistic husband in *Casablanca*, played the role of the kindly German professor, Mr. Staefel. The actor, a veteran of the Vienna stage before coming to London, had appeared in a number of Austrian films. *Goodbye, Mr. Chips* marked his American film debut. "Greer was extremely nervous about her ability," he recalled, "and came to Bob Donat and me in tears at least twice a week. 'I'm just not getting it.

What shall I do? Please, Paul, Bob—help me out.' And we did, and Sam Wood . . . helped her too. 'Be simple,' we all advised her. 'Just remember, you can be more effective by throwing away a line than by emoting over it.'"

Greer's anxieties about *Goodbye, Mr. Chips* turned to melancholy as Christmas approached. The Murrays, who had promised to visit, were forced to cancel when Uncle James became ill. As the cast and crew worked through the afternoon of the twenty-fourth, then dispersed for homes and parties, she faced the holiday alone. "I felt more terribly lonely than I ever had in my life," she recalled. But when Victor Saville stopped by with holiday farewells and learned of her situation, he invited her to his home. Greer accepted and never regretted it. For years she remembered that evening with special affection. "It was so jolly," she recalled, "a very big party, and after dinner we danced the Lambeth Walk till our legs gave way."

In January, shooting continued at Repton College, which doubled for the fictional Brookfield. Greer was snagged by a *Picturegoer* journalist one afternoon while the others attended an impromptu studio party honoring Donat's own headmaster from Manchester Central School. "My year in Hollywood was, quite frankly, the unhappiest of my life," she remarked candidly, displaying a rare public flash of temper. "Nobody is to blame, really. It's just one of those unfortunate things. But I can never make up for it. Time is very precious to me, you see."

Greer finished her performance on February 6 and planned to visit friends and enjoy a short vacation in Paris until her scheduled return on March 4 for the preview and re-takes. She appeared at numerous London parties, received and declined an invitation from Michael Barry to appear on television with Robert Donat, and enjoyed a brief, happy visit with her uncle, aunt, and cousins. Everyone was anxious to hear about her movie experience. Recalling her confusion before the camera, the distractions, disturbances, and worries, Greer told them, "It was like being comfortably at home in 'The Cabinet of Dr. Caligari.'"

Goodbye, Mr. Chips, produced at a final cost of $1,051,000, was previewed for the English press at Sam Eckman's little theater behind Cambridge Circus. Among the congratulatory notices that L.B. Mayer received in Culver City was a telegram from Greer. "I will gladly come and make a picture with you when you have one ready for me. But a repetition of the past eleven and a half months I spent in Hollywood would kill me. It was the most difficult and unhappiest year of my life. All I have to show for it is eighteen thousand miles of travel, a few tests, and an almost infinitesimal part in *Goodbye, Mr. Chips*. Now that I am fortunate enough to be away, it would take wild horses to drag me back."

Mayer was not about to lose the star of what appeared to be a box-office hit. He sent her a sharp order to return, softened with a collection of complimentary notices about her performance, and a solemn promise to renew her contract on more lucrative terms. He added that scripts were being prepared for her. She obediently packed her bags and sailed for New York. She was surprised to find a cluster of reporters awaiting her at the dock. *Goodbye, Mr. Chips* had been previewed in Los Angeles, and the press was already seething with excitement about MGM's latest female discovery. "No more laudable film has come out of England," proclaimed *Variety*. "In Greer Garson the picture introduces an attractive young English actress of outstanding talent and charm. . . . She plays her romantic assignment as the wife of Mr. Chips . . . with rare understanding and tenderness. The reticent love scenes are masterpieces of emotional power."

From her new friend Gabriel Pascal, whom she had met on the ship to England, she received a telegram of congratulations. In response she wrote, "I am not as depressed as I might have been for the attitude has changed completely here at MGM, which makes all the difference. Now the studio is as anxious to find a story for me as I was to have them, for they do not want me to be off the screen any longer than necessary, they assure me earnestly, after the success of *Chips*. Scripts are submitted to me and story conferences held and, whereas last year I had not been good enough for anything; now, nothing is good enough for me. I was given a dressing room in the building reserved for the stars. Mr. Benjamin Thau is charming, and takes me dining and dancing and to concerts and the opera. Miss Bette Davis invited me to dinner. Parties are given for me. I am, in short, no longer invisible." After adding her bold signature to the letter, she added a postscript. "Thank you for your lovely offer, but I shall have to decline it. I underestimated completely Mrs. Chips's influence on my career. For once, I am glad I was wrong."

Goodbye, Mr. Chips premiered at the Astor Theater on Broadway in New York on May 15, 1939. In his radio address, Alexander Woollcott proclaimed, "In a year in which the great nations of the world seem to be choosing partners for a dance of death this cavalcade of English youth becomes suddenly an almost unbearable reminder of something which in a mad and greedy world may be allowed to perish from the Earth. I am here only to testify that in my own experience, the most moving of all motion pictures is the one called *Goodbye, Mr. Chips*." "It is not necessary to agree with Alexander Woollcott that this is the best motion picture ever made, to be certain that it is a screen masterpiece," remarked the *New York Herald-Tribune*. "Greer Garson, as the woman who marries Mr. Chips in spite of himself, conspires with him to give a performance of enormous sincerity which makes her relatively brief appearance in the film electric and haunting."

The celebrated new movie star attended the star-studded Hollywood opening on May 22 at the Four Star Theater on Wilshire Boulevard. Hundreds of fans lined both sides of the street as the studio limousine carrying Greer and her mother arrived. Nina emerged with a smile, concealing her exasperation that her daughter had caused them to be late. Most of the stars had already gone inside. As Greer made her way down the red carpet, wearing a glamorous red velvet cloak with the hood hanging to her waist and feathers in her hair, the camera flashes suddenly stopped. The pressmen stared blankly at her. The following day, Alta Durant wrote in *Variety:* "Miss Garson stepped out of her car with her mother, but there was no cheer from the crowd . . . the fans didn't know her . . . photographers from the downtown papers also did not recognize the new luminary, but Metro flacks rallied the snapshooters and the latecomer to fame again marched down the lane of gawkers with the attention due her."

The belief that Nina, Lillian Burns, Sam Wood, and Sidney Franklin had shared that Greer was the ideal Katherine Chipping was proven to everyone in the audience that evening. Under the gentle support of her director and costars, Greer blossomed on screen. If she did not invest her part with the rich, assured emotion of her later film characterizations, she was irresistibly beguiling in scenes such as the Christmas Eve sequence that had touched Lillian Burns. At home before the fireplace, she tells her husband, "Never be afraid, Chips, that you can't do anything you've made up your mind to. As long as you believe in yourself you can go as far as you dream." None of the troubles that she had experienced on the set were evident in her portrayal of a woman who profoundly affects the life of the man she loves. In fact, so profound is her effect upon Chips and the picture that her abrupt passing makes the rest of the film seem overlong. The *Philadelphia Public Ledger* observed, "Miss Garson, somehow, and there must have been magic in her, has managed to present a Katherine who is, to the smallest detail, everything Mr. Hilton's broad description implied. The part of the film she shares is the richest, the sweetest, part of it. . . . That Miss Garson has beauty is obvious. That she has intelligence is apparent in her handling of a role that might have become cloying. That the Scotch-Irish actress will become one of MGM's brightest stars, we're ready to wager."

Afterward, as the gathering began to disperse, a reporter asked what it was like for the new star to see herself in a motion picture. Greer paused a moment. "I enjoy acting while I am doing it," she said, thoughtfully. "But it is an uncomfortable sensation to see myself on the screen. Like the Student of Prague who sold his shadow to the Devil whereupon it stepped away from him and went off to lead an independent, and probably deplorable existence of its own, so my image danced on the screen and does extraordinary things over which I have no control. I am helpless to twitch its skirt into place, rearrange its hair or tell it to change that silly expression. To see myself canned, disembodied, and distilled, upsets me." When asked for his impression of the film, James Hilton volunteered only one fault: less than the conventional three minutes had been allowed for the brewing of the tea.

Goodbye, Mr. Chips eventually grossed $3,252,000, among the highest of 1939. It earned seven Oscar nominations: for Best Picture, Best Direction, Best Screenwriting, Best Film Editing, and Best Sound Recording. Robert Donat was nominated for Best Actor, and Greer was nominated for Best Actress. The nomination sent her world spinning. Already crowded out of her small bungalow on North Walden, she was in the process of moving to 149 South Roxbury Drive when the publicity blitz struck. Still hardly believing that her part in *Goodbye, Mr. Chips* had been such a success, she was suddenly thrown into the Oscar limelight. It had been an incredible feat, earning a nomination for the industry's highest honor in her very first film. Only in 1931, when Helen Hayes was nominated for *The Sins of Madelon Claudet,* had an MGM actress earned such a status. Greer's competition within the category were all film veterans: Bette Davis (*Dark Victory*), Irene Dunne (*Love Affair*), Greta Garbo (*Ninotchka*), and Vivien Leigh (*Gone with The Wind*). It was not only a vindication for the tragedies and pain of her "lost year" but a recognition that her closest rivals, Luise Rainer (*Dramatic School*) and Myrna Loy (*The Rains Came*), did not receive. With one picture, Greer was suddenly on an equal footing with Greta Garbo, Metro's only other nominated star. To other hopeful starlets envious of her sudden fame, Greer offered this advice: "All I know about getting something that you want is that there are three essential things: wanting, trying—and getting the opportunity, the breaks. None works alone without the others. Wanting is basic. Trying is up to you. And the breaks—I do know this—they always happen."

The Academy Award ceremony was held on February 29, 1940, in the Ambassador Hotel's Cocoanut Grove. The *Los Angeles Times* published the winners in their 8:45 edition, so many latecomers to the Grove knew in advance who was going to win. Nevertheless, the audience was stunned into silence when Spencer Tracy announced that Robert Donat had won the Oscar over such incredible competition as Clark Gable for *Gone with the Wind*, Laurence Olivier for *Wuthering Heights*, and James Stewart for *Mr. Smith Goes to Washington*. Although controversy continues to linger to this day about who deserved the award—Clark Gable fans insist that he should have won—it is undeniable that Donat gave his most fondly remembered and best screen performance in *Goodbye, Mr. Chips*. To Lillian Burns, this was due in part to Greer: "She inspired him to be more human, more lovable, than he had ever been on screen before—just as Kathy influenced Chips." As news spread around the country that Vivien Leigh had won Best Actress honors for *Gone with the Wind*, the *Chicago Sunday Tribune* pointed out, "Greer Garson might have won an Oscar except for an error; she was nominated in the star performance division, but she was only a featured player. She might have won in the featured division."

Although pleased that her performance was making such a worldwide stir, Greer remained skeptical about the character who had made her famous. Asked for her opinion about one film review that praised her warm depiction of womanliness, she replied: "I have never thought of myself as particularly womanly." Thereafter she wrote a letter to James Hilton, asking, "And what do you intend to do, sir, to deliver me from this sweet wraith?" But as the Hollywood press began to circle and invade her private world for the first time, demanding to know more about "Mrs. Chips," she was proud of one fact. She had proven to the College of Cardinals that she was a star who did not require Hollywood's starmaking buildup. Most of all, as she told *Family Circle*, "If anything glowed through Mrs. Chips it was the deep delight in my heart that after fifteen months of miserable, humiliating idleness, I was working!"

Howard Strickling's office milked Greer's sudden fame for all it was worth. She recreated the part of Katherine Chipping in two radio broadcasts. The first costarred Basil Rathbone, on the "Gulf Screen Guild Theatre," on November 3, 1941, and the other featured Leslie Howard as Mr. Chips, in a live radio broadcast from Los Angeles to Washington, D.C., where King George VI and the Queen were visiting President Roosevelt. A contingent of Hollywood's English actors, including Vivien Leigh, Sir Cedric Hardwicke, Basil Rathbone, Merle Oberon, Brian Aherne, and David Niven were also featured. Niven's biographer, Sheridan Morley, related the outcome of the British tribute: "David happened to run into Queen Elizabeth . . . and asked what she and the late King had made of the proceedings. 'Wasn't it awful?' replied Her Majesty, and before he could take that as a verdict, she went on, 'President Roosevelt's radio battery ran out just before you all came on.'"

CHAPTER 11

"GREER GARSON, AS A SIGN OF HER accomplished stardom in *Goodbye, Mr. Chips* has been presented with a nice new dressing room by MGM," the *Sunday Times* reported on August 13, 1939. "A prelude we may hope to a nice new part in a nice new picture." By that time Louis B. Mayer, eager to cash in on the newfound popularity of his protégée, had already cast Greer in *Remember?* The slapdash screenwriting effort by Norman Z. McLeod, who would also direct the film, and Corey Ford concerned the effect of a memory-erasing drug called Memothene upon a young couple's marriage. Although it was typically silly 1930s screwball fare, Greer was complemented in the production by two of Metro's popular male stars, Robert Taylor and Lew Ayres, and a first-rate supporting cast that included Billie Burke, Laura Hope Crews, Reginald Owen, and Henry Travers. Thrilled to be back in the comfortable world of comedy and hopeful that she might equal Carole Lombard's Radio City success with *Nothing Sacred*, Greer told the press: "After all, I made my stage start in light comedy, and I entered film with the idea that I would find the same kind of parts—with some really nasty villainesses for good measure."

She enjoyed receiving the full glamor treatment from Gilbert A. Adrian, head of the studio's fabled wardrobe department. He had come to Metro-Goldwyn-Mayer in 1928 and had subsequently helped to create "the MGM look," outfitting the studio's stars to glamorous perfection. The Crawford shoulder pads, the Shearer hats, the sexy Harlow negligees, even the whimsical Munchkin apparel in *The Wizard of Oz*, bore the distinctive Adrian touch. He began by noting Greer's proportions: "Size 12, Bust 36½–30¼, Waist 26½, Hip 34-38." "I go to Adrian's for a fitting and I wreck his place," she once said. "We have such hilarious times together before we get serious about pins and seams and color charts."

Filming on *Remember?* began on July 31, 1939, and continued through the summer. It was a particularly happy time for L.B. Mayer's new English star. She enjoyed showing off her horsemanship during an on-location fox hunt that was shot in Santa Monica Canyon. Robert Taylor was amused to find that the dignified "Mrs. Chips" was delighted to perform a slapstick number involving a fall into a muddy pool. "I've always wanted to jump into the water fully dressed, but never dared to," she whispered to Taylor, barely stifling a giggle. Her only regret: "I spoiled a lovely riding habit!" "Greer Garson has been the biggest surprise to Robert Taylor as she has to Hollywood," observed a writer for *The Weekly Telegram.* "Far from being Mrs. Chips in real life, Miss Garson is a vivacious, vital, young actress with the sunny disposition of the Irish, a winning smile and an exciting voice."

In the late afternoons Greer invited Taylor and fellow costar Lew Ayres to join her for afternoon teatime. "Come what may the English must have their tea," reported a visiting journalist from the *San Francisco Examiner.* "Miss Garson has ordered it at the usual time of four o'clock, and when a tea kettle has to boil it boils regardless of movie scenes or what have you."

After a long day of work on *Remember?* on August 31, Greer drove home relieved that the Labor Day holiday lay before her. Although many members of the British colony chose to set sail for Catalina, Greer and Nina intended to enjoy a quiet vacation at home. Their plans were shattered the following morning. Great Britain and France had declared war on Germany. Although enveloped in the comfort of their California oasis, the Garsons had continued to pay attention to the storm gathering in Europe. Greer had been a struggling, not-too-successful London actress when Adolf Hitler became Germany's chancellor and withdrew the country from the League of Nations. She was enjoying her first success in *The Golden Arrow* when Mussolini invaded Ethiopia. She was rising to prominence in *Page From a Diary* and *Mademoiselle* when Germany reoccupied the Rhineland and civil war erupted in Spain. In 1938, while she was absorbed with her "lost year" in Hollywood, Germany had annexed Austria and Czechoslovakia's Sudetenland, with England's Prime Minister Neville Chamberlain's blessing. He had declared that he had successfully negotiated, at the

Munich appeasement conference, "peace in our time." Chamberlain realized his mistake in 1939 when Hitler swallowed the rest of Czecho-slovakia and invaded Poland, despite protestations from Britain. And now, World War II had begun.

Immediately, the two reclusive women at 149 South Roxbury Drive phoned the British consul for news. Should they take the next plane home? The weary voice at the other end of the line repeated the same message to hundreds: "No one is to return at this time, unless in the case of dire emergency. The consulate is awaiting more news from the British ambassador, Lord Lothian, in Washington, D.C."

The response among Hollywood's British colony was as diverse as its population. Some, such as David Niven and Leslie Howard, went home at once. Others, such as Basil Rathbone and Cedric Hardwicke, attempted to leave but were turned down for service because of age, while younger men such as Laurence Olivier and Cary Grant, torn between lucrative studio contracts and homeland loyalties, flew to Washington to see Lord Lothian. They returned, having uneasily accepted the ambassador's advice to make pro-British films instead of joining the war effort.

Greer and Nina felt helpless, for they had little communication with home. Los Angeles papers were worthless for international news, and New York papers were a day late. Radio was the prime source of information. When Greer returned to MGM she quickly replaced her phonograph and collection of favorite classical recordings with a portable radio. She became immediately aware of the changes in her adopted country. The isolationists accused all British actors of being spies, insidiously planning to persuade Americans to go to war. "It was a painful situation," recalled Laurence Olivier, "and wretchedly embarrassing with the Americans who were, for once, our not very enthusiastic hosts. Many of them seemed far from certain whose side they were on." The discrimination led to action. Cedric Hardwicke recalled: "Some of us actors met once a week in what we called the Ironing Board, to iron out any problems that arose in our relations with Americans as a whole and any criticisms directed against us on either side of the Atlantic."

To make matters worse, *Remember?* opened in New York at the Capitol Theater on December 14, 1939, to dismal reviews. "For the spectacle of a charming actress trying desperately to make good doing the things her employers unaccountably want her to do, we refer you to Greer Garson in *Remember?*" wrote Bosley Crowther in the *New York Times*. "Miss Garson, who is pretty enough in the half-British *Goodbye, Mr. Chips*, has been so formidably glamoured for her domestic debut . . . that one is tempted to say of her, in the present instance, with feelings of mingled sadness and regret, Goodbye, Mrs. Chips. We feel sure that Miss Garson will yet justify the high hopes which her first appearance excited, but in some other vehicle, in some season, perhaps. . . . As the moneyed jilt-flirt who ditches the pleasantly plausible Lew Ayres for the colorless and incredible Mr. Taylor, she seems to be slightly out of Greer."

Remember? proved to be an embarrassment for everyone involved at the studio. The conclusion of the movie had been a source of concern ever since it had been filmed. Lew Ayres's character, Sky Ames, has attempted to resolve the marital problems of his good friends, Jeff (Robert Taylor) and Linda (Greer), by giving them a dose of Memothene. Their troubles, as well as any memory of their relationship, are erased from their minds. As illogical as this solution seems, the fadeout is even more ridiculous when Linda announces that she is pregnant. It was a finale that threw all reason—as well as the already threadbare plot—to the winds. Greer was told that the film would cause controversy. "It did," she recalls. "It also caused me—and the studio—grave concern for while most of the reviewers brushed it off, asking, 'Why did they put Mrs. Chips in a thing like that?' others called me a 'One-picture star' and prophesied for me a speedy and total eclipse." The box-office gross for the film, which Greer would henceforth refer to as "Forgive and Forget," was $889,000, which meant a $32,000 loss for the studio. Greer's fellow "Neglected Imports" were sharing her fate. Hedy Lamarr appeared with Robert Taylor in *Lady of the Tropics*, another 1939 box-office dud. Ilona Massey costarred with Nelson Eddy in the musical *Balalaika* that year, but it would be another seven years before she made another film for Metro. The MGM career of Miliza Korjus began and ended with *The Great Waltz*. The College of Cardinals were beginning to doubt Louis B. Mayer's faith in his latest female protégées.

As Mayer hastened to rectify mistakes that had placed his "Imports" in such precarious positions, Greer became increasingly aware of the mogul's difficulty in finding film roles for her. At Metro, well-regarded as "The Women's Studio," she was competing with the most formidable array of female talent in Hollywood. Besides Greta Garbo, Norma Shearer, Joan Crawford, and Myrna Loy, there were Katharine Hepburn, Lana Turner, Ann Sothern, Margaret Sullavan, and Maureen O'Sullivan. The studio may have had more stars than the heavens, but there did not seem to be enough good parts to go around.

In early January 1940, Mayer thought he had found the perfect showcase for Greer Garson: Elizabeth Bennet in producer Hunt Stromberg's *Pride and Prejudice*. Greer heartily agreed. But Norma Shearer, the popular favorite in numerous MGM costume dramas such as *The Barretts of Wimpole Street, Romeo and Juliet,* and *Marie Antoinette,* was set to play it. When Shearer cast off the role of Susan Trexel in a screen version of Rachel Crothers's celebrated satirical comedy *Susan and God,* Mayer offered the part to Greer. "MGM has given her the keys to the city on a red velvet cushion," wrote journalist Max Breen. "In other words, Greer is playing the coveted title-role in the film version of *Susan and God,* in which Gertrude Lawrence has made a great stage success in New York." The play, which debuted on Broadway on October 7, 1937, had been a smash hit, running for 288 performances. Although concerned about appearing as the mother of a fourteen-year-old girl, Greer felt cast to perfection as Susan Trexel, an upper-crust European currently infatuated with evangelism. With plenty of witty lines and opportunities for the sort of bravura acting that she loved, Greer threw herself into the part and in early January began an intense regimen of makeup and hairstyling tests and dress fittings.

But then, in a sudden move, Norma Shearer, whose indecisiveness was beginning to wreak havoc with her career, decided to turn down *Pride and Prejudice.* Hunt Stromberg toyed with the idea of reuniting Clark Gable and Vivien Leigh, the famous costars of *Gone with the Wind,* as Fitzwilliam Darcy and Elizabeth Bennet or of pairing Gable with his longtime favorite Joan Crawford. But Gable hated costume pictures and refused to be a part of it. Vivien Leigh, who wanted the part, was considered with Brian Aherne, Robert Donat, Robert Taylor, Melvyn Douglas, and Errol Flynn. But she preferred Laurence Olivier, and Stromberg, who had seen Olivier's brilliant performance as Heathcliff in *Wuthering Heights,* agreed with her. However, Mayer felt that casting him opposite Vivien Leigh was dangerous. He argued that the couple's extramarital affair could bring adverse publicity to his "family studio" and condemnation from moviedom's Legion of Decency.

L.B. was now prepared to play his trump card. He again proposed Greer Garson for the part. Giving her a second look, Stromberg decided that she might indeed prove to be an inspired choice. MGM publicists broadcast the news. The *Baltimore Evening Sun* remarked, "*Pride and Prejudice* is believed to be more suitable for Greer Garson than for Norma Shearer. Maybe it is, but why wasn't Greer told in the first place instead of letting her get steamed up about the *Susan* role?" Although disappointed by the sudden change in roles, Greer was nonetheless pleased with the idea of reveling in her favorite period of history, the world of nineteenth-century England.

Meanwhile her old mentor, Laurence Olivier, was cast as Darcy, still believing that Vivien Leigh would be cast opposite him and that George Cukor would be directing. But that arrangement changed before the ink on his contract had dried. Vivien was persuaded to star in Mervyn LeRoy's production of *Waterloo Bridge* with the solemn promise that Olivier would play opposite her, and Cukor was forced to abandon the project in order to meet a contractual agreement to direct *Susan and God*. By the time the dust had cleared, Vivien Leigh and Robert Taylor were cast in *Waterloo Bridge*, Joan Crawford and George Cukor made *Susan and God*, and Greer Garson and Laurence Olivier were cast in *Pride and Prejudice*.

It was Irving Thalberg who first considered Jane Austen's "comedy of manners" as a production for MGM. On November 5, 1935, in New York at the Music Box Theater, he had seen a successful revival of the play, directed by Robert Sinclair and starring Adrianne Allen and Colin Keith-Johnston. For years he had made it a habit to study the latest Broadway productions as likely prospects for motion pictures. Envisioning MGM stars in each of the roles, he saw Jane Austen's story as a perfect vehicle for his wife, Norma Shearer. So, on March 17, 1936, he paid playwright Helen Jerome fifty thousand dollars for the screen rights. Although the book itself was in the public domain, Thalberg was cannily aware that Jerome's popular contemporary version would be instantly recognizable to the public and would serve as publicity for the film. He sought Victor Heerman and Sarah Y. Mason, a married team who had won an Oscar for their film adaptation of *Little Women*, to write a screen adaptation. But it was Aldous Huxley, the distinguished British novelist, who wrote the script, with the assistance of Jane Murfin, and created a rare classic that was faithful to Jane Austen despite extensive rewriting. The Meryton ball sequence is an example of their inspired technique, combining several scenes into one. Ernst Matray choreographed the scene to perfection, allowing the characters to deliver their dialogue while whirling around the dance floor. *Pride and Prejudice* originally began with an introductory foreword, which was later cut from the film: "This is a story that takes place in the days when pride was a virtue and fashionable . . . and prejudice the only defense of the spirited; when a kiss, however lightly given, meant a proposal of marriage; when young ladies were chaste and dutiful and had no careers except matrimony, and mothers pursued husbands for their daughters like baying hounds on the scent of a fox."

When two eligible, wealthy bachelors, Mr. Darcy and Mr. Bingley, come to visit Meryton, all the mothers in the English village hasten to introduce them to their daughters. Mrs. Bennet is the most competitive of them all, with her brood of five: Elizabeth, Jane, Lydia, Kitty, and Mary. Jane immediately falls in love with Mr. Bingley, but, through the intervention of Mr. Darcy and Bingley's sister, Caroline, who are strongly class-conscious, Bingley leaves town, ending the romance. Elizabeth is furious at the snobbery of Mr. Darcy and uses every opportunity to criticize his aristocratic behavior. Unwittingly, however, the pair are falling in love despite Elizabeth's pride and Darcy's prejudice. Meanwhile, a dashing fortune hunter named Wickham runs off with Lydia, intending to use the situation to blackmail her family. Darcy comes to the rescue, providing funds for Wickham so that he will marry Lydia and bringing Bingley back from London to his sweetheart, Jane. He then makes his peace with Elizabeth, and the couple profess their love for each other.

Producer Hunt Stromberg assigned Robert Z. Leonard to direct the film. Leonard was one of MGM's busiest and most successful directors, turning out such varied fare as torrid romances (*Susan Lenox, Her Fall and Rise*), lavish spectacles (*The Great Ziegfeld*), and popular musicals (*Maytime*). A Hollywood veteran since 1907, Leonard was renowned on the lot as a director who could manage big-budgeted productions. At a final cost of $1,437,000 and a large cast that included Mary Boland, Edna May Oliver, Maureen O'Sullivan, Ann Rutherford, Edmund Gwenn, Edward Ashley, Frieda Inescort, Heather Angel, Melville Cooper, and Karen Morley, *Pride and Prejudice* would prove to be such a project.

Marsha Hunt, a freelance actress who had worked at MGM, Paramount, RKO, Republic, and Grand National, was cast as Elizabeth's sister Mary Bennet. "I respected Greer as an actress greatly," she recalls, "but I never got to know her well. She was extremely private, didn't share herself, was very involved in her work. I don't mean she was cold. She was a very witty and articulate woman; I relished her intelligence." "Greer approaches each acting assignment as if preparing to write a master's thesis on the subject," observed the *Saturday Evening Post*. Her costars agreed. "She was such a perfectionist in all her scenes," recalls Edward Ashley, who played Wickham. Greer studied carefully with renowned archery expert Larry Hughes, who shot Elizabeth's bull's-eyes and had doubled for Errol Flynn two years earlier in *The Adventures of Robin Hood*. She sided with Adrian in his decision to advance the wardrobe fashions a few decades into the hoopskirted era that she had enjoyed in *Old Music*. Ann Rutherford, playing Greer's sister Lydia Bennet, recalls, "When the studio, in its infinite wisdom . . . changed the wardrobe from the wet-nightgown look, that Empire look, to the ship-in-full-sail Victorian—they did such a wise thing. Because the sight of Mary Boland bustling down the street with all of her little goslings behind her in their huge voluminous skirts, and all of them chattering at once—it wouldn't have been nearly as delightful a sight-gag."

Adrian's historically inaccurate costumes caused unforeseen problems when the actresses arrived on Cedric Gibbons's correctly designed, finely detailed period sets. "When they got all five sisters, and Mary Boland moving around with all of our petticoats," recalled Miss Rutherford, "we would naturally bump into those small tables. They would have little antique Meissen pieces on them . . . wonderful things . . . and if we would knock them over, I noticed, to my horror, that the prop man would just come with his dustpan on a stick and a broom and he'd sweep it up."

Greer continued her tea ritual with the largely British cast at four o'clock sharp. "All the women were wearing gorgeous hoop skirts," Greer explained, "Larry Olivier and all the men were dressed to the nines in frock coats. Tea seemed the natural thing to do—I suppose it was part of living in Jane Austen's world all day." "Greer held court with her afternoon tea in her dressing room," recalls Edward Ashley. "It was quite a thing to be invited. One afternoon, when she observed my appreciative glances at the many beautiful women in the cast, she said,

'Edward, are you aware that most of the girls are attached to staff members here?' I found it quite endearing that she was attempting to warn me." Ashley was also a guest for tea at Greer's home. "What impressed me most," he recalls, "was Mrs. Garson. She was a lovely woman, and extremely protective of Greer. I also recall in the living room they had this table absolutely covered with newspapers, books, and magazines. I always wondered where Greer found time to read them all!"

Laurence Olivier was another frequent tea partner. "We had not met, except briefly, since 'Golden Arrow,'" Greer told MGM publicists, "so that a vast amount of reminiscing and catching up went on between scenes and over our afternoon tea, to be sure. He amused himself and flattered me by telling everyone he was very proud of our early association and always added gravely, 'In fact, I invented Greer.'" Olivier, however, was not as happy with the turn of events. Neither was his desired screen mate, Vivien Leigh. Virginia Field, who was featured in *Waterloo Bridge,* recalled, "Miss Leigh was completely upset from start to finish of *Waterloo Bridge.* She was furious at having Mr. Olivier pulled from the cast to help out *Pride and Prejudice.*" His relationship with Greer was not eased by the fact that his former protégée was the star of the production. It was her name that preceded his own in the film credits and publicity releases. Thus there was an edge of condescension to his kindness. His envy got the better of his judgment when he later commented, "Darling Greer seemed to me all wrong as Elizabeth . . . [playing her] as the most silly and affected of the Bennet sisters."

Radio broadcasts concerning the escalating European war continued to emanate from Greer's dressing room. Karen Morley, who played Greer's close friend Charlotte Lucas in the film, recalled that spring of 1940 as a "terrible time. That's one of the reasons the picture is . . . strange in my memory. Hitler had begun his march through Europe. We'd come in, and one day it would be Belgium, and then the Netherlands. We would corner Karl Freund, that marvelous cinematographer, because he was German, and say, 'How could it have happened?' You know, what was it . . . And then we'd get into our stays, and . . . we'd go back to being 'ladies' and to that more brittle, charming period. But . . . Greer, who was (as she said) from the *north* of Ireland—'We're loyal, you know . . . I'm very worried about the anti-British feeling in America. I don't know what they expect of us. We're only a little island!' So it was really a fascinating time."

Principal photography wrapped up in April 1940, but retakes continued into May. On May 8, Greer entered the downtown Los Angeles courthouse to obtain a divorce degree from Alec Snelson. Attempting to hide her identity behind horn-rimmed glasses, a black tailored suit, and a wide-brimmed hat, she sat down beside Herman Selvin, of the studio's favored law firm, Loeb and Loeb. She took the stand and pleaded mental cruelty, testifying that her marriage had virtually ended after their honeymoon. "I found my husband was a man of very violent temper," she told Superior Judge Clarence Hanson, "unreasonably jealous, and possessive, and with a streak of penuriousness that was most eccentric and often very embarrassing. He objected to my expenditures and I think he would even have washed my personal laundry to save money. We separated in London, five days after we returned from our wedding journey." Finally, she presented a letter she had received from Alec in 1938, in which he told her of his love for another woman. Since Snelson was not present, the divorce was granted within a matter of minutes. "I have rarely mentioned my marriage to interviewers because it is painful to me to discuss or have any publicity about a situation that has been a source of unhappiness for many years," she told the *Los Angeles Times* in a rare moment of candor. "My greatest personal desire is to attain a sense of proportion and proper values. If ever I do, I may be able to view my marriage as an unfortunate episode in my life due to nothing more reprehensible than an error in judgement, and so feel less inhibited about it."

Greer's dream of a Radio City Music Hall premiere was realized on July 26, 1940, with *Pride and Prejudice*. The critics, once so doubtful that she could maintain her stardom, were now more laudatory than ever. It was obvious to all that, as Vivien Leigh was Scarlett O'Hara and Errol Flynn was Robin Hood, Greer Garson was the silver screen's most perfect embodiment of Elizabeth Bennet. She was, as Jane Austen described her character, "something more of quickness than her sisters," with "a lively, playful disposition, which delighted in anything ridiculous," and a face "rendered uncommonly intelligent by the beautiful expression of her dark eyes." "This, by your leave, we proclaim the most deliciously pert comedy of old manners, the most crisp and crackling satire in costume that we . . . can remember ever having seen on the screen," remarked Bosley Crowther in the *New York Times*. "Greer Garson is Elizabeth—'dear, beautiful Lizzie'—stepped right out of the book, or rather out of one's fondest imagination: poised, graceful, self-contained, witty, spasmodically stubborn, and as lovely as a woman can be." The *New Yorker* remarked, "Greer Garson seems a perfect choice to play Lizzie Bennet. A beautiful woman who is also intelligent, or at least looks intelligent, doesn't turn up every day in Hollywood—or, for that matter, anywhere else. She really deserves the compliment of being called a woman, too; most Hollywood actresses are girls, and remain girls to the bitter end. Oh, I could go on and on about Greer Garson." The box-office receipts closely matched the critical response. *Pride and Prejudice* played four weeks at the Music Hall and grossed $1,849,000. The Academy of Motion Picture Arts and Sciences awarded Cedric Gibbons and Paul Groesse an Oscar for Best Black and White Interior Decoration. It remains one of Greer's most fondly remembered and frequently reissued films. "None of us had any idea the film would be so popular," Marsha Hunt recalls. "Recently, Maureen O'Sullivan, who appears as my sister Jane, told me that when she met Olivier years later in England they expressed mutual surprise at the picture's success."

Always looking for a chance to return to the stage, Greer was pleased to join the cast of Noël Coward's *Tonight at Eight-Thirty,* at the El Capitan Theater in Hollywood. The benefit for the British War Relief, which ultimately raised twenty-five thousand dollars, boasted "The Greatest Cast Ever Assembled on Any Stage" and outdid Broadway for sheer popularity and glamor. Among the celebrities who appeared in the seven sketches were Douglas Fairbanks Jr., Constance Bennett, Basil Rathbone, Gladys Cooper, Dame May Whitty, Reginald Gardiner, Judith Anderson, Zasu Pitts, Joan Fontaine, and Clare Trevor. "Noël came to see us," Fontaine recalls. "The illustriousness of the cast was staggering. No producer could have hired a more star-filled one." August 19 through August 24, Greer appeared in the sketch "Ways and Means." It was the sort of racy, light comedy she adored. She and Brian Aherne played Stella and Toby Cartwright, house guests in the Villa Zephyre on the Cote d'Azur. When the couple loses all their money at the gambling tables, they find it difficult to find a way to exit the house and escape their formidable hostess, Olive Lloyd-Ransome, gracefully. Clad in a shimmering white chiffon nightgown—most of the play took place in a double bed—and appearing more beautiful and desirable than MGM had ever allowed, Greer brought down the house in a thunder of applause. One Los Angeles critic wrote: "With the memory of her hauntingly beautiful portrait of the gentle Mrs. Chips flitting about in their cerebellum, the sight of Greer Garson sharing a bed with Mr. Aherne and giving smart bedroom comedy a new refinement was enough to convince all present that here was Gertrude Lawrence doubled in hearts and available for celluloid. Columnists, critics, and paragraphers were unanimous about it: Louis B. Mayer should put Coward on handsome retainer and have him fashion a batch of conversation pieces for the 'new Garson,' something bright, bitter-sweet, and buoyant."

Elsa Maxwell, who played Olive Lloyd-Ransome, became one of Greer's closest friends during the period. "She helped my performance immeasurably," Elsa commented. "For instance, she said: 'Elsa, when you stoop to pick up anything from the floor why don't you turn your back to the audience?' Since my figure is one that always is very much in evidence this proved an excellent bit of business which brought howls from the audience throughout our run." She also enjoyed being invited to Greer's small house parties on Roxbury Drive. Watching Artur Rubinstein, the famous pianist; Lauritz Melchior, the Metropolitan tenor; and Greer pretend to orchestrate Wagner, was "one of the funniest things I have ever seen. Greer's hair became rumpled and her gown was awry. But, devoid of any pretensions of elegance, she isn't given to worrying about such unimportant things. Consequently, she's more fun than most women I know." "She made a point of speaking to everyone at parties," remarked one observer. "It was entirely unique because she could speak with anyone on any subject, and instantly make you feel at ease." Although Greer rarely attended big Hollywood functions, she was always very much in evidence when she did. "Flame-haired Greer Garson, never without her mother, always courageously wore scarlet or cyclamen," recalls Joan Fontaine. "She also carried her own thick red pencil in her evening bag. Her signature in the guest book was as much a standout as she was."

Flushed with her latest success and carrying her scrapbook bulging with the congratulatory notices from *Tonight at Eight-Thirty*, Greer made an appointment with L.B. Mayer. She pleaded with him to allow her to make another comedy—in Technicolor—preferably by Noël Coward. Instead, he sent her to the office of producer Irving Asher with the copy of a screenplay entitled *Blossoms in the Dust*. After the disastrous *Remember?* and the success of *Chips* and *Pride and Prejudice,* the mogul was certain that his first instinct about her, as a demure dramatic actress, was correct. Observing her patrician bearing and resemblance to Norma Shearer, he could not envision Greer as a comedienne. He intended to develop her stature at the studio by carefully choosing prestige roles for her in films such as *Blossoms in the Dust,* as Irving Thalberg had done for his wife. Indignant, Greer recalled, "When I first read the script for *Blossoms in the Dust* I rather jibed at doing it. I felt it was too similar to Mrs. Chips and that I should have a chance to prove versatility by doing a more glamorous and, perhaps, giddier part. But when Mr. Irving Asher, who produced the film, added that Mrs. Gladney, herself, had expressed the wish that I play the part, I was so flattered, I was speechless."

The development of *Blossoms in the Dust* from an inspiring true story to a celebrated motion picture was a unique one. In 1940, Ralph Wheelwright, an MGM publicist, and his wife wanted to adopt a baby girl. After they searched agencies nationwide, Edna Gladney of the Texas Children's Home and Aid Society in Fort Worth finally found a child for them. Inspired by Mrs. Gladney's selfless devotion to the Home, Wheelwright sketched out her life story and presented his manuscript to L.B. Mayer. Aware of the success of a previous studio biography on Father Flanagan of Boys Town, Mayer approved the project, paid Wheelwright ten thousand dollars, and sent for Edna Gladney to come to Hollywood. The "Lullaby Lady," as she was known to the Fort Worth orphans, arrived in November. As a guest of the studio, she was invited to confer about historical details and to help cast the picture. A check for five thousand dollars was bestowed upon the Texas Children's Home and Aid Society for screen rights to Edna's story.

Ralph Wheelwright's manuscript was adapted for the screen by one of Hollywood's best screen writers, Anita Loos. If the choice of a woman well known for writing hilarious and sassy dialogue for books like *Gentlemen Prefer Blondes* and films like *Red Headed Woman* seems odd, the assignment was even more of a surprise to Miss Loos. "It was a tough assignment," she recalls, "because there wasn't any plot. I went through weeks of the agony, frustration, trial-and-error that only an author can know. Several times I hit on a story line; followed it through with elation until, at the climax, the whole thing fell apart."

Irving Asher had in fact chosen Anita Loos because he knew she could write about women. More important, she could do it in a straightforward manner, avoiding the pitfalls of sentimental melodrama. Anita based her fictional screenplay on a precept of Edna Gladney's that "even the most perfect orphanage creates traumas that can harm children for life; they should be gotten into real homes just as soon as possible." Thus evolved the story of Edna's effort to find better, and quicker, means of matching orphans with parents. Because of the addition of numerous other fictional elements, a disclaimer was included in the opening credits: "Except for the roles of Edna Gladney and Sam Gladney, and except for the Texas Children's Home and Aid Society, all events, characters and institutions depicted in this photoplay are fictitious." The screenplay begins in 1903, when Edna Kahley and her adopted sister Charlotte prepare for a double wedding ceremony. Edna has been swept off her feet by a bank teller named Sam Gladney, a visitor from Texas with ambitious plans to build wheat mills, and Charlotte plans to marry Allan Keats. But when Allan's parents discover that Charlotte was a foundling, they forbid the marriage; and Charlotte, in despair, commits suicide. Edna is devastated but marries Sam and moves to Sherman, Texas. There, the couple prospers and have a son—the only child Edna can have. When the boy dies in a sledding accident one Christmas, Edna hides her grief by becoming a busy society matron. Sam and the family pediatrician, Dr. Breslar, give her a new direction in life by inviting an orphan girl into the home. Soon Edna has opened a day nursery for her husband's mill workers. When the Gladneys move to Fort Worth in 1918, her work expands with the Texas Children's Home and Aid Society. She especially devotes herself to a crippled foundling named Tony. Surviving the loss of her husband, Edna faces an even greater challenge: to strike the word "illegitimate" from all birth records. Though public opinion is against her, she delivers a stirring speech to the state legislature and gets the bill passed. It is a victory for Edna but one that she has won for Charlotte and Sam. On Christmas Eve she allows Tony to be adopted by a childless couple, realizing that her devotion to the home and its children is tantamount to sharing her life with only one child.

The man who had nearly produced Greer's film debut in *Dramatic School* was assigned to the picture. "If you have a message, let it cheer." Such was Mervyn LeRoy's viewpoint when it came to motion picture making. As his Warner Bros. hit *I Am a Fugitive from a Chain Gang* had explored the injustices of the prison system, he intended that *Blossoms* would detail the prejudice of illegitimacy. It had been one of Edna Gladney's greatest triumphs to pass a bill that prevented babies from being labeled illegitimate on their birth certificates, which often ruined their lives. Although the neophyte MGM producer had earned the respect of his peers with a string of hits—*Dramatic School, Stand Up and Fight, At the Circus,* and *The Wizard of Oz*—his true interest lay in directing. Mayer acquiesced to his wishes by dropping his salary to twenty-five hundred dollars and assigning him the director's chair for *Waterloo Bridge.* The film was a smash hit, and much the same was expected of *Blossoms in the Dust.* Walter Pidgeon once remarked, "Actors understood Mervyn LeRoy. Somehow he always managed to get his emotions across to us with very little words."

For the 1941 season, Metro-Goldwyn-Mayer announced that two of its features would be produced in Technicolor: Robert Taylor's *Billy the Kid* and *Blossoms in the Dust.* The latter film received advance publicity when the studio produced a short, *The Miracle of Sound,* which featured Greer's color test for *Blossoms* photographed by Karl Freund. Among the raves from movie audiences was this assessment from *Screenbook*: "Greer should be filmed in Technicolor to do her justice. Black and white gives no hint of the burnished copper tones of her mass of fine and fluffy hair, of the whiteness of her skin which portrays a natural red head or the oval depths of her eyes which she insists are the press agent green." Although flattered that Mayer had bestowed upon her the studio's first drama in Technicolor, Greer had reservations about the decision. "I know my limitations well," she told Karl Freund, "and color photography can do terrible things to you." There were many in Hollywood who were wary of the Technicolor process, which was not only costly but was barely six years old. Like most Hollywood studios, MGM had used early forms of color photography as a gimmick to enhance the prestige of pictures such as *Ben Hur, The Mysterious Island,* and *The Viking.* Despite the introduction of a markedly improved three-strip process in 1935 that combined three negatives sensitive to red, green, and blue, the studio used it only sparingly for special prestige films like *The Wizard of Oz, Sweethearts,* and *Northwest Passage.* If it had not been for the success of these pictures or the spectacular use of color in *Gone with the Wind,* L.B. Mayer would never have considered making *Blossoms in the Dust* the studio's fifth movie in full color.

Greer's unwillingness to play the role of Mrs. Gladney was in part because of her fear of working with children. The actor's unwritten rule never to work with scene-stealing babies or animals was magnified one-hundred-fold for this film. Indeed, Metro-Goldwyn-Mayer had never produced a picture that incorporated so many young children. "It was an extraordinary experience," Greer recalled. "Our set was full of babies, mothers, pots, cribs, bottles, and stand-by babies—and stand-by babies for the stand-by babies because you can only have the children work about five seconds under the heavy Technicolor lights."

One of Mervyn LeRoy's most time-consuming tasks was casting the role of little Tony. After innumerable tests with children who could not handle the number of lines Tony had to speak, the director, much to his relief, finally found an engaging four-year-old named Pat Barker. It was not until the film's premiere in Fort Worth, when little Pat came to join the festivities, that movie audiences learned that "Pat" was actually Patricia. "'Blossoms in Dust' Crippled Boy Is Here," announced the *Fort Worth Star-Telegram,* "But He Isn't a Cripple and He Isn't a Boy!" Hearing that his secret was out, Mervyn LeRoy shrugged his shoulders and said, "She looked like a boy after we had trimmed her hair a bit."

Principal photography began on January 27, 1941. With so many young actors and a nervous leading lady, problems were inevitable. "In the making of a movie, emotionalism often used to spill off the sound stages onto the side lines," observed Anita Loos. She was called to the set with the news that Greer had retired to her dressing room in protest after a heated argument with Mervyn LeRoy. The dispute had erupted over one of little Tony's key lines. In the scene in which Edna bids farewell to the orphan when he is adopted, the boy was supposed to say, "But I can cry inside, can't I?" Greer objected to the dialogue, not only because "it's not in the psychology of a child to ask a question," but because she feared the young actor was stealing the scene. "On the other hand it would be quite understandable for me to say 'But you can cry inside, darling,'" she told LeRoy. An emergency meeting was called in L.B. Mayer's office. Although Mayer listened carefully to Greer's argument, he awarded Pat Barker the line, which the girl uttered so well that he burst into tears. Marsha Hunt, who played Charlotte, had her own troubles with Mervyn LeRoy. In the scene in which she ascends a staircase to commit suicide, LeRoy insisted on keeping the camera at the foot of the stairs. She recalls, "I begged Mervyn, 'Please shoot it my way, with the camera observing my emotions as I mount the stairs. It will make the episode clearer to audiences. Then we'll try it your way.' 'No,' he answered. 'It will be more effective understated.' So, it was done his way. I still think I was right. In view of the fact that the sister's suicide propels Edna Gladney in all her subsequent activities, it should have been underlined."

The tensions on the set were eased by Walter Pidgeon, who was cast as Edna Gladney's husband. Shaking a finger at Greer, Pidgeon laughed and said, "I told you we would work together some day." "Walter had a great sense of humor," Greer observed. "There was nothing he enjoyed more than trying to break me up before a very serious scene. He was a great kidder." Studio publicists soon realized that here was another MGM pair displaying the same kind of magical screen chemistry that had made Myrna Loy and William Powell America's favorite married team on screen. The gags and practical jokes the mischievous pair would play on each other offscreen became legendary on the MGM lot. Nothing was sacred to Pidgeon, who made fun even of her perfume. "I don't know how I would live without my sense of smell," Greer told Hollywood writer Lydia Lane. "When I'm doing a picture they always laugh about the bottles of perfume I carry on the set. I try to wear a different perfume for every new picture. It's like a familiar song. Every scent I have revives a memory. There is a magic in the sense of smell that stirs emotions. Walter had names for my favorites. One he called 'Give Him a Chance' and the other, which he found particularly intriguing, was 'Show Him No Mercy.'"

In their first scene together, Pidgeon commented on the irony of playing Sam Gladney as a young bank teller. One of his earliest jobs, after being injured in World War I, had been as a bank messenger for the Shawmut Bank in Boston. Recalling that his doctor had advised him to find an easy job, he said "It was easy all right, and dull as toast. I knew I couldn't stick to it for long." Like Edna Gladney's husband, Walter Pidgeon held greater ambitions. After negligible parts in *The Shopworn Angel* and *Listen Darling* in 1938, the actor's career had received a major boost in 1939. To his and MGM's surprise, he came into his own in three B movies, playing Nick Carter, the master detective. "The kids loved it," Pidgeon recalled, "and don't ask me why—so did I!" As fan mail began to pour in, he was loaned to Twentieth Century-Fox for two important films: Fritz Lang's *Man Hunt* and John Ford's *How*

Green Was My Valley. He returned to MGM a critically acclaimed star, as popular on the set as on the screen. His patience and total equanimity surprised more highly motivated screen actors. One studio friend quipped, "He has as much temperament as a turtle."

As the filming schedule sped by, Greer discovered that she liked her first biographical role. It was "like being given the gift of another span of experience altogether," she said. "If the person you are playing is still alive, it is more of an ordeal than to impersonate someone who belongs to history but that, I found, adds to the challenge." As her interest grew, her feelings toward her young costars relaxed, and her performance was subsequently enriched. Some of the scenes in the orphanage are among the most moving that she ever performed. In one sequence she presents a young couple with a baby girl. "Why, Mrs. Gladney," the new mother observes, "you're crying." "I work like a fury to get them adopted," Greer admits, "and then cry like a fool when they go." The emotion that she projects was genuine. After completing the scene, she made this confession to the press: "If I don't marry, and soon, I'm seriously thinking of adopting a baby, possibly two babies. A child, you know, keeps you in touch with the stream of life. You've got to be natural, you've got to be honest and real with a child. I'd like to see no such things as a childless house or a homeless child in all America."

Greer's coworkers discovered that she was happiest when she was working the hardest. The star once known as "Greer Garson—The Leaper from Play to Play" surprised her coworkers, who were exhausted by the heavy demands of the factory-like studio system, with her energy and willingness to work late hours. She was studying Mrs. Gladney's life day and night, preparing for her next film, *When Ladies Meet*, and researching other projects she wanted to bring to Mayer's attention. "I'm happy because I'm working myself to skin and bone," she said. "I hate inaction. Well. I'm in action now. It's a fantastic life, really." "A fantastic amount of energy hums away inside her body," observed *Saturday Evening Post* writer Pete Martin, "although she occasionally feels called upon to stoke it with vitamins, which she munches like popcorn or has administered hypodermically. She is beset by a driving psychological need for work. An old back injury hurts her when she's idle; she forgets it when she's working. Her memory is a photographic plate; she never blows a line before the camera."

The opening sequence, the Kahley engagement party, presented an

unusual problem for Mervyn LeRoy when Walter Pidgeon had difficulty following the choreographed dancing patterns for the camera.
Improvising, LeRoy ordered the studio carpenters to construct a low
platform attached to roller skates. As couples danced around them on
the Kahleys' drawing room set, Greer and Walter, and the camera,
whirled about on the platform. As Greer later related: "We were the
first duet on a skateboard . . . I think I ran around the circumference,
and he stayed on the skateboard." "Be careful, Walter," LeRoy warned.
"If you ever kick Greer square in the shins with those number 13's of
yours, you'll break her leg!"

Despite a shaky start, the star and director of *Blossoms in the Dust*
were close friends by the end of shooting. "Greer Garson has the most
beautiful speaking voice of any actress the screen has ever seen," Mervyn
LeRoy said, "and she is an exquisite-looking woman." "Mervyn has a lot
of orderliness in him," Greer observed. "He is a very good thermometer
of audience reaction, and he knows his angles. The atmosphere is very
light-hearted, which is very good for me." She now freely admitted to
friends and the press that she had enjoyed essaying a biographical role.

After filming ended on April 10, 1941, Edna Gladney was invited
to a special preview screening. Afterward, she wrote to L.B. Mayer: "I
bow with humility to this extravagant praise of my small part in the
completion of this wonderful gem. . . . Walter Pidgeon is splendid as
Sam. Our love story, of course, is sacred ground to me, but not in any
way have you encroached, or handled the story in a melodramatic or
cheapened way. I am grateful for the recognition that this picture will
give to our cause. It will stimulate interest in children and child placement agencies."

Although there was a lavish opening for *Blossoms in the Dust* in
New York, Greer's second opening at Radio City Music Hall, it was the
premiere of the film in Fort Worth on July 18, 1941, that carried special significance. E.B. Coleman, manager of the MGM publicity office in
Dallas, organized the event and gathered pink and white gladioli, the
Gladneys' favorite flower, to adorn the Worth Theater. Katherine
Howard wrote in the *Fort Worth Star Telegram*: "It is going to be a great
thrill to the homefolk Friday evening when they find that one of their
own community has been given such recognition on the screen in as
tender and lavish a way as only Hollywood can do it. . . . There probably won't be a dry eye in the Worth Theater when the premiere is

over." Escorted into the theater by the mayor of Fort Worth, Edna Gladney was seated with John W. Herbert, the president of the board of the Texas Children's Home, and many of her foster parents. When asked after the screening what she thought of the film, Mrs. Gladney remarked, "It was all very wonderful. I am so happy and satisfied, but there still is work to be done."

At a cost of $1,110,983, *Blossoms in the Dust* grossed $2,658,000 in worldwide ticket sales. Mervyn LeRoy had made another box-office blockbuster and a beautifully realized, touching tribute to Mrs. Gladney. Besides standout performances by Marsha Hunt and Felix Bressart, as the dedicated Dr. Breslar, Greer etched a tender and believable portrait of the "Lullaby Lady." The maternal warmth of her characterization brought raves from the critics, another Academy Award nomination as Best Actress, and an I-told-you-so smile of satisfaction from L.B. Mayer. *Variety* commented: "For Greer Garson . . . it affords the greatest screen role of her career, and even at this early date there will be many who will insist that the Academy Award for the 1941-42 season is already settled." Britain's *Picturegoer* awarded her a gold medal for best actress of the year. But LeRoy's cheer of social commentary—so succinct in films like *Fugitive* because of the sparse, low-budget Warner Bros. style—was stifled by MGM's obvious intention to make the film a lavish showcase for Greer. Historical details, such as the fact that no one suggested that she utilize her gift for dialects to speak a true Midwestern accent, were secondary to the look of the film and its leading lady. Indeed, the only Academy Award the film earned was for Cedric Gibbons's plush Technicolor interior decoration.

The success of the film led Greer and Walter Pidgeon to an encore performance on February 16, 1942, on Cecil B. DeMille's *Lux Radio Theatre*. Grateful for the praise that she received and the boost in popularity that *Blossoms in the Dust* bestowed upon her, Greer was nonetheless concerned that L.B. Mayer was carving a niche for her at the studio as the supportive wife from which she might never escape. Walter Pidgeon, on the other hand, did not mind typecasting. Too old for military service when America entered World War II, he would become one of the most popular stars at MGM in the 1940s primarily because of his role as Greer Garson's husband. For him their partnership was "one of the happiest associations of a lifetime."

CHAPTER 12

A NEW CONSTELLATION OF STARS was appearing in the MGM heavens in 1941, displacing many of those who had been at the studio since the silent days. In a year when Greta Garbo departed the lot after sixteen legendary years, stars such as Hedy Lamarr, Lana Turner, and Judy Garland, who were featured in *Ziegfeld Girl* that year, were indicative of the future. New meteors such as Katharine Hepburn, in *Woman of the Year*, and Ingrid Bergman, in *Dr. Jekyll and Mr. Hyde*, were trailing stardust, while the careers of Jeanette MacDonald and Norma Shearer, MGM's still-reigning queen, had stagnated. Above them all was Greer Garson. The remarkable critical and popular success she had achieved in *Pride and Prejudice* and *Blossoms in the Dust* made her heir apparent to the throne at Metro as the queen of the studio's dramatic prestige pictures. For a woman of Greer's ambition, this position was both an intoxicating triumph after years of career frustrations and disappointments and a gilded trap that threatened to stifle her wish for versatile acting assignments.

There was, however, another actress who had struggled for over fifteen years to wear the crown of queen of Metro-Goldwyn-Mayer, and she did not intend for Greer, a mere newcomer, to take that honor away from her. Her name was Joan Crawford. The 1940s were "a rough period for us Americans at Metro because of what we called 'the British invasion,'" she complained. "Metro had a big studio in England, but when the war started it wasn't very practical to make pictures there, so they imported Greer Garson, Deborah Kerr, etc. God only knows how many good parts I lost. The more films geared for them, the fewer for us." In the *Dallas Morning News,* Philip Wuntch wrote: "Greer Garson describes most of her colleagues in glowing terms. Vivien Leigh was 'porcelain mischief.' Norma Shearer was 'an extremely lovely lady.' And Joan Crawford? Welllll . . ." Greer had learned from her earliest days on the lot to avoid the star, whose acting ambitions exceeded even her own. Although there were rumors circulating around the studio that Mayer was tired of her battles for better roles and was trying to get rid of her, everyone knew that Joan Crawford would not go without a fight. With the same fierce, single-minded determination that had turned an unknown chorus girl named Lucille LeSueur into an internationally famous movie star, she intended to rise and reign above her female contemporaries at MGM. During the summer of 1941 Crawford was particularly unhappy to learn that her next picture would be *When Ladies Meet,* the kind of dressy, drawing-room comedy that she had made once too often, with Greer Garson, the actress she considered her chief rival. The film's title was regarded as a suspenseful double entendre by the cast and crew of the picture, who waited nervously to see what would happen when these two volatile MGM ladies met.

The play, *When Ladies Meet,* had opened the Broadway season at the Royale Theatre in New York on October 6, 1932, featuring Frieda Inescort, Walter Abel, Spring Byington, Herbert Rawlinson, and Selena Royle. It told the story of Mary Howard, a successful novelist who gives up an admiring suitor, Jimmy, for her publisher, Rogers Woodruf, who is a married man. MGM producer Lawrence Weingarten paid Rachel Crothers forty-five thousand dollars for the screen rights in January 1933 and made a successful film adaptation with Myrna Loy, Ann Harding, Robert Montgomery, Martin Burton, and Alice Brady. Nearly eight years later, coproducers Orville O. Dull and Robert Z. Leonard dusted off the John Meehan/Leon Gordon screenplay with the help of S.K. Lauren and Anita Loos. Joan Crawford replaced Myrna Loy as Mary; Greer was assigned Ann Harding's role as the wife, Clare Woodruf; and Robert Taylor was cast in Robert Montgomery's shoes as Jimmy. In the most inspired piece of casting, Robert Z. Leonard, who also directed the picture, allowed Spring Byington to reprise her original role in the play as the hilariously feather-brained socialite Bridget, whose city and country homes are the settings for the film.

After two costume pictures in a row, Greer was pleased to be back in a contemporary comedy. The production also promised to be her most glamorous showcase. With a makeover from William Tuttle, a flattering new hairstyle from Sydney Guilaroff, and the full glamor treatment from Adrian's wardrobe department, the results were breath-taking. The *Chicago Sunday Tribune* would later state, "In *When Ladies Meet* MGM really found out what to do with Greer Garson. . . . She stood right in there with Joan Crawford and at least held her own—due not only to the fact that she can act but also to the fact that the studio has finally learned how to clothe her and dress her hair." Walking onto the set of Bridget's country home the first day of shooting, Robert Leonard reputedly looked her over approvingly, and said, "So that's what Mrs. Chips looks like without her bustle!"

The costume Greer wore in the boating sequence, in which she teaches an awkward Robert Taylor the art of sailing, was one of her favorites. Beneath the skirt was a pair of red-striped shorts. When Taylor gets knocked overboard, Greer was supposed to strip away the skirt, revealing the shorts, and dive in to save him. After the scene was shot in the MGM water tank on Lot One, Greer was disappointed to learn that the scene had been edited. The producers had decided that it wouldn't seem manly if Taylor couldn't swim. Having already told the press of her exciting moment, she vowed that she would reveal her legs in another picture. A year later she would keep her promise—in *Random Harvest*.

Although Greer enjoyed working again with Taylor and delighted in four o'clock teas with the inimitable Spring Byington, her relations with Joan Crawford were, as expected, another matter. "Joan was just completely nonplussed that I refused to feud with her," she recalled. "She tried very hard to feud with me because she felt it was natural for her to feud with every other actress on the lot. . . . She gave a dinner party in 1949. . . . Joan sat herself at the center table, surrounded by the most desirable men, including a certain Buddy Fogelson whom she knew I was dating. She placed me at the studio electricians' table, with the words, 'Oh Greer, dear, you get along with everyone.' Our table had more fun than any other, but by the end of the dinner, enough was enough. I got my plate of chocolate mousse, moved my chair next to Buddy's at Joan's table and said, 'I think I'll have my pudding with my fella.' There was nothing Joan could do about it."

As shooting progressed Crawford grew more incensed as she realized that Greer's almost supporting role of Clare Woodruf was not the thankless one it had appeared to be in print. Greer invested her part with a dash of humor and a glowing confidence that made her characterization in *Remember?* seem anemic. By now she was in complete command of the film medium and created a sparkling characterization that outshone Crawford's performance. Greer and Robert Taylor, whose comedic timing had also improved since *Remember?*, enjoyed the proceedings, and their delight shows on the screen. Their flirtation and Greer's dramatic confrontation with her errant husband, Herbert Marshall, and Crawford, are easily the highlights of the film. Years later Joan Crawford bitterly remarked, "I have nothing but the worst to say for *When Ladies Meet.* Terrible story, terrible script, and I doubt that any actress could have made the goddam thing believable. Adrian dressed me divinely, as usual, and that's the only good thing I can say for it." The acidity in her tone reflects her failure to stop the ascendancy of Greer Garson as the studio's most promising star.

Filming wrapped up on August 11, 1941, and a preview at the Alexander Theater in Glendale was held two weeks later. Opening at the Capitol Theater in New York on September 4, 1941, *When Ladies Meet* was a nationwide success, grossing $1,846,000. "This is entertainment deluxe," remarked the *Hollywood Reporter.* "Greer Garson, by virtue of the fact that most of the sympathy goes to her, stands out above the others. As the 'constant wife' in a marital quadrangle, her characterization is warmly appealing. The transaction from a happy young woman to victim of a very real situation, is beautifully handled."

Upon her return from the New York premiere, Greer was summoned to Louis B. Mayer's office. A screenplay entitled *Mrs. Miniver,* stuffed with multicolored revisions, lay on his desk. She shifted uncomfortably in her seat, aware that Sidney Franklin was behind this confrontation. His search for an actress to play Mrs. Miniver had become common gossip on the Culver City lot ever since his first choice, Norma Shearer, turned it down. Greer had enjoyed the book, published in 1939, about the lighthearted domestic adventures of an English housewife and her family on the eve of World War II. But the MGM screenplay that Franklin had presented her to read on the train to New York was a different matter. Not only had the story changed dramatically, the character, in her opinion, had changed as well. "I found that Mrs. Miniver, far from being a mouthpiece of stirring wartime sentiments, was a self-effacing creature," she said, "and to my further amazement, I discovered that one of her children had become a young man who brought home a daughter-in-law and nearly made me a grandmother!"

Having received this criticism from other possible Mrs. Minivers, Sidney Franklin had thrown up his hands in frustration. In his twenty-five years of experience in Hollywood he had learned that actresses were happy to play young girls or old hags, but never a middle-aged character with grown children. Greer left Mayer's office a short time later and alarmed his secretaries by fainting. He had appealed to her patriotism and used equal amounts of flattery ("Franklin and I think you are the ideal choice"), tenacity ("I brought you to America. Do it for me") and an overwhelming personal performance of the screenplay to get her to accept the role. "I fainted away," Greer recalled. "To this day, I still think Louis Mayer played Mrs. Miniver better than I did."

It seemed everyone at the studio was certain that Greer Garson was right for Mrs. Miniver—except Greer Garson. In exasperation, she showed the script to Lillian Burns and asked for an opinion. "Here she was about to do Mrs. Miniver—about an English lady, like Mrs. Chips," Miss Burns recalled. "I told her to do it. Greer was born to play Mrs. Miniver."

The author of *Mrs. Miniver,* Jan Struther, was born Joyce Anstruther in 1901 in Whitchurch, Buckinghamshire. After schooling in London, she married Anthony Maxtone Graham in 1923 and had three children. The Grahams' family life centered at 16 Wellington Square in London; the old Graham family estate, Cultoquhey, in Perthshire, Scotland; and a cottage near Rye in Sussex. In the 1930s her talent for writing emerged with a growing collection of stylish poems that were published in *Punch, The Spectator,* and *The New Statesmen.* To avoid confusion with her parents, Harry Anstruther and Dame Eva Anstruther, both writers, she changed her name to Jan Struther.

When Peter Fleming, whose famous brother Ian wrote the James Bond novels, requested that she write a continuing piece in the *London Times* court page, Jan came up with Mrs. Caroline Miniver. She derived the last name from English heraldry: the white fur used to trim robes. Although she originally intended to write the series in verse, she found that "I ran short of material just when my deadline was approaching, so I put the ideas into prose instead." Jan insisted that neither she nor her family were the models for the famous Miniver family, but it was obvious that her children, Jamie, Janet, and Robert, were the same ages as the Miniver children, and that even their homes, vacations to Scotland, and daily activities were reflected in the episodic pieces.

The parallels between Greer Garson and Jan Struther/Mrs. Miniver are unique. Both were from a Scotch heritage (Struther from Edinburgh) and both enjoyed long summer holidays in Scotland. The *London Times* review of the book brings forth another interesting similarity: "Mrs Miniver has the gift of expression—she says that words for her clarify expression—and both her charming and irritating qualities are probably derived from the fact that she can put into words so many of the thoughts about everyday matters that most people form in a dim and unspecified way. What Mrs. Miniver does possess is a combination of serenity and humour which carries her through major and minor crises with equal common sense and calm." Jan Struther's daughter, Janet Rance, once described her mother in terms that could also easily be applied to Greer Garson: "She dashed through life at full tilt, with gaiety, energy and grace. She loved words and would pause to net and examine them like a butterfly enthusiast." "Zest for life," Jan Struther once reflected, is "an accidental gift . . . impossible to acquire, and almost impossible, thank heaven, to lose." She shared that quality with Greer.

The best-seller immediately attracted attention in Hollywood. When Harcourt, Brace published the book in America in July 1940, MGM story editor Kenneth MacKenna sent a copy to Sidney Franklin. The producer was intrigued with the contemporary story and its already beloved characters and so was Eddie Mannix, who authorized a purchase of the film rights from Miss Struther for $32,500. With the funds, she immediately purchased two ambulances for the British war effort.

Of all the creative talent at Metro-Goldwyn-Mayer that gathered to create *Mrs. Miniver*, it was Sidney Franklin who provided the inspiring guiding hand throughout its long and turbulent production schedule. From the outset he believed that *Mrs. Miniver* could be made into a very human story of suffering and triumph—a topical prestige picture that could be perhaps the greatest that MGM had ever produced. "I had the notion that someone should make a tribute, a salute to England, which was battling for its life," he said. "Suddenly, I realized that I should be that someone." It is therefore all the more surprising to note that he almost did not make it at all. He had intended to focus his energies into *The Mortal Storm*, one of the studio's first anti-Fascist motion pictures, starring James Stewart and Margaret Sullavan. He began directing the picture in early 1940, but the strain from months of overwork forced him to retire, and he was replaced by Victor Saville. He turned to *Mrs. Miniver*. He placed the book upon the studio's assembly line, after throwing out most of the text, to be fashioned in the mold of *The Mortal Storm* and the Robert Taylor and Norma Shearer anti-Nazi thriller *Escape*, which were both prepared for release in 1940. Franklin's team of British writers (Arthur Wimperis, George Froeschel, James Hilton, Claudine West, R.C. Sherriff) spent six months adapting Jan Struther's work into a Hollywood screenplay. Within that time, *Mrs. Miniver* evolved from an episodic, lyrical study of family life in prewar London to a dramatic account of Britain's current wartime situation. The script begins in September 1939 as England declares war on Germany, where the original book ends. Except for the brief vignette about a new car, the ages of the Miniver children, and the fact that the family had homes in London and in the country, everything else was rewritten. Fortunately, Jan Struther had delineated her characters so well that the screenwriters had little trouble enlisting them into wartime duties. Mrs. Miniver catches a German pilot. Mr. Miniver lends himself and the family yacht to the Battle of Dunkirk. Their oldest son, Vincent, joins the RAF and marries the girl next door. The various townspeople of Belham were inventions of the screenwriters from the regal Lady Beldon and her granddaughter Carol Beldon, who marries Vin, to Mr. Ballard, the popular rose-growing stationmaster. "This film was made with complete integrity," Greer Garson remarked in 1989. "It was not, as I've heard it spoken of, a carefully concocted propaganda film. It was nothing like that. It was a study of an ordinary British family—upper-middle class family—and how ordinary, decent people behave under extraordinary circumstances and stress. The stress of a total blitz."

The work of two British scenarists was especially important. Arthur Wimperis had been an actual air-raid warden and a river patrolman in England, and his experiences lent authenticity to the emerging screenplay. He based the fictional Kentish town of Belham, in which the Minivers lived, on his own village and placed it on the banks of the Thames so that he could incorporate the dramatic Battle of Dunkirk, which many of his friends had witnessed, into the story. Although uncredited in the film, R.C. Sherriff also lent an integral hand, contributing the film's powerful bomb shelter sequence.

Louis B. Mayer received the screenplay on August 27, 1941, in what was becoming an uncomfortable era in which to be a motion picture mogul. Pictures like *Mrs. Miniver* required great delicacy in handling and treatment, not only because the United States still clung to an increasingly fragile neutrality but because he was trying desperately to hold on to a declining, war-torn international market for MGM films. In September he became even more concerned when a Senate subcommittee began to investigate ludicrous rumors of a Jewish conspiracy among the Hollywood moguls to encourage Americans to join the war effort through anti-Nazi films in order to protect their British interests. More inclined to approve family fare such as *Life Begins for Andy Hardy* or musical escapism such as *For Me and My Gal* during the summer of 1941, Mayer was alarmed at the large number of anti-German films filtering out of the Writers Building. There was *Reunion in France* with Joan Crawford and John Wayne; *Journey for Margaret,* in which Robert Young, Laraine Day, and a new tot named Margaret O'Brien faced the London Blitz; and *Somewhere I'll Find You,* in which Clark Gable and Lana Turner became war correspondents—albeit glamorous ones. Mayer grew even more nervous when he discovered that Sidney Franklin had brought William Wyler from the Goldwyn studio to direct *Mrs. Miniver.* For Wyler was no pacifist, still keenly aware that his birthplace, Alsace-Lorraine, had been overrun by Nazis. Realizing that the United States would face the totalitarian world alone if Britain were to fall, Wyler was determined to rouse British and American audiences alike with the film. "I was a warmonger," he admitted. "People say we should be making escapist pictures today. I say 'Why?' This is a hell of a time to escape from reality. We're in an all-out war—a people's war—it's the time to face it."

Despite Mayer's uneasiness with the project, Franklin and Wyler were more concerned with casting decisions. Walter Pidgeon seemed a likely candidate for Mr. Miniver considering his box-office success with Greer in *Blossoms in the Dust.* But Pidgeon did not want to play a Miniver either. "I had heard so many tales about William Wyler that I decided not to do it," he said. "I argued with Sidney Franklin about it. I could out-shout him and then I had to argue with Eddie Mannix. Mannix talked me into it." Sidney Franklin was prepared to cast James Stephenson, who had earned excellent reviews as Bette Davis's lawyer in *The Letter,* as a substitute if Mannix had failed to convince Pidgeon to take the part. Meanwhile, William Wyler was testing actors for the roles of Carol Beldon and Vincent Miniver. He chose Teresa Wright, a beautiful and talented ingenue from the Goldwyn studio, whom he had directed in *The Little Foxes*, to play Carol. When asked how he had chosen Richard Ney to play Vincent Miniver, however, Wyler remarked, "I picked him out of a bunch of silly kids because he seemed the silliest."

The director had his first meeting with Greer in October. Aware of the rumors of Wyler's perfectionist filmmaking methods, especially his notorious policy of shooting numerous retakes, Greer was cautious and nervous. She suggested that, in view of the ages of Mrs. Miniver's children, she should be aged for the role with wrinkles, graying hair, horn-rimmed glasses, and padded hips and stomach. Wyler disagreed, replying that she looked the right age as she was. That hit a nerve. As her face reddened, she indignantly replied that it would be ludicrous for a woman of her age to portray the mother of a son over twenty. Wyler hastily apologized by explaining that the character was really ageless and that the role should be as young and attractive as possible to audiences. The argument was not solved until Mayer intervened on behalf of Wyler.

Greer was also nervous when Joseph Ruttenberg, who had photographed her screen test, was chosen as cinematographer. Although he had lensed some of the studio's most acclaimed motion pictures, including *The Great Waltz*, for which he won an Academy Award, *Three Comrades, The Women, The Philadelphia Story*, and *Dr. Jekyll and Mr. Hyde*, she had hoped for Karl Freund, who had photographed her most attractively in *Pride and Prejudice* and *Blossoms in the Dust*. Ruttenberg was an unhappy reminder of her miserable first year in Hollywood. Of the incident, Ruttenberg recalls, "When I first started photographing Miss Garson on the *Miniver* picture, it took a little while to get the right lighting angles for her, as it would any cameraman. I had photographed Walter Pidgeon before in *The Shopworn Angel*, so I knew something about him. But she wasn't too sure about me—but after *Mrs. Miniver* it was a fight to get her to let anybody else photograph her!"

Completely unhappy with the project, her role, her director, and her photographer, Greer was in a bad humor when Ruttenberg began shooting tests of the Miniver cast members. On October 11, 1941, she was scheduled to test with the actor who would play her oldest son. Sidney Franklin invited Greer to his office that morning to meet Richard Ney. That moment would be romanticized beyond all resemblance of fact by the press. In her article, "Secret Romance," Beth Emerson wrote: "Greer, laughing with correct politeness, looked up, prepared to see the usual young actor. Instead, she observed a tall, very slender fellow with a sensitive, studious face. Richard Ney looked down, undoubtedly expecting the Greer Garson American movies have portrayed, an almost poisonously understanding, tolerant young matron. What he saw was a pale, humorous face framed in an incredible nimbus of red-gold hair. His startled blue eyes flashed to her slender ankles, even as Greer's startled green eyes took heed of the width of his shoulders; and then their delighted glances met again, met and locked and held." Of the actual event, Greer had a significant memory. "The Minivers were an odd family," she said. "As a mother, I had a small tot or two, then my brood skipped ten or fifteen years to a son just down from Oxford. The full force of this blow struck me when Sidney called me to his office, and said 'Miss Garson, here is your son.' 'Oh, that nice, little boy,' I said, momentarily forgetful of the liberties the scenarists had taken. 'How-how-how-how-how do you do,' I said, and not until the fifth 'how' did my eyes meet those of six-foot Mr. Richard Ney. Really, I thought, this is too much. So, giving him a very cold and disapproving stare, I added 'Sonny,' and walked out of the office."

Twenty-three-year-old Richard Ney was new to Hollywood. His only acting experience was a minor role as one of the sons in a road company version of Howard Lindsay and Russel Crouse's Broadway chestnut, *Life With Father*, starring Louis Calhern and Dorothy Gish. Interestingly enough, it was the same play in which Teresa Wright had also scored an early success in a New York stage presentation. A native of New York but raised in Lakeville, Connecticut, Richard was majoring in English at Columbia University and considering a career in journalism when he attended the New York World's Fair in 1939. He was asked to become a part of the RCA television exhibit, which sparked an interest in acting. He joined the *Life With Father* troupe promptly after graduation in 1940. When the tour reached Los Angeles, he stopped by MGM to visit his French professor from Columbia, who was acting as a studio technical advisor. He was overwhelmed by the scope of L.B. Mayer's dream factory. "It had the climate of Eden," he later recalled. "I was in paradise, eating apples everywhere." Visiting the casting office, he was granted an interview and a screen test, for which he was paid

$132.32. Uncertain that his effort would gain him anything more than that check, he was surprised when he was chosen by William Wyler to play Vincent Miniver for three hundred dollars a week for five months. On his MGM employment papers he listed Greta Garbo as his favorite actress. He had been married once, to a New York artist, Elden Hewitt, who divorced him in 1939.

The Garson/Wyler relationship continued to disintegrate as shooting began on November 1, 1941. On that very first day, she presented Wyler with a pair of black velvet gloves, which, from the inscription, were for "the iron hands of William Wyler." "He wore them with great panache on the first day of shooting," Greer recalled. "But they were soon put aside, both figuratively and actually." Wyler's method of shooting and reshooting scenes was a bewildering and frustrating experience for her. Noël Coward had directed her in a repetitive manner during *Mademoiselle,* but she felt he had compensated for it with an ingratiating sense of humor and a warm and comforting guiding hand, which Wyler lacked. Certain that her first performance was her best, she tried to charm Wyler into agreeing with her. "I wish you could have seen how Greer got her way with him," Teresa Wright recalled. "She'd be very sweet and charming and say, 'Don't you think, Willy, we ought to do it this way?'" But this tactic was not always successful. Wyler insisted that she light Walter Pidgeon's cigarette so many times in one sequence that she became ill from the smoke. When an interviewer asked her about rumors that Wyler required twenty-six takes for every scene, she snapped: "What do you mean twenty-six takes? He makes seventy-four!" Bette Davis, who had made three of her greatest films with the director—*Jezebel, The Letter,* and *The Little Foxes*—encouraged her friend to continue. "You will give the great performance of your career under Wyler's direction," she said. Greer did have to admit grudgingly that Wyler was a meticulous, master craftsman. During a particularly dramatic scene, she recalled, "Willy came over to me and said, 'The tears in your eyes. That was very good. But you let them spill over just a second too soon. Now, if you can get the tears again, I want you to hold them there. And then I want you to let that tear run down your cheek.' I got myself back in Mrs. Miniver's skin and into the moment, and I could feel the tears stinging my eyes. The camera moved in and, wonder of wonders, the tear obligingly and obediently rode out and down my cheek."

But one morning the director's methods caused Greer to lose her temper and walk off the set. "Wyler was a perfectionist," Joe Ruttenberg recalled. "He was so wrapped up in the picture that he was shooting that he wouldn't even say 'Good morning' when he walked on the set—not being snooty or anything, just intense concentration. And never, ever satisfied. Take after take after take. And if he didn't like the rushes, he'd go back and do it some more. It was tough on the actors and Greer Garson got more and more angry until one Saturday morning she blew her stack, told Wyler what she thought of him and walked off the set. It was quite a scene."

"Because I never make a film which does not absorb me from beginning to end, I cannot let it alone," Wyler said. "When all the possible paper work and thought has been poured into it, then it is necessary to experiment, to retake a scene several times until the scene tells the audience exactly what it is meant to tell. There are simpler, easier ways of making motion pictures, but not for me."

Wyler was summoned to L.B. Mayer's office, where the mogul brought out a list of grievances provided by a variety of MGM personnel. It seemed that Wyler, in his first film for the studio, had already made many enemies on the lot. The mogul was disturbed that his favorite actress was upset, and he criticized Wyler for irritating his art director, Cedric Gibbons, who resented the director's interference with his vision of the English sets. Sidney Franklin and Wyler had hoped to make the film as accurate as possible at the Denham Studio, but the wartime situation prevented it. Since the film was to be entirely made in Culver City, the production design was put in the very capable hands of Gibbons and his talented staff, who undertook the project in MGM's lavish style, creating a "chocolate box world of rose-strewn villages, landed gentry and old family retainers." that Wyler, in his quest for realism, despised.

Mayer was also concerned about the rushes, in which he saw that his worst fears about an anti-German bias in *Mrs. Miniver* were being realized. One sequence in particular bothered him. The original script contained a scene in which Mrs. Miniver encounters a downed Nazi pilot. The young man was depicted sympathetically, reminding Kay Miniver of her son, Vincent. Wyler thought it a touching scene but did not intend to portray Nazis in a positive manner. Mayer insisted that the character remain as originally written. A few weeks later, on December 7, 1941, when Pearl Harbor was bombed and America was suddenly at war, the mogul quickly changed his mind. Wyler was free to portray the Nazi as he wanted. "We all felt, and sought to convey, the profound determination that dramatized those days," Teresa Wright recalled. "It was a picture produced in the shadow of headlines, and those of us who appeared in it never forgot it."

As in the early days of shooting *Blossoms in the Dust*, Pidgeon helped keep confrontations between star and director at a minimum. He invited Greer to play the pin games on the English pub set and brought Wyler along when Greer invited him to tea. Tay Garnett, now a resident director at MGM, was the witness to another episode that relieved Greer's tense hours on the *Miniver* set. While directing *Cross of Lorraine* at MGM, he went to lunch one afternoon with one of his stars, Cedric Hardwicke. As they passed a soundstage where a crowd had gathered to watch Judy Garland perform a musical number, Greer, completely engrossed in her script, bumped into Cedric. Momentarily startled by the priestly costume Hardwicke was wearing, Greer bent her head and muttered, "I'm sorry, Father." Cedric grinned wickedly, pretended to bless her, and then began to dance in a highly suggestive manner to the music. "In his priestly costume," Garnett recalled, "it was outrageous. Greer caught her breath, glanced upward into Cedric's stern face, and almost popped her wig with laughter." In years to come, whenever Greer and Cedric met he would bless her solemnly, never bothering to explain his action to confused observers.

Above all, it was the intervention of Sidney Franklin that kept the *Miniver* set peaceful. He actively supported Greer's four o'clock tea, when others at the studio, including Wyler, considered it a needless extravagance. When Louella Parsons asked him about it one day, he replied, "It's selfish on my part. I like tea. Then, too, it brings all my people closer together, and because of it we get a good hour's work from the warmth and relaxation it gives us." Greer particularly enjoyed the company of Dame May Whitty, who played Lady Beldon; her daughter, Margaret Webster, had directed Greer in *Old Music*. During their afternoon tea they would chat about the England they remembered while Whitty knitted for the Red Cross. The seventy-six-year-old actress had enjoyed a long and distinguished career, which stretched back to the 1870s, in England. She made the first of many trips to America in 1895 with Ellen Terry and Henry Irving's repertory company. She enjoyed telling Greer about her proudest moment—when King George V made her a Dame Commander of the Excellent Order of the British Empire in recognition for her work in World War I as the head of the Women's Emergency Corps. In her motion picture career, which had begun in 1914 and would end in 1948, she appeared in such classics as *Night Must Fall, Conquest, A Bill of Divorcement,* and *Suspicion.* During the shooting Greer hosted a party at her home for Whitty and Ben Webster on their fiftieth wedding anniversary.

William Wyler considered Lady Beldon's flower show, in which Mr. Ballard enters a red rose in direct competition with Lady Beldon's white rose, *Mrs. Miniver's* most important sequence. From the very beginning of the film Wyler took great care in building up the suspense of this subplot, which, he believed, revealed the true heart of England. We are introduced to Mr. Ballard early in the film as Mrs. Miniver arrives by train to Belham. In one of the film's most memorable scenes, made all the more touching by the sincerity of Henry Travers's delightful performance as the stationmaster, Ballard shyly invites Kay Miniver to see his latest rose. In the original script, he asks, "Have you ever thought, Ma'am, how few people there are in the world with as much beauty and sweetness as there is in that rose? What goes to make a rose Ma'am is breeding and budding, and horse manure, if you'll pardon the expression. And that's where you come in. . . . I need a name for it." With quiet pleasure, Mrs. Miniver replies, "Oh, you want me to name it for you?" No, Ballard insists. "I've got a name for it, if you'll give me your permission. I want to call it the 'Mrs. Miniver.' I've watched you go in and out of town for years now—and you've always had time to stop and have a word with me—and I always waited for you to come home, and you remind me of the flower." Later, when a pessimistic friend remarks that if war comes there will be no flower show, Mr. Ballard expresses Wyler's sentiment with a key line of dialogue: "Don't talk silly. You might as well say goodbye England. There will always be roses." *Variety* would later note: "The rose festival becomes almost as important to the story as the war element. The rose is a symbol of the English countryside, its gardens, the homeland. A tremendous amount of concern and suspense is built up about the floral competition with its ritualistic implications and the class distinctions that are seen to wear away as the narrative proceeds into the common tasks of defense and morale. It is as if the authors of the tale, the director, the players are saying 'if battles aren't for gardens and roses and neighbors, old and young, gathering at a county fair, what are they for?'"

Wyler's attention to detail is also apparent elsewhere. With the aid of a literate script, he is able to capture quickly the audience's affection for the Minivers as a family much like their own. To the vicar of Belham Mrs. Miniver expresses the common pleasure in "nice things—things beyond my means sometimes . . . pretty clothes . . . good schools for the children . . . the garden . . . you know!" Her husband is proud of the new car he has purchased, while the youngest Minivers scamper under-foot with their amusing childish escapades and their pet cat, Napoleon. Every detail of life in the family household is carefully handled, right down to the family clock, which Clem and Kay Miniver are forever correcting. By the time war is declared, audiences cannot help but be touched by the poignancy of Kay Miniver's startled look when her son announces that he intends to join the RAF. "Isn't he young?" she asks her husband. "Even for the Air Force?" "Yes, he's young," Clem replies. Wyler believed the silence between the parents in this scene was more powerful than a subsequent scene he cut in which Mrs. Miniver criti-cizes war: "I'm all mixed up, thinking of Vin. Oh you men! What a mess you've made of the world! Why can't we leave other people alone!" Clem Miniver admonishes her with this stoic reply, "Darling, there's one thing we can do—not just you and I, but all the decent men and women in the world—we can make sure that this thing doesn't come twice in one generation to our children, as it has come to us." The last remark is in reference to an earlier scene depicting the Minivers' wed-ding amidst the horrors of World War I, which was also cut from the film. As James Parrish would later note, "What makes *Mrs. Miniver* work as super-screen entertainment and tangentially as allied propa-ganda is the solidarity of the Miniver family in the war crisis."

William Wyler's masterpiece, however, is contained in the film's final moments. In the screenplay, the vicar is supposed to deliver a stir-ring, patriotic address to his war-weary audience that would end the film on a triumphant note. "The homes of many of us have been de-stroyed," he says, "the lives of young and old have been taken, yet we gather here, those of us who have been spared, to worship God as our ancestors for a thousand years have worshipped Him under this roof—a damaged roof, but one through which the sun now shines as it never could before." Although he allowed the scene to be filmed, Wyler was not satisfied with the speech. The problem nagged him all during production until, finally, he knew the scene had to be rewritten and reshot. The fact that Henry Wilcoxon had already left MGM and enlisted did not deter Wyler. As the actor recalled: "The Navy gave me permission for two days' absence; I flew to Los Angeles. William Wyler and I stayed up all night rewriting that sermon, and finally, with coffee running out of our ears, we opened the curtains; it was broad daylight. It was about seven in the morning, and I had to be on the set at nine. I took a quick shave, got makeup and had the thing in the can by noon." In the revised speech, the vicar declares: "We, in this quiet corner of England have suffered the loss of friends very dear to us. Some close to this church . . . The homes of many of us have been destroyed, and the lives of young and old have been taken. There is scarcely a household that hasn't been struck to the heart. . . . And why? Surely you must have asked yourself this question . . . Children, old people, a young girl at the height of her loveliness. Why these? Are these our soldiers? Are these our fighters? Why should they be sacrificed? I shall tell you why. Because this is not a war of soldiers in uniform. It is a war of the people— all the people—and it must be fought not only on the battlefield, but in the cities and in the villages, in the factories and on the farms, in the home and in the heart of every man, woman, and child who loves freedom. . . . This is the people's war! It is our war! We are the fighters. Fight it then! Fight it with all that is in us! And may God defend the right!" President Roosevelt was so impressed with the message that he ordered it spread over Europe in leaflet form and broadcast on radio over Voice of America. Other filmmakers during World War II would attempt to capture the powerful nature of the scene and speech, most notably David O. Selznick in a similar sequence in his Americanized *Mrs. Miniver* classic, *Since You Went Away*, but none could match it.

Greer departed the studio on February 25, 1942, for a whirlwind bond-selling tour for Canada's second Victory Loans campaign. Traveling over eight thousand miles in two weeks with Nina, Sir Cedric and Lady Hardwicke, and James Melton of the Metropolitan Opera, Greer had a chance to tour the Royal Canadian Air Force fields, meet the Prime Minister, give a shortwave broadcast that stretched to England, and, in Montreal, deliver a radio address to the French Canadians in their native language. She was so popular that a Canadian journalist commented: "Morale soared sky-high wherever Miss Garson set her pretty foot." Her message to the Canadians was simple: "We can't escape the war, and we shouldn't try. *Mrs. Miniver* has been a constant reminder to me of the things that are happening and have happened to my friends and relatives in London. They are such good people—gentle people. There wasn't an ounce of hate in them. When I first got the news of the bombing of London, and I thought of them—a wave of fury broke over me. I thought of my men-folk, so peace-loving, so essentially gentle in spirit, and all of them in uniform." When Greer returned to Hollywood in March, the studio orders she had dreaded were waiting for her. There were to be more retakes, which ultimately lasted until April 13.

Aunt Evelyn continued to keep Greer and Nina updated with letters from home. Uncle James had joined the British navy in 1939 and served on a ship picking up refugees and supplies at various points between India and England. Both of his sons, Greer and David, had joined the war. Greer was a lieutenant-surgeon in the Royal Naval Volunteer Reserve, and David had given up his engineering courses at Glasgow University to join the Scots Guards. Aunt Lilian Garson was one of the thirty-one thousand casualties from the German bombs that were dropped on London. Nina's old home in Ilford was one of the first buildings destroyed in that neighborhood. Belfast received a devastating Nazi bomb raid in 1941 that almost completely leveled the city. "How wonderful it will be to gather all the clan together again," wrote her aunt, "when all this mess is cleaned up."

One evening, Greer returned home particularly exhausted. She had spent the day at the Twentieth Century-Fox Studio with Joseph Schenck as part of an Infantile Paralysis Drive of Movie Theaters, which raised $480,000. Nina was waiting for her with good news. Unhappy with their lodgings, now split between South Roxbury and 1300 North Crescent Heights Boulevard in Hollywood, she had spent weeks with a real estate agent in Beverly Hills and found an ideal home. Greer often romanticized the first glimpse she had of the beautiful 8200-square-foot Tudor-style manor house at 680 Stone Canyon Drive. "The moment I drove in through the wooden gates I said, 'This is it.' I knew it. I knew this was home. I bought it because it looked weathered and serene . . . the gardens not clipped and manicured but as if several generations had lived in them." She was surprised to find out that it was the home that Tay Garnett had described to her in London. He recalled, "We finally sold for thirty-five thousand; not long ago the person to whom I sold told me laughingly that she had been offered $350,000, but she wouldn't think of giving it up. Her name is Greer Garson. Proves what I've often said: Beauty and brains are frequently found together."

A press preview for *Mrs. Miniver* was arranged for May 14, 1942, in projection room one at the studio. A very nervous L.B. Mayer was there with the film's stars to await the reaction. When the screening was over and the lights came on, Mayer turned to Walter Pidgeon and remarked that it would be a marvelous prestige picture for the studio but would probably not make much money. Greer rose from her seat with the same opinion. She intended to concentrate fully on her next film, *Random Harvest*, and hoped to leave *Mrs. Miniver* and all the headaches involved with the production forever behind her.

CHAPTER 13

"THE SCREEN'S MAIN FUNCTION, I believe, is to give the world beauty and romance," Greer said in 1976, "to make us forget our own troubles for a time and send us out of the theater with a lift of the heart. For sheer make-believe romance you cannot top James Hilton's *Random Harvest*. It was the happiest film I ever made. I know I am prejudiced but I think it is one of the half dozen greatest love stories." After adapting *Goodbye, Mr. Chips* for the screen, Hilton had surprised his wife and English friends by settling permanently in California. After buying a home in Long Beach, he told MGM publicists, "When a writer says he's going to Hollywood, people crowd around him with far more solicitousness than if he were about to leave, say, for the Brazilian jungle. 'You will be disappointed,' they say. 'You will either be crushed by failure or ruined by success. Anyhow, you won't be happy.' Well, to be personal, I have been in Hollywood now for six months and none of those prophecies has come true. I am still happy, I am thinking of writing a book, and it won't be anything about Hollywood." The book emerged, with a title inspired by a German war report ("According to a British Official Report, bombs fell at random"), as *Random Harvest*. It was the story of Charles Rainier, a bewildered amnesiac who escapes an asylum in the small village of Melbridge, England, on Armistice Day. A vivacious showgirl, Paula Ridgeway, nicknames him "Smithy" and nurses him back to health. They fall in love and marry. When Smithy is hit by a taxicab on a business trip in Liverpool, his early memory is restored, but his idyllic years with Paula are forgotten. He returns to the family estate, Random Hall, and attempts to extinguish a nagging loneliness he does not understand by marrying Kitty, a close friend. But his shad-

owy memories of the past prevent it. Paula becomes his secretary, and
later his wife, with the hope that he will remember her. After many
lonely and frustrating years, her dream is finally realized at their
former honeymoon cottage, surrounded by flowering cherry trees.

Little, Brown published the novel with high expectations. No
one was disappointed. With its story of unrequited love, mystery, and
war, the novel sold in excess of a hundred thousand copies in six
weeks. Sidney Franklin snapped up the film rights for fifty thousand
dollars and began a collaboration on a screen version with Mervyn
LeRoy. Of their success with *Waterloo Bridge*, Franklin remarked,
"Trying to make good pictures isn't a one-man job. I could never
accomplish anything without writers, directors, camera men, and
soundmen. A picture is a jigsaw puzzle in which each one contributes a small section to make the perfect whole. Often, Mervyn and I
direct parts of a film together."

On January 27, 1942, Howard Strickling made the announcement that *Random Harvest* would be Greer Garson's seventh film for
Metro-Goldwyn-Mayer. Not since *Pride and Prejudice* was she so
utterly pleased with a new screen assignment, a film that happily
reunited her with the author who had made her a star and teamed
her with Ronald Colman, the screen idol of her youth. "One reason
I found Paula so interesting to play was that I believed in her," Greer
said. "She was as multi-faceted as most human beings are—the music
hall actress, gay and independent; the sympathetic, gentle girl; the
adored wife, happy Mrs. Smith; the efficient secretary, and finally the
influential Lady Rainier. But more important even than the variety
that gave color to the role was the fact that it was a sensitively written study of a woman's heart. Fidelity to human nature in such a story
is more important to any thoughtful player than opportunities for
showmanship." It was a character as perfectly suited to her as Elizabeth Bennet or Kay Miniver.

Ronald Colman had previously appeared in Columbia's *Lost
Horizon*, another screen classic based on a James Hilton novel. He
played a world-weary war correspondent who is transformed by true
love. His character in *Random Harvest*, Charles Rainier, was very
similar. Colman's own life and career remarkably paralleled the fictional character's as well. Born in England on February 9, 1891, in
Richmond, Surrey, not far from Rainier's fictional estate, Colman was

a studious and shy young man, like Charles. Both were World War I veterans. Serving with Kitchener's famed Contemptibles, the "first hundred thousand," Colman survived the bloody battle of Ypres only to have his ankle shattered by a shell explosion at Messines. Like Rainier, he was invalided out of the war and felt lost and bitter in its aftermath. He escaped his melancholia, like his fictional counterpart, through work. Colman got his first role on the stage in 1916 in *The Maharanee of Arakan.* His success led him to New York's Broadway and greater acclaim in silent motion pictures. Sound pictures revealed new depths of Colman's versatility. "When *Random Harvest* came along, Ronnie and Greer were the first choice for the role." Mervyn LeRoy recalled, "It could have been written for them. Between the two of them, the English language was never spoken more beautifully on film." James Hilton was so pleased with the casting and the screenplay treatment that he agreed to deliver the opening narration in the film.

For the pivotal role of Kitty, the young woman who almost marries Charles Rainier, Mervyn LeRoy cast an MGM ingenue named Susan Peters. He intended to take her under his wing during production and turn her into a major personality as he had transformed Lana Turner, Ginger Rogers, and Loretta Young. Peters's tremendous coup was Ann Richards's loss. Although the Australian actress was given the small role of a member of the Rainier family in *Random Harvest,* her recent arrival at MGM had not been early enough for Sidney Franklin. He told the actress: "If you had come to the lot earlier, you would have gotten the much more important role of Colman's fiancée, which Susan Peters is already signed to play. She is supposed to remind him of his first love, Greer Garson, whom you resemble much more than Susan does." Although disappointed, Ann was a good sport and, years later, expressed warm memories about the production. "Ronnie was extremely charming and made me feel very comfortable. In Australia, I had gone to school with his nieces, the children of his brother, Eric, and this formed a little bond between us." Ultimately, however, Susan Peters's triumph turned to tragedy. Her bright future at MGM, after her success with *Random Harvest* and a string of box-office hits, was shattered on New Year's Day in 1945 during a hunting trip with her actor-husband Richard Quine. After accidentally discharging her gun, she was rushed to a hospital where it was discovered that the bullet had lodged in her spine. She was permanently paralyzed from the waist down. Although she continued to make films and later worked on television, her MGM career was short-lived, and she died in 1952 at the age of thirty-one.

Like *Mrs. Miniver, Random Harvest* was shot entirely at MGM. When filming began on April 21, 1942, sets on Backlots Two and Three substituted for the streets of Liverpool and London, and Victoria Station. The studio's vast soundstages held Random Hall's elaborate interiors, the village of Melbridge, and portions of the English countryside. Commenting on the Culver City-bound environment of *Random Harvest,* English critic William Whitebait later wrote: "I rather enjoyed this film, though it reeks of the studio, and every landscape looks as though one could put one's foot through it. Devonshire, especially, is precarious." One idyllic set, complete with shady trees, a running brook, and trained fish, was constructed for a country picnic sequence in which Smithy proposes to Paula. It remains one of the most memorably romantic scenes in cinema history. "I've run after you from the very beginning," Paula admits. "I've never let you out of my sight since I first saw you in that little shop." "Never do it," Smithy replies. "Never leave me out of your sight." Greer entered the scene on a bicycle, and she wanted to use her own well-worn, three-gear "skimmer." But, for authenticity's sake, a vintage 1918 vehicle was used instead. At the end of production LeRoy presented her with a new bicycle that Greer happily pedaled through the streets of Beverly Hills and Bel Air, waving to passersby, as she had since her childhood in London. She enjoyed the surprised glances she received from her affluent neighbors. "Was that Greer Garson?" they would ask. "I can't imagine her on a bicycle!"

On February 19, 1942, the MGM publicity department released a bombshell. It read: "Greer Garson Drops Familiar 'Mrs.' Roles— Star's Shapely Legs to Be Revealed On Screen! Since she played 'Mrs. Chips' in 1939, Miss Garson's films have run to costume and period clothes, hardly revealing more than her ankles. The redheaded, green-eyed Irish star's lower extremities have recently been tested from every camera angle for a spirited, high-kicking song-and-dance number." From the beginning, *Random Harvest* screenwriters Claudine West, George Froeschel, and Arthur Wimperis had found it difficult to find a way to portray Garson's character as a showgirl. In the book, the character of Paula Ridgeway is described only once upon the stage, performing in the patriotic World War I play, *Salute the Flag*. In the end, it was Greer who suggested that she perform Harry Lauder's famous number, "She's Ma Daisy," in a kilt, the costume of her forebears. "I love to dance," Greer explained. "The Scotch and Irish are always dancing and their natural sense of rhythm was born in me. It seemed a wonderful opportunity to prove that I wasn't born with a bustle." The response from Franklin, LeRoy, and L.B. Mayer was tense deliberation. "The advisability of her appearance in a shimmering expanse of hose was weighed by her studio almost as carefully as was the Army's decision to drop the first atomic bomb," wrote Hollywood writer Pete Martin. Sidney Franklin recalled: "We felt it would be a mistake suddenly to throw her legs at the public, and we didn't want to have her 'go Hollywood' on the screen; so we had kilts made in three different lengths, and tried them all out. Finally we decided to use the medium-length ones." At first Greer was nervous about her new costume: "I was a bit embarrassed the first time I put on the kilt," she said. "I seemed to be all legs, and for once I wished there was a hoop skirt handy."

After three weeks in rehearsal with dance directors Ernst and Marie Matray, the show was ready to go on. On April 27 the theater set on Soundstages Five and Six was refitted to a 1918 vintage and filled with two hundred boisterous extras, swarms of publicists, and curious MGM employees. Greer stood in the wings. "Lights. Camera. Action!" "When I pranced out onto the sound stage wearing this abbreviated costume, I felt terribly shy and embarrassed," she said. "Then the extras and the gang gave out with long whistles and I must say, I felt pleasantly flattered." One of the onlookers was Lillian Burns. "What a delightful piece that was," she recalls. "That number was exactly what Greer really wanted to do—really enjoyed to do: musical comedy." As she finished the number, the extras, unprompted, launched forth with an exuberant version of "For She's a Jolly Good Fellow." It had been a memorable performance because, as Hilton had written of his heroine, "of her warm vitality that came over the footlights, and her own rich personality, full of giving—even to a twice-nightly audience." Sidney Franklin sent a telegram: "I was simply delighted with our Scotch number and your performance was beyond what I ever thought possible. I think it will add great color to the picture and great warmth will be given to the character of Paula."

The sequence caused an unforeseen controversy when the picture was released. A stocking manufacturer informed Don Iddon of London's *Daily Mail* and Earl Wilson of the *New York Post* that Greer had worn his special stockings for *Random Harvest*. She promptly cabled a bemused reply to both men:

> Your column about my legs just broke out here and caused quite a storm in the local tea cup. I don't know this Willy or his trick stockings and if he is trying to build up a business for himself I wish he would leave my name out of his publicity campaign. Recently he told a columnist that I was knock-kneed and had to order specially seamed stockings as a disguise. This is not the truth.
>
> > Say I'm dreary, say I'm sad
> > Say my acting doesn't please
> > Say my films are awfully bad,
> > But don't knock my knees.
>
> Now the horrid man tells you I'm bowlegged and wear padded stockings. Heavens to Betsy. Can't he even make up his mind so that I can arrange my quatrains accordingly? The next time you are out here you can check the evidence for yourself.

As she worked on *Random Harvest*, Greer had constant reminders of her girlhood in London. Besides the familiar English places in which the story took place, Greer had an amusing recollection one particular day on the set of Charles Rainier's office. Playing the devoted secretary, ordering scurrying aides about, and accepting flowers from a young suitor, she spoiled a take by laughing. It reminded her of the day when the head of LINTAS came into her office, which was crowded with flowers from admiring male coworkers, and informed her that the agency was not intended to be a florist's shop. A particular line of dialogue she delivered as Lady Rainier, which was later cut from the film, also reflected a message Greer would have liked to share with American moviegoers: "I'm not a great lady. I come of the people, too. I don't shout it from the housetops, because of Charles—but I was only a little actress in a third rate touring company." With a story steeped in English traditions, a friendly and utterly professional cast, and her favorite director and photographer, the making of *Random Harvest* was one of Greer's most satisfying experiences in Hollywood. "Playing the part of Paula was pure joy for me," she recalled. "Sometimes when working on a film, I come home utterly exhausted, but while playing this role I ended each day feeling fresh and lighthearted. The script flowed so beautifully, like a symphony. I would just sing going to the studio every morning. And that was at 4:45 A.M.!" The ideal conditions are reflected in *Random Harvest*. She has never appeared more convincing, more beguiling, or more lovely on film.

By now, Greer's daily schedule at MGM had become routine. It all began in William Tuttle's makeup chair at 7:00 A.M. "She was a brilliant woman," Tuttle recalls, "but hardly ever on time. She would rush into the makeup department late, jump in the chair, and declare, 'Give me one of your speediest this morning, Professor.' And I could just manage it. But then she would start another lengthy story and I would say, 'Greer, you had better go.' She was supposed to be on the set at nine." Sometimes, instead of chatting, she spent her morning reading mystery novels or poetry. She seldom joined in the gossip with the other actresses around her, which added to her image as an unapproachable grande dame.

"She was incredibly observant," says Tuttle. "We were dining at Jimmy's once, her favorite restaurant, after a magazine layout. She kept watching a waiter across the room, at least forty feet away. She called him over finally and told him his glasses were foggy and that he should clean them. I couldn't believe it." An impatient limousine driver, under strict orders to keep her on schedule, awaited Greer outside the makeup department to escort her to a soundstage. Once on the set she was a tireless worker who seldom socialized with her costars and never held up production except to knock off at four o'clock for tea. She avoided the studio's busy commissary and spent most of her mealtimes alone in her dressing room, lunching from a picnic basket that Nina and the cook had prepared.

During breaks in shooting, Greer was frequently driven by limousine to the portrait studio on Lot One ("a very ugly, uninspiring place," recalled MGM fashion editor Ann Straus) behind the sound-stages and in front of the machine shop for magazine and publicity layouts. Although Straus worked extra hard to make the experience pleasant by decorating the room with flowers and always providing a steaming pot of tea, Greer, who still hated being photographed in this way, was distant and unhappy. One day Greer emerged from her dressing room in an emerald nightdress and posed dramatically in front of the mirror. "What do you think?" she asked Straus. "Oh, Miss G., you look divine!" the editor declared. When Greer turned to her and asked, "Aren't you dishing it a bit?" Ann Straus replied, without the usual deference to the new Queen of the Lot, "I'm not dishing it. I'm shoveling it." Greer burst into laughter. "From that moment on," Straus said, "I could tell her to put on a lampshade and she'd do it." "On still portraits you can retouch wrinkles or blemishes on the face," Joe Ruttenberg once said, "but in motion pictures you don't have that opportunity." His use of glamorous soft focus, achieved by attaching very sheer ladies' stockings to the lens, made him a favorite with all of MGM's leading ladies, especially Greer. She was a firm believer that a girl's best friend was her cameraman and could frequently be found discussing photographic angles with Ruttenberg. "Greer had one good side, and I recognized what it was," he recalled. "Metro even built sets to favor her right side."

Since L.B. Mayer seldom allowed Greer to talk to the writers on her films (they were told to watch her films instead), she frequently rewrote her scripts, adding pages of dialogue suggestions. Instead of being annoyed, Sidney Franklin was impressed with her work and offered her—only half in jest—a position in the Writers Building. While many actors found the grind of moviemaking difficult, Greer found it comparable to the day-to-day play performance schedule in London. She tried to schedule her days at MGM in the same manner that she had worked in Birmingham—10:00 A.M. to 7:00 P.M. "All of the actors on the lot were behind her," Marsha Hunt recalls. "We cheered when she went to propose the idea to the front office. Unfortunately the answer was a firm no." At six o'clock when employees flew out the studio gate, Greer would stay to study the daily rushes. Returning home exhausted, she shampooed her famous red hair and rinsed it with a cup of California champagne, brushed it out one hundred strokes, and then tied it up in a net for the night.

Greer's last day of shooting for *Random Harvest* was May 8. On that day, Mervyn LeRoy shot the final sequence in the picture, with Ronald Colman. It was an emotional day for both actors. "We were meeting at our once beloved little cottage, in the country," Greer recalled. "All the lost years of our love, and all the hopes for the future are crowded into that one scene. It hit the deepest emotional point I've ever experienced in a picture—and it remains a thrilling memory." LeRoy recalled, "We all got on so well, it was a wonderful picture to make. When we did the last scene at the cottage gate, which was also the last scene we filmed, Ronnie said to me, 'This is one picture I hate to finish!'"

Meanwhile, excitement began to mount at MGM after the press screening of *Mrs. Miniver.* From the early, leisurely paced sequences in the Miniver household, which are filmed in the glossy manner typical of MGM, through the powerful later scenes depicting the dark days of war, which are uniquely William Wyler's, the audience laughed, suffered, wept, and fell in love with the Minivers. Under Wyler's guidance the film utilized its propaganda elements to the best advantage, especially in the kitchen sequence between Mrs. Miniver and the wounded Nazi pilot, and transcended similar wartime films made at Metro such as *The Mortal Storm* and *Escape* because it was a uniquely warm, poignant portrayal of a flesh-and-blood family. One member of the household stood out above the rest in the critics' estimation. *Variety* raved: "Greer Garson is always strange and distinctive and fascinating in each picture—never the same, never merely Greer Garson in this part or that. Here she is magnificently Mrs. Miniver, brave, wifely, maternal, and a pillar of civilian morale. In the production by Sidney Franklin, the direction of William Wyler, the un-affected performances by Greer Garson and Walter Pidgeon and their scarcely subordinate peers, an extraordinary amount of taste, discretion, and artistry has been displayed to make this one of the most important and beautiful film dramas of the season." But L.B. Mayer's optimism about the film's box-office prospects took a nosedive when Howard Strickling informed him that Greer Garson and Richard Ney were dating. His first thought, before panic set in, was—what had happened to Benjamin Thau?

Until 1942, Greer Garson's personal life had remained private, quiet, and uneventful. "There was nothing about Greer to attract the

Hollywood wolf pack," remarked one journalist. "She was neither a sweater girl nor a light of love. There was, in fact, everything about her to drive the eager wolf from her door. She reads books, lots and lots of books, on all subjects from economics to political strategy to the art of Renoir as contrasted to the music of Cesar Franck. Next, she did herself in by the very perfection of her portrayals."

Benjamin Thau had been her closest companion. As the liaison between studio management and the stars under contract, Thau had been a devoted friend to Greer since their first champagne toast at the Claridge's Hotel in London. He had helped her through her divorce, lunched with her at the Hillcrest Country Club, accompanied her to parties and premieres, and arranged for her to see L.B. Mayer when she needed to. Elsa Maxwell felt that Greer found Thau's "admiration and adoration warming." But whenever the question of marriage arose, one or both of them hesitated. Many at MGM were aware of the close relationship. "In fact," said Myrna Loy in her autobiography, "he was Greer Garson's great love before she married the actor who played her son in *Mrs. Miniver*."

When Richard Ney finished his work in *Mrs. Miniver* on February 10, Howard Strickling reported: "On the completion of his first screen role, Ney has launched into an intensive study of dramatics at the studio. He devotes considerable time to a study of experienced stars at work, visiting the sound stages when pictures are in production, at every opportunity." It was obvious to the cast and crew of *Random Harvest* that Richard Ney studied Greer Garson more than any other. One evening soon after starting his second film, *The War against Mrs. Hadley*, he invited her to dinner and dancing at the Club Gala on the Sunset Strip. To his delighted surprise, she accepted.

The news of their date spread through the film colony, as one journalist put it, "with a speed that makes wildfire look sluggish as a river of oatmeal." "I continued to be cool and distant to Mr. Ney throughout *Mrs. Miniver*," Greer told writer Gladys Hall, "which was a ridiculous piece of feminine pique on my part since, obviously, he had no more to say about the casting than I. So perhaps it was a form of retribution that when the picture was finished and our roles of mother and son safely canned and jelled, I went dancing with Mr. Ney and had a most beautiful time."

Mayer summoned them to his office. There sat Greer Garson,

one of MGM's supreme capital investments, and the unknown contract player named Richard Ney staring defiantly back at him. In his
typical fatherly manner, Mayer counseled Greer about the unfavor-
able publicity that could result from an actress falling in love with
her screen son. Turning to Richard, he explained the cruel fact that
marriage hurts the popularity of any star, male even more than female. Seeing no change in their expressions, no signs of repentance,
he got straight to the point. In terse tones he warned them that their
actions could irreparably damage the box office of *Mrs. Miniver*. They
must avoid being seen together off the lot. The couple quietly acquiesced and departed. Mayer breathed a sigh of relief. He was certain
that he had nipped the blossoming romance in the bud.

But, in defiance of Mayer's ultimatum, the couple continued to
meet—not dining and dancing on the Sunset Strip—but privately at
the Garson home. There they enjoyed quiet evenings playing four-
hand piano duets on Greer's magnificent Steinway grand pianos,
quietly chaperoned by Nina. In her article, "Secret Romance," Beth
Emerson wrote, "Richard Ney tells everyone he encounters how completely, utterly and devastatingly he is in love. Greer says nothing, but
her happiness is as luminous as a searchlight sweeping a blackout sky.
It is the glow of that happiness that lets you know how lonely Greer
has been until now, how much she has wanted this laughter and this
gaiety and this youth that have been brought to her."

As the premiere date for *Mrs. Miniver* neared, MGM publicists
were busy at their typewriters. The praise from President Roosevelt
and British Prime Minister Winston Churchill, who had demanded
early viewings of the film, was doing much of their work for them.
Churchill predicted that the film's contribution to defeating the Axis
powers would be more powerful than a fleet of battleships and urged
President Roosevelt to press for an immediate wide release—especially in England. Dispensing with original plans for exclusive show-
ings in major metropolitan areas and a gradual publicity buildup,
Louis B. Mayer did as he was told. In doing so, as Greer explained:
"It reached out not only to metropolitan cities but the rural areas,
and wherever *Mrs. Miniver* went she had quite an extraordinary
welcome."

The film premiered at Radio City Music Hall on June 4, 1942,
coinciding with the second anniversary of Winston Churchill's fa-

mous "We shall go on to the end. . . . We shall never surrender!" address to the English people. The centerpiece of the Music Hall lobby display was a "Mrs. Miniver Rose." Dr. Eugene Boerner, an American botanist, had produced the rose for MGM publicity purposes. In many of the major cities in which the movie would premiere, such roses were presented to women on the home front who had made significant contributions to the war effort. Jan Struther frequently presented the roses herself.

"It is hard to believe that a picture could be made within the heat of present strife which would clearly, but without a cry for vengeance, crystallize the cruel effect of total war upon a civilized people," remarked Bosley Crowther in the *New York Times*. "Yet this is what has been magnificently done in Metro's *Mrs. Miniver*. It is the finest film yet made about the present war, and a most exalting tribute to the British." The Radio City Music Hall engagement broke all previous box-office records, running an unprecedented ten weeks, drawing 1,499,891 theatergoers and grossing $1,031,500. *The Philadelphia Story* and *Rebecca* had held the record at six weeks. Although 158,000 people saw *Mrs. Miniver* in its final week, the theater reluctantly let the film go because of the backlog of films waiting to open there. The Los Angeles premiere, at the Carthay Circle Theater on July 22, 1942, was a lavish, star-studded benefit for the Voluntary Army Canteen. Elsewhere, extraordinary records were set. *Mrs. Miniver* ultimately made $5,358,000 in the United States alone and reaped a further $3,520,000 in its limited international release. The remarkable box-office total, $8,878,000, was a significant factor in MGM's $12 million profit for 1942. L.B. Mayer's foreign press corps jubilantly sent word that *Mrs. Miniver* was surpassing the box-office receipts of *Gone with the Wind*—from London to Cairo. "In fact," one journalist remarked, "it achieved the most significant validation a pop-culture icon is capable of receiving: It became as much a source of amusement as respect." Even Dr. Goebbels, Adolf Hitler's propaganda minister, admitted it was an "exemplary propaganda film for German industry to copy."

That summer of 1942 the romance of Greer Garson and Richard Ney finally hit the papers worldwide. Although theirs was the first publicized Hollywood war romance, it came to an abrupt halt on July 3 when Richard was shipped off to active service. "Since *Mrs. Mini-*

ver we have continued to see each other and to have beautiful times together and if it were not for the war we would, I am sure, be married now," she told the press. "For when Richard told me that he had volunteered in the U.S. Naval Reserve and was off to the Officers Training Unit at Notre Dame, Indiana, I was suddenly and acutely aware of how much I should miss him."

As Mayer had predicted, the news sparked controversy. From the start, Greer was on the defensive. Few approved of the match. As had been the case with other Hollywood couples such as Robert Taylor and Barbara Stanwyck, the obvious disparity in their ages was the cause of the most trouble. Although few could have guessed that there was actually fifteen years between them, Hollywood rumormongers hinted that Richard was growing a mustache to look older. "Greer Garson should know better," *American Weekly* editorialized, "for it is part of the common belief of all mankind that in marriage the man should be as old or older than the woman." To Greer and Richard's dismay, articles like this began appearing with regularity. Beth Emerson wrote: "They are moody souls, each of them, and their romance might evaporate with all the swiftness that characterized its reception. But regardless of the future, they are ecstatically, madly happy right now."

At first surprised to find she was flouting a rule of Hollywood society, Greer quickly grew defiant. "I want to marry him because he makes me feel that much younger—so there!" she told reporters, "and because we're in love." Elsa Maxwell was reached by the press to explain Hollywood's most talked-about romance. "Greer knew that Richard was in love with her," she said. "And she allowed herself to fall in love with him. She has not gotten ahead in pictures by being played as a favorite. She has earned her way, proved her worth. She is in a position to marry whom she wishes, when and how. And with all her heart she wishes to marry Richard."

English critics brought out their knives when *Mrs. Miniver* premiered in Great Britain at the Empire. Critic Eric Knight moaned, "It's tremendous. . . . It's hogwash. . . . It makes people cheer. . . . Oh. God, those Hollywood men with their funny ideas of what this war is about!" The *London Times* remarked: "It must be made clear that the Minivers on the screen are by no means the Minivers of the book, and the picture of England at war suffers from that distortion which seems inevitable whenever Hollywood cameras are trained on it. While, however, the fatal lack of precision in the camera's lenses is persistent, Miss Greer Garson is always at hand to cloak with the virtue of her acting the flaws in the production. She gives a performance which lifts the screen to the level of the best traditions of the stage, and Mrs. Miniver in her hands becomes a warm, human, and altogether admirable human being."

Greer attributed her success to Aunt Evelyn. "She is Mrs. Miniver in the way she works for her country, meets all the hardships and anxieties of war and continues to write to me amusingly of domestic trivia," she said. "I thought of her constantly while I was making *Mrs. Miniver*, and after the picture was released, I wrote and asked her how she liked her 'screen portrait.'" But unlike Caroline Miniver, Aunt Evelyn tragically lost her "Clem" in the war. Uncle James died in 1943 in Rangoon from a recurrence of the trench fever he had contracted during his service in World War I. He was buried in the Red Sea with full naval honors.

Whatever the reaction to *Mrs. Miniver* from overseas, it was the impact of the film on Americans that mattered most. Screenwriter Talbot Jennings, speaking at the Writers' Conference in October 1943, said, "*Mrs. Miniver* was just the right British for us, and came at just the right time, too—that critical time when many people in the country were, for one reason or another, indifferent to Great Britain, even hostile." Years later, Greer commented, "The impact of the film was exceptional, particularly in the United States. *Mrs. Miniver* appealed powerfully to Americans of all types—urban, rural, old, and young: 'What if it should happen here, to us?' I like to think *Mrs. Miniver* had something to do with dispelling the last traces of isolationism in America." She and Walter Pidgeon would reprise their roles on December 6, 1943, on *Lux Radio Theatre*.

As in the case of *Goodbye, Mr. Chips* in 1939, Greer Garson was once again caught by surprise as the star of the hour. Never before in the history of Metro-Goldwyn-Mayer had the perfect marriage of actress and role created a superstar who was also revered as an international heroine. As tributes flooded the studio, MGM publicists proudly declared: "Prizes and Awards Fall to Garson Like Plums." She was first on the annual Gallup poll of fifty-five thousand moviegoers for two consecutive years and winner of the English Picturegoer award for three. Readers' polls in *Country Gentleman*, *Woman's Home Companion*, *Screen Guide*, *Photoplay*, *Look*, *Modern Screen*, and *Redbook* put her at the top of their lists. She was named among the top ten moneymaking stars in the Motion Picture Herald Hall of Fame, a consistent annual honor until 1946. An American chrysanthemum was named for her. Along with Hollywood's sweater girls, she was voted by World War II soldiers "the woman we'd like to spend the rest of our lives in the nose of a bomber with." She received over a thousand fan letters a day. The Merrill Publication Company began producing a popular line of Greer Garson paper dolls, books, and coloring books. *Film Daily's* poll of the nation's critics voted her the top feminine star of the year. Thornton Delehanty, editor of *Redbook Magazine*, presented Greer and Walter Pidgeon with the Redbook Cup for *Mrs. Miniver*. Charles Skouras, of Fox West Coast Theatres, sponsored an honorary luncheon for *Mrs. Miniver* at the Ambassador Hotel. Before Los Angeles civic and business leaders, he presented awards of recognition to the stars, as well as to William Wyler and Sidney Franklin.

On July 23, 1942, Nina accompanied Greer to Grauman's Chinese Theater, where *Mrs. Miniver* granted her immortality in the cement forecourt. It is a unique memorial, for underneath the cement square that bears Greer's footprints and autograph, a time capsule was placed. With the help of sailors Dan Gleason and William Cobb, Greer also dedicated a plaque that was installed on the east wall of the theater. It was "Dedicated to the truly great Heroines of this War. . . . The millions of Mrs. Minivers in every democratic nation . . . the mothers, the wives, and the sweethearts of the men fighting for freedom, liberty, and justice, not alone for one people, but for all. Below the tablet with the signature of Greer Garson a print of the motion picture, *Mrs. Miniver*, a copy of the manuscript and of the book have been placed so that future generations may have a pictorial record of the fighting spirit of the people on the home front in 1942."

Even as MGM's former queen, Norma Shearer, retired from the screen in the spring of 1942, Louis B. Mayer was preparing a new coronation. He moved Greer into Shearer's lavishly appointed dressing room, Apartment D in the Stars Building, and gave her a thirty-thousand-dollar bonus. The ceremony concluded on August 27, 1942, when she signed an exclusive seven-year contract, with a raise to four thousand dollars a week without options. "After *Goodbye, Mr. Chips*," Greer declared, "my life was never the same. For a while, I was kind of the queen bee." Proud of his protégée, L.B. Mayer's generosity seemed boundless, including the gift of a five-thousand-dollar Continental convertible. Significantly, the mogul once compared Greer to his favorite racehorse, Busher, calling her "a classy filly who runs the track according to orders, and comes home with blue ribbons!" She was afforded the full star treatment, prompting Judy Garland to complain to her husband, director Vincente Minnelli: "Make them treat me like they do Greer Garson."

To escape the spotlight that summer, the Garsons purchased a cottage near Carmel in a recent subdivision of the vacation resort and art colony. The house, which they dubbed "Quail Haven," offered spectacular views of the Pebble Beach golf course and the ocean, while the area offered a variety of artists, writers, and theatrical presentations that they missed in Los Angeles. "There's a great danger in Hollywood," Greer said, "of becoming too cramped in outlook—and this makes for unhappiness and impatience." "The misty, cool northern California weather reminds her of earlier homes in Scotland and England," reported the *Chicago Sunday Tribune.* "Greer also bought the Del Monte house partly because of her pair of astonishing pets. There's plenty of room in their place up north for her giant poodles, Gogo and Cliquot."

In mid-August, Greer had a private conference with L.B. Mayer. She wanted to discontinue her MGM contract and return home to help the war effort. She argued that Laurence Olivier and many others had already departed. But Mayer, horrified at the thought and agonizing over the impending loss of such male stars as Clark Gable, Robert Taylor, and James Stewart, refused to consider it.

Greer did not intend to give up easily. On August 22 she set off on a nationwide bond selling campaign, visiting three hundred cities with fifty other celebrities including Hedy Lamarr, Ronald Colman, Irene Dunne, Joan Leslie, and Ann Rutherford, which concluded with a Washington, D.C., command performance. On September 12, 1942, she attended a special ceremony as the *Mrs. Miniver* script was presented to the Library of Congress. She also took the opportunity to meet with the British ambassador. Aware that England was hardly prepared to take back emigrants and find work and food for them, he offered the same diplomatic advice that he had given to dozens of others. "Stay in America." Greer recalled the conversation: "I said I'd drive a truck, be an air-raid warden, join the Red Cross, run a soup kitchen—whatever they could find for me I'd do. 'My dear young lady,' he said, 'your value to your country if you did that would be about two pounds ten shillings a week. But if you stay where you are and the studio continues to give you pictures like *Mrs. Miniver*, your value is incalculable.'" Greer also found an opportunity to meet First Lady Eleanor Roosevelt at the Waldorf Astoria, where they each spoke at the twelfth annual *New York Herald-Tribune* Forum on the subject of postwar rehabilitation.

Greer was an even greater success in the Hollywood Bond Cavalcade, the most ambitious all-star bond tour ever assembled, which ultimately raised $1,079,568,819. Greer wrote a song with Judy Garland and Lucille Ball entitled "I've Got Those Rooney-Skelton-Pidgeon Blues" which was a roaring success everywhere. *Los Angeles Times* columnist Charles Champlin wrote: "A journalist friend of mine in Cleveland remembered how Greer Garson had once come to town on a war bond tour and kept a press conference enthralled for over an hour while she talked of the comparative success of invasions from the east as compared to invasions from the west."

These public appearances were not easy for the shy actress who still broke into a sweat when she remembered her one and only speech for the Tomorrow Club. "My first Bond tour was inspiring, intimate, significant and stirring," she recalled. "Really rough stuff. I lost a pound a day, but for a shy girl who never opens her mouth if more than five people are present, I really felt I had done something." Although MGM writers prepared speeches for her, Greer invariably rewrote them. This was her favorite:

> Mr. Chairman, Ladies and Gentleman
> Those five words are all that you are going to hear from
> me today in the way of a formal speech. There isn't
> time! I've come a long way to be here with you for these
> few moments. So let's get down to the heart of the
> matter. I feel that you will not resent it if I address you
> as friends—your warm welcome has made me feel that I
> have friends everywhere I go in this blessed land—I am

here now at the request of your Government. I have
accepted this assignment with pride that I should be
called upon, but I have no idea how to get you to buy
bonds unless you already want to buy bonds; unless you
realize what it means to each of us. I believe you do
know. I know you are patriots. I speak to you from my
heart because I have come to love America and the
people of America. I have made my home here. I have
found happiness and opportunity beyond anything I
had hoped for. I feel I belong here as much as if I had
been born on this soil.

Of her World War II bond-selling years she would later write:
"I was one of those who pioneered on such tours alone. It was a
revelation to me—my personal discovery of America. . . . In every
village, every town, the spirit was the same—a complete awareness
of the international and personal meaning of this war, a simple determination to work, save and plan to bring victory nearer, and bring
the fighting men home again—home to the kind of life they're fighting to preserve. Somehow I feel that this activity, the bond tours, the
camp and hospital visits, the Canadian tour, is about the most useful
kind of fighting in this war that an actress can do."

Upon her return to Los Angeles in mid-November, Greer was
cast in a cameo role in *The Youngest Profession*. Based on Lillian Day's
popular short stories about the adventures of young autograph
hounds, the production was designed to feature Metro's most popular stars. Lana Turner, Walter Pidgeon, William Powell, and Robert
Taylor were all given amusing cameos in the picture. The two juve-
nile leads, Virginia Weidler and Jean Porter, waited to meet the guest
stars with the same excitement as the characters they were playing.
"The first big stars we worked with were Walter Pidgeon and Greer
Garson in a hotel room," recalls Jean Porter. "Greer surprised me, in
our scenes together, when she looked at the top of my head instead
of establishing eye contact. Virginia and I went aside and said, 'What
do we do about that?'" Mervyn LeRoy explained: "Joseph Ruttenberg
knew that Greer looks better with her chin raised. During rehearsals
they worked out private signals. Whenever Greer lowered her head,
Joe would signal her and she'd raise it again. Theirs was such a close

and successful relationship that she refused to make a picture unless he was her cameraman."

In a move that surprised the industry, L.B. Mayer chose to premiere *The Youngest Profession* at Radio City Music Hall. Never before had such a little picture enjoyed such a lavish opening. "Even with the great celebrities running interference, this glimpse into the workings of a teen-age movie fan club is at best flyweight fare," remarked the *New York Times*, "so slight on humor that it has a hard time making an impression in the vastness of the Music Hall. . . . Of course, Metro had every right to extol its own assets since it paid the bill, but it is a circumstance which makes *The Youngest Profession* appear too uncomfortably like a house ad." Despite the reviews, the film was a tidy profitmaker for MGM, grossing $1,546,000.

From the date of its first preview at MGM on November 27, 1942, *Random Harvest* was a spectacular success. The *Hollywood Reporter* considered it "one of the truly fine motion pictures of this or any year . . . Greer Garson, most gracious and feminine of stars, has a role in Paula, the music hall entertainer who becomes an aristocrat, which she makes magnificent. It is a performance of perfection by a great actress." The public flocked to the film in record numbers, stacking a staggering gross of $8,147,000. Once again, at Radio City Music Hall, a Garson picture broke every previous record, playing for eleven weeks and attracting 1,550,000 patrons. "It could have played longer," Mervyn LeRoy proudly observed, "but Nick Schenck wanted to have it played in all of the Loew's theaters, so they took it off after eleven weeks. But the Hall's Russell Downing told me that it could have stayed on for another ten weeks, it was such a big hit there." So many people were cramming Rockefeller Center to see *Random Harvest* that the management extended the daily schedule to seven showings a day for three days, beginning at 7:45 A.M. Commemorating the event, a celebratory luncheon was held in February 1943. Plaques were presented to Sidney Franklin, Mervyn LeRoy, George Froeschel, Claudine West, Joseph Ruttenberg, Ronald Colman, and Greer Garson. The unprecedented popularity of the story prompted Greer and Colman to rekindle the magic of their performances twice for *Lux Radio Theatre*: on January 31, 1944, and April 19, 1948.

But few of the accolades for *Random Harvest* matched the fan letters that she received from American and British soldiers. From the

USS *Augusta*, Navy officer James A. Ball wrote: "I have just come from seeing you and Mr. Colman in *Random Harvest*. In the words of the United States Navy 'well done,' and the praise of a former civilian 'excellent.' The picture was shown aboard ship and it is the first time I actually heard sailors openly applaud a film. At various other times, throughout the show they were moved to urging you by word of mouth to 'run to Smithy.' They got their fighting blood aroused when Charles Rainier hesitated as he bade you farewell at the train. They kept their seats on the deck and cheered until the film flickered off. And that, Miss Paula, is very unusual for this fighting ship. I, and I speak for the entire crew, wish to express my deepest sentiments and gratitude for a really splendid performance. Truly, your part typifies the sailor's dream: a happy home, a family, and a good wife."

Although consumed with the desire to switch from Mrs. Miniver and period roles on screen to the villainesses and comediennes of her London days, letters like this gave Greer pause. "One has to consider the present time and the fact that we are fighting for the retention of certain values in life," she admitted. "I wouldn't want to cause disappointment to the men in the service who have been so kind and appreciative." In the years to come, her affection for Mrs. Miniver would grow as she came to realize the character's crucial importance to war-weary movie audiences. Seven years later she would become instrumental in bringing Caroline Miniver back to the screen. She had capably filled a void at MGM with the departure of its key female stars, and now she was filling an even greater role as an icon of steadfast courage and an ambassador of peace to the world. Her contribution to the changing role of women on film was significant. "There had been what was called a Golden Age of movies," Greer said, "with great glamour. But about the time I came along war had made everyone a little more serious-minded. Family virtues, love of home and family, and feminine virtues, the good woman, suddenly were not such a bore after all."

CHAPTER 14

"HERE AM I, POSSIBLY THE ONLY NATURAL REDHEAD in Hollywood, mildewing away the years in shawls, shrouds, and chignons in unrelieved black and white," Greer complained in 1943. "I hope that *Madame Curie* will be my last heavy dramatic role I shall play for some time." The comment was not so much an indictment of the film, which fascinated her, as a sign of her growing antagonism toward Louis B. Mayer. She had run up against the barbed wire of Donington Hall that Constance Collier had complained about. She was trapped in a Hollywood stereotype and keenly aware that she was tied down to a studio contract. "I don't want always to represent nostalgic naphthalene to people's minds," she argued. "Playing in a picture of today brings you nearer to the public so much more quickly than one of yesterday." But Louis B. Mayer insisted that dramatic parts like Marie Curie displayed her talents to the best advantage—certainly the box-office receipts of *Goodbye, Mr. Chips, Blossoms in the Dust,* and *Mrs. Miniver* were proof of that. Gazing at her as she sat in his office uttering her complaints, he saw an immaculately dressed, impeccably mannered British lady whom he could not imagine as anyone else. He was also aware that, for all her criticisms about the pictures she was making at MGM, she was very much dependent on him as a mentor because she found decision-making difficult. The poor choices she had made as a London stage actress had only strengthened that belief.

Greer was particularly envious of a former RKO contract player named Lucille Ball, whom Sydney Guilaroff turned into a redhead as part of her star-making buildup at MGM. It was Ball who captured the sort of frothy, comic parts in *DuBarry Was a Lady* and *Best Foot*

Forward that Greer wanted. The studio's film trailers advertised Lucille as "The Screen's Best Romantic Red-head," a title Greer would have liked. And she could only enjoy vicariously, through her friendship with Katharine Hepburn, the career diversity of films like *Alice Adams, Sylvia Scarlett, Mary of Scotland, Bringing Up Baby,* and most recently *Keeper of the Flame.* Greer was impressed when she learned that Hepburn had abandoned a faltering Hollywood career in 1938 for Broadway's *The Philadelphia Story,* which she later brought to MGM. The film version, directed by George Cukor, rejuvenated her career and granted her a long-term Metro contract. "I admire Katharine immensely," Greer once confessed, "the way she has mapped out her career. She has such confidence."

When it came to *Madame Curie,* Greer assumed a disinterested attitude from the outset and expressed the regret that she would have to be aged into her sixties for the film. "It doesn't matter," she said. "When I'm 62, they'll probably cast me as an ingenue. At 70, I'll be in pigtails. Anyway I can dream can't I?" Eve Curie's biography of her mother, the celebrated woman who had discovered radium in 1898, had been published in the fall of 1937. By December it was a runaway international success, becoming both a Book-of-the-Month Club and a Scientific Book Club selection. Hollywood producers were immediately interested. Warner Bros. had realized the box-office and award-winning potential of scientific biographies with *The Story of Louis Pasteur* in 1936, starring Paul Muni. By the time *Madame Curie* was purchased by Universal, Twentieth Century-Fox was already preparing to star Don Ameche in *The Story of Alexander Graham Bell,* and Metro-Goldwyn-Mayer was preparing to make a double feature: *Young Tom Edison* and *Edison the Man* with Mickey Rooney and Spencer Tracy.

When Universal could not produce a satisfying script for its star, Irene Dunne, the story rights to *Madame Curie* were sold, along with the rights to *Show Boat,* to MGM in April 1938 for two hundred thousand dollars. Bringing *Madame Curie* to the screen would prove to be the greatest challenge of Sidney Franklin's career. In November 1942 he sent a memo to William Cannon, the production unit manager: "We have got to be authentic in every respect, as there are too many scientists who would ridicule our picture if we are not. This is of the greatest importance, and I think the matter should be given your close attention immediately. I imagine we will have to get a man like Dr. Langer from Cal Tech (whom we had help us on the script), to go through the entire picture and start at once to design the different instruments."

Dr. Rudolph Langer, a physicist, was hired as the official technical advisor for the production. Among his duties were detailed performances of the Curie experiments for the screenwriters. His greatest challenge, however, was convincing MGM personnel that the Curie laboratory should not resemble, as it was envisioned in an early screenplay, the elaborate Gothic set from *Frankenstein*. "Dramatically it would be false to science," he explained patiently to director Mervyn LeRoy.

When word of the production reached the ears of Eve Curie's sister, Irene, Sidney Franklin found himself in the middle of a family feud. Salka Viertel, one of *Madame Curie*'s eighteen screenwriters, who had gone to France for research, wrote: "Irene Jolliot-Curie dislikes, or rather, is very much hurt by the idea that the life of her mother should be shown in a motion picture. Confidentially, I found out from other people in Paris that Eve never told anybody that she had sold her book to the movies. Irene and her husband have great influence and are very much respected here in France. As she is not certain what our picture will be like, even if the intentions of my collaborators are the best, she refused any cooperation, since she would thereby lose the right to protest. . . . And, dear Sidney, when she refuses it is as if the Rock of Gibraltar were to refuse."

Meanwhile, the various departments of the studio went to work. In the typical MGM manner, studio screenwriters could—and did—romanticize the life of a historical personage such as Marie Curie, but the sets and costumes were thoroughly researched for authenticity. Personnel in makeup and wardrobe studied family photographs of the Curies, which were supplied by Eve. When possible, costumes were duplicated from these photographs. Among the historically accurate sets, designed by Cedric Gibbons and Edwin Willis, was a reproduction on Stage Twenty-one of the old shed at the School of Physics where radium was discovered. The MGM prop department obtained lab apparatus to furnish the shed from Cal Tech, UCLA, the Los Angeles County Museum, and private collections. In the case of Pierre Curie's Magnetic Balance, seen in the opening sequences in the picture, a carefully reproduced copy was built at the studio from Curie's own drawings. Greer observed this curious melding of Hollywood and science with interest. "There's a great deal of beauty in laboratory apparatus properly set up," she remarked. "I think it was very commendable of us that nobody blew his eyebrows off; nothing exploded; no one broke a single thing. Now I could get a job as a lab boy!"

By then she had done considerable research of her own. The challenge of portraying a world-famous personage was heightened by the fact that her role had originally been envisioned for Greta Garbo. After going head to head with Joan Crawford, she was now competing against Garbo's legend. "I read everything I could lay hands on in French and English," she said. "I even had a Polish woman translate whatever had been written in Polish. Even if my line was merely 'Good morning, Pierre.' I wanted to know how Marie would say it. . . . For months, and for nine to fifteen hours a day, Madame Curie was my main preoccupation . . . with the result that I feel I know and understand the wonderful woman better than anyone I have actually met."

Greer was intrigued by the similarities she shared with Marie Curie. "During my schooldays mother and I, by trimming our budget for months in advance, managed two or three Continental holidays," she recalled. "We would decide where to go by closing our eyes and sticking a pin in a map. One summer the pin sent us to L'Arcouest on the Emerald Coast of Brittany where, I discovered, Madame Curie used to spend a great deal of time. I loved it and considered 'retiring' there where I could write and become a famous author." The years Greer had spent in the British Museum helped her understand the sheltered, scholarly young scientist. "I spent long, happy, self-important days there," she recalled, "looking up books of reference, taking notes, surrounded by other students, mostly elderly, and all very solemn. When I played *Madame Curie* on the screen, I was glad I had those quiet months in that studious atmosphere. They helped me feel more at home in her way of life than I might otherwise have done." Another similarity was captured by the MGM screenwriters in the sequence in which Pierre Curie's mother, played by Dame May Whitty, makes this touching observation about young Marie: "You'll do well, whatever it is. I'm not paying compliments. I'm just telling

you what I see in your face. It's all there, in people's faces. . . . Look
at yours: stubborn, determined, obstinate; and of course, intelligent;
and then something also I don't quite know how to give a name to.
Fiery, is it? Flame-like? That's a little nearer. Flame-like, then. Something flame-like."

Surrounded by biographies and scientific textbooks, Greer studied long into the night. Often, there would be a familiar knock on
the door and Nina would appear with tea and a midnight snack.
"Mother is my best audience," she said, "a good and patient listener
and an excellent judge of dramatic values. I know that I caused her
to lose more sleep than ever before while I was portraying Marie. We
have such a rare, beautiful companionship. It's the kind that makes
me tell her to come and comb her hair in my room, just so I can be
with her." Among Greer's rarest historical discoveries was Marie
Curie's favorite poem, "To the Young," by Adam Asnyk. When the
screenwriters were unable to decide on the film's conclusion, her
solution was to incorporate the poem into Marie's speech upon the
twenty-fifth anniversary of the discovery of radium in 1923. As distinguished scientists gather from around the world to honor Madame
Curie, she encourages the world of science: "Leave, then, the dreams
of yesterday. You—take the torch of knowledge and build the palace
of the future."

By the time the lights on the Curie sets came on and the cameras were ready to roll, Greer admitted, "I can honestly say that once
I began work, Madame Curie has taken hold of my imagination and
thoughts as no other character I have played has done. The poor
student, haunted by dreams, the humble and obscure research worker
emerged from the shadows of anonymity into the blinding and un-
welcome limelight. She refused wealth, endured honors with indif-
ference and remained almost unaware of her astonishing destiny."

Sidney Franklin's first choice for Pierre Curie was Spencer Tracy,
who read for the part and loved it. But as *Madame Curie* went
through numerous production delays and endless script rewrites, he
moved on to other projects. In December 1942, the College of Cardinals suggested William Powell. Ultimately, Franklin chose Walter
Pidgeon, who had recently been miscast in the absurdly melodramatic *White Cargo* with Hedy Lamarr. The choice turned out to be
an inspired one, for the actor earned another Academy Award nomi-

nation for his poignant and sensitive portrayal of Pierre. It was, arguably, his finest performance at MGM. In trying to explain the undefinable quality that made this characterization one of Pidgeon's best, Greer referred to his beard, which MGM experts, after studying old photographs, had trimmed into a close facsimile of Pierre's. "Walter has never looked more handsome or romantic," Greer enthused. "I'll make a wager that women will find him more exciting with a beard. I did. It gives him a fascinating distinction." Ruth Pidgeon was not impressed, and laughingly told a reporter: "I'm going away for a vacation. I'll come back when he shaves off the beard!" It must have been a long stay, because Pidgeon kept it for eighteen weeks. Years later, Pidgeon recalled, "Everywhere in the world *Mrs. Miniver* is rated as my best and people always talk about it. I always like two other films as the best of my career. I thought *Command Decision*, with Clark Gable, and *Madame Curie* were my best. I still cherish that scene in *Madame Curie* when Pierre goes out to buy Marie jewelry and gets killed. Really touching."

The sequence is one of many classic romantic moments the MGM screenwriters incorporated into *Madame Curie*. Preparing for a formal presentation at which the Curies will be honored with a new, fully equipped laboratory by the president and faculty of the University of Paris, Marie buys a new dress. Proud of his wife's beauty, Pierre remarks, "It's a pity . . . Evening-dress becomes you so. But there it is, we just haven't got time." He adds that she ought to have "some kind of little ornament, hadn't you? Something bright. I've seen them on women and they look nice." Without her knowledge, he goes out to buy earrings and describes his wife to the jeweler: "I would say her face was—oval. And her hair is a sort of—gold—you know—! And her eyes are gray—very calm and gray—and nice delicate coloring— And—well, I don't know whether it'd be of any help to you, but I believe the lady is quite beautiful." Although his untimely death in a street accident prevents him from presenting the earrings, Pierre's precious gift later enables Madame Curie to emerge from mourning and continue her scientific studies.

Among the most memorable sequences in any Garson/Pidgeon film is the charming proposal scene. Pierre Curie has invited Marie to visit his family, and the evening before she is due to leave he bursts into her bedroom. Despite some nervous stammering, he makes an announcement: "I know how you feel about men—about love, I mean. And I respect that feeling. It is also my conviction. For the scientist there is no time for love. I have always believed science and marriage to be incompatible. But it is stupid to believe in generalizations. In our case, it would be a wonderful collaboration! A wonderful collaboration! Don't you feel it? It would be a very fine thing, I believe, to pass our lives together with our common scientific dream." Marie, startled at first by the interruption of her sleep, is sitting up, seemingly frozen, in bed. Only the tears in her eyes display the deep emotion she is experiencing. "I believe you are right," she replies. "I should like to remain in Paris—very much."

Among the superlative supporting cast of *Madame Curie*, which included the usual troupe of Henry Travers, Reginald Owen, and Dame May Whitty, were a number of new faces at MGM. Greer's films, now among the largest and most prestigious on the lot, were becoming training grounds for new talent. Robert Walker, playing Pierre Curie's eager young assistant, had just completed his first major film role in *Bataan*. Over at Twentieth Century-Fox his wife, Jennifer Jones, was performing her star-making role in *The Song Of Bernadette*. Playing the young Irene Curie was Margaret O'Brien, star of *Journey For Margaret*, who became the studio's most popular child star. An even younger member of the cast was Gigi Perreau, playing Eve Curie. Playing a family breakfast scene with the adorable infant, Walter Pidgeon quipped, "If Gigi has any more scenes, no one will care whether I'm in the picture or not." And finally there was another rising star who played the brief role of a newspaper reporter who is granted an interview with Marie Curie. "Before we filmed the scene, I asked who was going to play the reporter," Greer recalled. "Mervyn LeRoy replied, 'A young song-and-dance man named Van Johnson.' When he turned up, with that shining schoolboy face and ingenuous blue eyes, everyone on the set liked him very much. Since he had to play a rather ingenuous young man, it was nice casting." In subsequent pictures like *A Guy Named Joe, Thirty Seconds over Tokyo*, and *Thrill of a Romance*, Johnson would become one of the studio's most enduring and popular leading men.

On February 7, 1943, to top off 1942's movie season, dubbed "the year of Greer," the Academy of Motion Picture Arts and Sciences announced its nominations for the films of 1942. *Random Harvest* earned seven nominations for Best Picture, Director, Actor (Ronald Colman), Supporting Actress (Susan Peters), Screenplay, Black and White Interior Decoration, and Best Musical Scoring. *Mrs. Miniver* received twice as many. Besides Greer's nomination as Best Actress, the film received nods for Best Picture, Director, Actor (Walter Pidgeon), Supporting Actor (Henry Travers), Cinematography, Screenplay, Sound Recording, Film Editing, and Special Effects. Dame May Whitty and Teresa Wright were both nominated in the supporting actress category for *Miniver*. Greer was ambivalent, both about her role and her chances of winning at the ceremony on March 4. "It was a character part," she observed, "and I was young and didn't want to become a character actress before my time. I also thought I was crossing those mother-part bridges before I came to them." But when she did win and held the Oscar up before a blaze of flashbulbs and newsreel cameras at the Ambassador Hotel, the trials of *Mrs. Miniver*'s production were forgotten in a haze of triumph and gratefulness.

The following morning when she reported to the studio, the MGM press corps awaited her. Greer related an incident that had occurred earlier that morning. "When I awoke and there was no Oscar on my bedstand, I said to myself, 'So it was a dream after all.' Mother had taken him away while I was still sleeping, to show the cook!" But her good humor quickly changed in the days—and years—to come. The Academy's ceremony and their selections quickly came under attack. The *Hollywood Reporter* griped, "Probably no big event ever attracted more tiresome speakers voicing greater dullness and long-winded speeches, consuming with the Awards, the better part of three hours." The anti-British Hollywood faction had a field day with *Mrs. Miniver*'s extraordinary success. Hedda Hopper wondered why a film that was not even about Americans could win so many American awards, and word began spreading about Hollywood that Greer Garson had given the longest acceptance speech in the Academy's history. At a party thrown by Danny Kaye and his wife, Sylvia Fine, a few days after the ceremony, the couple presented "Oscars" to their guests. Actor Laird Cregar received Best Female Impersonation of the Year and stretched a mocking version of Greer's speech to an unendurable length. Other local jokes ("Her speech was longer than her part") and legends sprang forth, greatly exaggerating the duration to over an hour.

In an attempt to still the industry gossip, Greer did a rare thing. She went to the press. Her award had not been presented until after 1:00 A.M., she argued indignantly, in front of a tired and sleepy audience that had production calls early the following morning. She admitted that she had thanked many people, including the doctor in London who brought her into the world. ("Well," she said, "I wouldn't have gotten very far without him!") "I wasted all the happiness out of it by droning on too long accepting it," she continued. "I was so grateful to so many people, I wanted to thank them all. But it was *five* minutes. They said it was two hours. I don't think Winston Churchill could hold their attention for two hours!"

Later that month, when Richard Ney received a forty-eight-hour leave, the talk about Greer turned from award ceremonies to wedding bells. Gossip columnists discovered that the couple had tried to obtain a marriage license but were disappointed to learn that it was impossible to obtain because of California's three-day-wait law. New orders arrived, and Ensign Ney sailed for action in the Aleutians. Greer confided to Gladys Hall, "Richard and I thought, at first, that to be married might give us a sense of nearness and solidarity in spite of distance. But to wed on Tuesday only to be separated on Wednesday is, to me, an appalling idea. It may be that during one of Richard's leaves impulse will get the better of common sense, but I hope we are wise to wait until the war is over and then we can start our home, and our lives, together."

As shooting on *Madame Curie* continued into the spring of 1943, Walter Pidgeon kept his leading lady's spirits high with his typical jokes, crossword puzzles, thoughtful conversation, and pleasant teatimes. Mervyn LeRoy never forgot one incident. It was the most dramatic scene in the picture, when Pierre and Marie Curie glimpse the glow of radium for the first time inside their darkened workshed on New Year's Eve. "We rehearsed it and rehearsed it so the audience would have goosebumps when it flashed on the screen," LeRoy recalls. "I called for action, and the cameras were rolling—and then, from out of the darkness, I heard Greer laugh. 'Cut,' I yelled. 'Come on, Greer, what's so funny? Why the big laugh?' 'I couldn't help it,' she said. 'Walter just told me the funniest joke.'"

"In spite of my initial reluctance to do another serious screen character," Greer confided to reporters, "*Madame Curie* is one of the happiest pictures in the making! For I am working again with my favorite director, my favorite producer, and my favorite photographer, and his crew. In fact, actors, technicians, and studio workers in the various departments are old friends, so there is a wonderful family feeling." As shooting reached an end, Mervyn LeRoy insisted that the scene in which the Curies discover radium be re-shot. Unaware that the entire cast and crew had planned an elaborate surprise, Greer once again approached the glass bowl as the cameras rolled. Inside, she found a small package with the words: "To Our Best Girl, From the Crew." It was a gold ring with six ruby chips.

After ten months of duty, Richard Ney returned to Los Angeles. The couple made a surprise call on the man who had brought them together, Sidney Franklin. Because of the hot weather, he suggested a swim. "We had a wonderful time, marvelous," Greer recalled. In the evenings, she and Richard discussed wedding plans. They told no one, not even Nina, who was still not supportive of a union between her daughter and an actor. After the last day of re-takes, on Saturday, July 24, 1943, Greer met Richard and the couple drove to 680 Stone Canyon to break their wedding plans to Nina. If she was disappointed or uncertain of their future together, as many of their mutual friends were, she did not show it. Her daughter had made up her mind. There were not going to be any further postponements.

The ceremony was extraordinarily simple by Hollywood standards. "It was just another wedding, without pretensions, and very real," commented Rev. Richard Irving of the Santa Monica Presbyterian Church. "Instead of the bride being one of Hollywood's most glamorous actresses, she might have been just any ordinary young woman marrying her sailor." "I'm quite proud to be marrying a sailor," Greer explained to Reverend Irving, "because I come from a sailor's country!" The Neys spent a rushed honeymoon in New York, where a transport awaited Richard, and enjoyed the simple pleasures of the Staten Island Ferry, a visit to Grant's Tomb, and a ride in the elevator of the Empire State Building. All too soon Ensign Ney, U.S.N., whom Greer fondly dubbed "my long-legged husband," was gone, and the country's most famous Navy wife was riding the train back to Los Angeles.

From his ship, Richard wrote to Capt. Maurice M. Witherspoon, whom he had befriended on the naval transport bound for the Aleutian Islands the previous January: "If it hadn't been for you I might never have won Mrs. Ney. It was touch and go at the time I had the pleasure of reading your letters to your wife. They taught me a lot and I took the liberty of incorporating some of my newly gained knowledge in the letters I wrote to my fiancée."

The news of Greer's marriage ignited a powder keg in Hollywood. "There are many who claim that in wartime reason takes a holiday—that youth rushes into matrimony with little thought of post-war consequences," remarked the *Los Angeles Times*. "Take, for example, the case of Greer Garson and Richard Ney. Greer is as beautiful a woman as there is in Hollywood. Yet the fact remains that Ney is several years younger." But Greer was immune to criticism by then, happy in the knowledge that her dream of a family was finally coming true.

Almost at once Hollywood gossip columnists hinted that "Metro's Glorified Mrs." was going to have a baby. Furious, Greer granted a rare interview to Mary McCall. "She was red-headed mad," McCall informed her readers. "She feels a professional woman, who is to have a child, should retire from the screen until her baby is born, and that until she announces that retirement, it is bad taste to discuss her expectancy in print. 'But,' Greer adds, 'I wish it were true.'"

At a final cost of $1,938,000, *Madame Curie* was finally ready to be screened. At 8:00 P.M. on November 18, 1943, the press filed into projection room one at the studio. Once again the weight of an expensively mounted production was placed squarely on Greer's shoulders, and once again she rose magnificently to the challenge. Those at the studio who had been certain that only Greta Garbo could portray the great scientist changed their minds by the time the film was over. L.B. Mayer considered it the studio's finest film, second only to *The Human Comedy*. The following day, *Variety* voiced the opinion of all critics present: "Every inch a great picture, *Madame Curie* is not only a distinguished combination to the screen in that it absorbingly tells mankind of the struggle and heartaches that ultimately resulted in the discovery of radium but further than that, because it is a very poignant love story, its box office success is assured." Greer was not at the press screening. While participating in another Canadian War Loan Drive that month, she learned that her husband's ship had docked in Boston. She sent a cable and flew to meet him. But the telegram did not tell Richard where she was staying. Only by systematically checking each hotel in Boston was he able to find his wife. "I finally found her," Richard said, "but only after some kindly secretary had informed me that 'Miss Garson is travelling incognito—as Mrs. Richard Ney.'" The couple traveled on to New York, where Richard received his orders to report to a ship sailing from San Pedro, California. The Neys were able to share the train trip across the country.

Arriving home on December 2, the newlyweds settled into a brief period of happy domesticity and even performed on WTOP radio one evening in "Next Time We Love" for the *Screen Guild Players Drama*. "It was great to see Richard and Greer together," Elsa Maxwell recalled. "They have the same wonderful humor about everything, including themselves. They have the same gift for enjoying whatever comes their way whether it be tea at a little stand at the beach or a great symphony. It is downright exciting to see them laughing and loving and playing together."

The Neys attended the Hollywood premiere of *Madame Curie* on December 15 at Grauman's Chinese Theater, marking the forty-fifth anniversary of the discovery of radium. Greer seemed unaffected by the laudatory ovation she received after the film and distant to the celebrities who rushed up to congratulate her. Her only comment to the throng outside the theater was: "It was a very pleasant partnership, Walter's and mine, and we hope that MGM will find us a good comedy subject so that we may continue, but in a lighter vein for a time, as 'Mr.' and 'Mrs.'" The couple reprised their roles as the Curies for *Lux Radio Theatre* on September 16, 1946.

At the Radio City Music Hall opening the following night, the picture attracted more than 950,000 fans and went on to play seven weeks. "Mrs. Long-Run Is Back Again at Music Hall," declared the *New York Herald-Tribune*. The *New York Times* considered the film to be "a lasting inspiration. . . . [*Madame Curie*] makes the quest for knowledge a romantic and thrilling pursuit. Miss Garson, the invariable patrician, plays with that gentle, wistful grace which makes her a glowing representation of feminine nobility and charm." On December 20, *Time* magazine was issued with a portrait of Greer Garson on the cover. The cover's headline read: "Greer Garson: Hollywood discovered a radioactive element." Inside, the article began: "In an expert piece of sentiment called *Goodbye, Mr. Chips*, a young English actress, who looked rather like a goddess sculptured in butterscotch, made her brief screen debut, and without fair warning even to herself, stole the film. Though nobody clearly realized it at the time, she also started something new in screen history. The something new was to make *Mrs. Miniver* and *Random Harvest* two of the five greatest screen hits ever manufactured. . . . It was slowly to crystallize and congeal Miss Garson's vivid, rangy talent for acting, and to lift it to an eminence comparable to that of St. Simeon Stylites: high, conspicuous, and not without grandeur . . . which culminated this week in the soberly splendid scientific romance, *Madame Curie*. For Hollywood and for Greer Garson, the picture was one of the scariest jobs either had ever undertaken. But, given the fusion of their compensating formulas, success was almost chemically inevitable."

Certain that they had another hit of *Miniver*-like proportions, MGM publicists released an elaborate eight-page Oscar advertisement in the Hollywood trade papers. The members of the Academy of Motion Picture Arts and Sciences, who evidently agreed with the laudatory comments in the ad, bestowed seven nominations on *Madame Curie*, for Best Picture, Best Actor, Best Actress, Best Cinematography, Best Interior Decoration, Best Sound Recording, and Best Musical Scoring. Although the American Radium Society presented Greer with the prestigious Janeway medal for her performance and the film was listed in the *New York Times* as one of the ten best films of the year (the movie eventually grossed $4,610,000), no Oscars were forthcoming, a surprise and disappointment to everyone at Metro-Goldwyn-Mayer who had labored so lovingly on the ambitious project. For it was, as *Time* described it, "much graver and more deeply felt than *Mrs. Miniver*. It was more daring and more difficult to make. It devotes itself to dramatizing matters seldom attempted on the screen: the beauty, dignity and calm of a marriage earnestly, rather than romantically, undertaken, the binding and illuminating power of a rare intellectual companionship and of grinding work performed in common." L.B. Mayer, furious at the Academy for the slight, nevertheless gave Sidney Franklin a reward of another kind: a forty-thousand-dollar bonus for his extraordinary work on *Curie* and the Irene Dunne wartime hit *The White Cliffs of Dover*. Exhausted from his heavy schedule, Franklin took off for the East on a working vacation. Each stop on his itinerary, including New York, Lexington, Concord, Washington, and Williamsburg, was tied into his plans for his new film entitled *American Cavalcade*. He had brought the esteemed writer, Carl Sandburg, on board at MGM in 1942 to help him realize his vision. By April 1944 he and Sandburg had some forty thousand words of the script completed, beginning with the Pilgrims at Plymouth Rock, exploring the Revolution and Civil War, and concluding with the present day. Both men envisioned Greer Garson as the star, and believed it would be her greatest achievement to date.

Greer was interested, but weary of such heavy historical roles. She complained to Philip Scheuer of the *Los Angeles Times*, "The instant they find a story about an intelligent, suffering woman they come to me. I really envy Ginger Rogers such assignments as *Tom, Dick and Harry* and *Lady in the Dark*. Or, going back further, what a joy it would be to play in some delightful costume piece like Kermesse Heroique's 'Carnival in Flanders.' It's a pity Hollywood never approaches the past in the spirit of Boccaccio or of Henry VIII. Both writers and actors have a tendency to get 'heavy' in treating of anything that happened before the Gay Nineties. One exception, of course, was *Pride and Prejudice*—and how I loved doing it!"

When Scheuer mentioned that she had been voted the most noncooperative actress of 1943 by the Hollywood Women's Press Club, Greer's response was immediate. "I am for the days when actors, ostracized by more conventional folk, gathered in taverns and, under cover of night and enveloping cape, spoke privately together," she said. "They were more mysterious then and so, more provocative . . . for I may be fascinated by Mr. Nonesuch's Richard III on the stage but I do not want to know what brand of toothpaste he uses or by what pet name his wife summons him to dinner!"

Bob Thomas of the *Hollywood Citizen-News* came to her defense when the Women's Press Club announcement was made. "Greer has a reserve which some Americans don't understand," he wrote. "She is not actually shy, merely reserved. That is something as foreign in Hollywood as a happy screen writer. Greer is sensitive about the things that are written about her. . . . She is very meticulous about what appears concerning her in the fan mags." The controversy was another chapter in the uneasy seven-year relationship between Greer Garson and the Hollywood press.

CHAPTER 15

"WE ARE HERE TO INTERVIEW A LADY," announce a group of admiring pressmen to the butler of an imposing Hollywood household, "known to you because of her ability as the glamorous, amorous lady they call—" "She's expecting you, gentlemen," the butler interrupts. The scene is from "The Great Lady Gives an Interview," a classic musical send-up of a film star in Metro-Goldwyn-Mayer's 1945 film *Ziegfeld Follies*. Although performed by Judy Garland in the film, Kay Thompson and Roger Edens, two of the studio's top musical collaborators, had originally written it for Greer Garson. The witty satire of a haughty actress not only poked fun at Greer's recent complaints about her film roles ("Must the roles I play be tragic . . . full of Oscar-winning magic?") and *Random Harvest* ("Do you think it is permissible to be, for once, quite kissable and give them a peep of my legs?"), but also contained a direct pun on *Madame Curie* ("Madame Cremantante, gentlemen, will be a monumental, biographical tribute to a monumental, biographical woman"). Greer had refused the part under pressure from her disapproving mother and told the *Hollywood Reporter,* "Oh, it would have been fun, wouldn't it? But at the time I didn't think it was appropriate to be making fun of the hand that was feeding me, so to speak."

No one who ever interviewed Greer Garson could mistake the similarities of the experience with the *Ziegfeld Follies* sketch. "Greer is the complete show-off," Mona Gardner wrote in *Ladies Home Journal.* "Five minutes talk with her develops into a literal travelogue—since in one sentence she is quite apt to throw her vigorous lithe body from here to way over there. In the next, she's across the room, out a door, and back in through another one—with the shades of

Bernhardt, Duse and Fifi the Gorgeous Soubrette dogging her many footsteps." To Bob Thomas, she was "one of the most sparkling conversationalists in town . . . full of wit and gaiety [with] a mind that absorbs information like a blotter." "Miss Garson has the tongue of the Irish," another agreed. "You think you've got it pinned down, and lo! it mocks you from the other side of the fence." "Fortunately," Pete Martin observed in the *Saturday Evening Post*, "for those exposed to Greer's conversational flood, it is not turgid or muddy." Vina Windes of the *New Mexican* agreed, "Miss Garson is a person who has a great many things to say about a great many things. In a running dialogue with her, you not only have to run to keep up, you resort to leaps and skips, and fly round corners holding your hat!"

An opportunity to witness such a performance was, however, very rare. Greer preferred quiet evenings at home, visits to the theater in unobtrusive seats, and the simple pleasures of gardening, picnics on the beach, riding, and tennis. While Richard was away during the war, she and Nina were still the same hermitlike, self-sufficient pair they had been in London. They never attended the horse races at Santa Anita and did not belong to the fashionable beach clubs where, Greer declared, "to stroll across the sands is to be on parade." "She has yet to be mired in any scandal," admitted Pete Martin. "She doesn't have to maintain face by putting in an appearance at Romanoff's or Chasen's or Ciro's; she makes no cringing bows to those twin bugaboos the *Hollywood Reporter* and *Variety*; she sees socially only whom she pleases; she doesn't throw huge parties, and is therefore not obligated to attend those thrown by others."

"Although I had some preparation for it, having been on the stage, it was not until after *Mrs. Miniver* that I actually experienced the full glare of the spotlight," Greer complained. From that time the presence of the American press was completely unavoidable. Resigned to the task, she allowed a select few to slip past her quiet British reserve, and the forbidding wooden gates of 680 Stone Canyon. "You feel as if you were stepping into the Miniver home when you visit Greer Garson," Mary C. McCall remarked, "a gracious lady living in traditional English style." In an article entitled "Bundle from Britain" for his London readers, John Franchey reported: "It's a homey, mildly Tudor white brick manse secreted in its own little canyon through which a brook flows, with some artificial goading, under ancient sycamores. The rooms are comfortably luxurious, panelled in bleached oak, furnished in shades of green blending into the garden foliage through long French windows."

Many writers felt pressured to make a stop at the library before entering the Garson household. "She is the most erudite actress in Hollywood," J.B. Griswold observed, "leading the pack by seven five-foot shelves. As though I were to be a guest on *Information Please* I had brushed up on Shakespeare, dipped into *The Spectator* of Addison and Steele, which was reputed to be Miss Garson's favorite light reading. I was afraid she wouldn't talk unless I kept the conversation on an intellectual plane." A writer for *Time* remarked, "She is shy, and she takes out her shyness in polysyllables, parody, sentimentality and histrionics. She is voluble, with a remarkable memory and an intellectual ostrich's appetite for miscellaneous knowledge. (She once floored a shipmate of Ensign Ney's by asking if his ship used Worthington pumps.) She is playful. Occasionally she enriches the English language with lines like her description of a visiting businessman: 'The gentleman surprised me, young, gallant and full of schmaltz and flair and *je ne sais quoi* besides!'"

Guests were frequently treated to tea poolside or in the rose garden where the Greer Garson and Mrs. Miniver roses grew, bordered by a cascading lily pond. "Two years of life in the cinema Bagdad and she's still a bright bolt of English dimity," observed one writer, "amusing and engaging, especially when she tries to mingle the picturesque and leisurely folkways of suburban England with the urgent and chromium-plated life patterns which is Hollywood." Wherever the interview, Nina Garson was always present. "Mrs. Garson has the magnetic composure of a strong perceptive soul," John Franchey observed, "and you know her dark bright eyes are seeing through you. Though aware of clairvoyance you are not uncomfortable because she is wise and kind and therefore tolerant." On the pink enameled tabletop, Nina would dispatch china teacups, saucers, cream, sugar, and a platter of sliced cucumber and cress sandwiches, with cream cheese, Banbury tarts, and an assortment of marmalade rolls and Scotch scones. Greer prepared her own tea ("two bags, the cream goes in first"), while Nina poured for their guests and herself.

Teatime invoked a conversation about her favorite foods, both from the Old World and the New. Principally she enjoyed those from her childhood: porridge and haddock, fruit juices, buttermilk, oysters, potatoes, Irish stew, and haggis. She still enjoyed a bowl of stewed fruit, which reminded her of her childhood on the farm in County Down. Although she did not smoke, she proudly informed her guests that she was once named the Tobacco Queen at the National Tobacco Festival in Virginia.

Those rare journalists who became friends with the Garsons were invited on a house tour, which Greer decorated "for the effect of a woodland, with the walls the pale wood of silver birch, the rugs the green of the forest, and an old glass here and there, like pools of water." The interviewers were invited to sit on a twelve-foot green velvet divan that its owner described as "so cozy for two people to sit facing each other and read, or even cozier with two at one end." It faced an oversized fireplace, over which a massive eighteenth-century antique mirror, intricately carved with happy cherubs, hung. Greer filled the house with paintings by Renoir, the French moderns, and the works of Hungarian artist Csillig. The drapes covering the French windows were embroidered with red English roses and allowed the California sunshine to brightly illuminate an alcove with built-in shelves for her books and gleaming Academy Award statuette, and the twin Steinway grand pianos. When Greer had purchased them as the centerpiece for evening entertaining, the Beverly Hills salesman had explained that only one had ever been used, by Artur Rubinstein before a Los Angeles recital. Greer agreed to take them but warned that she expected a two-thousand-dollar discount if the famous concert pianist had played "Fire Dance" on them—even once. Rubinstein and Oscar Levant were frequent dinner guests, who would spontaneously dash off a duo-pianist concert program of classic and popular music. Among her most constant guests was Sydney Guilaroff. "We enjoyed half an hour or so of playing two-piano versions of favorite concertos," Greer recalled, "he the brilliant soloist, myself filling in the orchestral score as best I could—before adjourning for hair-doings and script study."

The tours and tea were all very nice, but the time came when the frustrated journalists wanted a story. Most departed with their questions left unanswered while others such as Hedda Hopper, who risked the Garson temper by asking more probing questions, were frequently banned from the house for long intervals. Of the mercurial Garson temperament, one frustrated reporter remarked, "Greer is sort of like grape squeezings—to some people she is sparkling champagne, to others just damned sour vinegar." John Franchey observed: "With British diffidence, Miss Garson refuses to take the interview seriously. One of the most intellectual women in Hollywood, she jumps from Grecian sculpture in the age of Phidias, to the opera technique of Verdi . . . from the Swedish ballet and novels of Thomas Wolfe, to the importance of the fleur-de-lis motif in early Frankish heraldry. But no personal history. A half-hour brush with the arts and sciences, and you remind the lady that all this is very nice indeed, but business is business and what about giving a fifteen-minute speech on The Life and Times of Greer Garson. She laughs a merry, proper little laugh, and promises to do better."

May Mann remarked in *Maclean's* magazine, "About the theatre, pictures, books, hobbies, travels, Greer Garson will talk to any length. Otherwise she is as communicative as the sphinx." Greer was particularly sensitive about her marriage. In a rare moment of candor after seeing *The Fighting Lady*, a Navy film that showed her husband's ship, she confided to Louella Parsons, "I didn't sleep for a week. I try not to think of Richard out there so far away. I have moments when I'm so worried I can hardly talk to people." "She thinks she'd like to act with her husband, Lieutenant Richard Ney, when the war is over," wrote Mary C. McCall. "She thinks so, but she's not positive. 'Maybe it wouldn't be good, at that,' she said. 'Maybe we'd get into one of those, "Darling, if you upstage me again, I'll kill you" businesses.'"

She discussed her passion for wearing gloves, collecting seashells, reading the poetry of John Donne, writing long letters, and having lengthy telephone conversations. Lillian Burns recalled, "If you got on the phone with Greer, forty-five minutes was not anything. And a letter. She never could finish a letter. The sentences would go up the side of the paper because she would have so much to say." One of the few questions she did enjoy answering was "Why did you become an actress?" "I think because I am fascinated by the variety and scope of human experience," she would say. "I am not content to live just one existence. I wish I could live a great many lives." One perceptive journalist wrote, "Her relentless driving force seems to be a fear, almost an obsession that she won't get all the things done she wants to get done, or see everybody, and be all the people she wants to be."

She criticized the studio's treatment of her at the slightest provocation, and insisted that her next film would be a comedy. "In self-defense," she would explain. "Before comedy for Garson becomes as indecent as if the Statue of Liberty got down and cut a rug in the middle of Harlem." She was always the first to make fun of her queenly Ideal Woman status, referring to herself as "Metro's Glorified Mrs.," "Metro's Golden Mare," "a walking cathedral," or "plushy-bustly-wifely." When Louella Parsons complained that Greer and Walter Pidgeon were in danger of becoming a ham-and-eggs combination, Greer quickly sent off a telegram: "Dear Walter: Which of us did she mean? Lots of love—Sunny Side Up Garson."

Journalists were intrigued with the Garsons' scrupulous attention to finances. Mike Levee had developed a system of accounts for them that Greer followed carefully. "In prodigal Hollywood," it was said, "she is rated extremely frugal, very conservative and quite, quite substantial."

"Sometimes at night when I run up these stairs," Greer would demonstrate in the entryway as journalists packed up their materials, "I stop about here, I run back and flash on the lights for one last look. I have always wanted to give my mother the sort of home my father, had he lived, would have given her. Oh, of course it's a fantastic, it's a fictitious thing for a girl on a limited income such as I had before I went on the stage in London—a girl with no rich relations or influence or prospects to come to this!" Smiling reflectively as she opened the heavy white oak door with its Scottish crest, she concluded, "You know, it's rather nice—and heartwarming—to feel that people are interested in me. I can only hope that when the pattern of my life is completed, I may have worked into it some of the beauty and skilled craftsmanship and perfection of my Grandmother Greer's patchwork quilts."

CHAPTER 16

IN JANUARY 1943 MGM'S COLLEGE OF CARDINALS gathered to decide on a Greer Garson picture for 1944. Among their choices were two recent bestsellers (Louis Bromfield's *Mrs. Parkington* and Marcia Davenport's *The Valley of Decision*), two remakes (*If Winter Comes*, an English tearjerker by A.S.M. Hutchinson, and *Gaslight*, a period thriller to costar Charles Boyer), as well as two Broadway plays (S.N. Behrman's swashbuckling satire *The Pirate* and Noël Coward's *Blithe Spirit*). When Benjamin Thau related the news to Greer, she was intrigued with Joseph Pasternak's desire to cast her and Cary Grant in *The Pirate* in roles that Lunt and Fontanne had performed on stage and the chance to return to the stylish comedy of Noël Coward. Marcia Davenport's novel also interested her with its tale of an Irish girl from the wrong side of the tracks. Ultimately, however, the Cardinals chose *Mrs. Parkington*.

In 1941 Louis Bromfield had written a one-page synopsis that he entitled *Mrs. Parkington*. The renowned author of twenty-two novels, including *The Green Bay Tree*, the Pulitzer Prize–winning *Early Autumn*, and *The Rains Came*, sent this brief sketch to Hollywood. His heroine, Susie Graham Parkington, is a survivor, a poverty-stricken boardinghouse keeper in Leaping Rock, Nevada, whose marriage to the ambitious Maj. Augustus Parkington sweeps her into the glittering and treacherous world of New York society. Among the actresses who admired Susie Parkington was Bette Davis, but on July 21, 1941, it was MGM's sixty-thousand-dollar offer that won the *Parkington* bidding war. Receiving his check, Bromfield retired to his Ohio farm to expand the story into a novel. By the time it appeared in bookstores, first as a popular serial in *Cosmopolitan* magazine and then as a runaway best-selling book, Louis B. Mayer had already employed Leon Gordon to produce the motion picture version and Robert Thoeren and Polly James to write the script. They centered their screenplay around Susie as an elderly matriarch who must curb the spoiled and shady business dealings of her children to teach them that family honor is more important than wealth. Interspersed throughout were flashbacks to Susie and the Major's tumultuous relationship.

When she read the script, Greer's temper flared. She informed Mayer, through Mike Levee, that she did not intend to play another old lady whose life is viewed in retrospect. "The studio powers are always looking for a story of today, promising that there will be one and then they end up by casting me as the bride of Tutankhamen," she complained. "I probably should say the mother of Tutankhamen after playing the octogenarian in *Mrs. Parkington*!" When word got back to L.B. Mayer that Greer was complaining to the press about her costume pictures, stating that she was so used to sitting on divans sidesaddle that she was developing a permanent list, he called a meeting. When threats of suspension failed to curb her rebellion, Mayer offered a compromise. He purchased the screen rights to *The Valley of Decision* for $76,000, the starring role to be developed for her at a later date.

"It took a lot of doing to get Mrs. Parkington and me together," Greer candidly informed *Photoplay* during preproduction tests in early February 1944. "Susie Parkington is good, of course, but I'll try to indicate that she just might, on occasion, be otherwise." In the following weeks, the studio hummed with activity. William Tuttle devised a new "aging" makeup that would age Greer from a naive Western girl of eighteen to a dignified matriarch of eighty-four. Leon Gordon chose Henrique Medina, a Spanish-Portuguese artist whose portraits of Mussolini and European royalty hung in the Paris Louvre, to paint Greer's portrait for the film and assigned Irene, who had replaced Adrian in 1942, to design the elaborate costumes. Tay Garnett, who was chosen to direct the picture, looked forward to finally working with Greer Garson. "Usually Greer's humor was packaged by her intellectual turn of mind," he recalled. "I relished it, but sometimes it left others cold. For *Mrs. Parkington* the great couturier Irene designed an elaborate period gown that dripped lace and fur-

Left, Arrival in America, November 22, 1937. Courtesy of Elizabeth Jones.
Below, Although she did not want to be in the movie, Greer smiles for the paparazzi after a long day on the set of *Goodbye, Mr. Chips* at the Denham Studio in London.

Above, Director Sam Wood (on Greer's right) and Robert Donat (on her left) supported the frightened young actress through the confusing process of making *Goodbye, Mr. Chips,* for which she received the Best Actress nomination in 1939. © Turner Entertainment Co. All rights reserved.

Left, Mother and daughter attend their first Hollywood premiere: *Goodbye, Mr. Chips* at the Four Star Theatre, May 22, 1939. © Turner Entertainment Co. All rights reserved.

Above, Greer and Robert Taylor take a plunge in *Remember?*
Right, Laurence Olivier and his protégée share a romantic moment in *Pride and Prejudice*. Both © Turner Entertainment Co. All rights reserved.

Greer and Edna Gladney, the woman she portrays in *Blossoms in the Dust,* for which she earned another Oscar nomination.

Spring Byington looks on as Joan Crawford confronts her rival at MGM, Greer Garson, in *When Ladies Meet.*

Right, Jan Struther, author of *Mrs. Miniver*, looks over her celebrated novel with Greer.
Below, A rose for Mrs. Miniver: Henry Travers and Greer in one of the film's most unforgettable scenes.

Left, Tensions are rising on the set of *Mrs. Miniver*. Greer and Walter Pidgeon squeeze into the Minivers' bomb shelter.
Below, Although Richard Ney played Greer's son in *Mrs. Miniver*, he later became her second husband.

Above, The marriage of Mr. and Mrs. Miniver during World War I. A rare production still from a scene cut from the picture.
© Turner Entertainment Co. All rights reserved.
Right, Greer plants the first registered "Miniver Rose Bush" at the headquarters of the Volunteer Army Canteen Service on Sunset Boulevard in Los Angeles. Mrs. L.B. Mayer attended the ceremony, which was part of the premiere festivities for the film. Security Pacific Historical Photograph Collection, Los Angeles Public Library.

Left, Accepting her Academy Award for *Mrs. Miniver* from Joan Fontaine at the 1942 Award ceremony.
© A.M.P.A.S.

Below, Director Mervyn LeRoy shoots the memorable final scene of *Random Harvest* with Ronald Colman and Greer. Of all her films, this was her favorite.

Above, Greer joins a host of celebrities on the Hollywood Cavalcade Train Tour to sell war bonds. © Turner Entertainment Co. All rights reserved. *Below*, Greer and the MGM team that made some of her finest films: (left to right) Cameraman Joseph Ruttenberg, director Mervyn LeRoy, and producer Sidney Franklin figure out a method of filming a delicate experiment in *Madame Curie*. She earned her fourth Academy Award nomination for the film. © Turner Entertainment Co. All rights reserved.

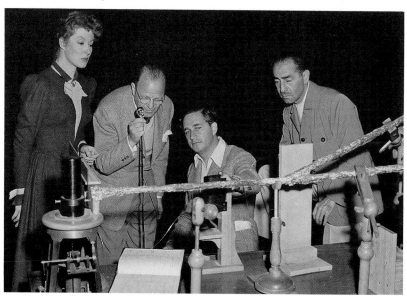

Above, "More Stars Than There Are In Heaven..." on MGM's twentieth anniversary. Greer occupies the seat of honor beside Louis B. Mayer. *Below*, Newlyweds Greer and Richard Ney take a stroll across the lawn of 680 Stone Canyon. Both © Turner Entertainment Co. All rights reserved.

Right, The most popular dramatic team at MGM and the best of friends— Garson and Pidgeon. *Below*, Author James Hilton and Greer try out the new water fountain in the backyard of her Bel Air home. Both © Turner Entertainment Co. All rights reserved.

Above left, The Queen of MGM, at the height of her career, kneels before the fireplace of her home for a glamour portrait.

Above right, "It took a lot of doing to get *Mrs. Parkington* and me together," Greer said of her tenth film, in which she earned another Oscar nomination for Best Actress. She is shown here with Agnes Moorehead.

Right, She co-starred with Gregory Peck and captured a sixth Oscar nomination for *The Valley of Decision*.

Above, In *The Valley of Decision* with frequent costar Marsha Hunt and Marshall Thompson. *Below left,* Director Tay Garnett is introduced to Greer's poodle, Gogo, on the set of *The Valley of Decision. Below right,* "Gable's Back and Garson's Got Him!" in *Adventure.* All © Turner Entertainment Co. All rights reserved.

Above, Making the disastrous *Desire Me* with Richard Hart. Only minutes after this photo was taken the actors narrowly escaped death when a huge wave hit the rocky Monterey shore. *Below*, Preparing for the bathtub sequence in *Julia Misbehaves*.

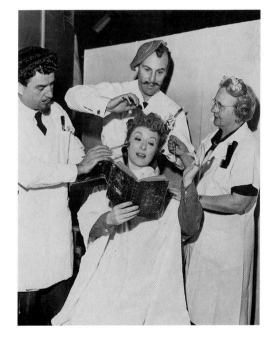

Above left, The Queen of Radio City Music Hall is crowned. Ultimately, thirteen of her pictures would play there, for a total of eighty-three weeks, a feat that remains unmatched by any other actress. Security Pacific. *Above right*, Greer tops the pyramid formed by the Ted De Wayne circus troupe with co-star Cesar Romero (center, bottom row) in *Julia Misbehaves*.
Right, "Art For Art's Sake": Clowning with (left to right) makeup man Don Robertson, Sydney Guilaroff, and hairdresser Edith Hubner. Both

belows and came to a climax with an enormous taffeta bow perched on the stomach. Greer tried on the dress. Doubt arched her eyebrows. Turning a full-length profile toward the mirror, she said solemnly, 'But Irene, it makes me look as if I had a marsupial pouch.' Rumor has it Irene was not amused."

Among the press notices for *Mrs. Parkington*, no story generated so much attention as the announcement that Greer would be a brunette. The dark color would allow her to age, she and Sydney Guilaroff reasoned, more clearly and dramatically in a black-and-white film. "Susie is different," Greer said, "and I want to be different in the role. An actress, to be interesting, must strive constantly for new effects." The Queen of the Lot had spoken. After photographic tests, she won her point and enjoyed the resulting publicity swirl immensely. "I had to do it," she would say. "All the other girls are getting red hair for Technicolor pictures and they're putting me out of business. Since MGM sees fit to keep me in black and white pictures, my only hope is to have black hair and if the trend to red continues, I'll be unique!"

Walter Pidgeon was once again Greer's costar in *Mrs. Parkington*, and among the distinguished lineup of supporting players was Gladys Cooper. As a struggling young performer in London, Greer had idolized the aristocratic Miss Cooper, whose superlative performances on the stage had earned her fame in England and America. In fact, it was at the Playhouse Theatre where Greer had starred in *Butterfly on the Wheel* that Cooper had begun her long and successful career as an actress, producer, and manager. She had appeared in films only intermittently since 1917. But after Alfred Hitchcock invited her to Hollywood in 1939 to appear in *Rebecca*, she bought a house in Pacific Palisades and settled into a comfortable career at MGM. She often invited Greer to her home, where many of the British colony could be found.

No actress was more pleased to join the *Mrs. Parkington* crew than Agnes Moorehead. An actress with a distinguished career in films (*Citizen Kane, Journey into Fear, Jane Eyre*), Agnes nevertheless had to mount a campaign to play the glamorous Aspasia Conti, Major Parkington's former lover and Susie Parkington's good friend. "I only got the role by the skin of my teeth," she recalled. "After all, she isn't one of those bitter, nasty, frustrated women I usually play. I was eager for a good, normal role." Although Leon Gordon was willing to cast her as the drunken Countess de Brancourt (which Gladys Cooper played), Agnes persuaded the producer to let her play Aspasia by borrowing a beautiful ball gown from the wardrobe department and wearing a blonde wig. "I found out that Greer Garson was wearing a dark wig, so I got a blonde one," she said. Gordon was impressed. In 1949 she told the *Saturday Evening Post,* "I thoroughly enjoyed being a worldly French baroness who was not only attractive and intelligent but who had great wisdom and heart. I also learned to know Greer Garson and formed a lasting friendship. So, all in all, the role was worth the battle I put up to get it, and I'm quite happy to name it as my favorite." "She's one of the finest actresses I've ever met," Greer remarked. "Someday I'd like to do a two-woman play with her."

The early sequences set in Leaping Rock, Nevada, were shot first on the sprawling western set on Lot Three. Al Block, the studio censor, nervously watched the boardinghouse sleeping porch scene in which the lusty, worldly-wise Maj. Augustus Parkington woos the innocent Susie, in her nightgown, with only a sheet hanging between them. The Hays Office had previously approved the script, but Block was on the sidelines to ensure approval. Tay Garnett was not pleased with the way things were going. He felt Greer was not yet reconciled to playing the part. "During the first scenes it became obvious that Greer had not yet caught onto the 'Susie Parkington' character," he recalled. "'Susie' was a bright, spirited, western mining town girl, bouncy and bubbling with vitality but without artifice. Greer was playing her too Great Lady, too British. Wise Walter Pidgeon saw the problem and—grinning wickedly—slapped Greer on the neatest derriere in Hollywood (a stunt he had used earlier in *Mrs. Miniver*) and said offhandedly, 'Relax, honey. It was LAST year that you won the Oscar.' Greer laughed and relaxed. End of problem."

Tay Garnett and Greer struggled again when it came to a running characterization gag that he invented for Susie. Whenever her character's temper got the better of her, she was supposed to exhale violently, blowing a stray curl of hair on her forehead. But the gag was not working, and the director knew why. "It looks as though you were amusing yourself, as if you were doing it to consciously BE funny," he told her. "You mean I'm wearing a spangle on my nose?"

she asked with amusement. "Neon," Garnett conceded. "After this," she replied, "when you see me getting a bit too Christmas-panto-mime, just place your forefinger on the tip of your nose and I'll get the message." "Such rapport is rare between director and star," Garnett said.

If the early sequences of Susie Parkington's life were difficult for Greer, she found that playing an octogenarian was much worse. "Playing an 80-year-old woman is a problem," she complained to Louella Parsons during an afternoon tea. "I do not know anybody of those years whom I can use as an inspiration in this particular pic-ture. The one or two I was acquainted with were very gay and spritely, which doesn't fit the story." Back at work with the screenwriters, she transformed old Mrs. Parkington into a lighthearted soul, bringing her own sense of humor to the grand old lady with knowing winks and an eye for handsome men. Louella Parsons observed approvingly that "Greer suddenly has become the wit of the MGM lot. She's no longer the dignified star who takes herself so seriously, but her ready Irish wit has become famous for the quips and gags she pulls. No one was more surprised than L.B. Mayer, her boss, when he came on the set during one of her 84-year-old sequences. 'Hello, Junior,' yelled Greer, 'How are you?' L.B., who hadn't seen the lovely red-head in her old-age makeup, really was taken aback, and wondered if the aged woman was a relative."

Production came to a close on May 31. The final cost of the production totaled $1,574,000. In peacetime, it would have been considerably more. "Motion pictures may still look lavish," said Tay Garnett, "but film studios are ingeniously practicing wartime thrift. Particularly when it comes to ration points." The most evident ex-ample is the Parkington ball. Upon the forty-foot buffet table were laid turkeys, hams, squabs, roasts, pheasants, and a tiered cake—all papier-mâche, plaster, or painted cardboard. That the full financial weight of the studio, despite its wartime thrift, was now behind the Garson/Pidgeon films is no more evident than in *Mrs. Parkington*, with its towering sets, elaborate costumes, and multiple locales.

After completing the film, Greer planned a six-week vacation. To George Cukor, who was planning to direct a future movie with her, she wrote, "If I'm lucky, I may live to have as much fun out of life as Mrs. Parkington did at 84. She was gay, witty, in good health.

She had a wonderful philosophy that enabled her to overcome misfortunes—the ones that make many of us 'martyrs.' Looking back on it now, it really was a very happy picture. While I haven't seen it yet, I know that some of this harmony and good spirits must have come through on the screen. And so, in these days of nervous strain, I hope that *Mrs. Parkington* will provide two hours of good escapist theater for everyone. The old girl was a hilarious but rather exhausting chore and I need a rest very badly!"

Greer returned to the studio on June 22 for a studio party attended by fifteen hundred studio employees, with a two-hour show by Metro talent (billed as "the greatest show on earth") marking the celebration of Metro's twentieth year. "The boys who pace the marble halls of Metro-Goldwyn-Mayer are pounding each others' backs today," remarked the *Los Angeles Times*, "celebrating the 20th anniversary of the world's biggest movie studio. They've got more stars under contract than any other studio, so many in fact that you find most of their dressing rooms in the old writers' building. Directors occupy the new, new writers' building, while the scriveners, themselves, function at desks all over the place, including the magnificent white Thalberg building for executives. It's quite a place, Metro-Goldwyn-Mayer, even unto the chicken noodle soup which has been on the luncheon menu at thirty-five cents a bowl for the full twenty years."

The Radio City Music Hall premiere of *Mrs. Parkington* on October 12, 1944, was particularly spectacular. To accompany an all-American family epic, the program included an "American Rhapsody," featuring a cavalcade of musical selections by George Gershwin played by the Music Hall's Symphony Orchestra and performed by the renowned Rockettes. But the critics were not impressed with the film. The sets and trimmings were luxurious, the family plot was intricate, and Greer and Walter Pidgeon once again displayed their superlative chemistry and high level of professionalism, but ultimately the film lacked heart. The dramatic scene in which Susie falls down the family staircase and suffers the miscarriage of her first child should have struck an emotional chord with the audience. Since the characters were not as carefully fleshed out as those in the earlier Garson/Pidgeon films, this scene, and many others throughout the film, seems merely to be elegantly choreographed. Greer succeeds best as old Mrs. Parkington. Her scenes with Pidgeon in England, where she goes to tighten the leash on her straying husband and meets a bemused Edward, Prince of Wales, are easily their best in the film. And for the second time L.B. Mayer had miscast his protégée. It was a film that required an actress who might have been born in such a town as Leaping Rock, like Joan Crawford or Lana Turner. In the *New York Times*, Bosley Crowther remarked, "Miss Garson performs with all the tricks of charm and dignified poise that have endeared her to the vast movie audience. That such breeding and manners came natural to a boarding-house slavey in a frontier town is one of the little allowances that you will have to make. . . . One might say that Metro has actually sold a sterling acting couple awfully short. Alongside the Minivers and the Curies, the Gotrocks Parkingtons are a smug and meaningless couple, for all their luxury and love." Nevertheless the star power of MGM's most popular dramatic team turned *Mrs. Parkington* into the studio's most profitable film of the year. It grossed $5,631,000 and earned Greer her fifth Academy Award nomination for Best Actress. The popularity of the movie would also lead to an encore performance with Walter Pidgeon on *Lux Radio Theatre* on January 25, 1946. "Some actresses have a certain spark that has nothing to do with training or acting experience," Tay Garnett observed. "It's there or it isn't. In Duse it was called 'the divine spark.' At what point it becomes divine and at what point it is just 'inspired human,' it is hard to determine, but whatever it is, Greer Garson has that spark."

By the summer of 1944 Greer was recognized as the world's most popular movie star. Dr. George Gallup's poll of 55 million theatergoers awarded her a second gold medal for being "the most popular star in the United States." Servicemen in the South Pacific, in a poll conducted by the Army Overseas Motion Picture Service, elected her best actress of 1944 and presented her with their G.I. Fuzzy-Wuzzy popularity award. She was named top actress in *Film Daily's* "Famous Five" contest and was elected "favorite star" in polls conducted by the Canadian army newspaper *Khaki*, the British service newspaper *Crusader*, and the Bengal, India, Journalists' Association. That year, in other polls, she was named favorite star in Mexico, Sweden, France, Portugal, Belgium, Africa, Australia, Argentina, and Tel Aviv, Palestine.

The preview trailer for *The Valley of Decision* celebrated Greer's past achievements while presenting a look at her newest film. As a gallery of scenes from *Goodbye, Mr. Chips, Pride and Prejudice, Mrs. Miniver, Random Harvest, Madame Curie,* and *Mrs. Parkington* came across the screen, MGM narrator Frank Whitbeck remarked: "Strange, isn't it, that the career of Greer Garson is so closely identified with the heroines of your most popular books. And now—a magnificent story—a best-selling novel—gives Greer Garson her best chance of all—Mary in Marcia Davenport's *The Valley of Decision!*"

The screenplay, as adapted by John Meehan and Sonya Levien from the 790-page epic, begins in the spring of 1873 when a spirited Irish lass named Mary Rafferty is hired to work as a servant at the William Scott home in Allegheny City, the fashionable district across the river from her home in Pittsburgh. The Scotts are steel manufacturers whose plant had accidentally crippled and embittered her father, Patrick. Mary quickly endears herself with the Scotts through her dedicated work and genuine affection for the family. Her feelings turn to love for the eldest son, Paul, and though the family gives its blessing, their happy future is threatened by a strike at the mill. Pat Rafferty and Paul's father, William, are killed during a confrontation brought upon by Pat's undying hatred for the family and the Scotts' mistake in hiring strikebreakers. The social gulf between Mary and Paul is wider than ever, and, in his loneliness, Paul marries the aristocratic Louise Kane. Louise bears him a son but despises the mill and Pittsburgh as well, for she knows it reminds Paul of Mary. When Paul's mother, Clarissa, dies, the future of the mill is uncertain. Younger brother William Scott Jr. wants to sell out, a desire agreed to wholeheartedly not only by sister Constance, who is debt-ridden, but by brother Ted, who is a drunken wastrel, and Louise. But Mary, who has inherited Clarissa's share, convinces the family to preserve its heritage. At this point the screenwriters were stuck. They had no satisfying conclusion. In the novel Mary and Paul are never reunited—and Louis B. Mayer demanded happy endings for MGM pictures.

To eliminate Louise from the picture Meehan and Levien considered divorce. However, the industry's all-powerful censor, Joseph Breen of the Motion Picture Producers and Distributors Association of America, would not accept it. It was the first serious case in which the Association, which pledged to maintain "the highest possible moral and artistic standards in motion picture production" with its list of eleven "don'ts" and twenty-seven "be carefuls," came down on a Greer Garson film. On September 22, 1944, Breen wrote: "We regret to advise you that the material, in its present form, seems not to be acceptable under the provisions of the Production Code. This unacceptability is suggested by the present indication contained in the closing scenes, that the marriage between Paul and Louise is to be broken up, and that Paul and Mary will later get together. This appears to us a condonation of the breakup of marriage, and because of this cannot be approved. It might be possible to indicate, with the insertion of dialogue, that, while the marriage of Louise and Paul may be broken up, there will be no marriage between Paul and Mary. This indication would be acceptable." To impose Mayer's happy ending, the screenwriters made it clear that Paul and Louise would divorce and then added a concluding scene in which Paul drives Mary home, thereby hinting, with Breen's approval, that they would eventually get married.

Although the characterization of Mary Rafferty shared many of the characteristics of Susie Parkington and the picture was another period piece, Greer was intrigued with *The Valley of Decision*. "I really believed in that girl," she said. "I tried to make her seem as realistic as possible. You know, it's much more difficult to play a good person than a bad one." It is among her most delightful performances and one she clearly enjoyed. She is effective both in the early sequences as the young, naive Irishwoman who sings some charming Irish ballads and as the older, wiser woman who holds the Scott family together in moments of crisis. In an early sequence as the spunky yet naive new servant girl, Greer teases Marshall Thompson, as Ted Scott, to delightful effect with a fable about her journey to America: "Oh, I didn't come steerage, sir. I'll tell you how I got here. Would you believe it—one night in Ireland I was strollin' and stepped into a Fairy-ring, unbeknownst. All at once I'm surrounded by the little people, the mischievous ones, and suddenly, in the midst of it all, the leprechauns raise me up and whisk me away over the clouds and out across the ocean—and here I am in the castle of my dreams!" Later, in the climactic final scene when the Scott family disagrees about the fate of their steel mill after the death of their parents, Greer and Jessica Tandy, as the shrewish Louise, clash in a brilliant confrontation.

When Louise learns that Mary has inherited a substantial share in the mill, she turns on her rival in a rage. "What a fool I've been!" she declares accusingly. "Two million dollars—that's what you wanted. And all the while I thought you were in love with Paul!" "You haven't been a fool, Louise," Mary replies with quiet intensity but equal venom. "I've loved Paul from the moment I walked into this house. I've loved the mill because it was part of the family—and as long as there is a breath in me I'll fight to preserve it." Greer could not deny that L.B. Mayer, who hoped to have another *Mrs. Parkington* hit, had surrounded her with the best: producer Edwin Knopf, director Tay Garnett, and the finest cast she had ever worked with at Metro-Goldwyn-Mayer: Donald Crisp and Gladys Cooper as William and Clarissa Scott; Gregory Peck, Dan Duryea, Marsha Hunt, and Marshall Thompson as their siblings Paul, William Scott Jr., Constance, and Ted; Lionel Barrymore as Pat Rafferty; Jessica Tandy as Louise; and Dean Stockwell as Paul Scott Jr.

"I learned quite a lot from that film," Jessica Tandy recalled. "Tay Garnett was a wonderful, meticulous director. I remember watching the scene one day, that I was not in, between Gregory Peck and Greer when they were sitting late at night over a kitchen table drinking cocoa and talking. And I thought, 'Oh, this is never going to do. Nobody's going to hear what they're saying. It's much too small and quiet.' And I was surprised when Tay Garnett said, 'Print it.' Well, then I went to see the rushes. And, of course, it was perfection. Both of them had the ability to be absolutely true with the greatest economy. And I said, 'Ah, that's the way screen acting is done.'"

Principal photography on *The Valley of Decision* lasted four months and cost $2,165,000. The street from *Meet Me in St. Louis* on Lot Three was refurbished to recreate Pittsburgh. Joseph Ruttenberg was once again the cinematographer. Of his successful partnership with Greer, Ruttenberg told *American Cinematographer*, "Miss Garson looks her best on the screen when given careful, individual lighting. When the same cameraman works with a star, picture after picture, as I have done with Miss Garson, he naturally improves upon the lighting and photographic technique established for that particular star with each successive picture." Gregory Peck, aware of the crew's deference to Greer, later reported: "When it came to viewing the rushes, I saw that every time I was in a scene with her, her face was a lovely luminous moon floating in the center of the screen and I was the rather dim figure beside her in semi-shadow. Not that I really minded, Greer was beautiful and all woman. I was impressed, a little intimidated at first, but soon I learned that she was, off her pedestal, a wonderfully warm and lovable woman. She was aware that the crew on the sound stage was a bit awestruck in Mrs. Miniver's presence. She had a way of cracking the ice with her quick sense of humor, straight from English Music Halls. We all felt that we were in on a well-kept secret. The Queen of MGM was a red-headed clown."

Peck was also impressed with Lionel Barrymore's acting method. "Lionel would rehearse a scene for hours before they would shoot it," he recalled. "By the time the scene was set, he had spent enough energy for 100 men. [Tay Garnett] once said to him, 'For God's sake, Lionel, stop that. You're going to give yourself a heart attack.' Lionel said, 'W-e-l-l, who gives a damn?'" When Greer learned that Barrymore was a classical music enthusiast on whom the studio's research department frequently depended to answer difficult questions, she invited him to four o'clock tea to enjoy her classical phonograph recordings of Shostakovich, Prokofiev, and Tchaikovsky.

However, Barrymore's performance in the film caused grave concern after an early preview in Pasadena. The audience's response was largely critical. One preview card read: "Junk it." The studio was in an uproar. Not only was Greer Garson's prestigious name threatened, but a large sum of MGM capital was wrapped up in the extravagant production. J.J. Cohn, the studio's general manager, whose motto was "Do everything as inexpensively as possible," was prepared to take drastic action. He dismissed editor Blanche Sewell and worked with another, Tommy Held, and Edwin Knopf to prepare the picture for national release. They discovered that Barrymore's acting in such crucial sequences as the bloody confrontation between the steelworkers' union and the strikebreakers was tending toward burlesque. They quickly reedited the scenes showing only the back of Barrymore's head and recalled Tay Garnett and the actors for additional retakes that lasted until February 23, 1945. Three days later, during a brief vacation from the studio, Greer was delighted to team up with *Valley* costar Donald Crisp in a *Lux Radio Theatre* version of the Loretta Young and Don Ameche comedy screen classic *Bedtime Story.* Cary

Grant played her egotistical playwright husband who goes to hilarious extremes to persuade her to star in his latest production.

The studio planned a special screening of *The Valley of Decision* for author Marcia Davenport. "I was sitting with Carol Brandt in the projection room," she recalled. "We had seen most of the film, and I was just beginning to relax in relief and reassurance over the fine cast and the faithful and gripping representation of the third of the book which had been used, when Howard Dietz made his way to us across the dark room, leaned over our shoulders and told us that President Roosevelt had just died."

After the picture premiered at Radio City Music Hall on May 3, 1945, L.B. Mayer, J.J. Cohn, and Edwin Knopf breathed a sigh of relief. The lines that wrapped around the massive theater were a happy portent for things to come. In fact, *The Valley of Decision* brought in $8,096,000, and Greer's sixth nomination for Best Actress. "With Greer Garson playing an Irish maid in a Pittsburgh steel magnate's family, the new Music Hall show has a radiant intensity which should make it a thumping boxoffice success," proclaimed the *New York Herald Tribune.* "Miss Garson's portrayal of Mary Rafferty . . . is sheerly brilliant. . . . She is profoundly convincing and dramatically effective." Another critic added, "Despite its convoluted and stylized plot, no one will ever view it without realizing the singularity of its star: the sheer energy, will and charisma Miss Garson brings to her craft."

The Irish press had a field day with *The Valley of Decision.* For the first time, they noted, Greer Garson was playing a character of her own nationality. In March 1947, the *Irish Digest* commented: "When a little girl from County Down rises so far above an army of the world's most talented and beautiful women that . . . she is called the 'First Lady Of Hollywood' and is earning in a single year something over £44,000, you can either put it down to the traditional luck of the Irish, or you can regard such glittering success as the due reward of hard work and determination. . . . Baby Greer's heritage on both sides was plain common sense and forthrightness, and that quality was later on to give her acting a sincerity that is unequalled."

Marsha Hunt, who played the delightfully spoiled Constance Scott, recently commented: "*The Valley of Decision* was another fine but, I think, underrated picture. It doesn't seem to have stayed with people the way it should have. . . . Greer was so lovely in it." Gregory Peck, who reprised his role with Greer in a *Lux Radio Theatre* version of *The Valley of Decision* on January 14, 1946, remarked in 1985: "Had we worked together again, my wish would have been for Greer Garson and [me] to do a comedy. In their excitement over Greer the beautiful and gracious lady, MGM sometimes overlooked Greer the comedienne, one of the most piquant, delicious and funny ladies ever to appear on the screen."

The critics were beginning to take note of this. "If ever a movie actress has been caught in an artistic rut, that actress is Metro's Greer Garson," complained Bosley Crowther in an article titled "Goodbye, Mrs. Chips," in the *New York Times*. "Take this rare and exalted female whom Miss Garson always plays. She is more than an ideal composite. . . . She's a wondrous and shining myth, a supernatural fancy of virtuous femininity . . . bearing no more actual resemblance to the variable and fascinating members of her sex than do those vaporous visions rapturously spun by swooning poets long ago. She's been creeping up on us for a long time—this monumental dame Miss Garson plays. And now, in *Valley of Decision* . . . this phantom of feminine magnificence is spreading her sweet essence again. Of course, when you come right down to it, there is nothing subversive about the myth, however deceptive and hypnotic it may prove to a lot of good folks. But the constant reiteration of the same righteous character not only makes movies tend to monotony but wastes the talents of a capable star."

Such reviews were the kind of ammunition that Greer intended to wield, with the full power of her prestigious position at Metro-Goldwyn-Mayer, to wrest control of her career. She was aware that a new picture titled *Adventure,* based on the novel *The Anointed* by Clyde Brion Davis, was being planned for Clark Gable upon his return from the war and that no expense or studio expertise was to be spared. She wanted the costarring role as Emily Sears, an introverted librarian in San Francisco whose life is profoundly changed by an affair with an adventuresome merchant marine, Harry, played by Gable. Although they enjoy a brief marriage in Reno, the marine eventually abandons Emily to return to find more adventure upon the sea. He has spent his life roaming the ocean in search of something he calls "it": a reckless and independent excitement that gives him reason for living. But his good friend Mudgin, to be played by Thomas Mitchell, bitterly criticizes Harry for giving up the finest thing that has ever happened to him—Emily's love. Deliberately suffering a serious injury so that Harry will return to Emily, Mudgin dies. Harry returns to Emily and finds that they have a child. Greer told L.B. Mayer that she could draw upon her years as a researcher for *Encyclopedia Britannica* and LINTAS for the part. Although horrified at the thought of Mrs. Miniver becoming a sailor's pickup, Mayer was getting tired of arguing with her and gave her the part.

But there were forces beyond even the formidable powers of Louis B. Mayer that Greer could not control. Already her fortunes and the fortunes of Metro-Goldwyn-Mayer were changing. By the time *The Valley of Decision* went into general release, the world was celebrating V-J Day and the end of World War II. Impromptu parades formed in cities and small towns throughout the country. In Los Angeles, crowds gathered at Broadway and Fifth Street and marched past the Crown Theater, which was playing the movie. It was a significant moment. Little did Greer and her proud mentor realize that their careers were about to take a startling, and dramatic, turn.

CHAPTER 17

LOOKING BACK ON IT while secluded within the peaceful confines of Quail Haven in early November 1947, Greer realized that the origins of the destructive forces that tore her marriage apart, seriously damaged her career, and even threatened her life could be traced to the spring of 1945.

She was in her dressing room at MGM. Apartment D in "Stars' Row" was described as "a swanky affair . . . all done in sea shells. The lamp is made of sea shells, and the backs of the chairs are decorated with sea shells, and over Miss Garson's couch is a fishing net." Elsa Maxwell and Rosalind Russell were with her for a small afternoon lunch when Katharine Hepburn and Benjamin Thau stopped by and asked to join them. "That request from Katie Hepburn—looking sweet in old slacks—in itself shows Greer's position," Elsa Maxwell recalled. "Stars aren't given to calling on each other at the studio. Katie especially. However, she adores Greer and Greer adores her."

Together the actresses discussed their latest film roles. Katharine Hepburn was making *Without Love* with Spencer Tracy. Rosalind had taken a year off to give birth to a son but was currently making a film at Warner Bros. called *Roughly Speaking*. Greer described her confrontation with L.B. Mayer about *Adventure* and his sudden interest in a redheaded newcomer to the studio named Deborah Kerr. The twenty-three-year-old Scottish actress had been discovered by Gabriel Pascal and was currently being groomed for stardom in an MGM/British effort entitled *Vacation from Marriage*, with Robert Donat. The women laughed amongst themselves at Mayer's none-too-subtle attempt to warn the Queen of the Lot that she was not the only demure, redheaded beauty who could work for the studio. "MGM in those days was constructed like something that was going to hit the beaches on D-Day," Rosalind once remarked. "There was a first wave of top stars, then a second wave to replace them in case they got difficult." Rumors were now circulating around the soundstages of MGM that L.B. Mayer now considered his favorite star "difficult."

On May 22, 1945, two weeks after principal photography had begun on *Adventure*, the studio held a press conference. It was crowded beyond capacity with newspapermen, publicists, photographers, and fans eager to welcome Metro's King, Clark Gable, back from the war and curious about his pairing with the studio's acclaimed Queen. It occurred at a particularly jubilant time for Metro-Goldwyn-Mayer, which was still the wonder of the industry and roaring proudly with a record $14.5 million profit. Applause overcame the noise of expectant voices as Gable and Garson entered and took their seats before the crowd. Greer happily announced that she was making a picture circa 1945. "Think of it," she said. "I get to wear modern right-up-to-the-minute clothes!" But the good feelings quickly deteriorated as Gable grew impatient with the questions being directed at him. He confessed that he had tried to avoid making *Adventure*. "I stalled as long as I could," he said. "I just couldn't get up what it takes to come back before these cameras. In uniform, a guy fast develops an unbeatable sense of confidence; but when you come back you have nothing but an overwhelming sense of uncertainty." It was evident to all present that the King was still mourning the loss of his wife, Carole Lombard, who had died tragically at the age of thirty-four in a plane crash in 1942. In his column for the *Daily News*, Erskine Johnson commented: "He looks different—older, with lines on his face. . . . The start of a new Gable picture when Carole Lombard was alive . . . would have been much different [and] resulted in some of Hollywood's prize gags." The press interview for Production #1352 significantly foreshadowed the difficult creation and the ultimate release of this controversial film.

In 1941, MGM producer Sam Zimbalist purchased the rights to *The Anointed* as a star vehicle for Spencer Tracy. But with Zimbalist's busy schedule, and Tracy's constant work in *Woman of the Year* and *Tortilla Flat*, the project was never realized. With Clark Gable's return from the war, the production was reactivated as his comeback picture. Zimbalist hoped that the production would be a fitting postwar film for Gable, allowing him to display his famous bravado and reveal a more serious, deeper acting level as well. Louis B. Mayer was especially eager to make Gable, who had worked for MGM for fourteen profit-making years, as comfortable as possible. Among the actor's friends chosen for the production were Victor Fleming, his favorite director, and Shug Keeler, the studio electrician who had worked with Gable since 1931. Screenwriter Luther Davis recalled, "Clark had come back from the Army without a contract at MGM, and his agents were being very coy. His first postwar film, *Adventure*, was done as a one-picture deal." Eager to gather Gable back into his studio family, L.B. Mayer wanted *Adventure* to be an unqualified hit.

The cast and crew had settled into a quiet and friendly filming schedule on May 9, 1945. Greer had been pleased with Victor Fleming, whom she affectionately dubbed "Mr. Vic." Despite his rough manner, she found him to be a thoughtful director who respected her talent. She also appreciated his sense of humor. One afternoon, after observing Greer's tea ritual, Gable's jugs of milk from his ranch, and Blondell's supply of coffee and Coca-Cola, Fleming exclaimed, "Try to get someone around here to do any work, and you have to bust up a picnic!"

But the good feelings evaporated as friction developed between Gable and his leading lady and when Zimbalist and Fleming observed the rushes. Despite the top production values, an excellent director, and a first-rate cast, *Adventure* was suffering from a bizarre, long-winded story and mismatched costars. Except for a brief romantic excursion into the country when their characters fall in love, Greer appeared stiff and Gable's famous bravado was merely unpleasant when the actors appeared together on screen. Apart, they both visibly relaxed and enjoyed interacting with the vivacious Joan Blondell. Greer also shared some poignant moments with Thomas Mitchell. In many ways, Greer may have reminded Gable of his uncomfortable experience with Vivien Leigh in *Gone with the Wind*. Refined and educated English ladies did not appeal to this Midwestern actor, who had been an oil-driller and lumberjack before breaking into the theater. He preferred women like former costars Jean Harlow and Joan Crawford, or Joan Blondell in this project. Greer's British habits, especially her afternoon tea ritual, annoyed him. But most of all he hated her need of canvas screens, called "blacks," which shut out everything from view except the necessary director, actors, lights, and crew members. "Playing a love scene requires a feeling of intimacy between the man and woman and intense concentration," she once explained. "I don't like to look over the shoulder of the man and see the long gloomy sound stage behind the camera, cluttered with equipment and pieces of sets from past pictures." "When she had the 'blacks' put up for *Adventure*, Clark Gable asked what the heck was coming off," Bob Thomas reported in the *Hollywood Citizen-News*, "which made her even more sensitive about it. It's not that she isn't friendly. The crew, which is always the same, adores her. But that's just the way she is." Lina Romay, who played Gable's Chilean girl-friend in the film, felt that "they were opposites. She'd insist on vel-vet slats around them when they acted, so no one could see them except the director Victor Fleming. Whereas Gable was a big, open guy who liked to use four-letter words."

"*Adventure* was not a good experience," Greer later recalled. "Clark was very taciturn and withdrawn and, I think, somewhat embarrassed at having to deal with things like wardrobe fittings and makeup after the war years. Despite his reputation, he was not really a ladies' man. I think he was most relaxed when he was out hunting with men." Her disillusionment with the film she hoped would open new opportunities for her at MGM turned to anger when she heard the publicity slogan that Howard Dietz was preparing: "Gable's Back and Garson's Got Him!" Dietz tried to appease her objections with an alternate: "Gable puts the arson in Garson." "They're ungallant," she indignantly replied. "Why don't you say, 'Garson puts the able in Gable?'" Gable's sour reaction to the fiasco was unprintable.

Greer did enjoy the premiere of *Adventure* at Radio City Music Hall on February 6, 1946. Gus Eyssel, Radio City's managing direc-tor, presented her with a red, yellow, gold, and topaz jeweled Cartier tiara in recognition of the fact that nine of her twelve motion pic-tures had opened at the Music Hall, bringing the total playing time to fifty-six weeks—a record unequaled by any other actress. Robert Osborne of the *Hollywood Reporter* later commented, "You get an indication of her boxoffice power when you realize the majority of those 6,200 seats had to be filled five times a day, seven days a week!" In her acceptance speech, Greer took the opportunity to remind

Howard Dietz of his comment to her upon her arrival in America: "My dear, only the biggest stars play Radio City Music Hall."

But her triumph was short-lived. Although *Adventure* grossed a healthy $3,478,000, it was a thorny bouquet that contained some of the worst reviews of her career. "It is really difficult to fathom what interests Metro thought it would serve with this embarrassingly foolish picture," wrote Bosley Crowther. "Did it figure to shock impressionable folks by having leathery Mr. Gable push the beauteous Miss Garson around. If it did, it was certainly reckoning on the lowest possible audience taste. Or did it figure to fool the general public with a whole lot of high-sounding talk about wisdom and man's immortality, all of which really says nothing at all? If you ask us, we'd guess that Metro simply said, 'Oh, boy—a Garson-Gable film! It can't miss!' and went right at it with just a so-what inspection of the script. And that, we say, is a deplorable exploitation of the 'star system.'" Gable was especially disappointed about the outcome of the film that critics were now calling "Misadventure." "He had to take an awful lot of ribbing on the golf course from his three pals, Howard Strickling, Eddie Mannix and Billy Grady," wrote Gable's biographer, Jean Garcean. "If Billy was losing, all he had to do when it was Clark's turn to play was to say, 'I just saw *Adventure* again,' and Clark would blow the shot." Luther Davis recalled, "When *Adventure* flopped, [Gable] announced, 'I won't re-sign until you get me a decent picture.'" Fortunately for all concerned, Gable's next film, *The Hucksters*, scripted by Luther Davis and costarring Deborah Kerr, was a hit. Gable took up residency at MGM for another nine years.

The nihilistic, serious tone of *Adventure* reflected the emergence of postwar realism at MGM, which threatened to end Greer's role as the studio's popular, romantic heroine. The film also revealed the problems that were beginning to surface at Metro and in the movie industry in general. One writer remarked, "The hollowness, fatigue and sexual fizzle that marked every frame of *Adventure* is symptomatic of many Hollywood pictures of the middle and late forties." L.B. Mayer was no longer the careful star groomer he had once been. Indeed, as the decade wore on, his struggles to maintain control of MGM, develop younger talent, and curb his obsession with horse racing threatened the career of his most prestigious female star.

Immediately upon her return from New York, Greer began work

on a new film, *Desire Me*, to be produced by Arthur Hornblow and directed by George Cukor—the team that had launched *Gaslight* into the box-office stratosphere in 1944. The gifted Cukor was renowned as a "women's director" who drew fine, sometimes Oscar-winning, performances from stars such as Greta Garbo (*Camille*), Norma Shearer (*Romeo and Juliet*), Joan Crawford (*A Woman's Face*), and Ingrid Bergman (*Gaslight*). Hornblow, who had also produced the highly successful all-star *Weekend at the Waldorf* with Ginger Rogers, Walter Pidgeon, Lana Turner, and Van Johnson, assured Greer and L.B. Mayer that they could polish her career back to its wartime luster.

The screenplay, based on Leonhard Frank's critically acclaimed novel, was a dark melodrama concerning a young Frenchwoman, Marise Aubert, who faces a moral dilemma when her husband, whom she believes to be dead, returns from a concentration camp. By then she is engaged to Jean Renaud, a man she believed to be her husband's best friend. In the climax Renaud reveals his true nature when he attempts to murder her husband in his psychotic desire to possess her. The fact that a stage version by the Theatre Guild in New York and two silent movie versions had not been particularly successful did not deter Arthur Hornblow, who had purchased the book for forty thousand dollars, nor George Cukor or Casey Robinson, who were hired to adapt it into a screenplay. But it soon became a challenging task to create a cohesive script. Much of the difficulty lay in censorship issues. Upon receiving the first draft of the screenplay in March 1946, Joseph Breen wrote: "It is basically a story of illicit sex and adultery, treated without the full compensating moral values required by the Code. In fact, it amounts practically to a condonation of adultery." Rewrites continued right up until the first day of shooting.

Arthur Hornblow had initially wanted Walter Pidgeon to play the role of the husband. But fearing the public would be outraged at the idea of "Mrs. Miniver" being unfaithful to "Mr. Miniver," the idea was dropped. Robert Montgomery, who had been with the studio since 1929 and had recently returned from wartime service as a Navy lieutenant, was chosen instead. Hornblow chose Robert Mitchum to play Jean Renaud. The popular wartime hero of *The Story of G.I. Joe* and *Till the End of Time* was under contract to David O. Selznick, who demanded twenty-five thousand dollars for Mitchum's services.

From the first day of shooting on March 19, 1946, the production was a nightmare for the cast and crew. George Cukor was so dissatisfied with the script and disliked Robert Mitchum so heartily (the feeling was mutual) that he closed down the picture after a week and enlisted three new writers—Marguerite Roberts, Sonya Levien and Zoë Akins—to repair the screenplay.

One calamity seemed to follow another. Because of the shooting delays, Robert Montgomery was removed from the picture to begin work on his directorial debut, *Lady in the Lake*. Robert Mitchum was recast as Marise's husband, and a search was on for another actor to play Jean Renaud. Arthur Hornblow signed Richard Hart, a talented New York stage actor who had impressed an MGM talent scout with his recent performance as the "Witch Boy" in the fantasy *Dark of the Moon*. Robert Mitchum considered this move intolerable. He recognized that Hart had the meatier role and that he was left with a rather insignificant, secondary part in the picture. The whole arrangement made his extravagant loan-out arrangement from David O. Selznick a ridiculous investment. Frustrated with his contractual obligations (he was shooting another MGM picture, *Undercurrent*, and RKO's *The Locket* simultaneously), Mitchum engaged in shouting matches with his director, which caused Greer, for the first time in her career, to yearn for the end of the day so that she could retreat to her quiet haven in Bel Air.

Fortunately, her crisis coincided with her husband's return from active service. Her good humor and enthusiasm were restored as she and Richard talked over their peacetime plans. "I knew I wanted to make my way in Hollywood strictly on my own," Richard told the *Hollywood Citizen-News*. "At Metro I felt I couldn't put up a stiff fight for good roles without embarrassing my wife. I know I'm right in this viewpoint, for I've seen, in other cases, the complications that can arise when husband and wife are under contract to the same studio." During the summer, he was signed by Darryl Zanuck at Twentieth Century-Fox to play the supporting role of John Apley in *The Late George Apley*, a gentle satire on the Boston upper class starring Ronald Colman, Peggy Cummins, and Vanessa Brown. "My wife has been reading Peggy Cummins' and Vanessa Brown's lines," he said, "and I, in turn, read the lines of the actors in her script. It works out wonderfully well for both of us." The Neys also enjoyed a brief vacation when the studio sent Greer to Rollins College in Florida to receive an honorary degree. At the convocation ceremony, she was given a doctor of humanities degree by Dr. Hamilton Holt, president of Rollins, and was selected as the Rose Sweetheart by the Kappa Alpha fraternity. Hollywood journalists were amused to report that, during her address to the students, a large rat scurried in front of her podium on the stage. Before the horrified faculty could react, Greer remarked, "Oh, that's nothing. We have much bigger ones in California!"

Meanwhile, tensions on the set of *Desire Me* increased. George Cukor's frustration with the project rose each day as exponentially as the temper of his leading man from RKO. Robert Mitchum resented the long overtime hours that the director insisted upon and, in turn, managed to alienate his costars with his eccentric behavior. Greer, in particular, dreaded her scenes with him because of his penchant for hamburgers smothered with onions and Roquefort dressing. "Her eyes would spin around and she'd offer me a Chiclet," he recalled. "I'd refuse. Gum? No thanks. It didn't occur to me my breath was spinning her out. Horses didn't seem to mind." She was not amused when Mitchum scrawled "Red" on the soundstage floor for her camera setups. But Mitchum's most infamous practical joke occurred late one evening when he and his stand-in, Boyd Caheen, raided the studio's makeup department. They filled their car with head forms, brushes, hair dryers, wigs, and beards, and drove away. A.Q. Hodgett, investigator for the MGM police department, threatened to prosecute the pair for grand theft. But MGM's bark was worse than its bite. Fearful of delaying two costly productions, L.B. Mayer dismissed the matter after RKO, Mitchum's home studio, supplied $52.40 for damages.

In mid-April the MGM company of 150 people moved on location to Monterey, at Victorine Ranch below Mal Paso Creek. Greer was delighted to work so near to her beloved Quail Haven and enjoyed escorting Richard Hart and his wife on local shopping trips and historical tours. On the morning of the nineteenth, she and Richard Hart were performing the "shrimping" sequence. Cukor had enlisted a local fisherman, Vincent Sollecito, to act as a technical advisor and teach the actors how to use the fishing nets. The scene begins as Greer appears on the porch of Marise's cliffside home and spots Jean down below. "Where did you learn to catch shrimp?" she called. "I'm just learning now," Hart replied on cue. "Come on down. Come on. You afraid of getting wet?"

The line was eerily prophetic, for as Greer descended a stone stairway to the beach and took up her net, ready to fish for the camera, a huge, eight-foot wave swelled up. Before any member of cast or crew could move, it had crashed down upon them. When the water subsided the camera was still rolling—and the actors had disappeared. Greer was pulled thirty feet along the rocky promontory. A second wave threatened to sweep her into the cove and out to sea. Hart, who had a heart condition and had barely managed to save himself, was in no condition to aid his leading lady. So the cameraman and Vincent Sollecito jumped in after her and, to the great relief of everyone, brought her in, covered with cuts and bruises and suffering from exposure. A local physician was notified, and she was taken to the Monterey Community Hospital. Emily Torchia, the MGM publicist chosen to cover the on-location work, quickly informed the studio about the accident, but to her surprise no one would believe such a story. In desperation, she phoned Ralph Jordou, the head publicity planter. "I can't get anyone to believe me, Ralph," she said, "and Miss Garson's in the hospital. She's torn to pieces!"

Jordou rounded up a planeload of pressmen and flew to San Francisco. From there they descended upon a story that made world headlines. "We had to get into the hospital to get Miss Garson made up," recalls Emily Torchia. "I remember photographer Virgil Apger pushing me up to the hospital window, so I could climb in. The doctor didn't want the press in taking pictures, but that's how the publicity department worked." Grasping Sollecito's hand ("We wanted the fisherman to save her," recalls Torchia), Greer received reporters and described her experience. To the *Los Angeles Times* she related: "I saw it coming and said to myself, 'Golly, not like this, please, I have a lot of things I want to do first.' Next thing I knew I was scraping along the rocks. I don't remember being frightened. But I certainly do remember hugging those sharp rocks with all my might even though they cut and bruised. Suddenly, painful as it was, that jagged ledge was the most precious thing in the universe. I was on the brink when strong arms caught and pulled me back." L.B. Mayer presented Sollecito with a thousand-dollar check for his rescue, and Greer bought him an engraved eighteen-karat-gold watch.

Greer returned to the beach for shooting on April 26. "She wanted to go right on with the picture," a member of the film company told curious reporters and tourists who began flocking to the scene. "She certainly has what it takes." While there was conjecture in newspapers about whether the film of the stars' near-fatal accident would be used in the picture, MGM executives tactfully dispensed with the footage.

But the life-threatening accident and injury proved to be more serious than anyone at the time imagined. The physical and mental reverberations would continue for years to come. Physically, Greer was ill. Injuries to her abdomen and back would require a series of operations in the next few years and would cause further delays in the making of the picture. Cukor sent reams of telegrams to Culver City explaining these delays: "Miss Garson still unable to work before 10 A.M. Complaining she doesn't feel well. Still continues to take back treatments each day approximately 5 P.M. Under these conditions simply impossible to accomplish a full days work. She said she would love to cooperate for longer day, but would be physically impossible at present time." Mentally, Greer was deeply shaken. Even when Richard interrupted his increasingly busy filming schedule— testing for *I Live Alone* and *Captain from Castile* and preproduction tests for *Ivy*, a new film costarring Joan Fontaine and Patric Knowles— to be with his wife, Greer could not be consoled. Depression had enveloped her. He returned to Los Angeles troubled and frustrated.

In May the weary *Desire Me* crew returned to the MGM soundstages. Despite the happy publicity stills that MGM manufactured— of George Cukor's birthday on the set and of the Neys' third wedding anniversary—Elliott Morgan, a friend of Cukor's, commented: "*Desire Me* was a fiasco altogether. I think George couldn't get on with Mitchum. That's where the trouble was." Marguerite Roberts observed: "Cukor was one of those directors who was usually quite good. But when he went bad, he went very bad."

When Arthur Hornblow observed the rushes, the skyrocketing budget, which had topped $4 million, and the low morale of cast and crew, he took matters into his own hands. He fired Cukor and commissioned Marguerite Roberts to rewrite portions of the script. Then, any available director was put in charge. Jack Conway, then Victor Saville, and finally Mervyn LeRoy, who completed the filming on August 1, 1946, worked futilely with the dramatically incoherent film. Of the whole debacle, Cukor would later state: "*Desire Me* was shot from a script that didn't really make sense, and when it was finished I was just removed from the picture, and another director reshot a good deal of it with the understanding that his name wouldn't appear on the credits. Since very little of the final footage was mine, I wouldn't allow my name to be on the picture either." Not only Cukor, but Marguerite Roberts and Sonya Levien tried to get their names removed from credits.

Almost everyone involved with the film avoided the press. But not Robert Mitchum. He candidly told reporters: "George Cukor and Mervyn LeRoy are exemplary directors in their own right, but together they don't spell mother. And I've stopped taking Hollywood seriously after it took Greer Garson 125 takes to say no." For his part, Mervyn LeRoy explained: "In 1946 I stepped in to reshoot much of a picture called *Desire Me*. They had a good cast, but a rotten script, a script that made absolutely no sense. I tried my best to make something out of it, but I failed, just as Cukor had failed. Both of us insisted that our names not appear on the screen, and so the picture came out without any director listed at all. It was a botch . . . the only major film ever issued without a director's credit."

Arthur Hornblow knew, however, that his name and the name of the studio's most valuable female star would appear on the picture. While Joseph Durvin struggled in the editorial room, Hornblow held emergency meetings with other studio executives. It was obvious the film was not going to be a good one no matter how it was edited. Delaying the inevitable, the College of Cardinals shelved the picture for fourteen months. Hornblow needed a scapegoat, and George Cukor was the obvious target. The days following his dismissal from *Desire Me* were not pleasant ones. Few MGM personnel besides his closest friends would even speak to him. "Now I know who will come to my funeral," the director said bitterly. His disappointment was sharpened when the Twentieth Century-Fox Tyrone Power/Gene Tierney epic *The Razor's Edge*, which was a project he had turned down to work on *Desire Me*, premiered as a resounding hit.

Things were not much better at 680 Stone Canyon, where the Ney marriage was unraveling in a mire of accusations and ugly quarrels. Greer's illness and the threat that *Desire Me* posed to her career could not have come at a worse time. Tired of being referred to as

Greer Garson's husband, Richard was disappointed when *The Late George Apley* was not the hit that he had hoped for. His frustration with living in a home owned by his increasingly withdrawn wife, across the hall from a mother-in-law he did not get along with, caused quarrels to erupt with disturbing regularity.

Greer was featured on the cover of the 1946 Christmas issue of *Photoplay*. When the editor asked her to write about how the Ney family celebrated the season, she chose instead to remember happier holidays of the past, with a tinge of melancholy. "To me, Christmas Days should be as individualized and distinctive as one's friends," she wrote, "each possessing a special brand of enchantment. My Christmases have had an amazing series of backgrounds. There have been my Scottish holidays, all set in snow and haggis. There were my London Yuletides, very posh as Londoners say, or very swank as we say in America, and now my Beverly Hills Christmases. Christmas is a home day, and it must be divine to be in huge families then. I wish I could expect to have one, sometime, with my forty-seven grandchildren gathered round my knee. But as that looks a little doubtful, I do wish there were some way of reaching the people who are stranded on Christmas and have them all come in. I think anyone in that position should be quite shameless as I was in 1938 in London, and latch on to someone else's family."

On January 27, 1947, Greer surprised the Hollywood community by declaring that she had separated from her husband. Not since the intense scrutiny following the premiere of *Mrs. Miniver* had her life received so much attention. On February 3, noting that Richard Ney was being considered for the romantic lead in Gene Tierney's *The Ghost and Mrs. Muir*, columnist Erskine Johnson fanned the flames with his editorial. "The reason for the Neys' marital discord is pretty obvious," he wrote. "When they were married, Ney was unknown. Now he is getting the big roles. It always happens that way in Hollywood."

When, in late March, the Neys attempted a reconciliation and were seen on the Sunset Strip, Hedda Hopper pounced on the story. "Greer Garson Goes Stepping with Husband!" blared the headline of her March 29 column. "It's spring," she wrote, "and perhaps that accounts for Richard Ney and Greer Garson stepping out once more at the Club Gala. Neither would say it was a reconciliation. But Greer did admit she had no plans for a divorce. Personally, I think they will reconcile, and soon. They're very much in love with each other."

But the reconciliation was short-lived. On August 18 Greer requested a two-week vacation. Although she told her friends at MGM that she was taking a rest after her Monterey ordeal, her boss knew differently. It was not a comfortable, quiet vacation at Quail Haven that she wanted. It was to put an end to her disturbing estrangement from Richard Ney. Mayer helped her begin divorce proceedings the following day. Filing the suit in Superior Court, attorney George W. Cohen of Loeb and Loeb charged, "The defendant has inflicted upon the plaintiff a course of great and grievous mental and physical anguish and suffering and extreme cruelty." On August 20, newspapers around the world publicized the news. Journalists waited hungrily for a court date to finally learn what had happened behind the closed doors at 680 Stone Canyon to cause Mrs. Miniver to dissolve her marriage.

A preview of the patchwork *Desire Me* was arranged in September. Apparently, nothing that Arthur Hornblow had attempted to do to save the picture had worked. Greer looked haggard and unhappy. Gone was any trace of the intensity that had made her earlier dramas so riveting. She seemed to be merely confused by the events surrounding her. The troubles that had plagued her through the production were evident in her behavior in every scene. Robert Mitchum's character seemed as unconcerned about the proceedings as the actor had off camera. Only Richard Hart appeared to be trying to add tension and excitement to the story and making sense of the directorless maelstrom. "Greer Garson is back for the first time since March of '46," announced *Motion Picture Daily*, "when she costarred with Clark Gable in *Adventure*. That makes it quite a span between attractions and also a cause for regret that her reappearance could not have been marked by more auspicious circumstances." *Variety* observed, "Miss Garson's role requires continual emotional stress that makes for a heavy job. [The] climactic fight scene of the film is laid in thick fog of the Breton coast and the same fog seems to have enveloped the script. There's some highly dramatic action and poignant emotion in the piece, but scripters show a tendency to 'back into them sidewise' and keep the audience waiting over-long for the thrills."

On September 25 Greer entered the downtown Los Angeles

Courthouse. She was a pale, unhappy figure in a gray silk gabardine suit and black French skullcap, supported by her secretary, Charlotte, George Cohen, and a phalanx of Metro's publicity men. It was the last day of her divorce proceedings. She paused, unsteady on her feet for a moment in the entrance hall, as she faced a seething publicity madhouse. Dodging reporters, she appeared in the designated courtroom. In a moment, Superior Judge Arthur Crum called her to the witness stand. Reporters in the back of the courtroom waited expectantly. Judge Crum requested that she explain her reasons for a divorce. "We separated in January after he became extremely moody, morose and refused to talk to me, destroying my feeling of security in the home," Greer said quietly, visibly shaken. "He disparaged my work and taunted me about being finished as an actress. It was destructive criticism, not constructive, and it undermined my self confidence to a great degree, and it made it hard for me to continue. He was constantly creating scenes. He had such an uncompanionable attitude that for the past year I have been under a doctor's care."

When Judge Crum requested her to be more specific in her allegations, Greer described a harrowing event that had occurred during the Christmas holidays of 1946. After a long, depressing day on the set of *Desire Me*, and wanting only to climb into bed with her script, she discovered that Richard's frustration with her distant manner had kindled into fury. As she retired to her dressing room and closed the door, he began to pound on it, demanding to be let in. "It is very difficult for me to give testimony," she admitted, momentarily unable to continue her story. "I said, 'Please, I must rest and go to bed or I shall not be fit to go to work tomorrow.' And he kicked down the door and made a great scene." After a moment she concluded, "I tried to make a success of our marriage—I can honestly say that."

Stepping down from the witness stand, Greer seemed to be in a daze. "She wandered three or four minutes around the filled courtroom," the *Hollywood Citizen-News* reported, "apparently unable to decide where to sit down." Not finding an empty chair, she fled the courtroom in tears. Outside, she was surrounded by blinding flashbulbs and the loud, questioning voices of the press. "George," she cried, looking about for her lawyer, "George! Make them let me alone." George Cohen came running up behind her, shielding her face and escorting her to a court reporter's room, while the studio publicity men forcibly backed the newsmen into a corner. Leaving the courthouse an hour later, she sharply chastised a photographer who rushed to take her picture: "This isn't acting, chum. This isn't part of my job!"

Greer refused to look at a newspaper for weeks afterward. For once, the coffee table in the living room was devoid of newspapers and magazines. And for good reason. Headlines like "Greer Garson's Divorce Plea Ends 'Ideal Marriage' to Ney" and "Mrs. Miniver's Heartbreak" were everywhere. "Greer Garson has portrayed few roles to equal the one she played in court where she sought a divorce from her youthful husband," remarked the *American Weekly.* "In this, Richard was betrayed by his youth; Greer, by her idealism. Thus Greer and Dick were divorced. But she can't view her marriage to Dick with detachment. At the drop of a word, an unguarded reference, or reminder of their life together, tears will fill her eyes."

In an editorial entitled "The Miniver Rose," one critic wrote: "Now comes the news that Greer Garson has sued for divorce. The popular mind will not allow such a heroine to be thought of in the ordinary sense that the neighbor girl is condemned for her failure at marriage, so divorce must be given a new dignity in the rationalization of Garson fans. Otherwise, the stable, wholesome, courageous Mrs. Miniver Garson would be no more, and we would have lost another illusion. Through logical transference, divorce as an acceptable device in Hollywood life, slowly becomes a 'natural' thing in life across the nation. Chosen as the easy way to solve the most difficult of problems, it has gradually penalized society with the soporific effects found in an excessive use of sedatives. Through the dazzling sunshine of Greer's prime as an actress and woman of the world, she is joined by her public in the demand that no difficulties exist along her happy way. Hence, divorce, to keep the Miniver rose fresh. But what of October, November, and December, during that season when deep roots are the only defense against the winds of time?"

L.B. Mayer took charge of his fallen star. He escorted her to the newest plays in downtown Los Angeles and sent cheerful letters when she entered the hospital for another series of operations necessitated by her Monterey injuries. The new seven-year contract, at five thousand dollars a week, which Greer signed on February 17, 1947, was Mayer's personal guarantee that, despite her personal troubles and the state of her increasingly precarious career, he was still solidly behind his famous star. On June 16, the contract was revised, with an additional seven-year nonexclusive period during which she could accept work from other studios, at a salary cut to $1,725 a week. The pension plan, which would become active when she reached sixty, provided 15 percent of her average annual earnings at Metro, plus 10 percent of such earnings over three thousand dollars. Greer's spirits were raised by the generous offer. "It looks like I'll be busy acting until I'm a little old lady," she said.

Then, she retreated to Quail Haven. On September 26, she received a letter from J. Robert Rubin, MGM's East Coast vice president: "Dear Greer, hope that all your troubles both professional and domestic are now over and from this time on you have nothing but domestic peace and happiness and professionally a succession of triumphs and success. Keep your chin up. Carry on." Greer would not return to the Culver City lot for four months. Many employees wondered if she would come back at all.

She and Nina did attend the premiere of *Desire Me* at New York's Capitol Theater on October 31, 1947. Inside, the posters read: "Metro-Goldwyn-Mayer presents Greer Garson, recipient of more honors and awards than any other actress in screen history in 'Desire Me' a timely and powerful romantic story of today." But the critics were merciless. "Greer Garson's back, folks," reported the *New York Times*, "and bravely shouldering a multitude of woes. [She] registers varying emotions chiefly by tilting her head and smiling, and sniffing the air much in the fashion of a haughty Pekingese. The only remarkable thing about *Desire Me*, is the fact that it has dispensed blithely with the services of a director." Alone on the train to Beverly, Massachusetts, the following day, where she intended to enter another hospital for still another operation, Greer found a note from Nina almost buried under the reviews. "Darling, you were so wonderful last night, so brave and cheerful. I was proud of you. Everything is going to be so much better now. All love, Mummy."

Desire Me eventually registered as a $2,440,000 loss for the studio, but most of those involved in its creation recovered. Arthur Hornblow got back on track within the year, producing *The Hucksters*. George Cukor bounced back at MGM in 1949 with Katharine Hepburn and Spencer Tracy in *Adam's Rib*. Robert Mitchum's subsequent success in films such as *Out of the Past, Rachel and the Stranger,* and *The Big Steal* swept aside his bad memories of working at Metro-Goldwyn-Mayer. Richard Hart made two more MGM films. He appeared in the Lana Turner epic, *Green Dolphin Street,* and Barbara Stanwyck's *B.F.'s Daughter* before a fatal heart attack in 1951 cut his career short. Greer's life and career, however, were profoundly changed. "*Desire Me* was a sad mistake," she told Hedda Hopper soon after her return to Los Angeles on November 26. "No alibis, though. I steeled my red head for the blows and they came, the cracks by the columnists and critics. I was a setup. Now, this period of comparative idleness has given me time to count my blessings. I've learned to relax and be at peace with myself and the world. I am not interested in a career just for the sake of itself. I want to do only those things in which I'm interested. I no longer have the momentum of career ambition to drive me. I'm grasping for a new philosophy of life. Nothing is ever going to worry me again."

CHAPTER 18

"I'VE ALWAYS LOVED THE LETTERS I get from fans," Greer said shortly after her reappearance at Metro-Goldwyn-Mayer in the winter of 1947. "One note read, 'Don't worry Greer, I am writing a Western for you that's sure to bring you back.' Well, it wasn't a Western I wanted after my Humpty-Dumpty. I wanted a rip-snorting comedy to play. No more queens; the queen's crown had slipped slightly." To gratify the wish of his emotionally fragile star, L.B. Mayer purchased a comedy, Margery Sharp's *The Nutmeg Tree,* for $18,490, provided a generous $2,706,000 budget, and surrounded Greer with a supportive creative team including producer Everett Riskin, who had helmed the popular Columbia comedy/fantasy *Here Comes Mr. Jordan;* director Jack Conway, famous for many of Metro's best comedies (*Red Headed Woman, Libeled Lady, The Hucksters*); and old friends such as Walter Pidgeon, Reginald Owen, Joseph Ruttenberg, Sydney Guilaroff, and Twentieth Century-Fox star Cesar Romero. "What I've wanted to do all along was make people laugh," Greer remarked. "Besides, the combination of Greer and drear was wearing thin!"

"When Greer Garson starts a picture in a bubble bath, that's news!" Such was the publicity that issued from Metro-Goldwyn-Mayer on January 16, 1948, as Greer prepared for the opening scene of *Julia Misbehaves.* As she sat, chatting gaily with the crew before a warm bathtub filled with Ardena Fluff Milk Bath while her hairdresser, Edith Hubner, swept her hair up into a curly mass, she seemed like her old self. She was pleased that despite a "No Admittance" sign on the soundstage door, a steady line of friendly well-wishers crowded their way into the eight-foot-square replica of an

English bathroom. While Jack Conway and Joe Ruttenberg prepared to film the scene, prop man Tony Ordoqui kept filling the tub with bubbles. Irene was there to check on Greer's skin-colored bathing suit. Al Block, the studio censor, moved about nervously, anxiously second-guessing the Production Code's view on modesty. Finally Conway shooed everyone out except for Walter Pidgeon. "After all," Pidgeon argued, "as an actor who has been married to Greer Garson four times, I should have some privileges."

In *Julia Misbehaves*, Greer played Julia Packett, a divorced vaudeville actress who receives a wedding invitation from her daughter, whom she has not seen since childbirth. Returning to her husband's estate in France, she finds that her daughter is actually in love with another man who is a local painter. Her matchmaking schemes and the interference of an itinerant family of acrobats cause chaos in the stuffy confines of the Packett household. The head of the acrobats, Fred Ghenoccio, played by Cesar Romero, falls in love with Julia, which inspires jealousy and reawakened love in her ex-husband. It seems that only the spirited Julia can set everything right. She sends the Ghenoccios packing and Susan off to elope with the painter. But even she cannot control the comic turn of events in which she and her husband are reunited happily, in the mud during a thunderstorm.

Elizabeth Taylor and Peter Lawford played the young lovers in *Julia Misbehaves*. Since Elizabeth was not needed for the first week's shooting, she took time off to visit with her friends. Among them was Gayle Fogelson, nephew and adopted son of Texas oil millionaire Col. Elijah E. "Buddy" Fogelson. Gayle and his two brothers and sister attended school in Los Angeles. Elizabeth knew that the colonel had many friends in Hollywood, including Humphrey Bogart and her father, and that since the death of his brother he had looked after his three nephews and niece. Peter Lawford was also an acquaintance of Buddy's, as a skeet shooting partner. It was inevitable that Colonel Fogelson, who was in Los Angeles that winter, would be invited on the set of Elizabeth and Peter's latest picture.

Peter Lawford brought Colonel Fogelson to Stage Five one morning. While screen extras were finding their seats on the theater set, Lawford told his friend that he intended to introduce him to the star of the picture.

"Who is Greer Garson?" the colonel asked.

As Lawford's mouth opened in surprised disbelief, Jack Conway called for silence. Buddy Fogelson gazed at a beautiful redhead posing in front of the cameras on stage. Although impressed with this actress that he assumed was Greer Garson, his eye was caught by another attractive carrot-top talking and laughing with a crowd of grips and electricians to his right. A stenographer or script girl, he assumed. Suddenly Conway stepped over to the group and disentangled the woman. "Greer is ready," he told Joe Ruttenberg.

After watching Greer perform the energetic musical number "Oh What a Difference the Navy's Made to Me," the colonel asked Lawford to be introduced to her. Learning of Buddy's mistake, Greer smiled and explained that it was her stand-in, Adele Taylor, who had been before the camera. Buddy was enchanted with Greer's merry laughter and warm personality. He asked her to Chasen's for dinner, but she refused with the explanation that she had to get up early the following day for work. "Buddy was shy, I was brash," Greer recalled. "Besides, I didn't think we had anything in common. But I thought about him later and invited him for cocktails. He was so delighted he sent the Lawfords a taxi-full of flowers."

A few days later, Greer invited Buddy Fogelson, Peter Lawford, and the Pidgeons to supper at her home. During after-dinner drinks, Greer got up and left the dining room to change a record. Buddy followed. Greer never forgot that moment. "He took my hand and said, 'I'm going to marry you some day'—just like that." The guests settled in the living room. Walter Pidgeon invited Buddy to join him at the piano. This would be the first of many such duets. Louella Parsons later observed, "Those two get together beside a piano, when nobody's around, and there isn't an operatic tenor aria that Buddy can't sing beautifully. Walter had begun his motion picture career singing, and Fogelson once considered an operatic career, with the encouragement of Enrico Caruso." Saying goodnight to Greer from the doorway, Buddy proposed dinner the following night at Chasen's. She accepted.

Soon, roses began filling the house and her dressing room at MGM. "There were so many roses that we ran out of vases," Greer recalled. Although in love at first sight, Buddy Fogelson quickly learned that Greer, after two failed marriages, was wary of an intimate relationship. But one date led to another, and the colonel took up a more permanent residence at the Shoreham in Beverly Hills.

The final sequence filmed for *Julia Misbehaves*, on April 9, 1948, was the acrobatic number in which Greer sings, à la Beatrice Lillie, "When You're Playing with Fire" from a balcony thirty feet above the floor of Stage Five. She insisted on doing her own stunts in the scene, which included being lowered down onto a human pyramid of acrobats. "Then, if I break my neck," she told publicists, "it won't matter. MGM will still have a picture to release." Rehearsed for more than a week with circus professionals, the number was shot without a hitch, and Greer retired to her dressing room happily exhilarated but tired. Edward Lawrence of the *New York Times* had observed her work that day and wrote: "The cool repose of her finely chiseled features is deceptive; she is no passive madonna, though occasionally she might have been painted by Raphael. It is only off-screen that one discovers that the films as yet have hardly revealed her electric vivacity."

During the final days of retakes, Greer's position as the film capital's most popular international ambassador reached its pinnacle. She made telephone calls of friendship to thirty countries, reaching over 77 million people listening to nationwide radio hookups and loudspeakers or reading the newspaper interviews.

She participated in the promotion of *Julia Misbehaves* with a verve she had seldom displayed on earlier occasions. At the press preview of the picture she said, "MGM calls it, 'The New Look on Garson' and nobody's kidding. One good picture and I'm happy as a lark again! We had so much fun making it, and when it was finished it was wonderful to go into the theater and hear people laughing at what that formerly staid and prim Greer Garson was doing up there on the screen." Unconcerned with the critics' view that the picture was not in the league of her classic Metro features of the early 1940s, she was pleased merely to be working again, and in the genre that she felt most comfortable. Taking Buddy Fogelson's arm, she smiled once more for the photographers and added, "I am happier than I have been in a long time. All my worries seem to have vanished. What more can one ask for?"

Julia Misbehaves premiered at Radio City Music Hall on October 8, 1948, and was a resounding hit, grossing $4,497,000. "The common misconception that Greer Garson was born with a bustle is hilariously disabused in *Julia Misbehaves*," remarked the *Hollywood Reporter,* "a slip of a comedy into which the first lady of Metro sails with evident relish and infectious zest. The result is a charmingly provocative performance which will inevitably delight the Garson fans. It is very much her own show as she runs the gamut from pratfalls to a mud-splattered finish with the fine artistry of a low comic." Shortly thereafter, on November 29, Greer switched back to drama in *Lux Radio Theatre's* version of *Brief Encounter,* based on David Lean's 1946 British film. She was intrigued with the poignant tale of two strangers who briefly meet at a train station and fall in love. Fellow MGM player and Academy Award winner Van Heflin played her lover.

At Buddy Fogelson's invitation, Greer and her mother spent a week relaxing at his Forked Lightning Ranch in Pecos, twenty-seven miles northeast of Santa Fe, New Mexico. "I'll never forget my first trip to the Forked Lightning Ranch," Greer recalled. "I was dressed in an organdy dress, light blue, with high-heeled blue shoes and a huge, willowy picture hat. I was so surprised. I thought it would be a farm with a picket fence and a duck pond and maybe a pony. I was immediately struck by the color of the earth, the sky and the people. It's a melting pot of three cultures: Indian, Spanish, and pioneer American. The wonderful thing is they all get on well together. It's historic. Spacious. Thrilling. It's not like the lush pasturage of, say, Virginia. Instead of eight cows to an acre it's more like eight acres to a cow! I felt so fragile and uncomfortable in that vast, rugged land."

As Colonel Fogelson gave the Garsons a tour of the ranch, he explained the region's rich history. The Forked Lightning Ranch was established in 1925 by rodeo celebrity Clarence Van Nostrand, who preferred to be known as Tex Austin. The "Daddy of Rodeo" bought parcels of the old Pecos Pueblo Grant, which amounted to 5,500 acres, and named the ranch after the numerous thunderstorms that frequently rolled through the region. Austin's brand still marked the dining and living room fixtures when Buddy purchased the site in 1941, expanding the Forked Lightning to thirteen thousand acres for his four hundred head of Santa Gertrudis cattle. Within the acreage lay the easternmost pueblo ever built in the United States. Known as "America's first apartment house," the ancient Pecos Pueblo, settled in 1100, was also the site of a mission begun by Coronado in 1541 and completed in 1615. During leisurely visits to historic sites, Greer quickly found there was much more to Col. Elijah E. "Buddy" Fogelson than her initial impression of "cowboy gallantries, oil wells and cattle."

Fogelson was born in College View, Nebraska, in 1900. He left school to become an adventuresome oil wildcatter in Texas, accumulating a variety of oil and natural gas financial interests. Returning to school, he earned degrees from Texas Christian University and the School of Military Government at the University of Virginia. During World War II he served with distinction for six and a half years as a colonel on General Eisenhower's staff and was largely responsible for the conception and implementation of the oil pipeline that made possible the Allied invasion and rapid advance in Europe. President Truman appointed him to the reparations commission in Moscow and at the Potsdam conference. By 1949 he was a prominent oilman, rancher, racehorse owner, and philanthropist with business interests in California, New Mexico, Kentucky, and Texas, and had collected an astonishing number of honors. He was awarded the Croix de Guerre avec Palme from General Charles de Gaulle and was knighted into the Order of the White Rose by the President of Finland, the home of his ancestors. He was a member of the Cowboy Hall of Fame, an accomplished performer of magic tricks, and a director of the Boys Clubs of America. He had found little time for movies.

"He had started life as a lawyer so we had something in common since I started as a lawyer," recalls his friend Herbert Hutner. "He was extremely bright and perceptive. We were driving one day in Santa Fe and he saw this doughnut shop. He said to me, 'Let's go in there. I have an idea that that company's going to do very well.' Well, we walked in and we ordered some doughnuts. It was pretty crowded. Later, we got out in the car and he said, 'Well, I'm calling my broker and I'm going to buy a good sized block of that stock.' It was Dunkin' Donuts. He did extremely well in the stock market by paying no attention to any advice from brokers or money managers. He was also one of the last outstanding independent oilmen."

The Fogelson-Garson romance grew swiftly and sparked nationwide publicity. For Greer, the romantic parallels of her own life with Edna Gladney's in *Blossoms in the Dust* must have been remarkable. Lillian Burns remarked: "Greer was a great lady. Beautiful vocabulary.

Well-read. Real intellect. But she was a lady who could kick up her heels if she wanted to and I think that Buddy Fogelson appreciated that in her." But there were complications. "We had a long and stormy courtship," Greer would recall. "I didn't want to get married, and we were from two different worlds."

Louella Parsons was among the first Hollywood columnists who tried to second-guess the couple's wedding plans. On her radio program she announced, "My lovely red-haired and good friend, Greer Garson, is making plans to marry Texas millionaire Buddy Fogelson early this winter. She has been out with him every night, and he has been her house guest at Pebble Beach twice. Moreover, he hasn't taken out any other girl since he met her and she hasn't gone with any other suitor."

Alarmed with the premature announcement, Greer invited Louella to 680 Stone Canyon. "If I marry again, it must be for forever," she declared. "Do you know I'm the only one in my family ever to be divorced? I could never go through again what I went through that awful day when I was kept at the courthouse for hours, being photographed and interviewed."

Meanwhile, in an attempt to surmount increasing financial crises, MGM acquired some new blood. On August 9, 1948, Dore Schary negotiated a long-term, fourteen-year contract to become vice president in charge of production at Metro-Goldwyn-Mayer. It was a post that had remained vacant since the death of Irving Thalberg. Schary immediately established the same cost-efficient cutback procedures throughout the bloated studio that he had maintained successfully at RKO. He had immediate ambitious plans, aiming to cut production costs by 20 to 25 percent with better script preparation and more efficient employment of personnel. Under his influence, MGM was slowly revitalized. By the end of 1949, he nearly doubled the studio's production output, from eighteen films to thirty-five.

The company's most ambitious plans were for the new studio facilities, Borehamwood, outside London. Located in Hertfordshire, a northern suburb of London, the newly refurbished, thirty-eight-acre facility had been opened with much fanfare in September 1948. It had been Mayer's intention ever since German bombers irreparably destroyed the Denham studio to reunite his corporation with Great Britain. In March 1944, Loews had purchased the seventeen-year-old studio after the land was de-requisitioned as a military supply depository. Alexander Korda was put in charge of the studio, but after eight months and only one film (*Perfect Strangers*), Korda had cited irreconcilable differences with his American partners and quit.

More eager than ever to keep a foothold in England with the release of the Films Act of 1948, Mayer put Ben Goetz in control. The Act lowered the tax on the import of American films to 30 percent. In return, a proportion of American earnings were to remain in England. American movie companies found it increasingly lucrative to make films in Great Britain and spend these otherwise frozen funds. Mayer outlined an ambitious schedule, including Sidney Franklin's production of *Young Bess,* the biography of young Elizabeth I; *The Conspirators* with Elizabeth Taylor; and two films for Greer Garson: *The Fortunes of Richard Mahoney*, based on Henry Handel Richardson's novel of the Australian gold fields, which would reunite her with Gregory Peck, and an elaborate adaptation of John Galsworthy's *The Forsyte Saga*. When *Mahoney* ran into production difficulties in August 1947, Galsworthy's work took center stage.

In the British Museum, three writings are grouped together in a special case: two authenticated pages written by Shakespeare, a letter from Lord Nelson to Lady Hamilton as he lay dying aboard his ship, the *Victory,* and the original manuscript of John Galsworthy's *The Forsyte Saga*. It was in 1906 that Galsworthy published *A Man of Property,* the first book in the celebrated trilogy. MGM purchased the screen rights to *The Forsyte Saga* in August 1937 for $32,188, and in the following years various producers such as David O. Selznick had considered filming the novel as a vehicle for John, Lionel, and Ethel Barrymore. Greer Garson was often considered for the key role of Irene Heron Forsyte, but it was not until the summer of 1948 that an acceptable script, which Robert Lord and Robert Nathan had worked on for over a year, was presented to her. For the first time Greer turned to Buddy Fogelson instead of her mother for career advice. He liked the story but urged her to have it altered so that she became more sympathetic, and the pivotal character. The studio agreed, and Jan Lustig, Ivan Tors, and James B. Williams revamped the screenplay, entitled *That Forsyte Woman,* specifically for her. The picture was scheduled as a Silver Jubilee Production in honor of MGM's twenty-fifth anniversary. It was one of an important list of films that included

Judy Garland's *In the Good Old Summertime,* Jennifer Jones's *Madame Bovary,* Gregory Peck's *The Great Sinner,* and Gene Kelly's *On the Town.*

The MGM version of Galsworthy's classic takes place in 1880s London, where the beautiful young Irene Heron is being courted by an arrogant and proud aristocrat named Soames Forsyte—a man determined to have what he wants. Although she is not in love with him, Irene accepts his proposal under his persuasive influence. Thus, she is introduced into the wealthy Forsyte family. Her only friend is June Forsyte, whose vibrant youth and friendliness are rare in the family's cold and materialistic world. June is in love with an itinerant architect, Philip, who is immediately attracted to Irene. Irene attempts to prevent an affair, but the reckless Philip is as determined to possess her as Soames is. She turns to gentle Jolyon Forsyte, June's father, who is the black sheep of the family. Fifteen years before, he had run away with the family governess to live in France, leaving his wife to die of a broken heart. Their child, June, had been raised by the Forsytes under the condition that Jolyon solemnly promise never to see his daughter again. When June finds out about Philip and Irene, she informs Soames, who discovers the pair at Philip's flat. His threats to ruin Philip are short-lived, for the architect is accidentally killed in a carriage accident on a foggy street. Irene leaves Soames and, one year later, marries Jolyon Forsyte.

When director Compton Bennett, a former interior decorator, began work on *That Forsyte Woman* on March 1, 1948, he intended to give the film an arresting visual style. His plans included the construction of some of the most lavish sets ever to grace an MGM film. Wimpole Street, on Lot Two, was completely renovated to make way for the imposing Forsyte homes. Some of the studio's most expensive set dressings and furniture were unearthed from the prop department warehouse for the production, including Greer's portrait as Mrs. Parkington, which was hung in Soames Forsyte's dining room. The wardrobe department received one of its largest orders for the film, including twenty-four elaborate gowns for Greer alone. Meeting with Greer and showing her his sketches of several key scenes, Bennett asked for her opinion. "Bring Joseph Ruttenberg on board," she replied. "Greer Garson's leading men come and go with each new picture," wrote Ralph Lawton, in *American Cinematographer,* "but the most important man in her cinematic life still is Joseph Ruttenberg, her cameraman."

Although *That Forsyte Woman* would be Greer's second feature in Technicolor, this was Joseph Ruttenberg's first. Shooting preproduction wardrobe and makeup tests gave the cameraman time to experiment. "It was a little difficult at first," he told *American Cinematographer*, "having done black and white pictures for so many years, then suddenly undertaking a new medium that requires about twenty percent more light. . . . It becomes a matter of knowing how to light each scene, or more correctly—how to balance the light to bring this color to the screen in the most natural and effective manner." He was especially concerned with shooting the opening and closing scenes, shrouded in London fog, which were the most dramatic ones in the picture. "You can't light fog scenes with top lighting," he discovered. "So when I reached this point in the *Forsyte* script, I had no idea how fog would photograph in Technicolor. The first day I didn't use any color in the fog scenes at all. The result was decidedly gray and lifeless; so the next day we put a little warmth into the lighting and got a very beautiful effect."

On April 13, 1948, Greer's wax image, as Mrs. Miniver, was unveiled at Madame Tussaud's in London by Metro's own Margaret O'Brien. It was a singular and noteworthy honor to be among the images of Sarah Bernhardt, Eleonora Duse, Marlene Dietrich, and Mary Pickford, whom she had admired as an ambitious young student at the University of London. She was also pleased to find a small role in *That Forsyte Woman* for her mother, marking their first appearance together in a film. Nina Garson played a member of the Forsyte clan under the screen name of Nina Ross and was paid $250. She had been on the MGM payroll as a character actress since March 1945 and had already appeared in *Lady in the Lake* and *On an Island with You.*

Although principal photography began on December 22, 1948, it was on January 1 that the set of *That Forsyte Woman* received international attention from the press. Errol Flynn had arrived at MGM. Originally considered for the romantic role of Philip Bosinney, Flynn found the complex role of Soames Forsyte irresistible. "I don't know whether I can convey how deep the yearning is of an actor who has been stereotyped," he later remarked, "who has that sword and horse wound about him, to prove to himself and to others that he is an actor. I worked hard for this role in *That Forsyte Woman*. I think that that picture was one of the few worthwhile vehicles in which I played."

In order to get Flynn for the film, L.B. Mayer traded William Powell, whom Jack L. Warner wanted for *Life with Father*. Flynn was notorious for his scandalous capers on and off screen, and the MGM publicists were primed for the confrontation between Don Juan and Mrs. Miniver. As intimidated as anyone by the formidable image of Greer Garson as Queen of the Lot, Flynn prepared carefully for his first meeting with his costar. "I primed myself with about three vodkas," he recalled. "When I was introduced, I adopted an air of bravado, the hearty Australian from the outback. I shook hands heartily, then I slapped her on the fanny. 'Hi yuh, Red!' I said. Everybody froze. There was a brief pause. Then she went into a torrent of laughter. That broke the ice."

"We stalked each other like terriers for a couple of days," Greer said, "and then found out we had a terrific lot in common." Flynn's father was once a professor at Queen's University in Northern Ireland, the same university that Aunt Evelyn had attended. Both Greer and Errol had begun their acting careers in British repertories—Flynn joined the Northampton Repertory Company in 1933. Like Greer, he performed in the West End of London and was subsequently signed by a major Hollywood studio—Warner Bros. Greer's first film under contract was made in England. Errol Flynn's first film, *Murder at Monte Carlo,* was made at the Warners' British Teddington studio. In their movie stardom, both resented their Hollywood stereotypes— hers as noble heroine and his as romantic swashbuckler.

Their sense of fun, completely at odds with the humorless characters they were playing before the camera, would make the shooting of *That Forsyte Woman* a pure delight. Janet Leigh, playing young June Forsyte, was as surprised as any of the featured players with Greer's behavior. "I had misjudged Greer Garson," she says. "I thought she would be staid, even somewhat uptight, probably because of the many serious roles she had portrayed. But she soon changed that notion. She immediately changed my calling her Miss Garson to Greer and proved her funnybone was well oiled." Janet was a witness to Flynn's shenanigans when he hid in Greer's bedroom closet for one scene. As the cameras rolled and Greer opened the door to put away a gown, he popped out. "He couldn't have asked for a better reaction," Miss Leigh recalls. "She screamed and fainted."

"The popular conception of Greer is that she is a kind of Mrs. Miniver: finely bred, the epitome of English cultured womanhood," remarked Flynn. "She is all this, but at the same time a mischievous imp. We were shooting a scene in a Victorian carriage. There came a time when I had to open the door and say, 'Now, my dear, shall we alight?' We didn't. But I sure as hell did. Because as I touched the doorknob the electric contact Greer had fixed right in the seat of my pants made me go through the air like a witch riding a broom."

It was not difficult for the cast and crew to realize the source of Greer's high spirits. She was in love. Newspapers and movie magazines across the country carried such headlines as: "Greer Garson's In Love Again," "Buddy Fogelson's friends in Texas are betting as high as $20,000 that he and Greer will marry before *That Forsyte Woman* starts," "Buddy Fogelson and Greer Garson hosting her mother at La Rue," and "Garson and her bridegroom-to-be Buddy Fogelson, buying X-mas pretties together at the silver shop next to Romanoff's." Hedda Hopper, who interviewed Greer on the set, wrote for her readers: "A change has come over Greer. . . . It's an undefinable, kind of cocky, assured look a woman gets who's in love. . . . She seems to love everyone else, too, more than she used to show it. She's pure peaches and cream to work with on the set . . . and even that eccentric Celt, Errol Flynn, who can cut a temperamental caper when he feels like it, is eating out of her hand."

Alexis Smith, a Warner contract player who had costarred with Errol Flynn in *Gentleman Jim* and *San Antonio*, was on the MGM lot making *Any Number Can Play.* Visiting her old screenmate in his dressing room one day, she heard a loud noise. Flynn explained that it was the call for everyone to come to the set. Watching everyone gather, Alexis observed the final lighting setups and Joseph Ruttenberg moving his camera into position. Only as everyone was prepared to shoot the scene did she hear a silver bell ring. It was Greer's Garson's signal to come on the set. "That was my first experience with the legendary MGM treatment of its First Ladies," she said. "And, evidently, Greer was the Queen of them all."

Production was halted on February 10, 1949, in honor of

Metro-Goldwyn-Mayer's twenty-fifth anniversary. A lavish luncheon was held in honor of eighty-one studio sales executives from thirty-two regional offices around the world. It was the culmination of a week-long sales conference. Greer and Errol were among the seven hundred guests who attended, and they were seated together, still in costume. After the meal Greer rose, as the still-reigning Queen, and presented Louis B. Mayer with a "silver key of opportunity," which harked back to the opening of the studio in 1924 when Will Rogers handed a similar key to Mayer and Irving Thalberg.

Outlining plans to reinvigorate the studio in Hollywood's current slump, Mayer told the gathering, "When MGM was formed in 1924, we had six stars and forty acres of land. Today we have thirty-one modern sound stages, sixty stars and five lots covering 176 acres. The motion picture industry will go forward in the years to come just as it has at this studio in the past twenty-five years. It is to entertainment what the game of baseball is to American sports. And I will remain head of this studio as long as Nick Schenck remains head of the company!"

Included in the sixty-seven productions the company planned to release in the 1949-50 season were a number of studio properties Mayer and Dore Schary considered for Greer Garson. Carl Sandburg and Sidney Franklin were still attempting to fashion a satisfying script for *The American Cavalcade.* Ben Hecht was writing a screenplay entitled *Europa and the Bull,* a comedy with a European background about an exiled princess, an American art collector, and a European dictator, to costar Cary Grant. "It has some of the brightest lines that you will ever hear," promised Dore Schary at the sales convention on February 8, 1949. Greer herself was working with scenarists to make a sequel to *Mrs. Miniver. The Chimes of Bruges,* published in France in 1896 as *Bruges La Morte,* by Georges Rodenbach, was also being considered.

Greer's merry demeanor during the making of *That Forsyte Woman* began to collapse as shooting wound up in mid-March. Few people were aware that her good humor actually belied some anxious worries. Her wedding preparations were constantly being undermined by the studio's ambitious plans for her and, a fact of which only Greer's mother and closest friends were aware, she was seriously ill. Intestinal problems had plagued her throughout the shooting of

That Forsyte Woman. Although she lived with the fear that she might share her father's fate and consulted physicians in Los Angeles as well as in the East, Greer avoided hospitals until production on *That Forsyte Woman* was completed.

Principal photography for the film officially ended March 18, but retakes dragged on into the summer. Meanwhile, preproduction tests began on *Europa and the Bull* in mid-May. But Greer could not keep up the pace. A memo was sent to Dore Schary from the wardrobe department that she was too "bloated and ill" to continue tests. On the seventeenth, Greer entered Good Samaritan Hospital for an emergency operation and remained there until the thirty-first, throwing the *Europa* schedule into serious peril. "Greer was sicker than anyone knew when she was in the hospital" reported Louella Parsons. "In the opinion of those closest to her, she will not marry until she has fully recovered from her illness." When she finally departed Good Samaritan, Buddy invited her to convalesce at the Forked Lightning Ranch for a weekend.

She went, causing Louella Parsons and practically every other Los Angeles gossip columnist to assume she was going to get married. Dining one evening in Santa Fe's historic Plaza at the La Fonda Hotel, they were sighted by the local press. Buddy chased them off by declaring that they would make an announcement about their future plans soon.

"When is Greer Garson going to marry Buddy Fogelson?" wrote an exasperated Louella Parsons. "That's the question everyone is asking. Greer is supposed to do a sequel to *Mrs. Miniver* in England after *Europa*, but in my opinion she and Buddy will not wait that long. He's very impatient and wants her to marry him immediately."

When she returned to Hollywood Greer concluded retakes for *That Forsyte Woman* on July 5 and began wardrobe tests for the *Miniver* film. Upon receiving word that she was scheduled to sail to Metro's Borehamwood studio on August 20 to begin shooting, she submitted her planned wedding date to Dore Schary's office. On July 12, as such future Garson vehicles as the *Miniver* sequel, *Europa*, and *The American Cavalcade* were in various phases of preproduction, Dore Schary sent off a memo to the College of Cardinals: "Hank Potter has been assigned to the *Miniver* film. He starts September 1st. Let Garson go now—test the rest of wardrobe when she returns."

Two days later, Greer was on the *Santa Fe Chief* en route to New Mexico for her wedding. Her mother was not with her. Nina had taken ill only a few days before and was unable to travel. With promises to join her daughter in Santa Fe after the honeymoon, she had prepared the large, beribboned parcel that lay beside Greer. It contained her wedding gown, a white linen suit lined in turquoise-blue chiffon and decorated with lace flowers, and a wide-brimmed straw hat with turquoise veil. Always a traditionalist for "something old," Greer clutched another important item in her hand as she gazed out upon the desert landscape. It was a family heirloom, a chiffon handkerchief embroidered with the name "Greer" in her mother's handwriting and dyed turquoise to match the trim of her wedding dress. Nina had enclosed a brief note inside the handkerchief: "Dearest Buddy and Greer, I hope you will enjoy every hour of this very special holiday. Congratulations, blessings and loving wishes for a long and happy married life. Think of you both. Love, Nina"

ACT THREE

Dallas (1949-1996)

Were her first years the Golden Age; that's true,
But now she's gold oft tried, and ever new.
That was her torrid and inflaming time,
This is her tolerable tropic clime."

—"The Autumnal," John Donne

CHAPTER 19

GREER ARRIVED AT THE TRAIN STATION in Lamy, New Mexico, at ten o'clock on the morning of July 15, 1949. Buddy was there with a welcoming committee of friends that included New Mexico Governor Thomas J. Mabry. Avoiding the publicity of a downtown church wedding, they took her to the Santa Fe home of Buddy's friend, Dr. Fletcher A. Catron, the former assistant U.S. attorney for the District of New Mexico. There, shortly before noon, she became Greer Garson Fogelson. Among the other guests who witnessed the wedding ceremony, conducted by New Mexico Supreme Court Justice James B. McGhee, were Santa Fe's mayor, Frank F. Ortiz; Slim Watson, foreman of the Forked Lightning Ranch; and best man Robert O'Donnell, vice president of Interstate Theaters from Dallas. An MGM representative, Ed Lawrence, was present along with Robert Taylor, who was on location in Santa Fe for an MGM Western called *Ambush*.

Driving back to Lamy, the Fogelsons were finally cornered by a gathering of Santa Fe reporters who immediately took note of a gleaming golden pendant, encircled with pearls, around the bride's neck. Greer explained that the gift from her husband was a medal of St. Genesius—the patron saint of actors, musicians, and, she added, Beverly Hills jewelers. She also made clear her new credo: "My career will not interfere with my marriage!" They managed to dodge the press and jump aboard the train bound for, they hoped, a secret location: the Swan Lake Ranch in Alcalde. "Buddy told me he'd booked honeymoon suites in about 88 hotels in such brilliantly original names like Mr. and Mrs. Smith or Jones to throw the press off the track," Greer recalled. "The only hitch was the fact that Buddy had forgotten most of the phony names under which he'd made the reservations." The following day the *Los Angeles Daily News* read: "Actress Greer Garson popped from the arms of Errol Flynn in a make-believe movie romance into the arms of a wealthy Texas oil man in a sure-enough romance yesterday!"

From the Swan Lake Ranch the Fogelsons headed for the Forked Lightning Ranch, where a round of parties awaited them. Among the festivities was an initiation ceremony for Greer by the Kiowan Indian tribe, making her an honorary princess. Nina was there with dozens of telegrams. "Welcome to the 49ers!" wrote David O. Selznick and his wife, Jennifer Jones, who had married only three days before in Genoa. Humphrey Bogart wrote to Buddy: "Will you please tell Mrs. Fogelson for me, that she could have done a great deal worse, and convey the wishes that she might find a greater happiness as Mrs. Fogelson than she did when she was married to Mr. Miniver." Aunt Evelyn said, "I'm so glad, darling, we wish you both every happiness. Love Eve and Clan Murray."

As she prepared for the trip back to Los Angeles and then on to London for *The Miniver Story*, Greer wrote a letter to Louella Parsons. "Buddy gave a delightful party for Nina, who has been visiting us at Forked Lightning Ranch. We had a Spanish orchestra and wonderful fun and music. Buddy is trying hard to arrange his affairs so he can go to Europe with me, but may not be able to come until ten days later. Nina also follows me there and will visit friends in Scotland before coming on to London. We hope to be back for a Merry Christmas in either California or Texas. I've taken to ranch life like a duck takes to water. I've switched from bustles and bows to Levis and boots, and I think it's definitely a change for the better. It's a great life and I hate to leave it even to renew acquaintances with dear Mrs. Miniver."

"When we first came to the ranch," Greer told reporters, "Buddy said, 'Don't fancy this place up, Rusty,' evidently afraid that I would bring Hollywood's glitter and glow. 'Don't worry,' I told him, 'I'll respect the local environmental harmonies.' The house was very plain and manly when I first saw it. Now, it's a little more Garson's style—nearly all white walls with brightly colored paintings and Indian rugs as accents." One of her first contributions was a British Union Jack, to be hoisted up the flagpole with the American and New Mexico state flags in the front yard each morning. "They have found their own personal Shangri-La," observed the *New Mexican*, "on a piñon-covered stretch of New Mexico high country, along the Pecos River. A Rolls Royce and a Lincoln Continental can be found parked behind the pink adobe main house, a big Spanish-type hacienda built around an inner garden filled with flowers and greenery. It is a place for entertaining as well as relaxing and enjoyment of living. Miss Garson is a non-stop talker (her husband claims he has been known as 'Silent Bud' since their marriage), but she peppers her conversation with wit, candor, and a gift for mimicry."

In mid-August Greer and Nina embarked on the Queen Mary for England. They unloaded their trunks at the Dorchester Hotel, where they were met by their old friend Douglas Fairbanks Jr. He escorted them along Shenley Road to the new MGM-British studio, Elstree, Borehamwood, where a presentation of a new breed of the Mrs. Miniver Rose and a cake inscribed "To the Lady of the Miniver Rose" awaited them. H.C. Potter, famed for *The Farmer's Daughter* and *Mr. Blanding Builds His Dream House,* was there to direct the movie. Walter Pidgeon, Henry Wilcoxon, and Reginald Owen, who would be reprising their respective roles as Clem Miniver, the vicar, and Belham's grocer, Mr. Foley, were also present. Only Sidney Franklin, who was too ill to travel to England, was absent. The studio facility was grander even than Denham, with ten soundstages, a vast backlot, twenty-seven cutting rooms, three preview theaters, still processing and printing services, a dubbing theater, one effects recording theater, a greenhouse, restaurants, a garage, and a water tank that rivaled the size of the Culver City lake on Lot Three. By the time Greer and Nina arrived, the excitement that had precipitated the grand opening had been dimmed by the lukewarm reception to the first MGM/Elstree efforts: *Edward, My Son*, with Spencer Tracy and Deborah Kerr, and *Conspirator*, with Robert Taylor and Elizabeth Taylor. Everyone hoped that the new *Miniver* picture would bring some prestige to the studio.

Sidney Franklin and Greer were excited about the possibilities of the production that they had intended, from its inception, to be more authentic than *Mrs. Miniver*. In numerous story sessions, Greer had taken an active role in creating the screenplay with Franklin, *Mrs. Miniver* screenwriter George Froeschel, and Ronald Millar. The story begins at the end of the war, as the Miniver family is brought together once more. Clem returns from construction work in Germany; Judy (Cathy O'Donnell) is back from Cairo, where she served as a WAAF; and Toby (James Fox) arrives home from the safety of the United States. Aware that recasting Richard Ney as Vincent Miniver in the film was out of the question, Greer suggested a lighthearted approach to disposing of the character. She told Franklin: "Well, we could have a scene in which Walter and I—he with his newspaper, I with my knitting—would be sitting at home one evening. I turn to him and say, 'Oh, by the way, I had a letter from Vinny today.' Walter looks at me absentmindedly, lights his pipe, and says, 'Who? Vinny?' 'Yes,' I reply. 'You remember Vinny, our son who went off to Hollywood and married Greer Garson.'" An early story synopsis, dated March 25, 1949, provides the ultimate fate of the character: "Five years ago the Minivers lost their eldest, Vin, an RAF pilot, in the Battle of Britain." After this reintroduction of the characters, the screenplay centers on Kay Miniver, who brings her family together with both happiness and apprehension in her heart. She harbors two secrets within her. First is her love for an American air force colonel (John Hodiak), who has been boarding with her and wants to return that affection. Discerning that theirs is merely a feeling of close companionship due to their mutual need for comfort during the horrors of war ("We have shared a lot of war together," he remarks), Kay sends the colonel back to his wife. The second secret is that she has been diagnosed with cancer and has only a year to live. But before she can reveal her secrets and can feel that she will leave behind a family that is safe and secure, she guides Judy through a dangerous infatuation with a married man (Leo Genn); reintroduces her daughter to Tom Foley (Richard Gale), the grocer's son who has always been in love with her; and helps Clem readjust to civilian life. Besides creating another warm and touching depiction of Kay and Clem Miniver ("We've had one of the rarest things in the world," Kay declares. "The perfect marriage."), the *Miniver Story* team attempted to correct the errors committed in the first film. After experiencing World War II firsthand, William Wyler had commented that *Mrs. Miniver* "only scratched the surface of war. I don't mean it was wrong. It was incomplete." Sidney Franklin strove for greater authenticity by making the movie on location and using more realistic sets and costumes, and he urged the screenwriters to introduce numerous examples of London's postwar privation and suffering into the Miniver household. He and Greer shared the belief that Mrs. Miniver should exemplify the experience the postwar English people, much as *Mrs. Miniver* had attempted to exemplify British solidarity and courage during the war. Greer knew about these experiences through her family in London and described them to Froeschel and Millar. "You've had quite a war, Mrs. Miniver," Clem observes in one scene, "and you're having quite a peace. Cooking, washing, scrubbing, standing in queues hunting for rations, finding the meals, reading the headlines and worrying about Judy . . . about Toby . . . about me. There are times, quite a number of times, when you feel so utterly and completely tired that you could sit down on the stairs and cry like a child." In another scene, Clem comments with amusement and exasperation upon the resourcefulness and deceit of English women: "You women are fantastic! It's the same thing every time. A foreigner comes to England having heard tales of our austerity and want, positively bursting with sympathy and understanding, and the minute he puts his foot in somebody's door what happens? You women start a conspiracy! You beg and you borrow and you scrape together a full-sized meal. Don't ask me how you do it or where it comes from. All I know is the poor, unsuspecting visitor staggers out of the house, his stomach bulging with four people's rations for a month, convinced we are all hypocrites and not half as bad off as we say we are. The tale spreads across the ocean. Highly delicate negotiations are compromised and the foreign policy of the country is seriously undermined—and it's all your fault!"

To inaugurate a festival celebrating Battle of Britain week, Greer and Walter Pidgeon made a visit to the men of the RAF on September 11. "From the stage of the Albert Hall, they looked out over a sea of faces belonging mainly to the men whose real life gallantry transformed their make-believe characters into figures of history," reported the *Daily Mail*. "Garson, her copper hair seemingly afire in the glare of the arc lights, spoke of the many Mrs. Minivers of the islands. She paid tribute to 'those beloved women who held the home front throughout the Battle of Britain and are still holding the home front in difficult conditions.' She gave thanks to every single man in the RAF and then altered that hastily 'to every man,' when the RAF saw the joke she had intended. Mr. and Mrs. Miniver retired from the stage in a storm of applause."

Reading some of her fan mail in her room at the Dorchester one evening, Greer was touched by a letter from a fifteen-year-old London school girl named Sheila Collings. Sheila never forgot their subsequent meeting: "I was an ardent fan and when I tremblingly approached her, bunch of pink roses in one hand and autograph book in the other, she turned and said, 'Are you little Sheila Collings who sent me that very sweet letter?'" It was the beginning of a forty-seven-year friendship. "She encouraged me in my desire to become an actress," Collings recalls, "and sent me, just for luck, when I was 16, the little, red Tyrolean jacket she had worn when she signed her first MGM contract in 1937." Greer's cousin, Commodore Robin Garson, who served on the HM submarine *Sea Wolf* during the war, remarked, "My own belief is that Greer, as she grew older, bitterly regretted having no children. She would have made a magnificent mother. It is entirely possible that when she first met young Sheila Collings it was the fact that she had no children of her own which drew them together. Their friendship was different and rare."

Meanwhile, *That Forsyte Woman* had opened in America. One critic from Texas sent his personal opinion of the film to Greer by Western Union: "I saw a picture tonight called *That Forsyte Woman.* The sympathy given to Irene has added a dramatic intensity that it lacked before. Lady playing leading role is the most gorgeous creature I ever saw. I am living in restless anticipation of meeting her again. It is difficult to visualize ever seeing a more fascinating girl. If I were a poet I would write about her the loftiest expressions and the most beautiful poetic tributes that man could give to woman. Good night, my darling. Buddy."

For Greer, the premiere of *That Forsyte Woman* in London on November 17 was the most rewarding one she had ever attended. Indeed, it was one of the proudest moments of her career, for the picture was to be honored as a Command Performance at the Odeon Cinema, Marble Arch, to benefit the Cinematograph Trade Benevolent Fund. Besides the king and queen, a great number of celebrities from British and American theater and motion pictures would be present. Her escort was Errol Flynn, who had arrived from location work in India for MGM's production of Rudyard Kipling's *Kim.* In a chauffeur-driven limousine, Greer recognized the city streets, packed with thousands of waving fans in the wintry dusk and sealed off from normal traffic for five hours, as those she had once trod as an ambitious but not very successful actress looking for work. The *London Times* reported: "After the white lights and the cheerful din outside, the waiting auditorium was decorously dim until their Majesties appeared, when floodlights in the proscenium wall suddenly illuminated the front of the balcony, the company rose and clapped, and the band played the National Anthem." The screening was followed by an elaborate live performance by a stellar array of MGM and British celebrities, including Jean Simmons, Richard Attenborough, Moira Lister, Sir Ralph Richardson, Jack Hulbert, Ann Sothern, George Murphy, Michael Wilding, Gregory Peck, and John Mills. Greer appeared with Walter Pidgeon in a comic version of *The Miniver Story.* "It was," the *London Times* observed, "an affair that delighted the audience, and would have seemed very heaven to the eager and fascinated throng outside. It was announced that some £30,000 had been raised for the trade charity."

Unfortunately *That Forsyte Woman* did not live up to the high expectations either in England or the United States, despite the beautifully realized, elegant visual style bestowed by Compton Bennett, Joseph Ruttenberg's superlative Technicolor camera work, and Bronislau Kaper's excellent musical score. Arguably this is the sort of film that, with all the lavish production values, a large cast, and an English flavor, would have been handled more sensitively by Sidney Franklin. As the *Times* remarked, "The answer must be as well as can be expected considering the variety of accents, the fact that few of the players bear any resemblance to the characters as Galsworthy's readers imagine them, and what appears to be deliberate willfulness in the casting. Miss Garson has a great deal to do as Irene, but somehow the graciousness and charm are lacking, and Mr. Pidgeon, as young Jolyon, has the ungrateful task of popping in and out and acting as a kind of commentator on the protracted proceedings. Tremendous trouble has been taken to get the details of the period right in costumes and furniture, and the film in general is frightened enough of the Forsytes to be solemn and conscientious to the point of extreme dullness. It has got all the adjectives right, so to speak, but the spirit of the phrases of which they are a part is missing." Errol Flynn delivered a powerful and underrated performance that managed to reveal the depths of Soames's desperate love for Irene and his despair at losing her, despite the thoroughly contemptible characterization imposed on him by the MGM screenwriters, who sought to sway the audience's affections completely toward Irene. Janet Leigh delivered a particularly fine performance as well, but Robert Young, who was too old and lacked the dashing and romantic spirit of Galsworthy's young Philip Bosinney, was miscast. His part would have been perfect for Flynn, whose screen chemistry with Greer was exemplary. As with Robert Donat, Laurence Olivier, and Ronald Colman, one wishes that Flynn could have been reteamed with Greer in another picture.

That Forsyte Woman grossed $3,697,000, but the enormous cost of the production resulted in a loss of $574,000. However, Dore Schary was optimistic about the movie's fate. After two films in which Greer did not seem to belong, her performance in *That Forsyte Woman* and the film itself were successful enough to put her back on the road to recovery at MGM as the studio's most esteemed dramatic actress. She and Walter Pidgeon were invited to reprise their roles in a *Lux Radio Theatre* version of the film on November 5, 1951. In the studio's sudden new flurry of interest in Greer Garson, a number of promising screen properties were considered for her. Among them was *The Chimes of Bruges*, a story in which Greer would play the dual role of a dignified beauty and an English actress of the music hall variety, to be filmed on location in Brussels and Bruges. Because of her hectic schedule, Greer had to turn down Frank Capra's offer to play the wife of Spencer Tracy in *State of the Union*. She also had to turn down Sidney Franklin, who was still attempting to get *Young Bess* and *American Cavalcade* off the ground. Other considerations included *Madame Bovary* and *Mogambo*, with Clark Gable. There was also a comedy called *The Saintly Miss Peters*, a tale about a schoolteacher who is sent to a state capital to lobby for a teachers' bill only to become involved with a motley crew of politicians and gangsters.

Buddy arrived in London in time for a weekend visit to the Murrays. "Buddy Fogelson was a fine man," recalled Sophia, "with a rich sense of humour. He is the only person I know who called Greer 'Rusty' with impunity." Her brother Greer, who had joined Sophia in the family's general practice, took the Fogelsons on a fishing trip on his wife's old cutter and showed Buddy Culyean Castle where the National Trust for Scotland had given General Eisenhower, Buddy's favorite golf partner and Palm Springs neighbor, a flat. Greer showed him Rob Roy's gravesite, but Buddy was most intrigued to see cattle grazing peacefully about—without fear of New Mexican coyotes! He asked Greer if he was now a member of the clan—or would he have to start his own? "Perhaps the MacFogelsons?" he asked.

Since the shooting schedule for *The Miniver Story* would keep her in England for the Christmas holidays, Greer hoped that Buddy would be able to join her. It seemed that the plan would work until December 11, when the frightening news came to her that Buddy had suffered a heart attack in New York. She called an emergency meeting with Hank Potter. "I feel responsible," she told him. "He worked so hard to be able to join me in London to spend Christmas with me. Nothing to me is as important as Buddy—my career or anything else." He agreed to delay shooting, and despite her fear of flying and studio protestations, she flew to New York and stayed with her recuperating husband for a week at Presbyterian Hospital. On December 14, the *Star* reported, "Mrs. Miniver, Greer Garson, made a dramatic air dash in fog to America to look after her sick husband. She has been given a room at the hospital. Hospital officials say he needs a long rest and will be there another week. Schedules have been reshuffled in order to shoot scenes in which she does not appear."

Greer returned to Borehamwood and spent Christmas Eve with her old mentor, George Bernard Shaw. Answering the doorbell, Shaw found an untidy redhead struggling with a giant fir tree. When he asked if she had brought lights for it, she felt like the amateur actress again under his gaze and apologized that she did not. At supper, he brought up her resemblance to Ellen Terry and asked if she had ever seen his play *Captain Brassbound's Conversion*. No, she had not. He admitted that, although he had written it for Miss Terry, she had never liked the heroine, Lady Cicely Waynflete, and he suggested that Greer should play it. "That's a part for a blonde," she teased. "Write me a play for a redhead." Shaw agreed to think it over. "I may not be a very good playwright," he said, "but I'm an excellent ladies' tailor."

In early January, Greer fell ill with a dangerous, but familiar, trio of illnesses: bronchitis, laryngitis, and flu. Hedda Hopper, in her column of January 17, wrote: "Greer Garson's *Miniver* picture being made in England has had nothing but bad luck. First Sidney Franklin, the producer, became ill. Greer flew to New York when Buddy

Fogelson was taken ill. On her return, she came down with laryngitis. Another director may be sent over to finish the picture because Hank Potter has almost used up his 180-day allotment from the British government. If he runs over, he'll have to pay two income taxes."

Since Christmas, Sidney Franklin had been sending urgent telegrams to Borehamwood, unhappy with the rushes he was receiving in Culver City. When he received a cable from Ben Goetz on January 18 with the message, "From our experience doubt whether Potter will meet our schedule," he sent his old friend Victor Saville as a replacement to London. Hearing of this, Greer cabled back on the twenty-sixth, "Distressed to hear from Ben your contemplated move. Nothing personal against anyone but we are happy with Hank Potter and much prefer finishing at least important scenes with him. A change now very hurtful to him and risks difference in texture of picture due different personality and taste. Also different handling and atmosphere on set. We are working hard. Please let us continue as is!"

But it was too late. Almost immediately, Saville and Greer clashed. The "pill scene" involved a typical confrontation. In a key bedroom sequence, Mrs. Miniver collapses in pain and dizziness due to her illness. Both Sidney Franklin and Victor Saville felt the scene, as Potter had directed it, was too dramatic. Saville insisted upon a retake. Greer refused. She liked it as it was. The argument went on for nearly a month. Finally, Saville cabled Sidney Franklin. On February 16, Franklin's response came back:

Dear Greer,
Sorry you are not in accord with retake. However would
appreciate your doing it the way I now think it should
be done. This way we have choice. Present attack of
pain so severe and crawling to couch so agonizing I am
most fearful. Once an audience gets an impression like
this scene gives it is almost impossible to get out of
their mind and could hurt most seriously the balance of
the picture as they would be expecting another attack
almost any moment and would not be paying attention
to the episodes as they unfold. Another point against
the severity of the attack is that I believe the doctor

scene which follows is dangerously hurt and this would be a real tragedy as it is so beautiful. I most earnestly hope you will bear with us. I know it has not been easy being away so long and alone. I just saw the scene on the staircase between you and Clem at the end of the picture which was beautiful and many other rushes. Generally speaking, I feel this will be one of your finest portrayals.

Although the scene was reshot on February 17, 1950, the last day of production, Potter's version was eventually selected for the final print. Aware of the difficulties of shooting, Franklin sent a final telegram to Saville. "Victor, I can not tell you how much I appreciate your helping us out on the picture and your cooperation in every respect. I can only say your attitude has been a fine thing and I want you to know I am deeply appreciative beyond words."

"*The Miniver Story* is finished and in the can," wrote an English correspondent for the *Hollywood Reporter* on March 6, 1950, "and the beautiful Mrs. Miniver has packed her grubs and departed these shores. Typical of the affection in which she was held by all the studio was a scene in which she had to wander about in a thin nightie before hopping into a bed on the set. The day was cold and she was shivering. When she eventually got between the sheets, she had found the boys had put a very welcome hot water bottle in the bed and attached to it was a tag that said, 'Our love will keep your warm, From the gang.' What struck me most about Greer Garson was her intense belief in the policy of interchange between American and English artists and technicians. She believes it would help a lot to get both our industries out of the current critical conditions more than it would aid in simmering Anglo-American good relations, and I think she is right."

As Greer sailed from Southampton, an item in the *Star* surprised all but her closest friends. "Presents taken by Greer Garson, who is on her way home on the Queen Mary, include some old china for her mother, some clothing material for a suit and silk for summer dresses for herself, and seven shorthorn heifers and a bull she bought for husband Buddy Fogelson's new ranch." She informed the *Shorthorn World*, official journal of the American Shorthorn Breeders

Association, of her plan to "carry out a long cherished wish to possess white shorthorns, a breed I have so much admired when motoring in England and through the pages of British papers. I phoned my husband in America and received his approval to go ahead. He presented me with a section of the ranch that I've named El Rancho Blanco! I considered a white hippopotamus—but my husband wired a firm 'no.' We were offered a white donkey and other white animals from people all over England. If I'd accepted all the offers I'd have come back like Mrs. Noah."

Greer had traveled up to the cattle show and sale in Perth, Scotland, to purchase the herd. Frank W. Harding, a Chicago importer of pedigreed stock, chose for her the six best purebred white shorthorn heifers and a bull named Philorth, White Knight, for the Forked Lightning Ranch. Although many were stumped by Mrs. Miniver's interest in cattle raising, those who remembered Eileen Evelyn Greer Garson understood. The New Mexican ranch life recalled Greer's happy days on her grandparents' farm in Ulster and provided the means to realize a cherished dream. The little girl who had enjoyed the Castlewellan county fairs was now a woman who happily dubbed herself "the darling of the Southwest fair circuit."

She had plenty of time to spend with her husband and her new purchases at the Forked Lightning Ranch because she asked L.B. Mayer for a six-month leave of absence without pay. It was a decision that was meant to express her disappointment in the studio's treatment of her. All the promising, elaborate projects that Mayer and Schary had offered her (*American Cavalcade, Europa and the Bull, The Saintly Miss Peters*) were collapsing as the studio rechanneled its resources into expensive but enormously successful musicals such as *On the Town, Show Boat,* and *An American in Paris.*

Among those who saw an early American preview of *The Miniver Story* was Lillian Burns. On June 7, 1950, she sent a note to Greer: "Congratulations Greer Garson, and I am going to presume, upon our old, and to me, very dear friendship to say welcome back the Great Greer Garson. I think your performance is as beautiful as I've ever seen you do anything and more beautiful than I have ever seen you do in a long time. Something so real is back in you that never for one instant did I feel any sense of death in the picture. You looked exquisite and if I had chosen which scene I liked the best and in which

I thought you were the greatest, I would find it difficult because in every scene I find something so superbly done that I look forward to seeing it again. Also, I thought Walter was wonderful. With deep affection and a great thank you for a wonderful Greer giving a wonderful performance. Always, Lillian."

The Miniver Story, at a final cost of $3,660,000, opened at the Empire in London on August 27, 1950. "Mrs. Miniver and her lot are set two problems," Punch explained, "to settle her husband's unrest with post-war Britain and to ensure that her daughter marries the former grocer's boy instead of a glamourous general. She achieves the first by shifting Mr. Miniver's office furniture into another room with a nicer view, and the second by confessing to the brass-hatted Steve that her family knows nothing about art, represented to her by Greggs, a minor concerto. She then dies off, ensuring that there will be no further sequels, for which on a whole we may be grateful."

Before traveling eastward to the New York premiere of the film, which Greer hoped would be received better than in London, the Fogelsons threw an enormous party at the Forked Lightning Ranch to celebrate Greer's return. The Santa Fe New Mexican called it an event "to be remembered. . . . A magnificent buffet had been set up decorated with ice carvings and flowers and loaded with a rich assortment of foods. Everything from stuffed lobsters to filet mignon was on the menu . . . prepared by the Fogelsons' chef. Almost the entire dining room staff at La Fonda had been moved to the ranch to serve the guests as well as the bartenders and orchestra. La Fonda orchestra played for dancing throughout the evening concluding with the popular Raspa and Varsoviana in which the Fogelsons were among star performers."

"Remember the Minivers!" proclaimed the MGM ads as the eleventh Greer Garson picture opened at Radio City Music Hall, on October 26, 1950. As Lillian Burns had enthused, Greer and Walter Pidgeon were back on track, registering another portrayal of the Minivers that is as poignant as their first attempt. The performances of Henry Wilcoxon, Reginald Owen, and Cathy O'Donnell and Richard Gale, who play the young lovers Judy Miniver and Tom Foley, were also excellent. "This picture . . . has been given a magnificent production, such as you will always see in any MGM picture," remarked the Hollywood Reporter, "but the story is a bit too sad, the ending too tragic, to be credited as superb creation and writing, and lacks the entertainment expected of this sequel. Greer Garson, as Mrs. Miniver, contributes a magnificent performance and lifts the picture's interest to a great degree." "Personally," the *Los Angeles Herald-Examiner* offered, "as with any friend (and thanks to author Jan Struther and actress Greer Garson, millions of movie-goers regarded Mrs. Miniver as just that!) I would have preferred to think of her as a warm, vibrant woman, still fighting today's battles than be faced with the unhappy finality of her death." Bosley Crowther added, "We can well understand why Jan Struther, who originally brought the lady forth, called up yesterday to mention simply that she had nothing to do with the writing of this film."

Jan Struther was so upset at MGM's cavalier treatment of her heroine that she refused to see the film, and she successfully sued the studio for terminating her beloved character. Audiences seemed to agree with her, and *The Miniver Story* lost $2,311,000 for Metro-Goldwyn-Mayer. The following year Struther was diagnosed with cancer and died in 1953 in New York's Presbyterian Hospital at the age of fifty-two.

Greer's disappointment with *The Miniver Story*'s outcome was dispelled in November 1950 when she attended the New Mexico State Fair. Her white shorthorns won nine blue ribbons and four out of five leading awards in the Beef Shorthorn classes. "I called William Tuttle at MGM," she told the *Los Angeles Times*, "and asked him 'What was that stuff you used on the blondes? Would you send me a 20-gallon drum of it railway express for my cows?' Then I painted their pails white with the Forked Lightning blue flash, made them blue show blankets piped in white and sent to Belgium for a set of bells—the eight notes of the octave. It was a beautiful sight and sound." Whatever the state of her acting career, *Shorthorn World* declared that "Greer Garson, MGM film star, is on her way to becoming the owner of one of the country's outstanding cattle ranches."

CHAPTER 20

ON AUGUST 23, 1950, *VARIETY* REPORTED: "Under Dore Schary's regime at the Metro studio, the day of the long-term contract for most producers, directors and scripters is in the twilight. Schary has already slashed the studio's overhead substantially by his policy of a strictly limited number of longterm pacts. In many cases, same policy applies to thespers as well as the production execs and technicians." By the end of the year, Schary allowed a number of MGM's brightest talents to depart the studio. Among them were Judy Garland, Ethel Barrymore, Frank Sinatra, Ann Sothern, Lena Horne, Angela Lansbury, Mary Astor, Edward Arnold, and Edmund Gwenn.

Greer, who celebrated her forty-sixth birthday upon her return to MGM in September, remained a valued asset in Culver City. But the choicest roles were being played by the studio's new generation of stars. Among them was Deborah Kerr, who drew praise in the box-office event of the year, *King Solomon's Mines*. In fact, Deborah had performed exceptionally well in *The Hucksters*, *If Winter Comes*, and *Edward, My Son*, which were originally intended for Greer. Born in Helensburg, Scotland, on September 30, 1921, but raised in Glasgow, the redheaded actress found herself molded in Greer's image. "All I had to do was to be high-minded, long-suffering, white-gloved and decorative," she recalled. The press, aware of the striking resemblances between the two actresses, attempted to create a rivalry between them. "The idea of a feud between us was pure poppycock," Deborah replied, "or rather, gossip writers' fabrication—the stuff that dreams were made of. Greer was going great guns all through the time of my contract at Metro, and our friendship has lasted from that time to the present day." Greer's response to all the fuss was: "We had a lot of fun out of it, Deborah and I. I think I invited her over once for arsenic sandwiches."

But the fact that her status at the studio was slipping was no laughing matter. Suddenly, Greer could appreciate what it had been like to be Greta Garbo when Mayer brought in rival Luise Rainer, and what Joan Crawford and Norma Shearer had experienced when she herself had arrived at MGM. Now she was the one who was waging the battles with the administrators in the Thalberg Building to play a wider array of roles. "On the London stage I often played a very flighty baggage," she said. "I even shot a husband now and then. But here the studio goes into an acute palsy if I even suggest a hoydenish gesture!" "The way people feel about you," Helen Hayes once told her, "it would be like Santa Claus taking off his beard before small children." The *Hollywood Citizen-News* remarked, "It is strange that in recent years Hollywood has had so little to offer Greer Garson. Her special qualities of womanliness and gentility . . . have reached an impasse insofar as good scripts are concerned. Certainly her abilities have been wasted recently on a series of saccharine stories." Among the barrage of story ideas that Greer sent to the College of Cardinals in a continuing effort to broaden her scope at the studio were Shakespeare's *As You Like It, The Rivals, She Stoops to Conquer,* and *Cyrano de Bergerac.*

But looking after Greer Garson's career had become less important to MGM by 1950. There were too many other problems. No one could ignore the fact that the studio's Oscar count had dwindled to only eight between 1945 and 1948; and in 1947, for the first time since the studio's inception, no MGM picture received a Best Picture nomination. The College of Cardinals had become profligate from years of incredible success. Too much money was being spent on too many executives and too few pictures. By 1947, the studio faced a deficit of $6.5 million and ranked fourth in profitability among the Hollywood studios. Dore Schary was clashing with L.B. Mayer regularly. Apart from ideological and political differences, their tastes in motion pictures were radically different. The downward slide of Metro-Goldwyn-Mayer had begun. And with it went Greer Garson's film career.

Greer's personal life was receiving more attention in the newspapers. On April 11, 1951, it was reported that she had received her final American citizenship papers in federal court in Abilene, Texas.

"I feel a deep and proud affinity with this country," she said, "which has given me so much that is fine materially and, even more treasured, spiritually." While Greer's career seemed uncertain, MGM celebrated her past by rereleasing *Blossoms in the Dust*. During the successful 1950 run, studio publicists reported that, in honor of the nearly ten thousand babies Mrs. Gladney had helped place in homes, the Texas Children's Home and Aid Society had become the Edna Gladney Home. In 1980, the *Fort Worth News-Tribune* noted: "In 1941 when Metro-Goldwyn-Mayer released the movie, *Blossoms in the Dust*, Edna Gladney became a household word. The motion picture based on Mrs. Gladney's life and her fight to protect children turned the Fort Worth woman into a legend. Unlike many films which quickly run their course, *Blossoms* has continued to be shown somewhere in the world every few weeks." Among those who had been inspired by the film was Joe Hawn of the House of Representatives of Dallas County. "Please permit me this opportunity to thank you for playing the role of Mrs. Edna Gladney in *Blossoms in the Dust*," he wrote to Greer. "I saw the picture many times both on the screen and on television, because the story was very close to my heart. I was a ward of the Gladney Home until adopted at the age of five, and was then raised in Sherman and had close association with Mr. Sam Gladney's Gladiola Mill on Lamar Street. So, you can see that I had close interest in both your role and that of Walter Pidgeon."

Producer Edwin Knopf thought he had the answer to Greer's dilemma. He was preparing just the kind of British drawing-room comedy that she adored. It was the story of a London servant, Jane Hoskins, who meets the charming but disreputable Nigel Duxbury. "You speak like Gladstone and look like Helen of Troy," he tells her. "Very surprising." "You look like a duke and act like the Artful Dodger," she replies. "Equally surprising." Under his influence, Jane embarks on a glamorous career as Lady Loverly and assists Nigel in cheating the wealthy out of their money at gambling casinos across Europe. Fleeing their infamous reputation, the couple land in San Francisco, where they attempt to steal the fabulous jewels of an eccentric multimillionairess, Mrs. Wortin. Although Lady Loverly is surrounded by numerous suitors, she falls for her charming accomplice on the eve of their greatest caper. It no longer matters when they are caught and must return to England to serve a jail term for their crimes, for they are in love. Knopf sent a screenplay treatment of *The Law and the Lady* to Greer for Christmas. He was right. Mrs. Fogelson was thrilled to accept the chance to appear once again in her favorite genre, and as an unscrupulous woman for a change. She developed a particular affinity for Jane Hoskins when she read of the character's ambitious plans, which she was amused to discover echoed her own early dreams. "All my life I've watched other people enjoying luxuries," Jane declares. "Now, I'm going to enjoy them. I shall be waited on, and served and catered to." "And where will you manage all this on two hundred pounds?" asks Nigel. "I shall emigrate to America! I have a cousin in a little village there called Brooklyn."

The production was scheduled to begin shooting January 29, 1951. Like *When Ladies Meet, The Law and the Lady* was a remake of an earlier Metro-Goldwyn-Mayer film. In fact, the 1925 Broadway stage hit, known as *The Last of Mrs. Cheyney,* had been made twice. It has served as an early talkie for Norma Shearer in 1929 and as an elegant showcase for Joan Crawford in 1937. Throughout the 1950s, as MGM sought to regain its former status by recycling its earlier hits, *The Law and the Lady* was one of many films, including *The Merry Widow, Scaramouche, Rose Marie, Kismet, The Student Prince,* and *Ben-Hur,* that were recast and refilmed within the decade. Walter Plunkett flew out to Texas for, in his own words, "one of the most peculiar costume design sessions in the history of Hollywood. All the discussions took place in a trailer, for Greer was with her husband, who was supervising the opening of a new oil well. Frequently there would be laborers coming in and out with dirty clothes and dirty boots. And in the midst of all that commotion was Greer Garson, chatting and joking, preparing coffee and sandwiches for the guys, doing dishwasher duty, and talking about movie costumes. It was unreal!"

For the role of Lady Loverly's dashing accomplice and mentor, played by George Barraud and William Powell in the earlier versions, Edwin Knopf cast Michael Wilding. One of the most popular actors in England and under personal contract to producer Herbert Wilcox and his wife, actress Anna Neagle, Wilding was ready to expand his reputation in America. On November 29, 1950, Knopf and Wilcox worked out an intricate arrangement that gave Wilding script approval on the proposed *Law and the Lady* project and eighteen thousand pounds for the thirteen-week production schedule. It seemed to be a profitable arrangement on both sides. MGM gained another noted British performer, and Michael Wilding was introduced to Holly-wood.

Among the supporting players in *The Law and the Lady* were Fernando Lamas and veteran character actress Marjorie Main, of Ma and Pa Kettle fame. Lamas, who had signed with Metro in July 1949, would be making his American film debut as a hot-blooded Califor-nia landowner, Juan Dinas, who falls for Lady Loverly. From the first day of filming, Marjorie Main kept everyone in a good humor. When Michael Wilding came to the set, having memorized the entire script instead of following the Hollywood tradition of studying only a day's work in advance, the crew was surprised when he asked, "What's the scene this morning?" Miss Main was the first to reply, patting him on the back, and confiding: "I never read the script either, Michael. It would spoil the preview for me."

For Greer, *The Law and the Lady* offered the opportunity to show off her horsemanship skills. The outdoor scenes were filmed outside Los Angeles at the Fontana Hog Farm in the grassy outskirts of California State Polytechnic College. In February Greer took a break from shooting to attend the thirty-seventh annual Cattle Grow-ers Association Convention in Albuquerque, New Mexico, as a guest speaker. It was the first time that a woman had been chosen to speak. "The best part of this life is the people," she said. "The cattle frater-nity is a fine breed. There is a common bond among them no matter what part of the world they are in. It seems to me that this might be a new basis for international understanding. As you know, I'm par-ticularly fond of one cattleman in particular. He's a great guy." Prin-cipal photography of *The Law and the Lady* concluded in little over a month, on March 3, 1951, at a cost of $1,194,000.

As preparations for a premiere in the summer unfolded, Metro-Goldwyn-Mayer was shaken to its very foundations. On June 23, 1951, the *Los Angeles Times* reported that L.B. Mayer had officially resigned from Metro-Goldwyn-Mayer. While shock and disbelief re-verberated about Hollywood, those left in command at the Culver City studio knew the action had been inevitable. The *Hollywood Reporter* remarked, "For nearly three years Hollywood has watched with consistent interest what, at least in the public view, appeared to be a struggle of power over the town's richest film studio between a rising young man and an entrenched old man." That struggle reached a climax when Mayer called up Nicholas Schenck in New York and delivered an ultimatum. Either Schary must go or he would. For Schenck, whose relationship with Mayer had ceaselessly crumbled since he took control of Loews as president in 1927, it was not a hard decision to make. Besides personal antagonisms, Schenck believed that Mayer's managerial tactics had lately become both old-fashioned and unprofitable. It was Dore Schary who was producing the box-office winners and prestige pictures now. On July 16, 1951, Schary was named successor as head of production and studio operations of Metro-Goldwyn-Mayer Studios. The appointment was announced by Schenck following a weekend executive conference at the Ambassador Hotel in Chicago. The power of the College of Cardinals was smashed. Instead, a smaller executive board consisting of Eddie Mannix, Benjamin Thau, and Louis K. Sidney was formed.

Greer's career seemed, at least temporarily, unaffected by the changing of the guard. *The Law and the Lady* premiered on schedule at the Capitol Theater in New York on August 15, 1951. The studio's publicity slogan for the film was "Remember her in *Julia Misbehaves?* Gorgeous Greer is misbehaving again! MGM laughingly presents *The Law and the Lady.*" Unfortunately it proved to be a disappointment for the studio when it only grossed $1,360,000, dipping $395,000 into the red. The *Hollywood Reporter* commented, "*The Law and the Lady* is, indeed, 'the last of Mrs. Cheyney.' The Frederick Lonsdale jewel thief heroine who served long and well in the theatrical capitals of the world, across the country in stock, and on the screen, comes a cropper, on the California Gold Coast, an ignominious fate for a lady who never dreamed there was land West of the Hudson. This curious transcription of 'The Last of Mrs. Cheyney' is typical of 'new adaptations' in that producer and writers blatantly ignore the qualities that made the original successful." *The Law and the Lady* is definitely a curiosity in the screen career of Greer Garson and is, at its best, a light, witty masquerade ball with numerous MGM players disguised in costumes but unable to give their screen characterizations the ring of truth. Greer appears in a beautiful array of gowns, but the black wig that she chose to wear for this film invites an unfortunate comparison with Susie Parkington. She is equally miscast in this film.

The plot for *The Law and the Lady* calls for a Jane Hoskins that is an unscrupulous, common woman who is not a lady but tries, without success, to be one. Although Greer is endearing in the part and tosses off the witty lines supplied by the screenwriters with maximum effect, it is apparent to any moviegoer that she is very much a lady from the first scene. Although Greer had enjoyed making the picture, Michael Wilding thought it was a "lousy movie. Greer tried to inject some humour into her role by attempting a Cockney accent. I saw the film again recently and the only funny thing about it, apart from my own lamentable performance, was Greer's concept of Cockney speech." *The Law and the Lady* is decidedly a film with flaws, but Greer and Milding Wilding, two professionals with a mastery for English wit, nevertheless make a delightful pair.

In January 1952 Dore Schary tried to revive the Greer Garson/ Walter Pidgeon box-office magic in a picture called *Scandal at Scourie,* based on a *Good Housekeeping* magazine story, "Good Boy" by Mary McSherry. He hoped the turn-of-the-century story of a Protestant couple who are criticized in their community for adopting a Catholic orphan would be as successful as his previous hits, *Crossfire* and *Intruder in the Dust,* which also dealt with religious intolerance and small-town racial bigotry. Schary had built his career at MGM with such socially conscious films, beginning as a writer in 1938 on *Boys Town,* which dealt with child welfare issues. He chose Jean Negulesco, the accomplished director of *Humoresque, Johnny Belinda,* and *How to Marry a Millionaire,* for the film. Child star Donna Corcoran was cast as the young orphan, Patsy.

"I hope this one proves to be a better story for Greer than *The Law and the Lady,*" Louella Parsons remarked in her column. "But perhaps that one wasn't entirely the studio's fault; I had the feeling when Greer was acting in it, that she was more interested in her happy marriage to Buddy Fogelson and in raising thoroughbred cattle than she was in the camera. With her old sidekick back with her, I expect Greer really will be her old self again."

March 20, 1952, marked the twenty-fourth Annual Academy Award ceremony. Greer was invited to participate as presenter of the Best Actor award. She was also notified that she might have to perform double duty. Vivien Leigh, nominated for her role as Blanche DuBois in *A Streetcar Named Desire,* was in the midst of *Antony and*

Cleopatra on Broadway in New York. The Oliviers requested that
Greer appear just in case. Escorted by Buddy, she appeared in a
stunning strapless pale-green gown with velvet overskirt over full
pleated taffeta. Around her throat she wore a fine chain of dia-
monds matched by diamond earrings, which were recent gifts from
her husband. Earl Wilson commented, "I've never been a guy to
bring my wife home a present, but after seeing the success of the
Greer Garson-Buddy Fogelson marriage, maybe I'll become a con-
vert. Just so the practice won't be taken too seriously, they refer to
presents as 'prezzies' and pretend to be surprised when they get any,
which seems to be constantly."

Shortly after handing the Oscar over to Humphrey Bogart for
The African Queen, Greer returned onstage when Ronald Colman
announced that Vivien had indeed won Best Actress honors. Grasping the golden statue, a memory flashed through her mind. "Well, this
is hardly the time to expand verbally," she told the audience with a
knowing smile. "We've been told to keep to a strict timetable. But if
anyone wants some extra material, I can let them have some five-and-
a-half minutes out of a speech I made on a similar occasion several
years ago, as you may remember." She received a warm standing
ovation.

Afterward, columnist Sheilah Graham observed the usual backstage commotion: "The lineup for the photogs looked like it happened a long time ago with Bette Davis, Greer Garson, and Ronald
Colman waving Oscars they hadn't won." When asked how she had
finally been able to joke about the speech that had caused her such
humiliation over the years, Greer answered, "It's the Fogelson influence. Now, I take everything in my stride . . . and enjoy it all!" After
dining with the Colmans that evening, Greer penned a telegram to
Leigh: "Congratulations, Vivien dear, on another bright jewel in your
crown. Much love to you both, Greer."

In late April, she joined such Hollywood personalities as Audrey
Totter, Victor Jory, Don Taylor, Sam Marx, and Archie Mayo on an
exhaustive thirty-two-city train excursion known as The Movietime
U.S.A. Tour. It was the Tour's cochairman, Harry Lamont, who convinced the gathering to join in the cross-country promotion of movies in an era when audiences were being lured away from theaters by
television. The facts were startling to Hollywood's moguls. At the

height of Greer's career in 1945, there had been more than 20,457 U.S. movie theaters, playing 350 movies, with a weekly attendance of 90 million. But by the mid-1950s the number of theaters had fallen dramatically to 19,200, with only 46 million attending 254 films. Buddy joined Greer on the trip, and she enjoyed it immensely. In New York she crowned the queen of the annual Cherry Blossom Festival in Brooklyn's Botanical Gardens and joined Buddy in seeing the latest plays. They met playwright Moss Hart, who revived Greer's old dream to appear on Broadway by remarking that he would write a play for her—if she could tear herself away from her servants and swimming pools in Hollywood. But with a busy film career—including a starting date of July 14 for *Scandal at Scourie*—her wish seemed unlikely.

When the Fogelsons returned to Los Angeles on June 3, the Pidgeons invited them to dinner. Over the borscht, filet of beef, and cheesecake tarts they discussed *Scandal at Scourie*. MGM was already promoting the film as "the hilarious story of a red-headed woman whose husband knew what he wanted—when she told him!" Greer was intrigued with the chance to play another Irishwoman, Victoria McChesney, who shared many of her own characteristics. Raised in Ulster, Victoria was also childless; and the film's best, and most poignant, moments stem from the character's desire to finally have a family. Greer also displayed a delightful, rare flash of redheaded temper in the film when Victoria vehemently slaps a towel at a man in a barber shop who criticizes her adoption of a Catholic child. "It's the Irish in me," she admits, "North Irish!" "I believe that *Scandal at Scourie* will appeal as a human story," she said, "and that it has novelty." As for Walter Pidgeon, he told reporters, "Greer and I have worked well from the first. She's a fine, professional actress—and a hell of a woman. I've done eight pictures with that gal and we never had a bad word between us. I went with her through her romances and her marriages. A great lady, I think."

With a budget of $1,148,000, Jean Negulesco directed the entire film cheaply on Lot Three, making the best of the surrounding greenery, the lake, and the western town left over from *Mrs. Parkington*. *Scourie* screenwriter Norman Corwin placed a note among the good wishes and flowers Greer received during production: "A rose is a rose is a rose and Greer is Greer is Greer and they are both things of beauty and a joy forever. I am happy and honored that the fortunes of McChesney will be carried on your shapely and superbly capable shoulders." The final sequence, in which she tackles a young runaway in the mud, received as much publicity as her long-ago watery plunge in *Remember?* The *Hollywood Citizen-News* reported, "Greer Garson, who has to tackle a small boy in the mud for MGM's *Scandal at Scourie,* says she's been sliding in the mud so much, she's being scouted by the Los Angeles Rams." Indeed, she proudly produced a letter signed by Tommy Prothro, the head coach: "We have been on a nationwide search for a head cheerleader for our football team. We have finally found one. Please get in shape for the season. We are training at Long Beach State College. . . . Would you be interested in rooming with the football team?"

Scandal at Scourie* finished up in a little over a month, on August 21. Walter Pidgeon performed his scenes in only four days. "I couldn't have had any leading man I would have liked better," Greer said. "He represented the kind of strong, yet gentle, warm, kind man that every woman thinks will make a wonderful husband." On that last day, Jean Negulesco wrote to Greer: "I know now why the people at your studio consider you the lady queen of MGM. Thank you, Vicki. Words cannot say the humble joy of being part of *Scourie,* and working with you. It was like getting the jackpot in every scene."

After numerous delays and reediting, *Scandal at Scourie* was screened for the press at the Egyptian Theater on April 16, 1953. Once again, the Garson/Pidgeon magic illuminated the picture. There is humor in the sequences in which Walter Pidgeon's character adapts to becoming a parent. "We continue to be good Protestants, and we bring up Patsy to be a good Catholic. Now what could be simpler?" Vicki McChesney asks. "Off hand, almost anything," is Mr. McChesney's reply. Discovering Nova Scotia salmon on the table one evening, he declares, "One of the first things that brought us together, Mrs. McChesney, was our mutual opinion that fish was a dish fit only for cats. Just why is there fish on this table?" Vicki replies that it is because little Patsy cannot eat meat on Fridays and assures her husband that it is the only dietary measure they will have to follow. "Except for the days when we don't eat anything at all," adds Patsy cheerfully. There are also effective sentimental moments. Discussing the fact that Patsy could fill a void in their childless lives, McChesney says to his wife, "It's been lonely for you, hasn't it? All right, we'll try it. But I must tell you frankly I'm not very hopeful. And above all else, I don't want it to break your heart if it doesn't work out." As she embraces him, it is obvious that both are aware that there is no going back. But despite such moments as these and the beautiful Technicolor photography by Robert Planck, *Scandal at Scourie* suffered the same fate as *The Law and the Lady*. Not even Metro's most famous dramatic team could hold together the simple-minded script and the inferior production values that the studio imposed upon them. "Like other Garson-Pidgeon pictures in which idealistic thoughts have been encouraged, this one is heavily injected with romantic attitudes and pretenses," criticized Bosley Crowther. "Miss Garson's infallible rightness is magnificent and unreal; Mr. Pidgeon's gentlemanly caution is as trim as the smoking jacket he wears." Critics found the film to be a pale copy of past Garson/Pidgeon efforts and considered the title completely misleading for such a mild family picture. Dore Schary could have explained that the title was supposed to reflect a volatile tale of small-town prejudice that had unfortunately been submerged in sentiment, but he was disappointed that the film posted a loss of $333,000 and didn't bother.

It was obvious that Dore Schary's MGM was growing less interested in its former Queen when *Scandal at Scourie* did not open at Radio City Music Hall as every previous Garson/Pidgeon film had. The legendary days when Greer Garson and Walter Pidgeon ruled Hollywood were over. Instead of glowing reviews and lavish premieres, critics paid little heed to the film, which opened quietly at the Little Carnegie Theater on June 12, 1953. It was the last time the famous couple would ever act together, and ironically it was in a film about orphans that harked back to their first pairing in *Blossoms in the Dust*. Their disappointment in the movie was shared by many other actors on the lot. In the mid-1950s, as the studio's fortunes continued to spiral downward, Clark Gable, Lana Turner, June Allyson, Esther Williams, and Elizabeth Taylor suffered through films like *Never Let Me Go*, *Flame and the Flesh*, *Battle Circus*, *Neptune's Daughter*, and *The Girl Who Had Everything*.

Buddy Fogelson was not happy with MGM's treatment of his wife and urged her to quit Hollywood for good. Immediately gossip columnists began to hint that the Fogelson marriage was in trouble.

In January 1953 Mike Connolly of *Photoplay* wrote: "It was rumored around these Hollywood hills that Greer and Buddy Fogelson weren't seeing eye to eye on Greer's career. It was said that Buddy didn't approve of his wife's making movies—that he wanted her to be plainly and simply Mrs. Buddy Fogelson. It was also whispered about that Greer's present strong upsurge in popularity at MGM would soon bring an open marital rift."

The "strong upsurge in popularity" of which Connolly spoke, referring to the still-busy schedule of films that Dore Schary was preparing for Greer, was the subject of discussion at an interview he conducted in the rose garden of 680 Stone Canyon. Dismissing the rumors with a wave of her hand, Greer handed him a cup of tea. "It's so untrue!" she insisted. "It's not that Buddy doesn't approve of my making pictures, it's just that he doesn't want me to make dull pictures! Buddy loves show people and they love him. He knows more people in the business than I do!"

But behind the laughter, Greer was aware that the rumors were truer than she cared to reveal. Decades later she would admit, "Buddy often said, 'Life would have been so much easier if you'd been the stand-in instead of the star.'" When the tug-of-war struggle to maintain their union—despite very separate and busy careers—threatened to snap, Greer took action. She refused Dore Schary's offers to appear in such promising roles as *The Romance of Henry Menafee*, a *Goodbye, Mr. Chips*–styled English drama, *The Fortunes of Richard Mahoney, Chimes of Bruges,* and an ambitious epic, *Magna Carta,* with a cast to include Stewart Granger, Michael Wilding, and Deborah Kerr. Schary received the following memo from Mike Levee: "Miss Garson is having trouble with her husband over extending her contract and in order to protect her marriage she doesn't want to make these pictures overseas."

On August 25, 1952, only four days after she had completed her role in *Scandal at Scourie*, Greer joined the prestigious cast of Dore Schary's ambitious filmization of William Shakespeare's *Julius Caesar*. She had requested to play Calpurnia and was signed on June 11, 1952. "I suppose I could jokingly say I couldn't bear to have a 'Mrs.' role come up at the studio that I didn't play," she said. "Truthfully, I've been a devotee of Shakespearean roles ever since I made my debut in a school play portraying Shylock, complete with beard. I wanted to be 'with it' even if I were only carrying a spear!" Deborah Kerr received a similarly small role as Portia. Of their brief scenes Greer commented, "We are just there to dress up the story. Our parts are so small that we felt like the producer's girlfriends while making it."

Schary had wrangled for priority screen rights to *Julius Caesar* with other studios, including First National and Twentieth Century-Fox, since 1948. In April 1952 the right combination of talent and legal clearances finally materialized. He bought the screen rights from English Film Incorporated for two hundred dollars and made John Houseman—the multi-talented writer, producer, and actor best known for his collaborations with Orson Welles—the producer. By Houseman's side was director Joe Mankiewicz, who had won four Oscars for his work on *A Letter to Three Wives* and *All About Eve*. All three men had different opinions about who should play Marc Antony. Stewart Granger and Paul Scofield were considered before John Houseman convinced his partners to make a different and more revolutionary choice: Marlon Brando. The triumvirate gathered together an unparalleled cast at Metro-Goldwyn-Mayer, including John Gielgud, James Mason, Louis Calhern, and Edmond O'Brien, but Schary imposed a modest budget—$1.7 million (the final cost would be $2,070,000)—and continued to keep a steady eye on the proceedings. The studio may have been able to afford a lavish Shakespearean prestige picture like Irving Thalberg's *Romeo and Juliet* in 1936, but not in 1952. Early plans for Technicolor were dropped in favor of black and white because, as Houseman explained, "*Caesar* is a tragedy of personal and political conflict; it calls for intensity and intimacy rather than grandeur; for direct, violent confrontations that do not benefit from a lush, polychrome background."

Julius Caesar, Production #1599, attracted the attention of the entire Hollywood industry. In his column, Sidney Skolsky wrote, "It's now: When at MGM do as the Romans do. Everyone, and this includes the movie stars, wants to get on the *Julius Caesar* set and watch Gielgud, Brando, Mason, Calhern and the other Romans do their stuff. But you practically need a pass from Shakespeare, or at least from his coworker, Director Joseph Mankiewicz, to get on. The door leading to the soundstage has a huge sign reading: 'No Admittance—Positively. Not even for an Earthquake.'" Behind the guarded doors of Soundstage Twenty-seven, *Julius Caesar* had begun in a flurry of controversy. Dore Schary refused to grant John Houseman's request for an expensive three-week rehearsal period, which Houseman insisted was necessary because the actors needed time to become comfortable with each other, their roles, and their Shakespearean dialogue. Schary finally capitulated after hearing the results of the first reading. "Gielgud . . . sailed through the part of Cassius with terrifying bravura," John Houseman recalled. "Mason, depressed and embarrassed by the brilliance of his compatriot, chose to read the entire role of Brutus with a pipe clenched tightly in his front teeth; Calhern, always at his worst at first readings, read Caesar with the meaningless flamboyance of a nineteenth-century provincial ham; O'Brien and Kerr were adequate; Miss Garson was very British and ladylike. Brando . . . whom everyone was dying to hear, gave a perfect performance as a stuttering bumpkin only remotely acquainted with the English language."

Pier Maria Pasinetti, a Venetian novelist and faculty member of the Italian Department at the University of California, Los Angeles, was enlisted to help. John Houseman believed that Pasinetti could help create a Rome that evoked "the living mood rather than the archaeological detail of a crowded Mediterranean town." Greer was, of course, fascinated with the historical details and Dr. Pasinetti's copious notes. After an afternoon tea with Pasinetti, she informed the cast that a pig could cross the forum in ancient Rome to witness Julius Caesar's funeral but that the privately chauffeured chariots of Cicero, Publius, and other senators were barred by traffic laws. The life of Calpurnia, Caesar's third wife, was of particular interest to her. She learned that marriage and divorce in upper-crust patrician circles were matters of political convenience or a means of cementing alliances among the important families. "Politically correct, perhaps," she told Pasinetti, "but hardly a model for domestic felicity!"

Julius Caesar was released during the summer of 1953, opening on an international scale in Australia, New York, London, and Los Angeles in stereophonic sound and 1.75-to-1 widescreen. The MGM publicity department sent Greer on a university lecture tour in England to promote the film's foreign release. Her itinerary included her alma mater, King's College, and the Birmingham Repertory Theatre. Manchester University proved to be her greatest challenge. There she faced an assembly of nine hundred students, many of whom were particularly hostile toward John Gielgud, who made no secret of his homosexuality. But Greer asserted that "it was very largely owing to his influence on the film's production that the conglomeration of players, from all sorts of backgrounds, have presented a unified style of speaking Shakespearean verse with freshness, intelligence and vision." Although she was booed, she refused to stop, and eventually won her audience over with humorous tales about working on the movie at MGM. "Even Esther Williams crawled out of her tank to come to see us," she told them, evoking whistles and applause.

Julius Caesar was the kind of prestigious smash hit that Greer's career desperately needed. The *London Sunday Express* declared: "'I come to bury Caesar, not to praise him.' So said Mark Antony. . . . So said the critics' faces, in the Empire, Leicester Square. Hollywood Shakespeare must, of course, be bad. So they moved in for the attack, ready to make a meal off Marlon Brando. Instead they had to eat their words. . . . *Julius Caesar* has defied the oracles—and triumphed. . . . It is not only the best Shakespeare Hollywood has ever done . . . it is also the best theatre that the Americans have ever sent to Britain." In Hollywood, Variety was enthusiastic: "To those normally allergic to Shakespeare, this will be a surprise—a tense, melodramatic story, clearly presented, and excellently acted by one of the finest casts ever assembled for a film. Miss Garson, as Calpurnia, shines in the scene where she warns Caesar not to venture forth on the Ides of March." The film grossed over $4 million during its first engagement and much more from continual revivals and a popular soundtrack album. For Dore Schary *Julius Caesar* was a proud achievement, and for the studio it was a chance to celebrate a resurgence of critical and popular acclaim. The Academy of Motion Picture Arts and Sciences nominated *Julius Caesar* for four Oscars—Best Picture, Best Black and White Art Direction, Best Dramatic Score, Best Actor (Marlon Brando)—and awarded the film the Oscar for Best Art Direction.

Greer was particularly happy as she made the voyage home to America after the *Julius Caesar* tour. Dore Schary was pleased with the results of her appearances, and she had enjoyed the satisfaction of being recognized as an honored celebrity when she spoke at her alma mater and in Birmingham. She had also received a citation as life governor of the Women's Hospital in Melbourne, Australia, in recognition of her "long-distance" support of the hospital since 1950. Her most recent Hollywood-to-Melbourne telephone appeal, broadcast over Australia's radio network, had raised nearly $250,000 for the hospital. But none of these laurels excited her so much as her next film project. After years of coaxing the executives in the Thalberg building, she had been promised a challenging starring role in a film that was anticipated to be one of the most important movie events of 1954.

CHAPTER 21

ON JUNE 25, 1951, AFTER FINISHING *The Law and the Lady*, Greer had treated Nina to a Hawaiian getaway. Although the press had been told it was merely a short vacation, the Garsons had visited Honolulu on business; they met with Marjorie Lawrence, the Australian opera singer whose meteoric career was nearly destroyed by a crippling attack of infantile paralysis in 1941. Although confined to a wheelchair, Miss Lawrence had inspired audiences with a triumphant comeback and a best-selling biography entitled *Interrupted Melody*. She had sent an advance copy to Greer, one of her favorite actresses, during the filming of *The Miniver Story*. Greer was inspired and intrigued by the similarities that they shared. Both women had been raised on a farm and shared an unquenchable desire to perform, despite family disapproval. But it was the opera star's triumph over debilitating illness, which Greer knew only too well, that made her want to portray Marjorie Lawrence on screen.

Prior to 1951, that dream, like her interest in performing works of Noël Coward or Shakespeare, seemed hopeless. But *The Great Caruso*, starring Mario Lanza, which MGM released in May at Radio City Music Hall, surprised Hollywood showmen by grossing nearly $4 million. Operatic musicals, it seemed, could indeed be big box office. In June 1952 MGM producer Jack Cummings purchased the screen rights to *Interrupted Melody* for twenty-seven thousand dollars. In July, Howard Strickling announced to the Hollywood press that the decision to cast Greer Garson as Marjorie Lawrence had been made "after receipt of petitions signed by hundreds of the great soprano's fans in more than a dozen countries." The *Star* proclaimed: "Greer gets her dream part! MGM has given her the starring role in

Interrupted Melody, the life story of Marjorie Lawrence!" Exhibiting more enthusiasm about a role than she had in years, Greer began her characteristically intensive research for the role in January 1953. In order to properly lip synch to the musical numbers, to be sung by Eileen Farrell, she studied some of her own favorite operas, including *Carmen, Tristan and Isolde,* and *Madame Butterfly,* in three languages with famed opera coach and conductor Wolfgang Martin. Utilizing her gift for dialects, she also perfected an Australian accent. Sonya Levien and William Ludwig (*Julia Misbehaves*) adapted the book into a screenplay.

But as the budget of *Interrupted Melody* escalated toward $2 million and the studio found it difficult to cast the role of Marjorie Lawrence's husband, Dore Schary began to have second thoughts about the expensive project. He had little interest in continuing to make the kind of women's pictures that had made Metro-Goldwyn-Mayer famous. He was not another Thalberg who could provide Greer with another *Goodbye, Mr. Chips* or *Pride and Prejudice.* Instead, he concentrated on gritty, realistic, all-male stories such as *Battleground, Take the High Ground,* and *Bad Day at Black Rock.* Former MGM contract star Angela Lansbury remarked: "Mr. Schary wasn't a movie man like L.B. Mayer. He wasn't interested in the glamour ladies; he preferred the more down to earth ones. So suddenly there was no place for quite a lot of people I think." Greer appeared to be one of Dore Schary's first casualties when the *Hollywood Reporter* announced on February 3, 1953, that "*Interrupted Melody* has been interrupted—permanently. The studio's trying to figure out a way to cut production cost on the biopic." Greer called her agent. Once again, as in 1938, her career had reached a critical point, and she depended on Michael Levee to save it.

As negotiations began, Dore Schary explained that *Melody's* budget was out of hand and that the studio had shut down production in order to consider shooting the film in Cinemascope or 3-D to attract more customers. He promised that production would resume before the end of 1953. In late February, as Greer prepared for a trip east to address three thousand Red Cross workers on behalf of their annual fund drive, she wrote to Schary: "I leave on Monday on my Boston safari with a much happier heart since being assured by you yesterday that we will definitely resume *Interrupted Melody* later this year with the same group of devoted enthusiasts. I'll eat all my hats if we don't bring you a few medals and plaques with this one!"

When she arrived back at Metro on March 9, Greer met with Dore Schary. Since *Interrupted Melody* was still postponed, he suggested that she make another film in the interim. Her choice was a project that Sidney Franklin had brought to her attention. In June 1952 he had purchased the rights to Louise Baker's story "Snips and Snails," which had been serialized in *Ladies Home Journal,* for thirty-five thousand dollars. Screenwriter William Roberts transformed the simple tale of the misadventures of a new female teacher at an exclusive boys' school named The Oaks into a script entitled *Her Twelve Men.* Since Franklin was involved with other projects at the time and was increasingly at odds with Dore Schary about what sort of films MGM should make, Greer chose John Houseman to produce the picture. Houseman was well aware of studio politics. "It was part of the accepted pattern of studio operation," Houseman explained, "that for every film you really wanted to make, you made one to please the studio." *Executive Suite,* based on Cameron Hawley's best-selling novel, was the picture he wanted to make, with director Robert Wise and an all-star cast headed by William Holden and Barbara Stanwyck. *Her Twelve Men* was the picture that he made to please the studio.

But busy with his *Executive* project, Houseman had little time to put his own personal mark on *Her Twelve Men.* He had a particular aversion to the story because of his negative experience in 1946 producing *Miss Susie Slagle's.* That sentimental film, with a story line similar to *Her Twelve Men,* had been a box-office disaster. So he hired scenarist Laura Hobson to help William Roberts write the screenplay. However, as Houseman commented, with obvious disapproval, "What astringency she might have given the subject was offset by the studio's selection of the veteran Robert Z. (Pop) Leonard to direct it. Contrary to custom I rarely went down to the set during shooting; after a few tedious arguments with Pop Leonard, I stopped checking on the directorial methods of this ancient, experienced man who had directed Miss Garson more than a dozen years before."

Houseman's other major contribution was in the casting department. Robert Ryan had risen to prominence after World War II in films such as *The Woman on the Beach, The Set Up,* and *Clash by Night.* By 1953 the actor was eager to stray from such dramatic fare and try comedy instead. Houseman obliged his friend by assigning him to *Her Twelve Men*. Among other notables in the cast was future *Gunsmoke* star James Arness. The six-foot-six actor, who had once been a real estate agent and had made his screen debut in Loretta Young's 1947 classic *The Farmer's Daughter,* had a small role as a gym teacher. The always delightful Richard Haydn, now best known as "Uncle Max" in *The Sound of Music,* played Dr. Avord Barrett, superintendent of The Oaks.

Principal photography for *Her Twelve Men* began on August 10, 1953, and continued into the fall. Throughout production, as Greer waged a losing battle to keep *Interrupted Melody* afloat, her relationship with Dore Schary grew more acrimonious. MGM lawyer F.L. Hendrickson sent a memo to Benjamin Thau: "The problem is that Miss Garson has been told by someone at the studio (Mike Levee thinks it was Lillian Burns) that *Interrupted Melody* is supposed to go into production. He said Miss Garson takes the position that it is embarrassing and very annoying to her that the studio won't let her do that particular picture and she feels that she doesn't want to give the studio any pictures unless she gets this, i.e. she wants to cancel out. He said if the studio makes it while she is at the studio, it will embarrass her and she doesn't want to be in that kind of a position."

Bitterly disappointed that she was losing a picture so close to her heart and with the potential to revive her career, Greer found little satisfaction making the tepid *Her Twelve Men.* She was pleased that the picture was set in the present day, which allowed Sydney Guilaroff to design a becoming new hairstyle for her. Because she had begun an intensive exercise regimen for *Interrupted Melody*, she appears particularly slim and lovely in the film, with a flattering wardrobe designed by Helen Rose. To escape her studio troubles, she joined her husband for a weekend trip to their cottage at the Eldorado Country Club in Indian Wells near Palm Springs. But their brief, happy hours enjoying golf, tennis, and dining out, frequently with their neighbors Dwight and Mamie Eisenhower, were spoiled when Greer's jewels, valued at over ten thousand dollars, were stolen from their home. They were never found.

Among her guests for tea on the set of *Her Twelve Men* was actor Barry Sullivan, who played the father of one of her most troublesome students. A busy Metro contract player, Sullivan was also appearing on television in a unique arrangement between MGM—which was attempting to join forces with television rather than continue to fight it—and NBC. Greer was intrigued with the opportunities and met with Benjamin Thau to discuss a similar arrangement. The meeting resulted in her American television debut on March 19, 1953, on the first televised Academy Awards show, at the RKO Pantages Theater on Hollywood Boulevard. Her role was deceptively simple—to present the Best Supporting Actor Award to Anthony Quinn for *Viva Zapata*— but in the chaos involved in Oscar's first telecast, it was a confusing affair. "They really threw me to the lions on that one," she said. "Cameras all over the place, hundreds of young men dashing in and dashing out, six different monitors to watch, directors arm-wagging frantically at me. Live television holds no more fears for me." Thereafter, she was an assured, perennial favorite at the annual ceremonies until 1977.

Her Twelve Men premiered in August at the Sixtieth Street Trans-Lux Theater in New York. A special screening was arranged on September 29, Greer's birthday, in Hollywood for the Crippled Children's Fund. But no one was impressed with the film, which displayed MGM's disinterest in Greer's career so obviously that it amounted to a B picture. *Variety* dubbed *Her Twelve Men* "an okay 90 minutes of family entertainment. The cast names and subject matter aren't commercially exciting enough to indicate much trade outside family patronage, and the latter may be confused by the title's implications since Miss Garson's film reputation is hardly synonymous with sin." The *Hollywood Reporter* was flabbergasted: "Ever since the great days of *Random Harvest* someone at Metro seems to have been laboring under the delusion that a refined, intelligent and cultured woman can't also be physically desirable and desiring. Miss Garson badly needs a transformation such as Deborah Kerr underwent in *From Here To Eternity.* As a paid-up card-carrying member of the Greer Garson Fan Club, I hope that she soon gets it." The movie grossed $1,418,000, posting a loss of $863,000.

Greer found more satisfaction with her work at the Forked Lightning Ranch. On August 19, 1953, the *Los Angeles Herald Express* reported an interesting item: "Those all white cattle of Greer Garson's are going to give her an entirely new claim to fame. The MGM redhead has sold all 20 of the snow-white shorthorns on her New Mexico property to a Texas rancher, Clint Murchison. The animals will be crossed with the white Brahmas to establish a new breed. It will take a number of generations, but when the new species is developed the cattle will be registered for posterity as 'white short-horned Greers.'"

On March 1, 1954, Greer's exclusive contract with the studio was at an end, and she chose not to continue with the nonexclusive portion. Bitterly disillusioned by the fiasco of *Interrupted Melody*, which was still shelved, and with MGM's treatment of her in recent years, she packed up her things in Apartment D and quietly departed the studio that had been her home for nearly seventeen years. She had hung on too long at the studio. Now it was time for her to freelance as so many of her friends, such as Katharine Hepburn and Rosalind Russell, were doing. Among the good-bye letters that she received from coworkers was one that read: "I can't believe I won't see your lovely red-head around the pickle factory anymore! Just want you to know that I, for one, will miss you. I know you'll be much happier wherever you go—whatever you do! God Bless You, Van [Johnson]." Greer's departure that year was part of a virtual caravan of MGM stars, including Clark Gable, Spencer Tracy, Esther Williams, Lana Turner, and Katharine Hepburn. Greer was the last of the original "Neglected Imports" to leave the studio. After *Rosalie* and *Balalaika*, Ilona Massey made only one movie, *Holiday in Mexico* with Walter Pidgeon and Jane Powell, before leaving the lot in 1946. Hedy Lamarr, who had started straying from MGM as early as 1945 to make films for United Artists and Paramount, left the studio permanently in 1950 after making thirteen pictures of variable quality for the studio.

Greer continued to keep in touch with Louis B. Mayer until his death in 1957. Whatever their disagreements at the studio, he remained a father figure who had, to a greater degree than anyone else, made her dreams of a successful acting career come true. She would always remember MGM under his direction to be "a wonderful place for creative people, not just actors, but writers, directors, producers, designers. There was a strong air of paternalism and it was genuine. I'm sure there was a good deal of nepotism too, but why not? If a man builds up a great corporation don't you think he'll want his neighbors and family in it too?"

On March 10 Greer signed a new contract to star in Mervyn LeRoy's production of *Strange Lady in Town* at Warner Bros. for ten thousand dollars. Since the release of its ground-breaking talkie, *The Jazz Singer*, in 1927, the sprawling Burbank studio, helmed by Jack

Warner, had been one of Metro-Goldwyn-Mayer's chief rivals. With its brassy style, searing gangster pictures and melodramas, and a rogue's gallery of stars including Humphrey Bogart, James Cagney, Bette Davis, and Errol Flynn, Warner Bros. was new territory for Greer Garson. But like former MGM stars such as Joan Crawford and Judy Garland, she hoped to forge a new career there.

The screenplay for *Strange Lady in Town* evolved at a Hollywood dinner party when Greer was seated next to Warner Bros. screenwriter Frank Butler. "I told him I read at least a dozen books about the early days of Santa Fe and love to question very old residents who remember what it was like in the last century," she recalled. "He must have caught some of my enthusiasm because a short time after that he told me he was writing a screen story laid in Santa Fe in 1880, about the time the railroad came through. I didn't know he was also writing in a role for me, and a red-headed woman at that."

Strange Lady was constructed as typical Warner's fare—colorful entertainment with a social consciousness. The script that Butler completed on April 22, 1954, told the story of Dr. Julia Winslow Garth, who leaves her Boston home to practice in Santa Fe. Hoping to avoid the prejudice against female physicians that ruined her career in the East, she is welcomed by her ne'er-do-well brother, David Garth, who is stationed with the U.S. Cavalry in town. She soon wins the town over, including the other doctor there, Rork O'Brien, who falls in love with her. Together they improve the local hospital and help a blind boy and a woman abused by her husband. Romantic complications ensue when O'Brien's daughter, "Spurs," falls in love with David. When he is killed by Santa Fe citizens for trying to steal cattle, "Spurs" is devastated, and Julia decides to leave town because of the scandal. But with the support of her friends and a marriage proposal from Dr. O'Brien, she decides to settle down. The script contained all the ingredients of a classic western: gunfights, gambling saloons, the railroad, and a picturesque fiesta. For good measure some historical New Mexicans were added, including Billy the Kid and General Lew Wallace, governor of the territory and author of *Ben-Hur.*

Frank Butler infused Dr. Garth with many of Greer's recognized qualities. Not only did Julia Garth have red hair, but she was a Protestant and schooled at the University of London. The sense of humor was there, as was the sense of adventure and the independence. Julia was not afraid to challenge intolerance and, as she argues, "men who resent the audacity of a woman daring to practice medicine— daring to crash the gates of a man's world." Consoling the local padre in the film when the future of his hospital looks bleak, Julia says: "The real sadness of a dream is its unfulfillment. To make something of it—even if it's only a beginning—why, that's real achievement!" Such was Greer's view of life, her career, and *Strange Lady in Town*.

The lavish production values that the film would necessitate made studio mogul Jack L. Warner uneasy. By 1954 the studio system was crumbling as revenues dropped, production costs increased, stars became independent, and competition with television tightened. Warner Bros. was also making huge investments in such trouble-plagued productions as Judy Garland's *A Star Is Born*. With this in mind, Warner returned the script for *Strange Lady in Town*, submitted to him by Mervyn LeRoy, with a cautionary memo: "So far as the script is concerned, it is everything we always said it would be. However, one thing that worries me is the cost. The location and work here will run into quite a big charge. Above all, the main thing is to adhere to the schedule once you set it. With the exception of a handful of pictures, in this past year there have not been many profitable ones."

To help ensure that *Strange Lady in Town* was profitable, Jack Warner ordered that the film be photographed in Cinemascope and WarnerColor. By the mid-1950s it seemed that the only way to lure audiences back into theaters was to provide alternatives to television. Cinerama was launched on September 30, 1952 (*This Is Cinerama*), and 3-D began on November 27, 1952 (*Bwana Devil*). But nothing was so successful as Cinemascope, which debuted with *The Robe* by Twentieth Century-Fox in September 1953 and grossed $3 million nationwide in only two weeks. Warner, like the other studio moguls, was eager to cash in on the new format, and Darryl Zanuck was happy to oblige, for a license fee of twenty-five thousand dollars.

After a three-month vacation with her husband, with France, England, Scotland, Spain, and North Africa on the itinerary, Greer reopened her Stone Canyon residence. She intended to use her time in California to the maximum by planning an extensive renovation of the house while staying at the nearby Bel-Air Hotel. She told

Louella Parsons: "My house was perfect for my mother and me before I married Buddy, but it definitely was not large enough for a dynamic man like Buddy. So the only sensible thing to do was to literally push out the walls so that he could have his own quarters. The elevator, too, is for Buddy's comfort so he doesn't have to walk upstairs." Much of the house was done over in Greer's favorite color, pink. Publicists had a field day when it was learned that she had spent twenty thousand dollars on her bathroom of rose marble with inlaid Italian mosaic tiles. She offered Warner Bros. the Forked Lightning Ranch for location shooting. But after scouting the ranch and Santa Fe, the studio turned down the idea in favor of an ideal western set near Tucson, Arizona, named "Old Tucson." As early as June 1954, months before actual production began, studio carpenters were on location constructing an additional thirty-four buildings of wood, tile, and adobe brick, creating a 150-acre site.

With the film's star already chosen, casting the rest of the roles was done with relative ease during the summer of 1954. Popular *Best Years Of Our Lives* star Dana Andrews, who had not made a western since Gary Cooper's *The Westerner* in 1940, was cast as Rork O'Brien. Many of Warner's young male stars, including Richard Egan, Tab Hunter, and Robert Stack, were considered for the role of Julia's brother before Cameron Mitchell was chosen. It was an easy choice for Mervyn LeRoy, who admired Mitchell's talent; he had helped the actor along the road to stardom by building up his role in MGM's *Homecoming*. For the pivotal role of "Spurs" O'Brien, LeRoy intended to utilize his star-making ability—and cast twenty-one-year-old Lois Smith, who had appeared with James Dean in *East of Eden*.

On August 3, 1954, Greer entered the gates of Warner Bros. studio at 4000 West Olive Avenue for the first time. After spending a week and a half reporting to Stage Eighteen for the Cinemascope wardrobe and makeup tests, she was treated to a "Welcome to Warner Bros. Tea" hosted by the Hollywood Foreign Press in the executive dining room. Greer was amused with the printed sign that hung over the fireplace: "The names of the persons, places, and incidents mentioned during conversation are purely coincidental and have no relationship to actual persons, places, or incidents."

The *Strange Lady in Town* cast and crew departed Los Angeles on Saturday night, August 14, for the five-week shooting stint in Tucson.

With her husband and her stand-in, Adele Taylor, Greer arrived on Sunday amidst a crowd of well-wishers. A committee representing the women of Tucson presented a fruit basket and gifts. Then the crowd followed Greer and Buddy to the Santa Rita Hotel, where they would be staying with the rest of the cast. The glamor, excitement, and money that the Warner Bros. crew brought with them caused the city to go movie-crazy. Local newspapers reported that 750 people jammed the hotel's lobby and parking lot when Mervyn LeRoy put out a call for extras.

Greer found a variety of diversions in her new locale. The University of Arizona in Tucson loaned the crew a collection of Indian relics from the state museum. Intrigued, Greer spent her days off at the university studying archaeology. She would take her newest passion back to the Forked Lightning Ranch, where she could inspect the Indian and Spanish ruins. Before leaving the company for work in Dallas, Buddy enjoyed a buying spree in Tucson, spending five hundred dollars on geological specimens for his rock collection.

Although acclimated to New Mexico, Greer was not prepared for the difficult assignment of working in the Arizona desert. In the afternoons, the temperature climbed dangerously high into the hundreds. Wardrobe designer Emile Santiago recalled: "Mouchete was used in the dress Miss Garson has on when making her first entrance into Santa Fe. She thanked me afterward for constructing this outfit so light. She had to sit in the buggy throughout an entire, scorching day." Water was a constant necessity. Greer took cakes of ice for the crew every day, but in the extreme heat she lost seven pounds. In the evenings she was required to have a hot-oil treatment in order to keep her hair WarnerColor red. The outdoor sets attracted more than just curious tourists. Every morning a "snake patrol" attempted to clear the area of scorpions, snakes, and other creatures, but it was not always successful. One morning, as the camera rolled, a large tarantula emerged from its hole not far from Greer and Dana Andrews. Although Andrews and the crew quickly backed off, Greer calmly shoved the hairy beast aside with a twig, explaining: "I have lots of tarantulas on my ranch in New Mexico. They don't bite unless you show aggressive intentions."

Years later, Mervyn LeRoy would describe the on-location shooting of *Strange Lady in Town* as "a mess. In those days, Andrews had a drinking problem ... that made my life difficult. We were shooting in Arizona, so we were all away from home, and I guess that let down the inhibition barriers. Possibly more serious was Greer Garson's health. She isn't the complaining sort, so when she said she felt poorly, I knew she must have felt rotten. We called the company doctor, and he got [four] doctors from the Tucson Clinic for consultation. It was unanimous; she had appendicitis. The doctors agreed she really should have the appendectomy immediately. 'No,' Greer said, with her red-headed stubbornness. 'I can't do it now. There is an entire company depending on me. They'd have to shut down for a few weeks. It wouldn't be fair to them.' She's what they used to call a trouper. Every night, they piled ice bags on her abdomen. Every day, they fed her pills and the nurse was there, sticking a thermometer in her mouth between every scene." Between visits to the Tucson clinic and doses of medication that her Beverly Hills doctor, Dr. Maynard Brandsma, sent to her, Greer remarked casually to the local press, "My body will be a battleground of opposing bacteriological forces for the next few weeks."

For Jack L. Warner, Greer's illness was the last straw. Fearing that the production, which was already behind schedule and over budget, would never be finished, he fired a memo off to Mervyn LeRoy: "I am enclosing Friday's production report, which tells its own story. You made thirteen starts on one scene of which seven were full takes and you marked the eighth 'hold.' In my opinion, this is one of the predominant factors of why you are four days behind plus the tremendous cost of the picture. As I told you before, we do not want to be making pictures just to be purchasing negative from Eastman. In my experience with pictures over the years, I damn near know what is going to happen. Stop being a perfectionist. If you hit it right on the first take, go to the next scene. I know that you know the score and know exactly what I mean. I don't know how we are ever going to make a buck unless we make pictures at a price within reason."

In early September, alarmed by reports of his wife's health, Buddy Fogelson returned to Tucson to take her back to California for the final weeks of shooting. Location work continued in the Santa Susanna Pass near Los Angeles into early October. A brush fire had recently ravaged the area, which created a perfect environment for the dramatic sequence in which David Garth is killed by a Santa Fe mob. The airy costumes that had been so comfortable in the desert were now chilly in the cool temperatures of the pass. Despite the cold and her ailment, Greer managed to maintain the pace, missing only one day during the entire shooting.

The crisis came on October 11 when she suffered another severe attack in her Bel Air home and was rushed to St. John's Hospital in Santa Monica. Doctors reported that an appendectomy was done just in time to save her life. While convalescing, she caught the flu, which lengthened her absence. The production was closed down for twenty-seven days. Despite his frustration, Jack Warner managed to send Greer his good wishes: "Please do not worry as getting well is the most important thing you can do. If you do not have good health, you do not have anything."

Shooting was resumed on Stage Two at Warner Bros. Mervyn LeRoy was under extreme pressure to finish *Strange Lady* and to complete *Mister Roberts* as a favor for his ailing friend John Ford. Scenes that had been planned showing Julia Garth's life in Boston, including selling her family's Beacon Hill mansion to open an office on the waterfront, were abandoned. Nick Adams, who was playing Billy the Kid and had not suffered the rigors of location shooting, attempted to lighten up the weary crew with his impersonations of the famous male stars at Warner Bros. His favorite gag was to answer the soundstage telephone as Marlon Brando, James Cagney, or Cary Grant. The confusion that resulted led studio employees to wonder just who was starring in the production on Stage Two. On November 30, after making two theater trailers—one for the Treasury Department's bond drive and the other for the Gonzales Warm Springs Foundation, a crippled children's hospital in Texas—Greer went home to the ranch for Christmas.

The song "Strange Lady in Town," written by Dimitri Tiomkin and Ned Washington for the film, was already a popular hit on radio and jukeboxes throughout the country when the movie was previewed in February 1955 in Huntington Park. Jack Warner was furious when the music and dubbing effects went awry. Although the errors could be corrected, he wanted more insurance that the film would be a hit. He persuaded Greer to go on a Texas tour with the film, to its premiere in Austin on April 12, 1955, at the Paramount Theater, and to subsequent openings in San Antonio, Houston, Dallas, and Fort Worth. She had never made such an exhaustive tour for a motion picture in her life, but, because of her own personal belief in the film, she accepted. She had designer Moss Mabry create six new satin gowns and jewelry for the events.

But before that, she flew to New York in March 1955 to begin rehearsals for "Reunion in Vienna," a television love story concerning an archduke, the inamorata of his youth, and her psychoanalyst. Fred Coe, producer of NBC's Producer's Showcase series, convinced Greer to perform her first televised dramatic assignment. "It's been so long since I've had a chance to do a little scenery chewing," she informed the New York press. Despite her experience with the BBC in the 1930s, the assignment was a challenging one. "The set reminded me of a huge chess board swarming with human chessmen," she recalled. "Everyone kept telling me to concentrate on the red lights of the cameras. Then a young fellow, wired for sound, slipped up to me. He was wearing a red vest. He told me to watch him and he would see that I was on the proper spot at the proper time. Rehearsals went fine. I followed the boy in the red vest. Next day at show time what happened? There were five young men—all wearing red vests!" Critics who wondered how the Queen of Radio City Music Hall would fare on the small screen were surprised and delighted with the results of her debut on April 4, 1955. *Variety* noted: "Greer Garson's television debut is on the triumphant side. Completely at ease, she sparkled and handled herself like a veteran TV trouper."

Greer arrived in Austin, Texas, for the April 12 premiere of *Strange Lady in Town* with a squadron of Hollywood notables, including Mervyn LeRoy and Austin native Dana Andrews. "From the standpoint of a theater manager, there must be little that's more embarrassing than being saddled with the world premiere of a mediocre picture," began John Bustin, in his review of the film in the *Austin American*. "Fortunately, for the management of the Paramount Theater, though, no such embarrassment is called for as a result of the local world premiere of *Strange Lady in Town*, because this is a film which could stand alone without benefit of sideshow come-ons or similar shots in the arm. The Mervyn LeRoy production neither pretends nor manages to be a really great picture. But this is hardly a discredit inasmuch as it is obviously designed more as a vehicle for entertaining a general audience than for shocking them out of their seats."

After the screening, Greer was invited to address the House and

Senate of the state legislature, as well as the Austin Women's Federation. "Unlike Dana, I was not born in Texas," she told them, "but at least I had the sense to come to Texas. And having married a Texan I feel I am an adopted daughter. As a new citizen, I am especially aware of the influence you have in the motion picture industry. I know you have the best interests of the American home and its young citizens at heart. I personally have taken a vow to never appear in a picture in which crime is the theme."

By the time Greer returned to Los Angeles, *Strange Lady in Town* was a hit, easily surpassing its $3 million cost and earning a certificate from the Southern California Motion Picture Council that proclaimed it "a delight to all." "Shot in Cinemascope, in mellow tones of WarnerColor, this expensive outdoor picture highlights the beauty, charm and graciousness of Greer Garson against the drowsy, sun-baked glamour of the old Southwest," commented the *Hollywood Reporter.* The *Los Angeles Herald-Examiner* encouraged its readers to see the film "because it's uncomplicated, unsophisticated and often completely unreal drama, excitement, and fun by turns. Because it has lovely Greer Garson being witty, fiery and tender as its heroine. Go see it and have some un-arty, un-depressing, important fun." Jack Warner wrote to Greer: "All your trials and tribulations were well worth going through as we saw the entire show last night and your performance was magnificent."

Interrupted Melody was also released in 1955. A month after Greer had left MGM, Dore Schary had cast Eleanor Parker as Marjorie Lawrence and Glenn Ford as her husband. The movie was a resounding success and earned Eleanor Parker an Oscar nomination for her performance. Although she would always regret losing the opportunities that *Interrupted Melody* could have offered her, Greer regarded *Strange Lady in Town* with personal satisfaction. It was, in her estimation, "a richly corny period story which interested me particularly because I've been a carpet actress all my life in Hollywood. I wanted to do an outdoor role, one with horses and sunsets. The result of my love for the life and history of old Santa Fe has been put on film, and I am proud of my little part in helping to create it."

When Mike Levee could find no other projects for her at Warner Bros., he engaged Greer in a series of television programs. It was a happy and welcome solution for her marital problems. The medium provided an outlet for her to continue her career, in varied roles, without a long movie production schedule that separated her from Buddy. "I like doing television," she said. "It's exciting. I guess I can best describe it as a stupendous, short, supercharged effort. When I was in high school I went out for girls' athletics. I always liked the sprints better than the distance runs. I guess that's why I like to do a TV show now and then." *TV Guide* commented: "Cut this girl loose on television, complete with a free choice of both shows and scripts, and she'll become to TV what Art Carney is to Jackie Gleason. Until one had heard this one-woman Irish rebellion change her voice and shout, 'It's the Jackie Gleason Show—and away we go!' there is no yardstick by which to measure her potential."

A good sport and prone to laughter, Greer was a favorite guest-star, eventually appearing on *Laugh-In, The Red Skelton Show, What's My Line? The Steve Allen Show, Toast of the Town, The Tennessee Ernie Ford Show, The Joey Bishop Show, The Donald O'Connor Show,* and *The Smothers Brothers Show.* On *The Bob Hope Show* she enjoyed performing a parody of the 1937 Cary Grant/Irene Dunne screwball classic *The Awful Truth.* She appeared on *Father Knows Best,* playing herself. Jimmy Durante was so excited to get her on his program that he prepared his crew in advance: "Miss Garson is a perfect lady—so watch yourselves." At rehearsals, he explained to her: "You say dis and den dere's a laugh. Den I say dis and den dere's a laugh." When Greer asked, "But what if they don't laugh?" Durante replied, "Den we go down the terlet."

Apart from an occasional all-star musical variety program such as *Dateline 2* in which Greer performed an "Electronic Trio" song-and-dance number with Janet Blair in New York and Peggy Lee in Hollywood ("as if the 3,000 mile gap didn't exist," *Variety* observed), *The Ford Show* with Reginald Gardiner, and *The Big Party by Revlon* in which she performed the death scene from *Camille,* she also handled a number of dramatic parts. Among them was an episode of *Star Stage,* entitled "Career," in February 1956 in which she played a movie star whose tumultuous lifestyle, involving scandalous headlines and romantic escapades, is changed with the adoption of a child. "I hope no one gets the idea that this is my life story," Greer laughingly told the press. Said *Variety:* "Miss Garson excels at her role, convincing at first as the cold-hearted and ruthless star; equally convincing as the icicle whose heart is melted by the kid." She also made a delightful appearance as a vigorous Irish schoolteacher in *General Electric Theater*'s fantasy "The Glorious Gift of Molly Malloy." Although television producers such as Aaron Spelling and Bing Crosby Enterprises would try to cast her in a weekly series in years to come, she always refused. "I just can't see tying myself down to thirty-nine shows, even for a year," she said.

Offers continued to descend on 680 Stone Canyon. Michael Barry wrote to convey an invitation from Henry Sherek to play *Candida* on tour through Edinburgh, Berlin, and London. She replied: "Esme Percy also wrote to me about Candida, for the Shaw centenary, but I have been dodging Candida for years—mainly because I seem to be playing lesser versions of that character for so long that I would like a change."

Samuel B. Harrison tried to lure her to New York: "Why keep doing another and still another television potboiler? You owe it to yourself to do one unforgettable play like Gertrude Lawrence in 'Lady In The Dark' and Miss Lynn Fontanne in 'The Guardsman.' Claudette Colbert, Olivia de Havilland, Deborah Kerr, and Rosalind Russell went to Broadway. You're an actress, create the role and stay in it for three months, and it will be yours for the screen too. If your heart is in it, surely Mr. Fogelson will give you his blessing." Although she doubted Buddy's approval of such a project, Greer could not deny that the lure of Broadway was growing irresistibly stronger. Her interest only increased when Ruth Pidgeon wrote to her that Walter was enjoying a road company version of Kyle Crichton's *The Happiest Millionaire* after playing the starring role on Broadway.

But once again Greer put her dream aside to appear in three television dramas. In December she made her first appearance in a *Hallmark Hall of Fame* telefilm, Lillian Hellman's *The Little Foxes*. Although she found the live show to be "hideously lit and photographed," Greer relished the opportunity to play the greedy Regina Giddens, who ruthlessly pursues wealth at the expense of her family. It was a plum role that had been played on the stage in 1939 by Tallulah Bankhead and on the silver screen in 1941 by Bette Davis. Thinking back over her demure MGM years, she exclaimed, "Thank heavens someone has given me a role like this!" Her venomous performance lent credence to James Agee's notion that she would have made an interesting Lady Macbeth. In January she made "The Earring," which concerned a desperate attempt to regain her jeweled earring from a blackmailer who threatens to expose her extramarital affair with it. Of "Revenge," which she made in September, *Variety* posed the question: "Anyone know a better way of kicking off a new season for a dramatic series than having Greer Garson give one of her peerless performances and busting open a cowtown at the seams? It . . . provided the viewers with a display of how acting should be done."

CHAPTER 22

AT DUSK, GREER, DRESSED IN a form-fitting fuchsia gown with a sable collar and gold slippers, finally sat down and relaxed in her favorite white armchair. It was January 18, 1958. The curtains of her thirtieth-floor Hampshire House suite were open, revealing a breathtaking view of the twinkling lights of New York's Central Park and the Wollman Memorial Ice Rink. She was prepared to meet a writer from *Cue* to discuss her latest project. Buddy was out of sight, quietly studying business reports in the bedroom. He had purchased two apartments in the building for Greer and Nina in the early 1950s. Mother and daughter had furnished the rooms with green carpets and white furnishings. Her cherished dream to appear on Broadway had at last come true. In 1955 Dore Schary had advised her to read the phenomenally popular novel *Auntie Mame*, by Patrick Dennis, and consider it as a screen vehicle. Greer immediately fell in love with the story of Dennis's spirited, fun-loving aunt who, with the aid of her equally adventurous and eccentric friends, transforms her introverted young nephew. "I like her courage and her ebullience," she said. "She promoted a general liveliness and kindliness, and isn't that the best one can do? I think there's a bit of Auntie Mame in every woman—a kind of counterpart to the Walter Mitty in every man."

But it was too late. Two weeks later the dramatic rights were snapped up by Robert Fryer and Lawrence Carr for a New York stage presentation starring Rosalind Russell. Three years later Rosalind left the long-running Broadway smash to make a film version for Warner Bros. Although Constance Bennett was playing the part in a successful road version, Fryer and Carr had another actress in mind for their replacement in New York. Russell had suggested that her old friend from Metro, Greer Garson, should play the part. After negotiations, Greer signed on for a four-and-a-half-month stint, for eight performances a week, on July 29, 1957.

Her *Auntie Mame* adventure had begun in November when she arrived in New York with Buddy and Nina. Rehearsals had begun two days before Christmas at the Broadhurst Theatre on Forty-fourth Street, with introductory blocking and integration with a crew that included Peggy Cass as Agnes Gooch, an introvert whom Mame takes under her wing; Jan Handzlik as the young Patrick Dennis; Polly Rowles as Mame's indestructible best friend Vera Charles; and Robert Smith as Mame's husband, Beauregard Jackson Pickett Burnside. On January 6 the play's director, Morton Da Costa, took over for final rehearsals, which lasted until January 13. "Rehearsals so far have been a lark—a strenuous lark," Greer told the *New York Post*. "I keep losing my wigs in the curtains. I can't see a thing in the blackouts, and they forgot to scrape my shoes, so I was slipping all over the stage. I suspect the real show will be backstage."

Upon his arrival at Hampshire House, Philip Minoff of *Cue* was surprised by what he found there. "Thirty floors below us, the lights of Central Park flickered. On the tiny, white skating pond that glared up at us through the chilly night, gaily-covered forms moved about like so many miniatures in slow motion. 'Look!' cried Greer Garson, her green eyes lighting up as if she were seeing it all for the first time. 'It's like a Grandma Moses scene come to life!' And it was, but just as exciting was Miss Garson's own breathless reaction to the scene, for as a woman who can just about buy Central Park, she might be fashionably blasé about such a setting. But Greer is blasé about nothing. Her overpowering eagerness about life is apparent from the moment an interviewer enters her suite. By the time he leaves, he's convinced that the whirlwind lady with the orangest hair this side of Lucille Ball is much more 'Auntie Mame' than *Mrs. Miniver*."

"I did hope to come to America by way of Broadway," Greer commented to Minoff. "I've played tense, dramatic parts, a lot of stuffy lavender-scented roles. It's wonderful to be able to touch people. But I love to hear laughter. There's something terribly healthy about laughter."

January 20, 1958, was opening night at the Broadhurst Theatre. *Variety* raved:

No need to worry about "Auntie Mame." However Greer Garson's characterization may differ from or be similar to Rosalind Russell's original, "Auntie Mame" remains "Auntie Mame." The frenzied change of costumes and wigs demanded of the actress endeavoring to get through the evening as Auntie Mame never intrudes upon Miss Garson's tranquility or spirited romping, whichever the scene may at the moment demand. From strawberry blonde and lounging pajamas of the opening cocktail party, to silver gray and sari of the close, Miss Garson is in personal command of herself, her performance and the play.

Knowing that a tour de force is demanded, she presents one, her own, and it's good. In fact, it's extremely pleasant to see Miss Garson in something other than her screen personality. At the Broadhurst, she is an actress of verve, style, chorus girl bite, a comedienne of perfect timing and extraordinary energy. No "Mrs. Miniver" this, and vive la difference.

"I have watched your performance and I think you are far superior to anybody else in the part you are playing" wrote theatrical legend J.J. Shubert, who managed the Broadhurst, to Greer. Hollywood columnist Mike Connolly wrote: "I saw Greer Garson in 'Auntie Mame' and liked her very much. She got a lot of humor that she has in person into the part—the kind we've seen so seldom on the screen because she's always a rather heavily-type-cast 'Mrs. Miniver.' She got laughs Roz Russell didn't get—in the switchboard scene for instance, which Roz hated doing and 'threw away' but which Greer milked for all it was worth—very funny!"

Although Buddy was unable to stay for the entire run of *Auntie Mame*, Greer intended to enjoy every moment of her Broadway experience. She attended the Tony Awards Dinner. On February 12, she joined Sir Laurence Olivier and the cast of his latest film, *The Entertainer*, for an evening supper at the Hotel Pierre. She appeared as a surprise guest on *What's My Line* on April 6, throwing the live audience into an uproar. She was a frequent guest at "21," often dining with MGM alumnus Ricardo Montalban and Claudette Colbert, who were performing in neighboring theaters. "I still picture in my mind arriving at '21' preceded by Venus in a white mink coat," one of her escorts recalls. "Nothing like it has ever been seen before or ever will be again. She probably did not notice the whole restaurant stopped eating; most people with their mouths open wide until she was surrounded by greeters—all together a remarkable incident in my life."

On May 23, as Greer's run as Auntie Mame was coming to an end, the management wrote: "Have happy summer of rest—though 'Auntie Mame' will not be nearly the same . . . not nearly so warm and appealing a character after you have left. What a real woman you made of her." Despite other Broadway offers, including *Beauty, Inc., My Indian Family, The Girl in the Swing,* and *Love Affair,* Greer returned to Santa Fe when her contract at the Broadhurst ended May 31. She had stuck by her statement: "My career will not interfere with my marriage." Buddy Fogelson was proud of his wife's achievements, and as her Hollywood career declined he introduced her to an entirely different role, as Mrs. Fogelson, that could absorb her high-powered energies. No longer was she "Ca-reer Garson," the reclusive celebrity behind the gates of 680 Stone Canyon, living only for her next film. For the first time in her life she could confidently say, "I wouldn't want acting full time anymore, I'm enjoying real life too much." Buddy gave her support and the chance to grasp at life as she never had before. "Life is so exciting that one life seems hardly enough to live," she told the *Los Angeles Times.* "Actors enjoy the illusion of living many lives. And after ten years of marriage to my mad Texan, I now have the privilege of living them all and dividing my time and interests between city and country, acting and my personal life!" Marsha Hunt, who met Greer again for the first time since 1946 at an Eleanor Roosevelt Foundation luncheon in the mid-1960s, remarked, "Greer was so effusively delighted to see me—as if we were long-lost close friends—that it took me aback. Our relationship when we made three films together had been strictly impersonal. It was obvious that some of that reserve from the old days at Metro had left her. She was a much more outgoing, bubbly personality."

The Fogelsons furnished a penthouse overlooking Dallas's beautiful Turtle Creek area with special care. The press soon descended upon the town's most famous newcomer. "Greer Garson has not changed much," columnist Julia Sweeney observed, "She is just as regal today as when she accepted the Academy Award for *Mrs. Miniver* during World War II. Her hair is as apricot souffle-red as when headlines screamed, 'Gable's Back and Garson's Got Him!' in 1945, after the war. Her face is just as arrestingly beautiful and her voice is just as richly theatrical as when she played the doomed wife of Mr. Chips in 1939."

Unlike Hedy Lamarr, who married oilman Howard Lee and found Texans "clannish, inhospitable and downright unfriendly," Greer observed that "Dallas is small enough to be neighborly, but still big enough to have many cultural activities. There is something about the gallantry of the men too, and their women have bloomed under it. They're all keen to get into the most exciting crap game in the world." She enjoyed dozens of civic duties there, serving on the board of the Civic Light Opera, the Dallas Free Shakespeare Theater, the Dallas Theater Center, and the Dallas Symphony and Museum among others. Her busy day-to-day schedule was well explained in a motto she had at the time: "Keep your horizons wide and your waistline narrow."

The Fogelsons made donations to create the downtown Pegasus Plaza, the Fogelson Fountain in the Dallas Arboretum, and the Fogelson Pavilion dining room in the Morton H. Meyerson Symphony Center. They also began a permanent endowment at the Dallas Theater Center for annual acting awards for two outstanding apprentices. On an international level, the Fogelsons were a force behind the British-American Theatre Institute, which brought English drama groups to the United States. They endowed a scholarship in Greer's name for promising students at the University of Ulster in Northern Ireland. In all these pursuits, Greer sought to continue, as exemplified by another of her mottoes, "Upward and Onward with the Arts—and Sideways in many other interesting directions!"

Buddy taught his wife about the oil industry and named an oil field for her in Palo Pinto County, Texas. "The oil and gas exploration business is like show business," she informed the *Los Angeles Times*. "You never know where it's going to be found. Like our farming life, I get a thrill out of the industry, its hazards and its triumphs. The expenses and risks are great. The ratio of dry holes to gushers is as high as Broadway flops to hits! Every oil well is a source of endless worry, but when it is a success the excitement is tremendous." Her great pride in Buddy's success sometimes surprised her old Hollywood friends. When she met Edward Ashley in a Los Angeles art gallery, she proudly took a small glass vial filled with black liquid from her purse and handed it to him with a question, "Do you want to hold my baby?" Staring at the strange sight, Ashley was speechless with confusion. With a laugh, Greer explained, "It's oil from the Greer Garson Fogelson oil well!"

Greer was quickly acquainted with her husband's circle of friends. Dr. B. Clayton Bell Sr., senior minister of Highland Park Presbyterian Church, recalled his first meeting with Buddy's famous new wife. "It struck terror in my heart," he said. "But one of the marks of great people is that they make little people feel important in their presence, and we became good friends." Greer also struck up a lifelong friendship with the concert pianist Van Cliburn, of Fort Worth. His mother, Rilda Bee Cliburn, whom Greer referred to as "Lady Precious," was also a frequent guest at the Fogelsons' home. "She was one of the loveliest people," Van Cliburn recalled. "A very youthful, healthy—despite her infirmities—vibrant, happy person. She was devoted to classical music. She stunned me over dinner one evening when she began discussing Franck's *Symphonic Variations.* I found it extraordinary that she knew it. Brahms's *Second Concerto* was a great favorite of hers." When Mrs. Cliburn died, Greer was at Van's side. "She called me," Cliburn recalls, "and said, 'Lady Precious may be gone from our sight; remember you are now released from the anxiety of her passing, and you are now brought into the comfort and presence of her beauty.'"

The respect and admiration Greer earned in Dallas led the Republican GOP leaders to ask her to run for Congress in the fifth district of Texas. Although she was briefly tempted when Jack Crichton, chairman of the county GOP Congressional Candidate Committee, formally approached her, she quickly declined the offer. As she wrote to George Cukor: "Personally, I think I'm still in a state of shock. That'd mean working with a script even more unpredictable than *Desire Me*—and no director to say, 'That was perfect. Now we'll do just one more.'" But the request—and her husband's own staunch Republican ideals—increased her interest in politics.

During the summer of 1958, Greer became a client of the William Morris Agency and explained her wishes for the future: "If you could think of a good stage property that would be effective for a long

TV dramatic program—either comedy or drama—I would like to do something like that either late this year or the beginning of next. I have talked with director Ralph Levy recently. He has recently married one of my best friends in Santa Fe, Miranda Masoco. He invited me to be on the opening program of the Garry Moore show. I am considering some interesting motion picture offers. Desi and Lucille asked me to do an hour show for them. I am having traction and physical therapy for a real crazy cervical condition. The x-rays indicated that I have recently been thrown from a horse or a Flying Purple People Eater and had landed on my head. I don't seem to remember such an episode at all, so it's quite mystifying. As soon as this clears up, we will probably mosey off to New Mexico and open up the main house at the ranch, if only for a short time."

But Greer's ambitious schedule collapsed on November 27, 1958, when Nina Garson suffered a heart attack. "Mrs. Fogelson was in Dallas at the time for Thanksgiving," Jack Evinger, the Fogelsons' chauffeur and bodyguard, recalls, "and she had a terrible time trying to get a flight out of Dallas. By the time she arrived in Los Angeles, her mother was dead. I don't think Dallas was ever the same for her after that." "During the first forty-eight hours I didn't know if I wanted to live or die," Greer confided to Van Cliburn. "But that was temporary. The spirit takes over, and the beautiful memories." Louella Parsons called it the end of "one of the sweetest mother-daughter relationships in our town." Aunt Evelyn Murray, visiting her son David and his family in Australia, was en route back to Scotland when she heard the news. She flew to California for the funeral. Greer invited her aunt to remain at her Bel Air home in Nina's old room.

Greer retreated to the Forked Lightning Ranch to regain, in her own words, "a sense of the continuous, the permanent. In watching the beauty and inevitability of the seasons in rotation, there is comfort and peace of mind. There is an almost mystical strength about New Mexico. The longer you stay it seems to be the center of the world and everything else peripheral." "Religion became very important to her," recalls Jack Evinger. "I used to drive her to church many times in Santa Fe, in Dallas, and Palm Springs. She told me religion was a wonderful anchorage. A necessary anchorage."

Of the healing powers of her New Mexico oasis, Greer remarked, "We never had a typical day at Forked Lightning. When you wake up in the morning you have the energy and enthusiasm of a 10-year-old. If we were expecting a cattle shipment we got up at 4 A.M. Otherwise, it's usually 7:30. We would have a serve-yourself hunt breakfast." She had a name for everything on the ranch. The Fogelson Fleetwood limousine became "the Queen Mary," while her horses were dubbed "Kissing Time" and "Ho-Hum Silver." While she disliked hunting—the ranch was an animal sanctuary—she learned skeet shooting from her husband. "I'm not very good," she remarked, "but I no longer faint when I hear the sound of a gun." Interested in all the local customs, she attempted to make Mexican bread in the stone oven in the backyard. "Of course," she admitted, "by the time I'm through, it's cost about $6 a loaf. But, I bake it!" She also enjoyed gathering the children from families who lived on the ranch and teaching them. "It would do my old grandmother's heart good to see me teaching like this once in a while," she would say.

"Listening to Greer and Buddy Fogelson talk about the ranch, it is difficult to tell who is the most enthusiastic about New Mexico," wrote George Fitzpatrick of the *New Mexican* upon his visit. "But then, she is an enthusiastic person generally, and whatever the subject, whether it's cattle, the ranch, New Mexico, the movies, or T.V., she exudes enthusiasm." "Give a redhead an inch, and she'll take a mile and a half," Greer often said. "You should see my articles in the *Beef Breeder's Gazette* and the *Shorthorn World*." When disbelieving reporters asked if "Mrs. Miniver" actively participated in the operation of the ranch, Greer truthfully replied: "I do help in the round-up, and I ride fence. That's checking on the fences for damage, due usually to flash floods. I've gone out with barb wire, but I'm not very good at it. I've helped herd the wild horses. Running the house is really my province. When we do business entertaining those are busy days for Ma Fogelson!"

"Running the house" did not include the art of cooking. From her earliest days of stardom, Greer had employed a butler, a maid, and a cook. "Her instructions were to cook everything raw," Jack Evinger recalls. "Lots of raw vegetables, just a little bit warm. She also loved a breakfast of orange juice with a raw egg in it. She tried cooking for Buddy a few times, but not often. We had to grab toasters and skillets to save the kitchen, save the house. You've got to time things, but time meant nothing to her. She would concentrate on one thing, and everything else would be afire. Mr. Fogelson would say, 'Rusty, get out of the kitchen. You'll burn the house down.'"

Along with Greer's shorthorns, Buddy Fogelson took particular pride in raising Santa Gertrudis cattle. After years of running Herefords on a profitable commercial basis, he bought the sire of a new herd, Gee-Gee, at the Rockefeller Winrock Farms auction in Arkansas in 1958. Although the Santa Gertrudis had been developed in the semitropical climate of Texas, he was certain that he could raise the breed in the mountain country of New Mexico. "We pioneered in bringing them to the high country," Greer reported. "Of course, we raise cattle only for breeding—you feel you're improving the world's nutrition by bringing up the size and quality of the herd." It had been a sizable gamble, since each of the several dozen cows cost three to four thousand dollars, and Gee-Gee cost ten thousand dollars. However, like the shorthorns, they soon became prizewinners. Gee-Gee earned "grand champion" honors at San Antonio and Fort Worth stock shows.

Gilbert Ortiz, manager of the Forked Lightning Ranch for three decades, recalled, "Mrs. Fogelson loved this country. She would say that, if she could, she'd make Pecos and the ranch her primary home. She was a good horsewoman, and with her husband she would ride around to look at the one hundred to two hundred head of Santa Gertrudis cattle and just enjoy her time."

"Greer had tremendous balance in her life," Miranda Levy recalled. "Her life was absolutely devoted to Buddy. He loved having people around and I think that's why she entertained a lot." The rambling ranch house, built around a patio filled with flowers and greenery, was ideal for parties. Chuck-wagon picnic lunches on the banks of the Pecos River were a house specialty, complete with denim-covered tables and red bandanna napkins. For evening entertainment, the Fogelsons would set out a fiesta buffet on the patio, which was transformed with dozens of colorful lanterns, candles, and bright flowers (usually a profusion of Greer's favorite pinks and reds). "An invitation to the Forked Lightning Ranch was a very good ticket to get," recalled Ralph Levy. "They gave marvelous parties with margaritas and mariachis. Greer was the epitome of the word lady. She's strong as hell, generous as hell and with great compassion."

Among the Fogelsons' most frequent guests was Greer's cousin,

Dr. Sophia Sloan, who had moved to Canada, the Gregory Pecks, the David O. Selznicks, and Art Linkletter and his wife. "One rare luxury of the ranch is that the Santa Fe train can be stopped at the tiny station nearby," Linkletter recalled. "It was part of the 'right of way' deal made by the original owner. Greer, a wonderful hostess, was there to meet us when we arrived. She was wearing a magnificent Western costume with lavish scarves of lime and orange blowing in the breeze. It was as if a great director had carefully arranged the scene and she was the cattle queen in some wild Technicolor movie. . . . Beneath the awe-inspiring beauty and regal persona Greer was a kid at heart. Rather than the 'Queen and the Cavalier,' I prefer to think of Greer and Buddy as the jesters; each loved to laugh and enjoy a good story and each was capable of telling a good story in his or her own style. I recall most social evenings with them as being small, cozy affairs with six to eight people for dinner, the guests full of marvelous anecdotes; there was wry, understated humor from Buddy and my own contributions in the form of loving 'leg-pulling.'"

"This is the quaintest town," Greer said of Santa Fe, "where a movie star gets special mail delivery at her beauty shop because the beautician's husband happened to process it through the post office. To give you an idea of the contrasts I'll mention that one night we took friends in to the Santa Fe Opera and as we were riding back over the dirt road to the ranch house we came upon a wolf. I have followed tangential detours all my life, but I have at long last learned to be interested in where I am." Miranda Levy observed, "She never stopped plugging Santa Fe. She thought this place was heaven." Among the local citizenry, Greer was known as "La Dama del Cabello Naranja" (The Lady with the Orange Hair).

Jack Evinger always accompanied Greer on her Santa Fe shopping sprees. "I got a kick out of the fact that she would put her dark glasses and a hat on to disguise herself," he recalled. "But the minute she opened her mouth and said something, everybody knew who she was!"

Her activities in Santa Fe and Pecos grew as limitless as in Dallas. She headed a cancer fund drive, became an Honorary Colonel and Governor's first aide in New Mexico, and a sheriff's deputy and member of the posse in both Santa Fe and San Miguel Counties, New Mexico. She maintained a college scholarship program for girls at

Pecos High School. Beginning in 1960, the residents of Pecos annually celebrated their movie star neighbor by naming the Sunday closest to the actress's birthday "Greer Garson Day." On that day, Greer was driven through town, her fiery hair matching the red fire engine in which she rode. She was also named an honorary Admiral of the State Navy of New Mexico. "I converted my wardrobe to navy and white," she recalls. "It was too bad, because before I got piped aboard, I lost my entire navy of two tankers to Prudential Insurance."

She watched David Susskind's remake of *Mrs. Miniver* for CBS. The ninety-minute telecast featured Cathleen Nesbitt as Lady Beldon, Paul Roebling as Vin, Juliet Mills as Carol Beldon, and Leo Genn as Clem Miniver. Greer had little to say about the show, and neither, apparently, did the critics. "Now that the deed is done," commented *Variety*, "it's still as much a mystery as before the performance why David Susskind chose to resurrect for television this Jan Struther heart tugger that warmed the home front during World War II. Maureen O'Hara was wholly convincing in the title role, but Mrs. Miniver still is Greer Garson, and vice versa."

In early March 1959, Greer received a phone call from Dore Schary at the Forked Lightning Ranch. Her former MGM boss, who had resigned from the studio in November 1956, was now the successful author and producer of Broadway's *Sunrise at Campobello*, which recounted the true story of Franklin D. Roosevelt's struggle back into the political arena after a crippling bout with polio. Leland Hirshan, Greer's agent from William Morris, had recently submitted her name as a candidate for the role of Eleanor Roosevelt in the upcoming film version. Having turned down all offers since her mother's death, Greer was prepared to turn down this one as well.

"He phoned to ask me if I'd do the role," she recalled. "There was a dead silence—I don't know what Dore thought—but several things ran through my mind. I thought, well, it's a small part and I had a lot of things to do. Then, suddenly, I decided I should and would do it." Even as she hung up the telephone she regretted the decision. Buddy did not like the idea either. He argued that the part was not the key role and did not offer any special acting opportunities. It would also mean a long separation. With her mind made up, Greer immediately sat down with pen and paper. "Since I lost my sweet mother I have found it very difficult to adjust to this strange vacuum in my life," she wrote to Schary. "At present I seem to need time to study and meditate and the performing arts have lost their lure. But later on I suppose I will turn to the therapy of work in some form." But Dore would not give up. He wrote back: "I understand so well your feeling of disorientation since you lost your mother. I felt the same thing for months after my mother passed away. But life calls on us to function and I am sure that is what you will be doing very soon."

Soon after, she decided to sign the Warner Bros. contract, at $150,000 for four months' work. "She possesses the same Rooseveltian energy," Schary reported to Warner Bros. publicists, "the same rare ability of being intensely interested in everybody she meets." Vincent Donehue, who had directed the play and was now prepared to direct the film, was equally pleased, recalling the fine work Greer had done for him in "Reunion in Vienna" in 1955. "I realized she was a much better actress than she had ever been given a chance to be," he said. "She was scared to death, but there's a lot in her like Mrs. Roosevelt. The same ramrod up her back, that same kind of code—if you're going to cry, you go into your bedroom by yourself."

Upon her return to Los Angeles, Greer became painfully aware that five years away from motion pictures had affected her status in Hollywood. One afternoon as Jack Evinger drove her down Sunset Boulevard, they stopped at the intersection of Highland and Sunset. A group of students from Hollywood High School waved at them. Greer rolled down the window to wave back. "Those kids hollered back, 'Look, it's Lucille Ball!'" Jack Evinger recalls. "Mrs. Fogelson was furious."

Sunrise was the catalyst to pursue other work. She narrated children's stories for an MGM record album, performed on radio in "Stand-in For Murder" for *Lux Playhouse*, and accepted the lead in another *Hallmark Hall of Fame* telefilm, *Captain Brassbound's Conversion*, to be directed by George Schaefer at the NBC studios in Burbank. She played the role that George Bernard Shaw had thought ideally suited to her talents: Lady Cicely Waynflete, a globe-trotting charmer who converts Captain Brassbound, a cynical pirate, and prevents him from murdering her brother. Life seemed to imitate art on the set. For playing opposite her as Captain Brassbound was a Canadian newcomer to Los Angeles named Christopher Plummer. "No one could have been kinder or more loving than the lady in question when she welcomed me to that strange and distant town," Plummer recalled. "I fancied myself a bit of a rebel then, and was eager to impress her with my new found smouldering 'Anger,' but her quiet serenity and contagious humour reduced me at once to 'humble pie' and in an instant I was putty in her hands! Professionally she treated me as her equal, as she did all the others, and personally, she made me feel I had known her all my life. The charity, the ease, the graciousness of her nature were completely unforced and came as no surprise but seemed as natural and as inevitable as the day is long. It was all so clear that for her, Life and Work had long since come together and the devotion, the joy and the humanity with which she graces them both have made them one and the same."

When the show reached the air on May 2, *Variety* declared, "It doesn't fall to the lot of just any actress to play a Shaw comedy on television. George Schaefer, who has a long and illustrious string of credits as producer-director in this series, chose Greer Garson for this production. A better choice for the fiery adventuress could only come out of a dream. Miss Garson gives a commanding performance, so stylish in technique that one suspects the notable cast must have felt inferior."

The therapy of work allowed Greer to discuss with the press, for the first time, Nina's death. "I discovered the importance of prayer after the death of my wonderful mother," she told Louella Parsons. "I turned down script after script, didn't want to work, and had very little interest in anything. But I found that my prayers brought me out of that unhappy state of mind, and gave me a realization that I must not give way to my own personal feelings, and make other people unhappy. I only hope that I can radiate some of that belief in a motion picture some day."

Greer decided to fly to Mexico with her husband to make a cameo appearance in Columbia's all-star musical *Pepe* because, as she told reporters, "If ever there is a Mrs. role they think of me—even in Mexico!" Arriving in Vista Hermosa in early April 1960, she met Cantinflas, the star of the picture. The ambitious comedian, with more than twenty well-received Mexican films to his credit, had recently made his American debut in Mike Todd's *Around the World in Eighty Days*. *Pepe* was planned as his most lavish showcase, closely patterned after *Around the World in Eighty Days*. He was Pepe, a "little tramp" not unlike the character created by Charlie Chaplin, who travels to many exotic locales, including Hollywood and Las Vegas, in search of his beloved horse, which he has been forced to sell. Along the way he meets an incredible roster of American film stars. Greer Garson, Edward G. Robinson, and Dan Dailey were the first three introduced in the opening reel of *Pepe*. He meets them at a horse and cattle show where they are trying to buy Pepe's horse. As they watch Pepe engage in a bullfight in the arena, Robinson attempts to interest Greer in making a film with him. "Eddie, that's a lovely idea, but you know today I'm not Greer Garson the actress. I'm just Mrs. Buddy Fogelson, private citizen. And something tells me we may be competing for the same horse." As Greer sat in the arena and the cameras rolled, a surprise awaited her in the crowd. Sitting in the row behind her was her husband. "You should have seen Greer's face when she turned around," said director George Sidney to a reporter of the *Los Angeles Mirror-News*. "First time in twelve years of marriage she's ever been surprised about anything!" Buddy said with delighted satisfaction. Obviously enjoying his film debut, he told the *Los Angeles Mirror-News*: "I'm the only movie extra in the world in the 92 percent tax bracket. You know, I've become antagonistic toward big, solvent characters. Since becoming an actor, big businessmen seem like the dullest people in the world."

That evening, Cantinflas invited the Fogelsons to dinner at his luxurious home in Cuernavaca. "He was a warm and genial host, obviously adored by his household staff," Greer reported to *American Weekly*. "He superintended everything personally. Seasoned the cooking in the kitchen, made a strike in the bowling alley, danced like a leprechaun, was expert at tennis, billiards, swimming and enjoyed showing us his considerable art collection."

The three-hour film, catapulted by a powerful publicity blitz around the country, opened with a lavish premiere in New York on December 21, 1960, and earned impressive box-office returns. "The travels of a simple-souled little Mexican peon through the never-never world of motion pictures forms the narrative foundation of the long and eagerly awaited *Pepe*," remarked *Film Daily*. "It is a picture of charm, delight and surprise." Greer was not present at the all-star premiere. She was, by then, entirely immersed in the most challenging cinematic project of her career.

CHAPTER 23

"I ALWAYS HEDGED WHENEVER a member of the press asked me what I considered the greatest moment of my career, " Greer remarked in the spring of 1960. "But since filming *Sunrise at Campobello* I no longer hedge about the answer. The role of Eleanor Roosevelt has intense, personal meaning for me. I consider portraying her to be a great privilege."

The play, *Sunrise at Campobello,* produced by the Theatre Guild, originally opened at the Cort Theatre in New York on January 30, 1958, and featured Ralph Bellamy as Franklin Roosevelt, Mary Fickett as Eleanor Roosevelt, and Henry Jones as Louis Howe. The play begins in 1921, when FDR is stricken with polio while vacationing with his family at their summer retreat on Campobello Island, New Brunswick, Canada. He loses the use of his legs, and the family moves back to Hyde Park, New York, where Franklin's mother, Sara, intends to look after him. But Roosevelt is not content living as a semi-invalid and merely running the estate. He dreams of re-entering the world of politics. With the support of his wife, Eleanor, and his best friend, Louis Howe, he begins a comeback. His future looks bright when he takes ten fateful steps to the podium at the Democratic National Convention to make a speech during Al Smith's gubernatorial campaign in 1924. "I always thought there was a dramatic story in this portion of Roosevelt's life," Schary told the press on opening night. "I didn't write the play as a tribute to the President. That wouldn't be good drama. I wrote it because I think it is a tremendously gripping story of a man's fight against overwhelming odds." The play ran for eighteen months and won five Tony Awards, including Best Play, Best Director, and Best Actor.

Schary sold the screen rights to Warner Bros. for $500,000 with the proviso that he could produce the film and earn an extra $125,000 to write the screenplay. He intended to cast many of the original Broadway cast and crew in the movie. Despite Jack Warner's urgings to cast Marlon Brando as FDR and to utilize Robert Wise, John Sturges, or Vincente Minnelli as a director, Schary insisted on Ralph Bellamy, who had not missed one of his 857 stage performances, and Vincent Donehue. Greer Garson and Hume Cronyn, playing Louis Howe, and *Singing in the Rain*'s Jean Hagen, playing FDR's secretary Missy LeHand, were among his Hollywood additions.

Neither Dore Schary nor the Warner Bros. publicity department was prepared for the widespread belief in Hollywood that Greer Garson was all wrong for the part of Eleanor Roosevelt. "Ever since the original announcement that the lovely redhead would play Mrs. F.D.R . . . there have been many raised eyebrows," reported the *Los Angeles Mirror-News*. "Greer Garson and Mrs. Roosevelt would seem to have no physical similarities." "Leave it to Hollywood—they've got an Eisenhower Republican playing Eleanor Roosevelt!" wailed the *Beverly Hills Citizen*.

Greer and the Warner Bros. makeup department went all out to prove the critics wrong. The transformation involved a three-step process. First came the exhaustive research that Greer invested in each of her biographical roles. "I think one of my primary aims was not as much to create a photographic image of Mrs. Roosevelt but to obliterate the Greer Garson image," she said. "I think that an actor must really study and live a part, and the problem of projecting Mrs. Roosevelt's love, dignity, wisdom and compassion to her husband was foremost in my mind." For the second step, Greer brought one of her favorite makeup artists from MGM, Keester Sweeney, to apply the makeup contrived by the studio's own Gordon Bau. Her dentist from MGM, Dr. Scott Christensen, provided the finishing touch: a specially constructed dental mouthpiece. He was an ideal choice for this, since Mrs. Roosevelt had once been his patient. For the finishing touch Greer selected Noel Taylor, who had recently designed Ingrid Bergman's costumes for *Turn of the Screw,* to design her costumes. Of the result, one critic wrote: "Her beautiful face deformed by buck teeth, her mellifluous voice distorted into a semblance of Mrs. Roosevelt's speech impediment, Garson shed her screen persona with a virtuosity not always apparent during her years of stardom."

Schary took extreme pains to make the film historically authentic. He intended to shoot the movie on location, at the actual Roosevelt residences, with only the carefully reproduced interiors on the Warner lot. He sent daily memos to the Warner Bros. research department. What were the correct prices of vegetables and fruits at a roadside stand near Hyde Park? What was the exact seating plan for delegates at the 1924 Democratic Convention? How do you build a Roosevelt wheelchair? How had Eleanor Roosevelt dressed her hair in the 1920s? Schary went directly to the source on one question. He phoned Eleanor to find out if she had bicycled back in the 1920s, and the seventy-five-year-old replied: "I most certainly did ride a bicycle. I still can!" Proud of his attention to accuracy, Schary talked constantly about his project with associates in the Warner Bros. commissary. He was not amused to hear one employee remark: "Oh, yeah, 'Sunrise at Campanella.' Isn't that the story of former Dodger catcher, Roy Campanella?"

Principal photography got under way on April 20, 1960, at the Shrine Auditorium in Los Angeles. There, Schary gathered 3,150 extras to film the 1924 Democratic Convention. He even got into the act himself, portraying the delegate from Connecticut. Assistant director Russell Saunders was in charge of the sequence. "It was an incredible sight," recalled actor Tim Considine, who played FDR's son James. "As I wheeled Ralph Bellamy onto the set, I saw hundreds of extras packed into that massive room, cheering as we entered. I'll never forget it."

As they moved to Warner Bros. soundstages, Ralph Bellamy watched Greer's emerging performance with interest. "Greer Garson is an actress of the 'Old School,'" he observed. "And I hasten to say that doesn't mean 'Old Age.' It means complete research and study of physical characteristics for each part, as in the part of Eleanor Roosevelt." Like his costar, Ralph Bellamy had begun his career on the stage. An ambitious teenager, he had undertaken an intensive schedule—playing four hundred roles with fifteen different stock companies in a ten-year period. After 1930 he had worked in films, then abandoned Hollywood for the stage again in 1945. He considered his role as FDR to be one of his most difficult. "Great physical effort is involved in walking with stiff braces," he told Warner Bros. publicists. "If you falter you literally fall flat on your face. I did myself many times. Roosevelt's one fear was that of fire. To be able to escape a fire unaided, he taught himself to crawl. To do this, Roosevelt sat upright and then literally walked on his hands. He would do it with a joke to distract you from what he was doing."

The intensive location shooting schedule began in June 1959. First stop was the Roosevelt home at 47-49 East Sixty-fifth Street, New York City. Filming the exterior, the crew closed off the one-way street to traffic. On June 7, the cast and crew filmed the sequences at the Roosevelts' Hyde Park estate. Eleanor Roosevelt met with Donehue, Bellamy, and Garson and gave them a full tour. On their inspection of the spacious lawns, Greer found a four-leaf clover and took it as a fortunate sign for the company.

While lunching and renewing her acquaintance with the former First Lady, Greer used the opportunity to study Eleanor's unique speech pattern. "Mrs. Roosevelt's diction is much more English than it is American," she observed. "All the people who come from the New England states talk with a marked British accent. Besides, Mrs. Roosevelt attended school abroad for many years. Actually, I think she has more of an accent than I have." She was amused when a tourist, visiting the estate during the filming, remarked: "Mrs. Roosevelt sounds exactly like Greer Garson!"

After Hyde Park, the company moved on to Bangor, Maine, and Canada for the final ten days of shooting. "I've never seen a group of actors so eager to give the best possible performances," Donehue told New York reporters. "They reincarnated the Roosevelt family in the happy home life depicted in the motion picture. Why, Greer Garson actually received Mother's Day cards from her five screen children. And between scenes Ralph Bellamy could be found giving some fatherly advice to the youngsters or playing catch with them."

After the day of shooting in Bangor, the *Campobello* crew took a bus to Lubec, where a ferryboat provided transportation to Campobello Island, New Brunswick, off the Canadian coast. Once on the island, it was immediately obvious to everyone that little had changed there since the 1920s. For authenticity's sake, it was fortunate. However, for the Hollywood crew, who had stayed at the Warwick Hotel in New York and in comfortable motels near Hyde Park, the island's living conditions were primitive. Since there were no inns or restaurants, the Hammer family, who currently owned the historic Roosevelt cottage, helped arrange for accommodations in local homes. Meals were served in the meeting hall of St. Anne's Anglican Church by a Maine catering service.

Greer and Jean Hagen were housed a mile away from the Roosevelt cottage at the 135-year-old residence of Mrs. Wayne B. Morrell. Jutting off a cliff overlooking the Bay of Fundy and with some of its rooms lit only by candlelight, the house allowed Greer's romantic imagination to soar. She delighted in exploring the house's antiques, bathing in the evenings by firelight, and learning the island's history. A quiet summer retreat for the people of New Brunswick and Maine, Campobello was part of Charlotte County, New Brunswick, located near the entrance of Passamaquoddy Bay in the Bay of Fundy, one mile from the American coastline. It had been granted by George III in 1770 to Admiral William F. Owen, a Welshman of the Royal Navy who brought settlers to populate the isle. The Morrell home had been built by the grandson of Admiral Owen. And the forty-two-room Roosevelt cottage, which had been built by FDR's father, was a Roosevelt museum, with many of the family's furnishings still intact.

Dore Schary had the best accommodations of all. He slept nights in the bedroom used by FDR. One particular day of shooting at Campobello was especially memorable for Schary. "When Roosevelt was carried from the Campobello house on a homemade stretcher after his polio attack," he said, "people were certain that his career was ended. The opposite was the case. His sun was rising. Only twelve years later he returned to Campobello as President of the United States."

When location production ended, the crew returned to the studio in Burbank on June 20 to shoot the final interior scenes of Campobello on Stage Four, and the Hyde Park sequences on Stage Six. Greer performed the scenes in which Eleanor Roosevelt gave her first public addresses. "I can certainly understand Mrs. Roosevelt's nervousness during her first speeches," Greer said. "I could draw from my own experience for this scene. I remember the ordeal of my first talks during World War II bond drives and government tours of factories, shipyards and hospitals. I had never given a public speech before. When my turn came, only the fact that my knees had turned to jelly prevented me from racing to the nearest exit. I gradually discovered that thinking about the good cause helped me forget my nervousness."

She told cast and crew of the time she was supposed to address the National Federation of Press Women at New York's Waldorf Astoria. Following the directions of a helpful bellman who knew a "shortcut," she came upon a startled usher and explained that she was not on the program but was only supposed to bring greetings from the movie colony. She was introduced onto the stage, gazed out into the darkened audience pit, and began: "Ladies of the press . . ." She was practically done with her speech when she discerned the audience to be almost entirely male. "Who are you?" she finally asked. "We thank you, Miss Garson. We are the Radio Directors of America."

Sunrise at Campobello premiered at the RKO Palace Theater in New York City on September 28, 1960. Greer was unable to attend but sent a telegram to the box office from Santa Fe: "Dear Dore, May the Sunrise come up happy and glorious this evening. Love and best wishes from this far outpost. Greer and Buddy." Running over two and a half hours with intermission and a six-minute overture of popular songs from the 1920s, the film was distributed by Warner Bros. on a roadshow, reserved-seat basis.

On October 10, Greer wrote a letter to her friend Radie Harris, the entertainment columnist: "The *Reporter* for October 1st just reached us in this remote hacienda. It must have flown in on especially speedy wings as it brought me your lovely account of the New York premiere of *Sunrise at Campobello*. As you can imagine, all of us concerned are in a real glow about the fine reception given to the picture by critics and audiences. It was such a happy picture in the making. A wonderful group of people—and I think we all felt a sense of responsibility and more than a touch of inspiration. Personally, I had a double responsibility, wanting not to break the wonderful illusion that Ralph Bellamy manages to create in his portrait of FDR and also hoping, most earnestly, to convey an honest and fair impression of the great lady herself. It has been for me personally, a great inspiration to study her life and character. I do admire her so much and working in the picture has been a great tonic for me after the long unhappiness of last year. Buddy, too, enjoyed your page so much. He laughed and said, 'Well, it couldn't be nicer! That gal certainly can pour it on when she wants to, can't she!'"

On November 3, Dore Schary wrote to Greer: "I realized that I had never written you after the picture opened and by now you're probably whispering to totem gods and Buddy has probably named a tarantula after me. As I ask your forgiveness for my total preoccupation of the past few weeks, again let me recite to you the overwhelming reception that you have received all over—in New York and Boston, Los Angeles, Cleveland, Washington, Detroit, and hamlets beyond my ken—for the fabulous Eleanor that you put on the screen. I told you early in the game what I felt would happen with the magic you put up there, and it's all come true or will come true."

The screenplay of *Sunrise at Campobello* allowed adequate moments for each of the stars in the cast to shine, from Ralph Bellamy's FDR, reaching beyond the incapacities of a wheelchair to realize a fulfilling political career; to Hume Cronyn's passionate Louis Howe, Franklin's most supportive friend who predicted his presidential future before anyone else; to Ann Shoemaker, who, as Franklin's strong-willed mother, Sara, attempts to take command of her son with overprotective measures all the while cloaking a broken heart when it seems crippling disease has shattered his life. Greer's poignant portrayal of Eleanor is unique. She is still Mrs. Miniver, the supportive wife with a sense of humor, but for the first time on screen she reveals the overwhelming strain of being the family's pillar of strength. Everyone in the Roosevelt family looks to her when Franklin is bedridden, and she has few opportunities to let her guard down. "Mommy, you look tired," her children observe, but Eleanor will only admit, "Well, I am a little, darling." And then, in one startling scene when she attempts to comfort her children by reading to them, she bursts into tears and runs from the room. "I don't know anyone who's more entitled to a good cry," Louis Howe says to her when she attempts to hide her loss of control. The raw emotion that Greer displays in this scene may well have stemmed from the loss of Nina, her source of strength and comfort from her earliest babyhood. Certainly it is a level of emotion she never displayed before or after. Slowly, she collects herself in the sequence and, as her strength returns and her back straightens, she informs Howe, "I won't ever do that again. Not ever." Significantly, Greer was the only member of the cast who earned an Academy Award nomination—her seventh, for Best Actress. She also received a Golden Globe and Best Actress honors from the National Board of Review of Motion Pictures. Film critics were unanimous in their praise of Greer's new level of maturity in her screen acting. "If *Campobello* opened a new career for Schary, as a playwright in 1958," declared *Variety*, "then it can be said with equal confidence that this film should mark the beginning of a new, if she chooses to pursue it, brilliant career for Greer Garson. She comes through with a deeply moving, multifaceted characterization that reveals an understanding of emotions which transcends the point beyond which it seems possible for a director or writer, with all due respect, to assist in the creation of a performance. Miss Garson succeeds astonishingly in submerging her own personality and, considering the distinctive voice of Eleanor Roosevelt, the total impression is all the more remarkable. Miss Garson is a major source of interest, emerging from a shy introspective wife and mother to suggest, as the film ends, the positive, humane and politically conscious woman now so well known to the world."

Academy Awards night on April 17, 1961, was the culmination of Greer's *Sunrise* experience. Besides the recognition that she had received from the Academy, *Sunrise at Campobello* was also nominated for Best Art Direction, Best Sound, and Best Costume Design. Others in the Best Actress category were Shirley MacLaine (*The Apartment*), Melina Mercouri (*Never on Sunday*), Elizabeth Taylor (*Butterfield 8*), and Deborah Kerr (*The Sundowners*). As Greer got out of her limousine and approached the Santa Monica Civic Auditorium where the ceremony took place, a reporter asked her about the competition. Her reply was one she had repeated for years. "I don't feel that I'm in competition with anyone but myself," she said. "I compete with my own limitations, and knowledge and ability." Dore Schary, who accompanied her, was in a bad humor. Although pleased by the critical reception of his picture, he was aware that the film was not a big box-office attraction. Even Greer had written to him in dismay, asking, "How is the picture doing nationwide? While I was in Dallas I was able to observe the booking and business situation there, which I hope was not typical. The picture opened a few days before the election. Dallas is strongly Republican in sentiment and feelings were running pretty high. And everyone was staying at home, as you know, glued to TV during the last days of the campaign. The theatre 'starved to death' they told me and the picture was yanked the day after the election! The reviews had been excellent and everybody was completely taken by surprise at the short stay. Innumerable people came up to me and said: 'I hear the picture is simply wonderful, we've been meaning to go and see it.'" Certainly *Sunrise at Campobello* was not the box-office hit that another Warner Bros. film, *The Sundowners*, starring Kerr and Robert Mitchum was. Furious that the studio was supporting *Sundowners*, presumably because it was a moneymaker, Schary had fired off a memo to New York colleague William Fitelson: "Warners were plugging *Sundowners* all the way, and even now they are paying no attention to the fact that Greer Garson very likely has the best chance to win the Best Actress award next to Elizabeth Taylor, and conceivably could beat her for the award if some effort was made. I think the Warners are continuing to do an injustice to a good film, and that certainly they are doing an injustice to a fine lady and brilliant actress." In the end, Elizabeth Taylor won the Oscar that evening, and neither *Sunrise at Campobello* nor *The Sundowners* won any Academy Awards.

Although unwilling to do a follow-up motion picture to *Sunrise* because of the long separation from Buddy that it would entail, Greer continued her television work. In a *Dupont Show of the Month* titled "The Shadowed Affair," she finally grabbed the opportunity to act with Douglas Fairbanks Jr., who played a Nobel Prize-winning writer that she, as his wife, controls with pathological rigidity. In *General Electric Theater's* "R.S.V.P.," she played a glamorous Broadway actress who visits old friends and repairs their deteriorating marriage by flirting with the husband and making the once-distant wife jealous.

In 1963, Greer appeared in another *Hallmark Hall of Fame* production, *The Invincible Mr. Disraeli*, in New York. A *Daily News* writer found her and costar Trevor Howard "rehearsing with producer George Schaefer and the cast in a ballroom above Ratner's Delicatessen in the Bowery—a place that smells of goose-grease, old age and dirt. Even in these surroundings, Miss Garson moved with her chin high and nostrils flared and a kind of decency about her that sparkles." Greer enjoyed her supporting role as Mary Disraeli, who was fifteen years her husband's senior. "From what I have been able to learn, their marriage was a very warm and poignant relationship," she said. "This will be my third role for Hallmark and I am beginning to feel like one of the family."

During the summer of 1964, the Fogelsons embarked on another international vacation. Greer wrote to Louella Parsons: "Buddy and I celebrated our fifteenth anniversary and had a charming small party on the terrace of the Hotel De Paris at Monte Carlo. We were disappointed Jennifer and David Selznick couldn't make it as they celebrated their anniversary a couple of days earlier. They sent showers of beautiful roses. Princess Grace was looking lovely right after the official announcement that she and Prince Rainier are expecting another addition to their fairy-tale family. Back in New York we had a day at the Fair and an evening of 'Hello, Dolly.' Visiting backstage with Carol Channing, she told us that the color of her bright tousled wig had been copied from a color photograph of me and that they call it 'Garson pink'! Now we are again enjoying life at our Forked Lightning Ranch. Buddy getting much work done, and I'm reading scripts. Ray Stark sent me a play and a film, *Night of the Iguana,* that we are discussing."

Although she turned both scripts down ("They weren't my cup of tea"), Greer did make a memorable Christmas appearance on *The Red Skelton Show* on December 21, 1965. "The Plight Before Christmas" was the title of the story about a hobo (Skelton) who invites Greer, playing herself, to his shack for Christmas when he mistakenly assumes she is homeless. Among the admirers of a musical number she performed on the show was Bing Crosby, who wrote to the Fogelsons: "I saw Greer on the Skelton show and she was just delightful. I had no idea you could sing and dance like that, Greer. I suppose your dancing skill goes back to your younger days on the boards, but I'm confident that Buddy must have coached you in the singing phase of your performance. He must have taught you placement, breathing and projection. He was a master—Always your friend, Bing."

There is a significant moment in *The Red Skelton Show* when Greer is asked, "Who in show business does more for charity than you, Miss Garson?" She replies, "We all do our share with the benefits and the donations for all the good causes. But that, for some reason or another, is rather remote or impersonal. On Christmas Eve, I begin to wonder how much I'm giving of myself." Although it was a scripted response, Greer was in fact beginning to shift her energies from acting to philanthropy. She was inspired to do so by Buddy. "It's my husband who does the doing," she often remarked. "I just do the talking. He's the most self-effacing do-gooder in the world." That Christmas, after twenty-five years, a long-standing dream of Buddy Fogelson's was coming true. He had always been concerned about the historic fourteenth-century Pecos Indian Pueblo and seventeenth-century Franciscan Mission on the Forked Lightning Ranch. In December 1964, the National Park Service Director, George B. Hartzog Jr., proposed spending five hundred thousand dollars in five years to restore the ruins and build trails and a visitor center for tourists. He was backed by President Lyndon Johnson, who signed a bill making the ruins a National Monument. The Fogelsons transferred 382 acres of land to the federal government for the proposed site. The New Mexico Museum gave an additional sixty-two acres. "We now have a resident historian, an archaeologist, and three students directing excavation," Greer reported. "It's a fresh source of pride and income for the village of Pecos." "Despite her international fame and her golden Oscar statuette, Greer Garson didn't put on airs when she lived in New Mexico," observed the *Albuquerque Journal.* "She . . . became part of the New Mexico community."

As Mrs. Buddy Fogelson, the philanthropy that she had practiced in Los Angeles and Dallas broadened to Santa Fe. In the 1960s their attentions turned to St. Michael's College when its president, Brother Cyprian Luke Roney, approached Buddy Fogelson for a donation. Although St. Michael's had first opened its doors in the fall of 1947 with 148 students and a faculty of 15 Christian Brothers in the army barracks of the old Bruns General Army Hospital, the history of the small liberal arts college stretched back to 1874 when a territorial charter was established by the Christian Brothers, making it New Mexico's first college. Buddy's response to Brother Roney's offer was a challenge. He would provide five thousand dollars, but only if New Mexico's Archbishop Edwin Byrne matched the amount. "I doubt whether Mr. Fogelson realized how big a challenge that was," Brother Roney said, "but also I suspect he greatly relished the humor in the situation."

When the Archbishop matched the gift, Buddy kept his word and delivered the five thousand dollars. Soon after, the Fogelsons invited Brother Roney to the Forked Lightning Ranch for Greer's birthday. "On this first meeting I was impressed by Miss Garson's graciousness, charm and beauty," he recalls. "And I distinctly remember the twinkle in Mr. Fogelson's eyes. That first meeting had many happy sequels." In years to come the Fogelson money provided scholarships and funds to build a new science building and liberal arts center. When Buddy heard that the center would include a theater, he suggested that it bear his wife's name. "I'll never forget the day I brought her in my office, closed the door and asked her," Brother Roney recalls. "She looked out the French windows and said, 'You know, Roney, with every honor comes a responsibility. I'll have to think about it.'"

On June 5, 1964, Greer wrote to her old friend, George Cukor: "Quant à moi, I am glad to report that after quite a protracted period of domestic preoccupations there are four pictures being discussed now that I think might be interesting to do. I am keeping my fingers crossed that there will be no hitches as it would be fun to get out my makeup box again. High time, in fact!" One of these projects, *The Singing Nun*, came to fruition.

While learning French, producer Hayes Goetz had come across the true story of Sister Luc-Gabrielle. The young Dominican nun, known as Soeur Sourire, or "Sister Smile," was working in a Belgian settlement house in the slums of Antwerp when her musical talents were discovered by Phillips Records and led to a recording contract. The first album, including the famous "Dominique," sold half a million copies by 1963. Listening to the inspirational lyrics, Goetz became convinced that her story would make an excellent motion picture in the fashion of *Going My Way* or the more recent blockbuster *The Sound of Music*. He convinced a fellow producer, John Beck, to make the film with him and obtained the motion picture rights from Sister Luc-Gabrielle's home, the Monastery of the Dominicans of Fischermont on the outskirts of Waterloo, Belgium, with the provision that the nun's story be fictionalized.

Returning to Hollywood, Goetz made arrangements with MGM president Robert H. O'Brien and vice president Robert W. Weitman to produce the picture with the studio. Henry Koster, a veteran of religious pictures (*Come to the Stable, The Robe, A Man Called Peter*), was chosen to direct. After negotiations throughout the spring of 1964, they selected the final cast that represented Metro's past (Debbie Reynolds, Agnes Moorehead, Ricardo Montalban, and Tom Drake) as well as its present (Katharine Ross and Chad Everett). Television host Ed Sullivan, who reenacted his interview with Sister Luc-Gabrielle, rounded out the cast. Greer was signed to a five-week production schedule, for ten thousand dollars per week, to play the convent's prioress.

Although *The Singing Nun* was to begin shooting in less than two weeks, Greer was adamant about being present at St. Michael's College on September 10, 1965. The final phase of construction of the new nine-hundred-thousand-dollar Liberal Arts Center, which might yet bear her name, was taking place. Touring the site with Brother Luke, Jerome Monks, the college development director, and Brother Denys, the dramatics director, Greer told the *New Mexican*, "While this building was ingeniously conceived, featuring the most modern, contemporary design, its bricks, mortar and steel will not make a theatre. Only ideas reflected in music, dance and drama will give it life."

On September 20, 1965, Greer reentered the gates of Metro-Goldwyn-Mayer to begin work. It was a nostalgic homecoming, tinged with melancholia. For although a few of her old friends on the lot welcomed her back, many that she remembered were no longer there. In the nearly twelve years that she had been gone, the last vestiges of the studio system had crumbled. No longer was there an all-powerful mogul in control with a pool of talent at his disposal. Now producers, writers, and stars brought their projects to MGM. Instead of streets filled with "More Stars Than There Are in the Heavens," the lot looked sadly vacant. In contrast to the forty-six pictures that were being made in 1937 when Greer first arrived at MGM, only twenty were in production in 1965—and most of those were done on location or abroad. Financially, the studio was in a precarious situation, still suffering from a $17 million loss in 1963.

The studio's polished treatment of its stars was also a thing of the past. Elva Martien, in charge of the costumes for *The Singing Nun*, remembers Greer's first day on the lot. "I thought Greer was treated very shabbily," she recalls. "I was down on Stage Four putting the costumes in the dressing trailers. When I walked into Greer's dressing room I was shocked, because it was the filthiest thing I had ever walked into. We just got finished cleaning it up when she walked in. I breathed a sign of relief, thinking that if she had come five minutes earlier she would have walked into a disgraceful mess."

During filming that summer Greer received a number of honors. In July, at the forty-eighth annual convention of Lions International, she was presented an award for her contributions to CARE's service of food, education, and medicine around the world. "I do believe that this people to people project must convince even the most skeptical of our neighbors that we are . . . eager to share our blessings," she said. She was also named a "Woman of the World" by the Los Angeles Chapter of International Orphans. She was given Philadelphia's Fashion Group Award for being a continuing influence on American fashion. But none of them meant so much as the announcement in the *New Mexican*: "Liberal Arts Theatre Named after Actress Greer Garson." Included in the article was Greer's letter of acceptance to Brother Roney.

It is a great honor that you offer. In deciding to accept it I am mindful that no honors in this life come without attendant obligations. If the theatre bears my name, I will hold myself ready to serve wherever and however I can, the instructors and students who will be associated with it through the years.

Since my first visit to the college, I have watched with growing interest and admiration the development of this fine foundation and the spirit of dedication to those highest standards and ideals which alone can make a college, not merely an intellectual but also a spiritual influence . . . a force to enrich and ennoble the lives and characters of all who come in contact with its ambience. Moreover I love New Mexico, and this identification with St. Michael's College makes me very happy and very proud.

"When Buddy wanted it to be named after me I said 'Oh, no!'" she told *The Singing Nun* crew at teatime, "but then I indulged in the feminine privilege of changing my mind. Why not, when you're still around to enjoy it? Usually these things are terribly posthumous! I'm going to be able to bring my two lives together soon."

Philip Scheuer of the *Los Angeles Times* witnessed the filming of Ed Sullivan's sequence in *The Singing Nun*. "I watched Miss Garson in a scene in which Ed Sullivan was endeavoring to persuade her to give permission for Sister Ann to sing for his television show," he wrote. "He argued that she would be made visible to millions who had only heard her recordings . . . and he was seconded by Father Clementi (otherwise Ricardo Montalban), who had helped bring about the recording contract. Miss Garson only shook her head; then as Koster called 'cut,' she turned to Sullivan and ad-libbed, 'I should have asked you what your rating is!'"

During the filming, Greer confided to another *Times* writer that she still found acting in motion pictures to be complex. "It's very difficult, this mosaic work," she said. "To me acting is an exchange. But it explodes like a kaleidoscope. Then we go to lunch and it's very difficult to get the same rapport." By the end of October, Greer was finished with her brief scenes and departed MGM for the last time on October 27. She was not sorry. The haunted place was but a shadow of the exciting, busy film factory she remembered.

CHAPTER 24

WHEN GREER ARRIVED BACK IN SANTA FE on October 29, her melancholy reverie about the fate of Metro-Goldwyn-Mayer faded into excited anticipation. On the eve of the opening of the Greer Garson Theatre, the college announced the formation of a Theatre Guild, with its patroness as the honorary chairman. The final architectural touches were still being added to the theater, as a variety of performances began inside. There was a U.N. Day program and a concert by the Santa Fe Symphony. The official 1965-66 theatrical season began with *All by Myself* on November 15, starring Anna Russell. In honor of the Guild's new chairman, the opening included red roses for all the female patrons.

The theater's opening coincided with a rededication of St. Michael's and its coeducational facilities as The College of Santa Fe. On the point of coeducation Greer wrote to Brother Brendan, the chief librarian: "The College is certainly doing its part in helping to right a wrong attitude that has hampered women's opportunities and development for far too long. Frankly I could not have continued to feel such an interest and admiration for C.S.F. if an enlightened order and local faculty (especially dear Brother Luke) had not decided to make it a coeducational center of education!"

The formal dedication of the Greer Garson Theatre and the Liberal Arts Center took place on a cool Thursday evening, December 9, 1965. Santa Fe radio station KTRC and television reporters from Albuquerque were there to broadcast the event live. "We are all aware of the need for communication in today's world," Greer wrote in the program. "We have here a great opportunity and also a great responsibility. May we in this place, dedicated to the Arts and Sciences of communication, be inspired in all our endeavors to interpret and influence the minds and hearts of men."

Master of ceremonies Jerome Monks, chairman of the Development Council, opened the event. Rev. Arthur Kinsella, O.P., former chaplain of the college, delivered the invocation; the new hundred-seat lecture hall in the Liberal Arts Building bore his name. Then Brother Luke took the stage and introduced Greer Garson. "She is not only a successful actress," he said, "but a symbol of American womanhood, with intense personal concern and interest in her fellow men." As Greer mounted the podium, the audience of over five hundred rose to its feet in a standing ovation.

"Words are the tools of my trade," she began, visibly shaken, "but I am at a loss to speak after the beautiful tribute Brother Luke has just conferred upon me. I am so thrilled to have my name attached to such an edifice during my lifetime." Applause began once more, and she wiped away a tear. She thanked everyone behind the theater project and reminded the crowd that "brick and steel alone does not make the building, but the spirit in which it is used. One can learn the elements of performing arts by standing in front of a mirror and practicing lines but it isn't until the practice is put on the stage that one can make it work."

"Greer Garson, who has thrilled untold millions in her career as an actress, probably reached another zenith of her life Thursday night, with the dedication of the Greer Garson Theatre in the Liberal Arts Building at St. Michael's College," wrote Ralph Dohme in the *New Mexican.* "Without the aid of a script, she added an accent of beauty and emotion to a ceremony that often has been labelled as 'boring and cornball.' In a lighter vein, she . . . went on to [mention] some other things that have been named after her—such as a rose, tulip, a mountain, a dog and a jail. Of the Pecos jail, she said that she didn't think it was a bad jail and they do have good coffee—'I go there often for coffee.'" "St. Michael's officially became The College of Santa Fe that night," reported *New Mexican* writer Cheryl Wittenauer. "It was almost as though the institution had found a new patron saint."

In March, Greer made a guest appearance on *The Art Linkletter Show.* She brought with her a personal discovery, flamenco dancer Vincente Romero. "Buddy and I discovered Vincente when he danced at a party we gave at the ranch in New Mexico," she told the television audience. "He's really talented. I'm delighted to introduce him nationally. Years ago I recall seeing a very funny young man in a smoke-filled nightclub in Boston and urging my Hollywood producer pals to look him over. They didn't. His name? Oh, just Jerry Lewis!"

On March 4, 1966, Herbert G. Luft, vice president of the Hollywood Foreign Press Association, wrote to Greer: "I saw last night at MGM the motion picture, *The Singing Nun* and hasten to congratulate you on the wonderful portrayal as the Mother Prioress. Rarely, if ever, do I come out with such praise, but I feel your performance radiates so much warmth and human dignity, that I must drop you this line. Keep up the good spirit and keep making more pictures." Audiences seemed to share Luft's sentiments, and *The Singing Nun* made a healthy profit. Although the film did not match either the artistry or box office of *Going My Way* or *The Sound of Music,* as producer Hayes Goetz had hoped, it was a charming and entertaining vehicle for Debbie Reynolds, who displayed her characteristic verve as the determined, idealistic young nun. *The Singing Nun* also produced a best-selling soundtrack album. Although she had a subordinate role and once would have refused to play this latest variation of her saintly characterizations at MGM, Greer was pleased to be a part of the production. "We shouldn't lose sight of the fact entertainment should lift people," she said. "Years ago, I gave up my Church, my God. I was young. I began to doubt and to challenge the traditional faith. But as life went on for me, I realized, slowly, but surely, that I needed my Church back, and my God. Faith is the most essential thing in anyone's life, and especially for an actress, who needs it every day."

Greer arranged for a screening of *The Singing Nun* in Santa Fe for the benefit of St. Vincent's Hospital and The College of Santa Fe. She turned over her own salary and royalties from the film to CSF as well. *The Singing Nun* opened on a Thursday evening, April 14, at the Lensic Theatre. "Greer Garson Sweeps into Santa Fe for Premiere!" headlined the *New Mexican*. Vina Windes wrote: "Greer Garson is the kind of person who in movies, and by reputation, seems larger than life. When you meet her in person, you discover, with a pleasant sort of shock, that she is. Miss Garson swept into the Lensic Theatre on a wave of 'Ohs' and 'Ahs,' flashing cameras and smiling greetings, to

open the state premiere. Backstage, standing among Santa Fe's singing nuns, she made jokes about having freckles—'those are frown
wrinkles, you know'—and laughed. Asked to mingle with the guests
for a TV news shot, Miss Garson moved gaily into the glare of the
camera light, inviting 'Please mingle with me everybody, don't leave
me stranded here.' And she began to walk talking up and down the
scale, 'mingle . . . mingle . . . mingle . . .'"

During the evening's festivities New Mexico's Lieutenant Governor Mack Easley presented Greer with a proclamation of Greer
Garson Day, and Santa Fe Mayor Pat Hollis gave her a key to the city
and roses. "I think it's a Miniver rose," Greer said, "and I hope it's the
key to your hearts. This premiere has not only the sparkle and brilliance of other premieres I have attended, but warmth. And that is
uniquely Santa Fe!" After the show, as Greer departed the theater, she
admitted that she was not going to participate in the Academy Awards
ceremony on the eighteenth. "I think it's time I stayed home, put my
feet up and watched it in comfort." But it was not at the ranch that
she would relax but rather in Los Angeles, where she planned to make
her twenty-fifth film, *The Happiest Millionaire*.

Walt Disney considered the true story of Col. Anthony J. Drexel
Biddle, one of the most distinctive men in early twentieth-century
America, ideal screen fare and a worthy successor to *Mary Poppins*.
Cordelia Biddle had written a biography of her father in 1955, and
Kyle Crichton, who had cowritten the book, had adapted it for the
stage in 1958. Biddle was the patriarch of one of Philadelphia's oldest
and most influential families. He held Biddle Bible classes and jujitsu
and boxing lessons at his home at 2104 Walnut Street in Rittenhouse
Square. A novelist, avid explorer, and patron of the arts, Biddle was
also involved in American politics. He believed strongly in armed
preparedness during both World Wars, teaching hand-to-hand com-
bat to the Marine Corps and writing their manual, "Do or Die." If all
this did not disturb his aristocratic neighbors, the fact that he kept
live alligators as pets did. The marriage of his only daughter to the
equally wealthy Angier Duke and the comedic chaos it causes in the
aristocratic households was the focus of the stage play and the screenplay written by A.J. Carothers.

Mary Poppins songwriters Richard and Robert Sherman added
a musical score. Each song enhanced the characterizations and the

plot. For example, "There Are Those" was written to point out the differing opinions of the matriarchs—Angier's mother, Mrs. Duke, and the Biddles' Aunt Mary—while "Are We Dancing" furthered the romance of Cordelia and Angier Duke. Norman Tokar, who had directed Disney films since 1961 and had recently completed *Follow Me Boys*, was assigned as director. Walter Pidgeon had hoped to be cast in the leading role, but Walt Disney chose Fred MacMurray. The supporting cast included Greer's old friend, Dame Gladys Cooper, and three talented newcomers: Tommy Steele, John Davidson, and Lesley Anne Warren.

Bill Anderson, vice-president in charge of production at Disney, offered Greer the part of Angier Duke's mother. Already familiar with the story after seeing Walter Pidgeon perform in *The Happiest Millionaire*, she looked forward to playing the flamboyant matriarch of New York City society who had established Duke University. Vivien Leigh, Helen Hayes, and Geraldine Page had also been considered for the part but had turned it down. Anderson was pleased when Greer communicated her interest and wrote Walt: "With Garson and Cooper playing those roles, we should have an outstanding 'There Are Those' scene." A contract was drawn up. Greer would receive seventy-five thousand dollars for an eight-week production schedule behind the walls of movieland's most fabulous fantasy factory.

On the morning of May 5, 1966, Greer made her first visit to the Disney Studio in Burbank. Walt Disney invited her to lunch in the executive dining room with director Norman Tokar and A.J. Carothers. Afterward, the Sherman brothers played the score for her on the piano in Walt's office. It was a thoroughly enjoyable experience, and Greer left for a short stay in Palm Springs before her starting date on June 8.

In the meantime, Geraldine Page reconsidered her refusal to play Mrs. Duke. Norman Tokar went out to Greer's desert home and explained the situation. Would she consider playing Mrs. Biddle? Greer was hesitant. A gentle, aristocratic Mrs. Miniver character was far less interesting than another Auntie Mame. But when Tokar reminded her that the Shermans had written a song for Mrs. Biddle, "It Won't Be Long 'Til Christmas," which Greer loved, she agreed to the switch. This was fine with A.J. Carothers, since he had written the part of Mrs. Biddle with Greer in mind.

Upon her arrival back in Burbank she was welcomed by the cast and crew on Stage Two. A.J. Carothers observed that Greer was "very much the star, in the best sense. . . . She really took her work seriously. But she also had a real spirit and sense of humor about herself and life in general. I recall overhearing a fan remark to her, 'Oh, I wish I could look like Greer Garson,' and she replied, 'Oh, my dear, so do I!'" Greer arrived at the studio every day in a white Rolls Royce with a fresh rose in a vase inside. On that first day she dispersed tiny stuffed teddy bears among cast and crew. She performed all her scenes on an elaborate 28,340-square-foot, nine-room re-creation of the Biddle mansion designed by art director Carroll Clark and set decorator Emile Kuri, which was furnished with $450,000 worth of crystal chandeliers, walnut paneling, and antique furnishings. Principal photography got off to a shaky start on May 23, 1966. In rehearsals, Fred MacMurray had sprained his ankle preparing for the "I'll Always Be Irish" musical number. Then, a faulty twenty-thousand-dollar mechanical alligator specially made for the film had to be junked. The twelve live alligators that were brought to the studio from trainer Ken Earnest's California Alligator Farm in Buena Park, which had been supplying the creatures to movie studios since 1907, caused more trouble. One of the largest, eight-foot-long "George," ruined take after take of the "Fortuosity" dance number with Tommy Steele when he snapped his jaws and struck out at the actor.

The fact that Greer did not have to pretend to be a rich woman for *The Happiest Millionaire* was evident to cast and crew when she brought such wealthy friends from Dallas as H.C. Hunt and Stanley Marcus to visit the set. Since her marriage to Buddy Fogelson, Hollywood had never ceased to be amazed by her wide circle of distinguished acquaintances. Press agent David Resnik recalls, "She asked me once to show some friends around town. It turned out to be the Shah of Iran and his entourage!" "But who would ever suppose that my role as millionaire's wife would call for alligator handling?" she asked the press. "At first I had my doubts . . . but it really wasn't so bad. As I told Lesley Anne, I just pretended my gator was a $400 handbag from I. Magnin's. And filming the scene turned out to be great fun!"

When she joined rehearsals for the "I'll Always Be Irish" number, A.J. Carothers was on the set. "While all the other actors were off

Greer weds Col. E.E. "Buddy" Fogelson, July 15, 1949. She considered her life with him "the greatest adventure." Security Pacific.

Greer and Nina pose in costume for their roles in *That Forsyte Woman*. © Turner Entertainment Co. All rights reserved.

Above, A picturesque moment between the Minivers in the ill-advised sequel, *The Miniver Story. Left,* As Lady Loverly, the notorious jewel thief in *The Law and the Lady.* Both © Turner Entertainment Co. All rights reserved.

With costar Marlon Brando and MGM "rival" Deborah Kerr on the set of *Julius Caesar*. © Turner Entertainment Co.

Greer appeared with costars Robert Ryan and James Arness in *Her Twelve Men*. Bitterly disappointed that she had not made *Interrupted Melody* instead, she left MGM soon afterward. © Turner Entertainment Co. All rights reserved.

No one in Hollywood loved gardening as much as Greer did. Here she is watering flowers on the set of *Scandal at Scourie*.

"You should see my articles in the Beef Breeder's Gazette and the Shorthorn World," Greer said of her new interests at her husband's Forked Lightning Ranch.

Above, Greer proudly displays her catch from the Pecos River to Hans, the cook at Forked Lightning. *Below*, She was more at home outside the kitchen, here with herdsman Kay Lee Skipworth, looking after the prize-winning white shorthorns she brought from Scotland. Both © Turner Entertainment Co.

Frances Bergen, wife of Edgar and mother of Candice, is amused to read about Greer's adventures in Santa Fe outlined in the cover story of *New Mexico*.
© Turner Entertainment Co. All rights reserved.

Left, In the 1950s, like many other stars, Greer became a Hollywood freelancer. From the author's collection.
Below, Cameron Mitchell, Dana Andrews, and Lois Smith appeared with Greer in *Strange Lady in Town*.

Above, Tea at Hyde Park with Eleanor Roosevelt during production of *Sunrise at Campobello.* Hearst Newspaper Collection, University of Southern California. *Below*, Greer and Cantiflas in *Pepe.* From the author's collection.

Above, Greer joins (from left to right) Vivien Leigh, Laurence Olivier, Danny Kaye's wife Sylvia, Tallulah Bankhead, Kaye and Artur Rubenstein at Hedda Hopper's Hollywood home. A.M.P.A.S. *Below,* Greer enjoyed television work, such as an appearance on *The Bob Hope Show* with Vivian Blaine in a parody of "The Awful Truth", March 21, 1956. Hearst Collection.

One of Greer's finest portrayals: Lady Cicely Waynflete in George Bernard Shaw's "Captain Brassbound's Conversion." She loved it so much she played it on stage and television. Security Pacific.

Above, Celebrating her sixty-second birthday with Debbie Reynolds and Ricardo Montalban on the set of *The Singing Nun*. *Below*, Jim Gould, managing director of Radio City Music Hall, and Walt Disney visit Greer on the set of *The Happiest Millionaire*.

Above, Horse racing at Hollywood Park: (left to right) Jack Evinger, Dr. and Mrs. Bernstein, Zann Taylor, Greer, Buddy, Mervyn LeRoy, Cary Grant, and Charley Wittingham. Jockey Lafitt Pincay Jr. rode the Fogelson's horse, Noholme Jr., to a $54,650 victory. Courtesy of Jack and Marilyn Evinger. *Below,* Roddy McDowall, Greer's lifelong friend, took this photo of her in 1990. © Roddy McDowall.

Greer Garson
Theatre
Department Of
Performing Arts

The College of Santa Fe
GREER GARSON THEATRE
presents

THE MADWOMAN OF CHAILLOT

by Jean Giradoux
starring GREER GARSON

OCTOBER 1 • Governor's Benefit Performance

OCTOBER 2-7, 1975

ARMS AND THE MAN

by George Bernard Shaw
NOVEMBER 13-16, 1975

BUS STOP

by William Inge
FEBRUARY 12-15, 1976

ANYTHING GOES

by Cole Porter
APRIL 15-18, 1976

The program for Greer's final stage appearance, "The Madwoman of Chaillot."
Courtesy of The College of Santa Fe.

The Lady of the Miniver Rose. Courtesy of Elizabeth Jones.

in their dressing rooms, Greer would go up and down the family staircase, again and again. I finally said something about it to her, and she said, 'You see, I would have lived in this house for many years and I would know the stairs by touch. I would never have to look down. So when I come down the stairs I don't ever want to lower my eyes.' This professionalism was very expressive of her attitude during the picture."

While shooting *The Happiest Millionaire*, Greer kept a busy schedule and collected a number of awards. She recorded a record album, "The Royal Family of the Theatre," about the Barrymore family. The Long Beach Chamber of Commerce announced "Greer Garson Week" from June 19 to 25, during which she was presented with the annual Delba Award for her "outstanding contributions and high ideals in motion pictures." In the Grand Trianon Ballroom of the Beverly-Wilshire Hotel, Mrs. Fogelson and her old friend Walter Pidgeon were honored by the Alliance Francaise of Los Angeles for their contributions to French culture and world unity. She told the gathering: "I hope you will not be impatient if I try to express my thanks in very rusty French. I am very happy to be here tonight to meet with the members and friends of the French-American colony of Southern California. This occasion revives for me so many happy memories. I recall my student days at Grenoble University, and many delightful journeys and vacations spent in France, in little villages like Cassis on the Cote D'Azur, and L'Ile de Brehat in Brittany, and in the great cities, especially of course in Paris. All of us who work in the universal medium of communication that is film for cinema and television are grateful to you our Alliance Francaise for your recognition and encouragement of our individual efforts, however small, to help towards better understanding between the nations and the unity we all desire for the 'Family of Man.'"

A few days later, Greer wrote to Walter Pidgeon: "Dearest Walter, In my book you have always been Number One Wonderful Partner, Actor and Friend and as such I think of you as far above all the very transitory ratings of the multiple annual citations. I felt such a pang, however, when I heard your acceptance speech—so modest and touching—last Sunday at L'Alliance Francaise Awards. You should have a bookcase filled with such baubles, but indeed you don't need such trivial symbols—you must know that everyone loves, admires and likes you just enormously. And I'm your original One Woman Fan Club!"

On July 18, Geraldine Page made her appearance on Stage Two of the Disney lot. Watching her on the set, Greer realized what a fun part Mrs. Duke really was. "It's frustrating standing around and watching all the others saying those witty lines," she complained, "but Norman tells me that the mother is the eye of the hurricane. Well, I must say, it's pretty quiet there."

"We shot Geraldine Page's scenes pretty much back to back," A.J. Carothers recalls, "and you could see Greer dealing with the fact that Page was getting all the lines and all the flash as Mrs. Duke. One day I asked her how she was, and she said, 'Oh, fine. Of course, the snake has all the lines.' Lest that sound more severe than intended, there was a very popular book out at the time by Jean Kerr. It dealt with children putting on a play—a sort of Adam and Eve-type play in which one of the players complained that 'The snake has all the lines.'"

Greer prerecorded "It Won't Be Long 'Til Christmas" on June 2. The song had a troubled history. It was originally conceived by the Sherman brothers to take place during a train station sequence in which Mr. and Mrs. Biddle watch their sons depart for college. "The song made better sense in this part of the script—it was more integral," A.J. Carothers recalls. "Besides, it would have been a beautiful sequence," he recalls, "with the steam and an ornate, glass-ceilinged Victorian train station." But Walt Disney insisted that it be placed at the end of the film, when the last of the Biddles' children have left home. "Walt liked to put his favorite songs at the end of the picture so that the audience was sure to remember it when they left the theater," said Carothers. "The train set would also have been an extra expense. Of course Walt won his point." The controversy about the song would continue even after the film was released.

Although Greer completed her performance before the Disney cameras on August 2, she returned on the ninth and tenth to film a preview trailer for the film as well as charity spots for Diabetes Week and Toys for Tots on the Biddle mansion set. A.J. Carothers prepared a special script for the trailer. In it, Greer welcomes the audience into her home ("You'd like to see my house? I'd be delighted"); tours them about the parlor, kitchen, and conservatory; introduces them to the alligators; and invites them for tea on the terrace. All the while she introduces the Biddle family and friends through film clips.

In September, Greer and Buddy were back in Santa Fe to attend the Para los Niños Ball benefit at the La Fonda Hotel in honor of visiting Vice President Hubert H. Humphrey. Among the other guests were George Montgomery and New Mexico's Governor Campbell. The Fogelsons also attended the opening of the 1966 Greer Garson Theatre season, with *Bell, Book and Candle*.

When she heard that Walt Disney had been hospitalized with a recurring lung condition on December 11, Greer sent a telegram to St. Joseph's Hospital in Burbank: "Dear Walt, Not sure if you are still there being improved but if so hope you will very soon be graduating and returning home to flex your muscles around the Christmas tree. At this season of love and kindliness and rejoicing we want you most especially who gives the world so much of these things to be feeling well and happy." Four days later, Disney was dead. In honor of their friend, the Fogelsons established a memorial endowment at St. John's College library in Santa Fe. "St. John's offers a liberal arts curriculum based on 100 great books," Greer explained. "They hold seminars instead of classes. There's too much specializing too early nowadays. We can lose our heritage in two generations while trying to land a man on the moon." She received a thank-you note from Mrs. Disney: "Your gift in memoriam of Walt is greatly appreciated by my daughters and me. He got so much pleasure from the little stuffed bear and the flowers which you sent him while he was in the hospital. He was proud to include you in what he liked to call his studio 'family' and I'm sure must have told you how pleased he was with your performance in *The Happiest Millionaire*."

Following Disney's wishes, *The Happiest Millionaire*'s premiere was planned on a lavish scale as a benefit for Cal Arts, the professional school of performing and creative arts that Walt had helped to found. The Pantages Theater on Hollywood Boulevard was chosen to host the event and decorated to resemble the Biddle estate. The theater was closely linked with Disney history. As a showcase for RKO's films, the Pantages had handled many of Disney's cartoons and animated features, and between 1949 and 1960, when the theater had been the site of the Oscar ceremony, Walt Disney had accepted fifteen of his thirty-two Academy Awards on its stage. Greer and Buddy attended the premiere on June 23, 1967, riding up to the theater with the other *Millionaire* stars in an antique automobile. After the film, guests were entertained by the Disneyland Band as they were escorted to the

Hollywood Palladium for the post-premiere party.

The Biddle family hosted another premiere in Philadelphia. "I think *The Happiest Millionaire* is just divine," said Cordelia after the screening. "Dear, wonderful Walt Disney has done such a marvelous job of bringing the old Philadelphia back to life. Greer Garson is great. She has really captured mother's spirit. I was so pleased that she took the role." Although they attacked the picture as being over-produced and overlong, the critics agreed with this assessment. "Greer Garson, in a welcome return to films, is as warm and lovely as ever as Mrs. Biddle," remarked the *San Diego Union*. "Greer Garson as Mrs. Biddle is too lovely for words," added the *San Jose Mercury News*. "What a breathtakingly gracious woman she is and what charm she lends to the overworked script." Greer's response to the reviews was: "Gracious is a word that has haunted me all my life. I abhor it. The only things I'm allergic to are the words 'gracious' and caraway. I would much rather be thought of as zesty, mischievous or serene, although I'm not at all serene, I'm afraid."

By then, as *The Happiest Millionaire* opened throughout the country in the fall of 1967, it was obvious that her Disney experience had soured. After exhibitors complained about the running time and with Walt Disney no longer around to defend his film, studio editors cut the original 164-minute roadshow version to 144 minutes for general release, and down further to 141 minutes in some theaters. "It Won't Be Long 'Til Christmas," which was easy prey for the editors because of its placement at the end of the picture, was one of the first cuts. By the time the film opened in Houston, the song had permanently disappeared. "It was assumed that Greer would attend the Houston opening," recalls A.J. Carothers, "But she didn't, and I'm sure the reason was that her favorite sequence had been cut. I couldn't blame her."

It was not until November 1983 that Disney archivists restored *The Happiest Millionaire* to its original length by editing together two incomplete prints. Included was the "It Won't Be Long 'Til Christmas" sequence. The restored movie then received a new premiere November 6, 1984, on the Disney Channel and has enjoyed a successful afterlife on television and home video. The film was only moderately successful upon its opening in 1967, however, and barely recouped its $6 million cost. It was the thirteenth of Greer's motion pictures to play during the Christmas season at Radio City Music Hall. That brought the total to eighty-three weeks, a feat unmatched by any other actress.

Vivien Leigh succumbed to tuberculosis on July 8, 1967. In March of the following year, Greer attended "An Appreciation of Vivien Leigh" sponsored by the Friends of the Libraries at the University of Southern California. It was a nostalgic occasion to celebrate the life of one of her oldest friends and to renew friendships with Dame Gladys Cooper, Brian Aherne, George Cukor, and Mervyn LeRoy. Introduced to the gathering by Chester Erskine, she remarked upon the "warm and wonderful atmosphere here tonight. How Viv would love it—does love it." Of her association with Vivien over the years from London to Culver City, Greer added, "I think there's probably nobody in this room tonight who has known her longer than I have. Her debut in the London theatre took place just a few months before my own, so naturally I watched her career progress with more than average interest." Her concluding remarks about the Hollywood of the 1930s and 1940s were as much a personal comment on her own career as her friend's: "Looking back on those days when it was customary for actors and others under contract to be strongly critical of the studio's handling of their careers, I wonder if perhaps the moguls after all didn't know what was right for all of us. Because, as far as Vivien was concerned, time has proved that although she was enchanting in light comedy . . . her true quality and personal kind of artistry . . . will always be remembered in her interpretation of romantic heroines, with their fragile dignity, their need for love, their vulnerability and inevitable heartbreak."

On Wednesday, August 14, 1968, Winifred Blevans of the *Los Angeles Herald-Examiner* slipped into the Hollywood Masonic Hall. Prepared to do a story on the play that would open the second theatrical season at the Ahmanson Theatre, she was taken aback by the dramatic appearance of Elliot Martin. The director of the Center Theatre Group swept her inside with a excited cry, "Look at this cast! Have you ever seen anything like it?" Blevans recognized George Rose, Tony Tanner, Paul Ford, John Williams, and Darren McGavin. "George is going to play Reverend Rankin," Martin began, brimming with enthusiasm as he introduced her to each actor. "Tony is Drinkwater, Paul is Captain Kearney, John is Sir Howard Hallam, and

Darren will be *the* Captain. And then—" a woman emerged from behind the men, and made an exaggerated curtsey "—there is Greer Garson, as Lady Waynflete!" As Greer's giggle broke the group up into laughter, Elliot bowed and concluded with a flourish, "Welcome to the first day of rehearsal of 'Captain Brassbound's Conversion!'"

"Greer's Back, In Glitters of 'Brassbound'" read the headline in the *Los Angeles Herald Examiner.* In the article, Blevans wrote, "Elliot Martin hastened to insist that the glitter of the names in the *Brassbound* cast is not the only cause of his excitement. It is rather, the beginning of the realization of the concept behind the Center Theatre Group . . . to be able to make free use of the largest and most capable group of resident actors in this country . . . The capture of Miss Garson, an Academy Award winner, and film and television veterans like Darren McGavin and Paul Ford, represents a dramatic reversal for Martin. . . . The comedy, directed by Joseph Anthony, will be girded by the Center Theatre Group's most elaborate production to date."

"We tend to think of a classicist like Shaw heading for the library," Greer remarked, "but his humor and themes are very modern. In *Brassbound,* the theme of converting a man who lets his past dictate his life—opening him up to a future and releasing him from entanglements of the past—is like a psychological drama." She was eager to step back into Shaw's heroine. "I just love Lady Cicely," she said. "She has a vocabulary and a manner that is off-putting for a lady of today, but she has the right attitude toward people and events. She goes out to meet people, convinced that they will like her. She approaches people expecting things to go well. She anticipates the best from them and from circumstances, so she helps to make them that way. More people should be like that! And what a welcome relief 'Brassbound' will be for audiences! So much of what we see on the stage today is hopeless and despairing."

One hot afternoon, straight from rehearsals, Greer met with Joyce Haber of the *Los Angeles Times* for a lunch interview at the Hollywood Roosevelt Hotel. "She is a rare creature," Haber wrote, "looking cool and composed in a dress of chartreuse silk, an orange scarf knotted smartly around her neck . . . the kind who can get away with wearing white gloves in the afternoon in Hollywood, a town where white gloves are regarded as the fictional aberration of a man named Lewis Carroll and the prerogative of the rabbit in *Alice in*

Wonderland. Unlike so many stars of today, she is willing, nay, eager to conform to her onscreen image."

The play opened on a warm Tuesday evening, September 24, 1968. Among the good wishes Greer received that evening was a telegram from Lillian Burns and her husband, director George Sidney: "Our thoughts are with you back and front stage. As they say in Merry London Town—Break a Leg. With All Love." A last-minute switch was made when Paul Ford became ill and Jim Backus, with only three days of rehearsal, went on as Captain Hamlin Kearney.

After the performance, Greer, in a pale pink Victorian gown (the *Herald-Examiner* described her as "a pink rose among the thorny ship's crew"), departed the stage amid a standing ovation and emerged at the after-theater party a dazzling figure in a Norman Norell silver-sequined gown, a turquoise chiffon stole, and a topaz necklace, carrying a nosegay of tea roses. Before her in the Founders' Room of the Music Center, a fabulous array of Hollywood celebrities applauded her entrance and came forward to congratulate her. Kirk Douglas and his wife reached her first. "Congratulations, darling," Mrs. Douglas said, embracing her. The James Stewarts and the Charlton Hestons were there, as well as Art Linkletter, the Sinatras, the LeRoys, George Cukor, and Benjamin Thau. A phalanx of actresses including Jennifer Jones, Rosalind Russell, and Anne Baxter greeted her. As they expressed happy wishes, Greer's eyes filled with tears when she caught sight of a distinguished-looking gentleman and his wife moving through the crowd toward her. It was Walter and Ruth Pidgeon. "Congratulations, honey," he said, with a giant bear hug. "We had some trouble getting in here," Ruth laughed. "I just kept telling that mob of reporters out there that we had to get in to see someone special!" Suddenly, there was another stir in the crowd as someone attempted to make his way toward Greer. It was Jim Backus. "Darling, I knew you would save the day," she told him. "I'm just glad you were here tonight," he told her, "because tomorrow night I might not remember a line!"

Once again Greer Garson had taken Hollywood by storm. "Tuesday was a gala night at the Ahmanson Theatre for two of the best reasons in the entertainment world of Los Angeles," wrote Charles Faber in the *Citizen-News.* "Greer Garson, one of the great

Hollywood personalities, made her Los Angeles stage debut, and the Center Theatre Group began its second season at the Ahmanson. . . . Lady Cicely Waynflete is so incredibly well-bred, ruthlessly charming, and royally condescending in her belief that all men are equally susceptible to her benevolently despotic personal brand of democracy that only an actress of enormous personal charm would dare essay the role. Miss Garson has that charm in abundance, and the truly sparkling moments occur when a part of the minimal truth in the character makes contact with some portion of the elusive truth in her portrayal." The *Los Angeles Times* found Greer "an utterly delectable man-eater. She tosses about Shavian wit in a fine throaty growl, dismissing the idea witnesses should tell the whole truth with 'Nonsense—as if anybody ever knew the whole truth about anything!' She flits through the Moroccan desert with a steely, stylish charm like a pastel butterfly with an atomic warhead, scattering brigands and murderous Moors before her."

The *Los Angeles Times* declared Greer the "Woman of the Year." "There's one word I must ask you please not to use in describing me," Greer informed *Times* writer Kevin Thomas as she offered a cup of tea. "Whatever you do, don't sum me up as charming! Satirical! Ironic! Even menacing! Or enigmatic! Ah, that's it! Enigmatic!" Bowing to her wishes, he titled his article "Greer Garson: Mischief and Miniver" and concluded that: "To describe her as merely charming is like saying she is one and the same with Mrs. Miniver. True, she has her most famous character's graciousness and gallantry, but she herself is much more than that. The movies have often overlooked her wit and sense of mischief. Satirical and ironic she could be in . . . Shaw's 'Captain Brassbound's Conversion' . . . and menacing she has been . . . in 'The Little Foxes' on TV. . . . Enigmatic she is in that she makes you wonder how she could have achieved so much professional success, and assumed so many responsibilities—she's a member of sixty-three boards around the world—without sacrificing an ounce of her femininity."

The Fogelsons attended a subsequent Ahmanson production of *My Fair Lady* in May 1969. Greer's old friend Douglas Fairbanks Jr. was playing Henry Higgins. He wrote: "It was so terribly kind of you to send the candy clown and balloons on opening night. It's so amusing—and still is the showpiece of my dressing room. I take a particular pride in it, as being your frustrated 'movie discoverer,' and I have long taken pride in the friendship of you both."

In March 1970 Greer read the Easter story for the Sunrise Service at the Presbyterian church in Palm Desert. It was an experience no one ever forgot. "She had spoken at several services," Jack Evinger recalls, "but she always needed glasses to read the Bible. I remember she was running late for that particular service. She was always late, and she expected me to make up the difference. So we went speeding down there, and the preacher was out in the road waiting for us. Greer jumped out and walked directly to the pulpit. The Bible was open, and ready for her, but she couldn't read one word because she had forgotten her glasses. Everyone was standing at attention, waiting. She composed herself, like a trouper, and started ad-libbing. She went on and on for I think nearly an hour. The preacher said, 'I've never heard anything like that before in my life. It was beautiful.'"

Buddy Fogelson's interest in expanding the educational opportunities in New Mexico were rewarded on October 18, 1970, with the dedication of the E.E. Fogelson Library at The College of Santa Fe. Asked to speak before the gathering, Greer said:

> My husband is a very modest man and I was afraid I would never get him to this moment without having him disappear unaccountably and so I finally hit on a marvelous device. I said, "Well now, Fogelson, I just want you to know that in case you have a sinking spell or a sprained ankle, I'm all ready with a script of my own, because I was in on the typing of your notes and I know all your salient points and both your jokes. So, if you don't feel quite up to the moment, I'd be happy to be your understudy and step on blindly." Well, you'd be surprised how that sharpened him up.
>
> This is a wonderful, happy time. I hope that Brother Luke, the staff, and the friends of the College will always keep at least one of those wooden army barracks, just to remind us of the early beginnings of the College. I thought it was beautiful when our Brother Luke said, "These are only the outward and visible signs

of what is obviously a very powerful and inward spiritual grace, in which you have all shared."

That same month Greer received an honorary Communication
Arts Doctorate from The College of Santa Fe. The award did not have
the worldwide prestige of an Oscar, and the ceremony may have
lacked Hollywood glamour, but for Greer it was priceless. Seldom in
her acting career had she felt so fulfilled and satisfied as she read the
words on the beribboned scroll: "A star may be born, but only a
person's willingness to sacrifice, to study again and again, to give of
self when giving seems impossible, to live with empathy and sympathy as kin, then, truly, the star shows its light to the world."

CHAPTER 25

ON JANUARY 29, 1973, at 7:30 P.M., on CBS Television, Greer and Gil Stratton hosted "The Thoroughbreds," a nostalgic thirty-minute look back at Holly-wood's love affair with Santa Anita's racetrack. Stratton talked about the great riders, horses, and races, while Greer provided a glimpse of the movie colony of the 1930s and 1940s at the track and the fashions that they had inspired there. Although she admitted that she could not speak with authority on the subject, "I speak with beginner's enthusiasm!" Don Page, in his review in the *Los Angeles Times*, wrote: "The show does its job. If you aren't a racing fan, chances are you'll want to be after tonight!"

Although she had been raised to ride English-style and loved her travels over the rugged terrain of the Forked Lightning Ranch with her part-Arabian stallion, Ho-Hum Silver, Greer was not a born horse-race observer. In December 1942 she had informed Joseph Henry Steele of *Photoplay*: "I dislike bullfights, political arguments, bouillabaisse, hamburgers—they give me indigestion—and horse-racing." Buddy Fogelson, however, had a passion for it. Although he shrugged his shoulders over his wife's opinion at first ("I wasn't thinking about horses when I met her," he would remark with a smile), the colonel was determined to interest her in his hobby.

Buddy Fogelson had gathered a stable of thirty gray racehorses (his favorite color) prior to World War II. When he returned from the service he found that his lawyer, Fletcher Catron, had gotten rid of many of them. "I asked him why he'd done it," Buddy told the *Blood-Horse* in 1971. "He said he'd had to. Most of them were walking on their knees." He sought out more grays, much to his friend's consternation. "That was long before Native Dancer or Decidedly made that color a little more fashionable," Buddy said. "Back then, a lot of people believed a gray couldn't be a top horse. Well, mine weren't. 'Get a good one, and paint it gray,' a friend kept advising me." His luck changed in the ensuing decades with horses like Deck Hand, Noholme Jr., Colorado King, Race the Wind, Cara the King Jr., and Bargain Day. The victories of Deck Hand, winner of the Discovery, Pomona, and San Marcos Handicaps; and Bargain Day, who, Fogelson's trainer Charley Whittingham said, "has always been in there giving his best . . . picking up some substantial paychecks," pushed the Forked Lightning earnings toward $240,085.

But it was not until the advent of five-year-old Ack Ack, whom Buddy purchased from Capt. Harry F. Guggenheim on January 22, 1971, for five hundred thousand dollars, that Greer was lured to the racetrack to stay. From his first dramatic race under the Forked Lightning colors on February 6, in which the handsome dark bay stumbled badly but then leaped ahead to win the San Pasqual Handicap, she was hooked. "All of a sudden I found myself in a race to get the sports pages in the morning," Greer admitted. "I love to watch Ack Ack. . . . My British cool, I blew it completely. What a wonderful name to yell—Ack Ack Ack Ack Ack!" Thereafter, she referred to herself as Ack Ack's fan mail secretary and began to compile a garageful of scrapbooks and press clippings.

Greer's new hobby amazed her Southern California friends. After a brief stay in a hospital under the care of her cardiologist, Dr. Corday, she mentioned to reporters that she had used the same bed vacated by Gen. Omar Bradley and sent him a note: "I'm sleeping in your bed (signed) Goldilocks." A few days later she received a thank-you note from Lt. Col. John P. Dodson on behalf of the Bradleys, which mentioned her recent appearance on *The Johnny Carson Show*. They thought she was "as always, beautiful, vivacious and witty and the best ad for stud service they have ever seen in action. So good, in fact, that Mrs. Bradley was quite ready to take the next flight into Kentucky."

Ack Ack was indeed a remarkable animal. At three, he won the Arlington Classic, earned first place in the Withers Stakes, and set a new track record of 1:34 2/5 at Churchill Downs in the one-mile Derby Trial Stakes. He scored in a division of the Bahamas Stakes and finished third in the Jersey Derby. At the age of four he won the Los

Angeles and Autumn Days Handicaps. But his record at five, under trainer Charley Whittingham and jockey Willie Shoemaker, was unprecedented. In seven months he scored four more consecutive stakes victories in the San Antonio Stakes, Santa Anita, Hollywood Express, and American Handicap. In his greatest achievement, he won the Hollywood Gold Cup Handicap under 134 pounds—the heaviest weight ever carried to victory in that event. "While Southern California has been suffering through a weird and wild winter of record brush fires, record winds, record heat waves, record cold waves, and a devastating earthquake which wrought a lot of physical and mental damage," Leon Rasmussen remarked in the *Thoroughbred Record*, "Forked Lightning Ranch's Kentucky-bred Ack Ack has been a brilliant, consistent force in this land of seething uncertainty." Greer's old butler in Los Angeles won enough money on the horse to buy a retirement home on the Isle of Wight in England. "He bet by the thousands of dollars," recalls Jack Evinger, "because Ack Ack never lost a race!"

After the victorious San Antonio stakes, Greer presented Bill Shoemaker with a congratulatory kiss. She had almost arrived too late because she had been part of the committee welcoming the Queen Mary to her final mooring place in Long Beach. She was tossed a ceremonial line to tie up the legendary ship and told reporters, "The Queen Mary and I have a lot in common. We are both from England and were both invited to the United States. I hope she will be as happy here as I have been."

At the track, Greer usually bet two dollars on the horse with the longest tail. When it was a Fogelson racer, she upped the ante to ten dollars. "That was her theory," recalled Jack. "Of course, she lost along with all the rest of us." She also took it upon herself to decide the Forked Lightning racing colors. At first she chose flaming red racing silks and then switched to pink and powder blue. Frequently the Fogelsons showed up color coordinated as well, with Greer in a red jacket and white pants by Givenchy and Buddy in a red tattersall jacket from his tailor. "Living with Buddy has broadened my life," she once said. "I've shared the excitement of sitting up with him all night waiting for a gusher to come in answering fan mail for a horse."

By now both Fogelsons were active members of the Thoroughbred Racing Association. Buddy was elected to the boards of the Hollywood Turf Club and Hollywood Park. As "The Thoroughbreds" had indicated, they found themselves in familiar society. There Greer could chat with Mervyn LeRoy, President of Hollywood Park, Cary Grant, Carroll O'Connor, Mrs. Jule Styne, Gen. Omar Bradley, and Jim and Henny Backus. Meanwhile, Buddy and Herbert Hutner watched the races: "Two gentlemen who take their racing seriously," observed Jody Jacobs of the *Los Angeles Times*. "Not much chitchat or food for them." "The Fogelsons were both horse people," Jack Evinger recalls. "Don Pierce or Willie Shoemaker were their jockeys. We were always out at either Santa Anita or Hollywood Park or Del Mar. At Hollywood Park we would always go up to [LeRoy's] table in the Director's Room for a massive lunch and sit up there and eat until they had to roll us to the car." "We used to go with them to the races," said Julie Hutner, "and travel around to see Ack Ack race. At Santa Anita, we were generally the guests of the owners of the track. I remember a speech Greer made once. She said, 'Ack Ack is to us like a mountain. He's there for everyone to see and enjoy. We only have the care of Ack Ack for awhile, but he is for everyone's pleasure.'"

On a seemingly unbeatable winning streak, Buddy and Charley Whittingham planned a bid for Ack Ack in the Woodward Stakes in the East. But it was not to be. Ack Ack developed colic and an impaction, which required a VEE vaccination. "It became impossible to get him up to the Woodward," Whittingham told the press. "I would have had to run him cold turkey, and that's pretty difficult to do over at Belmont Park without a race in your horse."

In November 1971 the Fogelsons retired Ack Ack to stud, for a fee of $15,000, at A.B. Claiborne Farm, a breeding farm in Paris, Kentucky, famed for its internationally renowned stallion roster. Greer took special care to look after the horse, even choosing a pet cat to keep him company. "It's been a happy privilege to be Ack Ack's custodian," she said. "It's like a trust. We have tried to help him meet his potential. It is fun awaiting his first crop of champion children."

In January 1972 the Fogelsons sold the house at 680 Stone Canyon, or "Garson's Gardens" as they had affectionately called it, for $250,000. For their new home they combined two apartments into a five-bedroom suite at Wilshire Terrace. Originally built in 1961, it was one of the first residential buildings on the Wilshire Boulevard Corridor. "I am in the middle of moving our Los Angeles base from the rambling, roomy hacienda that has been my California home for twenty-five years to an apartment not far from here on the west side," she wrote to Edward Purrington, the chairman of Performing Arts at The College of Santa Fe. "The amount of moss I seem to have accumulated is incredible and the operation is quite a challenge physically and mentally, but when completed will add immeasurably, we hope, to the simplification of our design for living."

"That move from 680 Stone Canyon was a nightmare," Jack Evinger recalls. "Every clothes closet was full, everything was full. The butler and I hauled a lot of things in the big station wagon to their new apartment. But the interior decorator, one of Beverly Hills' finest, would tell me, 'Jack, you'll have to take that back to 680. It does not fit into my arrangement here. The place looks like a warehouse instead of a beautiful place to live.' But Mrs. Fogelson overruled him, telling him she would not get rid of her things, and he threw up his hands in defeat. She gave me so much stuff I had to build another wing onto my house!"

On January 26, Buddy and Greer were special guests at the Eclipse Awards Winners' Circle Dinner in the grand ballroom of the Waldorf-Astoria in New York. It was the first time horse racers had been brought together to honor a season of champion horses. That evening the Fogelsons received three Eclipse Awards for Ack Ack, as champion sprinter, champion handicapper, and Horse of the Year, having earned a total of $636,641. "Miss Garson's speech was longer than anticipated," reported Leon Rasmussen for the *Thoroughbred Record,* "and it involved a number of clichés, but they certainly sounded better than we ever had heard them sound before. Her presence added a sparkle to the ceremony."

In June 1972, Greer received a letter from Edward Purrington at The College of Santa Fe. "I have a notion that has been rattling around in my head for some time," he wrote, "which I want to share with you: would you consider being 'guest artist' in a production by the Performing Arts Department, say, as the Madwoman of Chaillot, either next year or the following year? It would be a particularly fine experience for our drama majors as well as for all of those interested in the College. I realize there are mammoth problems in trying to work out a schedule (which is why I include 73-74 as a possibility). You may very well have other ideas of a vehicle, but I think you would be a delicious Madwoman!"

Intrigued with the possibilities, most of all to perform on stage again, Greer considered the offer during a busy award season. In late October 1972 she was honored with the Presbyterian Hospital Center Foundation's fourth Award for Excellence for "personal achievements to benefit mankind," presented at the center's annual dinner in Albuquerque. Later, she accepted an Honorary Doctorate in Music from the Cleveland Institute of Music. Her Commencement Day address was entitled, "Of People, Performers and Push-Buttons."

Today is a lovely day for me as it must be for all of you in the graduating class. I regard this diploma as a most delightful and unexpected award for work done in all the good years I've enjoyed in the acting profession since I first launched the frail barque of my fortunes on the choppy waters and dangerous currents of a career in the theatre. There will be many barques bravely launched by you out of this fine harbour after today. They are not in the least frail for you start out well equipped and should be full of confidence as you set sail.

There are many similarities between the actor's life and the musician's. For example I can't resist warning you from my own experience that it may not be all lollipops and roses for those of you who will be making a livelihood as well as a career in music. If it is as precarious a living as the actor's, you will be advised, as I was, to have a second string to your bow, learn a marketable skill in case there are long, dry runs between engagements. That's probably a good idea, unless you have a wealthy family behind you, which is an even better idea. Better still, is to have confidence in yourself—even if it's misplaced! And above all, someone who believes in you, even before you have proved yourself. That's one of the greatest things I could wish for an artist. In my case family and friends predicted doom. They were certain that even with some training and talent, I couldn't possibly make it without money, influence or connections. My mother was the only person who encouraged me to follow my dream, not for any thought of fame or fortune, but simply because she believed that everyone has the right to try to find occupational happiness in life. And through the bad times, and there were plenty of them, she always told me, "Have faith in your star." So, especially to those of you who will be making music your career, I say, "Have faith in your star."

Here in this beautiful school you are all blessed with occupational happiness and I hope nothing will ever prevent or impede your continuing in it. The world needs music. And the world needs people who are happy. I am thinking of two of the happiest people I ever met. Both are well known to all of you—those exquisite artists and dear human beings, Vitya Vronsky and Victor Babin. I know the idea of inviting me here originated with them and I am very grateful to your chairman and directors for following through. Strange how paths cross and meet again in life. Years ago when I was still a student I was a fan of the great duo-pianists from Europe. Vronsky and Babin were then concertizing and recording in Europe. Years later, we met again. By many tangents I had arrived at a new pattern of lifestyle, spending part of every year with my husband on his historic cattle ranch in the mountains of New Mexico. Imagine my surprise and delight to find echoes of the Old World in the New. . . . Dr. and Mrs. Babin were living quite near in an idyllic summer retreat they called (what else?) 'Rancho Piano' . . . though why not 'Rancho Dos Pianos'? I often wondered. What an oasis of friendship, with laughter, warmth, good company, good talk, great cooking and glorious music! How I envied the students when I heard that these two inimitable artists were going to be associated with the Cleveland Institute of Music! This is how, through a friend's happy thought, I came to be in Cleveland today. Maybe now you are wondering why! Certainly my virtuosity as a practicing musician would not qualify me to be among you. My early romance with the piano ended abruptly with concentration on college courses. My flirtation with the guitar and later with African drums was exhilarating but brief. I can claim that when I was first imported to Hollywood from the London theater, I brought with me a rare treasure-trove, collected in Ireland and Scotland, of most unusual folk-songs (also a most unusual singing voice!). Alas! I was ten years ahead of the popular rediscovery of such music in America and could inspire no interest at the studio. Otherwise I might have been the Bobbie Gentry of motion pictures and a bonafide part of the music scene. But it was not to be. I did think today of bringing along my two-inch harmonica, given to me years ago by Larry Adler, but my repertoire would hardly be appropriate in this classical milieu. . . . Somehow everything I play on it, from Bach to Bacharach, comes out sounding like "Old McDonald Had a Farm." I'm afraid the directors might un-doctorate me on the spot. Evidently then, I am here because I am an actor and because as fellow performers we have much in common. The arts are direct channels of human communication, and music is perhaps the greatest international language since time began. You will be part of this God-given medium for increasing understanding between races and nations. I hope you will be traveling often to bring music and joy where it is needed. You can be a great and powerful influence for good, and you will be helping to keep the lively arts lively in our electronic, push-button world.

After Ack Ack's retirement, the Fogelsons remained a familiar sight at the track. But the golden age had passed. There were horses such as Rising Arc and Barbazon Jr., who won ten thousand dollars in July 1971, and Born American, who won six thousand dollars that same month. In January 1972 Yes, Of Course won seven thousand dollars. Yes, Of Course won again at Santa Anita in February 1974. But of this horse's variable record, Greer remarked "We're thinking of changing the name to Yes, Perhaps." The last triumph was Really

Somebody, who earned twelve thousand dollars and first-place honors on May 10, 1979, at Hollywood Park. Although she learned to love the excitement of the racetrack, the glittering social whirl of the glamorous Turf Club, and caring for the horses, Greer was bemused by all the publicity Ack Ack won. "All sorts of people—in restaurants, in stores—come up to Buddy and me and say, 'How's our horse?' They never say, 'How's our wife?' And I used to be something of a movie idol."

CHAPTER 26

ON JULY 23, 1974, the Fogelsons celebrated their silver wedding anniversary at Chasen's in Beverly Hills. Mervyn and Kitty LeRoy were there, and Aunt Evelyn. "When I left Hollywood to marry Buddy, and live with him on a working cattle ranch, our friends gave us six months," Greer said. "We came of such different worlds, he with his business affairs and loving the life of his ranch in New Mexico, and I the bloomin' movie star." When an article had appeared in the *National Enquirer* declaring that the Fogelsons were about to get a divorce, Greer had been furious. "She immediately wanted to sue," Jack Evinger recalled. "But her lawyer, John Roach, insisted that it would only cause more trouble." There had been concern on Buddy's part that her career, revitalized by *Sunrise at Campobello* and *Captain Brassbound's Conversion,* would strain their marriage as in the 1950s. "I wish she weren't involved in so many things in such a big way," he had grumbled on the set of *Pepe.* "But all actresses want to act and they're not quite happy if they do not."

By 1970, when it became obvious to film and theater critics and her fans that she did not intend to take advantage of her new success, they assumed she had sacrificed her career for her marriage. In fact it was true that she turned down an array of stage offers, including Emlyn Williams's *The Corn Is Green,* Ibsen's *Ghosts,* James Goldman's *The Lion in Winter,* and Noël Coward's *South Sea Bubble,* but Greer Garson Fogelson was discovering new avenues of interest and increasingly preferred the quiet serenity of the Forked Lightning Ranch, philanthropy, and marriage to the fast-paced Hollywood lifestyle. "I now do only the projects which excite me particularly," she explained. "It doesn't mean my interest in acting has waned. Fewer

film and play performances have actually sharpened my love of acting. I hope I'll always continue to act."

But there were fewer opportunities in the 1970s for her. Filmmakers rarely made the sophisticated, romantic comedies or dramas
that she preferred, and she refused to join her Hollywood peers like
Joan Crawford, Olivia de Havilland, and Bette Davis who were making horror films like *Whatever Happened to Baby Jane, Lady in a Cage,*
and *Hush Hush Sweet Charlotte.* "I've been offered nymphomaniacs,
kleptomaniacs, pyromaniacs, homicidal maniacs and just plain maniacs," she reported. "I think producers felt that after playing a long
series of noble and admirable characters there would be quite a lot
of shock value in seeing me play something altogether different. But
I prefer upbeat stories that send people out of the theater feeling
better than they did coming in. It's my cup of tea."

During interviews, she frequently and sharply criticized current
films and filmmakers. "I'm not a keyhole peeper in real life, so why
should I go to the cinema to be a keyhole peeper?" she said. "Producers should have more courage. People will respond to stories with love
and courage and happy endings instead of shockers. I think the mirror should be tilted slightly upward when it's reflecting life—toward
the cheerful, the tender, the compassionate, the brave, the funny, the
encouraging—and not tilted down to the troubled vistas of conflict."

Greer also chastised reporters who assumed that she had retired.
"Old? No, I'll never be old," she would say. "I'm a creature of impulsive enthusiasms. I'll be taking flying lessons or skiing or off on a trip
to the moon. If I cease to want to learn I'll be under the daisies. Life
is full of challenges, and its every stage is wonderful." In Los Angeles
there were "Random Readings" for her to do at the Love Gift Tea for
the Women's Association of the Beverly Hills Presbyterian Church.
She participated in the mayor's conference on Action for Community Beauty, or "Operation Flowerpot." In Santa Fe she brought the
Royal Shakespeare Company to visit the Greer Garson Theatre three
times, as well as members of the National Theatre, and helped launch
the British-American Theatre Institute. In Dallas she did radio spots
for the Symphony Orchestra, spoke at the University Club of Speech
Arts, and was present at the unveiling of her wax image in the Southwestern Historical Wax Museum. She was made an honorary chairwoman of the Bash for the Bard, a benefit for the Shakespeare Festival

of Dallas, and the Shakespeare Globe Center. As a member of the Dallas Free Shakespeare Theater, she raised money for "Free Shakespeare in the Park." She also received the Distinguished Women's Award from the Northwood Institute in Detroit, Michigan, for her contributions to the arts.

She was named the "Ambassador of Good Will for California, New Mexico, and Great Britain" by Texas Governor William P. Clements for her continued pursuits as an "ambassador of the world." She attended numerous White House political dinners with her husband, including a particularly memorable one in the Nixon White House to honor Harold Wilson, the prime minister of Great Britain. She hosted Rachid Badri of Tunisia at a tea party for the governor of Texas, as well as Madame Hsieh Hsi teh from Shanghai's Fudan University. She was made an honorary Admiral in the Texas Navy and an Aide-de-Camp for the state of New Mexico. She was the Texas State Chairwoman for Easter and Christmas Seals, and headed the Salvation Army's Christmas Campaign and the Cancer Crusade in Los Angeles. She found time to star in a two-part radio presentation of *Evangeline,* based on the life of Evangeline Booth, the former commander of the Salvation Army, and to attend the annual George Bernard Shaw Festival in Dublin.

In the years to come, Greer could be found more frequently behind the scenes instead of front and center. The Fogelsons became theatrical producers. During the run of *Auntie Mame,* Greer had befriended Arthur Cantor, a New York theatrical producer. Together, Cantor and the Fogelsons brought Alec McCowen's one-man show, *St. Mark's Gospel,* to America from London. That was just the beginning. They produced *The Kingfisher,* starring Rex Harrison and Claudette Colbert, and *Souvenir* at the Shubert Theatre, with Deborah Kerr and Tony Musante. *On Golden Pond* and *Playboy of the Western World* were others. "I can't think of a nicer way of losing my money," Greer told the *New York Times.* "I like to do offbeat things though, things that can be offered in small theaters. I don't want to get involved with gigantic, big-budget productions." If Greer and Buddy were not backstage, they were out front as an enthusiastic audience. Greer saw Myrna Loy in *Relatively Speaking* in Dallas. Myrna recalled: "Greer Garson appeared backstage with an exquisite carrying case of perfume from Gucci. I was bowled over by her gracious gesture. I never knew her terribly well in Hollywood, but closer friends often did far less when I hit their bailiwicks."

When Greer made her final appearance for the *Hallmark Hall of Fame* in April 1974 as Queen Mary in "Crown Matrimonial," English journalist Colin Barnes interviewed her at Wilshire Terrace. "About the little things in life, Greer Garson at least remains meticulously English," he observed. "Her sixth-floor flat does its best to evoke the interior of a manor house in Sussex. The walls are covered with paintings and the living-room is dominated by a large, open hearth. Robert, the English butler, serves champagne, enquires about the Chelsea Football Club and confides his hopes of retiring to the Isle of Wight. At 65 [*sic*], she is still striking. She is visibly very much the actress who, in 1940, Hollywood chose to project as the essence of English womanhood—genteel, thoroughbred, carefully-spoken but liable to be 'awfully-strong' when danger looms. An image manufactured for America, but greatly relished by us in the austere war years and after."

"Crown Matrimonial," based on Royce Ryton's play, dealt with the abdication of King Edward VIII. The show was taped in London, and once again she enlisted William Tuttle as her makeup man. "It is one of the most exciting, challenging and inspiring assignments ever given to me as an actress," she told the English press. "I love to do biography, it is more interesting than fiction. I found it interesting to go back to the country of my childhood, and portray a woman who was a wonderful, shining beacon in a changing world. I never met her, though I used to rub shoulders with Edward VIII when he was Prince of Wales, dancing in nightclubs. But I saw Queen Mary on a number of occasions. She came to the theatre to see 'Mademoiselle.' We stumbled over our lines peeking up at her in the royal box. Who would have thought that one day . . ."

Although she enjoyed her nostalgic visit to London, Greer contracted a serious case of pneumonia that worried the Hallmark Hall of Fame crew, as well as her husband. "I had brought some longjohns from California but they didn't keep me warm at all," she admitted, "and I missed several rehearsals. What an admiration I have for the British people, the way they put up with things. They are so courageous and good-humoured."

After the broadcast on April 3, 1974, she received two fan letters that she treasured. Her old BBC mentor, Cecil Madden, wrote: "My dear Greer, I have of course just seen your beautiful performance of Queen Mary in 'CM.' It was all so real and true. I am sure you are in as good form as you were in those splendid days when you did Yasmin in Hassan and the Sheridan with Campbell Gullan. Those were happy days when the theatre too was at its best in London." The other note was from Claudette Colbert. "I was so discomfited that I couldn't see your TV special—the photos I did see in the newspapers were smashing—you actually made yourself look like the old girl—and she was one of my favorites. They don't make queens like that anymore."

In the midst of her acting schedule, Greer received a gold medallion, carved with the familiar masks of the Performing Arts, from members of the Greer Garson Theatre Guild in September 1974. "My dear Friends and Team-mates," she wrote, "I was really deeply touched by your thought and this charming gift will be among my very special personal treasures. I just wish we could have a large scale reproduction by the same artist (though it would have to be in gilded papier-mâché or plaster rather than 14 carat gold, I'm afraid!) to install above the proscenium arch or somewhere else in the Theatre. It is very true, as I said, that you are our bridge from the College to the Community. I have experienced first hand—for example, at the Dallas Theater Center, the wonderful surge of interest and participation that a Guild can accomplish by enlisting personal interest in each member's circle of friends, which gradually builds to a good solid subscription list and a sort of club feeling that creates a basic and continuing audience, not only for the public performances but all the activities in-between-times that go on in the Performing Arts Department. Believe me, everything you do in the Guild will pay off in increased enthusiasms so that our little Theatre will gradually, I hope, acquire a fine reputation and become known to a wide public."

In November Greer was featured in a costarring role on an episode of the NBC series *The Men From Shiloh* entitled "Lady at the Bar." "Do I dispense booze or justice?" Greer reportedly asked Universal executive Leslie Stevens before accepting the part. "Justice." was the reply. Greer was disappointed, "I was already thinking of myself in spangles and tights." She was also a narrator in "My Father Gave Me America," a documentary about the immigrant experience that aired on December 31, 1974, and costarred Kirk Douglas, Ossie Davis, and Mamie Epstein. Greer told the story of a matriarch of the Jones family in Savannah, "where slavery had been forced on the landowners by state edict."

That winter Greer performed the narration of the Christmas program of the Los Angeles Master Chorale and Sinfonia Orchestra entitled "Joys of Christmas," in the Dorothy Chandler Pavilion. Between renditions of songs like "The Seven Joys of Christmas" and "Carols from Foreign Lands," she read with a special poignancy, for Aunt Evelyn had passed away that month and was interred next to Nina in the Great Mausoleum at Glendale's Forest Lawn. Two spaces for Greer and Buddy remained nearby. "I feel so secure to know that I'm going to eventually have all my family around me right out there," Greer said. In a letter of welcome to John Weckesser, who replaced Edward Purrington at The College of Santa Fe in December, she wrote: "I wish very much that circumstances would allow me to be in the Santa Fe area more often so that I could have the great pleasure and interest of keeping in closer contact with the Theatre work, but anytime that you feel like telephoning me (collect, please, as I would not wish to cause the College any extra expenses), or write me occasionally to let me know how plans are going, I would be very grateful to keep up with things in that manner, for, as you know, I have a great personal interest in the progress of the theatre center. I hope all is well with you and that the Christmas vacation will give you time to draw a few long breaths and make plans. Our home is shattered, alas, at this time by the loss of my very dear Aunt who made her home with us the last fifteen years. She leaves a great emptiness." She enclosed a gift, a piece of paper with a circle drawn in the middle, entitled: "A Round Tuit." Within the circle she wrote : "At long last I have a sufficient quantity for each of my friends to have his own. Guard it with your life; these tuits have been hard to come by—especially the round ones. It will help you become a much more efficient worker. For years, I have heard people say, 'I'll do this as soon as I get a round tuit.' Now that you have a round tuit of your very own, many things that have been needing to be accomplished will now get done." The page was inscribed, "To John Weckesser, who probably doesn't need it at all . . . From Greer Garson, who does, very definitely!"

Weckesser met Greer a short time later. "Being in the presence of Greer Garson could be very intimidating," he said. "There was a diva aspect to her. She was so intelligent. Of all the famous people I have known, she was by far the most literate and certainly the most eloquent, well-spoken. Unless you're talking about English royalty in this day and age there's nobody like her." Determined to get her more involved than ever in theater work, he continued to pursue Purrington's offer of doing a play. "And that took some doing," he recalls. "She was very generous with her money, but she always said, because of her ancestry, that she was 'tight.' When I needed a thousand dollars or two from her, I really had to make a case and justify it. One time I called her and explained we needed money. I could hear Buddy in the background, and he was getting tired of her being on the phone. 'Tell him he can expect a thousand dollars from me,' he said. Then there was a pause, and then she said, 'Excuse me, Buddy says O.K.'"

The Fogelsons responded to John Weckesser's efforts by attending the first performance of each new season, and Greer became his "Ace Clipping Service" by sending a regular barrage of useful and informative handwritten notes and clippings from around the country. "Every one was notated and highlighted," Weckesser recalls. "She would write detailed playbills of theater she saw in Dallas and Los Angeles, especially if she thought it was something we could do. There was never an opening night that Greer did not personally send a bouquet of flowers for the lobby or personal notes of encouragement to the cast members. The Performing Arts Department was her child. She told me that once."

For the tenth anniversary of the theater and to kick off the Artists-in-Residence program, Greer agreed to consider appearing in Jean Giraudoux's 1948 play, *The Madwoman of Chaillot*. It was not an easy decision for her to make. She preferred the venerable Miss Moffat in *The Corn Is Green*, but John Weckesser wanted *Madwoman* because it offered a wider variety of roles to the students. "It took me months to get her to agree to do that particular play," he recalls. "The main reason for her reluctance was because the Madwoman condemned a group of promoters and oil prospectors—who were plotting to destroy the city of Paris—to their deaths. She didn't like the idea. She wanted to find a way for them to redeem themselves. Only after I convinced her that the character was actually preserving beauty in the world did she begin to come around." Still uncertain about her decision in late May 1975, Greer wrote cautiously to John Weckesser: "Knowing your anxiety to be reassured about 'The Madwoman,' at this point I do dare to think all will be O.K. And if a bit out of my reach, you know I'll find you a lovely alternative. If it becomes necessary in your opinion to announce your program, why not include my name but not the title of the play—which I think might engender some suspense, curiosity and interest rather than showing all our cards at this time."

Finally she accepted. "Greer really loved the students and enjoyed working with them," recalled John Weckesser. "The play attracted national attention. Planes were chartered from various cities to bring fans here to see the play. People literally called from around the country, asking 'What can we do to help?'" During the early September rehearsals, a steady string of curious members of the press observed the crew's progress. "I gave up an offer to perform at the Shubert, and to star in a Neil Simon movie, *Murder By Death*, with David Niven," Greer told the *New Mexican*. "I had a promise to keep in Santa Fe. I made it ten years ago, and I knew the time had come. My husband asked me why the first play I did in Santa Fe happened to have oilmen as the villains. I said to him, 'Darling, would you like a part?'"

"Toward the end of rehearsals, she was having vocal problems because of pneumonia," Weckesser recalls. "And I told her 'We can do other things. You can take a day or two off.' 'No, no,' she'd say, 'I have to be here.' When it came to the point that she would come in with towels around her neck and Buddy told me, 'If you don't do something, you're not going to have your star for opening night,' I knew something had to be done." Weckesser and *Madwoman*'s director, William Pappas, decided to pretend that the lighting system had gone out. "She stayed awhile anyway," Weckesser recalled, "and worked lines with the other students. She was so meticulous. I remember one morning, for a matinee, I got in really early to get things done. And there she was, telling me that some of the posters needed to be rearranged."

On the evening of October 1, 1975, 450 people crowded into the Greer Garson Theatre for the black-tie preview of *The Madwoman of Chaillot*. To the delight of all, the play was a spectacular success. Anne

Hillerman of the *New Mexican* wrote: "*The Madwoman of Chaillot* has kicked off the 1975-76 College of Santa Fe season with fireworks and glitter as well as solid talent. The show . . . not only lived up to the advance publicity but offered some nice surprises on top of that. It should be no surprise, however, that the best thing about the show was its leading lady. Miss Garson was the focus of attention from her first appearance in the first act. Her vitality rang through both words and actions, perfectly in character for the Countess Aurelie."

At the governor's reception after opening night, New Mexico's Jerry Apodaca presented Greer with a bouquet of roses and carnations and a copy of the state seal. After the play's run, producer Arthur Cantor tried to persuade Greer to take the play on tour, or perhaps to Broadway, but to no avail. *The Madwoman of Chaillot* was Greer Garson's final bow as a stage actress.

On November 4, 1975, John Weckesser wrote to Greer:

Dear Greer,
I've been racking my mind to come up with some imaginative, sparkling way to say thank you for working with us in *The Madwoman of Chaillot.* Your appearance here literally turned this Department around. Educationally, it established a wonderful precedent for student-professional interaction. Your open friendliness with our people throughout the strenuous rehearsal period and performances is an example we must venerate with each future guest artist.

In terms of developing an audience for our work the statistics speak for themselves: 1003 season subscribers where there were less than 200; an unprecedented interest among individual ticket buyers that will have an effect for seasons to come. Also we were able to contradict at last the widespread belief that "Santa Fe is not a theatre town." Thank you again.

Among Greer's activities during the fall of 1975 was a benefit for the Eisenhower Medical Center in Southern California and another for the Philharmonic Association of Kansas City—in the city's stockyards. Bob Hope appeared on stage with her and later wrote:

"You not only looked beautiful, but how many leading ladies can you send out in the round, in front of 12,000 people to ad lib for ten minutes. You are something else and I know everyone really got a smash out of your appearance. You swing a mean tea bag!"

On March 9, 1976, Greer, Walter Pidgeon, and many MGM stars were on hand to salute William Wyler when he received the American Film Institute's Life Achievement Award. Pidgeon recalled: "One thing that would have been a terrific regret in my life is if I had succeeded in getting out of doing *Mrs. Miniver*. Paul Lukas was over to dinner the night I accepted the part. He said, 'You will find working with Wyler to be the most delightful experience you ever had,' and that's the way it turned out.'"

Meanwhile, Greer's contributions to The College of Santa Fe continued. In 1976 she donated the funds for the construction of a fountain in front of the library in honor of her husband's birthday. Its shape symbolized the tricultural heritage of Santa Fe. On June 4, she wrote to Brother Luke: "Fountains and landscaped pools of any description are unfailingly fascinating—soothing—poetic." That year she also attended the first Greer Garson Scholarship Awards banquet, on May 1 at the College. Five scholarships totaling $5,250 were awarded to four students for excellence in the areas of acting and design-technical. In 1979, she dusted off her college credentials and briefly became an adjunct professor of the Performing Arts. "She would come in and give talks," recalls Weckesser. "She would talk about her film career and the determination it takes. She talked with students individually at various get-togethers. She really cared about them. I think more than the money, was her name association with the institution that gave the whole college a higher distinction."

Although she refused stage offers, Greer was still available for television. In 1977, she narrated twenty-six hour-long episodes of *The Pallisers* series, and the following year played Aunt March in *Little Women* at Universal Studios. Of the lavish four-hour NBC miniseries, *TV Guide* noted that "*Little Women* offers, if neither revelation nor fascination, at least the pleasures of a classic revisited. Susan Dey is adequately feisty as Jo, but it's Greer Garson, as bossy Aunt March, who steals the show." She cohosted Christmas specials in 1978 and 1979. The first was a tribute to Radio City Music Hall, with Gregory Peck, Alan King, Beverly Sills, and Ann-Margret, which aired on

December 14, 1978. Vincent Canby later wrote, "Greer Garson was emblematic of everything the Music Hall stood for. In her high-toned MGM pictures, she was invariably serene, polite, elegant in a slightly unreal way, too good to be true, always prepared to meet any emergency and staunchly middle-class. Her pictures were neither inhibited by the Hall nor did they ever look tacky amidst all that splendor. Actress and theater were one." In *Perry Como's Christmas in New Mexico* on December 14, 1979, Greer introduced the world to Santa Fe. Performing a segment on "Christmas for American Pioneers," she also recited a poem, "Christmas Eve in Santa Fe." "She was on the set, which was the train station at Lamy, before anyone else," recalls television producer Bob Banner. "I found her rehearsing with two goats who were in the show. She was talking to them, and, looking up, she told me, 'They are born actors. Look, they know just where the camera is!'" With the flurry of activity, the *Los Angeles Herald-Examiner* quipped: "It's a slow season at the racetrack. That's why Greer is so television-minded these days."

CHAPTER 27

IN APRIL 1980 THE FOGELSONS were in Los Angeles. Greer had been invited to serve as president and host of the D.H. Lawrence Festival that took place in Taos, New Mexico, that summer. It was a celebration of the distinguished British author's visits to the state in the 1920s and his literary legacy. The woman who had invited him, Mabel Dodge Luhan, who owned a ranch fifteen miles north of Taos, had inspired Neil Adams to write a screenplay based on her life and the various artists and writers that she had brought to New Mexico. It was a project he had initially hoped to interest Greer in. "It certainly is a subject that could make for a colorful story line," she replied in her polite refusal. "You know an actress never quite finally gives up working but always hopes that the irresistible script will appear someday." Among those who planned to attend the festival were a number of Hollywood celebrities: Elizabeth Taylor, E.G. Marshall, Tony Randall, Dennis Hopper, Julie Harris, Trevor Howard, Richard Crenna, Jane Alexander, and Anne Baxter. In the midst of her preparation, letter-writing, and phone calls, Greer suddenly collapsed on the floor of her Wilshire Terrace apartment.

She had suffered a heart attack. After a week's recovery in the UCLA Medical Center, she admitted to the press that "the main works rather ground to a stately halt." To the folks in Taos, Greer wrote: "It is with deep regret that I have to resign from the D.H. Lawrence Festival presidency. However, all I can think of, really, is the basic fact that the Lord has been good to me, and I'm back from the very edge of beyond." With a pacemaker implant, Greer retired with Buddy to their desert home in Palm Desert. On May 5, Greer wrote to Walter and Ruth Pidgeon: "I'll cherish this super gift of Coral Azaleas with special care. It was a frightening experience but with the Pacemaker I am going to feel so much better. I insisted on going home two days earlier than the doctors expected, so I have been a bit shaky, but so thankful to be here. Buddy sends very best. Now you and Ruth take care, be of good cheer and let's all make a hundred. Fondest affection to you both. Yours as ever (plus a little extra equipment), Greer."

Although she promised her husband to slow down her social whirl of civic activity and public appearances, before the year was out Greer was already making plans to coproduce with Arthur Cantor a new play, *Jitters,* on Broadway and to participate in the Screen Actors Guild Conservatory Legacy Program. She also made a television appearance in "A Gift of Music," a musical salute for the Bicentennial of Los Angeles that featured Natalie Wood, Donald O'Connor, Eve Arden, Twiggy, Dionne Warwick, and Rosemary Clooney.

One hot August afternoon in 1981, Greer entered the Haagen-Dazs ice-cream shop in the bustling plaza of Santa Fe. As she ordered a chocolate ice cream cone, she became aware of a stranger in line behind her. Joseph Dispenza recalls their conversation to this day.

"My doctor says I'm not to have chocolate," Greer said, taking a bite of ice cream. "You won't tell anyone, will you?"

"Your secret is safe with me, Miss Garson."

"Oh, a gentleman!"

"At your service," Dispenza said, with a bow. "We were beginning to sound like characters from an old movie," he recalls.

"In that case, perhaps you'd like to join us."

"I did—and a friendship blossomed. Of all the movie stars I've met, she was really the most intelligent. She was a couple of inches from becoming an Oxford don. When you were in her presence, you toed the line. You never told an off-color joke, and you watched how you carried yourself. She was one of a small handful of top-drawer movie stars that have since become Hollywood icons."

At a party at the Forked Lightning Ranch, Dispenza, the chairman of the Communication Arts department at The College of Santa Fe, sat with Greer on the shady front porch. When their discussion turned to her career, she sighed, looked out over the expanse of rocky New Mexican terrain, the piñon trees, and the river, and said, "In a way it's too bad I had to be a 'movie star,' because it didn't allow me to be the actress I wanted to be."

In June 1982 Her Royal Highness Princess Anne visited The College of Santa Fe and the Greer Garson Theatre. "I hope Her Royal Highness and all who were with her on that whirlwind tour are rested and recovered by now," Greer wrote to Buckingham Palace after the visit. "It must have been a gruelling schedule, as I know from my own experiences as a movie star constantly on government, charity and promotional p.a. tours. Just want you to know—and I hope Princess Anne is aware—that her tour was a smashing success, not only for the Save-the-Children Fund, but also in ever-widening circles of happy personal impressions and influence for friendship and good will. There cannot be a more important cause than *that* in all this troubled world. Being British-born, I particularly like to invite British theatre people to come over and teach and perform at our center. Though brief, Princess Anne's visit was a great honor for the little college and has given much inspiration to our remote outpost of culture! P.S. I have met four generations of our wonderful Royal Family. They, especially the ladies, have a magic aura about them that inspires and warms all hearts. May God bless them, every one."

Greer was back in Los Angeles that summer at the Warner Hollywood Studio on Santa Monica Boulevard to make a guest appearance on Aaron Spelling's *The Love Boat*. Reporting to work on August 1, she told the press, "Being asked eleven times, in four years, to be on the show was endearing. It's always nice to be wanted." Nolan Miller designed her gowns, and she persuaded William Tuttle to do her makeup. After finding her dressing room, she met with the cast, her director, Richard Wells, and costar, screen veteran Howard Duff. Playing a suave ladies' man who falls in love with Greer's character, who has a gift of ESP, Duff was making a break from the usual gritty roles he made famous in 1950s films such as *Spy Hunt*.

During a break from shooting, Greer met with Jeff Silverman of the *Los Angeles Herald-Examiner*. Seated outside her dressing room on Stage Two in her gossamer costume, she poured out tea while Bill Tuttle repaired her makeup. "It's nice to get out my makeup box and get to work again," she said, gazing thoughtfully at the case that had been given to her by the employees of LINTAS so many years ago. "It brightened me up considerably, recharged my batteries. I've always been impressed with the romance of a cruise ship since reading a story, when I was a little girl, by Prosper Merimee." She confided to

Silverman that she had turned down Aaron Spelling's offer to play Joan Collins's evil, conniving mother on *Dynasty*. When he promised to give her a relaxed schedule with plenty of time to visit her husband, she had replied, "Oh, come on Aaron. When I start working, it will be Monday to Friday."

On Monday, August 9, the last day of shooting, *Love Boat*'s executive producer, Doug Cramer, hosted a cast-and-crew party in honor of Greer. Among the luncheon guests in Aaron Spelling's boardroom were many friends, past and present, including George Cukor, Dana Andrews, Cesar Romero, and Vincente Minnelli. Roaming about the studio lot, which had once been the Samuel Goldwyn Studio, the old friends sipped their drinks and fell to reminiscing. Romero recalled that it had been nearly fifty years since he started out there, in *Cardinal Richelieu* and *Clive of India*. Dana Andrews had made *The Best Years of Our Lives* there. "Greer, you look as beautiful as ever," George Cukor remarked, admiring the brightness of her red hair in the late afternoon sun. "Dear George," she replied, pointing at his glasses, "I'm afraid you're looking at me through rose-colored lenses! Did I ever tell you boys how George nearly drowned me during the making of *Desire Me*?" Laughter echoed through the shadowy stone canyons of sound stages as the small group returned to the party.

Over the weekend, before Greer returned to Santa Fe, Jack Evinger drove her along Sunset Boulevard toward 220 Strada Corta Road, the home of Walter and Ruth Pidgeon, in her old Bel Air neighborhood. The Pidgeons had been unable to join Doug Cramer's studio party because of illness, and Greer had promised to visit. As she gazed out the limousine's window, she realized that for all the excitement of being before the cameras again, Hollywood depressed her. She had regretted a nostalgic drive past the Metro-Goldwyn-Mayer lot, which looked neglected and unprosperous—hardly what she had remembered it to be in that golden autumn of 1937. The people had changed as well. "I can't imagine why so many young people today with their beautiful bodies and their lives in front of them would risk their health with drugs and other abuses," she remarked. "If they knew illness and pain as I have had, they would value every day they feel well and every night they can sleep soundly." Each street name and each home that she saw along the way harked back to the past.

So many of her friends in Los Angeles were dead: Louis B. Mayer, Benjamin Thau, Dore Schary, Sidney Franklin, and costars such as Robert Donat, Dame May Whitty, Robert Taylor, Gladys Cooper, and Errol Flynn. And now Walter Pidgeon was ailing. After sticking with MGM until his contract ended in 1956 and then freelancing at Twentieth Century-Fox, Columbia, Paramount, and Disney, he had taken a fall from a ladder at home in 1977, and a blood clot had developed on the brain. Although the medication that was administered saved his life, it damaged his inner ear. At the age of eighty-four, without the sense of balance, he was unable to walk and had become a virtual recluse. But despite his infirmity, he welcomed Greer as warmly and energetically as ever. His strength, like hers, rested in his optimism. They spoke of MGM, and Pidgeon's strength seemed to leave him as he recalled his return to the lot in 1972 to make *Skyjacked.* "Believe me," he said, "my homecoming was no sentimental affair. Everybody's gone except for a few old-timers on the technical crews. My favorite lot, number three, has been turned into a housing development. The difference from the old days is fantastic, and very sad. In the good old days I'd go to someone's suite—Lionel Barrymore's, Gable's, Fred Astaire's—have a couple of belts and hash over how things had gone. It was like a club." During dinner his good humor returned, and, as he said goodbye to Greer, he said, "I've had a lot of fun. There were a lot of other acting projects I suppose I might have done. Did quite a few of 'em, too! But I was lucky. I managed to remain an actor for most of my life."

Two days after Walter's eighty-seventh birthday, on September 25, 1984, Ruth Pidgeon telephoned Greer from St. John's Hospital in Santa Monica. After a series of strokes, her husband was dead. "It was a quiet and gentlemanly end to a quiet and gentlemanly life," eulogized the *Los Angeles Times.* Eighty-three-year-old Mervyn LeRoy was asked for comment. "He was a fine actor and a very fine person," he said. "He knew what he was doing and I enjoyed every minute of our association." From her desert retreat, Greer released the following statement: "My heart turned over when I heard from Mrs. Pidgeon on the phone today. I've lost a dear friend and a wonderful partner. He was a solid gold gentleman. Even on the difficult days on the set I looked forward to working because he was such a delightful man and a splendid actor. This is a sad, sad day." Soon after, she wrote to

Ruth Pidgeon: "Dearest Ruth, So many clippings about Walter came in from our press cutting service. People everywhere in England loved him. And everywhere else too, wherever his films were shown. As you say, he probably never realized his own stature and great popularity with the film-going public. But I do believe that in some way he knows now. ('And I shall know them, each as I am known' . . . Am not sure of the Testament words. But I always feel our loves are in touch with us here.)" Greer continued to send letters to Mrs. Pidgeon, enclosed with her favorite candied peaches, until her death in 1993.

During the summer of 1982 Buddy was diagnosed with Parkinson's disease. "He had a collapse in 1982," John Roach, the Fogelsons' lawyer, recalls, "and he was never well after that." It was as if Greer was suddenly living through her own version of *Sunrise at Campobello.* In that film Louis Howe makes a comment to FDR's mother about Eleanor: "Mrs. Roosevelt, this girl has worked like a whole squad of trained nurses." Like Eleanor, Greer frequently ordered that a cot be placed by Buddy's sickbed so that she could stay with him overnight. "It was very touching how Greer rallied to her husband's side during that very difficult time," Dr. William Tschumy of Dallas Presbyterian Hospital recalls. "I told her once that of all the awards she had received in her life, she deserved one for the way she looked after Buddy. It was very hard for her." "I remember one visit that Greer paid to my home in April of 1983," Van Cliburn recalls. "She was her usual spirited, lovely self all evening until she was at the door, saying goodbye. She took my hand and confided, 'Buddy is not doing well. Pray for us.'"

More aware than ever of her own mortality, she paid a visit to Dr. Corday, who installed a new pacemaker. "He told me I was harboring an antique, a Model T of a pacemaker," she told friends. "I'm assured that this one is quite up to date." Apart from her care of her husband, Greer continued to look after her extended family in Santa Fe. In 1984, she donated money to The College of Santa Fe for a new entrance on St. Michael's Drive and attended the gala opening of Santa Fe's Villa Linda Mall benefit for the college the following year.

On September 13, 1985, Buddy was able to escort his wife to a glittering "Tribute to Greer Garson: The MGM Years" at Southern Methodist University's Bob Hope Theater. It was as much a celebration of her film career as a recognition of her contributions to the university's Meadows School of the Arts. On the Fogelsons' thirtieth wedding anniversary, at a group luncheon in the Brook Hollow Country Club, Buddy had presented a gift in honor of his wife: the fifty-thousand-dollar Greer Garson Award for outstanding junior and senior theater students. Executive producer Bob Banner, a professor at SMU, and the Meadows' dean, Eugene Bonelli, had designed the tribute. "Dallas may have been overcast and gloomy this weekend, but stars were shining at the Meadows School of the Arts to honor Academy Award-winning actress Greer Garson" observed the *Daily Campus*. Among those who attended or sent video tributes were Sir Laurence Olivier, Gregory Peck, Art Linkletter, Cesar Romero, Fred MacMurray, Hume Cronyn, Jessica Tandy, Brian Aherne, Lew Ayres, William Tuttle, Sydney Guilaroff, George Schaefer, Ralph Levy, William Frye, and Arthur Cantor. President Ronald Reagan remarked, "The sons and daughters of the Emerald Isle have made many splendid contributions to the arts in America, and we were never more blessed than when Greer Garson reached these shores." Representing MGM was the current president and chief operating officer, Alan Ladd Jr., and the former music director, Johnny Green. "Throughout the decades, people have always kept a special place in their hearts for the name MGM," Ladd remarked. "During Hollywood's Golden Age, movie fans and filmmakers knew Metro-Goldwyn-Mayer as the studio where dreams really came true—the studio where the world's most talented artists defined, captured and sustained the highest qualities in entertainment for the motion picture screen. At the heart of MGM's success story were its performers—a roster which, the studio fondly boasted, contained 'More Stars Than There Are in the Heavens.' Today, none of the stars, past or present, shines more brightly than Greer Garson. Southern Methodist University's tribute to Ms. Garson is a salute to one of our most illustrious and beloved alumni." Mervyn LeRoy added, "If it's true as some people say about the older movies, 'they don't make them like that anymore,' then it can also be said about Greer Garson: they don't have movie stars like her any more." Film critic Charles Champlin remarked: "I've thought often of the time Mervyn LeRoy was being honored during the USA Film Festival at SMU and she had come to the Bob Hope Theater of a morning to chat with us after a screening of *Random Harvest*. When the lights came up, she was discovered in tears, the makeup in some slight need of repair. As often as she had seen the film, she said, it still made her cry. It seemed quite in character, and very affecting, that you should be moved by so romantic and idealistic a story."

"All this was most edifying and impressive," wrote Cynthia Rose in her review of the evening in the *Dallas Times Herald*. "Yet it began to make real sense when Garson appeared at the microphone. Swathed in a swirl of violent scarlet by Victor Costa, that 'human touch' for which so many had just lauded this star was immediately apparent. Her personality crackled straight into the audience, electrifying what could have been a too-solemn evening." During her thank-you speech which, as usual, went on much longer than expected, she brought down the house when she lost an earring, grinned, and spoke to her husband in the audience: "It fell off just like you said it would, Buddy!" She used the occasion to bring up other humorous anecdotes, including the time she broke a dental cap in Trader Vic's restaurant and had to "reassemble the bits" with gift-shop adhesive. "I don't know how to start to thank you all for this wonderful, once-in-a-lifetime experience," she said. "I have been so nervous and excited about it and it has turned out to be so beautiful. I do so wish my good friend and partner Walter Pidgeon could have been standing with me here tonight. That's the way work should be: with exceptionally lovely partners as I have had. I'm so surprised and grateful when I'm waiting for the traffic light to change and somebody taps me on the shoulder and says, 'Mrs. Miniver?'" Before Eugene Bonelli presented her with a Medal of Distinction, she summed up her movie career with a quote from Charles Champlin: "film which still speaks to the best in us—of hope, courage, persistence in adversity and generosity in triumph." Of the event, Champlin later wrote: "There was no question what L.B. Mayer had seen in her; a radiant intelligence, a rare and patrician red-haired, green-eyed beauty; an elegance, lightly worn. . . . Garson was something special, a well-educated cosmopolitan woman who was a skilled actress of warmth and depth and, not least, a dazzling and indefatigable talker. . . . It is all, one way and another, a very long distance from County Down, from the Encyclopedia Britannica and from Culver City. But what the story suggests is that MGM's happy endings were not always confined to the screen."

Although increasingly reluctant to be away from her husband's bedside in Dallas Presbyterian Hospital, Greer flew to Los Angeles to be the guest of honor for the thirty-fifth annual Ruby Ball in the Beverly Hilton Hotel on April 5, 1986. It was sponsored by the philanthropic "Lifelighters," with proceeds donated to the Exceptional Children Foundation and the John Wayne Cancer Clinic at UCLA. Resplendent in an appropriately red beaded gown, she told the gathering: "This kind of evening is not achieved by sitting in the shade and fanning oneself. To the volunteers—you make the world happier . . . thank you angels, cherubs, seraphs and archangels." Gazing around her at the walls adorned with her MGM photographs with Ronald Colman, Walter Pidgeon, Errol Flynn, and Laurence Olivier, she said "How nice it is to see through the rosy lenses of nostalgia. I have no sense at all of time. When I'm happy I may go on for hours and hours." "Everyone wished she had," remarked the *Los Angeles Times*, "for with her regal warmth, she seems to bathe the world with Mrs. Miniver courage, and erase the fist-shaking image of barbarism."

On August 12, 1986, Greer wrote to John Weckesser:

> Dear John:
> This summer has been a difficult time with our continuing health problems and now an unexpected complication has arisen. I have been increasingly tired and Sunday night I was hit with a minor stroke, struggled into Santa Fe yesterday for hours of tests and have to go to Dallas tomorrow for a consultation and probably surgery to follow. This is not something to enjoy, but I must be very thankful.
>
> I'm in no shape for letter writing or telephone calls but wanted to send a brief note to keep in touch. Hope you and the family are well and all is A-OK in your corner.

That fall, Brother Luke Roney retired as president of The College of Santa Fe. Amidst the administrative duties outlined to James Fries, the new president, was information about the college's most famous benefactress. "I was told to be watchful for and especially nice to any redhead pulling weeds," he recalled, "especially if there's a limousine nearby!" One of his first duties was to meet her for lunch at the Petroleum Club in Dallas. "From all the stories I had heard about her," Fries recalls, "it was very clear to me that Greer Garson Fogelson was larger than life and a legend, and the Petroleum Club was a seat of significant power and influence so it was a bit intimidating. Well, of course it took about thirty seconds to dispel all that. She was just a gracious, immediately charming person." President Fries's most immediate concern was enrollment declines at the college. While they discussed a variety of programs, including a new video, film, and television communication arts program and future plans to build a professional sound stage facility, Greer passed on a donation of twenty-five thousand dollars to the Theatre Center for operating expenses and remodeling.

The Fogelsons made plans to attend the dedication of the E.E. Fogelson Visitor Center at the Pecos National Historical Monument on August 2, 1987. The Center, built at Buddy Fogelson's expense, provided a screening room, large exhibit areas, computer technology, rest rooms, and a small bookstore. "The government was very slow about building that visitor center," Jack Evinger recalls. "Mr. Fogelson finally got impatient and said, 'Well, I want to see this center built while I'm still around.' So he donated the money. Greer was very involved in the construction and plans, and donated an authentic Wells-Fargo stagecoach." "The Rockefellers are responsible for the Grand Tetons," remarked John Bezy, the superintendent of the monument. "The Pecos National Monument is because of the Fogelsons. They had a goal, a dream, a vision. It was a personal commitment of the most significant kind. Their lives show the individual can make a difference." Doug Schwartz, the monument's archaeologist, observed, "Other people would have said, 'The bureaucratic machinery is too difficult to work with, let's go to Florida.' They said, 'Let's get a better design, a better location.'"

"She knew what she wanted for the Center," said Pecos park ranger Ann Rasor, "and it was only the best. She narrated the instructional film and got Ricardo Montalban to come from Los Angeles to narrate the Spanish version. She was so proud of this place—always bringing in friends, walking around, greeting guests, or watching the movie with them. Once, a woman came in after reading the plaque outside the Center, dedicated to Mr. and Mrs. Fogelson. 'I thought Greer Garson was dead,' she said. Mrs. Fogelson, who happened to be there that day, came up to her and said, 'Well, that's not quite true.' The poor lady was mortified."

On dedication day, Buddy's illness took a turn for the worse, and he was rushed to St. Vincent's Hospital in Santa Fe. Greer appeared alone for the dedication in a ceremony keynoted by Governor Carruthers and William Penn Mott, director of the National Park Service. Afterward, a procession of well-wishers made their way to the hospital to see Buddy, and Greer presented him with an honorary gold shovel. "It was a very difficult time," recalls Jack Evinger.

On October 16, 1987, Greer received the New Mexico Governor's Award, for which John Weckesser had nominated her the previous spring. Unwilling to leave Buddy, she wrote to Governor Garrey Carruthers from her husband's sickbed in Dallas.

> We are truly disappointed that we are not able to be there tonight. Please accept this written expression of our delight and gratitude at being nominated for this wonderful honor.
>
> Due to our having a ranch at Pecos we have become fascinated by and involved for nearly half a century in Education and the Arts in this area. It is the icing on the cake for us to be officially rewarded for things we enjoyed doing. We have been rewarded all along really, for these developments have brought so much interest and happiness into our lives, and so many cherished friendships.
>
> Our professional careers, His and Hers, in two very different fields, have meant a good deal of traveling, and necessitated living in more than one location . . . a restless lifestyle that has been stimulating and eventful, but somehow I think we both feel more at home here in New Mexico than anywhere.
>
> May I just say that it is Buddy's hope and mine that after we have left the scene, you will think of us sometimes and continue to keep alive and growing the good things that have been started. Our hearts are full of love for the Land of Enchantment and for our friends and neighbors who live there.

In November, Greer wrote to President Fries and John Weckesser: "Reports from the Colonel's physicians were encouraging today, relatively that is. Though he remains very, very ill, he has stabilized sufficiently that they are hopeful of moving him into a rehabilitation wing. When, or if, he will ever be able to leave the hospital remains most uncertain. I will of course, keep you both posted." Greer kept a round-the-clock vigil at Dallas Presbyterian Hospital. "For several months she had a room with a cot where she could stay right there at the hospital," Brother Luke Roney recalls. "The day I was there was near the end. We stood at the bedside for a moment in silence. Then, Greer requested that I recite her favorite Psalm. When I told her I did not have my Bible with me, she recited it very reverently, very beautifully. I'll never forget that. That was the real Greer Garson. Not cameras and movie sets but a very religious person, with a deep trust in God, facing a very painful experience magnificently."

Col. Elijah Fogelson died on December 1, 1987, at the age of eighty-seven. "Being married to Fogelson was something else," Greer told the press. "He led five lives at once, and there was never a dull day. I couldn't have survived the death of my mother without Fogelson. There was always an undercurrent of chuckles in our relationship. Oh, he could make me laugh. I think that's what makes a good marriage, the ability to laugh together." Following her husband's wishes, Greer had Buddy interred at Sparkman Hillcrest Memorial Park in Dallas. Although she acknowledged his close ties with the city, she was disappointed that her plans for Forest Lawn would not be fulfilled. She gave up the site next to her mother and aunt and made plans to be buried with Buddy in Dallas.

The funeral was held on December 3 at the Highland Park Presbyterian Church in Dallas. "I think everybody in the city was there," recalls Jack Evinger. John Roach delivered the eulogy. "We have only begun a discussion of Buddy's life until we reflect on his life of the past thirty-eight years with a remarkable lady of equal talent and ability and similar interests," he said. "Only persons of such equal ability and energy could have maintained the pace of the other. Together they enjoyed the ranch, the arts and their program of continuous giving; but what they truly enjoyed was each other, and the passing years have exhibited to all of us a deepening of their mutual affection and dependence on the other."

"Greer was never quite the same after Buddy's death," recalls John Weckesser. "She was really devoted to him, especially in her later years." The strain of keeping vigil at Dallas Presbyterian Hospital took its toll, and she collapsed with another heart attack. Among her visitors as she convalesced was Radie Harris. "Greer is terribly ill," she told the *Globe*. "She was absolutely devastated by Buddy's death, and nothing has been the same for her since. They were an absolute love match."

After being released from the hospital, Greer secluded herself in the Turtle Creek penthouse, which she referred to as her "ivory tower." "Her penthouse apartment in Dallas was bright and airy," Joseph Dispenza recalls, "tastefully appointed in an eclectic mixture of things she had picked up in the course of travels, with a predominance of her favorite, Southwestern furniture and art." In the afternoons she took walks along Lakeside in Turtle Creek with her personal maid, Francisca Lucas. "She loved to bring bread to feed the ducks and pigeons," Francisca recalls. "At the ranch she had hummingbird feeders around the place. In Palm Desert, I had to buy twenty-five pounds of bird seed every week. Each morning she sat at the breakfast table and watched them."

As Christmas approached, Greer did not make her usual holiday reservations to dine at the Brook Hollow Country Club, as she had done with Buddy for many years. It was as if the years had rolled back to the winter of 1938 when she was making *Goodbye, Mr. Chips* in London and faced Christmas alone. But this time it was not Victor Saville who invited her to dine with him. It was a Turtle Creek neighbor a few floors down, retired Army Air Corps Colonel James P. Caston, who learned that she had made no plans at all. "Greer was very, very hard to get close to," recalls Colonel Caston. "Very gracious—but what an Iron Curtain. She had been bombarded by people for years who wanted something out of her when she was in show business. I could see when she first met me she thought, 'Now what is he up to?' I realized that and worked very hard to destroy that curtain. She tested you at teatime. When you left, she understood you better than you had ever known yourself!"

"She was very down that Christmas," he recalls. "Her two most important motivations in life—her husband and career—were gone, finished. Of course, she never complained but I had known the

Fogelsons since they moved to Turtle Creek and I understood. I decided that what she needed was to see that the public, and specifically the people of Dallas, still remembered and loved her." Caston made a dinner reservation at the Fairmont Hotel, promising the manager, with an air of mystery, that he would bring an Academy Award-winning star on Christmas Day if a few conditions were met. He wanted the staff to be awaiting her at the entrance with two dozen pink roses, ready to escort her up the private elevator to the grand ballroom and center table. All the conditions were met, and as Colonel Caston drove up to the hotel he recalls, "Greer, who had thought we were having a small, quiet dinner, turned on me and declared, 'Jim, what have you done!' The whole night was just like a fantasy out of a movie. It was quite a production. The staff of the Fairmont went all out for her, and when the people in the dining room recognized her they came over to visit, including the resident Santa Claus. At first I thought she might not be ready to see people again like that, but she insisted on meeting everyone, and taking every child on her lap. When we got back in the car I didn't know what to expect from her. She turned to me and said, 'Jim, this is one of the best Christmases I've ever had. Thank you.'"

That Christmas was the inspiration to continue her husband's philanthropic work. She met with John Roach to discuss her financial affairs. "At first, her express words were, 'I'm going to use it to immortalize Buddy, because he's the one who made the money,'" Mr. Roach recalls. "I told her that was fine, but her name was not exactly an unknown one. So, I said let's do something permanent and proper and fitting for Greer Garson. We talked a lot about building a theater. At first, I thought of Southern California, where she made her name and fame, but she wanted to concentrate on Dallas. 'Buddy's buried here and I'll be buried here,' she said, 'so let's do something here.'" Eugene Bonelli recalls that "She had discussed giving SMU 'a little theater' for some time, but when Buddy's health deteriorated, she spent all her time with him. After his death she approached us again, and by that time we had a different approach in mind—a theater and film archives. So we got an architect, Milton Powell and Partners, to draw up the plans."

When the news of her $10 million donation to build a theater in Dallas became public, Greer explained, "Well, after all, I do lead a quiet life and have no children. And then, when I started out in the theatre no one helped me. I'm always suspicious of people who say they had it tough starting out and add that they wouldn't have it any other way. Believe me, I would have had it some other way. So maybe that's why I'm doing this, to give young aspiring artists some sort of helping hand."

In April, Greer made a gift of $1.5 million to the Southwestern Medical Foundation to endow the Fogelson Distinguished Chair in Urology to honor one of Buddy's physicians, Dr. Paul C. Peters, professor and chairman of the Division of Urology at the University of Texas Southwestern Medical Center at Dallas. Among the division's projects were studies in kidney transplantation, prostate and kidney cancer, adrenal transplants for Parkinson's disease, and the physiology of smooth muscle.

"About a year after Buddy died, we took her on a European vacation," Laura Roach recalls. "She had worn black ever since the funeral, so I took her shopping at Nieman's and we bought a lot of bright clothes. Because she had five pieces of luggage for that trip, we had to have two limousines at every airport. We went to France, Switzerland, and England, and Dr. Sophia Sloan came with us, to take care of Greer. We went to all her favorite spots in London and to Stonehenge, which she had never seen."

In April 1988 Greer received the Masters Screen Artists Award during the USA Film Festival gala in Dallas. The black-tie event included a film retrospective. Francisca recalled, "She stayed until 2:30 in the morning signing autographs. When I told her it was too much, she replied, 'Oh, no. I'm not going to let these people down. Not one. They're here for me.'"

Greer spent the summer at Wilshire Terrace in Los Angeles. On June 15, 1988, the Builders of Scopus, the American Friends of the Hebrew University of Jerusalem, honored her with a luncheon at Chasen's California Room for her humanitarian efforts for education. The event, celebrating the life of Golda Meir on the tenth anniversary of her passing, featured guest speaker Jehan Sadat, widow of the late Egyptian President Anwar Sadat. "Mrs. Meir and Miss Garson shared the belief that an international exchange of students and artists contributes to the cause of peace," she said. As Greer received the Golda Meir Fellowship Award from Barbara Sinatra, she said: "To meet and listen to Madame Sadat is a privilege and an inspiration, and to be linked with Golda Meir is a precious honor indeed. Our Presidents have their Oval Office, British Prime Ministers 10 Downing Street, but Golda . . . Golda had her kitchen. . . . She had her glass of tea. . . . She had her perambulator for walks with her grandchildren. Golda, in her relationship with the Hebrew University of Jerusalem, has been an example to each of us. We cannot turn our backs on gifted young men and women . . . on bright young scholars . . . whether at The College of Santa Fe, to which I have such close ties, or Golda's beloved Hebrew University, or Madame Sadat's alma mater at Cairo. We must not waste a single mind." To reporters outside she added, "I think that women can be a tremendous force in the world. If it were up to women there would always be peace . . . women don't want war. Squabbles maybe, but not war!"

Immediately after the luncheon, Greer entered Cedars-Sinai Hospital with severe chest pains and underwent triple-bypass surgery. Postoperative complications ensued when she developed pneumonia. "I realized what a trouper she had been on our European vacation," Laura Roach recalls. "Three-fifths of her heart was inactive all that time!" After recovering once more, Greer flew back to Dallas.

After years of philanthropic contributions to Dallas Presbyterian Hospital, which included placing park benches around the hospital's Walnut Hill campus with plaques quoting Nina's favorite Scottish proverb, "Rest and be thankful," December 14, 1988, marked the groundbreaking ceremony of Greer's largest gift. The Fogelson Forum had grown out of her initial desire to build a fountain, fashioned like the water-filled pie pans her mother had placed outside their homes for the birds, in front of a conference center that Douglas D. Hawthorne, president and CEO of Presbyterian Healthcare System, wanted. "She understood physicians and their need for ongoing education," said Carol Burrow, vice president of the Presbyterian Healthcare Foundation. "She wanted the Forum, and the Fogelson Lectureship Series that takes place there, so that the doctors would not have to travel far from their patients. She was very involved in the planning—from the floor color, which she wanted to reflect the colors of the Santa Fe desert, to the addition of a Green Room. She chose her favorite color of red—the shade of roses that Buddy Fogelson had given her—for the upholstery of all the chairs." After viewing the architect's miniature mockup of the center, Greer inserted a tea biscuit under the building's dome and exclaimed, "There now! The proportion is much better. What will that cost me?" "That is how the building grew to three floors," Carol Burrow recalls, "housing a medical library, an audio/visual support center, classrooms, and an auditorium."

At the ceremony Rev. Clayton Bell invoked a prayer that became one of Greer's favorites. "Our Heavenly Father, indeed we do thank you for the gift of laughter. And Lord, as the creation of this center continues to unfold before our eyes in the weeks and months before us, may it ever make visible the special love that Greer and Buddy had for each other. Bless us each and every one."

In March 1989, Greer suffered another minor stroke, and although she became increasingly reclusive in her "ivory tower," it seemed impossible for her to keep a low profile. Movie fans, spurred by releases of her films on television and home video, continued to write and greet her on the street. "It is rather remarkable," Greer told the *Dallas Morning News*. "I get letters from people who have just seen *Mrs. Miniver* on television. I reckon I'm on my third generation of fans by now. It's so nice when someone slightly middle-aged comes up and says, 'Oh, Miss Garson, I've loved your films since I was this high.' But when an old wizened gray-bearded man comes up with that. . . . People say, 'Is she still around?' I'm a theatrical landmark."

The Fogelson Forum at Dallas Presbyterian Hospital opened in September 1990. A festive gala was planned, hosted by Doug Hawthorne and cochairwomen Caroline Rose Hunt and Margot Perot. "Greer asked for a barstool to sit on during the ceremony," Carol Burrow recalls. "She wanted to be at eye level with everyone in the receiving line—which was the most extraordinary one I had ever seen. She spoke for hours with everyone. It was incredible." Greer's philanthropic works for the hospital now totaled $4 million, including the William O. Tschumy Jr., M.D., Chair of Internal Medicine to support the hospital's medical residency program. "Ms. Garson once wryly described herself as the MGM studio's 'glorified missus'" remarked the *Dallas Morning News*. "Fittingly, since leaving the stage and screen, she's become the maternal philanthropist."

The previous year Greer had gone back to The College of Santa Fe to unveil a portrait of her late husband to be displayed in the library. At that time she had also taken the opportunity to examine the progress being made on an ambitious project for the college that she would consider her crowning achievement.

CHAPTER 28

IN 1989, JOSEPH DISPENZA faced a major problem. "I had approached the College about starting a film program as part of its undergraduate liberal arts curriculum in 1986," Dispenza recalls. "The College agreed, and in the fall of the next year I took nine students into the world of the cinema. The program grew rapidly; by the end of the first two years fifty students were film majors. The sudden expansion in enrollment meant we would need more space."

On the far side of the campus, beyond the Greer Garson Theatre and the E.E. Fogelson Library, stood the physical education complex, which housed two gymnasiums. President Fries admitted that it was underused and acknowledged Dispenza's dream by planning to rebuild it as a communications center and studio, which would combine professional film and video production with Dispenza's academic program. If the complex could attract motion picture locationing companies to shoot at the Garson Studio, students would be able to get valuable production experience. Plans called for a fifty-four-thousand-square-foot building with two state-of-the-art soundstages, video production facilities, offices, wardrobe, and dressing rooms.

Once again, like facing a new acting challenge to be researched and met, Greer became involved in every phase of the ambitious undertaking. She donated the $3 million necessary for the renovation, remarking that "This gift is especially rewarding to me because it will bring together two dominant interests in my life—the academic study of the moving image and the professional management of the art. Many of the world's problems are the result of man's failure to communicate. I hope the Garson Communications Center will build bridges of better understanding." Illness pulled her away from the project during the summer of 1989. She entered the cardiac care unit of Santa Fe's St. Vincent's Hospital in August to undergo a two-and-a-half-hour blood-vessel surgery. As she recuperated, the Christian Brothers of The College of Santa Fe awarded her Affiliation status for her devotion to the school. She was back at work at the college until Christmas approached, and then she flew to Dallas. There, she entered Dallas Presbyterian Hospital for tests after the series of illnesses she had suffered the past year. It was then she was told that, because of the high altitude risk to her heart, she could never return to Santa Fe.

On Christmas Eve Greer was watching CNN from her hospital bed when it was reported that the Wilshire Terrace apartment complex in Los Angeles was ablaze. Reporters announced that the fire had started in a neighboring construction site. "Jack Roach called and asked us to go and check on the place," Jack Evinger recalls, "and when we reached the fire lines we were told that the apartment had been completely gutted. When we got up there we found that everything she had—including her grand piano and Academy Award—were down to dust." His wife, Marilyn, recalls that "Hardly anything survived. Greer called me and said, 'Marilyn, do you know the nightstand next to my bed?' And I said, 'Yes.' She said, 'I was thinking of a picture of my mother. Were you able to salvage that?' I would have given anything to have told her 'Yes.' But everything was ashes. We rescued only a few pieces of silver flatware, some Oriental bowls, and two gravy bowls from a dinnerware set that had once belonged to Napoleon."

A lifetime of personal memorabilia was gone. "I feel like a nonperson," Greer told reporters. "Everything is gone—my earliest pictures and family silver included." But she rallied, flashed her famous smile, and thanked everyone for their concern over her health, saying: "I'm the bionic woman. The Shepherd has walked with me through the valley of death so many times. In the end, I have to think it was fate for me to reach this point. I believe that He still has things for me to do, and I pray He gives me time to follow through on some good projects Buddy and I had planned. It's still a wonderful life."

In early 1990 Greer put the Forked Lightning Ranch up for sale and oversaw an auction of many of the ranch's furnishings. Buddy's prize Santa Gertrudis cattle had long since been sold to Governor Winthrop Rockefeller. "Unfortunately, I have to sell," she told *Variety's* Army Archerd, "It's beautiful, but its 7,300 feet up on the head waters of the Pecos River and it's become too tough for me." Remembering her promise to Buddy to respect the "environmental harmonies" of the land, she was careful in her selection of a buyer. Eventually the Richard King Mellon Foundation purchased 5,500 acres of the property, including the residence, for $4.5 million, and made it part of the Pecos National Historical Park. "We were fortunate to have an opportunity to transfer our ranch to a private trust," she told the *Dallas Morning News*, "which donated it to the US government, so the land will remain in its beautiful, natural state."

That Thanksgiving, in Dallas, Greer felt too ill to go out. "I had invited her to come down to my place for dinner," Colonel Caston recalls, "but Bobbie, her cook, phoned that morning to say that she was too ill. Well, I took the food upstairs to her apartment. I went in her bedroom, and she said, 'Oh, Jim, I'm so sorry I couldn't come down. It's a terrible thing to do to you.' But I told her that we were going to have Thanksgiving dinner right there. I told her, 'How many men can really truthfully say that they had Thanksgiving dinner in Greer Garson's boudoir?'"

In early October 1990, Greer sent a congratulatory telegram to the Greer Garson Theatre Center. "To everyone there may I express happy congratulations on the occasion of our 25th Anniversary at the Greer Garson Theatre. To all the splendid teachers, guest artists, current students and patrons who have been part of the life story of our Theatre including the critics, who have encouraged us, and the wonderful Steering Group . . . may I express my deep appreciation. I am truly proud of what has been achieved in our small but classy corner of the Muse's garden." She also sent her regrets that illness prevented her from coming to see the Greer Garson Communication Center and Studios. Already two film production companies, Vestron (*Enid Is Sleeping*) and Castle Rock Pictures (*City Slickers*), had moved into the nearly completed studio.

Friday, October 19, marked the three-day opening ceremonies. The festivities included a star-studded screening of *Julia Misbehaves* in the Greer Garson Theatre, and film clips from *Pride and Prejudice, Blossoms in the Dust, Mrs. Miniver, Madame Curie,* and *The Valley of*

Decision. In cooperation with the Academy of Motion Picture Arts and Sciences, a duplicate *Mrs. Miniver* Oscar was sent to the college to be presented via an amplified phone call by Master of Ceremonies Art Linkletter. That evening she told the gathering: "Today we should remember it is really Buddy Fogelson's long years of hard work and high achievement that have made it possible for me to make this gift, and I do so as from both of us. The world's problems are the result of man's failure to communicate. The Garson Communications Center will build bridges of better understanding." Among the speakers were Governor Garrey Carruthers, President James Fries, and Joseph Dispenza, who referred to Greer as "a hauntingly lovely presence, a firmly-rooted, self-possessed woman who can draw upon enormous reserves of courage. Her screen image stays in the mind as a woman beset, but triumphant. She is one moment the calm center of a storm and in the next a gorgeous gale unleashed upon an insufferably stuffy world." "While we enjoy her films," Garrey Carruthers remarked, "her philanthropy is what will endear New Mexicans to her." "Greer Garson has given us a rose that will bear many blossoms in years to come," concluded President Fries.

A question arose about what to do with the replacement Oscar. Finally, it was packed into a black leather case and sent back to the Academy in Los Angeles. Months later, Joseph Dispenza was in Dallas on a recruiting trip. He called Greer. "She said to me, 'Dear man, you must come to tea.' With Greer, such a line was more than an invitation; it was a summons." He arrived, was given a cup of "strong English Breakfast," and noticed the empty mantel. "I made a mental note to write the Academy," Dispenza said, "and ask whatever had become of the replacement Oscar." A few weeks later, he received a reply. After months of trying to schedule the proper "in person presentation," the Academy promised to mail the Oscar to Dallas. In the fall of 1993, on a trip to New York, Dispenza stopped in Dallas for Greer's eighty-ninth birthday. "I think you had better come over quickly," she told him. "A large box has arrived and I will need some help opening it." He unwrapped the mysterious black package and she saw a glint of gold. "I held the Oscar out to her," Dispenza recalled, "cleared my throat, and lowered my voice to match the gravity of the moment. 'For the role of Mrs. Miniver, the Academy Award for Best Actress of 1941 goes to—Miss Greer Garson.'" Greer was misty-eyed with delight. With a conspiratorial wink, she said, "You know, the last time I accepted one of these I gave the longest speech on record. I promise I'll be brief this time! Thank you." "The first time she accepted the Oscar, it was for a brilliantly executed acting assignment," Dispenza remarked, "the second time she accepted it, a world away from the bright lights of Hollywood, she seemed to be acknowledging something else—a life beautifully lived, and fully given."

Other awards were forthcoming. The American-Scottish Foundation presented her with the Wallace Award for Excellence, and she received the James K. Wilson Award for her contributions to the arts in Dallas. She also earned the *Dallas Times Herald* Jim Chambers Newsboy Award. The Meadows School of the Arts added an honorary Doctor of Arts degree to her staggering collection of prizes in the penthouse.

Meanwhile, plans went forth for Southern Methodist University's Greer Garson Theatre. "For her $10 million," the *Dallas Morning News* noted, "Greer Garson asked for a fountain that wouldn't dribble, large women's bathrooms and a touch of romance on the exterior." "She told us the fountain could not be one of those things that looks like a leaking pump," recalls Eugene Bonelli. "She wanted her fountain to spew high up in the air. She said, 'When I was a kid in Scotland, we had a leaking pump and I don't want anything that reminds me of that!' Referring to the women's bathrooms, she added, 'I can't stand the way we women have to wait for restrooms at intermission at the theater.'" Greer was as interested in every phase of design and construction of the theater as she had been with the Garson Studio. "My goal is to have the building itself inspire and challenge those who will study and perform in it," she said, "as well as pleasing our audience." When architect Milton Powell brought his original blueprints to her Turtle Creek apartment, she told him, "It's very handsome, Milton. But it's not very interesting. Go back and romanticize it." The second set of blueprints, with a revised exterior, met with her approval. "It's much better now," she said. "You see? I was rude and I was right." Next Powell showed her his "Laugh-In wall," an oak wall with removable panels, and nervously asked if she had ever seen the old television show that had inspired it. Greer replied, "My dear Milton. I starred in two episodes!" "So much for that problem," he recalls.

For the fiftieth anniversary of *Mrs. Miniver* in the summer of 1992, special screenings were arranged and a commemorative postage stamp was issued in Great Britain. "You know, whenever I went abroad, I was always addressed as, 'Ah! Señora Miniver!'" Greer remarked. "Or a London cabbie would exclaim 'What do you know, it's Mrs. Miniver herself!' This used to bother me a great deal at first, being identified with only one part. But as the years have passed and I have done many other quite different things, I confess I now get quite a thrill to have so many people around the world remember Mrs. Miniver. It was the very greatest triumph of my career. I am still proud of what I could do as a public servant during the war. I was sent on more bond-selling tours than any other actress. That was wonderful."

In mid-August, as construction of the 386-seat, five-floor theater was nearing completion, Eugene Bonelli conducted Greer on a wheelchair tour of the building. An SMU student, Joe Nemmers, was there to recite a speech from *Romeo and Juliet* from the classical thrust stage, the first in the Southwest. "I was thrilled when I saw the completed Garson Theatre," she later told reporters. "Milton Powell, the architect, whom I call my 'boy genius,' perfectly executed the plans we worked on over the last two years." She was touched by the porcelain Greer Garson rose that she found on permanent display in the theater's lobby. "We have created roses for Queens and Princesses," wrote Helen Boehm, of Boehm International Creators of Porcelain Art. "But to create a rose for my favorite actress, a stunningly beautiful person who has given so much of herself to the entertainment world both in war time and peace time, is a commission of joy."

Greer intended to be at the theater's inauguration on September 12, 1992. "Up to the very last minute we hoped Greer would be able to appear," recalls Eugene Bonelli. "But she wasn't strong enough." "We were so disappointed," Laura Roach recalls. "She was not in good health, but we were going to let her rest that day and then have her dressed, dim the lights of the theater, and have her come out. We had strict orders at her Dallas apartment. No visitors. But all those well-meaning visiting citizens of Santa Fe wanted to see her, and she let them all in. She was completely exhausted afterward. She couldn't even get out of bed."

Art Linkletter was once again the host for the Greer Garson

Theatre Fortnight Festival and introduced tributes from a brilliant cluster of Hollywood stars, Van Cliburn, and SMU performers and alumnus. Of her screen persona, film critic Rex Reed remarked: "She had pride and she had humility. She had passion and a daring openness of emotion. She was courageous and she was vulnerable. She had a joy and an awareness that was brave and honest and true. Greer Garson didn't just visit her films the way many actresses do. She lived them." The British ambassador delivered this bouquet from Queen Elizabeth II: "The Greer Garson Theatre will be a permanent reminder of Miss Garson's devotion not only to the acting profession but to the fellowship and well-being of mankind. She is remembered with particular affection for her role in the classic wartime film, *Mrs. Miniver*. And for her other contributions in support of the war effort. Her subsequent philanthropic works in the United States and the United Kingdom have made her an outstanding ambassador for Anglo-American friendship."

"I must say that in my fifty years in show business I was never acquainted with Mrs. Miniver or Madame Curie," said Art Linkletter. "But I knew a lady named Greer Garson—who was a Scottish minx. She was mischievous. She was flirtatious. She was someone full of life and hearty laughter. Incidentally, I spoke with Greer this afternoon at great length. Those who know her well know that is the only way you can talk to her—at great length."

The theater officially opened its first season on September 17 with *A Midsummer Night's Dream* at Greer's special request. The Meadows School of the Arts also sponsored a conference of distinguished Shakespearean scholars, theatrical practitioners, and critics from around the world the weekend of September 17 to 19. The Southwest Film/Video Archives celebrated its new quarters in the 3,800-square-foot lower level with a retrospective of Greer's films and a showing of *The Pleasure Garden*, Alfred Hitchcock's first film.

Greer's birthday in 1992 was celebrated at Dallas Presbyterian Hospital. While she clutched a new, pink-ribboned black poodle, Chi-Chi, Van Cliburn delivered the toast. "I know I speak on behalf of all of us here," he said, "when I say how much we all love Greer Garson, not only as the celebrated, world-famous lady that she is but also a very sensitive, wonderful, caring friend that we all know. She does indeed 'walk in beauty,' as Byron said. Since she is Irish, I will issue the Irish toast. May bad luck follow all of us all the rest of our days but never catch up with us."

That autumn, Greer had moved permanently into the two-room Blue Bonnet Suite on the ninth floor of the hospital, which had been converted into a "hotel" for long-term patients. "Although she occasionally missed her Turtle Creek penthouse and often wished she could see Quail Haven and the ocean again, she felt more safe and secure at the hospital than anywhere else," recalls Julie Hutner. Beyond the door of Room 939 was a small living room furnished with a table and chairs, small kitchen, dressing table, and bathroom, and beyond, in a small alcove, was her four-poster bed. On a table beside it was a picture of Buddy Fogelson and a pillow that read, "Age is a number, and mine is unlisted." From her room, letters, flowers, and financial contributions continued to flow out to friends and family. To those who were ill, a basket of flowers with a card inscribed "Feel Fine Fast My Friend" became a trademark. She also donated seven and a half acres of land worth $1.5 million to The College of Santa Fe and provided funds to help with the restoration of Westminster Abbey in London.

For her visitors, Greer often put on a performance that belied her fragile condition. She had a lifetime of practice of pretending to be healthier than she actually was. She expected that her guests, whether they be a new acquaintance or an old friend, wanted to see Greer Garson, and she intended to give them nothing less. She prepared in advance, storing up her energy, requiring a full makeup and hair treatment, and ordering tea with lunch. "She would put on the full act for any visitor," recalled James Caston. "You thought that she was just playing the part of an old lady in the hospital. I bought a big paper star and I said, 'If you're going to continue this charade of staying in the hospital I'm going to put this silver star on your door.' I made the accusation that she stayed there only as a big publicity stunt. She loved that."

Colonel Caston visited on Sunday afternoons, often bringing some of her favorite fruits and vegetables from the local farmers' market. "One time she was very low, very ill," he recalls. "So I told her I had the greatest idea in the world: to get her out of the hospital, and into the finest theater in London to give a 'Farewell Evening for Greer Garson.' I told her she should go back to where she had started and make that full circle. 'We'll get the best looking man on the stage to escort you to a big, beautiful gold gilded chair for you to sit down in,' I told her, and her face would light up. 'And there will be a pink spotlight on you,' I went on, 'that will make you look seventeen again. You will sit down and say, 'Oh, how nice of you to come to see me and what a lovely opportunity for me to say goodbye.'" Although Greer accused Caston of "using those rose-colored glasses again," his fantasy sparked her imagination. The years seemed to fade away, and she was once again the ambitious, bedridden little girl from 88 First Avenue, Manor Park, Essex, using her imagination to conjure up the glamor of London's West End and the splendor of the theatrical presentations in which she would appear.

From Santa Fe, Joseph Dispenza kept Greer updated on the Garson Studio. He could cite with pride the New Mexico Film Commission's report that the studio had helped generate nearly $48 million in business for Santa Fe. John Weckesser recalls, "Once she told me, 'When I think about dying it is nothing to worry about. It happens, but it is not truly the end of the world.' It was a life enhancing, one-of-a-kind, beautiful experience."

On July 7, 1993, Greer Garson's name and photograph were back before the public eye on an international scale. That day she received the insignia of an Honorary Commander of the Order of the British Empire from the British Consul-General Bernard Everett in Dallas. The award honored her work in improving relations between England and the United States, inspiring patriotism, working for the causes of conservation and wildlife protection, and providing endowments to universities worldwide. Holding up the blue enamel cross for photographers, Greer declared, "I'm so excited. I've lost nights of sleep. I can't tell you how much it means to find you're not forgotten in Great Britain and I humbly thank her gracious and beloved majesty."

That Christmas, Greer took part in the holiday festivities in the hospital. "Over a two-week period different employees volunteered to play the piano in the lobby," Carol Burrow recalls, "or we would have school groups come and sing to provide the patients and visitors with some cheer during the holiday. And Mrs. Fogelson came down when she knew the children were there. She asked for them to come over individually, and talked to them about their school and such. It was very touching. They didn't have a clue who the elegant lady in the wheelchair, wrapped in a bathrobe, was." "She would have made such a wonderful mother," Julie Hutner remarked. Although many had echoed such sentiments to Greer before, she had come to terms with the lost opportunity. "I'm afraid I have no children," she told a reporter. "But no life has everything and I think it would be very unbecoming for me to complain about something that was withheld, when so much has been given to me"

"She never had any extraordinary requests," recalls Ann Harper, public relations spokeswoman for the hospital, "and in fact never wanted to bother anyone." "She would not permit herself to be the ill patient," said Carol Burrow. "To be in that lovely room, away from the pressures of managing her own health and a staff, brought her an incredible relief. She was grateful for that."

On September 24, 1995, the Women in Film held their Topaz Awards and Scholarship Luncheon in Dallas. Greer Garson Fogelson, just about to celebrate her ninety-first birthday, was honored at the event. Although unable to attend, she remarked, "I don't believe in total scholarships. You need some incentive to keep working hard. But it was so difficult for me to get started. I wasted so much time. And time is all an actor has, time and health. You have only a certain number of years to be productive. I envy young people who can go right to their goals."

If anyone forgot that the former Queen of Metro-Goldwyn-Mayer was living in room 939 of the hospital, the date of September 29 provided a reminder. "Doug Hawthorne arranged to have a lovely cake made," recalls Carol Burrow of Greer's ninety-first birthday. "When it was finished, we took it up the back elevator. But before it reached Mrs. Fogelson, we were alerted to come down to the lobby. In the front door came the most exquisite piece of pastry, larger than any wedding cake I had ever seen, with red roses cascading over it. And out of marzipan was an 8½" x 11" card that said, 'Happy Birthday Greer, From Van Cliburn.' We quickly retreated our cake back down to the kitchen."

Soon after Greer's birthday, her health began a serious decline. "She really wanted to be brave," said Laura Roach. "A lot of nights she didn't sleep. But she was remarkable. She would feel just terrible and next thing you knew she would snap back." "We came for our usual visit," Marilyn Evinger recalled, "and she was very tired. When we walked to the door, I turned around and she had the most beautiful smile on her face. Her face was all lit up and she told us she loved us. That was the last time we ever saw her." Gregory Peck paid a visit to the Blue Bonnet Suite in November 1995. "She was very tranquil and very lovely," he recalls. "She joked that it was only the doctors who kept her there. I had no idea the end was so near."

"We continued to plan her farewell performance in London through the following spring," Colonel Caston recalls. "Week after week we'd have something new to plan and talk about. I told her about the grand finale: she would throw a kiss to the audience and the whole crowd would start to sing her favorite song: 'I'll Be Seeing You.' Then I'd walk out the hospital door singing that song, and she'd sing too. Three days before she died, I took her hand and said, 'Let me have that Garson smile,' and she did. I kissed the hand and kissed her on the cheek and began singing that song. I finished and said, 'That's all, darling,' and I put my arms around her and then walked out."

On Friday evening, April 5, 1996, Van Cliburn arrived at Dallas Presbyterian Hospital. He had been alerted by John and Laura Roach of Greer's critical condition and had cut short a concert tour in Tokyo. "I held her still-beautiful hands," Cliburn recalls. "It took my breath away how much she reminded me of the vigil for my own mother. She looked so lovely." The following morning, at 1:30 A.M., Greer died in her sleep of congestive heart failure. John Roach released a statement. "Until the last few days, when she became critical, she was very lucid and very bright. It was very peaceful."

EPILOGUE

Clem's Voice: "The house is still here and we're still here, the Minivers, if you chance to be passing this way. Kay isn't here anymore. I mean—you can't see her—but she's here for me. Close to me. She'll always be here. In a thousand ways. In the house, in the garden—everywhere."

—*The Miniver Story*

IN A 1991 INTERVIEW with Philip Wuntch of the *Dallas Morning News*, Greer had offered this reflection upon her life: "I've always lived by a few golden rules. Do as you would be done by. Be of good cheer. Strive to be happy. If you want to do it, you can do it. You just have to be open to life's surprises at every age. I know I've been blessed. My mother always said that no one has the automatic right to riches or beauty. But she felt everyone had the automatic right to occupational happiness. We can choose to do what we want to do professionally. I've had both occupational happiness and personal happiness. You can't get luckier than that."

"She was a great lady," said Van Cliburn after her death. "Life for her was an art."

After Greer's death, "Goodbye, Mrs. Miniver" was the universal salute in newspapers nationwide. But in Dallas it carried a more personal message, for the city had lost a benefactress who had looked after and improved its culture and welfare much as Kay Miniver had protected her brood from privation and enemy shells. Her will provided that, aside from the eight hundred thousand dollars going to family and friends and the books and theatrical memorabilia that she left to The College of Santa Fe, the remainder of the estate went to the E.E. Fogelson and Greer Garson Fogelson Charitable Foundation. From this wellspring, institutions associated with the Fogelsons could continue to draw funds for years to come.

"Dallas bid farewell to its star-dusted Lady Bountiful," observed the *Dallas Morning News* on April 9, "and even Louis B. Mayer in all his glory could not have produced a more fitting final tribute." "It was really beautiful," recalled Julie Hutner of that bright Tuesday morning service at the Sparkman Hillcrest Memorial Park. "Jack and Laura Roach had arranged everything and they must have gotten every rose in Texas because they were everywhere; magnificent roses of coral, pinks, and red—all the colors that Greer loved. The weather was just lovely, but it was those beautiful flowers that I shall never forget." On the pink-tinged headstone was carved the words, "A dignified lady of grace and beauty. Her wit, charm and talent thrilled the world and touched all who knew her."

At the memorial service, more than three hundred people filled the flower-strewn Highland Park Presbyterian Church. Dr. B. Clayton Bell Sr. spoke of Greer's "talents, charm, and grace," as well as the "friendship she shared and the wit we enjoyed." John Roach concluded that "this occasion would be incomplete unless we of this community and Greer's friends from New Mexico reflect on the extent of our debt to Buddy Fogelson, because he was the man who brought Greer to us and made her such an important, lasting part of our lives." Van Cliburn told the gathering a story that Sydney Guilaroff had once confided. The hairdresser was once asked by Louis B. Mayer, "Who do you think is the most brilliant and glittering of my stars?" Guilaroff replied, "Greer Garson." "You are correct," Mayer said. "She has the best education, she's the most cultured and, if she were a man, she could be the prime minister of England." "I will always cherish the years I spent with her to plan and build the Greer Garson Theatre at SMU," Eugene Bonelli said. "I've seen her again and again, working with students and inspiring them to do their best. We've really lost an era with her passing. She was unique."

On Sunday morning, April 21, The College of Santa Fe held "A Celebration of Generosity" at the Greer Garson Theatre. "The point of today's gathering is not sorrow," James Fries told the assembly, "but instead to say: 'Greer, we're glad we knew you.' She is the heroine of our story. What success we as an institution of higher learning have achieved; what eminence we hold in the higher education community is largely due to her involvement over the past 35 years. The qualities Greer embraced in her own personal life were quiet courage, generosity of spirit, grace, intelligence and strength. This is what she wanted to cultivate in our students, as well." John Weckesser also spoke that day. "For twenty-two years Greer Garson kept in touch with me through hundreds of handwritten letters, telegrams, phone calls and clippings. At one point she identified herself as my number one Ace Clipping Service. It is the generosity of her spirit which overrides her monetary contributions to the Department that will live with me, our faculty and our students forever."

Janet Wise, the director of Public Relations released a statement: "Greer Garson's association with The College of Santa Fe was marked not so much by buildings, business and money, but by genuine friendship, enjoyed and celebrated year after year. She loved people, and it showed. The theme for the Greer Garson Communication Center gala borrowed a line from her 1943 film *Madame Curie*: 'Take the torch of knowledge and build the palace of the future.' On April 6 in Dallas, the torch dimmed. But at The College of Santa Fe, it continues to burn brightly in the lives and the hearts of all who participate in Greer Garson's legacy."

Elsewhere in the United States, including Los Angeles, that most transitory of realms where an ambitious young Englishwoman had stepped off a train and been swept into a meteoric seventeen-year career at Metro-Goldwyn-Mayer, she was recalled as an all-but-forgotten symbol of Hollywood's Golden Age and World War II. "If there were flags at Radio City Music Hall, they would be at half-staff this week at the corner of 6th and 50th—or should be, in honor of the glorious Greer Garson," wrote Robert Osborne in the *Hollywood Reporter*. Charles Champlin summed up her contribution to the film industry in the *Los Angeles Times*:

> Greer Garson is known to a generation or more largely
> in the histories of a Hollywood that already seems, a
> half-century after her great successes, almost as remote
> as the silents.
>   It is too bad—and the generation's loss—because

Greer Garson brought grace, wit, elegance, charm and a lively Irish vigor to a place and an industry. The films she made were of their day—the wartime fervor of *Mrs. Miniver*, the powerful sentiment of *Random Harvest* and *Blossoms in the Dust*. But there was a lot to be said for the films of that day—and their messages of courage, caring and optimism—and, gifted actress that she was, Greer Garson gave the messages the ring of truth.

James Parrish wrote: "Elders who sigh, 'They don't make movies like that anymore,' can recall when the promise of a new Garson-Pidgeon feature meant a leisurely, plush excursion into a world of nobility, gentility, and tear-inducing emotions, refinements long gone."

The circle of tributes ended where her life had begun, in London, on the afternoon of July 4, 1996. To the strains of hymns from *Mrs. Miniver* and *Random Harvest,* more than 250 people crowded St. Paul's, Covent Garden—the actors' church. "It is for *Mrs. Miniver* that Greer will go down in cinema history," Sheila Collings said. "The scenes in the air raid shelter have become synonymous with the courage displayed by ordinary civilians during the war. She is, I think, unique among performers in having two theatres names after her. . . . At the peak of her career, in the forties, she was an amazingly beautiful woman, with her high, sculpted cheekbones, flame-coloured hair and milky white skin. She had a smile which lit her from within and that she kept to the end. In 1993 she was awarded an honorary CBE and of all the many honours which she received, this one gave her the most pleasure as it showed she was not forgotten in her own land. George Bernard Shaw once called her 'The Ellen Terry of Today,' and she did indeed seem to have that legendary magic—one of the truly great stars, whose like will not be seen again." Although there were many touching tributes presented that day at St. Paul's, by a diversity of people who reflected Greer's two worlds of theater and cinema, one of the most appropriate and poignant English epitaphs to Eileen Evelyn Greer Garson is the one engraved on the headstone of Jan Struther, which the author had penned for herself, at Whitchurch near Aylesbury. For it was Struther who transformed the ambitious young Englishwoman, who escaped the invalidism and closeted existence of her childhood to pursue "the gift of another span of experience," into a screen immortal.

> One day my life will end and lest
> Some whim should prompt you to review it,
> Let her who knows the subject best
> Tell you the shortest way to do it:
> Then say, "Here lies one doubly blest."
> Say, "She was happy." Say, "She knew it."

The Performances of Greer Garson

Theater Performances

Street Scene   (Elmer Rice) Birmingham Repertory Theatre, January 30, 1932; produced by Maxwell Wray. Featured Henry Fielding (Abraham Kaplan), Winifred Hindle (Greta Fiorentino), John Gordon (Elderly Man), Alfred Burton (Man with Peanuts), Mary Marvin (Emma Jones), Dorothy Dickens (Olga Olsen), Vincent Springett (Willie Maurrant), Sybil Arundale (Anna Maurrant), Robert Masters (Man in Dinner Jacket), William J. Rea (Frank Maurrant), Oswald Dale Roberts (George Jones/An Old Clothes Man), Graham Stuart (Steve Sankey), Mary Eames (Woman with Baby Carriage/A Girl), Mary Richards (Agnes Cushing), Reginald Gatty (Carl Olson), Eileen Garson (Shirley Kaplan), Charles Victor (Filippo Fiorentino), Freda Gaye (Alice Simpson), Aileen Wood (Laura Hildebrand), Dorothy Wall (Mary Hildebrand), Donald Hancock (Charlie Hildebrand), Ronald Kerr (Samuel Kaplin), James Hill (Man with Club Foot), Michael Barry (Man Following Girl/Second Policeman), Sydney Groom (Officer Harry Murphy), Mary Williams (Rose Maurrant), Jon Godfrey (Harry Easter), Mrs. Wiggs (Queenie), Basil Bartlett (Daniel Buchanan), Muriel Forbes-Robertson (Mae Jones), Philip

Howard (Dick McGann), Richard Caldicott (Vincent Jones), Felix Irwin (Dr. John Wilson).

Ten Nights in a Barroom (William W. Pratt) Birmingham Repertory Theatre, March 5, 1932; produced by Maxwell Wray. Featured Henry Fielding (Mr. Jackson), Basil Bartlett (Pianist), Graham Stuart (Mr. Romaine), Charles Victor (Sample Swichel), Oswald Dale Roberts (Simon Glade), Jon Godfrey (Frank Slade), Richard Caldicott (Harvey Green), Philip Howard (Willie Hammond), Winifred Hindle (Mrs. Slade), William J. Rea (Joe Morgan), Jocelyn Huband (Mary Morgan), Mary Marvin (Mehitable Cartwright), Sybil Arundale (Mrs. Morgan), Mary Williams (Sadie), Eileen Garson (Maidie).

The Constant Nymph (Margaret Kennedy and Basil Dean) Birmingham Repertory Theatre, March 26, 1932; produced by Maxwell Wray. Featured Basil Bartlett (Lewis Dodd), Sybil Arundale (Linda Cowland), Eileen Garson (Kate Sanger/Erda Leyburn), Felix Irwin (Kiril Trigorin/An Usher), Muriel Forbes-Robertson (Paulina Sanger), Mary Williams (Teresa Sanger), Jon Godfrey (Jacob Birnbaum), Freda Gaye (Antonia Sanger), Charles Victor (Roberto), Jocelyn Huband (Susan), Mary Marvin (Florence Churchill), William Rea (Charles Churchill), Aileen Wood (Millicent Gregory), Henry Fielding (Sir Bartlemy Pugh), Michael Barry (Peveril Leyburn), Oswald Dale Roberts (Dr. Dawson), Norma Wilson (Lydia Mainwaring), Graham Stuart (Robert Mainwaring), Philip Howard (A Fireman), Ronald Kerr (A City Clerk), Winifred Hindle (Madame Marxse).

Many Waters (Monckton Hoffe) Birmingham Repertory Theatre, April 23, 1932; produced by Maxwell Wray. Featured William J. Rea (Henry Delauney/A Registrar in Bankruptcy), Muriel Forbes-Robertson (Secretary/Another Nurse), Oswald Dale Roberts (Compton Schloss/Mr. Clinchpole), Graham Stuart (James Barcaldine), Mary Marvin (Mabel Barcaldine), Henry Fielding (An Old Gentleman/Stanley Rosel), Jon Godfrey (Another Old Gentleman/Captain Bovill/Dr. Hinchcliff), Michael Barry (A Youth/A Waiter/Official Receiver), Winifred Hindle (A Charwoman/Mrs. Rosel), Ronald Kerr (A Register Office Junior/Ticket Collector), Charles Victor (A Register Office Clerk/A Clerk), Freda Gaye (A Woman/A Nurse), Felix Irwin (A

Registrar/Dr. Sangster/An Usher), Mary Williams (Freda Barcaldine), Basil Bartlett (Philip Sales), Eileen Garson (Dolly Sales), Norma Wilson (A Maid), Philip Howard (Godfrey Marvin/Mr. Everitt), Jocelyn Huband (A Typist).

Jane's Legacy (Eden Phillpotts) Birmingham Repertory Theatre, May 21, 1932; produced by Maxwell Wray. Featured Mary Marvin (Ivy Mortimore), Oswald Dale Roberts (Jack Mortimore), Charles Victor (Sergeant Merryweather Chugg), Michael Barry (John Ford), Winifred Hindle (Mrs. Susan Thorn), Philip Howard (Ned Thorn), Eileen Garson (Emmeline Coode), Sybil Arundale (Jane Mortimore), Basil Bartlett (Tom Sparrow), Mary Williams (Daisy Ford), Ronald Kerr (Rupert Sparrow), Felix Irwin (Rev. Philip Ryle), Freda Gaye (The 'and of Providence).

Road to Rome (Robert Sherwood) Birmingham Repertory Theatre, September 10, 1932; produced by Herbert M. Prentice. Featured Philip Howard (Varius), Mary Williams (Meta), Rita Daniel (Fabia), Stanley Drewitt (Fabius Maximus), Barbara Francis (Amytis), Eileen Garson (Tana), Geoffrey James (Cato), Basil Atherton (Scipio), Vernon Harris (Sertorius/Thothmes), Sydney Groom (Drusus), Reginald Gatty (Tibullus/Bala), Geoffrey James (Corporal), Frederick Webb (First Guard), Alfred Burton (Second Guard), Harry Chappell (Third Guard), Bertram Edwards (Fourth Guard), Alfred Corfield (Fifth Guard), Gordon Bailey (Sergeant), Richard Caldicot (Hasdrubal), Douglas Quayle (Carthalo), Graham Stuart (Maharbal), Charles Victor (Mago), Vernon Sylvaine (Hannibal).

Too True to be Good (George Bernard Shaw) On Tour; produced by H.K. Ayliff. Featured Norman Claridge (The Monster), Greer Garson (The Patient), Mrs. F. Marriott-Watson (The Elderly Lady), David N. Steuart (The Doctor), Eileen Beldon (The Nurse), Donald Wolfit (The Burglar), F. Ambrose Flower (Col. Tallboys, D.S.O.), William Hartnell (Private Meek), Arthur Hambling (Sergeant Fielding), Gerald Kay-Souper (The Elder).

Musical Chairs (Ronald McKenzie) Birmingham Repertory Theatre, February 18, 1933; produced by Vernon Sylvaine. Featured

Vernon Sylvaine (Mr. Wilhelm Schindler), Basil Bartlett (Mr. Joseph Schindler), Eileen Garson (Irene Baumer), Mary Williams (Mary Preston), Norma Wilson (Anna), Isabel Thornton (Mrs. Schindler), Graham Stuart (Geoffrey Preston), Vernon Harris (Samuel Plagett).

When the Crash Comes   (Beverley Nichols) Birmingham Repertory Theatre, March 11, 1933; produced by Herbert M. Prentice. Featured Mary Williams (Ivy Maxwell), Marjorie Chard (Lady Poole), Douglas Quayle (Hon. Robert Poole), Isabel Thornton (Mrs. Maxwell), Eileen Garson (Hon. Celia Poole), Vernon Harris (Forester), Graham Stuart (Maj. Vernon Ash).

Infinite Shoeblack   (Norman MacOwan) Birmingham Repertory Theatre, April 1, 1933; produced by Herbert M. Prentice. Featured Vernon Sylvaine (Andrew Berwick), Mary Williams (Lizzie), Douglas Quayle (Ralph Mayne), Isabel Thornton (Mrs. Willis), Vivienne Bennett (Mary), Vernon Harris (Dr. Ralston), May Howard (A Guest), Marie Dean (A Guest), Harry Chappell (Waiter), Awdry Burnard (A French Civilian), Kay Dukes (First V.A.D.), Nora Bedford-Williams (Second V.A.D.), Paul Smythe (French Officer), Graham Stuart (Second Officer), Francis Drake (Italian Officer), William Geeve (Staff Officer), Leslie Frazer (Subaltern), Mary Mills (A Nurse), Eileen Garson (Austrian Lady), Gordon Crier (R.F.C. Officer), Norma Wilson (A Girl), Gordon Bailey (Brigadier-General Driver), Godfrey Kenton (Captain Chesney), Marjorie Chard (Mrs. Smart).

The Tempest   (William Shakespeare) Open Air Theatre, June 5, 1934; general director Sydney W. Carroll, produced by Robert Atkins. Featured Dennis Hoey (Alonso), Jack Carlton (Sebastian), John Drinkwater (Prospero), Clifford Evans (Antonio), Hubert Gregg (Ferdinand), J. Leslie Frith (Gonzalo), Frank Drew (Adrian), Eric Dance (Francisco), Robert Atkins (Caliban), Andrew Leigh (Trinculo), and Edward Rigby (Stephano). Greer Garson was billed thirty-second, as Iris.

The Comedy of Errors   (William Shakespeare) Open Air Theatre, June 12, 1934; general director Sydney W. Carroll, produced by Maxwell Wray. Featured Dennis Hoey (Solinus, Duke of Ephesus), Ben Greet (Ageon), Robert Eddison (Antipholus of Ephesus), R. Kerr

Carey (Antipholus of Syracuse), Andrew Lee (Dromio of Ephesus), Frank Tickle (Dromio of Syracuse), and Ivor Harries (Balthazar). Greer Garson and Iris Hoey played Courtesans.

A Midsummer Night's Dream (William Shakespeare) Open Air Theatre, June 19, 1934; general director Sydney W. Carroll, produced by Robert Atkins. Featured Ion Swinley (Theseus), Dennis Hoey (Egeus), Clifford Evans (Lysander), Jack Carlton (Demetrius), Hubert Gregg (Philostrate), Nigel Playfair (Quince), Michael Martin-Harvey (Snug), Robert Atkins (Bottom), Henry Hewitt (Flute), A.B. Imeson (Snout), Clement Hamelin (Starveling), Leslie French (Puck), Mary Sheridan (Hippolyta), Margaretta Scott (Hermia), Martita Hunt (Helena), Phyllis Neilson-Terry (Oberon), Pamela Stanley (Titania). Greer Garson appeared as an uncredited extra.

Androcles and the Lion (George Bernard Shaw) Open Air Theatre, July 17, 1934; general director Sydney W. Carroll, produced by Robert Atkins. Featured Nigel Playfair (Emperor), Andrew Leigh (Androcles), George Carr (Lion), Arthur Hambling (Centurion), Leslie French (Captain), Peter Dearing (Lentulus), Robert Eddison (Metellus), Robert Atkins (Ferrovius), Valentine Rooke (Spintho). Greer Garson was billed as one of thirty-two female extras.

The Six of Calais (George Bernard Shaw) Open Air Theatre, July 17, 1934; produced by Maxwell Wray. Featured Hubert Gregg (Black Prince), Leonard Thorne (John of Gaunt), Charles Carson (Edward III), Vincent Sternroyd (Eustache de St. Pierre), Leonard Shepherd (Piers de Rosty), Clement Hamelin (Piers de Wissant), Frank Tickle (Jean d'Aire), Derek Prentice (Gilles d'Oudebolle). Greer Garson was billed nineteenth as a Court Lady.

Romeo and Juliet (William Shakespeare) Open Air Theatre, August 7, 1934; general director Sydney W. Carroll, produced by Robert Atkins. Featured Dennis Hoey (Escalus), Eric Dance (Paris), R. Kerr Carey (Montague), Henry Baynton (Capulet), Griffith Jones (Romeo), Leslie French (Mercutio), Hubert Gregg (Benvolio), Terence de Marney (Tybalt), Ben Greet (Friar Lawrence), Sydney Bromley (Balthasar), Frank Tickle (Sampson), Laura Smithson (Nurse),

Marjorie Stewart (Lady Montague), Alison Pickard (Lady Capulet), Margaretta Scott (Juliet). Greer Garson was billed as an extra.

Androcles and the Lion   (George Bernard Shaw) Winter Garden Theatre, September 20, 1934; produced by Robert Atkins. Featured Oscar Asche (Emperor), Andrew Leigh (Androcles), Michael Martin-Harvey (Lion), Arthur Hambling (Centurion), Leslie French (Captain), Peter Dearing (Lentulus), Ian Atkins (Metellus), Robert Atkins (Ferrovius), Valentine Rooke (Spintho). In London, Drury Lane, three-tiered auditorium seating 1,581. Among the extras playing soldiers, Christians, slaves, and pages was Greer Garson, playing a Vestal Virgin.

The Golden Arrow   (Sylvia Thompson and Victor Cunard) Whitehall Theatre, May 30, 1935; produced by Laurence Olivier, stage direction by Maxwell Coburn, scenery by Peter Luling. Featured Helen Haye (Lady Harben), Nan Munro (Caroline Percival), Cecil Parker (Philippe Fayard), Denys Blakelock (Sebastien Lee), Laurence Olivier (Richard Harben), Greer Garson (Fanny Field), Lindesay Baxter (Butler/Waiter), Margery Caldicott (Labor Member's Wife), Molly Lumley (Her Friend/Proprietress of Service Flat), Peter Copley (Valet/Younger Journalist), Robert Craven (Chef de Reception), Robert Ashby (Elder Journalist), Joan Miller (May Stokes), Pauline Vilda (Blonde).

Vintage Wine   (Sir Seymour Hicks and Ashley Dukes) Victoria Palace Theatre, June 22, 1935; produced by Sir Seymour Hicks, stage direction by George Desmond. Featured Julia Neilson (Josephine Popinot), Seymour Hicks (Charles Popinot), Hayley Bell (Lissa), Sonia Somers (Rosa), Edna Mills (Maria), John Hooker/George Desmond/Morris Harper (Luigi), Greer Garson/Phyllis Thomas (Nina Popinot), Ronald Waters/Thane Parker (Leonardo Volpe), Oliver Gordon/Terence Downing (Hon. Richard Emsley), Richard Fairfax (Gallichan), Stanley Vilven (Henry Popinot), Arthur Bromley Davenport/John Hooker (Pierre), Alfred Smith (Footman), Patrick Baring (Benedict Popinot), Judy Gunn/Audrey Martyn (Blanche Popinot), Audrey Martyn/Gemma Fagan (Suzanne Favert), Phyllis Thomas/Barbara Deane (Stephanie Popinot).

Accent on Youth (Samson Raphaelson) Globe Theatre, September 3, 1935; produced by Samson Raphaelson, stage direction by Henderson Storie. Featured Mary Grey (Miss Darling), Ernest Lawford (Frank Galloway), Robert Flemyng (Dickie Reynolds), Greer Garson (Linda Brown), Nicholas Hannen (Steven Gaye), Archibald Batty (Flogdell), Mary Glynne (Genevieve Lang), James Hoyle (Chuck), Kenneth Buckley (Butch).

Butterfly on the Wheel (E.G. Hemmerde and Francis Neilson) Playhouse Theatre, October 16, 1935; produced by Arthur Hardy. Featured S.J. Warmington/George Relph (The Right Hon. George Admaston, M.P.), John Stuart (Roderick Collingwood), Arthur Hardy (Lord Ellerdine), Aubrey Mallalieu (Sir John Burroughs), Franklin Dyall/D.A. Clarke-Smith (Sir Robert Fyffe, K.C., M.P.), Frank Woolfe (Gervaise McArthur, K.C.), Garrett Hollick (Stuart Menzies, K.C.), John Clare (Foreman of the Jury), Andrea Malandrinos (Jacques), Philip Cunningham (Mr. Parks), George Hollman (Footman), John Clarkson (Detective), Mary Merrall (Lady Atwill), Selma Vaz Dias (Pauline), and Greer Garson (Peggy Admaston).

Page From a Diary (Charles Bennett) Garrick Theatre, January 16, 1936; produced by Campbell Gullan, stage direction by George Desmond. Featured Ernst Deutsch (Boris Vetier), Andrea Malandrinos (Riccio), George Elton (Mr. Benger), Greer Garson (Vivienne Maitland, Vivienne Glennie), Evan Thomas (Bobby Latimer), John Mortimer (Tony Trent), Isobel Wake-Clark (Joan Marmont), Nicholas Hannen (Col. Victor Maitland, Captain Victor Glennie), Murri Moncrieff (A Commissar of Gendarmerie), Frank Attree (Alphonse), John Clare (Mahomet Ali), Oliver Gordon (Lieutenant Martyn), George Manship (Chunda Singh), H.A. Saintsbury (The Mullah Pir Mahomet Sharriff), Godfrey Bond (A Native Cavalryman).

The Visitor (Nicholas Monsarrat) Daly's Theatre, July 7, 1936; produced by Ellen Pollock, stage direction by Lewis Broughton. Featured Lewis Broughton (Simmonds), Margaret Scudamore (Mrs. Markham), Greer Garson (Diana), Guy Middleton (Richard Armstrong), Aubrey Dexter (Mr. Markham), Louis Borell (Karl Novak), Nadine March (Dorothy).

Mademoiselle (Audrey and Waveney Carten [adaptation of Jacques Deval's play]) Wyndham's Theatre, September 15, 1936; produced by Noël Coward, stage direction by Gerard Clifton. Featured Isabel Jeans (Alice Galvoisier), Cecil Parker (Lucien Galvoisier), Ann Farrer (Helene), Greer Garson (Christianne Galvoisier), Victor Boggetti (Jean), Madge Titheradge (Mademoiselle), Nigel Patrick (Maurice Galvoisier), Laidman Browne (George Boutin), Dorothy Lane (Therese), Edward MacCormack (Edouard), Willeen Wilson (Juliette).

Old Music (Keith Winter) St. James Theatre, August 18, 1937; produced by Margaret Webster, general stage direction by Lewis Allen, settings designed by Rex Whistler, costumes by G.K. Benda. Featured Robin Maule (Master Nicholas Decker), Geoffrey Keen (Brian Decker), Marjorie Fielding (Mrs. Decker), Celia Johnson, (Judith Cameron), Greer Garson (Geraldine), Margaret Hood (Grace), Hugh Williams (Tony Yale), Gyles Isham (Edward Tresham), Bryan Coleman (Philip Tresham), Margery Caldicott (Mabel), Leonard Sachs (First Footman), Peter Blackmore (Second Footman).

Tonight at 8:30 (Noël Peirce Coward) El Capitan Theater, August 5, 1940; produced by the Theatre Guild of Southern California and staged by Edmund Goulding, George Cukor, Gladys Cooper, Dudley Murphy, Robert Sinclair, Margaret Webster, Peter Godfrey, and James Whale. A series of nine short plays: *We Were Dancing* (Douglas Fairbanks Jr. and Constance Bennett), *Astonished Heart* (Basil Rathbone and Gladys Cooper), *Red Peppers* (Reginald Gardiner and Binnie Barnes), *Fumed Oak* (Roland Young and Dame May Whitty), *Hands Across the Sea* (Judith Anderson and Zasu Pitts), *Family Album* (Joan Fontaine and Clare Trevor), *Shadow Play* (Dorothy Stone and Georges Metaxa), *Still Life* (Rosalind Russell and Una O'Connor), and *Ways and Means* (staged by James Whale). Featured Greer Garson (Stella Cartwright), Brian Aherne (Toby Cartwright), Elsa Maxwell (Olive Lloyd-Ransome), Claude Allister (Lord Chapworth), Cissie Loftus (Nanny), Montagu Love (Murdoch), John Loder (Stevens), Rafaela Ottiano (Princess Elena Krassiloff), Peter Bronte (Gaston).

Auntie Mame (Jerome Lawrence and Robert E. Lee) The Broadhurst Theatre, January 20, 1958; produced by Robert Fryer and Lawrence Carr, directed by Morton Da Costa. Featured Beulah Garrick (Norah Muldoon), Jan Handzlik (Patrick Dennis as a boy and Michael Dennis), Yuki Shimoda (Ito), Polly Rowles (Vera Charles), Grant Sullivan (Ralph Devine), John O'Hare (M. Lindsay Woolsey), Greer Garson (Auntie Mame), Geoffrey Bryant (Mr. Waldo), Robert Allen (Mr. Babcock), Robert Smith (Beauregard Jackson Pickett Burnside), Ann Summers (Sally Cato MacDougal), Spivy (Mother Burnside), Peggy Cass (Agnes Gooch), James Monks (Brian O'Bannion), Joyce Lear (Gloria Upson), Dorothy Blackburn (Doris Upson), Walter Greaza (Claude Upson), Patricia Jenkins (Pegeen Ryan).

A Midsummer Night's Dream (Shakespeare/Mendelssohn) Southern Methodist University McFarlin Auditorium, October 16, 1967. Excerpts performed by narrators Greer Garson and Michael Allinson and sopranos Sung Sook Lee and Anita Larson, the Southern Methodist University Choral Union (directed by Lloyd Pfautsch), and the Dallas Symphony Orchestra (directed by Donald Johanos).

Captain Brassbound's Conversion (George Bernard Shaw) Ahmanson Theatre, September 24, 1968. Produced by the Center Theatre Group of Los Angeles, directed by Joseph Anthony. Featured George Rose (Rev. Leslie Rankin), Alfredo Valentino (Houseboy), Tony Tanner (Drinkwater), Mario Aniov (Hassan the Porter), Joe Cellini, Franco Cuva (Krooboys), Greer Garson (Lady Cicely Waynflete), John Williams (Sir Howard Hallam), Darren McGavin (Captain Brassbound), Len Lesser (Marzo), Stanley Tackney (Redbrook), Bruce Gordon (Johnson), Saadoun Bayati (Osman), Joseph Mascolo (Sheik Sidi el Assif), Mina E. Mina (The Cadi), John Nealson (Bluejacket), Paul Ford (Captain Hamlin Kearney).

Joys of Christmas Dorothy Chandler Pavilion, December 21, 1974. Christmas carol program performed by the Los Angeles Master Chorale and Sinfonia Orchestra under the musical direction of Roger Wagner with Dorothy Wade as concert mistress, Thomas Harmon as organist, and Greer Garson as narrator. Included "O Magnum

Mysterium," "A Hymn to the Virgin," "Rejoice in the Lamb," "Seven Joys of Christmas," "Carols from Foreign Lands," and "The Christmas Story."

The Madwoman of Chaillot   (Jean Giraudoux, English adaptation by Maurice Valency), Greer Garson Theatre, College of Santa Fe, October 1, 1975; directed by William Pappas. Featured Chris White (The Waiter), Tony Chilelli (The Little Man), Henry Mustelier (The Prospector), Al Houseworth (The President), Stephen Reynolds (The Baron), Wendy Wilkinson (Therese), Wayne Sabato (The Street Singer), Lei Ramsey (The Flower Girl), Tom Fitzpatrick (The Ragpicker), Regina McBride (Paulette), Anna Pacheco (The Deaf-Mute), Linda Bearman (Irma), Michael Ter Maat (The Shoelace Peddler), Ted Cole (The Broker), John Delaney (The Street Juggler), Jake Brockwell (Dr. Jadin), Greer Garson (Countess Aurelie), Lawrence Campos (The Doorman), John Constantine (The Policeman), Tom Hoesten (Pierre), Joe Manuel (The Sergeant), Lynn Miller (The Sewer-Man), Laura Klein (Mme. Constance), Mickey Crocker (Mlle. Gabrielle), Franny Parrish (Mme. Josephine), Al Houseworth, Ted Cole, John Constantine (The Prospectors), Tony Chilelli, Julie Frank, Edward Blatchford (The Press Agents), Wendy Wilkinson, Regina McBride (The Ladies), Paul Whitson (Adolphe Bertaut).

Major Television Appearances

Play Parade, **"Twelfth Night"**   May 14, 1937, BBC; produced by George More O'Ferrall. Starring Greer Garson, Henry Oscar, Hilary Pritchard, South African actress Dorothy Black.

Play Parade, **"School for Scandal"**   May 19, 1937, BBC; produced by George More O'Ferrall. Starring Greer Garson, Campbell Gullan, Denys Blakelock, Earle Grey.

Theatre Parade, **"Hassan"**   June 8 and 14, 1937, BBC; produced by George More O'Ferrall. Starring Greer Garson, Frank Cellier, John Wyse, D.A. Clarke-Smith, Ivan Samson. Music by Frederick Delius conducting the BBC Television Orchestra.

How He Lied to Her Husband   July 7, 1937, BBC. Produced by George More O'Ferrall. Starring Greer Garson, D.A. Clarke-Smith, Derek Williams.

Producers Showcase, **"Reunion in Vienna"**   April 4, 1955, NBC; produced by Jean Dalrymple and directed by Vincent Donehue. Starring Greer Garson, Brian Aherne, Peter Lorre, Robert Flemyng, Cathleen Nesbitt, Lile Darvas, Herbert Berghof, George Voskovec, Frederick Worlock, Tamara Daykarhanova.

Star Stage, **"Career"**   February 24, 1956, NBC; directed by Sidney Lanfield. Starring Greer Garson, Patric Knowles, Stephen Bekassy, Richard Erdman, Sarah Selby, Douglas Evans, Mandie Prickett.

GE Theater, **"The Glorious Gift of Molly Malloy"**   September 23, 1956, CBS; produced by William Frye and directed by Herschel Daugherty. Starring Greer Garson, John Hoyt, John Abbott, J.M. Kerrigan, Ludwig Stossell, John Galludet, Charles Herbert, Jimmy Fields.

Hallmark Hall of Fame, **"The Little Foxes"**   December 16, 1956, NBC; produced and directed by George Schaefer. Adaptation of the Lillian Hellman play by Robert Hartung. Starring Greer Garson, Franchot Tone, Sidney Blackmer, E.G. Marshall, Eileen Heckart, Georgia Burke, Mildred Trares, Peter Kelley, Lauren Gilbert, Lloyd G. Richards.

GE Theater, **"The Earring"**   January 13, 1957, CBS; produced by William Frye and directed by Jules Bricken. Starring Greer Garson, Eduard Franz, Philip Reed, Norman Lloyd, Barney Phillips, Ruth Lee, Clark Howat, Frank Wolff.

Telephone Time, **"Revenge"**   September 10, 1957, ABC; produced by Jerry Stagg and directed by Lewis Allan. Starring Greer Garson, Florenz Ames, Grant Richards, Olive Blakeney, Clark Gordon, Jimmy Fields, Warren Parker, Mason Curry, Jim Heyward. Hosted and narrated by Dr. Frank Baxter.

GE Theater, "R.S.V.P." January 12, 1960, CBS; produced by Joseph T. Naar and directed by Richard Irving. Starring Greer Garson, Virginia Grey, Donald Woods, Virginia Gregg, Angela Greene, Noreen Nash, Joe Cranston, James Seay, Clark Howst, Ralph Dumke.

Hallmark Hall of Fame, "Captain Brassbound's Conversion" May 2, 1960, NBC; directed and produced by George Schaefer. Adaptation by Theodore Apstein. Starring Greer Garson, Christopher Plummer, Loring Smith, Felix Aylmer, Liam Redmond, George Rose, Henry Brandon, Howard Caine, Robert Carricart, Henry Ellerbe, Chris Gampel, Douglas Henderson, William Lanteau, Robert Redford, Patrick Westwood, Joseph Abdullah.

Dupont Show of the Month, "The Shadowed Affair" November 4, 1962, NBC; directed by Fielder Cook. Starring Greer Garson, Douglas Fairbanks Jr., Lois Nettleton.

Hallmark Hall of Fame, "The Invincible Mr. Disraeli" April 4, 1963, NBC; produced and directed by George Schaefer. By James Lee. Starring Trevor Howard, Greer Garson, Kate Reid, Hurd Hatfield, Denholm Elliott, Frederic Worlock, Eric Beery, Geoffrey Kean.

The Men from Shiloh, "Lady at the Bar" November 4, 1970, NBC; produced by John McLiam and directed by Russ Mayberry. Starring James Drury, Doug McClure, Stewart Granger, Lee Majors, John McLiam.

The Little Drummer Boy December 14, 1971, NBC; produced by Arthur Rankin Jr. and Jules Bass. Featuring the voices of Jose Ferrer, Teddy Eccles, and the Vienna Boys Choir. Narrated by Greer Garson. A sequel was made, *The Little Drummer Boy, Book II,* also narrated by Greer Garson, which premiered on December 13, 1976.

Hallmark Hall of Fame, "Crown Matrimonial" April 3, 1974, NBC; coproduced by David Susskind, Arthur Cantor, E.E. Fogelson, and directed by Alan Bridges. Starring Greer Garson, Peter Barkworth, Andrew Ray, Amanda Reiss, Bernard Archard, Maxine Audley, Anna Cropper.

The Pallisers   January 13 to June 20, 1977, BBC (shown in America on HBO and PBS); produced by Martin Lisemore and directed by Hugh David. Starring Susan Hampshire, Philip Latham, Roland Culver. Narrated by Greer Garson for twenty-six hour-long episodes.

Little Women   October 2 and 3, 1978, NBC; produced by David Victor and directed by David Lowell Rich. Adapted by Suzanne Clauser from the book by Louisa May Alcott. Starring Susan Dey, Meredith Baxter Birney, Ann Dusenbery, Eve Plumb, Dorothy McGuire, William Shatner, Cliff Potts, Richard Gilliland, Greer Garson, Robert Young, William Schallert, Virginia Gregg.

Perry Como's Christmas in New Mexico   December 14, 1979, ABC; produced by Ron Miziker, Stephen Pouliot, and directed by Sterling Johnson. Starring Perry Como, Joyce DeWitt, Anne Murray, Greer Garson.

The Love Boat, "The Tomorrow Lady"   December 4, 1982, ABC; produced by Art Baer and directed by Richard Wells. Starring Gavin MacLeod, Bernie Kopell, Fred Grandy, Ted Lange, Lauren Tewes, Jill Whelan; guest stars Greer Garson and Howard Duff.

Movies

Goodbye, Mr. Chips   Producer, Victor Saville; director, Sam Wood; screenplay, R.C. Sherriff, Claudine West, Eric Maschwitz; from the book *Goodbye, Mr. Chips* by James Hilton; photographed by Freddie Young; production manager, Harold Boxall; art director, Alfred Junge; recording, A.W. Watkins and C.C. Stevens; film editor, Charles Frend; special music, Richard Addinsell; musical director, Louis Levy. Premiere, May 15, 1939, Astor Theater, New York; running time, 113 minutes; black and white.

   Cast   Robert Donat (Charles Chipping), Greer Garson (Katherine Ellis Chipping), Terry Kilburn (John Colley, Peter Colley I, II, III), John Mills (Peter Colley as a young man), Paul Henreid (Mr. Staefel), Judith Furse (Flora), Lyn Harding (Wetherby), Milton Rosmer (Charteris), Frederick Leister (Marsham), Louise Hampton (Mrs.

Wickett), Austin Trevor (Ralston), David Tree (Jackson), Edmund Breon (Colonel Morgan), Jill Furse (Helen Colley), Scott Sunderland (Sir John Colley).

Song "Brookfield School Song" (Richard Addinsell, Eric Maschwitz).

Remember? Producer, Milton Bren; director, Norman Z. McLeod; original story and screenplay by Corey Ford and Norman Z. McLeod; art director, Cedric Gibbons, Urie McCleary; set decoration, Edwin B. Willis; musical score, Edward Ward; recording director, Douglas Shearer; director of photography, George Folsey, A.S.C.; film editor, Harold F. Kress. Premiere, December 14, 1939, Capitol Theater, New York; running time, eighty-three minutes; black and white.

Cast Robert Taylor (Jeff Holland), Greer Garson (Linda Bronson), Lew Ayres (Sky Ames), Billie Burke (Mrs. Bronson), Reginald Owen (Mr. Bronson), George Barbier (Mr. McIntyre), Henry Travers (Judge Milliken), Richard Carle (Mr. Piper), Laura Hope Crews (Mrs. Carruthers), Sara Haden (Miss Wilson), Sig Rumann (Dr. Schmidt), Halliwell Hobbes (Butler), Paul Hurst (Policeman), Brandon Tynan (Judge Sherman), Syd Saylor (Taxi Driver), Armand Kaliz (Marcel), Thomas Louden (Butler), Billy Taft (Train Announcer), Sarah Edwards (Lady in Revolving Door), Harry Lash (Cab Driver), Nell Craig (McIntyre's Secretary), Lee Phelps (Truck Driver), Norman Ainsley (Boat Steward), Edwin Stanley (Newbert).

Song "Try to Remember" (Edward Ward, Earl Brent).

Pride and Prejudice Producer, Hunt Stromberg; director, Robert Z. Leonard; screenplay, Aldous Huxley and Jane Murfin; based upon the dramatization of Jane Austen's novel written by Helen Jerome; musical score, Herbert Stothart; recording director, Douglas Shearer; art directors, Cedric Gibbons and Paul Groesse; set decorations, Edwin B. Willis; gowns by Adrian; men's costumes by Gile Steele; hair stylist, Sydney Guilaroff; makeup created by Jack Dawn; director of photography, Karl Freund, A.S.C.; dance direction, Ernst Matray; technical advisor, George Richelavie; film editor, Robert J. Kern. Premiere, July 26, 1940, Radio City Music Hall, New York. Running time, 117 minutes; black and white.

Cast Greer Garson (Elizabeth Bennet), Laurence Olivier (Mr.

Darcy), Mary Boland (Mrs. Bennet), Edna May Oliver (Lady Catherine DeBurgh), Maureen O'Sullivan (Jane Bennet), Ann Rutherford (Lydia Bennet), Edmund Gwenn (Mr. Bennet), Edward Ashley (Wickham), Frieda Inescort (Caroline Bingley), Heather Angel (Kitty Bennet), Melville Cooper (Mr. Collins), Karen Morley (Charlotte Lucas), Marsha Hunt (Mary Bennet), Bruce Lester (Bingley), Marten Lamont (Denny), E.E. Clive (Sir William Lucas), May Beatty (Mrs. Phillips), Marjorie Wood (Lady Lucas), Gia Kent (Miss DeBurgh), Gerald Oliver-Smith (Fitz William), Vernon Downing (Captain Carter), Buster Slaven (Beck's assistant), Wyndham Standing, Lowden Adams (Committeemen), Clara Reed (Maid in Parsonage).

Songs "The Assembly Waltz" (Herbert Stothart), "Flow Gently Sweet Afton" (Spilman).

Blossoms in the Dust Producer, Irving Asher; director, Mervyn LeRoy; screenplay, Anita Loos (contributions by Dorothy Yost and Hugo Butler); story by Ralph Wheelwright; directors of photography, Karl Freund, A.S.C., W. Howard Greene, A.S.C.; color director, Natalie Kalmus, Henri Jaffa; musical score, Herbert Stothart; recording director, Douglas Shearer; art director, Cedric Gibbons, Urie McCleary; set decorations, Edwin B. Willis; special effects, Warren Newcombe; gowns by Adrian; men's costumes, Gile Steele; hairstyles by Sydney Guilaroff; makeup created by Jack Dawn; film editor, George Boemler. Premiere, June 26, 1941, Radio City Music Hall, New York. Running time, ninety-nine minutes; color.

Cast Greer Garson (Edna Kahley Gladney), Walter Pidgeon (Sam Gladney), Felix Bressart (Dr. Max Breslar), Marsha Hunt (Charlotte Kahley), Fay Holden (Mrs. Kahley), Samuel S. Hinds (Mr. Kahly), Kathleen Howard (Mrs. Keats), George Lessey (Mr. Keats), William Henry (Allan Keats), Henry O'Neill (Judge), John Eldredge (Damon McPherson), Clinton Rosemond (Zeke), Theresa Harris (Cleo), Charlie Arnt (G. Harrington Hedger), Cecil Cunningham (Mrs. Gilworth), Ann Morriss (Mrs. Loring) Richard Nichols (Sammy), Pat Barker (Tony), Mary Taylor (Helen), Marc Lawrence (La Verne), Oscar O'Shea (Dr. West), Clarence Kolb (Senator Cotton), Edith Evanson (Hilda), Harry Allen (Gus, the Groom), David Clyde (Frederick, the Butler), Hope Landin (Olga, the Cook), Jimmy Spencer (Mr. Dirk), Anne O'Neal (Lena), Nora Perry (Mary), Carroll Nye

(Mr. Loring), Kay Linaker (Mrs. Bedlow), Janet Shaw (Tess), Tristam
Coffin (Mr. Howard), Jane Drummond (Mrs. Howard), Edward
McWade (Darrow), Harry Worth (Rader, Shyster Lawyer), Roy Gor-
don (Craig, Edna's Lawyer), Byron Shores (Mr. Eldridge), Fay Helm
(Leta Eldridge), Grace Stafford (Grace), Willa Pearl Curtis (Sarah),
Margaret Bert (Helen), Harrison Greene (Mr. Piggott).
  Song "Blossoms in the Dust," (Nacio Herb Brown, Eddie
Heyman).

When Ladies Meet Produced by Robert Z. Leonard and Orville O.
Dull; director, Robert Z. Leonard; screenplay, S.K. Lauren, Anita Loos;
based on the play by Rachel Crothers, produced by John Golden;
director of photography, Robert Planck, A.S.C.; musical score,
Bronislau Kaper; recording director, Douglas Shearer; art directors,
Cedric Gibbons, Randall Duell; set decorations, Edwin B. Willis;
gowns by Adrian; hairstyles created by Sydney Guilaroff; film editor,
Robert J. Kern. Premiere, September 4, 1941, Capitol Theater, New
York. Running time, 105 minutes; black and white.
  Cast Joan Crawford (Mary Howard), Robert Taylor (Jimmy
Lee), Greer Garson (Clare Woodruf), Herbert Marshall (Rogers
Woodruf), Spring Byington (Bridget Drake), Rafael Storm (Walter
De Canto), Mona Barrie (Mabel Guiness), Max Willenz (Pierre), Flo-
rence Shirley (Janet Hopper), Leslie Francis (Homer Hopper).
  Song "I Love Thee" (Edward Grieg, Auber Forestier).

Mrs. Miniver Producer, Sidney Franklin; director, William Wyler;
screenplay, Arthur Wimperis, George Froeschel, James Hilton,
Claudine West; based on *Mrs. Miniver* by Jan Struther; musical score,
Herbert Stothart and St. Luke Choristers, Ripley Dorr, director; di-
rector of photography, Joseph Ruttenberg, A.S.C.; recording director,
Douglas Shearer; art directors, Cedric Gibbons, Urie McCleary; set
decorations, Edwin B. Willis; special effects, Arnold Gillespie, War-
ren Newcombe; gowns by Kalloch; men's wardrobe, Gile Steele; hair-
styles for Miss Garson by Sydney Guilaroff; film editor, Harold F.
Kress. Premiere, June 4, 1942, Radio City Music Hall, New York.
Running time, 134 minutes; black and white.
  Cast Greer Garson (Kay Miniver), Walter Pidgeon (Clarence
Miniver), Teresa Wright (Carol Beldon), Dame May Whitty (Lady

Beldon), Reginald Owen (Mr. Foley), Henry Travers (Mr. Ballard), Richard Ney (Vincent Miniver), Henry Wilcoxon (Vicar), Christopher Severn (Toby Miniver), Brenda Forbes (Gladys, Maid), Clare Sandars (Judy Miniver), Marie De Becker (Ada, Cook), Helmut Dantine (German Flyer), John Abbott (Fred), Connie Leon (Simpson), Rhys Williams (Horace), Miles Mander (German Agent's Voice), Mary Field (Miss Spriggins), Paul Scardon (Nobby), Ben Webster (Ginger), Aubrey Mather (George, Innkeeper), Forrester Harvey (Huggins), John Abbott (Fred, Porter), Connie Leon (Simpson, Maid), Billy Bevan (Conductor) Florence Wix (Woman with Dog), Bobby Hale (Old Man), Alice Monk (Lady Passenger) Ottola Nesmith (Saleslady), Douglas Gordon (Porter), Gerald Oliver Smith (Car Dealer), Alec Craig (Joe), Clara Reid (Mrs. Huggins), Leonnard Carey (Beldon's Butler), Leslie Vincent (William), John Burton (Halliday), Eric Lonsdale (Marston), Guy Bellis (Barman), Charles Irwin (Mac), Ian Wolfe (Dentist), Charles Bennett (Milkman), Arthur Wimperis (Sir Henry), Peter Lawford (Pilot), Thomas Louden (Mr. Verger), Walter Byron (Waiter), Harold Howard (Judge), David Clyde (Carruthers), Colin Campbell (Bickles), Herbert Clifton (Doctor), Frank Baker (Policeman), Gene Byram, Virginia Bassett, Aileen Carlyle, Irene Denny, Herbert Evans, Eula Morgan, Vernon Steele, Vivie Steele, Marek Windheim, Tudor Williams (Glee Club Members), Kitty Watson, Hugh Greenwood, Sybil Bacon, Flo Benson (Contestants), John Burton, Louise Bates (Miniver Guests).

Songs "Midsummer's Day," (Gene Lockhart), "Children of the Heavenly King" (Pleyel, Cennick), "O God Our Help in Ages Past" (Croft, Watts), "Onward Christian Soldiers" (Sullivan, Baring-Gould).

Random Harvest Producer, Sidney Franklin; director, Mervyn LeRoy; screenplay, Claudine West, George Froeschel, Arthur Wimperis; based upon the novel by James Hilton; director of photography, Joseph Ruttenberg, A.S.C.; musical score, Herbert Stothart, "She's Ma Daisy" staged by Ernst Matray; recording director, Douglas Shearer; art directors, Cedric Gibbons, Randall Duell; set decorations, Edwin B. Willis, Jack Moore; gowns, Kalloch; hairstyles by Sydney Guilaroff; makeup created by Jack Dawn; film editor, Harold F. Kress. Premiere, December 31, 1942, Radio City Music Hall, New York. Running time, 126 minutes; black and white.

Cast Ronald Colman (Charles Ranier/"Smithy"), Greer Garson (Margaret Hanson/Paula Ridgeway), Philip Dorn (Dr. Jonathan Benet), Susan Peters (Kitty), Henry Travers (Dr. Sims), Reginald Owen ("Biffer" Briggs), Bramwell Fletcher (Harrison), Rhys Williams (Sam), Una O'Connor (Tobacconist), Aubrey Mather (Sheldon), Margaret Wycherly (Mrs. Deventer), Arthur Margetson (Chetwynd), Melville Cooper (George), Alan Napier (Julian), Jill Esmond (Lydia, Chet's Wife), Marta Linden (Jill), Ann Richards (Bridget), Norma Varden (Julia), David Cavendish (Henry Chilcotte), Ivan Simpson (The Vicar), Marie deBecker (Vicar's wife), Charles Wadron (Mr. Lloyd), Elisabeth Risdon (Mrs. Lloyd), Edmund Gwenn (Prime Minister), John Burton (Pearson), Alec Craig (Comedian), Henry Daniell (Heavy Man), Helena Phillips Evans (Ella, Charwoman), Mrs. Gardner Crane (Mrs. Sims), Montague Shaw (Julia's Husband), Lumsden Hare (Sir John), Frederic Worlock (Paula's Lawyer), Wallis Clark (Jones), Harry T. Shannon (Badgeley), Hilda Plowright (Nurse), Arthur Space (Trempitt), Jimmy Aubrey (Attendant), Harold deBecker (Milkman), Terry Kilburn (Newspaper Boy), Ian Wolfe (Registrar), Keith Hitchcock (Commissionaire), Arthur Shields (Chemist), Forrester Harvey (Cabby), Matthew Boulton (Policeman), Olive Blakeney (Woman), Lilyan Irene (Waitress), Major Harris, Herbert Evans, Eric Wilton, Ernest Hilliard, Al Hill (Members of House of Commons), George Kirby (Conductor), Peter Lawford (Soldier).

Songs "Oh Perfect Love" (J. Barnby, Gurney), "It's a Long, Long Way to Tipperary" (Jack Judge, Harry Williams), "She's Ma Daisy" (Harry Lauder, J.D. Harper), "Voice That Breathed O'er Eden" (Gauntlett, Keble).

The Youngest Profession Producer, B.F. Zeidman; director, Edward Buzzell; screenplay, George Oppenheimer, Charles Lederer, Leonard Spigelgass, Fredrick Kohner, Anna Lee Whitmore, Thomas Seller, Ethel Frank, Jan Fortune, Lillian Day; based upon the book by Lillian Day; director of photography, Charles Lawton, A.S.C.; musical score, David Snell; recording director, Douglas Shearer; art directors, Cedric Gibbons, Edward Carfagno; set decorations, Edwin B. Willis, Helen Conway; costume supervision, Irene, Shoup; film editor, Ralph Winters. Premiere, July 16, 1943, Radio City Music Hall, New York. Running time, eighty-two minutes; black and white.

Cast   Virginia Weidler (Joan Lyons), Edward Arnold (Burton V. Lyons), John Carroll (Dr. Hercules), Jean Porter (Patricia Drew), Ann Ayars (Susan Thayer), Marta Linden (Edith Lyons), Dick Simmons (Douglas Sutton), Agnes Moorehead (Miss Featherstone), Marcia Mae Jones (Vera Bailey), Raymond Roe (Schuyler), Scotty Beckett (Junior Lyons), Jessie Grayson (Lilybud), Sara Haden (Salvation Army Lass), Beverly Jean Saul (Thyra Winter), Marjorie Gateson (Mrs. Drew), Thurston Hall (Mr. Drew), Patricia Roe (Polly), Aileen Pringle (Miss Farwood), Nora Lane (Hilda), Dorothy Christy (Sally), Mary Vallee (Mary), Gloria Tucker (Gladys), Jane Isbell (Jane), Hazel Dawn (Hazel), Beverly Boyd (Beverly), Randa Allen (Randa), Ann MacLean (Ann), Gloria Mackey (Gloria), Bobby Stebbins (Richard), Mark Daniels (Les Peterson), William Tannen (Hotel Clerk), Ann Codee (Sandra's Maid), Dorothy Morris (Secretary), Eddie Buzzell (Man in Theater), George Noisom (Delivery Boy), Alice Keating (Governess), Leonard Carey (Valet), Herberta Williams (Hortense), Ray Teal (Taxicab Driver), Roland Dupree, Robert Winkler (Mail Room Boys).

Guest Stars   (in order of their appearance) Lana Turner, Greer Garson, Walter Pidgeon, Robert Taylor, William Powell.

Song   "Our Autograph Book" (Sammy Fain, Oliver Garver— cut from final release print).

Madame Curie   Producer, Sidney Franklin; director, Mervyn LeRoy; screenplay, Paul Osborn, Paul H. Rameau; based on the book *Madame Curie* by Eve Curie; narration spoken by James Hilton; musical score, Herbert Stothart; director of photography, Joseph Ruttenberg, A.S.C.; recording director, Douglas Shearer; art directors, Cedric Gibbons, Paul Groesse; set decorations, Edwin B. Willis, Hugh Hunt; special effects, Warren Newcombe; costume supervision, Irene; associate, Sharaff; men's costumes, Gile Steele; makeup created by Jack Dawn; film editor, Harold F. Kress. Premiere, December 15, 1943, Grauman's Chinese Theater, Hollywood; December 16, Radio City Music Hall, New York. Running time, 124 minutes; black and white.

Cast   Greer Garson (Marie Sklodowska Curie), Walter Pidgeon (Pierre Curie), Henry Travers (Eugene Curie), Albert Basserman (Prof. Jean Perot), Robert Walker (David LeGros), C. Aubrey Smith (Lord Kelvin), Dame May Whitty (Mme. Eugene Curie), Victor

Francen (President of University), Elsa Basserman (Mme. Perot), Reginald Owen (Dr. Henri Becquerel), Van Johnson (Reporter), Margaret O'Brien (Irene Curie at age five), Lumsden Hare (Professor Roget), Charles Trowbridge, Edward Fielding, James Kirkwood, Nestor Eristoff (Board Members), Moroni Olsen (President of Businessman's Board), Miles Mander, Arthur Shields, Frederic Worlock (Businessmen), Alan Napier (Dr. Bladh), Ray Collins (Lecturer's Voice, Eustace Wyatt (Doctor), Dorothy Gilmore (Nurse), Gigi Perreau (Eve at age eighteen months), Marek Windheim (Jewelry Salesman), Lisa Golm (Lucille), Linda Lee Gates, Marie Louise Gates (Perot Grandchildren), Howard Freeman (Prof. Constant's Voice), Francis Pierlot (Monsieur Michaud), Almira Sessions (Mme. Michaud), Dickie Meyers (Master Michaud), Leo Mostovoy (Photographer), Williams Edmunds (Cart Driver), Ilka Gruning (Seamstress), Harold deBecker (Professor), George Meader (Singing Professor), Ruth Cherrington (Swedish Queen), Wyndham Standing (King Oscar), James Hilton (Narrator).

Mrs. Parkington   Producer, Leon Gordon; director, Tay Garnett; screenplay, Robert Thoeren, Polly James; based on the novel *Mrs. Parkington* by Louis Bromfield; director of photography, Joseph Ruttenberg, A.S.C.; musical score, Bronislau Kaper, St. Luke Choristers; recording director, Douglas Shearer; art direction, Cedric Gibbons, Randall Duell; set decorations, Edwin B. Willis, McLean Nisbet; special effects, A. Arnold Gillespie, Warren Newcombe, Danny Hall; costume supervision, Irene, Marion Herwood; men's costumes, Valles; makeup created by Jack Dawn; hairstyles created by Sydney Guilaroff; film editor, George Boemler. Premiere, October 12, 1944, Radio City Music Hall, New York. Running time, 124 minutes; black and white.

Cast   Greer Garson (Susie Graham Parkington), Walter Pidgeon (Major Augustus Parkington), Edward Arnold (Amory Stilham), Agnes Moorehead (Aspasia Conti), Cecil Kellaway (Edward, Prince of Wales), Gladys Cooper (Alice, Duchess de Brancourt), Frances Rafferty (Jane Stilham), Tom Drake (Ned Talbot), Peter Lawford (Lord Thornley), Dan Duryea (Jack Stilham), Hugh Marlowe (John Marbey), Selena Royle (Mattie Trounson), Fortunio Bonanova (Signor Cellini), Lee Patrick (Madeleine), Harry Cording (Humphrey),

Celia Travers (Belle), Mary Servoss (Mrs. Graham), Rod Cameron (Al Swann), Helen Freeman (Helen Stilham), Tala Birell (Lady Norah Ebbsworth), Hans Conried (Mr. Ernst), Gerald Oliver Smith (Taylor) Ruthe Brady (Bridgett), Byron Foulger (Vance), Wallis Clark (Captain McTavish), Ann Codee (Mme. Dupont), Frank Reicher (French Doctor), George Davis (French Policeman), Kay Medford (Minnie), Edward Fielding (Rev. Pilbridge), Alma Kruger (Mrs. Jacob Livingstone), Rhea Mitchell (Mrs. Humphrey), Ivo Henderson (Albert), Charles Pecora (Head Waiter), Mary Zavian (Can-Can Girl), Myron Tobia (Boy), Eugene Borden (Drunk), Erin O'Kelley (Can-Can Girl), Lee Tung-Foo (Sam), Marek Windheim (Gaston), Johnny Berkes (Beggar), Franco Corsaro (Gypsy Fiddler), Anna Marie Stewart (French Maid), Marcelle Corday (Mme. De Thebes), Robert Greig (Mr. Orlando), Gordon Richards (James the Butler), Warren Farlan (Herbert Parkington, age two and one-half), Howard Hickman (Dr. Herrick), Maurice Cass (Shopkeeper), Wyndham Standing (Butler), Major Douglas Francis (First Groom), Harvey Shepherd (Second Groom), Brandon Hurst (Footman), Tiff Payne (Billiard Expert), Billy Bletcher, Harry Tyler, Vernon Dent, Bud Jamison (Quartette Members).

The Valley of Decision   Producer, Edwin H. Knopf; director, Tay Garnett; screenplay by John Meehan, Sonya Levien; based on the novel by Marcia Davenport; musical score, Herbert Stothart; director of photography, Joseph Ruttenberg, A.S.C.; recording director, Douglas Shearer; art direction, Cedric Gibbons, Paul Groesse; set decorations, Edwin B. Willis, Mildred Griffiths; special effects, A. Arnold Gillespie, Warren Newcombe; costume supervision, Irene, Marion Herwood Keyes; makeup created by Jack Dawn; hairstyles created by Sydney Guilaroff; film editor, Blanche Sewell. Premiere, May 3, 1945, Radio City Music Hall, New York. Running time, 119 minutes; black and white.

  Cast   Greer Garson (Mary Rafferty), Gregory Peck (Paul Scott), Donald Crisp (William Scott), Lionel Barrymore (Pat Rafferty), Preston Foster (Jim Brennan), Marsha Hunt (Constance Scott), Gladys Cooper (Clarissa Scott), Reginald Owen (McCready), Dan Duryea (William Scott Jr.) Jessica Tandy (Louise Kane), Barbara Everest (Delia), Marshall Thompson (Ted Scott), Geraldine Wall (Kate Shannon), Evelyn Dockson (Mrs. Callahan), John Warburton

(Giles, Earl of Moulton), Russell Hicks (Mr. Laurence Gaylord), Mary Lord (Julia Gaylord), Arthur Shields (Callahan), Dean Stockwell (Paulie), Mary Currier (Mrs. Laurence Gaylord), Norman Ollestead (Callahan's son), Connie Gilchrist (Cook), Willa Pearl Curtis (Maid), Jesse Graves (Sweeper), William O'Leary (O'Brien), Richard Abbott (Minister), Bryn Davis (First Maid), Anna Q. Nilsson (Nurse), Joy Harrington (Stella), Lumsden Hare (Dr. McClintock), Wayne and Warren Farlow (Timmy), Sherlee Collier (Clarrie).

  Songs "Molly Baun" and "Young Rory O'Moore" (traditional Irish ballads).

Adventure Producer, Sam Zimbalist; director, Victor Fleming; based on a novel by Clyde Brion Davis; adaptation, Anthony Veiller, William H. Wright; screenplay, Frederick Hazlitt Brennan, Vincent Lawrence; musical score, Herbert Stothart; director of photography, Joseph Ruttenberg, A.S.C.; film editor, Frank Sullivan; orchestration, Murray Cutter; recording director, Douglas Shearer; art direction, Cedric Gibbons, Urie McCleary; set decorations, Edwin B. Willis; special effects, Warren Newcombe; costume supervision, Irene, Marion Herwood Keyes; hair designs by Sydney Guilaroff; makeup created by Jack Dawn. Premiere, Radio City Music Hall, February 6, 1946. Running time, 126 minutes; black and white.

  Cast Clark Gable (Harry Patterson), Greer Garson (Emily Sears), Joan Blondell (Helen Malohn), Thomas Mitchell (Mudgin), Tom Tully (Gus), John Qualen (Model T), Richard Haydn (Limo), Lina Romay (Maria), Philip Merivale ("Old" Ramon Estado), Harry Davenport (Dr. Ashlon), Tito Renaldo ("Young" Ramon), Pedro de Cordoba (Felipe), Chef Joseph Milani (Rudolfo), Martin Garralaga (Nick the Bartender), Jack Young (Captain), Dorothy Granger (Cashier), Gladden James (Barber), Billy Newell (Barber), Esther Howard (Blister), Florence Auer (Landlady), Harry Wilson (Big Mug), Myron Geiger (Bartender), George Suzanne (Barfly), Eddie Hart (Milkman), Lee Phelps (Bartender), Richard Abbott (Clerk), Aileen Carlyle (Matron), Jack Sterling, Paul Stador (Bouncers), Frank Hagney (Boss), Betty Blythe (Mrs. Buckley), Pierre Watkin (Mr. Buckley), Charles La Torre (Tony), Dorothy Vaughan (Mrs. Ludlow), Morris Ankrum (Mr. Ludlow), John Harmon (Taxi Driver), James Darrell (Officer), Garry Owen (Jabbo), Ralph Peters (Joe), Joseph Crehan (Ed), Ray Teal

(Rico), Marta Linden (Ethel), Audrey Totter (Littelton), Harry Tyler (Doctor), Rex Ingram (Colored Preacher).
Songs "Norah Girl" (Herbert Stothart, Frederick H. Brennan).

Desire Me Producer, Arthur Hornblow Jr; director, no credit (George Cukor, Mervyn LeRoy, Victor Saville, Jack Conway); screenplay, Marguerite Roberts, Zoë Akins; adaptation, Casey Robinson; from a novel by Leonhard Frank; musical score, Herbert Stothart; director of photography, Joseph Ruttenberg, A.S.C.; art directors, Cedric Gibbons, Urie McCleary; film editor, Joseph Durvin; recording director, Douglas Shearer; set decorations, Edwin B. Willis, Paul Huldschinsky; special effects, Warren Newcombe, A. Arnold Gillespie; hairstyles created by Sydney Guilaroff; costume supervision, Irene; men's costumes, Valles; makeup created by Jack Dawn. Premiere, October 31, 1947, Capitol Theater, New York. Running time, ninety-one minutes; black and white.
Cast Greer Garson (Marise Aubert), Robert Mitchum (Paul Aubert), Richard Hart (Jean Renaud), Morris Ankrum (Martin), George Zucco (Father Donnard), Cecil Humphreys (Dr. Andre Leclair), David Hoffman (Alex, the Postman), Max Willenz (Dr. Poulin), Clinton Sundberg (Salesman), Tony Carson (Youth), Mitchell Lewis (Old Man), Fernanda Eliscu (Old Woman), Sid D'Albrook (Assistant), David Leonard (Cobbler), Edward Keane (Baker), Belle Mitchell (Baker's Wife), Hans Schumm, Frederic Brunn (German Voice), John Maxwell Hayes (Church Dignitary), Lew Mason (Sailor), Josephine Victor (Woman), Jean Del Val (Older Man), Nick Kobliansky, Jose Portugal (Soldiers), Hanz Tranzler (German Guard), Maurice Tauzin (Boy), Stanley Andrews (Emile), Harry Wood (Joseph), Sam Ash (Master of Ceremonies), Earle Hodgins (Barker), Bert LeBaron (Bear Trainer), Tom Plank (Clown), Gil Perkins (Soldier to resemble Mitchum), Albert Petit (Tinsel Wreath Vendor), Pietro Sosso (Jewelry Vendor), Grace Lord (Candle Seller), Duke Johnson (Juggler), Jack Shafton (Puppet Operator), Iris Shafton (Puppet Assistant).

Julia Misbehaves Producer, Everett Riskin; director, Jack Conway; screenplay by William Ludwig, Harry Ruskin, Arthur Wimperis; adaptation by Gina Kaus, Monckton Hoffe; based upon the novel *The Nutmeg Tree* by Margery Sharp; musical score, Adolph Deutsch; director of photography, Joseph Ruttenberg, A.S.C.; art directors, Cedric Gibbons, Daniel B. Cathcart; film editor, John Dunning, recording director, Douglas Shearer; set decorations, Edwin B. Willis, Jack D. Moore; special effects, Warren Newcombe; Miss Garson's costumes by Irene; hairstyles designed by Sydney Guilaroff; makeup created by Jack Dawn. Premiere, October 8, 1948, Radio City Music Hall. Running time, ninety-nine minutes; black and white.

Cast   Greer Garson (Julia Packett), Walter Pidgeon (William Sylvester Packett), Peter Lawford (Ritchie Lorgan), Elizabeth Taylor (Susan Packett), Cesar Romero (Fred Ghenoccio), Lucile Watson (Mrs. Packett), Nigel Bruce (Colonel Willowbrook), Mary Boland (Ma Ghenoccio), Reginald Owen (Benjamin Hawkins), Henry Stephenson (Lord Pennystone), Aubrey Mather (Vicar), Ian Wolfe (Hobson), Fritz Feld (Pepito), Phyllis Morris (Daisy), Veda Ann Borg (Louise), Edmund Breon (Jamie), Winifred Harris (Lady Pennystone), Ted DeWayne, Henry Monzello, William Snyder, Ray Saunders, Michael Kent (Acrobatic Troupe), Elspeth Dudgeon (Woman in Pawn Shop), Stanley Fraser (Pawn Shop Clerk), James Logan (Moving Man), Jimmy Fairfax, Harry Allen, Cyril Thornton, Jim Finlayson (Bill Collectors), Victor Wood (Postman), Herbert Wyndham (Piano Player in Pub), Sid D'Albrook (Waiter in Pub), Jimmy Aubrey (Drunk), Roland Dupre (French Messenger), Alex Goudavich (Bell Hop), Andre Charlot (Stage Doorman), Joanee Wayne (The Head), Mitchell Lewis (Train Official), Jean Del Val (Croupier).

Songs   "When You're Playing with Fire" (Jerry Seelan, Hal Borne), "Oh! What a Difference the Navy's Made to Me" (Leslie Alleyn, Ralph Stanley), "My Wonderful One" (Whiteman and Grofe).

That Forsyte Woman   Producer, Leon Gordon; director, Compton Bennett; screenplay, Jan Lustig, Ivan Tors, James B. Williams; additional dialogue, Arthur Wimperis; based on Book One of *The Forsyte Saga* by John Galsworthy; musical score, Bronislau Kaper; director of photography, Joseph Ruttenberg, A.S.C.; Technicolor color consultants, Henri Jaffa, James Gooch; art direction, Cedric Gibbons, Daniel B. Cathcart; film editor, Frederick Y. Smith; recording supervisor, Douglas Shearer; set decorations, Edwin B. Willis, Jack D. Moore; women's costumes, Walter Plunkett; men's costumes, Valles; hairstyles designed by Sydney Guilaroff; makeup created by Jack Dawn. Premieres, November 3, 1949, Penn Theatre, Pittsburgh, Pa.; November 11, Radio City Music Hall, New York; November 17, Command Performance, Odeon Theatre, London, England. Running time, 114 minutes; color.

Cast Errol Flynn (Soames Forsyte), Greer Garson (Irene Heron Forsyte), Walter Pidgeon (Young Jolyon Forsyte), Robert Young (Philip Bosinney), Janet Leigh (June Forsyte), Harry Davenport (Old Jolyon Forsyte), Aubrey Mather (James Forsyte), Gerald Oliver Smith (Wilson), Lumsden Hare (Roger Forsyte), Stanley Logan (Swithin Forsyte), Halliwell Hobbes (Nicholas Forsyte), Matt Moore (Timothy Forsyte), Florence Auer (Ann Forsyte Hayman), Phyllis Morris (Julia Forsyte Small), Marjorie Eaton (Hester Forsyte), Evelyn Beresford (Mrs. Taylor), Richard Lupino (Chester Forsyte), Wilson Wood (Eric Forsyte), Gabrielle Windsor (Jennie), Renee Mercer (Martha), Nina Ross (Louise), Constance Cavendish (Alice Forsyte), Isabel Randolph (Mrs. Winthrop), Tim Hawkins (Freddie), Reginald Sheffield (Mr. McLean), Frank Baker (Lord Dunstable), Jean Ransom (Amelia), Herbert Evans (M.C.'s Voice), Charles McNaughton (Attendant), Wallis Clark (Cabby), Conin Kenny (Constable), Leland Hodgson (Detective), Rolfe Sedan (Official), Andre Charlot (Director Braval).

The Miniver Story Producer, Sidney Franklin; director, H.C. Potter; screenplay, Ronald Millar and George Froeschel; based on characters created by Jan Struther; music by Herbert Stothart; adapted by Miklos Rozsa; Muir Mathieson conducting the London Philharmonic Orchestra; director of photography, Joseph Ruttenberg, A.S.C.; art director, Alfred Junge; film editors, Harold F. Kress, Frank Clarke; recording director, A.W. Watkins; photographic effects, Tom Howard, f.r.p.s.; Miss Garson's costumes designed by Walter Plunkett; additional costumes designed by Gaston Mallet. Premieres, August 30, 1950, Empire Theater, London, England; October 26, 1950, Radio City Music Hall, New York. Running time, 104 minutes; black and white.

Cast Greer Garson (Kay Miniver), Walter Pidgeon (Clem Miniver), John Hodiak (Spike Hartford), Leo Genn (Steve Brunswick), Cathy O'Donnell (Judy Miniver), Reginald Owen (Mr. Foley), Anthony Bushell (Dr. Kanesley), Richard Gale (Tom Foley), Peter Finch

(Polish Officer), William Fox (Toby Miniver), Cicely Paget-Bowman (Mrs. Kanesley), Ann Wilton (Jeanette), Henry Wilcoxon (Vicar), Eliot Makeham (Mr. Farraday), Brian Roper (Richard), Paul Demel (Jose Antonio Campos), Alison Leggatt (Mrs. Foley).

Songs "Ilkley Moor" (traditional), "Knees Up Mother Brown" (traditional), "Coffee Isn't My Girl," "Coffee and Andy Jitterbug" (Earl Brent), "When the Lights Go On Again" (Marcus, Benjemen), "Old Man River" (Jerome Kern, Oscar Hammerstein), "The Girl that I Marry" (Irving Berlin), Grieg's Piano Concerto.

The Law and the Lady Produced and directed by Edwin H. Knopf; screenplay, Leonard Spigelgass, Karl Tunberg; based on the play *The Last of Mrs. Cheyney* by Frederick Lonsdale; director of photography, George J. Folsey, A.S.C.; art directors, Cedric Gibbons, Daniel B. Cathcart; film editors, James E. Newcom, A.C.E., and William Gulick; music, Carmon Dragon; recording supervisor, Douglas Shearer; set decorations, Edwin B. Willis, Jack D. Moore; special effects, Warren Newcombe; women's costumes designed by Walter Plunkett; men's costumes designed by Gile Steele; hairstyles designed by Sydney Guilaroff; makeup created by William Tuttle. Premiere, August 15, 1951, Capitol Theater, New York. Running time, 104 minutes; black and white.

Cast Greer Garson (Jane Hoskins/Lady Loverly), Michael Wilding (Nigel Duxbury/Lord Minden), Fernando Lamas (Juan Dinas), Marjorie Main (Mrs. Wortin), Hayden Rorke (Tracy Collans), Margalo Gillmore (Cora Caighn), Ralph Dumke (James A. Caighn), Rhys Williams (Inspector McGraw), Phyllis Stanley (Lady Minden), Natalie Schafer (Pamela Pemberson), Soledad Jiminez (Princess Margarita), Lelo Rios (Panchito), Stanley Logan (Sir Roland Epping), Holmes Herbert (English Colonel), John Eldredge (Assistant Manager), Colin Kenny (Servant), James Aubrey (Coachman), David Dunbar (Driver), Andre Charlot (Maitre d'Hotel), Jean Del Val (Dealer), George Renevant (French Manager), Eugene Borden (French Detective), Antonio Pilauri (Italian Hotel Manager), Victor Sen Yung (Chinese Manager), Phil Tead (Assistant Manager), Tim Graham, Lester Dorr (Newspapermen), Matt Moore (Senator Scholmm), Anna Q. Nilsson (Mrs. Scholmm), Stuart Holmes (Mr. Bruno Thayer), Bess Flowers (Mrs. Bruno Thayer), Nikki Juston (Miss Belpayasa), Betty

Farrington (Miss Belpayasa), Spencer Chan (Servant), Richard Hale (Sheriff).

Songs "The Sari Waltz" (Emmerich Kalman), "Twelve Days of Christmas" (Traditional).

Scandal at Scourie Producer, Edwin H. Knopf; director, Jean Negulesco; screenplay, Norman Corwin, Leonard Spigelgass, Karl Tunberg; based on a story by Mary McSherry; music by Daniele Amfitheatrof; color by Technicolor; director of photography, Robert Planck, A.S.C.; Technicolor color consultant, Henri Jaffa; art directors, Cedric Gibbons, Wade B. Rubottom; film editor, Ferris Webster, A.C.E.; assistant director, Jack Greenwood; recording supervisor, Douglas Shearer; set decorations, Edwin B. Willis, Hugh Hunt; color consultant, Alvord Eiseman; special effects, A. Arnold Gillespie; costumes designed by Walter Plunkett; hairstyles by Sydney Guilaroff; makeup created by William Tuttle. Premiere, June 15, 1953, Little Carnegie Theater, New York, also at Loews Theater and the Egyptian in Los Angeles. Running time, ninety minutes; color.

Cast Greer Garson (Vicki McChesney), Walter Pidgeon (Patrick J. McChesney), Agnes Moorehead (Sister Josephine), Donna Corcoran (Patsy), Arthur Shields (Father Reilly), Philip Ober (B.G. Belney), Rhys Williams (Bill Swazey), Margalo Gillmore (Alice Hanover), John Lupton (Artemus), Philip Tonge (Fred Gogarty), Wilton Graff (Mr. Leffington), Ian Wolfe (Councilman Hurdwell), Michael Pate (Reverend Williams), Tony Taylor (Edward), Patricia Tiernan (Second Nun), Victor Wood (James (Motley), Perdita Chandler (Sister Dominique), Walter Baldwin (Michael Hayward), Ida Moore (Mrs. Ames), Rudy Lee (Donald), Ivan Triesault (Father Barrett), Joann Arnold (Sister Maria), Peter Roman (Freddie), Maudie Prickett (Mrs. Holohan), Ivis Goulding (Mrs. O'Russell), George Davis (Bartender), Vicki Joy Ereutzer (Edith), Claude Guy (Joseph), Jill Martin (Isabella), Coral Hammond (Cecelia), Alex Frayer (Wormsley), Eugene Borden (Old Man), John Sherman (Mr. Pringle), Matthew Moore (Kenston), Nolan Leary (Conductor), Charles Watts (Barber), Archer McDonald (Barber Apprentice), Robert Ross (Doctor Parker), Roger Moore/Al Ferguson (Ad Libs).

Songs "Green Sleeves" "Frere Jacques" (traditional airs).

Julius Caesar   Producer, John Houseman; director, Joseph L. Mankie-
wicz; based on William Shakespeare's play; music by Miklos Rozsa;
director of photography, Joseph Ruttenberg, A.S.C.; art directors,
Cedric Gibbons, Edward Carfagno; film editor, John Dunning,
A.C.E.; assistant director, Howard W. Koch; recording supervisor,
Douglas Shearer; set decorations, Edwin B. Willis, Hugh Hunt; spe-
cial effects, Warren Newcombe; costumes designed by Herschel
McCoy; hairstyles by Sydney Guilaroff; makeup created by William
Tuttle; technical advisor, P.M. Pasinetti. Premiere, May 11, 1953,
Sydney, Australia. U.S. premiere, June 5, 1953, Booth Theater, New
York. Running time, 121 minutes; black and white.

   Cast   Marlon Brando (Marc Antony), James Mason (Brutus),
John Gielgud (Cassius), Louis Calhern (Julius Caesar), Edmond
O'Brien (Casca), Greer Garson (Calpurnia), Deborah Kerr (Portia),
George Macready (Malrullus), Michael Pate (Flavius), Richard Hale
(Soothsayer), Alan Napier (Cicero), John Hoyt (Decius Brutus), Tom
Powers (Metellus Cimber), William Cottrell (Cinna), Jack Raine
(Trebonius), Ian Wolfe (Ligarius), Morgan Farley (Artemidorus), Bill
Phipps (Servant to Antony), Douglas Watson (Octavius Caesar),
Douglass Dumbrille (Lepidus), Rhys Williams (Lucilius), Michael
Ansara (Pindarus), Dayton Lummis (Messala), Edmund Purdom
(Strato), Paul Guilfoyle, John Doucette, Lawrence Dobkin, Jo Gilbert,
Ann Tyrrell, John O'Malley, Oliver Blake, Alvin Hurwitz, Donald
Elson (Citizens of Rome).

Her Twelve Men   Producer, John Houseman; associate producer,
Jud Kinberg; director, Robert Z. Leonard; screenplay, William Roberts, Laura Z. Hobson; from a story by Louise Baker; photographed
in Ansco Color, print by Technicolor; director of photography, Joseph Ruttenberg, A.S.C.; color consultant, Alvord Eiseman; art directors, Cedric Gibbons, Daniel B. Cathcart; film editor, Goerge Boemler,
A.C.E.; women's costumes designed by Helen Rose; set decorations,
Edwin B. Willis, Keogh Gleason; special effects, A. Arnold Gillespie,
Warren Newcombe; montage sequences by Peter Ballbusch; assistant
director, Al Jennings; music by Bronislau Kaper; recording supervisor, Douglas Shearer; hairstyles by Sydney Guilaroff; makeup by
William Tuttle. Premiere, August 11, 1954, Trans-Lux Theater, New

York, also at the Palace and the Hawaii in Los Angeles. Running time, ninety-one minutes; color.

Cast Greer Garson (Jan Stewart), Robert Ryan (Joe Hargrove), Barry Sullivan (Richard Y. Oliver Sr.), Richard Haydn (Dr. Avord Barrett), Barbara Lawrence (Barbara Dunning), James Arness (Ralph Munsey), Rex Thompson (Homer Curtis), Tim Considine (Richard Y. Oliver Jr.), David Stollery (Jeff Carlin), Frances Bergen (Sylvia Carlin), Ian Wolfe (Roger Frane), Donald MacDonald (Bobby Lennox), Dale Hartleben (Kevin Clark), Ivan Triesault (Erik Haldeman), Stuffy Singer (Jimmy Travers), Peter Votrian (Alan Saunders), Dee Aaker (Michael), Peter Roman (Tim Johnson), Timothy Marxer (Tommy), Patrick Miller (Pat), Aurelio Celli (Tony), Peter Dane (Pete), Robert Clarke (Prince), Larry Olsen (Edgar), Gary Stewart (Stanley), Kate Lawson (Maid), Sarah Spencer (Mrs. Travers), Vernon Rich (Mr. Travers), Sandy Descher (Little Sister), Peter Adams (Mr. Saunders), John Dodsworth (Mr. Curtis), Phyllis Stanley (Mrs. Curtis), Jean Dante (Mrs. Saunders), Norman Gilestad (Attendant), Ed Dearing (Fire Chief), Robert Carson (Doctor), Jo Gilbert (Nurse), Mary Adams (Martha), Chris Warfield (Official).

Song "Oh! Mighty Oaks!" (Bronislau Kaper, Charles Wolcott).

Strange Lady in Town Producer and director, Mervyn LeRoy; story and screenplay, Frank Butler; director of photography, Harold Rosson, A.S.C.; in Cinemascope, WarnerColor; art director, Gabriel Scognamillo; film editor, Folmar Blangsted; sound by Stanley Jones; set decorator, Ralph Hurst; wardrobe by Emile Santiago; special effects, H.F. Koenekamp, A.S.C.; makeup artist, Gordon Bau, S.M.A.; special effects, H.F. Koenekamp, A.S.C.; makeup artist, Gordon Bau, S.M.A.; choreography for fiesta by Peggy Carroll; assistant directors, Russell Saunders, William Kissel; music composed and conducted by Dimitri Tiomkin. Premiere, April 12, 1955, Paramount Theater, Austin, Texas. Running time, 112 minutes; color.

Cast Greer Garson (Dr. Julia Winslow Garth), Dana Andrews (Dr. Rork O'Brien), Cameron Mitchell (David Garth), Lois Smith (Carlotta Isabel "Spurs" O'Brien), Walter Hampden (Father Gabriel Mendoza), Pedro Gonzales-Gonzales (Trooper Martinez-Martinez), Joan Camden (Norah Muldoon), Anthony Numkena (Tomasito Diaz), Jose Torvay (Bartolo Diaz), Adele Jergens (Bella Brown), Bob

Wilke (Karg), Frank de Cova (Anse Hatlo), Russell Johnson (Shadduck), Gregory Walcott (Scanlon), Douglas Kennedy (Slade Wickstrom), Harry Hines (Chicken Feathers), Jack Williams (Ribstock), Joey Costarello (Alfredo), Nick Adams (Billy the Kid), Bob Faulk (Joe), Julian Rivers (Manuel), Frank Rodriguez (Mexican Peon), Stafford Repp (Macaneer), Pat Lawless (Bartender), Jerry Sheldon (Man at Bar), Ruth Whitney (Brunette), Abel Fernandez (Apache), Charles Sedillo (Mexican Peon), Jose Lopez (Pueblo Indian), Robert Cabal (Young Vaquero), Lilian Molieri (Sister Delphine), Helen Brown (Sister Muriel), Felipe Turich (Esteban), Belle Mitchell (Catalina), Ralph Moody (General Lew Wallace), Louise Lorimer (Mrs. Wallace), Helen Spring (Mrs. Harker), Joe Hamilton (Mr. Harker), Howard Hoffman (Judge), John Stephenson (Captain Taggart), William Boyett (Lieutenant Keith), Ray Bennett (Deputy at Bank), Phyllis Stanley (Mrs. Clegg), George Wallace (Curley), Marshall Bradford (Sheriff), Antonio Triana, Luisa Triana (Flamenco Dancers).

Song "Strange Lady in Town" (Dimitri Tiomkin, Ned Washington; performed by Frankie Laine, with Mitch Miller and His Orchestra).

Sunrise at Campobello Producer, Dore Schary; director, Vincent J. Donehue; screenplay, Dore Schary; based on the play by Dore Schary as produced by the Theatre Guild and the author; director of photography, Russell Harlan; art director, Edward Carrere; film editor, George Boemler, A.C.E.; sound by M.A. Merrick; costume design, Marjorie Best; associate producer, Walter Reilly; production supervisor, Joel Freeman; music composed and conducted by Franz Waxman; makeup supervision, Gordon Bau, S.M.A.; supervising hairstylist, Jean Burt Reilly; set decoration, George James Hopkins; assistant director, Russell Saunders. Premiere, September 28, 1960, RKO Palace Theatre, New York City. Running time, 143 minutes; color.

Cast Ralph Bellamy (Franklin Delano Roosevelt), Greer Garson (Eleanor Roosevelt), Hume Cronyn (Louis Howe), Jean Hagen (Missy LeHand), Ann Shoemaker (Sara Roosevelt), Alan Bunce (Al Smith), Tim Considine (James Roosevelt), Zina Bethune (Anna Roosevelt), Frank Ferguson (Dr. Bennett), Pat Close (Elliott Roosevelt), Robin Warga (Franklin Roosevelt Jr.), Tommy Carty (Johnny Roosevelt), Lyle Talbot (Mr. Brimmer), David White (Mr. Lassiter), Herb Anderson (Daly), Frank Ferguson (Dr. Bennett), Walter Sande (Captain Skinner), Janine Crandel (Marie), Otis Greene (Edward), Ivan Browning (Charles), Al McGranary (Senator Walsh), Jerry Crows (Speaker), William Haddock (Mr. Owens), Floyd Curtis (Mailman), Jack Henderson (Joe), Ruth March (Miss Garroway), Ed Prentiss (Barker), Francis DeSales (Riley), Craig Curtis (Newsboy), Don Dillaway (Sloan), Fern Barry, Mary Benat, Jack Perrin (Campaign Workers).

Pepe Producer and director, George Sidney; screenplay, Dorothy Kingsley, Claude Binyon; based on a story by Leonard Spigelgass and Sonya Levien from the play *Broadway Magic* by Ladislas Bush-Fekete; associate producer, Jacques Gleman; general music supervision and background score by Johnny Green; music conducted by Andre Previn; choreography, Eugene Loring, Alex Romero; recording supervisor, Charles J. Rice; music editor, Maury Winetrobe; sound, James Z. Flaster; script supervisor, Marshall Wallins; gowns, Edith Head; hairstyles, Larry Germaine, Myrl Stoltz; makeup supervisor, Ben Lane, S.M.A.; "Pepe" and "Mimi" special material and routines by Roger Edens; art direction, Ted Haworth, Gunther Gersys; set decoration, William Kiernan; director of photography, Joe MacDonald, A.S.C.; photographic lenses by Panavision; Eastman color by Pathe; special sequences in Cinemascope; film editor, Viola Lawrence, A.C.E., Al Clark, A.C.E.; assistant director, David Silver; Las Vegas sequences photographed at the Sands Hotel, the Tropicana Hotel; bullfight and fiesta scenes photographed at Hacienda Vista Hermosa, Mexico; A George Sidney-Posa Films International Production. Premiere, December 21, 1960, Criterion Theatre, New York. Running time, 195 minutes; color.

Cast Cantinflas (Pepe), Dan Dailey (Ted Holt), Shirley Jones (Suzie Murphy), Carlos Montalban (Auctioneer), Vicki Tuckett (Lupita), Matt Mattox (Dancer), Hank Henry (Manager), Suzanne Lloyd (Carmen), Stephen Bekassy (Jewelry Salesman), Carol Douglas (Waitress), Francisco Reguerra (Priest), Joe Hyams (Charro), Shirley DeBurgh (Senorita Dancer), James Bacon (Bartender), Jimmy Cavanaugh (Dealer), Jeanne Manet (French Woman), Bonnie Green (Dancer), Lela Bliss (Dowager), Ray Walker (Assistant Director), David Landfield (Announcer), Fred Roberto (Cashier).

Guest Stars   Joey Bishop, Billie Burke, Maurice Chevalier, Michael Callan, Charles Coburn, Richard Conte, Bing Crosby, Tony Curtis, Bobby Darin, Ann B. Davis, Sammy Davis Jr., William Demarest, Jimmy Durante, Jack Entratter, Col. E.E. Fogelson, Zsa Zsa Gabor, Judy Garland, Greer Garson, Hedda Hopper, Ernie Kovacs, Peter Lawford, Janet Leigh, Jack Lemmon, Dean Martin, Jay North, Kim Novak, Andre Previn, Donna Reed, Debbie Reynolds, Carlos Rivas, Edward G. Robinson, Jane Robinson, Cesar Romero, Frank Sinatra, Buddy Walters.

Songs   "September Song" (Kurt Weill, Maxwell Anderson), "Mimi" (Richard Rodgers, Lorenz Hart), "Pennies from Heaven" (Johnny Burke, Arthur Johnston), "Hooray for Hollywood" (Johnny Mercer, Richard Whiting, new lyrics by Sammy Cahn), "South of the Border" (Michael Carr, Jimmy Kennedy), "Let's Fall in Love" (Ted Koehler, Harold Arlen), "Lovely Day" (Augustin Lara, Maria Teresa Lara, English lyrics by Dory Langdon), "Pepe" (Dory Langdon, Hans Wittstatt), "That's How It Went All Right," (Dory Langdon, Andre Previn), "Faraway Part of Town" (Andre Previn, Dory Langdon), "The Rumble" (Andre Previn), "Suzie's Theme (Andre Previn).

The Singing Nun   Producer, Jon Beck; coproduced by Hayes Goetz; director, Henry Koster; music score by Harry Sukman; director of photography, Milton Krasner, A.S.C.; art direction, George W. Davis, Urie McCleary; set decoration; Henry Grace, Jerry Wunderlich; film editor, Rita Roland; assistant director, Kevin Donnelly; makeup by William Tuttle; music supervisor, Harold Gelman; associate producer, Hank Moonjean; choreography by Robert Sidney; recording supervisor, Franklin Milton; screenplay, Sally Benson, John Furia Jr.; story by John Furia Jr. Premiere, April 2, 1966, the Beverly Theater, Los Angeles. Running time, ninety-eight minutes; color.

Cast   Debbie Reynolds (Sister Ann), Ricardo Montalban (Father Clementi), Greer Garson (Mother Prioress), Agnes Moorehead (Sister Cluny), Chad Everett (Robert Gerarde), Katharine Ross (Nicole Arlien), Ed Sullivan (Himself), Juanita Moore (Sister Mary), Ricky Cordell (Dominic Arlien), Michael Pate (Mr. Arlien), Tom Drake (Fitzpatrick), Larry D. Mann (Mr. Duvries), Charles Robinson (Marauder), Monique Montaigne (Sister Michele), Joyce Vanderveen (Sister Elise), Anne Wakefield (Sister Brigitte), Pam Peterson (Sister

Gertrude), Marina Koshetz (Sister Marthe), Nancy Walters (Sister Therese), Violet Rensing (Sister Elizabeth), Inez Pedroza (Sister Consuella).

Songs "Dominique" (Soeur Sourire, English lyrics by Randy Sparks), "Sister Adele" (Soeur Adele), "It's a Miracle" (Une Fleur), "Beyond the Stars" (Entre les Etoiles), "A Pied Piper's Song" (Petit Pierrot, music by Soeur Sourire, lyrics by Randy Sparks), "Brother John" (Randy Sparks), "Lovely" (Randy Sparks), "Raindrops" (Randy Sparks, inspired by "Chante Rivièr" by Soeur Sourire), "Je Voudrais" (Soeur Sourire), "Mets Ton Joli Jupon" (Soeur Sourire), "Avec Toi" (Soeur Sourire), "Alleluia" (Soeur Sourire).

The Happiest Millionaire Producer, Walt Disney; coproducer, Bill Anderson; director, Norman Tokar; screenplay, A.J. Carothers; based on the play by Kyle Crichton; suggested by a book by Cordelia Drexel Biddle and Kyle Crichton; produced for the New York Stage by Howard Erskine and Joseph Hayes; director of photography, Edward Colman, A.S.C.; color by Technicolor; music and lyrics, Richard M. Sherman and Robert B. Sherman; music supervised, arranged, and conducted by Jack Elliott; film editor, Cotton Warburton, A.C.E.; art directors, Carroll Clark, John B. Mansbridge; set decoration, Emile Kuri, Frank R. McKelvy; choreographers, Marc Breaux, Dee Dee Wood; costumes designed by Bill Thomas; costumers, Chuck Keehne, Neva Rames; sound supervisor, Robert O. Cook; sound mixer, Dean Thomas; makeup, Gordon Hubbard; hairstylist, Vivienne Zavitz; special effects, Eustace Lycett, Peter Ellenshaw; assistant to the producer, Tom Leetch; assistant director, Paul Cameron; music editor, Evelyn Kennedy; titles, Alan Maley. Premiere, June 23, 1967, Pantages Theater, Hollywood. Running time, 164 minutes; color.

Cast Fred MacMurray (Mr. Anthony Biddle), Tommy Steele (John Lawless), Greer Garson (Mrs. Cordelia Biddle), Geraldine Page (Mrs. Duke), Gladys Cooper (Aunt Mary), Hermoine Baddeley (Mrs. Worth), Lesley Anne Warren (Cordelia Drexel Biddle), John Davidson (Angier Duke), Paul Peterson (Tony Biddle), Eddie Hodges (Livingston Biddle), Joyce Bulifant (Rosemary), Sean McClory (Sergeant Flanagan), Jim McMullan, William Wellman Jr., Jim Gurley (Marine Lieutenants), Aron Kincaid (Walter Blakely), Larry Merrill (Charlie Taylor), Frances Robinson (Aunt Gladys), Norman Grabowski (Joe Turner).

Songs   "Fortuosity," "What's Wrong with That?" "Watch Your Footwork," "Valentine Candy," "Strengthen the Dwelling," "I'll Always Be Irish," "Bye-Yum Pum Pum," "Are We Dancing?" "Detroit," "There Are Those," "Let's Have a Drink on It," "It Won't Be Long 'Til Christmas" (Richard M. Sherman, Robert B. Sherman).

Notes

Preface

ix "A radiant rose of a woman . . ." Cobey Black, *Honolulu Star Bulletin,* June 9, 1967.

x "You're not who I thought you were . . ." Diane Jennings, *Dallas Morning News,* Sept. 23, 1984.

x "So perhaps it's not surprising . . ." Henry Sheenan, *Orange County Register,* April 12, 1996.

xi "a romantic, tempestuous beauty . . ." Beth Emerson, "Secret Romance," *Photoplay-Movie Mirror,* Aug. 1942.

xi "A rose is a visual paradox . . ." Sally Brompton, *Times,* March 30, 1990.

xii "desperately romantic . . ." Ibid.

Prologue

1 "You made us feel more brave . . ." Queen Elizabeth letter to G.G., undated, SMU G.G. collection.

2 "It was a very emotional evening . . ." Teresa Wright, Turner Classic Movies interview, 1996.

4 "I suppose I always believed in fairy tales . . ." Jennings, *Dallas Morning News,* Sept. 23, 1984.

Chapter 1

5 "Destined, as I was . . ." Gladys Hall, *Silver Screen,* July 20, 1942.

7 "Tea with Greer Garson . . ." Porter Anderson, *Dallas Magazine,* Aug. 1992.

7 "I was born . . ." Hall, *Silver Screen.*

7 "rather horridly . . ." Ibid.

7 "Mother seems to have outgrown . . ." Ibid.

7 "Legendary film star . . ." Eddie McIlwaine, *Belfast Telegraph,* April 9, 1996.

10 "From the composite picture . . ." Hall, *Silver Screen.*

10 "one of those charming men . . ." Ibid.

11 "Aunt Alexina was a very strict Presbyterian . . ." Ibid.

11 "small, dark and narrow . . ." Ibid.

11 "[the phrase genteel poverty] is more attractive . . ." Ibid.
11 "By the time . . ." Ruth Waterbury, "Redheaded Rebel," *Photoplay–Movie Mirror,* Feb. 1941.
11 "I lived the characters . . ." Kitty Callahan, *The Family Circle,* Jan. 28, 1944.
12 "I think I was pretty until I lost my teeth . . ." Hall, *Silver Screen.*
12 "I was an odd kid . . ." Ibid.
12 "I loved my Saturday mornings . . ." Ibid.
12 "with my brow . . ." Ibid.

Chapter 2

13 "We had some kind neighbors . . ." Waterbury, *Photoplay-Movie Mirror,* Feb. 1941.
14 "Although Celtic by birth and temperament . . ." Hall, *Silver Screen,* July 20, 1942.
14 "running about like a happy little ragamuffin." Ibid.
15 "If Grandmother had been of this generation . . ." Ibid.
15 "I remember playing under blue skies . . ." McIlwaine, *Belfast Telegraph* obituary, April 9, 1996.
15 "a great fur, fish and feather man . . ." Mona Gardner, *Ladies Home Journal,* Sept. 1944.
15 "On two occasions . . ." Hall, *Silver Screen.*
15 "unconsciously great." G.G., "Christmas Story," *Photoplay,* Jan. 1947.
15 "She was not a very good sailor . . ." Dr. Sophia Sloan to author.
15 "it's rather mortifying . . ." Dorothy Drake, *Program,* June 1935.
15 "a gentle sport . . ." Ibid.
15 "Ahoy . . ." G.G. letter, SMU G.G. collection.
16 "It always smelled wonderful . . . Consistent with the biographies . . ." G.G., "Christmas Story."
16 "My two brothers and I . . ." Commodore Robin W. Garson to author.
17 "I would throw myself . . ." G.G., *Photoplay,* Jan. 1947.
17 "She was always brilliantly clever . . ." Dr. Sloan to author.
17 "I wish you could have seen my Shylock . . ." Waterbury, *Photoplay-Movie Mirror.*
17 "I must have looked over a cloud . . ." Hall, *Silver Screen.*

Chapter 3

18 "dark and powerful looking . . ." Hall, *Silver Screen,* July 20, 1942.
18 "It was delicately understood that Alec admired me . . ." Ibid.
18 "Only the very young . . ." Lydia Lane, *Los Angeles Times,* Aug. 22, 1954.
18 "I was an introvert . . ." G.G., *Modern Screen,* Jan. 1949.
18 "Acting was in the family . . ." Commodore Robin W. Garson to author.
19 "Mother had given my childish talk . . ." Hall, *Silver Screen.*
19 "My grandmother Garson . . ." G.G. letter to Norma Wilson, Feb. 27, 1956, SMU G.G. collection.

19 "Apparently I 'gave satisfaction' . . ." Howard Sharpe, *Modern Screen,* 1947.
19 "to be in the city . . ." Hall, *Silver Screen.*
20 "that hateful neighborhood." Ibid.
20 "the prettiest in Ilford . . ." Ibid.
20 "So thrilled was I . . ." Ibid.
20 "Marguery sauce . . . summons up . . ." Gardner, *Ladies Home Journal,* Sept. 1944.
21 "scholastic and sartorial triumph . . ." Hall, *Silver Screen.*
21 "There is inspiration . . ." G.G., Honorary Doctorate in Music speech, Cleveland Institute of Music, May 31, 1973.
21 "I often visited there . . ." Dr. Sloan to author.
21 "I did not go to Grenoble . . ." Hall, *Silver Screen.*
21 "I like women . . ." G.G. letter, 1927, SMU G.G. collection.
22 "I played the part of the young business executive . . ." Ibid.
22 "I never lacked for excuses . . ." Sanders, *Memoirs,* p.38.
22 "A thousand little candles . . ." Hall, *Silver Screen.*
22 "With my hair smoothed back . . ." Ibid.
23 "I hear you have an excellent job . . ." Ibid.
23 "Then . . ." Ibid.
23 "Where is the girl . . ." Ibid.

Chapter 4

24 "a trim little theatre . . ." Hardwicke, *Irreverent Memoirs,* p. 112.
24 "to enlarge and increase . . ." J.C. Trewin, *Birmingham Repertory Theatre,* p. 10.
25 "A constantly changing repertory . . ." Ibid., p. 104.
25 "Another red-head?" Hall, *Silver Screen,* July 20, 1942.
25 "probably very bad . . ." Ibid.
25 "There will be no standing her . . ." Ibid.
25 "It was a bad half-hour . . ." Ibid.
26 "He tried in every way to make me unhappy . . ." Ibid.
26 "The first-nighters laughed and cried . . ." Ibid.
26 "I lived like a troglodyte . . ." Ibid.
27 "a very poetic young man . . ." Ibid.
27 "I'm flattered by your proposal . . ." Ibid.
28 "Experience is what you need . . ." Ibid.
28 "Michael was someone with whom I might have been very happy . . ." Ibid.
28 "She had never really . . ." Commodore Robin W. Garson to author.
28 "In Oxford . . ." G.G. letter, 1932, SMU G.G. collection.
29 "I'll never forget . . ." Dr. Greer C. Murray to author.
29 "There is a tradition in the English theatre . . ." Hall, *Silver Screen.*
30 "Somehow . . ." Ibid.
30 "Sarah Bernhardt broke one's heart . . ." Milton Bracker, *New York Times,* April 3, 1955.
30 "As soon as my infection . . ." Hall, *Silver Screen.*
30 "Then, the nurse made the horrible mistake . . ." Ibid.

Chapter 5

32 "When a young man has money and leisure . . ." Hall, *Silver Screen,* July 20, 1942.
32 "There I was in bed . . ." Ibid.
32 "We were very congenial . . ." Ibid.
32 "You've proved that you can entertain an audience . . ." Ibid.
33 "Is this 'India'?" Ibid.
33 "But as the evening went on . . ." Ibid.
33 "You will be dependent . . ." Ibid.
33 "The country was beautiful . . ." Ibid.
33 "possessive to the point of being medieval." Ibid.
33 "India is . . ." Peter Stales-Corernam letter to G.G., undated, SMU G.G. collection.
34 "That two weeks . . ." Dr. Sloan to author.
34 "Skeleton gone a little wrong . . . an idiotically understated diagnosis . . ." Hall, *Silver Screen.*
34 "Nobody was ever lower in luck . . ." G.G., *Modern Screen,* Jan. 1949.
34 "from the knife . . . but divided like a fork." Hall, *Silver Screen.*
35 "I don't think . . ." Ibid.
35 "A striking girl . . ." Sydney W. Carroll, *Daily Tribune,* Sept. 19, 1935.
36 "Where the hell have you been?" Hall, *Silver Screen.*
37 "It was well for me . . ." Ibid.
37 "This sort of thing . . ." *Sunday Express,* 1935.
38 "Kind of odd charm . . ." Hall, *Silver Screen.*
38 "He was a strange one . . ." Ibid.
39 "Having Larry as a friend . . ." Ibid.
39 "To try out little things . . ." Spoto, *Laurence Olivier,* p. 84.
39 "with his usual enthusiasm . . ." Hall, *Silver Screen.*
39 "Babylon-on-the-Pacific." G.G., *Los Angeles Times,* Dec. 11, 1968, and *Austin American,* April 13, 1955.
39 "like a whiskbroom." Hall, *Silver Screen.*
39 "a signature . . ." Ibid.
40 "To say thank you . . ." Laurence Olivier letter to G.G., May 30, 1935, SMU G.G. collection.
40 "It is a pleasure . . ." Hall, *Silver Screen.*
40 "In his capacity as impresario . . ." James Agate, *Sunday Times,* May 31, 1935.
40 "Miss Garson is to be congratulated . . ." *Bystander,* May 31, 1935.
41 "too slender to survive." Hall, *Silver Screen.*

Chapter 6

42 "exactly like a film . . ." Hall, *Silver Screen,* July 20, 1942.
42 "I have made arrangements . . ." James Bunting, June 18, 1935, SMU G.G. collection.
43 "Sir Seymour was a terror . . ." Hall, *Silver Screen.*

43 "Although I lost eight pounds . . ." Ibid.
43 "Greer Garson is a most important newcomer . . ." *Daily Telegraph,* June 24, 1935.
43 "The revival . . ." *Daily Mail,* June 24, 1935.
43 "Miss Garson . . ." *London Times,* June 24, 1935.
43 "Miss Greer Garson has a personality . . ." Dorothy Drake, "The Stage of the Present Day," *Program,* June 1935.
44 "He had a little of the quality . . ." Hall, *Silver Screen.*
44 "By the first word she spoke . . ." *Stage,* Sept. 4, 1935.
44 "Miss Garson and Mr. Nicholas Hannen . . ." *London Times,* Sept. 4, 1935.
44 "The lovely young red-blonde actress . . ." *Star,* Sept. 1935.
44 "Experiment . . ." G.G., *Star,* Sept. 1935.
45 "I have always regretted my oversight . . ." Carroll, Daily Tribune, Sept. 19, 1935.
45 "A very backhanded compliment . . ." G.G., theater scrapbook, SMU G.G. collection.
45 "It was a sprightly comedy . . ." *Daily Mirror,* Sept. 17, 1935.
45 "It seems my white-haired . . ." Hall, *Silver Screen.*
46 "kept my interests varied . . ." Ibid.
46 "He and his sister . . ." Ibid.
46 "a most beautiful example . . ." Ibid.
46 "When you are . . ." Ibid.
46 "Is Pleasure What It Was" speech; SMU G.G. collection.
47 "It's no good . . ." Eric Braun, *Deborah Kerr,* p. 57.
47 "Greer always had . . ." *Daily Express,* Oct. 15, 1935.
48 "She started rehearsing . . ." *Play Pictorial,* Oct. 1935.
48 "Miss Greer Garson . . ." *Observer,* Oct. 17, 1935.
48 "Greer Garson lent her vivacity . . ." *New York Times,* Nov. 10, 1935.
48 "My dear . . ." Trevor Blakemore letter to G.G., Nov. 30, 1935, SMU G.G. collection.
49 "Have you a nice, simple taste in plays . . ." *Bystander,* Jan. 29, 1936.
49 "Mr. Monsarrat's play is better . . ." W.A. Darlington, *Sketch,* July 22, 1936.
49 "Miss Garson's intelligent and persuasive charm . . ." *London Times,* July 8, 1936.

Chapter 7

50 "Fame built on failures . . ." *Star Spotter Backstage,* Feb. 1936.
50 "Of course I'm disappointed," *Daily Express,* April 1936.
51 "She is so piss-elegant . . ." Noël Coward, *The Noel Coward Diaries,* p. 175.
51 "I never have to tell you what to do, Greer . . ." Ibid.
51 "Noël was a very exacting and painstaking taskmaster . . ." Ibid.
51 "Let me tell you . . ." Madge Titheradge, *Evening Times,* March 2, 1937.
51 "If being directed by me . . ." letter from Noël Coward, SMU G.G. collection.
52 "It is not so long ago . . ." *Evening News,* Sept. 19, 1936.
52 "She responded . . ." Garnett, *Light Your Torches,* p. 203.

52 "We promptly arranged for a comprehensive screen test." Garnett, *Light Your Torches*, p. 203.
52 "flustered and fluttery . . ." Fairbanks, *Salad Days*, p. 263.
52 "It was a smash . . ." Garnett, *Light Your Torches*, p. 203.
52 "all very lighthearted and charming . . ." Hall, *Silver Screen*, July 20, 1942.
53 "It was so nice . . ." Fairbanks, *Salad Days*, p. 264.
54 "Douglas Fairbanks Jr.'s . . ." *New Chronicle*, Dec. 12, 1936.
54 "What? . . ." Hall, *Silver Screen*.
54 "Noël Coward was very angry . . ." Ibid.
54 "My dear Douglas . . ." Noël Coward letter, Oct. 28, 1936, SMU G.G. collection.
55 "I have spent my time profitably in films . . ." Samson Raphaelson letter, Nov. 27, 1936, SMU G.G. collection.
55 "If you have any choice . . ." G.G. letter, undated, SMU G.G. collection.
56 "But it was not to be settled . . ." *Los Angeles Times*, May 9, 1940.
56 "The night . . ." Hall, *Silver Screen*.
56 "Some of the towns . . ." Ibid.
57 "Miss Garson brilliantly defines the minx . . ." *Manchester Guardian*, Feb. 1937.
57 "Noël Coward's production . . ." *Sunday Mail*, Feb. 1937.
57 "I'm enjoying a rest . . ." G.G. letter, April 1936, SMU G.G. collection.
57 "To date, televisionary results . . ." Flanner, *London Was Yesterday*, p. 42.
58 "Miss Garson gives an entirely original rendering . . ." *Evening Times*, May 15, 1937.
58 "The camera technique . . ." Hall, *Silver Screen*.

Chapter 8

59 "London's hotels . . ." Flanner, *London Was Yesterday*, p. 40.
60 "a gold-digger . . ." James Agate, *London Times*, Aug. 19, 1937.
60 "They're such fun . . ." *Evening News*, July 10, 1937.
60 "The play . . ." Agate, *London Times*, Aug. 19, 1937.
60 "Why 'Old Music'?" *Observer*, Aug. 19, 1937.
60 "What is presently . . ." Agate, *London Times*, Aug. 19, 1937.
62 "Excuse me . . ." Jennings, *Dallas Morning News*, Sept. 23, 1984.
62 "Hyphens and all?" *Time*, Dec. 20, 1943.
62 "But don't sign . . ." Hall, *Silver Screen*, July 20, 1942.
63 "We can do wonders with your face in Hollywood." Ibid.
63 "There's nobody who can't be photographed." *Time*, Dec. 20, 1943.
63 "What made up my mind . . ." Pete Martin, *Saturday Evening Post*, Dec. 26, 1946.
63 "Are you engaging me for a specific part?" Hall, *Silver Screen*.
63 "I can't tell you how awfully sorry I am . . ." David O. Selznick letter, Sept. 27, 1937, SMU G.G. collection.
64 "I don't think you want to come to work with us . . ." Hall, *Silver Screen*.
64 "Heartfelt thanks . . ." G.G. telegram, undated, SMU G.G. collection.

64 "It was all very gay and charming . . ." Hall, *Silver Screen.*
65 "You must naturally . . ." letter to Herbert de Leon, Oct. 25, 1937, SMU G.G. collection.
65 "We sold some of the furniture . . ." *Evening News,* Nov. 13, 1937.
65 "Around noon . . ." Hall, *Silver Screen.*
65 "Mother was happy . . ." Ibid.
66 "Is Miss Garson happy?" Telegrams in SMU G.G. collection.

Chapter 9

67 "People are always asking me . . ." Bob Porter, *Dallas Times Herald,* Sept. 8, 1985.
69 "like a hibernating bear . . ." Hall, *Silver Screen,* July 20, 1942.
69 "like a fairyland . . ." Ibid.
69 "My fame . . ." Ibid.
70 "My dear Miss Garson . . ." G.G.," MGM Spot News," Feb. 11, 1946.
71 "so much huger . . ." Hall, *Silver Screen.*
73 "Up to a certain point . . ." *Hollywood Examiner,* Feb. 6, 1949.
74 "The earliest native word for Ireland . . ." Howard Strickling memo, G.G. file, MGM/Turner Entertainment archives.
74 "Ranking high among my favorites . . ." G.G., *Saturday Evening Post,* June 16, 1945.
74 "She called me 'Professor' . . ." William Tuttle to author.
74 "What a magnificent creature . . ." Sydney Guilaroff to author.
74 "Studio experts teach you to streamline yourself . . ." Hall, *Silver Screen.*
75 "The moment the light was put on Miss Garson . . ." Ralph Lawton, *American Cinematographer,* Sept. 1949.
75 "Duchess . . ." Hall, *Silver Screen.*
75 "She has a sense of humor . . ." *Los Angeles Times,* Sept. 26, 1984.
76 "It has a most beautiful garden . . ." Hall, *Silver Screen.*
76 "It's an old English custom . . ." John Franchey, "Bundle from Britain," *Picturegoer,* 1941.
77 "The palette of Nature . . ." Hall, *Silver Screen.*
77 "The English colony is so large . . ." Taylor, *Strangers in Paradise,* p. 97.
77 "There is something in it . . ." Ibid., p. 90.
77 "There is more actual positive reality . . ." Ibid.
77 "Hugh, this place is just like Donington Hall . . ." Ibid., p. 91.
78 "Everybody was always conscious they were English . . ." Ibid.
79 "I was a star in London . . ." Hall, *Silver Screen.*
79 "She came to me after testing with Luise Rainer . . ." Lillian Burns Sidney to author.
79 "the hot mush had cooled off . . ." Dorothy Manners, *Los Angeles Herald-Examiner,* Feb. 15, 1953.
80 "If you're a painter or writer . . ." Hall, *Silver Screen.*
80 "A strange face was murder . . ." Davis, *Glamour Factory,* p. 307.
80 "The trouble . . ." G.G., *Los Angeles Times,* April 7, 1996.

81 "During that disappointing . . ." G.G., *Picturegoer*, Aug. 27, 1942.
83 "At last . . ." J.B. Griswold, *American Magazine*, 1942.

Chapter 10

85 "Suddenly I knew what I had to do . . ." Griswold, *American Magazine,* 1942.
85 "Tell him . . ." James Reid, *Photoplay-Movie Mirror*, 1940.
85 "Greer was having a very difficult time . . ." William Tuttle to author.
86 "Greer came in . . . It must have put . . ." Lillian Burns Sidney to author.
87 "A small, elfin-like man . . ." Hall, *Silver Screen*, July 20, 1942.
88 "I don't think . . ." James Hilton, *Picturegoer*, Nov. 4, 1939.
88 "the most profoundly moving story . . ." *Goodbye, Mr. Chips* MGM film
     trailer.
89 "I am optimistic . . ." James Hilton, *Entertainment World*, Nov. 7, 1969.
89 "I would rather . . ." Hilton, *Picturegoer.*
89 "Sam's been around . . ." Hedda Hopper, *Los Angeles Times*, July 11, 1943.
89 "Franklin and I . . ." *Picturegoer.*
90 "MGM has been tempting me . . ." Barrow, *Robert Donat*, p. 108.
90 "I'm not coming back . . ." Hall, *Silver Screen.*
91 "She was heartsick . . ." Hedda Hopper, *Chicago Sunday Tribune*, July 16,
     1950.
91 "womanly and warm . . ." Hall, *Silver Screen.*
91 "London has the greatest reservoir . . ." Wood, *Picturegoer.*
91 "The publicists were wonderful to me . . ." Ibid.
92 "Someone must have known I was going to play Mrs. Chips . . ." Ibid.
92 "He'd say, 'Look here, my lovely . . .'" Jennings, *Dallas Morning News*, Sept.
     23, 1984.
92 "Since there are split scenes . . ." Hall, *Silver Screen.*
92 "Bob was the dearest man . . ." Barrow, *Robert Donat*, p. 108.
92 "Greer was extremely nervous . . ." Henreid, *Ladies Man*, p. 69.
93 "I felt more terribly lonely . . .It was so jolly . . ." G.G., *Photoplay,* Dec. 1947.
93 "My year in Hollywood . . ." Ibid.
93 "It was like being comfortably at home . . ." Hall, *Silver Screen.*
93 "I will gladly come and make a picture with you . . ." Ibid.
94 "No more laudable film has come out of England . . ." *Variety*, May 1939.
94 "I am not as depressed as I might have been . . ." Hall, *Silver Screen.*
95 "In a year in which . . ." *Goodbye, Mr. Chips* MGM film trailer.
95 "It is not necessary . . ." *New York Herald-Tribune*, May 1939.
95 "Miss Garson . . ." Alta Durant, *Variety,* May 16, 1939.
96 "Miss Garson . . ." *Philadelphia Public Ledger*, May 1939.
96 "I enjoy acting . . ." Hall, *Silver Screen.*
97 "All I know . . ." G.G., *Modern Screen*, Jan. 1949.
97 "She inspired him . . ." Lillian Burns Sidney to author.
97 "Greer Garson might have won . . ." John Chapman, *Chicago Sunday Tri-
     bune*, Feb. 15, 1942.
97 "I have never thought . . ." Callahan, *Family Circle*, Jan. 28, 1944.

97 "And what do you intend to do, sir . . ." Frank Daugherty, *Christian Science Monitor,* May 9, 1942.

98 "If anything glowed through Mrs. Chips . . ." Callahan, *Family Circle.*

98 "David happened to run into Queen Elizabeth . . ." Sheridan Morley, *The Life of David Niven,* p. 97.

Chapter 11

99 "After all . . ." *Los Angeles Times,* April 7, 1996.

99 "I go to Adrian's . . ." Hall, *Silver Screen,* July 20, 1942.

100 "I've always wanted . . . I spoiled . . ." Ibid.

100 "Greer Garson . . ." *Weekly Telegram,* Aug. 1939.

100 "Come what may the English must have their tea . . ." *San Francisco Examiner,* Aug. 13, 1939.

101 "No one is to return . . ." Hall, *Silver Screen.*

101 "It was a painful situation . . ." Laurence Olivier, *Confessions of an Actor,* p. 111.

101 "Some of us actors . . ." Hardwicke, *Irreverent Memoirs,* p. 234.

101 "For the spectacle . . ." Crowther, *New York Times,* Dec. 15, 1939.

102 "It did . . ." Hall, *Silver Screen.*

103 "MGM has given her the keys to the city . . ." Max Breen, "Welcome, Mrs. Chips!" from unnamed magazine in author's collection, July 1, 1939.

104 "*Pride and Prejudice* . . ." *Baltimore Evening Sun,* Jan. 17, 1940.

106 "I respected Greer . . ." Marsha Hunt to author.

106 "Greer approaches each acting assignment . . ." Martin, *Saturday Evening Post,* Dec. 26, 1946.

106 "She was such a perfectionist . . ." Edward Ashley to author.

106 "When the studio . . ." Ann Rutherford, "Persuasions," published by the Jane Austen Society.

106 "When they got all five sisters . . ." Ibid.

106 "All the women . . ." Hall, *Silver Screen.*

106 "Greer held court . . ." Edward Ashley to author.

107 "What impressed me most . . ." Ibid.

107 "We had not met . . ." G.G., *Pride and Prejudice* pressbook.

107 "Miss Leigh was completely upset . . ." McClelland, *Forties Film Talk,* p. 260.

107 "Darling Greer . . ." Laurence Olivier, *On Acting,* p. 262.

107 "terrible time . . ." Karen Morley, "Persuasions."

108 "I found my husband . . ." G.G., *Los Angeles Times,* May 9, 1940.

108 "I have rarely mentioned . . ." Ibid.

108 "something more . . ." Jane Austen, *Pride and Prejudice,* p. 4.

108 "a lively, playful . . ." Ibid., p. 9.

108 "rendered uncommonly intelligent . . ." Ibid., p. 17.

108 "This, by your leave . . ." Crowther, *New York Times,* July 27, 1940.

109 "Greer Garson seems . . ." *New Yorker,* Aug. 17, 1940.

109 "None of us . . ." McClelland, *Forties Film Talk,* p. 90.

109 "Noel came to see us . . ." Joan Fontaine, *No Bed of Roses,* p. 130.

110 "With the memory . . ." Franchey, "Bundle from Britain," *Picturegoer,* 1941.
110 "She helped my performance . . ." Elsa Maxwell, "Gold Medal Lady," *Photoplay,* 1944.
110 "one of the funniest things . . ." Ibid.
110 "She made a point . . ." Robert Osborne to author.
110 "Flame-haired Greer Garson . . ." Fontaine, *No Bed of Roses,* pp. 148-49.
111 "When I first read . . ." Hall, *Silver Screen.*
111 "It was a tough assignment . . ." Loos, *Kiss Hollywood Goodbye,* p. 171.
112 "even the most . . ." Ibid.
113 "Actors understood . . ." Walter Pidgeon, *Blossoms in the Dust* pressbook.
113 "Greer should be filmed in Technicolor . . ." Kay Proctor, *Screenbook,* Dec. 19, 1939.
113 "I know my limitations . . ." Callahan, Family Circle, Jan. 28, 1944.
114 "It was an extraordinary experience . . ." G.G., taped interview, SMU G.G. collection, Sept. 1985.
114 "'Blossoms in Dust' . . ." *Fort Worth Star-Telegram,* July 18, 1941.
114 "She looked like a boy . . ." Ibid.
114 "In the making of a movie . . ." Loos, *Kiss Hollywood Goodbye,* p. 172.
114 "I begged Mervyn . . ." McClelland, *Forties Film Talk,* p. 90.
115 "I told you . . ." Hall, *Silver Screen.*
115 "Walter . . ." Nancy Hill-Holtzman, *Los Angeles Herald-Examiner,* Sept. 26, 1984.
115 "I don't know . . ." Lydia Lane, unnamed article in author's collection, Aug. 11, 1952.
115 "It was easy all right . . ." Ted Thackrey Jr., *Los Angeles Times,* Sept. 26, 1984.
115 "The kids loved it . . ." Ibid.
116 "He has as much temperament . . ." Ibid.
116 "like being given . . ." Ibid.
116 "If I don't marry . . ." *Blossoms in the Dust* pressbook.
116 "I'm happy . . ." Hall, *Silver Screen.*
116 "A fantastic amount of energy hums away inside her body . . ." Martin, *Saturday Evening Post,* Dec. 26, 1946.
117 "We were the first duet . . ." Parish, *Best of MGM,* p. 32.
117 "Be careful . . ." *Blossoms in the Dust* pressbook.
117 "Greer Garson has the most beautiful speaking voice . . ." Ibid.
117 "Mervyn has a lot of orderliness in him . . ." Ibid.
117 "I bow with humility . . ." Ibid.
117 "It is going to be a great thrill . . ." Katherine Howard, *Fort Worth Star Tele119* "It was all very wonderful . . ." Ibid.
118 "For Greer Garson . . ." *Variety,* June 27, 1941.
118 "one of the . . ." Thackrey, *Los Angeles Times,* Sept. 26, 1984.

Chapter 12

119 "a rough period . . ." Newquist, *Conversations,* p. 48.
119 "Greer Garson . . ." Philip Wuntch, *Dallas Morning News,* March 10, 1991.

121 "In *When Ladies Meet* . . . So that's what Mrs. Chips . . ." Chapman, *Chicago Sunday Tribune*, Feb. 15, 1942.
121 "Joan was just completely nonplussed . . ." Wuntch, *Dallas Morning News*.
122 "I have nothing but the worst to say . . ." Newquist, *Conversations*, p. 88.
122 "This is entertainment deluxe . . ." *Hollywood Reporter*, Aug. 27, 1941.
122 "I found that Mrs. Miniver . . ." Hall, *Silver Screen*, July 20, 1942.
123 "I fainted away . . ." Ibid.
123 "Here she was . . ." Lillian Burns Sidney to author.
123 "I ran short . . ." Jan Struther, "What Music Means To Mrs. Miniver," unnamed magazine in author's collection, June 1943.
124 "Mrs Miniver has the gift of expression . . ." *London Times*, Oct. 27, 1939.
124 "She dashed through life . . . Zest for life . . ." Janet Rance, *Mrs. Miniver*, 1989 edition, p. xi.
124 "I had the notion . . ." Sunshine, *Lovers*, p. 114.
125 "This film . . ." G.G., 1989 BBC interview.
126 "I was a warmonger . . ." Herman, *Talent for Trouble*, p. 234.
126 "I had heard . . ." Don Alpert, *Los Angeles Times*, Aug. 27, 1961.
127 "I picked him out . . ." Eleanor Ringel, *Atlanta Journal*, April 7, 1996.
127 "When I first started . . ." McClelland, *Forties Film Talk*, p. 284.
128 "Greer, laughing . . ." Emerson, *Photoplay-Movie Mirror*, Aug. 1942.
128 "The Minivers were an odd family . . ." Hall, *Silver Screen*.
128 "It had the climate of Eden . . ." Davis, *Glamour Factory*, p. 7.
129 "He wore them with great panache . . ." Herman, *Talent for Trouble*, p. 231.
129 "I wish you could have seen . . ." Ibid.
129 "What do you mean . . ." William Wyler, interview with Ronald L. Davis, July 19, 1979, Academy of Motion Picture Arts and Sciences, Margaret Herrick Library collection.
129 "You will give . . ." Whitney Stine, *Mother Goddam*, p. 141.
129 "Willy came over to me . . ." Ibid, p. 236.
130 "Wyler was a perfectionist . . ." McClelland, *Forties Film Talk*, pp. 284-85.
130 "Because I never make a film . . ." William Wyler, *Mrs. Miniver* pressbook.
130 "chocolate box world . . ." *London Times*, April 8, 1996.
131 "We all felt . . ." Teresa Wright, *Coronet*, Sept. 1949.
131 "I'm sorry, Father . . ." Garnett, *Light Your Torches*, p. 259.
131 "It's selfish on my part . . ." Sidney Franklin, *Mrs. Miniver* pressbook.
132 "The rose festival . . ." *Variety*, May 13, 1942.
133 "What makes *Mrs. Miniver* . . ." Sunshine, *Lovers*, p. 118.
134 "The Navy gave me permission . . ." McClelland, *Forties Film Talk*, p. 294.
135 "Morale soared . . ." Theodore Strauss, *New York Times*, March 15, 1942.
135 "We can't escape the war . . ." Frank Daugherty. *Christian Science Monitor*, May 9, 1942.
135 "How wonderful it will be . . ." Hall, *Silver Screen*.
135 "The moment I drove in . . ." Ibid.
136 "We finally sold . . ." Garnett, *Light Your Torches*, p. 258.

Chapter 13

137 "The screen's main function . . ." Bob Porter, *Dallas Times Herald*, April 8, 1976.

137 "When a writer . . ." Hilton, *Entertainment World*, Nov. 7, 1969.

138 "Trying to make good pictures . . ." Sidney Franklin, *Random Harvest* pressbook.

138 "One reason . . ." Martin, *Saturday Evening Post*, Aug. 16, 1947.

139 "When *Random Harvest* came along . . ." Parish, *Best of* MGM, p. 176.

139 "It could have been . . ." LeRoy, *Take One*, p. 150.

139 "If you had come to the lot . . ." McClelland, *Forties Film Talk*, pp. 151-52.

139 "Ronnie was extremely charming . . ." Ibid.

140 "I rather enjoyed this film . . ." Parish, *Best of* MGM, p. 176.

140 "Was that Greer Garson?" Nancy Winslow Squire, *Modern Screen*, Aug. 1944.

141 "I love to dance . . ." Hall, *Silver Screen*, July 20, 1942.

141 "The advisability . . ." Martin, *Saturday Evening Post*, Dec. 26, 1946.

141 "We felt it would be a mistake . . ." Ibid.

141 "I was a bit embarrassed . . ." Hall, *Silver Screen*.

141 "When I pranced out . . ." Martin, *Saturday Evening Post*, Dec. 26, 1946.

141 "What a delightful piece that was . . ." Lillian Burns Sidney to author.

141 "of her warm vitality . . ." Hilton, *Random Harvest*, p. 217.

141 "I was simply delighted . . ." telegram from Sidney Franklin, April 28, 1942, SMU G.G. collection.

142 "Your column about my legs . . ." G.G. telegram to Earl Wilson, Feb. 21, 1945, SMU G.G. collection.

143 "Playing the part . . ." Bob Porter, *Dallas Times Herald*, Sept. 8, 1985.

143 "She was a brilliant woman . . ." William Tuttle to author.

143 "She was incredibly observant . . ." Ibid.

143 "a very ugly, uninspiring place . . ." Davis, *Glamour Factory*, p. 154.

144 "What do you think . . . I'm shoveling it." Ibid.

144 "From that moment on . . ." Ibid.

144 "On still portraits . . ." Ibid., p. 236.

144 "Greer had one good side . . ." Ibid., pp. 236-37.

144 "All of the actors . . ." Marsha Hunt to author.

145 "We were meeting . . ." McClelland, *Forties Film Talk*, p. 265.

145 "We all got on so well . . ." Parish, *Best of* MGM, p. 176.

145 "Greer Garson is always strange . . ." *Variety*, May 13, 1942.

145 "There was nothing . . ." Emerson, *Photoplay-Movie Mirror*, Aug. 1942.

146 "admiration and adoration . . ." Maxwell, *Photoplay*, 1944.

146 "In fact . . ." Myrna Loy, *Being and Becoming*, p. 208.

146 "On the completion . . ." Howard Strickling publicity release, undated, MGM/Turner Entertainment Co. archives.

146 "with a speed . . ." Emerson, *Photoplay-Movie Mirror*.

146 "I continued to be cool . . ." Hall, *Silver Screen*.

147 "Richard Ney . . ." Emerson, *Photoplay-Movie Mirror*.

147 "It reached out . . ." G.G., 1989 BBC interview, and *Toronto Star*, Aug. 10, 1986.

148 "It is hard to believe . . ." Crowther, *New York Times*, June 5, 1942.

148 "In fact . . ." Henry Sheenan, *Orange County Register*, April 12, 1996.

148 "exemplary propaganda . . ." Parish, *Best of MGM*, p. 142.

148 "Since *Mrs. Miniver* . . ." Hall, *Silver Screen*.

149 "Greer Garson should know better . . ." *American Weekly*, March 14, 1948.

149 "They are moody souls . . ." Emerson, *Photoplay-Movie Mirror*.

149 "I want to marry him . . ." Maxwell, *Photoplay*.

149 "Greer knew . . ." Ibid.

149 "It's tremendous . . ." Eric Knight, untitled newspaper review in author's collection, July 8, 1942.

149 "It must be made clear . . ." *London Times*, July 8, 1942.

150 "She is Mrs. Miniver . . ." Hall, Silver Screen.

150 "*Mrs. Miniver* was just the right British . . ." Talbot Jennings Writers' Conference speech, 1943, *Mrs. Miniver* file, Margaret Herrick Library.

150 "The impact of the film . . ." G.G., 1989 BBC interview.

152 "After *Goodbye, Mr. Chips* . . ." G.G., program for the opening of Garson Studio, Oct. 20, 1990.

152 "a classy filly . . ." Parish, *MGM Stock Company*, p. 270.

152 "Make them treat me . . ." Minnelli, *I Remember It Well*, p. 221.

152 "There's a great danger . . ." Manners, *Los Angeles Herald-Examiner*, Feb. 15, 1953.

152 "The misty . . ." Chapman, *Chicago Sunday Tribune*, Feb. 15, 1942.

153 "Stay in America . . ." Jennings, *Dallas Morning News*, Sept. 23, 1984.

153 "A journalist friend . . ." Charles Champlin, *Los Angeles Times*, April 10, 1996.

153 "My first Bond tour . . ." Callahan, *Family Circle*, Jan. 28, 1944.

153 "Mr. Chairman . . ." G.G. speech, undated, SMU G.G. collection.

154 "I was one of those who pioneered . . ." G.G., *This Week Magazine*, 1942.

154 "The first big stars . . ." Jean Porter to author.

154 "Joseph Ruttenberg . . ." LeRoy, *Take One*, p. 150.

155 "Even with the great celebrities . . ." Crowther, *New York Times*, July 17, 1943.

155 "one of the truly fine motion pictures . . ." *Hollywood Reporter*, Nov. 25, 1942.

155 "It could have played longer . . ." LeRoy, *Take One*, p. 150.

156 "I have just come . . ." James A. Ball letter, Dec. 27, 1942, SMU G.G. collection.

156 "One has to consider . . ." Edwin Schallert, *Los Angeles Times*, Nov. 5, 1944.

156 "There had been . . ." G.G., "A Tribute to Greer Garson: The MGM Years," SMU documentary, 1985.

Chapter 14

157 "Here am I . . ." Hall, *Silver Screen*, July 20, 1942.

157 "I don't want . . ." Schallert, *Los Angeles Times,* Nov. 5, 1944.

158 "I admire . . ." Hall, *Silver Screen.*

158 "It doesn't matter . . ." G.G., *Screen Album Magazine,* No. 23, Summer Edition, 1943.

158 "We have got to be authentic . . ." Sidney Franklin memo, Nov. 9, 1942, USC Archives.

159 "Dramatically it would be false to science." MGM *Lion's Roar,* 1942.

159 "Irene Jolliot-Curie dislikes . . ." Salka Viertel, Aug. 21, 1939, USC Archives.

160 "There's a great deal of beauty . . ." Callahan, *Family Circle,* Jan. 28, 1944.

160 "I read everything . . ." Ibid.

160 "During my schooldays . . ." Hall, *Silver Screen.*

160 "I spent long, happy, self-important days there . . ." Ibid.

161 "Mother is my best audience . . ." MGM *Lion's Roar,* 1942.

161 "I can honestly say . . ." Ibid.

162 "Walter . . ." MGM *Lion's* Roar, 1942.

162 "Everywhere in the world . . ." *Los Angeles Times,* June 14, 1966.

162 "I'm going away . . ." Ibid.

163 "If Gigi has any more scenes . . ." Walter Pidgeon, *Madame Curie* pressbook.

163 "Before we filmed the scene . . ." G.G. film interview, "Greer Garson: The MGM Years," SMU, 1985.

164 "It was a character part . . ." Martin, *Saturday Evening Post,* Dec. 26, 1946.

164 "When I awoke . . ." MGM publicity, April 7, 1943.

164 "Probably no big event . . ." *Hollywood Reporter,* March 5, 1942.

165 "Well . . . I wasted all the happiness . . ." Joseph Dispenza, "Greer Garson and the Other Oscar," unpublished article in author's collection; Jennings, *Dallas Morning News,* Sept. 23, 1984.

165 "Richard and I thought . . ." Hall, *Silver Screen.*

165 "We rehearsed . . ." Parish, *Best of* MGM, p. 128.

165 "In spite of my initial reluctance . . ." Hall, *Silver Screen.*

166 "We had a wonderful time . . ." Ibid.

166 "It was just another wedding . . ." *Los Angeles Examiner,* July 25, 1943.

166 "I'm quite proud . . ." Maxwell, *Photoplay,* 1944.

166 "my long-legged husband." Hall, *Silver Screen.*

167 "If it hadn't been for you . . ." Richard Ney, *Los Angeles Times,* Dec. 1, 1943.

167 "There are many who claim . . ." *Los Angeles Times,* July 26, 1943.

167 "She was red-headed mad . . ." Mary C. McCall Jr., "America's Ideal Woman," undated article in author's collection, circa 1943.

167 "Every inch a great picture . . ." *Variety,* Nov. 19, 1943.

168 "I finally found her . . ." Philip Scheuer, *Los Angeles Times,* March 5, 1944.

168 "It was great to see Richard . . ." Maxwell, *Photoplay.*

168 "It was a very pleasant partnership . . ." Hall, *Silver Screen.*

168 "Mrs. Long-Run Is Back . . ." *New York Herald-Tribune,* Jan. 23, 1944.

168 "A lasting inspiration . . ." *New York Times,* Dec. 17, 1943.

168 "In an expert piece of sentiment . . ." *Time,* Dec. 20, 1943.

169 "much graver . . ." Ibid.

170 "The instant they find a story ..." Philip Scheuer, *Los Angeles Times*, March 5, 1944.
170 "I am for the days ..." Hall, *Silver Screen*.
170 "Greer has a reserve ..." Bob Thomas, *Hollywood Citizen-News*, Feb. 16, 1946.

Chapter 15

171 "Oh, it would have been fun, wouldn't it?" Robert Osborne, *Hollywood Reporter*, April 9, 1996.
171 "Greer is the complete showoff ..." Gardner, *Ladies Home Journal*, Sept. 1944.
172 "one of the most sparkling conversationalists ..." B. Thomas, *Hollywood Citizen-News*, Feb. 16, 1946.
172 "Miss Garson ..." Franchey, "Bundle from Britain," *Picturegoer*, 1941.
172 "Fortunately ..." Martin, *Saturday Evening Post*, Dec. 26, 1946.
172 "Miss Garson is a person ..." Vina Windes, *New Mexican*, Apr. 15, 1996.
172 "to stroll across the sands ..." Hall, *Silver Screen*, July 20, 1942.
172 "She has yet ..." Martin, Saturday Evening Post.
172 "Although I had some preparation for it ..." Hall, *Silver Screen*.
172 "You feel as if ..." McCall, "America's Ideal Woman," 1943.
172 "It's a homey, mildly Tudor white brick manse ..." Franchey, "Bundle from Britain."
173 "She is the most erudite ..." J.B. Griswold, *American Magazine*, 1941.
173 "She is shy ..." *Time*, Dec. 20, 1943.
173 "Two years of life ..." Franchey, "Bundle from Britain."
173 "Mrs. Garson ..." Ibid.
174 "for the effect of a woodland ..." Hall, *Silver Screen*.
174 "so cozy for two people ..." Franchey, "Bundle from Britain."
174 "We enjoyed half an hour or so of playing ..." G.G. letter, Susan Goldenberg, Aug. 17, 1987.
175 "Greer is sort of like grape squeezings ..." *Look*, April 4, 1944.
175 "With British diffidence ..." Franchey, "Bundle from Britain."
175 "About the theatre ..." May Mann, "The Woman with Woman's Digest," *Maclean's*, Aug. 1944.
175 "I didn't sleep for a week ..." Louella Parsons, *Los Angeles Examiner*, March 11, 1945.
175 "She thinks she'd like to act ..." McCall, "America's Ideal Woman."
175 "If you got on the phone with Greer ..." Lillian Burns Sidney to author.
175 "I think because I am fascinated ..." *Screenland*, June 1945.
175 "Her relentless driving force ..." Ibid.
176 "In self-defense ..." Rosemary Laing, unnamed and undated article in author's collection, 1944.
176 "Dear Walter ..." Gardner, *Ladies Home Journal*, Sept. 1944.
176 "In prodigal Hollywood ..." Ibid.
176 "Sometimes at night ..." Hall, *Silver Screen*.
176 "You know ..." Ibid.

Chapter 16

178 "The studio powers . . ." Schallert, *Los Angeles Times,* Nov. 5, 1944.

178 "It took a lot of doing . . ." G.G., *Photoplay,* Feb. 1944.

178 "Usually Greer's humor . . ." Garnett, *Light Your Torches,* p. 261.

179 "Susie is different . . ." MGM *Lion's Roar,* 1944.

179 "I had to do it . . ." Frederick C. Othman, *Hollywood Citizen-News,* March 15, 1944.

179 "I only got the role . . ." Agnes Moorehead, *Chicago Sunday Tribune,* Nov. 26, 1944.

180 "I found out . . ." Moorehead, *Saturday Evening Post,* May 7, 1949.

180 "I thoroughly enjoyed . . ." Ibid.

180 "She's one of the finest actresses . . ." G.G., *Mrs. Parkington* pressbook.

180 "During the first scenes . . ." Garnett, *Light Your Torches,* p. 260.

180 "It looks as though . . ." Ibid.

181 "Playing an 80-year-old woman . . ." Parsons, *Los Angeles Examiner,* March 11, 1945.

181 "Greer suddenly has become the wit of the MGM lot . . ." Ibid.

181 "Motion pictures may look lavish . . ." Tay Garnett, *Mrs. Parkington* pressbook.

181 "If I'm lucky . . ." G.G. letter to George Cukor, 1944, Margaret Herrick Library.

182 "The boys . . ." Frederick C. Othman, *Los Angeles Times,* June 22, 1944.

183 "Miss Garson performs . . ." Crowther, *New York Times,* Oct. 13, 1944.

183 "Some actresses have a certain spark . . ." Garnett, *Mrs. Parkington* pressbook.

185 "We regret to advise you . . ." Joseph Breen letter, Sept. 22, 1944, Margaret Herrick Library MPPA collection.

185 "I really believed in that girl . . ." G.G., *Dallas Morning News,* March 10, 1991.

186 "I learned quite a lot . . ." Jessica Tandy, SMU Celebration of Greer Garson, Sept. 12, 1992.

186 "Miss Garson looks her best . . ." Joseph Ruttenberg, *American Cinematographer,* Sept. 1949.

186 "When it came to viewing the rushes . . ." Freedland, *Gregory Peck,* p. 66; and McDowall, *Double Exposure,* p. 172.

187 "Lionel would rehearse a scene . . ." Molyneaux, *Gregory Peck,* p. 75.

188 "I was sitting . . ." McClelland, *Forties Film Talk,* p. 255.

188 "With Greer Garson . . ." *New York Herald Tribune,* May 4, 1945.

188 "Despite its convoluted and stylized plot . . ." Cynthia Rose, *Dallas Times Herald,* Sept. 16, 1985.

188 "*The Valley of Decision* . . ." McClelland, *Forties Film Talk,* p. 255.

189 "Had we worked together again . . ." Gregory Peck, "A Tribute to Greer Garson: The MGM Years," Sept. 13, 1985.

189 "If ever a movie actress . . ." Crowther, *New York Times,* May 20, 1945.

Chapter 17

191 "a swanky affair . . ." Sidney Skolsky, *Photoplay,* April 1945.

191 "That request . . ." Maxwell, *Photoplay,* 1944.

191 "MGM in those days . . ." Parish, MGM *Stock Company,* p. 632.

192 "Think of it . . ." Bob White, *Los Angeles Times,* June 17, 1945.

192 "I stalled as long as I could . . ." Ibid.

192 "He looks different . . ." Erskine Johnson, *Daily News,* May 23, 1945.

193 "Clark had come back . . ." McClelland, *Forties Film Talk,* p. 37.

193 "Try to get someone . . ." White, *Los Angeles Times,* June 17, 1945.

194 "Playing a love scene . . ." Hall, *Silver Screen,* July 20, 1942.

194 "When she had the 'blacks' put up . . ." B. Thomas, *Hollywood Citizen-News,* Feb. 16, 1946.

194 "they were opposites . . ." McClelland, *Forties Film Talk,* p. 158.

194 "*Adventure* was not a good experience . . ." Wuntch, *Dallas Morning News,* March 10, 1991.

194 "They're ungallant . . ." Martin, *Saturday Evening Post,* Dec. 26, 1946.

194 "You get an indication . . ." Robert Osborne, *Hollywood Reporter,* April 9, 1996.

195 "It is really difficult to fathom . . ." Crowther, *New York Times,* Feb. 10, 1946.

195 "He had to take . . ." Jean Garcean, *Dear Mr. G—,* p. 186.

195 "When *Adventure* flopped . . ." McClelland, *Forties Film Talk,* p. 37.

195 "The hollowness . . ." Carey, *All the Stars in Heaven,* p. 273.

196 "It is basically a story of illicit sex . . ." Joseph Breen letter, March 12, 1946, Margaret Herrick Library MPPA collection.

197 "I knew I wanted . . ." Lowell E. Redelings, *Hollywood Citizen-News,* Aug. 28, 1946.

197 "My wife has been reading . . ." Ibid.

198 "Oh, that's nothing . . ." *Hollywood Citizen-News,* June 11, 1953.

198 "Her eyes would spin around . . ." Eells, *Robert Mitchum,* p. 78.

199 "I can't get anyone to believe me . . ." Davis, *Glamour Factory,* p. 150.

199 "We had to get into the hospital . . ." Ibid.

199 "We wanted the fisherman to save her." Ibid.

199 "I saw it coming . . ." Paul Bretch, *Los Angeles Times,* April 20, 1946.

199 "She wanted to go right on . . ." *Los Angeles Daily News,* April 20, 1946.

200 "Miss Garson still unable to work . . ." George Cukor, MGM memo, May 13, 1946, MGM/Turner Entertainment Co. Archives.

200 "*Desire Me* was a fiasco altogether . . ." McGilligan, *Double Life,* p. 179.

200 "Cukor was one of those directors . . ." Ibid., p. 180.

200 "*Desire Me* was shot . . ." Levy, *George Cukor,* p. 162.

201 "George Cukor and Mervyn LeRoy . . ." Roberts, *Robert Mitchum,* p. 64.

201 "In 1946 . . ." LeRoy, *Take One,* p. 196.

201 "Now I know . . ." Levy, *George Cukor,* p. 162.

202 "To me . . ." G.G., *Photoplay,* Jan. 1947.

202 "The reason for the Neys' . . ." Erskine Johnson, *Los Angeles Times*, Feb. 3, 1947.

202 "It's spring . . ." Hedda Hopper, *Los Angeles Times*, March 29, 1947.

203 "The defendant . . ." *Los Angeles Times*, Aug. 20, 1947.

203 "Greer Garson is back . . ." *Motion Picture Daily*, Sept. 26, 1947.

203 "Miss Garson's role . . ." *Variety*, Sept. 26, 1947.

204 "We separated in January . . ." G.G., *Los Angeles Times*, Sept. 26, 1947.

204 "It is very difficult . . ." *American Weekly*, March 14, 1948.

204 "She wandered . . ." *Hollywood Citizen-News*, Sept. 25, 1947.

204 "George, George . . .This isn't acting . . ." *Los Angeles Times*, Sept. 26, 1947.

205 "Greer Garson has portrayed few roles . . ." *American Weekly*, March 14, 1948.

205 "Now comes the news . . ." *Illinois State Journal*, 1947.

206 "It looks . . ." G.G., *Modern Screen*, Jan. 1949.

206 "Dear Greer, hope . . ." J. Robert Rubin letter to G.G., undated, SMU G.G. collection.

206 "Greer Garson's back, folks . . ." *New York Times*, Nov. 1, 1947.

206 "Darling . . ." letter from Nina Garson, undated, SMU collection.

207 "*Desire Me* was a sad mistake . . ." Hedda Hopper, *Chicago Sunday Tribune*, Nov. 2, 1947; G.G., *Modern Screen*, Jan. 1949; and *Screen Album*, 1948.

Chapter 18

208 "I've always loved . . ." G.G., *Modern Screen*, Jan. 1949.

208 "What I've wanted to do . . ." Ibid.

208 "When Greer Garson starts a picture . . ." MGM News, Jan. 16, 1948.

209 "After all . . ." Edward Lawrence, *New York Times*, Feb. 1, 1948.

210 "Buddy was shy, I was brash . . ." Anderson, *Dallas Magazine*, Aug. 1992.

210 "He took my hand . . ." Joseph Dispenza, "Greer Garson and the Other Oscar," unpublished article in the author's collection.

210 "Those two get together . . ." Hedda Hopper, *Modern Screen*, April 1949.

210 "There were so many roses . . ." Dispenza, "Greer Garson and the Other Oscar."

211 "Then, if I break my neck . . ." Lawrence, *New York Times*, Feb. 1, 1948.

211 "The cool repose . . ." Ibid.

211 "MGM calls it . . . I am happier . . ." G.G., *Modern Screen*, and *Los Angeles Examiner*, Dec. 26, 1948.

211 "The common misconception . . ." *Hollywood Reporter*, Oct. 11, 1948.

212 "I'll never forget . . ." DeBlasio, Modern Screen, Feb. 1961.

213 "cowboy gallantries . . ." Ibid.

213 "He had started life . . ." Herbert Hutner to author.

213 "Greer was a great lady . . ." Lillian Burns Sidney to author.

214 "We had a long and stormy courtship . . ." Colin Barnes, unnamed article in author's collection, April 1974.

214 "My lovely red-haired and good friend . . ." Parsons, "New Life, New Love," *Photoplay*, 1949.

214 "If I marry . . ." Ibid.
216 "Bring Joseph Ruttenberg on board . . ." Ralph Lawton, *American Cinematographer*, Sept. 1949.
217 "It was a little difficult . . ." Ibid.
217 "You can't light fog . . ." Ibid.
217 "I don't know . . ." Flynn, *Wicked Ways*, p. 256.
218 "I primed myself . . ." Ibid.
218 "We stalked each other like terriers . . ." Jennings, *Dallas Morning News*, Sept. 23, 1984.
218 "I had misjudged Greer Garson . . ." Leigh, *There Really Was a Hollywood*, p. 83.
219 "He couldn't have asked . . ." Ibid.
219 "The popular conception . . ." Flynn, *Wicked Ways*, p. 257.
219 "A change has come over Greer . . ." Hedda Hopper, *Modern Screen*, April 1949.
219 "That was my first experience . . ." Alexis Smith, *That Forsyte Woman* pressbook.
220 "When MGM was formed . . ." Louis B. Mayer, *Los Angeles Examiner*, Feb. 11, 1949.
220 "It has some of the brightest lines . . ." Dore Schary, *Hollywood Reporter*, Feb. 8, 1949.
221 "bloated and ill." Dore Schary MGM memo, May 1949, University of Wisconsin archives.
221 "Greer was sicker than anyone knew . . ." Parsons, *Los Angeles Examiner*, June 15, 1949.
221 "When is Greer Garson . . ." Ibid.
221 "Hank Potter . . ." Dore Schary MGM memo, July 1949, University of Wisconsin archives.
222 "Dearest Buddy and Greer . . ." Nina Garson letter, July 15, 1949, SMU G.G. collection.

Chapter 19

225 "My career . . ." Hedda Hopper, *Los Angeles Times*, July 16, 1950.
225 "Buddy told me . . ." Hedda Hopper, *Chicago Sunday Tribune*, July 16, 1950.
226 "Actress Greer Garson . . ." *Los Angeles Daily News*, July 15, 1949.
226 "Welcome to the 49ers!" David O. Selznick telegram, July 22, 1949, SMU G.G. collection.
226 "Will you please tell Mrs. Fogelson . . ." Humphrey Bogart telegram, July 16, 1949, SMU G.G. collection.
226 "I'm so glad . . ." Evelyn Murray telegram, July 27, 1949, SMU collection.
226 "Buddy gave a delightful party . . ." Parsons, *Yorkshire Evening News*, Aug. 23, 1949.
226 "When we first came to the ranch . . ." *Albuquerque Journal*, April 9, 1996.
226 "They have found their own personal Shangri-La . . ." George Fitzpatrick, *New Mexican*, Jan. 1960.

228 "Well, we could have a scene . . ." Hedda Hopper, *Modern Screen,* Jan. 1949.

228 "only scratched the surface . . ." Herman, *Talent for Trouble,* p. 237.

229 "From the stage of the Albert Hall . . ." *Daily Mail,* Sept. 12, 1949.

230 "I was an ardent fan . . ." Sheila Collings, *The Stage,* April 19, 1996.

230 "She encouraged me . . ." Ibid.

230 "My own belief . . ." Commodore Robin Garson to author.

230 "I saw a picture . . ." Buddy Fogelson telegram, Oct. 22, 1949, SMU G.G. collection.

231 "After the white lights . . ." *London Times,* Nov. 18, 1949.

231 "It was an affair that delighted the audience . . ." Ibid.

231 "The answer must be as well as can be expected . . ." Ibid.

232 "Buddy Fogelson was a fine man . . ." Dr. Sloan to author.

233 "Perhaps the MacFogelsons?" Hedda Hopper, *Chicago Sunday Tribune,* July 16, 1950.

233 "I feel responsible . . ." Parsons, *Los Angeles Herald-Examiner,* Dec. 13, 1949.

233 "That's a part for a blonde . . ." Joyce Haber, *Los Angeles Times,* Sept. 1, 1968.

233 "Greer Garson's *Miniver* picture . . ." Hedda Hopper, *Los Angeles Times,* Jan. 17, 1950.

234 "From our experience . . ." Ben Goetz telegram, Jan. 18, 1950, MGM archives.

234 "Distressed . . ." G.G. telegram, Jan. 26, 1950, MGM/Turner Entertainment archives.

234 "Dear Greer . . ." Sidney Franklin telegram, Feb. 16, 1950, MGM/Turner Entertainment archives.

235 "Victor . . ." Sidney Franklin telegram, Feb. 23, 1950, MGM/Turner Entertainment archives.

235 "Presents taken by Greer Garson . . ." *Star,* Feb. 25, 1950.

236 "carry out a long cherished wish . . ." *Shorthorn World,* March 25, 1950.

236 "Congratulations Greer Garson . . ." Lillian Burns Sidney letter, June 7, 1950, SMU collection.

237 "Mrs. Miniver and her lot . . ." *Punch,* Sept. 13, 1950.

237 "to be remembered . . ." Calla Hay, *New Mexican,* Sept. 12, 1950.

237 "This picture . . ." *Hollywood Reporter,* Sept. 29, 1950.

238 "Personally . . ." *Los Angeles Herald-Examiner,* Sept. 29, 1950.

238 "We can well understand . . ." Crowther, *New York Times,* Oct. 27, 1950.

238 "I called William Tuttle . . ." Kevin Thomas, *Los Angeles Times,* Dec. 11, 1968.

238 "Greer Garson . . ." *Shorthorn World.*

Chapter 20

239 "All I had to do . . ." Parish, MGM *Stock Company,* p. 400.

239 "The idea of a feud . . ." Braun, *Deborah Kerr,* p. 135.

239 "We had a lot of fun out of it . . ." G.G., *Modern Screen,* Jan. 1949.

240 "On the London stage . . ." Gardner, *Ladies Home Journal,* Sept. 1944.

240 "The way people feel about you . . ." Martin, *Saturday Evening Post,* Dec. 26, 1946.

240 "It is strange . . ." *Hollywood Citizen-News,* June 11, 1953.

241 "I feel a deep and proud affinity . . ." Manners, *Los Angeles Herald-Examiner,* Feb. 15, 1953.

241 "In 1941 when . . ." *Fort Worth News-Tribune,* undated article in author's collection, 1980.

241 "Please permit me . . ." Joe Hawn, House of Representatives, Dallas County District 33, April 11, 1969.

242 "one of the most peculiar costume design sessions . . ." Walter Plunkett, *The Law and the Lady* pressbook.

243 "What's the scene this morning . . ." Fredda Dudley Balling, *Silver Screen,* April 12, 1951; and Scheuer, *Los Angeles Times,* March 5, 1944.

243 "The best part . . ." G.G., *Midland Reporter-Telegram,* Feb. 5, 1951.

243 "For nearly three years . . ." *Hollywood Reporter,* June 26, 1951.

244 "*The Law and the Lady* . . ." *Hollywood Reporter,* July 6, 1951.

245 "lousy movie . . ." Wilding, *Wilding Way,* pp. 62-63.

245 "I hope this one . . ." Parsons, *Los Angeles Times,* Oct. 21, 1951.

246 "I've never been a guy . . ." Earl Wilson, *Daily News,* April 29, 1952.

246 "Well, this is hardly . . ." Michael Connolly, *Photoplay,* Jan. 1953.

246 "The lineup for the photogs . . ." Wiley, *Inside Oscar,* p. 218.

246 "It's the Fogelson influence . . ." Connolly, *Photoplay.*

246 "Congratulations, Vivien dear . . ." G.G. telegram, March 20, 1952, SMU G.G. collection.

247 "I believe that . . ." Schallert, *Los Angeles Times,* Feb. 10, 1952.

247 "Greer and I . . ." Walter Pidgeon, *Los Angeles Times,* June 14, 1966.

247 "A rose is a rose . . ." Norman Corwin, SMU collection.

248 "Greer Garson . . ." *Hollywood Citizen-News,* Sept. 5, 1952.

248 "We have been on a nationwide search . . ." Tommy Prothro, undated, SMU G.G. collection.

248 "I couldn't have had any leading man . . ." Nancy Hill-Holtzman, *Los Angeles Herald-Examiner,* Sept. 26, 1984.

248 "I know . . ." Jean Negulesco, SMU G.G. collection.

249 "Like other Garson-Pidgeon pictures . . ." Crowther, *New York Times,* June 13, 1953.

250 "It was rumored . . ." Connolly, *Photoplay.*

250 "It's so untrue . . ." Ibid.

250 "Buddy often said . . ." Jennings, *Dallas Morning News,* Sept. 23, 1984.

250 "Miss Garson . . ." Michael Levee memo to Benjamin Thau, undated, University of Wisconsin Dore Schary collection.

250 "I suppose I could jokingly say . . ." Manners, *Los Angeles Herald-Examiner.*

251 "We are just there . . ." *Star,* Jan. 16, 1953.

251 "*Caesar* is a tragedy . . ." Houseman, *Front and Center,* pp. 392-93.

251 "It's now . . ." Sidney Skolsky, *Hollywood Citizen-News,* Sept. 17, 1952.

252 "Gielgud . . . sailed through the part . . ." Houseman, *Front and Center*, p. 390.

252 "the living mood . . ." Ibid., p. 395.

252 "Politically correct . . ." G.G., *Julius Caesar* pressbook.

253 "it was very largely owing to his influence . . ." *Variety,* Nov. 17, 1953.

253 "Even Esther Williams . . ." G.G., *Daily Express,* Nov. 13, 1953.

253 "I come to bury Caesar . . ." *Sunday Express,* Nov. 2, 1953.

253 "To those . . ." *Variety,* June 2, 1953.

Chapter 21

255 "after receipt of petitions . . ." Howard Strickling, MGM News, July 21, 1952.

255 "Greer gets her dream part . . ." *Star,* July 16, 1952.

256 "Mr. Schary wasn't a movie man . . ." Angela Lansbury, "Inside The Dream Factory," broadcast Aug. 8, 1995.

256 "I leave on Monday . . ." G.G. letter to Dore Schary, Feb. 27, 1953, MGM archives.

257 "It was part . . ." Houseman, *Front and Center*, p. 422.

257 "What astringency . . ." Ibid.

258 "The problem is . . ." F.L. Hendrickson memo, Aug. 31, 1953, MGM/Turner Entertainment archives.

259 "They really threw me to the lions . . ." *TV Guide,* April 2, 1955.

259 "an okay 90 minutes . . ." *Variety,* June 24, 1954.

259 "Ever since the great days . . ." *Hollywood Reporter,* June 24, 1954.

260 "I can't believe . . ." Van Johnson letter, 1954, SMU G.G. collection.

260 "a wonderful place . . ." *Los Angeles Mirror-News,* May 27, 1955.

261 "I told him . . ." *Strange Lady in Town* press release, 1954, University of Southern California Warner Bros. archives.

262 "So far as the script is concerned . . ." Ibid.

263 "My house was perfect . . ." Parsons, *TV View,* Feb. 6, 1955.

264 "Mouchete was used . . ." Warner Bros. press release, USC Warner Bros. archives.

264 "I have lots of tarantulas . . ." Ibid.

264 "a mess . . ." LeRoy, *Take One*, pp. 196-97.

265 "My body . . ." Warner Bros. press release, 1954.

265 "I am enclosing Friday's production report . . ." Jack L. Warner memo, 1954, University of Southern California Warner Bros. archives.

266 "Please do not worry . . ." Ibid.

267 "It's been so long.." *TV Guide,* April 2, 1955.

267 "The set reminded me . . ." Walter Ames, *Los Angeles Times,* Feb. 19, 1956.

267 "From the standpoint of a theater manager . . ." *Austin American,* April 13, 1955.

268 "Unlike Dana . . ." *Austin American,* April 12, 1955.

268 "Shot in Cinemascope . . ." *Hollywood Reporter,* April 28, 1995.

268 "because it's uncomplicated . . ." *Los Angeles Herald-Examiner,* April 28, 1955.

268 "All your trials and tribulations . . ." Jack L. Warner telegram, 1955, USC Warner Bros. archives.

268 "a richly corny period story . . ." G.G. letter to Norma Wilson, Feb. 27, 1956, SMU G.G. collection.

269 "I like doing television . . ." Ames, *Los Angeles Times*.

269 "Cut this girl loose . . ." *TV Guide*, April 2, 1955.

269 "Miss Garson is a perfect lady . . ." Boller, *Hollywood Anecdotes*, p. 262.

269 "as if the 3,000 mile . . ." *Variety*, Nov. 13, 1955.

269 "I hope no one gets the idea . . ." Ames, *Los Angeles Times*.

269 "Miss Garson excels at her role . . ." *Variety*, April 4, 1955.

270 "I just can't see . . ." *TV Guide*, April 1955.

270 "Esme Percy . . ." G.G. letter to Michael Barry, 1956, SMU G.G. collection.

270 "Why keep doing another . . ." Samuel B. Harrison, Sept. 20, 1956, SMU G.G. collection.

270 "hideously lit and photographed." G.G. letter to Bernie Seligman, Nov. 26, 1958.

270 "Thank heavens . . ." Val Adams, *New York Times*, Oct. 7, 1956.

271 "Anyone know . . ." *Variety*, Sept. 10, 1957.

Chapter 22

272 "I like her courage . . ." *New York Times*, Jan. 19, 1958.

273 "Rehearsals so far have been a lark . . ." Frances Herridge, *New York Post*, Jan. 20, 1958.

273 "Thirty floors below us . . ." Philip Minoff, *Cue*, Jan. 18, 1958.

273 "I did hope to come to America . . ." Ibid.

274 "No need to worry . . ." *Variety*, Feb. 26, 1958.

274 "I have watched your performance . . ." letter from J.J. Shubert, Feb. 6, 1958, SMU G.G. collection.

274 "I saw Greer Garson . . ." Mike Connolly letter, Jan. 28, 1959, SMU G.G. collection.

275 "I still picture in my mind . . ." letter from Lord Brabazon, 1958, SMU G.G. collection.

275 "Have happy summer of rest . . ." May 23, 1958, SMU G.G. collection.

275 "I wouldn't want acting full time anymore . . ." K. Thomas, *Los Angeles Times*, Dec. 11, 1968.

275 "Life is so exciting . . ." Fay Hammond, *Los Angeles Times*, April 14, 1961.

275 "Greer was so effusively delighted . . ." Marsha Hunt to author.

275 "Greer Garson has not changed much . . ." Julia Sweeney, *Park City News*, Sept. 10, 1992.

276 "clannish . . ." Lee Belser, *Los Angeles Mirror*, Jan. 12, 1961.

276 "Dallas is small enough to be neighborly . . ." K. Thomas, *Los Angeles Times*, Aug. 12, 1966.

276 "Keep your horizons wide . . ." Manners, *Los Angeles Herald-Examiner*.

276 "Upward and Onward with the Arts . . ." program for the opening of the G.G. Studio, Oct. 20, 1990.

276 "The oil and gas exploration business . . ." Thomas, *Los Angeles Times*, Aug. 12, 1966.

277 "Do you want to hold my baby?" Edward Ashley to author.

277 "It struck terror in my heart . . ." Dr. B. Clayton Bell Sr. to author.

277 "She was one of the loveliest people . . ." Van Cliburn to author.

277 "She called me . . ." Ibid.

277 "Personally, I think I'm still in a state of shock . . ." G.G., letter to George Cukor, Jan. 6, 1966, Margaret Herrick Library.

277 "If you could think of a good stage property . . ." G.G. letter to Bernie Seligman, Aug. 26, 1958, SMU G.G. collection.

278 "Mrs. Fogelson . . ." Jack Evinger to author.

278 "During the first forty-eight hours . . ." Van Cliburn to author.

278 "one of the sweetest mother-daughter relationships . . ." Parsons, *Los Angeles Herald-Examiner*, Nov. 29, 1958.

278 "a sense of the continuous . . ." G.G., *Screenland*, June 1945, and *Los Angeles Times*, Oct. 24, 1965.

278 "Religion became very important . . ." Jack Evinger to author.

278 "We never had a typical day . . ." K. Thomas, *Los Angeles Times*, Dec. 11, 1968.

279 "I'm not very good . . ." Ibid.

279 "Of course, by the time I'm through . . ." Art Ryon, *Los Angeles Times*, Jan. 8, 1960.

279 "It would do . . ." DeBlasio, *Modern Screen*, Feb. 1961.

279 "Listening . . ." George Fitzpatrick, *New Mexican*, Jan. 1960.

279 "Give a redhead an inch . . ." Earl Wilson, *Los Angeles Daily News*, April 29, 1952.

279 "I do help in the round-up . . ." K. Thomas, *Los Angeles Times*, Aug. 12, 1966.

279 "Her instructions . . ." Jack Evinger to author.

280 "We pioneered . . ." K. Thomas, *Los Angeles Times*, Aug. 12, 1966.

280 "Mrs. Fogelson loved this country . . ." Gilbert Ortiz to author.

280 "Greer had . . ." Cheryl Wittenauer, *New Mexican*, May 12, 1989.

280 "An invitation . . ." Ibid.

281 "One rare luxury of the ranch . . ." Art Linkletter, *Women Are My Favorite People*

281 "Beneath the awe-inspiring beauty . . ." Art Linkletter, *Park City News*, 1981.

281 "This is the quaintest town . . ." Windes, *New Mexican*, April 15, 1966.

281 "She never stopped plugging Santa Fe . . ." Wittenauer, *New Mexican*.

281 "I got a kick out of the fact . . ." Jack Evinger to author.

282 "I converted my wardrobe . . ." K. Thomas, *Los Angeles Times*, Aug. 12, 1966.

282 "Now that the deed is done . . ." *Variety*, Jan. 13, 1960.

282 "He phoned . . ." Lee Belser, *Los Angeles Mirror*, Jan. 12, 1961.

282 "Since I lost . . ." G.G. letter to Dore Schary, July 10, 1959, University of Wisconsin archives.

283 "I understand so well . . ." Dore Schary letter to G.G., Aug. 26, 1959, University of Wisconsin archives.
283 "She . . ." Dore Schary press release, 1960, USC Warner Bros. archives.
283 "I realized . . ." William Glover, *Los Angeles Times*, Sept. 25, 1960.
283 "Those kids hollered back . . ." Jack Evinger to author.
283 "No one could have been kinder . . ." Christopher Plummer, "Tribute to G.G.: The MGM Years," Sept. 13, 1985.
284 "It doesn't fall . . ." *Variety*, May 4, 1960.
284 "I discovered the importance of prayer . . ." Parsons, *Los Angeles Herald-Examiner*, April 24, 1960.
284 "If ever there is a Mrs. role . . ." Erskine Johnson, *Los Angeles Mirror-News*, April 9, 1960.
285 "You should have seen Greer's face . . ." Ibid.
285 "First time in twelve years of marriage . . . I'm the only movie extra . . ." Ibid.
285 "He was a warm and genial host . . ." *American Weekly*, April 2, 1961.
285 "The travels . . ." *Film Daily*, Dec. 22, 1960.

Chapter 23

286 "I always hedged . . ." *Hollywood Citizen-News*, Oct. 15, 1960.
286 "I always thought . . ." Dore Schary press release, USC Warner Bros. archives.
287 "Ever since . . ." Dick Williams, *Los Angeles Mirror-News*, June 8, 1960.
287 "Leave it to Hollywood . . ." Vernon Scott, *Beverly Hills Citizen*, June 7, 1960.
287 "I think one of my primary aims . . ." Phil Glickman, *Los Angeles Herald-Examiner*, Feb. 12, 1961.
287 "Her beautiful face . . ." Thomas, *Actors and Actresses*, p. 237.
288 "I most certainly did ride a bicycle . . ." Warner Bros. press release, 1960, USC Warner Bros. archives.
288 "Oh, yeah, 'Sunrise at Campanella.' . . ." Ibid.
288 "It was an incredible sight . . ." Tim Considine to author.
288 "Greer Garson is an actress . . ." Ralph Bellamy, program for the opening of the Garson Studios, Oct. 20, 1990.
288 "Great physical effort . . ." Ralph Bellamy press release, 1960, USC Warner Bros. archives.
289 "Mrs. Roosevelt's diction . . ." Parsons, *Los Angeles Herald-Examiner*, April 24, 1960.
289 "Mrs. Roosevelt . . ." WB press release, USC Warner Bros. archives.
289 "I've never seen a group of actors . . ." Vincent Donehue press release, 1960, USC Warner Bros. archives.
290 "When Roosevelt was carried . . ." Dore Schary press release, 1960, USC Warner Bros. archives.
290 "I can certainly understand . . ." G.G. press release, 1960, USC Warner Bros. archives.
291 "Ladies of the press . . ." Joyce Haber, *Los Angeles Times*, Sept. 1, 1968.

291 "Dear Dore . . ." G.G. telegram, Sept. 28, 1960, University of Wisconsin archives.
291 "The *Reporter* . . ." G.G. letter to Radie Harris, Oct. 10, 1960, author's collection.
292 "I realized . . ." Dore Schary, letter to G.G., Nov. 3, 1960, University of Wisconsin archives.
293 "If *Campobello* opened a new career for Schary . . ." *Variety*, Sept. 29, 1960.
293 "I don't feel . . ." Phil Glickman, *Los Angeles Herald-Examiner*, Feb. 12, 1961.
293 "How is the picture . . ." G.G. letter to Dore Schary, Dec. 5, 1960, University of Wisconsin D.S. archives.
294 "Warners were plugging *Sundowners* . . ." Dore Schary letter, March 15, 1961, University of Wisconsin Dore Schary archives.
294 "rehearsing with producer George Schaefer . . ." *Ludie (Calif.) Daily News*, April 27, 1963.
294 "From what . . ." Ibid.
295 "Buddy and I celebrated . . ." Parsons, *Los Angeles Herald-Examiner*, Aug. 25, 1964.
295 "They weren't my cup of tea." Ibid.
295 "I saw Greer . . ." letter from Bing Crosby, Dec. 30, 1964, SMU G.G. collection.
295 "Who in show business . . ." *The Red Skelton Show*, Dec. 21, 1965.
295 "It's my husband . . ." K. Thomas, *Los Angeles Times*, Dec. 11, 1968.
296 "We now have a resident historian . . ." K. Thomas, *Los Angeles Times*, Dec. 11, 1968.
296 "Despite her international fame . . ." *Albuquerque Journal*, April 9, 1996.
296 "I doubt . . ." Brother Luke Roney, program for the opening of Garson Studio, Oct. 20, 1990.
296 "On this first meeting . . ." Ibid.
297 "I'll never forget . . ." Wittenauer, *New Mexican*, May 12, 1989.
297 "Quant à moi . . ." G.G., letter to George Cukor, June 5, 1964, Margaret Herrick Library.
298 "While this building . . ." *New Mexican*, Sept. 14, 1965.
298 "I thought Greer was treated very shabbily . . ." Elva Martien to author.
299 "I do believe . . ." *Los Angeles Times*, July 9, 1965.
299 "It is a great honor . . ." *New Mexican*, Sept. 14, 1965.
299 "When Buddy . . ." K. Thomas, Los Angeles Times, Dec. 11, 1968.
299 "I watched Miss Garson . . ." Scheuer, *Los Angeles Times*, Oct. 13, 1965.
300 "It's very difficult . . ." Don Alpert, *Los Angeles Times*, Oct. 24, 1965.

Chapter 24

301 "The College . . ." G.G. letter, College of Santa Fe G.G. collection.
302 "She is not only a successful actress . . ." Ralph Dohme, *New Mexican*, Dec. 10, 1965.
302 "Words are the tools of my trade . . ." Ibid.
302 "Greer Garson . . ." Ibid.

302 "St. Michael's . . ." Wittenauer, *New Mexican,* May 12, 1989.

303 "I saw last night at MGM . . ." Herbert G. Luft, March 4, 1966, SMU G.G. collection.

303 "We shouldn't lose sight . . ." DeBlasio, *Modern Screen,* Feb. 1961, and Parsons, *Los Angeles Herald-Examiner,* April 24, 1960.

303 "Greer Garson . . ." Windes, *New Mexican,* April 15, 1996.

304 "I think it's a Miniver rose . . ." Ibid.

304 "I think it's time . . ." Ibid.

305 "With Garson and Cooper playing those roles . . ." Bill Anderson to Walt Disney, March 24, 1966, Walt Disney Archives.

306 "very much the star . . ." A.J. Carothers to author.

306 "She asked me once . . ." Al Martinez, *Los Angeles Times,* Jan. 10, 1995.

306 "But who would ever suppose . . ." John Connor, Walt Disney Productions Publicity Director, press release, 1967, Walt Disney Archives.

306 "While all the other actors . . ." Ibid.

307 "I hope you will not be impatient . . ." May 22, 1966, G.G. Alliance Awards acceptance speech, SMU G.G. collection.

307 "Dearest Walter . . ." G.G. letter, May 22, 1966.

308 "It's frustrating . . ." K. Thomas, *Los Angeles Times,* Aug. 12, 1966.

308 "We shot . . ." Carothers to author.

308 "The song . . ." Ibid.

308 "Walt liked . . ." Ibid.

309 "Dear Walt . . ." G.G. telegram, Dec. 11, 1966, SMU G.G. collection.

309 "St. John's . . ." K. Thomas, *Los Angeles Times,* Dec. 11, 1968.

309 "Your gift . . ." Mrs. Walt Disney letter, Feb. 17, 1967, SMU G.G. collection.

310 "I think *The Happiest Millionaire* is just divine . . ." Cordelia Biddle Duke Robertson, *Philadelphia Sunday Bulletin,* Oct. 15, 1967.

310 "Greer Garson, in a welcome return to films . . ." *San Diego Union,* Oct. 15, 1967.

310 "Greer Garson as Mrs. Biddle . . ." *San Jose Mercury News,* Oct. 15, 1967.

310 "Gracious is a word that has haunted me all my life . . ." Sweeney, *Park City News,* Sept. 10, 1992.

310 "It was assumed . . ." Carothers to author.

311 "warm and wonderful . . ." G.G., "An Appreciation of Vivien Leigh," Friends of the Libraries, March 17, 1968.

311 "Look at this cast!" Winifred Blevans, *Los Angeles Herald-Examiner,* Aug. 14, 1968.

311 "George is going to play Reverend Rankin . . ." Ibid.

312 "Greer's Back . . ." Ibid.

312 "We tend to think . . ." Norman Dash, *Los Angeles Herald-Examiner,* Sept. 22, 1968.

312 "I just love . . ." Joyce Haber, *Los Angeles Times,* Sept. 1, 1968.

312 "She is a rare creature . . ." Ibid.

313 "Our thoughts . . ." telegram from George and Lillian Burns Sidney, Sept. 24, 1968, SMU G.G. collection.

313 "a pink rose . . ." Gloria Walls, *Los Angeles Herald-Examiner,* Sept. 26, 1968.

313 "Congratulations . . ." Ibid.
313 "Congratulations, honey . . ." Ibid.
313 "Darling . . ." Ibid.
313 "Tuesday was a gala night . . ." Charles Faber, *Hollywood Citizen-News,* Sept. 26, 1968.
314 "an utterly delectable man-eater . . ." Cecil Smith, *Los Angeles Times,* Sept. 26, 1968.
314 "There's one word . . ." K. Thomas, *Los Angeles Times,* Dec. 11, 1968.
314 "To describe her . . ." Ibid.
314 "It was so terribly kind of you . . ." Douglas Fairbanks Jr. letter, May 16, 1969, SMU G.G. collection.
315 "She had spoken . . ." Jack Evinger to author.
315 "My husband . . ." G.G. speech, College of Santa Fe collection.
316 "A star . . ." Honorary Communication Arts Degree presented to G.G., Oct. 18, 1970.

Chapter 25

317 "I speak with beginner's enthusiasm!" Mary Lou Loper, *Los Angeles Times,* Jan. 29, 1973.
317 "The show does its job . . ." Don Page, *Los Angeles Times,* Jan. 29, 1973.
317 "I dislike bullfights . . ." Joseph Henry Steele, *Photoplay,* Dec. 1942.
317 "I wasn't thinking about horses . . ." Loper, *Los Angeles Times.*
317 "I asked him why he'd done it . . ." Gerry Strine, *Blood-Horse,* Dec. 13, 1971.
318 "has always been in there giving his best . . ." Leon Rasmussen, *Blood-Horse,* April 10, 1971.
318 "All of a sudden . . ." Ibid.
318 "My British cool, I blew it completely . . ." *Newsweek,* Feb. 7, 1972.
318 "I'm sleeping . . ." G.G. letter, undated, SMU G.G. collection.
318 "as always . . ." Lt. Col. John P. Dodson letter to G.G., Feb. 3, 1972, SMU G.G. collection.
319 "While Southern California . . ." Leon Rasmussen, *Thoroughbred Record,* March 6, 1971.
319 "He bet by . . ." Jack Evinger to author.
319 "The Queen Mary and I . . ." Rasmussen, *Thoroughbred Record,* March 20, 1971.
319 "That was her theory . . ." Jack Evinger to author.
319 "Living with Buddy . . ." Loper, *Los Angeles Times.*
320 "Two gentlemen who take . . ." Jody Jacobs, *Los Angeles Times,* July 17, 1972.
320 "The Fogelsons . . ." Jack Evinger to author.
320 "We used to go with them to the races . . ." Julie Hutner to author.
320 "It became . . ." Gerry Strine, *Blood-Horse,* Dec. 20, 1971.
320 "It's been a happy privilege . . ." Loper, *Los Angeles Times.*
320 "I am in the middle of moving . . ." G.G. letter to Edward Purrington, April 25, 1972, College of Santa Fe collection.
321 "That move . . ." Jack Evinger to author.

321 "Miss Garson's speech . . ." *Thoroughbred Record*, Feb. 7, 1972.
321 "I have a notion . . ." Edward Purrington letter, June 16, 1972, College of Santa Fe collection.
322 "Today . . ." G.G., Honorary Doctorate in Music speech, Cleveland Institute of Music, May 31, 1973.
324 "We're thinking of changing . . ." Loper, *Los Angeles Times*.
325 "All sorts of people . . ." Ibid.

Chapter 26

326 "When I left Hollywood . . ." *Los Angeles Herald-Examiner*, July 22, 1974.
326 "She immediately wanted to sue . . ." Jack Evinger to author.
326 "I wish she weren't involved . . ." Erskine Johnson, *Los Angeles Mirror-News*, April 9, 1960.
326 "I now do only the projects . . ." WB press release, 1960, USC Warner Bros. archives.
327 "I've been offered . . ." Joyce Haber, *Los Angeles Times*, Sept. 1, 1968.
327 "I'm not a keyhole peeper . . ." Ed Moreno, *Santa Barbara News-Press*, Oct. 14, 1990.
327 "Old? No . . ." Milton Z. Esterow, *New York Times*, Jan. 19, 1958.
328 "I can't think . . ." *New York Times*, July 28, 1978.
328 "Greer Garson . . ." Loy, *Being and Becoming*, p. 352.
329 "About the little things . . ." Colin Barnes, unidentified article in author's collection, April 1974.
329 "It is one . . ." Cecil Smith, *Los Angeles Times*, April 3, 1974.
329 "I had brought . . ." Ibid.
330 "My dear Greer . . ." Cecil Madden letter, Dec. 24, 1974, SMU G.G. collection.
330 "I was so discomfited . . ." Claudette Colbert letter, April 8, 1974, SMU G.G. collection.
330 "My dear Friends and Team-mates . . ." G.G. letter, Sept. 18, 1974, College of Santa Fe collection.
330 "Do I dispense booze or justice? . . ." Morton Moss, *Los Angeles Citizen-News*, June 4, 1970.
331 "I feel . . ." Jack Evinger to author.
331 "I wish very much . . ." G.G. letter, Dec. 10, 1974, College of Santa Fe collection.
332 "Being in the presence . . ." John Weckesser to author.
332 "And that took some doing . . ." Ibid.
332 "Every one was notated and highlighted" Ibid.
332 "It took me months . . ." Ibid.
333 "Knowing your anxiety . . ." G.G. letter, May 21, 1975, College of Santa Fe collection.
333 "Greer really loved . . ." Weckesser to author.
333 "I gave up an offer . . ." Anne Hillerman, *New Mexican*, Sept. 14, 1975.
333 "Toward the end of rehearsals . . ." Weckesser to author.

333 "She stayed awhile . . ." Ibid.
334 "'The Madwoman of Chaillot' . . ." Hillerman, *New Mexican,* Oct. 2, 1975.
334 "Dear Greer . . ." Weckesser letter, Nov. 4, 1975, College of Santa Fe collection.
335 "You not only looked beautiful . . ." Bob Hope letter, Nov. 17, 1975, SMU G.G. collection.
335 "One thing . . ." Walter Pidgeon, *Los Angeles Times,* Aug. 27, 1961.
335 "Fountains and landscaped pools . . ." G.G. letter, June 4, 1976, College of Santa Fe collection.
335 "She would come in . . ." Weckesser to author.
335 "*Little Women* . . ." *TV Guide,* Sept. 30, 1978.
336 "Greer Garson was emblematic . . ." Vincent Canby, *Times-Picayune,* April 7, 1996.
336 "She was on the set . . ." Bob Banner to author.
336 "It's a slow season . . ." *Los Angeles Herald-Examiner,* Dec. 10, 1975.

Chapter 27

337 "It certainly is a subject . . ." G.G. letter to Neil Adams, July 13, 1981, SMU G.G. collection.
337 "the main works . . ." Jeff Silverman, *Los Angeles Herald-Examiner,* Aug. 11, 1982.
337 "It is with deep regret . . ." *Hollywood Reporter,* June 30, 1980.
337 "I'll cherish this super gift . . ." G.G. letter, May 5, 1980, author's collection.
338 "My doctor . . . Of all the movie stars . . ." Joseph Dispenza, "Greer Garson and the Other Oscar," unpublished article in author's collection.
338 "In a way . . ." Ibid.
339 "I hope Her Royal Highness . . ." G.G. letter, June 25, 1982, College of Santa Fe collection.
339 "Being asked eleven times . . ." Silverman, *Los Angeles Herald-Examiner.*
339 "It's nice to get out my make-up box . . ." Silverman, *Los Angeles Herald-Examiner.*
340 "Oh, come on Aaron . . ." *Dallas Times Herald,* Sept. 8, 1985.
340 "Greer . . . Dear George . . ." Army Archerd, *Variety,* Aug. 10, 1982.
340 "I can't imagine . . ." Silverman, *Los Angeles Herald-Examiner.*
341 "Believe me . . ." Parish, MGM *stock company,* p. 564.
341 "I've had a lot of fun . . ." Walter Pidgeon, *Los Angeles Times,* Sept. 26, 1984.
341 "It was a quiet and gentlemanly end . . ." *Los Angeles Times,* Sept. 26, 1984.
341 "He was a fine actor . . ." Nancy Hill-Holtzman, *Los Angeles Herald-Examiner,* Sept. 26, 1984.
341 "My heart turned over . . ." Ibid.
342 "Dearest Ruth . . ." G.G. letter, Nov. 1984, author's collection.
342 "He had a collapse . . ." John Roach to author.
342 "It was very touching . . ." Dr. William Tschumy to author.
342 "I remember . . ." Van Cliburn to author.

342 "He told me . . ." Champlin, *Los Angeles Times*, Oct. 13, 1985.

343 "Dallas may have been overcast . . ." Susan Evans, *Daily Campus*, Sept. 17, 1985.

343 "The sons and daughters of the Emerald Isle . . ." President Ronald Reagan, "Tribute to Greer Garson" program, Sept. 13, 1985.

343 "Throughout the decades . . ." Alan Ladd Jr., "Tribute To Greer Garson" program, Sept. 13, 1985.

343 "If it's true . . ." Mervyn LeRoy, "Tribute To Greer Garson" program, Sept. 13, 1985.

343 "I've thought often . . ." Champlin, *Los Angeles Times*, Oct. 13, 1985.

344 "All this was most edifying. . ." Cynthia Rose, *Dallas Times Herald*, Sept. 16, 1985.

344 "It fell off . . . reassemble . . . film which still speaks . . ." Champlin, *Los Angeles Times*, Oct. 13, 1985

344 "There was no question . . ." Ibid.

345 "This kind of evening . . ." *Los Angeles Times*, May 4, 1986.

345 "Dear John . . ." G.G. letter, Aug. 12, 1986, College of Santa Fe collection.

345 "I was told . . ." James Fries to author.

346 "From all the stories . . ." Ibid.

346 "The government was very slow . . ." Jack Evinger to author.

346 "The Rockefellers . . . Other people . . ." Jennings, *Dallas Morning News*, Sept. 23, 1984.

346 "She knew what she wanted . . ." Ann Rasor to author.

347 "It was a very difficult time." Jack Evinger to author.

347 "We are truly disappointed . . ." G.G. letter, Oct. 16, 1987, College of Santa Fe collection.

348 "Reports . . ." G.G. letter, undated, College of Santa Fe collection.

348 "For several months . . ." Brother Cyprian Luke Roney to author.

348 "Being married to Fogelson . . ." Wuntch, *Dallas Morning News*, March 10, 1991.

348 "I think everybody in the city . . ." Jack Evinger to author.

348 "We have only begun . . ." John Roach eulogy for Buddy Fogelson, Dec. 3, 1987, in author's collection, courtesy of Zann Taylor.

349 "Greer . . ." Weckesser to author.

349 "Greer is terribly ill . . ." Radie Harris, *Globe*, Oct. 1988.

349 "Her penthouse apartment in Dallas . . ." Joseph Dispenza to author.

349 "She loved . . ." Francisca Lucas to author.

349 "Greer was very . . ." Col. James P. Caston to author.

340 "She was very down . . ." Ibid.

350 "Greer . . ." Ibid.

350 "At first . . ." John Roach to author.

350 "She had discussed . . ." Eugene Bonelli to author.

350 "Well, after all . . ." Wuntch, *Dallas Morning News*.

351 "About a year . . ." Laura Roach to author.

351 "She stayed until 2:30 . . ." Lucas to author.

351 "Mrs. Meir and Miss Garson . . ." Jehan Sadat, *Los Angeles Times,* June 16, 1988.
351 "To meet . . ." G.G. speech, June 15, 1988, SMU G.G. collection.
352 "I think that women . . ." Kim Mitchell, *Variety,* June 16, 1988.
352 "I realized . . ." Laura Roach to author.
352 "She understood physicians . . ." Carol Burrow to author.
353 "Our Heavenly Father . . ." Rev. Clayton Bell Fogelson prayer, Dec. 14, 1988, SMU G.G. collection.
353 "It is rather remarkable . . ." Jennings, *Dallas Morning News.*
353 "Greer asked for a barstool . . ." Burrow to author.
353 "Ms. Garson . . ." Jerome Weeks, *Dallas Morning News,* Aug. 30, 1992.

Chapter 28

355 "I had approached . . ." Joseph Dispenza to author.
355 "This gift . . ." G.G., *Los Angeles Times,* May 15, 1989.
356 "Jack Roach . . ." Jack Evinger to author.
356 "Hardly anything survived . . ." Marilyn Evinger to author.
356 "I feel like a nonperson . . . I'm the bionic woman . . ." Army Archerd, *Variety,* Jan. 12, 1990; Jon Bowman, *New Mexico Magazine,* Nov. 1990; and G.G. letter to Mike Nevard, *Globe,* Nov. 4, 1988, SMU G.G. collection.
357 "Unfortunately, I have to . . ." Army Archerd, *Variety,* June 18, 1990.
357 "We were fortunate . . ." Weeks, *Dallas Morning News,* Aug. 30, 1992.
357 "I had invited her . . ." Caston to author.
357 "To everyone . . ." G.G. letter, undated, College of Santa Fe collection.
358 "Today we should remember . . ." Wittenauer, *New Mexican,* May 12, 1989.
358 "a hauntingly lovely presence . . ." Ibid.
358 "While we enjoy her films . . ." Kay Bird, *New Mexican,* Oct. 21, 1990.
358 "Greer Garson has given us a rose . . ." Ibid.
358 "She said to me . . ." Dispenza to author.
358 "I think you had better come over quickly . . ." Ibid.
359 "You know . . ." Ibid.
359 "The first time she accepted the Oscar . . ." Ibid.
359 "For her $10 million . . ." Weeks, *Dallas Morning News.*
359 "She told us . . ." Bonelli to author.
359 "My goal . . ." Weeks, *Dallas Morning News.*
359 "It's very handsome . . ." Anderson, *Dallas Magazine,* Aug. 1992.
359 "My dear Milton . . ." Weeks, *Dallas Morning News.*
360 "You know . . ." Minoff, *Cue,* Jan. 18, 1958.
360 "I was thrilled . . ." Ibid.
360 "We have created roses . . ." Helen F. Boehm, "Greer Garson Theatre Fortnight Festival," Sept. 12, 1992.
360 "Up to the very last minute . . ." Bonelli to author.
360 "We were so disappointed . . ." Laura Roach to author.
361 "She had pride . . ." Rex Reed, "Greer Garson Theatre Fortnight Festival," Sept. 12, 1992.

361 "The Greer Garson Theater . . ." Queen Elizabeth II, Greer Garson Theatre Fortnight Festival, Sept. 12, 1992.
361 "I must say . . ." Art Linkletter, Greer Garson Theatre Fortnight Festival, Sept. 12, 1992.
361 "I know . . ." Van Cliburn to author.
362 "Although she occasionally missed . . ." Julie Hutner to author.
362 "She would put . . ." Caston to author.
362 "One time she was very low . . ." Ibid.
363 "Once she told me . . ." Weckesser to author.
363 "I'm so excited . . ." *Dallas Morning News,* July 9, 1993.
363 "Over a two-week period . . ." Burrow to author.
364 "She would have made . . ." Julie Hutner to author.
364 "I'm afraid I have no children . . ." Mitchell Smyth, *Toronto Star,* Aug. 1, 1986.
364 "She never had any extraordinary requests . . ." Ann Harper to author.
364 "She would not permit . . . One year . . ." Burrow to author.
364 "I don't believe . . ." Champlin, *Los Angeles Times,* Oct. 13, 1985.
364 "Doug Hawthorne . . ." Burrow to author.
364 "She really wanted to be brave . . ." Laura Roach to author.
364 "We came for our usual visit . . ." Marilyn Evinger to author.
365 "She was very tranquil . . ." Gregory Peck to author.
365 "We continued to plan her farewell performance . . ." Caston to author.
365 "I held her still-beautiful hands . . ." Van Cliburn to author.
365 "Until the last few days . . ." John Roach to author.

Epilogue

366 "I've always lived . . ." Wuntch, *Dallas Morning News,* March 10, 1991.
366 "She was a great lady . . ." Van Cliburn to author.
367 "Dallas bid farewell to . . ." Jane Sumner, *Dallas Morning News,* April 9, 1996.
367 "It was really beautiful . . ." Julie Hutner to author.
367 "talents . . . friendship . . ." Dr. B. Clayton Bell Sr. to author.
367 "this occasion . . ." Sumner, *Dallas Morning News.*
367 "Who do you think . . ." Van Cliburn to author.
367 "I will always cherish . . ." Bonelli to author.
367 "The point of today's gathering . . ." James Fries, *New Mexican,* April 22, 1996.
368 "For twenty-two years . . ." John Weckesser, College of Santa Fe's *Vistas,* Spring 1996.
368 "Greer Garson's association . . ." Janet Wise, *Vistas,* Spring 1996.
368 "If there were flags at Radio City Music Hall . . ." Robert Osborne, *Hollywood Reporter,* April 9, 1996.
368 "Greer Garson is known . . ." Champlin, *Los Angeles Times,* April 9, 1996.
369 "Elders who sigh . . ." Sunshine, *Lovers,* p. 123.
369 "It is for *Mrs. Miniver* . . ." Sheila Collings, *The Stage,* April 18, 1996.

BIBLIOGRAPHY

Books

Anderegg, Michael A. *William Wyler.* Boston: Twayne, 1979.

Austen, Jane. *Pride and Prejudice.* New York: Random House, 1995.

Barrow, Kenneth. *Mr. Chips: The Life of Robert Donat.* London: Methuen, 1985.

Bellyss, Connie, with Arthur Pierce. *Lux Presents Hollywood.* Jefferson, N.C.: MacFarland, 1995.

Bezy, John V., and Joseph P. Sanchez, eds. *Pecos: Gateway to Pueblos and Plains.* Tucson: Southwest Parks and Monuments Association, 1988.

Boller, Paul F., Jr., with Ronald L. Davis. *Hollywood Anecdotes.* New York: Ballantine, 1989.

Braun, Eric, *Deborah Kerr.* New York: St. Martin's Press, 1978.

Campbell, Grace. *Highland Heritage.* New York: Duell, Sloan and Pearce, 1962.

Carey, Gary. *All the Stars in Heaven: Louis B. Mayer's MGM.* New York: E.P. Dutton, 1981.

———. *Cukor and Company: The Films of George Cukor and His Collaborators.* New York: Museum of Modern Art, 1971.

Colman, Juliet Benita. *Ronald Colman: A Very Private Person.* New York: William Morrow, 1975.

Crowther, Bosley. *Lion's Share: The Story of an Entertainment Empire.* New York: E.P. Dutton, 1957.

Davis, Ronald L. *The Glamour Factory: Inside Hollywood's Big Studio System.* Dallas: Southern Methodist Press, 1993.

Donaldson, Gordon. *Scotland: The Shaping of a Nation.* London: David and Charles, 1974.

Eames, John Douglas. *The MGM Story: The Complete History of Fifty Roaring Years.* New York: Crown, 1982.

Eells, George. *Robert Mitchum.* New York: Franklin Watts, 1984.

Fairbanks, Douglas, Jr. *The Salad Days.* New York: Doubleday, 1988.

Flanner, Janet, edited by Irving Drutman. *London Was Yesterday, 1934-1939.* New York: Viking Press, 1975.

Fleming, Mary. *A History of the Thoroughbred in California*. Arcadia: California Thoroughbred Association Breeders Association, 1983.

Flynn, Errol. *My Wicked, Wicked Ways*. New York: G.P. Putnam's Sons, 1959.

Fontaine, Joan. *No Bed of Roses*. New York: William Morrow, 1978.

Francisco, Charles. *Radio City Music Hall: An Affectionate History of the World's Greatest Theater*. New York: E.P. Dutton, 1979.

Frank, Leonhard. *Desire Me*. Originally published under the title *Carl and Anna*, 1930. Translated by Cyrus Brooks. New York: Triangle Books, 1947.

Freedland, Michael. *Gregory Peck*. New York: William Morrow, 1980.

French, Warren. *Joseph I. Mankiewicz*. Boston: Twayne, 1983.

Garcean, Jean, with Ivey Cocke. *"Dear Mr. G—": The Biography of Clark Gable*. Boston: Little, Brown, 1961.

Garnett, Tay, with Fredda Dudley Ballington. *Light Your Torches and Pull Up Your Tights*. New Rochelle, N.Y.: Arlington House, 1973.

Graham, Sheilah. *Hollywood Revisited*. New York: St. Martin's, 1984.

Guilaroff, Sydney, as told to Cathy Griffin. *Crowning Glory: Reflections of Hollywood's Favorite Confidant*. Santa Monica, Calif.: General Publishing Group. 1996.

Hardwicke, Sir Cedric, as told to James Brough. *The Irreverent Memoirs of Sir Cedric Hardwicke*. New York: Doubleday, 1961.

Hay, Peter. MGM: *When the Lion Roars*. Atlanta: Turner Publishing, 1991.

Henreid, Paul, with Julian Fast. *Ladies Man: An Autobiography of Paul Henreid*. New York: St. Martin's, 1984.

Herman, Jan. *A Talent for Trouble: The Life of Hollywood's Most Acclaimed Director, William Wyler*. New York: G.P. Putnam's Sons, 1995.

Higham, Charles. *Merchant of Dreams: Louis B. Mayer, M.G.M., and the Secret Hollywood*. New York: Donald I. Fine, 1993.

Hilton, James. *Goodbye, Mr. Chips*. New York: Bantam Books, 1986.

———. *Random Harvest*. Boston: Little, Brown, 1941.

Hirschhorn, Clive. *The Warner Bros. Story: The Complete History of Hollywood's Great Studio*. New York: Crown, 1980.

Hoopes, Roy. *When the Stars Went to War: Hollywood and World War II*. New York: Random House, 1994.

Houseman, John. *Front and Center*. New York: Simon and Schuster, 1979.

Jarlett, Franklin. *Robert Ryan: A Biography and Critical Filmography*. Jefferson, N.C.: MacFarland, 1990.

Kobal, John. *Hollywood Glamor Portraits: 145 Photos of Stars, (1926-1949)*. New York: Dover, 1976.

Lambert, Gavin. *Norma Shearer: A Life*. New York: Alfred A. Knopf, 1990.

Leigh, Janet. *There Really Was a Hollywood*. Garden City, N.Y.: Doubleday, 1984.

LeRoy, Mervyn, as told to Dick Kleiner. *Mervyn LeRoy: Take One*. New York: Hawthorn Books, 1974.

Levy, Emanuel. *George Cukor, Master of Elegance: Hollywood's Legendary Director and His Stars*. New York: William Morrow, 1994.

Linkletter, Art. *Women Are My Favorite People*. Garden City, N.Y.: Doubleday, 1974.

Loos, Anita. *Kiss Hollywood Goodbye.* New York: Viking, 1974.

Loy, Myrna, with James Kilsilibus-Davis. *Myrna Loy: Being and Becoming.* New York: Donald I. Fine, 1987.

Madsen, Axel. *William Wyler: The Authorized Biography.* New York: Thomas Y. Crowell, 1973.

Martin, Pete. *Hollywood without Makeup.* New York: Bantam, 1949.

Marx, Samuel. *Mayer and Thalberg.* Hollywood: Samuel French, 1988.

McClelland, Doug. *Forties Film Talk.* Jefferson, N.C.: MacFarland, 1992.

McDowall, Roddy. *Double Exposure: Take Three.* New York: William Morrow, 1992.

McGilligan, Patrick. *George Cukor: A Double Life.* New York: St. Martin's, 1991.

Meyer, William R. *The Warner Brothers Directors: The Hard-Boiled, the Comic, and the Weepers.* New Rochelle, N.Y.: Arlington House, 1978.

Minnelli, Vincente, with Hector Arce. *I Remember It Well.* New York: Doubleday, 1974.

Molyneaux, Gerard. *Gregory Peck: A Bio-Bibliography.* Westport, Conn.: Greenwood Press, 1995.

Neville, Peter. *A Traveller's History of Ireland.* New York: Interlink, 1992.

Newquist, Roy. *Conversations with Joan Crawford.* Secaucus, N.J.: Citadel, 1980.

Olivier, Laurence. *On Acting.* New York: Simon and Schuster, 1986.

———. *Confessions of an Actor.* New York: Simon and Schuster, 1982.

Osborne, Robert. *50 Golden Years of Oscar: The Official History of the Academy of Motion Picture Arts and Sciences.* Los Angeles: Ese California in association with AMPAS, 1979.

Parish, James Robert, with Gregory Mank. *The Best of* MGM: *The Golden Years: 1928-1959.* Westport, Conn.: Arlington House, 1981.

Parish, James Robert, with Ronald L. Bowers. *The* MGM *Stock Company: The Golden Era.* New Rochelle, N.Y.: Arlington House, 1973.

Perry, George. *The Great British Picture Show.* New York: Hill and Wang, 1974.

Quirk, Lawrence. *The Films of Robert Taylor.* Secaucus, N.J.: Citadel, 1975.

Reynolds, Debbie, with David Patrick Columbia. *Debbie: My Life.* New York: William Morrow, 1988.

Roberts, Jerry. *Robert Mitchum: A Bio-Bibliography.* Westport, Conn.: Greenwood Press, 1992.

Sanders, George. *Memoirs of a Professional Cad.* New York: G.P. Putnam, 1960.

Schary, Dore. *Heyday.* Boston: Little, Brown, 1979.

Spoto, Donald. *Laurence Olivier: A Biography.* New York: HarperCollins, 1992.

Stokes, Sewell. *Without Veils: The Intimate Biography of Gladys Cooper.* London: Peter Davies, 1953.

Stine, Whitney, and Bette Davis. *Mother Goddam: The Story and Career of Bette Davis.* New York: Hawthorn, 1974.

Struther, Jan. *Mrs. Miniver.* 1939. London: Harcourt Brace Jovanovich, 1989 and 1990 editions.

Sunshine, Linda. *Lovers.* Atlanta: Turner Publishing, 1992.

Taylor, John Russell. *Strangers in Paradise: The Hollywood Emigres, 1933-1950.* New York: Holt, Rinehart and Winston, 1983.

Thomas, Bob. *Marlon: Portrait of the Rebel as an Artist.* New York: Random House, 1973.

———. *Thalberg: Life and Legend.* Garden City, N.Y.: Doubleday, 1969.

Thomas, Tony, with Rudy Behlmer and Clifford McCarty. *The Films of Errol Flynn.* Secaucus, N.J.: Citadel, 1969.

Tomkies, Mike. *The Robert Mitchum Story: "It Beats Working."* Chicago: Henry Regnery, 1972.

Tornabene, Lyn. *Long Live the King: A Biography of Clark Gable.* New York: G.P. Putnam's Sons, 1976.

Trewin, J.C. *The Birmingham Repertory Theatre (1913-1963).* London: Barrie and Rockliff, 1963.

Unterburgen, Amy L., ed. *Actors and Actresses.* Vol. 3 of *International Dictionary of Film and Filmmakers.* Detroit: St. James Press, 1992.

Walker, Alexander. *Elizabeth: The Life of Elizabeth Taylor.* New York: Grove Weidenfeld, 1990.

———. *Vivien: The Life of Vivien Leigh.* New York: Weidenfeld and Nicolson, 1987.

Wayne, Jane Ellen. *Robert Taylor: The Man with the Perfect Face.* New York: St. Martin's, 1973.

West, John G., Jr. *The Disney Live-Action Productions.* Milton, Wash.: Hawthorne and Peabody, 1994.

Wilding, Michael. *The Wilding Way: The Story of My Life.* New York: St. Martin's, 1982.

Wiley, Mason, with Damien Bona. *Inside Oscar: The Unofficial History of the Academy Awards.* New York: Ballantine, 1986.

Significant Articles and Programs

Anderson, Porter. "The Life and Theatre of Greer Garson." *Dallas Magazine,* Aug. 1992.

Dispenza, Joseph. "Greer Garson and the Other Oscar." Unpublished manuscript in author's collection.

Gardner, Mona. "The Glorified Mrs." *Ladies Home Journal,* Sept. 1944, 20, 90, 92, 94, 95, 101-6.

Garson, Greer. "Christmas Story." *Photoplay,* Jan. 1947, 30, 31, 100, 101.

"The Greer Garson Theatre Fortnight Festival." Southern Methodist University, Sept. 12, 1992.

Martin, Pete. "Hollywood's Fabulous Female." *Saturday Evening Post,* Dec. 26, 1946.

"MGM Lion's Roar." Studio publication, 1940-1946.

"The Opening of the Greer Garson Communications Center and Studios at the College of Santa Fe," Oct. 20, 1990.

"Persuasions." Jane Austen Society, Dec. 16, 1989.

"A Tribute to Greer Garson: The MGM Years." Southern Methodist University, Sept. 13, 1985.

INDEX